The Middle East Reader

The Middle East Reader

Edited by

MICHAEL CURTIS

Transaction Books
New Brunswick (U.S.A.) and Oxford (U.K.)

All essays previously appeared in *Middle East Review.*

Library of Congress Catalog Number: 86-11211
ISBN: 0-88738-101-4 (cloth); 0-88738-648-2 (paper)
Printed in the United States of America

Library of Congress Cataloging in Publication Data

The Middle East reader

A selection of articles from the last ten years of the Middle East review.

1. Near East—Politics and government-1945-
I. Curtis, Michael, 1923- . II. Middle East review
(New York, N.Y.)
DS63.1.M544 1986 956′.04 86-11211
ISBN 0-88738-101-4
ISBN 0-88738-648-2 (pbk.)

Contents

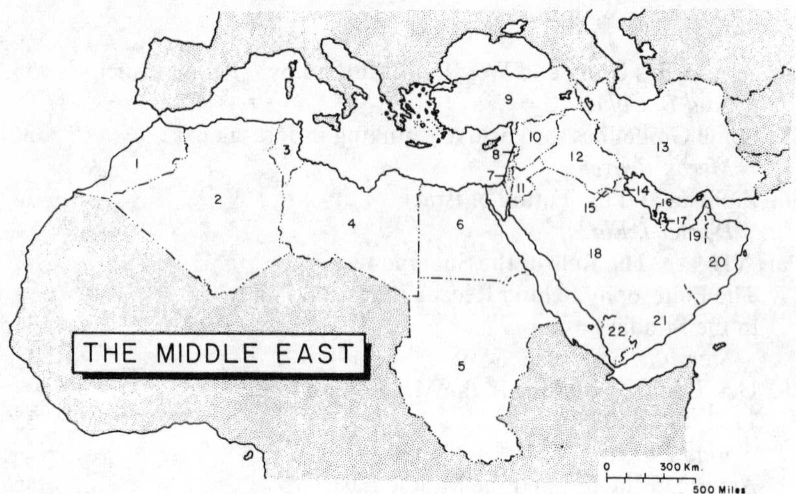

Map prepared by Dr. Norman Dlin, Associate Professor of Geography, Department of Social Sciences, Louisiana State University, Shreveport.

Countries of the Middle East

1. Morocco
2. Algeria
3. Tunisia
4. Libya
5. Sudan
6. Egypt
7. Israel
8. Lebanon
9. Turkey
10. Syria
11. Jordan
12. Iraq
13. Iran
14. Kuwait
15. Iraq-Saudi Arabia Neutral Zone
16. Bahrain
17. Qatar
18. Saudi Arabia
19. United Arab Emirates [No defined boundary]
20. Oman [No defined boundary]
21. People's Democratic Republic of Yemen (South Yemen) [No defined boundary]
22. Yemen Arab Republic (North Yemen) [No defined boundary]

Preface

This book consists of a selection of articles drawn from the *Middle East Review*, a quarterly journal devoted to eliciting new ideas and approaches for the solution of conflicts in the Middle East, and to the achievement of a just and lasting peace in the region.

The articles, written over the last decade, analyze the major factors and political forces in the contemporary Middle East. The subjects include Arab nationalism, Islamic fundamentalism, pan-Arabism, political rivalries, significant minorities, oil, Judaism and Israel, and the role of the superpowers and other external parties. The articles also discuss some aspects of the individual countries in the region as well as the political concerns of Israel, and the Palestinian issue.

No single book can possibly provide complete coverage of the complex issues and tensions in the Middle East today. This book is presented for both specialists and general readers in the hope that its wide coverage will lead to greater understanding of a region that is politically volatile but which is so important for the rest of the world.

Introduction

The term *Middle East* is of twentieth century origin, having been coined in 1902 to refer to the general area between Arabia and India. Geographical references with political overtones have often been derived from the Western view of the world with Europe as the center. The area to the east of Europe was thus logically regarded as the *East* and political issues relevant to it were part of the *Eastern Question*. In the nineteenth century, when West Europe became concerned with the affairs of Asia in a more substantial way, that area was viewed as the *Far East*. The term *Near East* had already been used first to refer to Southeast Europe, then under Ottoman rule, and later was applied to the other parts of the Ottoman Empire in Asia and Africa.

Beginning in World War II this term began to be replaced by *Middle East*, though some still use the older phrase, and some non-Western countries often prefer the term *Southwest Asia*. Definition of *Middle East* has been elastic. Sometimes it has been used for a large area, spanning three continents and largely dominated by Islamic culture, stretching from North Africa to Central Asia, the Horn of Africa, and Pakistan. But the term is most familiarly used to depict the triangle from the Nile Valley to the Muslim area of central Asia to the Persian Gulf, an area containing about 120 million people and the lands of Egypt, the Fertile Crescent (which now includes the countries of Israel, Jordan, Lebanon, Syria, and Iraq), Iran, Saudi Arabia, and the Persian Gulf countries.

The present map of much of the area dates from the breakup of the Ottoman Empire after World War I, when new states were constituted under the League of Nations mandates administered by France and Britain. For this purpose, these Western powers revived names long obsolete, including *Palestine*, a term that had been used by the Romans, but that had disappeared by the time the Crusaders arrived.

The Middle East has been the location of ancient civilizations of the world—Sumerian, Babylonian, Assyrian, Egyptian, Iranian, Jewish, and Arabic—and of the three great monotheistic religions, Judaism, Christianity, and Islam. Its geographic setting between the land masses of Europe, Africa, and Asia made the Middle East the crossroads of the world, thereby engendering trade and a mixture of people and cultures, but also leading to continual conflict and waves of invasion. The Middle East in whole or in part has been subjected to the control of a variety of rulers throughout history up to the Turks in the twentieth century. Religious enthusiasm produced the spread of Islam from its Arabian homeland into what were then Christian countries, and the unsuccessful attempt at a Christian reconquest by Crusaders from Western Europe in the eleventh and twelfth centuries. The strategic importance of the area has long been recognized. Napoleon Bonaparte invaded the Middle East to block British control of India. In its turn Britain supported the Ottoman Empire, which lasted until 1918, to prevent Russian expansion southward. Germany, before World War I, competed with the other powers at the time to obtain a foothold in the area. In the post–World War II era the vital importance of the area has been enhanced by the Western dependence on the area for oil—two-thirds of the world's known resources lie in the area—and by the rivalry between the United States and the Soviet Union for influence in the area.

The geography of the Middle East—desert, river valleys, mountains and fertile plain—has given rise to a diversity of cultural and behavioral patterns. Much of the area is desert, resulting primarily from lack of rainfall but also to some degree from past misuse, and only 5 percent is cultivable. Not much more of the area is likely to be under cultivation in the near future. Under present conditions the area cannot feed itself, a situation that will be aggravated by the increase in population. The desert has been a barrier to unity. The consequence of this and other geographical factors has been the clustering of families around places where water was available, thus creating isolated self-sufficient settlements adhering to particular ways of life. Historic rivalry has existed between herdsmen living in the desert and those living from agriculture. At an early stage rulers had to provide for the policing of desert borders and the security of desert routes.

The mountain ranges have been barriers to unified control, protecting religious and ethnic minorities and linguistic differences. For this reason, religious groups—including the Druse, Maronites, Yezidis and Alawites—tribes, such as the Bakhtiari in Iran, and a people, such as the Kurds in Iran, Turkey, and Iraq, have survived in the midst of an overwhelming Arabism or Islam. Persian has remained as a separate language in Iran. The historic rivals, Egypt and Iraq, result from river valleys and the area surrounding them. Both are ancient civilizations, skilled at agricultural production and in the use of artificial irrigation, and experienced in the art of centralized government. The geographic boundaries of modern day Turkey and Iran coincide approximately with the great plateaus. By contrast, the modern states of Israel, Jordan, Syria, and Lebanon are political entities whose geographic features do not correspond with the natural geography of the region.

The largest linguistic group in the Middle East is the Semitic language group. Most in this group speak Arabic, though a relatively small number—about 3.5 million—speak Hebrew. For centuries the area has been dominated by Islam and by Arabs. As is often the case in political analysis, terms of this kind do not lend themselves to easy definition.

One can talk of an Arab people as composed of individuals who are bound together by the Arabic language and civilization with a distinctive culture and literature, though it may include individuals of different races and religions. Arabs do not constitute a single physical type or race; and, though nine-tenths of Arabs are Muslim, they do not belong to a single religion, since there are Christians and Jews among them as well. As a corollary, Arabs constitute only about one-fifth of the world's 800 million Muslims. Language was therefore the most important single factor binding together the approximately 100 million in the Middle East geographical triangle who are regarded as Arab. Nevertheless, if Turkey is included in the definition of Middle East, about half of the population in that extended area speak Turkish or Persian.

For some 400 years, from the seventh to the eleventh century, the Arabs were the center of political power, commerce, and learning in the area. Yet a single Arab state has never existed in political terms which included all the Arab people. The Arabs have always been nationals of a number of countries, including, since 1948, Israel. The Arab-dominated Middle East has always been and remains the setting for fierce competition and rivalry among the individual states.

Two proposals for the creation of an Arab nation have been made. One is to weld existing states together to form a larger Arab union. Though a number of such attempts have been made, such as the United Arab Republic of Egypt and Syria between 1958 and 1961, all have quickly failed.

The other argument is to create a pan-Arabic state, based on the idea that all Arabic speakers form one nation with rights and aspirations and possess particular national attributes. By contrast, in this view each territorial nation is only a partial representative of the Arab people, often being based on the ambitions of the political rulers. As a political movement, pan-Arabism dates from the late nineteenth century, largely originating from Christian Arab thinkers. At first pan-Arabism was directed against the Ottoman Empire. After World War I, the new targets were the European countries, Britain and France, which had entered the area, and the increasing immigration of Jews into Palestine.

As a language, Arabic only became important with the emergence and rise of Islam. For many centuries identities such as Arab and Islamic consciousnesses were difficult to distinguish. Not until the late nineteenth century were the arguments made by Christian Arabs that Arab identity was not synonymous with religious identification, and that national loyalty should be given higher priority than adherence to Islam. The dialogue continues in the contemporary world between those advocating the primacy of the Islamic religion and those arguing that nationality should be the bond among Arabs.

The problem is complicated by the fact that in all Arab states except Lebanon, Islam is the established religion of the state, that religious instruction is given in the schools, and that religious institutions are financially supported by the state. Islam, the dominant faith for thirteen centuries in the Middle East, has provided a sense of common identity, resting on the fundamental principles that "God is one and Muhammed is his prophet," and that the Koran, the messages revealed to Muhammed in the early seventh century, and the traditions of the prophet should form the basis not only of theology but also of law, though commentators differ on interpretation of that law or *sharia*. For Islam, the sole source of political legitimacy is God, and the state and military power are to be employed in the service of God. In this view the world is seen as divided into the House of Islam, those lands in which the *sharia* is dominant, and the House of War, those lands that did not accept or resisted Islam. In theory, Islam is pledged to a *jihad*, or holy war, against those territories not under Muslim rule. Islamic theory also suggests that the ruler, whose main obligation is to implement religious law, is absolute; the notion of popular participation as in representative democratic systems is unfamiliar.

In spite of any clear distinction in Islam between the religious and the secular, two factors are pertinent to contemporary affairs. The first is the division within Islam itself between the majority group, the Sunnis, and the minority Shiites who honor Ali, the fourth caliph after Muhammed. Constituting 80 million in all, outside as well as within the Middle East, the Shiites constitute about 10 percent of the total Muslim population and are at the present time its most fundamentalist and militant part. In the Middle East, they form the dominant majority in Iran, a nondominant majority in Iraq, the largest single community in Lebanon, and constitute important groups in Yemen and other places.

The second factor is the existence of other religious affiliations. The Druse, an Islamic sect, exist in Lebanon, Syria, and Israel. The Alawites, holding certain deviant religious views but nonetheless regarded as being close to the Shiites, currently form the ruling group in Syria, though they constitute only 12 percent of the total population. Christianity, the majority religion in medieval times, has now dwindled to a small and largely powerless minority except in Lebanon, where numerous sects—Maronites,

Greek Orthodox, and Greek Catholics—remain. The largest Christian group, the Copts, form about 10 percent of the Egyptian population. Christianity is also the faith of many blacks in southern Sudan, whose position in that country has sometimes been made difficult. In Iran, small groups of Zoroastrians and Bahais remain.

Judaism is the oldest surviving faith in the region. Jews live primarily in Israel now that ancient Jewish communities in Arab countries have almost come to an end. Though dispersed by the Babylonians, the Assyrians and by the Romans in 70 A.D., and at times persecuted by both Christian and Muslim rulers, Jews have always been present in varying numbers in the area of the Holy Land. Jewish immigration from the Mediterranean countries in the sixteenth century led to an increase of intellectual as well as religious activity in towns such as Jerusalem and Safed. At the turn of the nineteenth century, Zionists from Central and Eastern Europe began immigrating as pioneers and settlers on the land. By 1914 this immigration by Zionists of different kinds led to about 85,000 Jews residing in Palestine, a number that had grown to half a million when the state of Israel was established in 1948. With the new state came the recognition of Hebrew, together with Arabic, as the official language and the accepted form of communication.

Despite the religious divisions, a pan-Islamic movement, whose political goal was the unity of all Muslims, emerged in the latter part of the nineteenth century among the Young Ottomans, who saw the Ottoman Empire as the natural center of such a union to ward off European influence. A more militant form of pan-Islamism in other countries after World War I, when there was a more active concern with religion, argued that Islam should be united as a world power, reasserting Islamic principles and values, against Western power and culture. But it was not successful in leading to an effective political organization based on religious solidarity. After World War II, the reassertion of Islamic principles, appealing to the lower classes, resulted in the creation of religious leagues, the most important of which has been the Muslim Brotherhood, originally founded in 1928 by Hasan al-Banna. The Brotherhood is part of the larger Islamic fundamentalist movement which attempts to transform the Muslim world by religious revival and return to the ethics of Islam. Since 1948 a major factor in the Islamic movement has been hostility to Israel. Strong in Egypt in the 1930s and 1940s, the Brotherhood provided a focus for opposition to economic and political control by foreign powers as well as for attack on the Egyptian monarchy. Suppressed by President Nasser in 1954, the Brotherhood reemerged under President Sadat, who saw it as helpful in the internal fight against communists. Saudi Arabia also viewed the Brotherhood as such, and has provided it with financial assistance.

The contemporary Middle East is marked by a number of political characteristics: a low level of political community; authoritarian governments of various kinds in almost all systems; political instability, conflict and frequent resort to violence; and unpredictability.

The low level of political community and the unlikelihood of a common national loyalty is partly the result of the perpetuation of ethnic, tribal or communal-religious divisions, and partly the heritage of boundaries laid down by colonial powers. In Lebanon, political positions have, since 1943, been allocated on the basis of religious affiliation; politics is therefore marked by fierce tribal disputes and the primacy of religious sects and clans. The Muslim perception of its position and perquisites as unjustifiably inadequate underlies the internal disarray in Lebanon that began in 1975. Ethnic groups, residing next to or within each other, see others as rivals. Lacking legitimacy through popular election, rulers have frequently appointed relatives, members of their extended family (*hamula*), and tribal allies to senior political and military positions as in Syria, Iraq and North Yemen where those appointed may not be representative of the majority of the population.

The boundaries of a number of Middle Eastern states were shaped in the early twentieth century by decisions of Britain and France, and were more the result of their strategic interests than of local ethnic or religious factors. The ensuing individual state may not therefore be the recipient of national support. In any case, most of the states are relatively new; only Saudi Arabia and Yemen predate 1936 as fully, rather than formally, independent states in their present limits.

Economic and social changes, such as movement in employment away from agriculture where only half the population now works, have not yet greatly altered the pattern of adherence to ethnic and religious loyalty in favor of loyalty to the state. Even the growing urbanization—the rapid move to the cities has led to about 45 percent of the population being urban—has not altogether weakened the local bond because rural migrants to the cities have tended to move close to other migrants from similar backgrounds.

In general, political power tends to be exercised in the Middle East in autocratic, often highly personalized, fashion. The very lack of national loyalty has been one factor explaining the continuation of authoritarian systems in which the dominant political and economic decisions are in the hands of traditional type monarchs or of leaders, most of whom have emerged from the military hierarchy, aided by a bureaucracy and security service, whose rule is limited only by respect for religious law. Most recently, a religious elite in Iran has exercised power. Except in the political democracy of Israel, in Turkey intermittently (since democracy there has been interrupted by military coups three times in the last 25 years), and, to some extent, in Lebanon, representative democracy and the idea of popular participation in the sharing of power have been unsuccessful in the region. At best, informal assemblies (*majlis*) have been the traditional way for demands to be considered. Where they do exist, parliaments have not been significant bodies, nor has meaningful opposition been tolerated. Lacking legitimacy in the Western sense of rules on popular election, some rulers have been tempted to strengthen their internal support by foreign adventures as with Libya's incursions, under Qadhafi, into neighboring African countries, or with Iraq's invasion of Iran in 1980.

The consequence of the fact that political activity is largely confined to the entourage of the ruler is that those outside the elite can only challenge the regime through insurgency, conspiracy and assassination. Recent predecessors of four of the current Middle East rulers, in Jordan, Egypt, Saudi Arabia and Lebanon, were assassinated; other rulers have survived assassination attempts. In 1982, Saddam Hussein of Iraq eliminated the town and inhabitants of Ad Dujayl after such an unsuccessful attempt.

The authoritarian regimes take different forms. Dynastic monarchies of the traditional kind still exist in Jordan, Saudi Arabia and the Gulf countries, and existed in Iran until 1979, with political power shared among the royal family and its advisers. Some regimes came into being as a result of military coups as in Egypt in 1952, Iraq in 1958, Libya in 1969 and the Sudan in 1985. The core of these regimes is the military which is a highly politicized unit and often the body that decides on political succession. Rulers in these regimes have often used organizations, such as unions, militias, the press and media, to bolster their rule and to prohibit any competing organizations. These military regimes have sometimes evolved into a third type in which a party or a movement is based, or purports to be based, on some ideological concept.

Examples of this third type are regimes in Egypt, Syria, Iraq and South Yemen. In 1962 President Nasser of Egypt created the Arab Socialist Union, with a doctrine called Arab socialism, to become the instrument of power and the basis for the mobilization of his people. Syria since 1966 and Iraq since 1968 have had an ideology of Arab Baath socialism which stresses the need for unity, the mission of the Arab nation in the fight against colonialism and the need for a new Arab consciousness, as well a claim that public utilities and natural resources be in the hands of the state. Some who participated in the overthrow of the Shah of Iran in 1978-79 hoped that the new regime under the Ayatollah Khomeini and the mullahs would embody a kind of Islamic socialism, a combination of socialist ideals and Islamic principles. Except in Israel, communist parties in the Middle East have been outlawed, though some intellectuals have been attracted to Marxism, but South Yemen now claims to have a Marxist orientation and is allied with the Soviet Union.

Though the Arab-Israeli dispute has received most regional and international attention, it is only one of the many conflicts and potential conflicts in the area. Historic animosities, conflicting ambitions, personal rivalries, religious differences, and territorial disputes have all played a role in the pattern of continuing violence. They account for the considerable proportion of gross national product spent on defense.

Some conflicts stem from differences over the demarcation of borders and territorial issues. A number of boundaries are loosely defined or may not be fully accepted by other countries. Syria and Iraq dispute the distribution of the Euphrates Dam waters and the pipeline for the transport of oil. Syria claims the Hatay province incorporated into Turkey in 1939. North Yemen has not given up its claim to the fertile Asir region of Saudi Arabia which it lost in 1934. Border clashes between North and South Yemen erupted in war in 1972. Islands in the Persian Gulf have been the subject of disputes and sometimes hostilities between Bahrain and Qatar, Qatar and Abu Dhabi, and Iran and Iraq. The destiny of the whole area of mandatory Palestine has not yet been resolved.

Other disputes arise out of rivalry for leadership, both national and personal, in the region. In recent years Egypt, Syria and Iraq have competed for domination of the Fertile Crescent or for controlling influence in the Middle East. These three countries differ from others in their ability to take initiatives and introduce new policies, though dependence on Saudi Arabia for financial aid may place some limit on this. Sadat in going to Jerusalem and then making peace with Israel, Iraq in attacking Iran in 1980, and Syria in supporting Iran against a fellow Arab state, all showed independence of action. Other states, however, such as Jordan and Saudi Arabia, are more likely to take account of existing local factors, align with the mainstream Arab position, and rarely move in important matters except in accordance with an Arab consensus, which thus would bestow legitimacy on any action. Since 1948 opposition to Israel has provided such consensus; a deviation such as the initiative by Sadat in reaching peace with Israel subjected Egypt not only to criticism but also to rupture of diplomatic relationships and exclusion from the Arab League.

A third type of dispute arises over religious differences or over the question of priority to be accorded the secular Arab nation or Muslim identity, or over interpretation of the *sharia*, religious law. The continuing Iran-Iraq war begun in 1980 is a struggle between the Sunni ruling group in Iraq and the militant Shiite regime in Iran, though it is also both a contest between an Arab state (Iraq) and a non-Arab state (Iran), and a war over disputed territory. The civil war and ongoing hostilities in Lebanon since 1975 have involved all the religious groups in differing combinations. In the Arab intellectual world, particularly in the Universities, clashes between adherents of religious fundamentalism and secular radicals have sometimes caused violence. Tensions cannot easily be resolved between advocates of allegiance to Islam, loyalty to the individual territorial state and concern for its national interest, and arguments for the creation of a greater Arab nation, transcending present national states.

As in other Third World countries, conflicts and social tensions have occurred as a result of the different levels reached in economic modernization and political development. The Middle East countries are differing mixtures of modernity and tradition, Oriental and Western cultures, wealth and poverty, with enormous disparity in resources, varying from per capita gross national product of $425 in the People's Republic of Yemen to $30,000 in the United Arab Emirates. The region is marked by rapid economic change in some countries largely due to the wealth stemming from the discovery and production of oil, a high rate of population growth, and migration, internally from rural to urban areas, and externally from the poorer to the richer countries. These factors have already brought social dislocation and the downfall of the Shah's regime in Iran. They may, similarly, imperil the social order or destabilize existing institutions in other countries, particularly the major oil producing lands in the Gulf. These lands have a very high per capita income and GNP, but do not have politically developed institutions, and they depend on expatriates from other countries for their economic modernization.

Political relations in the Middle East have often been fluid, and political actions unpredictable. Alliances between the countries have normally been loose and short-lived, especially those that involve Libya. Syria intervened in the civil wars in Lebanon from 1975 on, supporting first one side and then the other. Jordan in the 1970s allied with Syria against Iraq, then in the 1980s adopted a more nuanced position. Saudi Arabia supports some North Yemen tribes that oppose the central government in Sana'a. Yet it also finances the deficit of the central government which has often taken positions critical of Saudi Arabia.

Some of this unpredictability arises out of contradictions within the societies, some from changing events, and some from external pressures. If there have been a return to the veil by women in certain countries, the installation of a religious elite in power in Iran, and a high rate of illiteracy in most countries except Israel and Lebanon, there have also been an unprecedented increase in wealth, accumulation of modern sophisticated weapons, rapid increases in the general educational level, the establishment of advanced social services, and competing ideologies of territorial nationalism, socialism and Marxism from the West to compete with Islamic fundamentalism. If radicalism of the left seemed to gain support between the mid-1950s and the mid-1960s, religious militancy has been more significant in the 1970s and 1980s. If there is greater insistence on national self-interest, there have also been attempts at Arab cooperation in joint economic ventures and development and monetary funds.

Even the consensus on opposition to Israel ended with the unexpected initiative by Sadat in going to Israel and starting the process which led to the Egyptian-Israeli peace treaty of 1979, and which caused the division, which fluctuates from time to time, among Arab states and within the Palestine Liberation Organization into moderates and hard-liners on the issue of Israel and the destiny of the Palestinian area.

Relations between the individual Middle Eastern countries and the superpowers, who have sought to influence the area, have also fluctuated over the last 30 years. These changing relations may not reflect or be as dramatic as the kaleidoscopic picture of internal affairs. Nevertheless, the shifts in Egyptian attitude toward the Soviet Union up to 1955, between 1955 and 1972, and since then, and in the relation of Iran with the United States at different times, indicate that these relationships are not completely predictable or to be taken for granted. In studying the Middle East it is wise not to oversimplify a complex reality.

PART I
THE MIDDLE EAST POLITICAL ENVIRONMENT

1 Sources of Arab Nationalism: An Overview

By William L. Cleveland

When Sa'ad Zaghlul, Egypt's leading political figure in the early 1920s, was asked his opinion on Arab unity, he is alleged to have replied, "What is the sum of zero plus zero, plus yet another zero?"[1]. This attitude on the part of the leader of the state which was the center of both Arabic literary culture and Islamic reformism expresses the factionalism which has tormented inter-Arab political relations in this century. Arab unity, while trumpeted as the objective of Arab nationalist aspirations, has never been achieved. Part of the difficulty in establishing such a political union has been the diverse, and sometimes contradictory, origins of modern Arab nationalism. In part, too, it has been related to the political situation which prevailed in the Eastern Arab states in the years between the two world wars, a situation which gave a defensive and localized coloring to the nationalism then in the process of formation.

This essay attempts to examine the sources of Arab nationalism in the two distinct formative periods of its development — the decade or so preceeding World War I and the period between the two world wars — through representatives of various trends. It is intended to show that the concepts formed in the first period fulfilled different needs than were later required, forcing the ideologues of the post-World War I years to build new theories in the face of new circumstances. This, in my opinion, explains much of the uncertainty which is associated with the evolution of Arab nationalism.

The sources of Arab nationalism cannot be identified as having a single, common origin. Both loyalty and hostility to the Ottoman Empire, both religious intensity and rational secularism, helped generate the sentiments which led to nationalism. It is generally acknowledged that the three most dominant of these currents in the decade before the outbreak of World War I were Islamism, Ottomanism, and a growing sense of Turkish and Arab cultural distinctness which developed into two exclusive nationalisms.

By the turn of the century, an active Islamic reformist movement was underway in the Ottoman Middle East. Although its center was Egypt, it had its proponents in other major Arab cities of the Empire. The movement has been termed the 'defense of an injured self-view' in that it was a response to the political and cultural threat of Christian Europe.[2] Throughout the second half of the nineteenth century, the Tanzimat reform program of the modernizing Ottoman statesmen looked to Western European institutions as models. From the adoption of constitutionalism and new commercial codes, to permitting non-Muslims to serve in the army, the course of reform appeared to undermine the institutions of a divinely ordained society. And, if Westernizing bureaucrats failed to undermine it from within, the direct presence of European imperialism would certainly do so from without. It was as a reaction to these currents that Islamic reformism was born. Largely an effort to prevent the encroachment of Europe and the erosion of the Ott ,man Islamic system, the movement sought a revitalization of Islam both politically and intellectually.

For students of the modern Middle East, the names of Jamal al-Din al-Afghani (1838-1897) and Muhammad Abduh (1849-1905) have come to represent a watershed in the redirection of Islamic

Dr. Cleveland is Professor in the Department of History at Simon Fraser University. Among his publications are *The Making of an Arab Nationalist: Ottomanism and Arabism in the Life and Thought of Sati' al-Husri,* (Princeton University Press, 1971), and *Ataturk Viewed by His Contemporaries.*

thought. The former, a somewhat mysterious, itinerant anti-imperialist, saw in the revival of an Islamic consciousness the catapult with which to expel the contaminating Western presence from the lands of Islam. His doctrine mixed various reforming trends, and he blended them with "religious feeling, national feeling, and European radicalism."[3] While al-Afghani wrote little, his presence inspired young Muslims in the various lands where he resided, and these disciples carried on his program of activism after his death. Among them, the Egyptian, Muhammad Abduh is usually recognized as the most significant.[4] After an early phase of political activism, Abduh adopted a more restrained approach to Islamic reform than had his mentor. Working within the established system, he sought a spiritual purification of Islam which would strip it of its superstitions and lead to a reconciliation of divine revelation and independent reasoning, thus making the social principles of the religion compatable with the contemporary demands for change. In undertaking their reformist activities, both Abduh and al-Afghani recognized the threat from Western Europe. But they did not accept the long-term superiority of European civilization. It was the vigor of their response, the sense of possibility they had about them, that attracted young Muslims and gave to Islamic religious sentiment a politically-charged coloring. This Islamic activism played a significant part in the early formulations of Arab nationalism and, as recent events in the Middle East have shown, continues to be a reservoir from which all classes of Muslims draw strength in times of uncertainty.

In both British occupied Egypt and the Syrian provinces of the Ottoman Empire, Islamic reformism and Ottoman patriotism coalesced into a vision of the independent Ottoman caliphate as vital to the preservation of Islamic solidarity and the independence of Islamic territories from European imperialism. Ottomanism represented an attempt to evolve a sentiment of Ottoman nationalism which would embrace all the subject peoples of the multi-national Empire. But repeated Balkan revolts showed that the union could, at best, apply only to the predominantly Muslim peoples of the Empire, Arabs and Turks. The sentiment of Ottomanism, with its links to Islamism, was best expressed by one of its staunchest defenders, the Lebanese Druze, Amir Shakib Arslan:

> O' Ottomans of the protected kingdom, call upon God for your continued existence and for the removal of the [imperial] noose from your necks . . . O' Easterners, call upon God for the prosperity of one imperishable state so that the Middle East will never fail to have a government equal to those of Europe . . . O' Muslims, call upon God in all regions of the caliphate for the preservation of the spark of life of Islam.[5]

Although this vision would have to be altered with the collapse of the Ottoman Empire in World War I, it nevertheless served as the animating force for the majority of politically aware Arabs until the end of the war. It is important to realize that the late Ottoman period had an internal viability. One cannot view it merely as a prelude to Arab nationalism. Because nationalism was not seen by the Arab leadership as politically necessary, it was not debated; and it was for that reason that the Arabs found themselves without a nationalist ideology in the crucial decade after the war.

However, it is also true that the debates on Islamic reform and the nature of Ottomanism did give rise to sentiments which could later be developed into theories of nationalism. Two distinct sources of nationalist feeling can be discerned in the period before World War I, one of them historically consistent, the other seemingly paradoxical. Among the Arab Christians of Greater Syria, a sustained educational effort by European and American missionaries had produced a small but active new Christian intelligentsia in the region. One of the more enthusiastic observers of these activities, George Antonius, has remarked that they "paved the way, by laying the foundations of a new cultural system, for the rehabilitation of the Arabic language as a vehicle of thought."[6] It may be that the success was more measured than Antonius' assessment would indicate. Nevertheless, it is evident that in the wake of the new educational institutions came a rediscovery of interest in the classical literary tradition leading, in turn, to a Christian-dominated experimentation with new literary forms and to what has been termed *al-nahdah,* 'the awakening.' In addition to the aesthetic impulse, Syrian Christians demonstrated a receptivity to certain European attitudes not shown among Muslims. Syrian Christian scholars did not need to approach European concepts through the barrier of divinely revealed Islamic norms — for them, Europe was "not a threat to ward off, but a model to copy."[7] Thus, the secular constitutionalism which many Syrian Christians perceived as the explanation for European success could, they felt, be transferred to the organization of their own society. This, in turn, led some of them to disparage Islamic institutions and to formulate in their place a doctrine of Arab secularism which viewed Islam as one of several components of the Arab cultural heritage. This emphasis on Arab elements external to Islam can be seen as an effort to end the marginality of Arab-Christians in Islamic lands; it shows their desire to formulate a type of society in which a divinely ordained social order is replaced by a rational, secular one allowing Christian Arabs a full political role.[8]

The other formulation of a distinctly Arab component of cultural identity came from an unexpected source. The Islamic reformist movement described above raised many questions about the reasons for the current weakness of the Islamic world. It was only a matter of time before political rather than strictly theological answers were found. It was in the works of the Aleppine journalist and sometime administrator, Abd al-Rahman al-Kawakibi (1849-1902), that the nationalist possibilities in Islamic reformism were first expressed. For, in seeking to solve the problems of Islam in his day, al-Kawakibi concluded that it was the Turkish management of the religion which had corrupted it. To al-Kawakibi, the strength of earlier Islam was its close identification with the Arabs, most obviously its language, its Prophet, its geographical origin. This emphasis on the Arab role in Islam led al-Kawakibi to denigrate the Ottoman-Turkish contribution and finally to make the step from praising the Arabs' role in Islam to glorifying the virtues of all Arabs, both Muslim and Christian, which transcended Islam:

> Let the wise men among us tell the non-Arabs and the foreigners who instigate ill-will among us: allow us to manage our own affairs, understanding each other with the Arabic language, having for each other the compassion of brotherhood, consoling each other in adversity, and sharing alike in prosperity. Permit us to manage our affairs in this world, and make religions rule only the next. Let us come together around the same declarations: Long live the nation! Long live the fatherland! Let us live free and strong.[9]

Hence, in the defense of universalist Islam was found the source of a distinctly Arab cultural and political identity.

However, political action on the basis of al-Kawakibi's doctrines did not develop before World War I. Whatever Islam might show of Arab distinctness, it also showed that when combined with Ottomanism, it touched more deeply the majority of Arabs than did appeals to secular nationalism or political separatism. The pre-war ferment did give birth to various secret societies and loose political organizations. Increasingly active after the Young Turk revolt of 1908, these societies demanded more autonomy for the Arab provinces, especially in matters of education, language, policy and the selection of local officials. Their major achievement was to identify particularly Arab grievances and to cause the Ottoman government to respond to some of their reform proposals. In so doing they may have added to the tensions between a government which saw itself increasingly as Turkish and a minority which frequently asserted its cultural rights as Arabs. Yet, with the exception of certain Christian groups, their objective was not political separation. The name chosen by the most prominent of them, the Ottoman Decentralization Society, shows the desire for accommodation on the part of the Arab leadership, and suggests that Arab opinion, while urging reform and decentralization, favored continued existence within an Ottoman framework.[10]

This was changed by the events of 1914-1918. By treating the Arab provinces as potentially disloyal, the government alienated broad segments of the population from Ottoman policy and stirred vague hopes of an Arab existence separate from the Turks. At the same time, the Arab Revolt, proclaimed in Mecca in 1916, provided a more specific focus for those intent on gaining an independent Arab state. Yet even that Revolt was proclaimed in the name of preserving Islam, not in the name of Arabism or the Arab nation.[11] The titular leader of the Revolt, Hussein, the Sharif of Mecca, sought dynastic security and a permanent power base against his enemies in the Arabian peninsula. British gold and promises of post-war support appeared to offer better chances for Hussein than continued loyalty to the Ottoman government which had appointed him. No matter how much the Revolt has subsequently been sanctified as the cornerstone in the edifice of Arab nationalism, it did not, at the time, mobilize the Arab masses or their local leaders. Direct participation was limited to tribal levies and a few former Ottoman Arab officers. The affair was, to be sure, a revolt, but it was most definitely not a revolution. By rebelling against the Caliph of Islam, Hussein made himself unpopular among the very Arab circles in whose name he claimed to speak.

When the Ottoman Empire surrendered in November 1918, most of its Arab provinces had been captured by British forces supported by the levies of Prince Feisal (Hussein's son) from the Arab Revolt. In what appeared to be the final sequence in the dismemberment of the Ottoman Empire into its national components, an independent Syrian kingdom was proclaimed in Damascus, with Feisal as its monarch. Leading personalities from all over the Arab world, whatever their wartime loyalties may have been, were attracted to this new state in which their national destiny appeared to rest. Yet, in a story that has often been told, the decisions of the peace conference and the implementation of wartime agreements reversed the process which had led to the creation of the Syrian Kingdom. When the territories were finally apportioned in 1920 and 1921, France was in possession of Syria, Britain held the mandates for Palestine (including what was to be called Transjordan), with its accompanying obligation to implement the promise of the Balfour Declaration, and Iraq, as well as continuing to occupy Egypt. The pledges made to Hussein were sacrificed to inter-allied harmony and European security. For any student of Arab nationalism, the sense of bitterness and betrayal which accompanied the expulsion of Feisal from Damascus, the division of the former Arab provinces between Britain and France, and the encouragement of Zionist immigration, on however limited a scale, must form a constant backdrop to the character of the national ideology which took shape in the ensuing decades.[12]

•

As the first portion of this essay has shown, Islam and Ottomanism served as the principal factors of political solidarity among the Arabs before the war. But by the early 1920s, Ottomanism was irrelevant while Islam was suffering ever deeper humiliation at the secularizing hands of Ataturk and through the presence of European occupiers in the major cities of Arab Islam. It is not surprising, therefore, that Arab attention was devoted mainly to obtaining political independence from European control, and not to far-reaching discussions on social reform or the adoption of particular political systems. To the extent that this anti-imperialism was pervasive, it is correct to characterize Arab nationalism as negative during the inter-war period. However, even in seeking to organize their people for resistance to the foreign occupations, the Arab leadership generated an ongoing debate over what special elements of the Arab heritage could best be used as national symbols around which to organize the resistance and to shape the image of the independent Arab State. As Arab intellectuals had not created a clearly defined concept of Arabism before the war, it is natural that they confronted the changed circumstances as divided ideologically as they were politically.

The search to overcome these divisions led to a variety of proposals, none of which were fully realized, but all of which have contributed to the formation of Arab nationalism and continue, in one form or another, to appeal to most sectors of Arab opinion. In action that tended to crystallize the mandate boundaries, the special cultural heritages of certain regions within the Arab world were defined and political loyalty to them was demanded. The externally imposed political borders encouraged such localism, especially in Syria, where the French administration divided the region into four separate states (Syria, Greater Lebanon, The Jabal Druze, and the state of the Alawites) based on ethnic or sectarian concentrations. Representative of this regional trend in Arab nationalism was Antun Sa'adah (1904-1949), a Lebanese Christian, who founded the Syrian Social Nationalist Party in Beirut in the 1930s.[13] Although Sa'adah sought to overcome the divisions within Greater Syria, he belongs to the regional current of nationalism for his outspoken belief that Syria was a distinct and complete entity which should not be part of a larger Arab nation. In reaching this position, Sa'adah deplored the use of Arab history, religion, and culture as symbols of a modern, national revival. Instead, he proposed that Syrian history transcended Arab history and that Syria, as a distinct nation, was tied to the particular geographical and historical features which had interacted in the region from the beginning of human history. Here then, was one voice, one proposed resolution of the conditions created by the collapse of the Ottoman Empire and European occupation.

Further complicating the emergence of a pan-Arab ideology was the disinterested stance adopted by the majority of Egyptian intellectuals. Often, in the past quarter century, the Egyptian and Arab causes have seemed synonymous and of long standing. However, it was only the comparatively recent policies of the late Gamal Abd al-Nasser which thrust Egypt into the vortex of pan-Arabism. In the period between the world wars, Egypt was engaged in its own struggle for independence from Great Britain, and the foundations of Egyptian nationhood did not emphasize primarily Arab symbols. At the same time that Egyptians did not identify with Arabism, they were not seen as part of any projected Arab nation by Syrian or Iraqi politicians. Rather than Arabism, Egyptian patriotism was being focussed on a number of different cultural legacies. Although Islam was at the center of this, there was also an emergent fascination with the rich pre-Islamic past. The major symbol of Egyptian territorial nationalism, the great river which flows through the country, was eulogized along with the pharaonic civilization to which it had given birth. No writer of the time captured this sentiment more aptly than Hafiz Ibrahim, 'the poet of the Nile.' His Egypt declares:

I am the East's fair crown,
And grace her brow as she with myriad pearls
Adorns my throat. Can any thing be named
Whose loveliness the Western peoples boast
Wherein I have no share?

. . . Have ye not stood
Beneath the Greater Pyramid, and seen
What I have laboured? Have ye not beheld
Those magic carvings which defeat the art
Of any rival craftsman? Centuries
have not assailed their pigments, though the day
Itself turn color.[14]

In the face of these regional nationalisms, some Arab writers continued to assert the primacy of Islamic bonds in the formation of an Arab political unit. The uncertainty created by Ataturk's abolition of the caliphate and the increasing adoption of secular legislation in the mandated Arab territories made this issue one which aroused much concern. Two of the most prolific writers on the subject were Rashid Rida and his friend Shakib Arslan. Rida (1865-1935), through his Cairo-based journal, *al-Manar,* gained a wide readership for his ideas on Islamic reform. But he was also something of a transitional figure, a man whose starting point for social reform and political organization was Islam, but who, like al-Kawakibi before him, could not but emphasize the close bond between the religion and Arabness:

> My Islam is the same in date as my being Arab . . . I say, I am an Arab Muslim, and I am brother in religion to thousands upon thousands of Muslims, Arabs and non-Arabs, and brother in race to thousands upon thousands of Arabs, Muslims and non-Muslims.[15]

Shakib Arslan (1869-1946) was a Lebanese Druze who passed most of the inter-war period as an exile in Europe. Like Rida and others of his generation, Arslan could never completely forget his earlier loyalties to the Ottoman Empire and to the caliphate which symbolized the binding of Muslims under a single authority. But Arslan's approach to Islamic, and hence Arab, revival was not so concerned with theological points as was Rida's. His was a call for action, and he promulgated a militant Islam charged with political and moral assertiveness. In this, he is reminiscent of al-Afghani.[16] Although he stressed the Arabic core of Islam as the first political unit which should be created, Arslan was not a convincing Arab nationalist. He wrote essentially, and more persuasively, of the spiritual necessity of retaining the Islamic bond among the Arabs, arguing that it, and it alone, would prevent the collapse of the moral quality which gave, in the long run, a superiority to Eastern over European civilization. When Arslan asked, "Should our renaissance be essentially religious?" it was obviously a rhetorical question:

> If Muslims will resolve and strive, taking their inspiration from the Qur'an, they can attain the rank of the Europeans, the Americans, and the Japanese, in learning science and making progress . . . If we derive our inspiration from the Qur'an, we would be better qualified for progress than others . . . With constant discipline, with will and determination to march onward, and with correct understanding of the essentials of *Iman* — true faith — taught by the Qur'an, let us strive and continue to strive.[17]

In this is manifested the defensiveness so often associated with Arabic thought over the past century, the assertion that the imbalance so evident in the relationship between Europe and the East was not due to any inherent defect in Islam. Indeed, Arslan saw that a recognition of true Islamic principles would lead to a moral regeneration of the Eastern peoples which, in turn, would be translated into a political union of Muslims, with an Arab core, millions strong. In the face of this numerically and spiritually superior force, the shallow materialism of European civilization would be overwhelmed. Because of Arslan's insistence that activity would produce results, and perhaps because of his own appealing role as a sharp critic of European imperialism at the core of a European institution, the League of Nations, his message had a wide appeal and he received much adulation in certain quarters of the Arabic press in the late 1920s and 1930s. Yet, his version of an Arab renaissance looked to a bygone age for its inspiration and his impact was greatly diminished by the time of his death.

The third major expression of Arab political and cultural identity was formulated by those who rejected regionalism and Islamic sentiments in favor of secular pan-Arab nationalism. Their writings have kept alive the idea of a unified Arab nation bound by ties of Arab culture. This doctrine received its clearest exposition from the ideologue and educator, Sati' al-Husri (1880-1968). Although al-Husri himself had been a supporter of the Ottoman cause until the end of World War I, he adjusted to the changed circumstances by putting his Ottomanism behind him, joining King Feisal in Syria, and later in Iraq, and gaining a reputation as the most outspoken and consistent proponent of what has been termed a 'pure' theory of Arab nationalism. What has made al-Husri particularly significant in the development of Arab nationalist thought is his emphasis on the secular components of the Arab cultural heritage and his insistence that the consequence of recognizing these components is to admit the existence of an Arab nation similar to the nations of Europe which, like them, ought to be politically unified.

For al-Husri, the essential factors in establishing national identity were language and history. He wrote, "language is the life and spirit of the nation; it is like the heart and spine of nationalism, the most important of its components and characteristics."[18] If linguistic unity distinguished the nation, the unity of a shared history created the special personality of the nation, leading to "a mutual faith in the awakening and to mutually shared hopes for the future."[19]

From this general theory, al-Husri elaborated a more specific doctrine on the existence of an Arab nation. This nation was principally distinguished by its language and was thus composed of all who spoke Arabic — a vast region from Morocco to Iran. Al-Husri found unacceptable the regional stance of Antun Sa'adah or the anti-Arabism proposals contained in some of the Egyptian Taha Husayn's writings. For al-Husri, history had shown that shared language and cultural memories led inexorably to political nationhood and the power and dignity associated with that status. He was in the forefront of the pan-Arabists, and the full extent of his feelings are reflected in this refutation of Egyptian regionalism:

> Arabism is the strongest and most important of the ties which bind Egyptians to each other. This is because all Egyptians speak Arabic. We can therefore be certain that Egypt is Arab and that its future will be bound by the strongest of ties to Arabism.[20]

Nearly a quarter of a century after al-Husri inaugurated his journalistic campaign on the Arabness of Egypt, that country and Syria merged to form the United Arab Republic in 1958. Al-Husri claimed it was the happiest moment of his life.

Finally, al-Husri's stance on Arab nationalism was noteworthy for its uncompromising secularism. By refusing to approach the problem of Arab divisiveness from the perspective of Islamic civilization under attack, al-Husri naturally came to conclusions for the solution of that divisiveness which opposed those reached by Shakib Arslan and Rashid Rida. Arabic as a national language existed before Islam, he argued, and the loyalties contained in that language were the same for all Arabic speakers, be they Musli[illegible] those loyalties were to the Ara[illegible]

His vision stands in marked co[illegible] that of Shakib Arslan: "I believe only i[illegible] national tie which is based on language and history, and I regard the words 'East and Eastern and West and Western' only as geographical terms."[21] What al-Husri strove to do in his frequent articles was to prod his fellow Arabs into an awareness of their Arabism, their common cultural heritage. If this awareness could be generated, he felt that the hard political questions of how actually to achieve political unity would be capable of solution. Yet, while al-Husri's type of romantic nationalism came to have a great appeal and to represent the ideal toward which all Arabs should strive in a common cause, the reality has been disappointing to those who have felt as he did.

•

In the decades since the collapse of the Ottoman Empire, there has been tension among the proponents of these various alternatives to Arab political association. Each doctrine has contained a bit of the other and few have been as forceful in their disassociation of Islam from Arabism as al-Husri. Regional pride is a part of any group, but with the creation of the mandate territories, regional nationalisms — to say nothing of local administrative machinery — were generated to the extent that it became virtually impossible to subordinate them fully to the unity that men like al-Husri so ardently sought. The break-up of the UAR in 1961 may have represented the final failure of genuine political commitments — as opposed to propaganda campaigns — to the ideal of Arab unity. National interest has come to be defined in the individual terms of each of the several political states in the region, not by their shared cultural heritage. Events of the last four years in Lebanon, and of recent months elsewhere, would indicate that even within the borders of the Arab states, cultural pluralism, nurtured by social and economic grievances, has expressed itself more forcefully than have any sentiments toward unity. Amidst the sectarian [illegible] ies, and the [illegible] change, with [illegible] oriums, a con- [illegible] ms of all social [illegible] out to Islam. It is [illegible] nation of belief so [illegible] Islam of the variety espo[illegible] Arslan or, more recently an[illegible] rcefully, the Muslim Brotherhood. It [illegible] s though, given the apparent failure of pan-Arabism, there is a turning to the force which was linked with Arab greatness and respect in the past.

There certainly appears to be more expression of this sentiment at the moment than any serious talk about pan-Arab unity, despite the much-publicized discussion between Syria and Iraq. Plans for Arab brotherhood and cooperation may survive, but unification of the cultural Arab nation into a single political state remains an elusive dream, espoused by fewer and fewer public figures. Representative of this trend is the way in which Egypt is turning away from pan-Arab concerns toward its own internal affairs and a new affirmation of its own regional ties and symbols. A poignant example of this was provided by the extensive participation of the intellectual community in a recent debate in the pages of *al-Ahram* about the sources of Egyptian identity. That the debate had to occur at all is significant. That it included the following remarkable statement is even more revealing: "Egyptians are not Arabs, but they cannot disregard the Arab component of their destiny — shared culture and language."[22] Nothing better illustrates the still uncertain identities of the several Arab peoples whose cultural heritage embraces Islam, Arabism, and regional histories of great richness.

FOOTNOTES

1. Quoted in Sati al-Husri, *al-'Urubah Awwalan,* Beirut, 1965, p. 60. Throughout this discussion, the focus is on the Eastern Arab World.

2. For elaboration of this theme, see C. Ernest Dawn, *From Ottomanism to Arabism* (Urbana and Chicago: University of Illinois Press, 1973), esp. pp. 184-185. Other useful surveys of this movement are Albert Hourani, *Arabic Thought in the Liberal Age, 1798-1939* (London: Oxford University Press Paperbacks, 1970), Chaps. V, VI, VII; and Majid Khadduri, *Political Trends in the Arab World* (Baltimore: The Johns Hopkins Press, 1970), pp 55-69.

3. Hourani, *Arabic Thought,* p. 108; for a thorough biography, including a comprehensive bibliography, one should consult Nikki R. Keddie, *Sayyid Jamal ad-Din "al-Afghani"* (Berkeley and Los Angeles: University of California Press, 1972).

4. In addition to the works cited in note 2, Abduh's contribution is examined in Jemal Mohammad Ahmed, *The Intellectual Origins of Egyptian nationalism* (London: Oxford University Press, 1960); and Charles C. Adams, *Islam and Modernism in Egypt* (London: Oxford University Press, 1933).

5. Shakib Arslan, writing in the Egyptian newspaper, *al-Mu'ayyad,* 11 January, 1912.

6. George Antonius, *The Arab Awakening* (New York: Capricorn Books Ed., 1965), p. 40.

7. Hisham Sharabi, *Arab Intellectuals and the West: The Formative Years, 1875-1914* (Baltimore: The Johns Hopkins Press, 1970), p. 57. See also Robert M. Haddad, *Syrian Christians in Muslim Society: An Interpretation* (Princeton: Princeton University Press, 1970).

8. Haddad, *Syrian Christians,* pp. 5-6; 86-87.

9. Quoted in Khaldun S. al-Husry, *Three Reformers* (Beirut: Khayats, 1966), p. 104. In addition to al-Husry's fine study, an excellent analysis of al-Kawakibi and the developing currents of Arab consciousness is Sylvia Haim, *Arab Nationalism: An Anthology* (Berkeley and Los Angeles: University of California Press, 1964), esp. pp. 15-34.

10. See, Zeine and Zeine, *The Emergence of Arab Nationalism,* (Beirut, 1966); Haim, *Arab Nationalism,* pp. 31-4; and, for an interpretation which gives to the societies a more prominent and activist role, Antonius, *The Arab Awakening,* pp. 101-126.

11. Dawn, *Ottomanism to Arabism,* Chaps. i and iii.

12. The Arab perspective on these developments is eloquently presented by Antonius, *The Arab Awakening;* a useful synthesis is Elizabeth Monroe, *Britain's Moment in the Middle East 1914-1956* (London: Chatto and Windus, 1964), chaps. i and ii.

13. The most thorough treatment of Sa'adah is Labib Zuwiyya-Yamak, (Cambridge, Mass.: Harvard University Press, 1966); a useful summary of his ideas is found in Khadduri, *Political Trends,* pp. 186-194.

14. Quoted in A.J. Arberry, *Aspects of Islamic Civilization* (Ann Arbor: The University of Michigan Press, 1967), p. 363. See also Mounah Kouri, *Poetry and the Making of Modern Egypt* (Leiden: E.J. Brill, 1971); Nadav Safran, *Egypt in Search of Political Community* (Cambridge, Mass.: Harvard University Press, 1961).

15. Quoted in Hourani, *Arabic Thought,* p. 301

16. Arslan's ideas are summarized in Khadduri, *Political Trends,* pp. 181-182; the present author is currently preparing a manuscript on Arslan, tentatively entitled *Shakib Arslan and the Politics of Islamic Nationalism.*

17. Amir Shakib Arslan, *Our Decline and Its Causes,* trans. by M.A. Shakoor (Lahore: Sh. Muhammad Ashraf, 1944), pp. 134-135.

18. Quoted in William L. Cleveland, *The Making of an Arab Nationalist: Ottomanism and Arabism in the Life and Thought of Sati' al-Husri* (Princeton: Princeton University Press. 1971), p. 100.

19. *Ibid.*, p. 102.

20. *Ibid.*, pp. 137-138.

21. *Ibid.*, p. 161.

22. *The Middle East,* December, 1978, p. 14. The debate was begun in March 1978.

2

Arab Nationalism Today

By Carl Leiden

I

Nationalism, whether Arab or any other kind, is a conceptual matter of continuing controversy. It is of course largely ideological in nature and its diffusion among a populace is facilitated by such things as common language and culture. But the existence of such common features does not in itself produce nationalism. Nationalism seems best described as a *reaction* to threats or dangers, real or imagined; it is a sharing of discontent. Those who articulate its message react by intensifying the feeling of common qualities, particularly of common suffering and common exploitation; consequently it is an integrative process. But it is also a highly separative process since it requires a target group (or an alien ideology) for its full fruition. It should be emphasized that all sorts of groups, large and small, religious, class and so on, can assume the characteristics of a *nationalist* group, although it is true that we generally apply the term to large political populations. As an ideology, nationalism provides a rationale for action. Action covers the spectrum of target-directed vituperation, from verbal animosities to riots, demonstrations, terrorism and perhaps active warfare. Like all things political, it assumes less chaotic forms under the guidance of competent and perhaps charismatic leadership.

II

It is well to point out that the Arab world is not entirely an homogeneous body. Geographically, it stretches from the Atlantic Ocean to the Persian Gulf; it is difficult to *focus,* in a nationalistic sense, all Arab populations simultaneously and in identical directions. Political divisions continue to characterize the Arab world. Arabs differ somewhat among themselves, ethnically, religiously and in myriads of other little ways. The most obvious common feature of the Arab world is its language, but it is also fair to say that not all Arabs speak precisely the same Arabic and like fragments of the English-speaking world, they do not always take each others' quarrels to heart merely because of language.

But Arabs have shared two things in this century. They have shared a colonial past, at first Ottoman, and then French, British or Italian. And more recently, since the end of the First World War and specifically since 1948 when the state of Israel was formed, they have shared in their hatred of the Israelis. (But as we shall note below, even this hatred varies in intensity in the Arab world.) Moreover, for a few years, from the middle 1950s to the middle 1960s the Arabs possessed a remarkable leader in Gamal Abdel Nasser. These were the major ingredients in the modern form of *Arab* nationalism.

III

The Arabs themselves have for some time distinguished different forms of what they have meant by nationalism. *Umma* is the Arabic for nation (really *Arab* nation with the emphasis on Arabs as a people; originally the word had religious connotations) and *qaumiyya,* the sense of loyalty and attachment to the *umma* (hence Arab nationalism). *Watan* means the country of one's birth and *wataniyya* would be the equivalent sense of loyalty and attachment to that country and its people. It is assumed that the country (*watan*), in the sense of

---

Dr. Leiden is Professor of Government in the Center For Middle Eastern Studies at the University of Texas at Austin. His latest publication, co-authored with Dr. James A. Bill, is *The Politics of the Middle East,* Little, Brown & Co.

people, is a fragment of the *umma*.[1] Loyalty and attachment can be extended of course to domains smaller or at least different from both *watan* and *umma* and the Arabs have words for them. But what is important to us here is *wataniyya* (as exemplified in the expression "Egyptian nationalism") and *qaumiyya* which is that force, varying in intensity from time to time, bringing a large portion of all Arabs together as a united whole, sharing agonies and resources. It is the basis of that Arab unity that many Arabs have pursued with energy for such a long time.

IV

To properly trace the roots of Arab nationalism in *modern* times we must at least return to the period before the First World War when considerable restiveness under one colonial yoke or another characterized the Arab population. George Antonius has written the classic work *The Arab Awakening*[2] describing in detail the forces of this restiveness. Yet it is questionable whether, outside a minority of intellectuals and writers, the idea or concept of Arab nationalism was very widespread in those very early days. Egypt was certainly gripped in *wataniyya* nationalism (exemplified by Mustafa Kamil). But Egypt had proper boundaries with an identity — along with a British occupation — whereas the eastern Arab world was divided into Ottoman administrative districts (sanjaks and vilayets) that were not always very logically constructed. Terms such as Syria, Lebanon, Iraq and Palestine (let alone Jordan) did not exist as we know them today but were vague delineations for portions of Arab populated territory. It would be too much to expect to find even *Iraqi* nationalism (as we would understand it today) or Syrian nationalism at that time. But discontent and nationalism were there just the same; it remains to find a proper name for it. For the lack of something better this nationalism (such as existed in Syria before 1914) has been very commonly termed Arab nationalism but it was not quite the same Arab nationalism that existed in the Arab world in, say, 1958 (with the formation of the United Arab Republic) or for that matter today.

Much has been made of the so called Arab Revolt and the role of Sharif Hussein and his ambitious family in it. Despite our obsession with the Lawrence myth and an enormous mountain of literature the subject is still shrouded with some mystery and ambiguity. Without the space to document and justify my assertions let me simply state some conclusions that may be rejected by some of my readers. Lawrence was more of a charlatan (if sometimes unwittingly so) than anything else; militarily in any case the Arab Revolt was of little consequence. Hussein and his sons Abdallah and Feisal were primarily opportunists and did not properly represent legitimate strains of Arab nationalism so much as they did other personal, family, religious and local ambitions.[3] It is significant that if one separates two things from the mass of writing about what Robert Stookey has termed the "much promised land" — British promises to the Hashemites, to the French, to the Zionists and to others — one finds only a very small residue of Arab *qaumiyya* type nationalism. We must extract first of all primarily the anguish over the Balfour Declaration (1917) as it began to be understood in the 1920s by Arabs in Palestine and its immediate vicinity, and secondly, the emerging *wataniyya* nationalisms in the 1920s directed primarily against Great Britain and France. There was little then that generated the *common* sharing of discontent that is essential in my conceptualization of nationalism and Arab nationalism in particular. It is not insignificant that George Antonius first published his book in 1938, only a year away from the outbreak of the Second World War; already by this time the bankruptcy of British and French colonial policy in the Middle East was apparent, and in particular the agony of Palestine, with its struggle between Arabs and Jews there, had become paramount. What Antonius did was to write a beautiful and compelling rationale for the Arab *umma*; he talked about Arabs *qua* Arabs, he earmarked their enemies, he gave his *imprimatur* at least by implication to the later *idée fixe* of Arab unity. But his main thrust is about Palestine and Zionist ambitions there; indeed all his generalizations about Arabs seem to focus on the rights and fate of the Palestinian Arabs.

V

The major themes of this brief paper are simply told. Arab nationalism (*qaumiyya*) required two things before it could become a powerful force. It required a more compelling target than the old colonial powers. That target began to be formulated with the rising tide of Jewish immigration into Palestine during the 1920s and 1930s; it assumed its very real form in the middle of May 1948 when the state of Israel was founded. In addition to this, Arab nationalism required able Arab leadership. The roll call of available but inadequate men for this position is revealing. In Egypt there were King Farouk and Hasan al-Banna (the supreme guide of the Muslim Brotherhood). There was in Palestine the Mufti of Jerusalem, Hajj Amin al-Husseini. King Abdallah of Jordan was an eager candidate; so were Abdul Ilah, the prince-regent of Iraq and also Nuri al-Said, its perennial prime minister. All these and others had their ambitions to lead the Arab world to some sort of victory over the Jews (later Israelis) but the result of the 1948-49 war was not favorable to any of them. It was only in the aftermath of this war that *the* leader emerged; Gamal Abdel Nasser of Egypt. In short, Nasser and Israel were the symbiotic catalysts for the Arab nationalism that bloomed with fervor and excitement in the 1950s and 1960s and which still exists although in diminished form.

VI

Nasser did not come to his role quickly or even easily. However complex he later turned out to be he was in some fashion the simple soldier he claimed to be, the lieutenant-colonel who had led Egypt to a coup d'êtat in July 1952. It is well to recount some of the events in his early career as strongman, which gave him complexity (or at least revealed it) and ambition and opportunity beyond his earlier dreams. He consolidated his rule in Egypt and became in the process immensely popular. At first concerned about cutting down the old ruling classes by such things as land reform and selective nationalization and sequestration he was moved ultimately to concoct a social and political revolution that became in the Arab world a viable export commodity. In 1954 he finally got the British to agree to remove their troops from the Canal Zone. He dreamed of high dams but he also needed arms — as all strongmen do — to refurbish his army. He traveled to Bandung in 1955 where he was feted by those with heady names — Nehru and Chou en-Lai for example. In Bandung he discovered not only that he had *world* popularity (at least among those who were at Bandung) but that there were other arms merchants besides the United States and its Western allies. In 1955 then, came the famous Soviet arms deal with Egypt; it was to lead to the nationalization of the Suez Canal in late summer 1956 and was also to lead to the most fateful event of all, the second Arab-Israeli war, that with Egypt in October 1956.[4]

On the eve of the war Nasser was the incredible hero to Egyptians. He had given them identity and dignity. He had defied Egypt's traditional enemies and in one confrontation after another he emerged stronger than ever. Not unnaturally John Foster Dulles thought ill of him; Anthony Eden, the British prime minister, termed him a second Hitler, bent on "world" domination; and Guy Mollet, his French counterpart, worried about Nasser's activities in Algeria (in fact they were few) could only think of him as *merdeux*. Ben Gurion's views were more complex and were compounded of fear and uncertainty.

The British, French and Israelis attacked Egypt in October, 1956 (each with individual motives) and made Nasser the hero to all Arabs, at long last the leader for whom Arabs had been searching. Militarily he lost the war but he won it in every sense politically. What is important is this: already tempted to assume a role of Arab leadership (as distinct from Egyptian leadership) Nasser had little choice after 1956. Israel was the Palestinian Arabs' enemy; it was by now the enemy of Arab nationalists everywhere. It now became Nasser's enemy, for it had attacked Egypt and had humiliated the Egyptian armed forces.[5] There is considerable evidence for the assumption that the Nasser of 1952-56 gave Palestine low priority in his scheme of things. Had there been no war it is entirely possible (perhaps probable) that he would have moved to an eventual showdown with the Israelis in any event. But it is not certain. What is certain is that the Israeli attack in Sinai gave him no alternative. Now he could champion the Palestinian (by extension the Arab) cause while he sought revenge for the Israeli attack. Of course all historical reconstructions of this sort suffer from the charge of being simplistic. But had there been no war with the Israelis (especially the Israelis in conjunction with the French and British) there almost certainly would have been significant differences in the subsequent history of these two countries.

In any event, there is no uncertainty about Nasser's leadership after 1956 in the Arab world. He was wildly popular everywhere; his picture was the honored possession of Arab households throughout the Arab world. His attractiveness cut across class and group lines and the top rungs of Arab leadership in other countries were not immune to his charms. By early 1958 Syria had insisted upon union with Egypt (to be called the United Arab Republic). Backward Yemen wanted to join and in the early days of the July 1958 revolution in Iraq it was expected that this country too would join the UAR.

This was the peak of Arab nationalism and of Nasser's leadership. Things quickly began slipping. General Kassem in Iraq decided to maintain himself in power as well as Iraq in independence. Syria withdrew from the UAR in 1961 and Yemen was expelled from its associate status. Yemen itself broke out into civil war in 1962 and Nasser committed Egyptian troops there; it was his Vietnam. His disastrous war with the Israelis in 1967 sealed Nasser's personal fate as *the* Arab leader; even the Palestinians realized in increasing numbers that he was now a slender reed upon which to lean in their struggle for regaining Palestine. Nasser himself died in September 1970, just after King Hussein in Jordan had fought and expelled the major armed units of the Palestinian guerrilla forces. Certainly, Arab unity at that time was in tatters.

No *Arab* leader has emerged since Nasser's death. Anwar al-Sadat is unquestionably an Egyptian (*wataniyya*) leader, despite his frequent pious talk about Arabism. His trip to Jerusalem in late 1977 and his separate peace with the Israelis a year later underline this. Even the 1973 war with Israel (although Syria was an ally) was fought for Egyptian, not Arab ends. But the recent Baghdad rejectionist summit (November 1978) shows the bankruptcy of *Arab* leadership. Few decisions were made beyond denouncing Sadat and funding continued support for the Palestinians. Iraq's Ahmad Hasan al-Bakr is no *Arab* leader (in the sense that Nasser was); nor is Hafez al-Assad of Syria, nor King Khalid of Saudi Arabia, nor Mu'ammar Qadhafi of Libya, nor King Hussein of Jordan, nor King Hassan of Morocco (who seems more interested in Angola than Palestine in any case). Arab nationalism in a truncated form wanders, like Pirandello's actors, in search of something, in this case a leader. But the Arab world in late 1978 is split into so many factions and fractures that it is absurd to speak of a viable and unified political movement that could be termed Arab nationalism. Yet, the idea is not dead; it still possesses force and it is possible that it can be resurrected at some later time. But it is simply not what it was. Without leadership, it is also finding that the nature of its target has changed. The Israelis after all have come to be accepted by the Egyptians. Some other Arabs (and their leadership) are lukewarm in their eagerness to carry on continued warfare with Israel. Some, like Saudi Arabia in late 1978, are worried about other enemies that seem more real. All this is true in spite of the fact that the Palestinians have never been so strong nor so well funded (nor the Arabs in general so able to fund them). Undoubtedly, the

ficult to generate; specifically *Arab* nationalism in contrast to Egyptian nationalism (as an example) requires leadership of a high order plus a target group that all Arabs can single out as their enemy. That leader in the modern Arab community has been Gamal Abdel Nasser and the target has been Israel. This means that the full blossoming of Arab nationalism could only occur sometime after 1952 and before Nasser's death in 1970; probably it reached its apogee between 1956 and 1967 (the dates of two Arab-Israeli wars).

Today Arab (*qua* Arab) nationalism is largely leaderless. Moreover, Israel in the process of making peace with Egypt, is no longer the compelling target it was; it remains of course a very compelling target for Palestinian nationalism.[10] Troubles elsewhere, for example currently in the Persian Gulf, tend to dilute the forces of nationalism capable of being focused on Israel.

Arab nationalism is not likely to disappear but its peak in the twentieth century seems to have been passed; other nationalisms have taken its place while the turbulent politics of the Middle East continues.

FOOTNOTES

1. See Sylvia G. Haim (ed.), *Arab Nationalism. An Anthology* (Berkeley: University of California Press, 1962), p. 39.

2. George Antonius, *The Arab Awakening. The Story of the Arab National Movement* (Beirut: Khayat's College Book Cooperative, 1955).

3. At one time Sharif Hussein termed himself "King of the Arabs" to the embarrassment of the British. This claim had no basis in fact.

4. One thing always leads to another. Probably the most compelling factor in the Israeli decision to attack Egypt in 1956 (of course in concert with France and Great Britain) was the almost irrational Israeli fear of an Egypt that had been *rearmed*. The assumption was made that an Egyptian attack was inevitable once the arms to make it were available; therefore Israel should pre-empt. Today the inevitability of all this in 1956 seems less certain.

5. I am not unaware of pre-1956 Nasserite denunciation of Israel. But I am also not unaware of Nasser as a political craftsman, indeed a master craftsman, who used words and slogans for purposes that were not always congruent with his intentions.

6. They became surrogate targets for window smashing or the burning of embassies and information libraries (after all, there are no Israeli embassies in the Arab world).

7. Marshall G.S. Hodgson in his *The Venture of Islam. Conscience and History in a World Civilization* (3 volumes. Chicago: The University of Chicago Press, 1974) makes this point convincingly and beautifully.

8. For an interesting and unusual attempt to coordinate Islam and art see Keith Critchlow, *Islamic Patterns. An Analytical and Cosmological Approach* (New York: Schocken Books, 1976).

9. Particularly of course the martyrs of terrorism. In general see William B. Quandt, Fuad Jabber and Ann Mosely Lesch, *The Politics of Palestinian Nationalism* (Berkeley: University of California Press, 1973).

10. Many Arabs (and many Israelis too!) believe that Zionism is moribund if not dead in Israel. The Israelis have not been successful in attracting many present-day Jews in the Diaspora — and notably those in the Soviet Union — to settle in Israel. There is much evidence that this situation will continue. To the degree that it is true, Israel is less of a threat to Arabs other than Palestinians.

3

Pan-Africanism Versus Pan-Arabism:

A Dual Asymmetrical Model of Political Relations

By Opoku Agyeman

In the Fall of 1977, *Foreign Policy* observed that "... Africa is now at the center of the news. On most lists of potential world crises, it is second only to the Middle East as the possible scene of a bloody East-West confrontation."[1] Another publication, *Plain Truth*, echoed this opinion: "No parts of this unstable — and potentially unstable — world are more critical than the Middle East and Southern Africa."[2] And Robert McNamara, President of the World Bank from 1968 until 1981, titled an article in *The New York Times* of October 1982: "South Africa: The Middle East of the 1990's."[3]

In all, the designated source of this explosive potentiality is that "by a quirk of geography, these two regions contain the two most critical resources for the industrial world — oil and minerals."[4] What the Middle East in general and Saudi Arabia in particular is to petroleum, it is argued, Southern Africa, and specifically the Republic of South Africa, is to nonfuel minerals. Indeed, in terms of such strategic minerals as chrome, manganese, cobalt, platinum and gold, it is, as *Business Week* has observed, no exaggeration to call the highly mineralized region of Africa stretching from Shaba province in Zaire southward into South Africa's Transvaal Province "the Persian Gulf of Minerals", with South Africa as its "Saudi Arabia."[5]

From the standpoint of macro-politics or of super-power global calculations, the potential Southern African combustion is certainly both real and ominous. Viewed from the regional vantage, however, there is another potential source of commotion, bred by the same geographic variable — the relations between Africans and Arabs — and these have so far not been accorded proper attention.

On the strength of the nature and consequences of the historical links between Africans and Arabs over the last twelve centuries, it is the hypothesis of this paper that the two ideological-political movements of Pan-Africanism and Pan-Arabism are antithetical and that, in the final analysis, there is no room for the coexistence of the two on the African continent. An underlying premise of this hypothesis is that African-Arab relations have, to date, been woefully unbalanced and that this asymmetry, expressed in dualistic dimensions of internation and inter-racial political relations, has been weighted in favor of the Arabs and woefully to the disadvantage of the Africans.

It needs to be emphasized that the terms "Africans" and "Arabs" are used here as racial, not cultural, categories.

Dr. Agyeman is Assistant Professor in the Department of Political Science at Montclair State College, N.J. His essays have appeared in *Journal of Modern African Studies, Presence Africaine, Transition,* and other American and international journals.

THE DYNAMICS OF PAN-AFRICANISM AND PAN-ARABISM

According to the anthropologist and historian Chancellor Williams, the Arabs are "a white people, the Semitic division of Caucasians and, therefore, blood brothers of the Jews against whom they are now arrayed for war."[6] J. S. Trimingham's concept that the term Arab "has significance in a linguistic and cultural, rather than in a racial sense" and is therefore to be properly used in reference "to the result of the recent admixture" of Arabs and non-Arab peoples,[7] is not ethnographically accurate. The acculturated African in Northern Sudan is no more Arab than the Black American is white. "In studying the actual records" in the history of the races, then, as William counsels, "the role of White Arabs must not be obscured either by their Islamic religion or by the presence of the Africans and Afro-Arabs among them."[8] Indeed, the Arabs themselves insist that blood ties constitute the essence of their identity.

The Arab invasions and conquests wrought destruction on the ancient Ethiopian empire (which had incorporated Egypt and its north-eastern portion)[9] and had a negative impact on the successor black states of Ghana, Mali and Soughai.[10] Their slave trading in Africa was a destructive force that raged from the 9th through the 19th centuries on the Eastern seaboard of Africa, both preceding and even outlasting the transatlantic slave trade on the West Coast[11]. The wreaking depredations on the Sudan were the result of the murderous campaigns of Muhammed Ali at the beginning of the nineteenth century.[12] And not forgotten by Africans is the Arab complicity in the West's scramble for Africa in the latter part of the same century, in an effort once again to carve out an African empire for themselves[13]. Through this nexus of social, economic and political assaults, the relations between Arabs and Africans took on the confirmed asymmetry of perpetrator and victim.

Despite their awareness of the glaring disproportion in the exchanges between the two races, the Africans, supposedly on the basis of geopolitical considerations flavored with presumptions of Third World solidarity, argued their way vigorously, in the post World War II era, into a political alliance with the Arabs. As Kwame Nkrumah of Ghana put the case, Africa's freedom "stands open to danger just as long as a single country on the continent remains fettered by colonial rule and just as long as there exist on African soil puppet governments manipulated from afar."[14] The construct involved here is one of a "marriage" founded on the premise that both the Africans and the Arabs on the continent shared identical interests in the independence of Africa — that together they shared the aspiration of liberating Africa from, as Nkrumah saw it, the imperialist encroachments of the Boers to the South and the Israelis in the Middle East.

To analyze what is, essentially, a "marriage of expediency," and the nature of this "marriage," we must examine the dynamics of the two ideological-political movements of Pan-Africanism and Pan-Arabism.

Pan-Africanism

In its fundamentalist, Garveyite expression, Pan-Africanism calls upon "all people of...... African parentage" to join in a crusade to "rehabilitate" the race by establishing a "central nation" for it in Africa — "a country and government absolutely their own."[15] Drawing on the glory of Black civilization in ancient times, it proclaims the total possibility of Black achievement in the present. In Garvey's words: "Up, you mighty race, you can accomplish what you will!"[16] More elaborately:

> **We are the descendants of a suffering people...determined to suffer no longer. We shall now organize the 400 million Africans of the world into a vast organization to plant the banner of freedom on the great continent of Africa.**[17]
>
> **...We are determined to redeem our Motherland Africa from the hands of alien exploiters and found there a government, a nation of our own, strong enough to lend protection to the members of our race scat-**

tered all over the world, and to compel the respect of the nations and races of the earth.[18]

Wake up Ethiopia! Wake up Africa! Let us work toward one glorious end of a free, redeemed and mighty nation. Let Africa be a bright star among the constellation of nations.[19]

A cardinal tenet of this ideology is that "a race without authority and power is a race without respect."[20] Or, in Chinweizu's words: "Those who allow themselves to be weak have no dignity to claim... Those who want dignity must pay for it in the proper currency — power."[21] It goes without saying, Garvey emphasized, that the "white man" has the U.S. and the USSR, the "yellow man" has China, and the "brown man" has India. Where, he asked, was the black man's "massive and monolithic" political entity? Where was the African superstate equipped with modern weaponry and disposing massive military force?"[22]

Garvey's Africa-centeredness, or Africentricity, found expression in his Back-to-Africa Movement and was a logical development of his conviction that black people could expect no permanent or meaningful progress in any land dominated by whites or any other race. Indeed, he thought they could expect genocide.[23] It is no wonder, then, that in Pan-Africanist thought, the notion of Africentricity refers exclusively to the Africa of the Africans, of black people, and not to any continental mystique of a geographical area which includes Africa's invaders — whether they be the Arabs who set foot on it thousands of years ago, or the Dutch who made their incursion some five hundred years ago. In Chinweizu's observation: "The Arab world, even if part of it shares the same land mass with us (Africans), is still the Arab world. Their preoccupation is Pan-Arabism."[24]

Pan-Arabism

And what is Pan-Arabism? In a word, it is an ideological-political movement representing a conscious effort to create a united Arab nation. Its underlying principle is that the Arab states are parts of one indivisible Arab nation. Abd-el Nasser articulated this principle, for example, in justification of the then United Arab Republic's (of Egypt and Syria) interference in Iraq's internal affairs:

We are one Arab nation. Both our constitution and the Iraqi Provisional Constitution provide in their articles that we are one Arab nation. Accordingly, every Arab state has the right to defend Iraq's Arabhood and independence from Britain, the USA, the USSR, and all other countries. We are one Arab family in a boat caught in the tempest of international politics...[25]

There is no question that the concept of Arab "peoplehood" in play here is a racial one. Nasser himself affirmed this and made it clear that all other bases of identity among the Arabs — religious, geographic, etc. — are of secondary importance. Of the three circles he envisioned Egypt to be at the center of — Arab, Islam and Africa — the first, the Arab circle, stood out in pre-eminence. "There can be no doubt," he stressed, "that...(it) is the most important, and the one with which we are most closely linked."[26]

The Arabs are, of course, also very much bound together by a common religious heritage. Indeed, Islam is a core ingredient of Pan-Arabism. At the same time, being a more inclusive basis of identity, Islam embraces Turkey, Iran, Pakistan and other Islamic states which, Beling explains, by virtue of their non-Arabic languages, as well as their racial and other differences, are "excluded from the Pan-Arab concept."[27]

Even so, the crucial role of Islam as an instrument of Pan-Arabism should not be missed. In this regard, it is necessary to remind ourselves that the religion of Islam arose partly in answer to the indictment of Jews and Christians (according to Maxime Rodinson) that Arabs were "savages who did not even possess an organized church",[28] and partly in response to the state of feuding, separatism and decadence in which the Arabs were then mired.[29] By launching the new religion, by permeating the nature of his fellow Arabs with an autochthonous religious impulse, the genesis, instrumentality and language of which they could readily relate to,[30] Muhammad not only went a long way toward asserting the Arabs' creative genius, but also succeeded in transforming his fellow Arabs, replacing their jealousies and divisiveness with a spirit of mutual defense designed to promote common political and material interests. His success in this was indeed staggering, for almost at once Islam proved to be "the most important force" in the Arabs' political and social rejuvenation.[31]

Nor was this all. In its external ramifications, Islam soon triggered Arab empire-building as proselytizing brotherhoods "with an uncompromising aggressiveness unmatched in the history of religions" soon pierced into the heartland of Africa and beyond into Europe and Asia.[32] The essentially imperialistic, rather than beneficent or missionary role of Islam, is underscored by the fact, for instance, that it featured as an instrument of the Arab slave trade, for the slave trade and the religion were "companions throughout, with the crescent following the commercial caravan,[33] is further underlined by the fact that, revealingly, following the Moroccan invasion of Songhai in 1664, the African Muslims who had built and ruled the empire were not spared destruction by the Arab Muslims.[34]

To the non-Arabs, therefore, the utility of Islam, from the first, was seen to lie in its potential as a weapon for indoctrination, domination and, thereby, the augmentation of Arab power around the globe. In Nasser's own words:

> **When I consider the 80 million Muslims in Indonesia, and the 50 million in China, and the millions in Malaya, Siam and Burma, and the nearly 100 million in Pakistan...and the 40 million in the Soviet Union, together with the other millions in far-flung parts of the world — when I consider these hundreds of millions united by a single creed, I emerge with a sense of the tremendous possibilities which we might realize through the cooperation of all these Muslims...[35]**

From such a trajectory, it comes as no surprise that the remaining circle in Nasser's orbital schema, Africa, which he characterized as "the remotest depths of the jungle," featured as merely a candidate for Egypt's "spread of enlightenment and civilization" via Islamization-Arabization.[36]

At this juncture, it is well to sum up the essence of the Pan-Arabist ideology by noting that it is founded on the Arabs' belief, "illustrated by the jihads through which, in the 7th and 8th centuries, they spread Islam" into North Africa, Iberia and South Asia,

> **that in a rightly ordered world, dominion should belong to Muslims, and preeminently to the Arabs who gave Islam to the world. Since they not only lost dominion to the West, but found themselves overrun by the West, they have suffered from a feeling that the universe is out of its proper order. They have therefore, as Muslim Brotherhoods demonstrate, longed for a restoration of dominion to the faithful so [that] the world will be set right again.[37]**

In terms of goals, the cross-purposes of the two movements are self-evident. And this meant that any "alliance" between them could only be one of convenience and limited utility, confined to collaboration of sorts in the purely methodological realm of the adoption of means geared toward the elimination of the perceived obstacles (i.e., South Africa and Israel) and thereby, in the long haul, toward the attainment of what are fundamentally opposed ends.[38] The point cannot be overlooked, in this connection, that, outside the obligations of the "alliance," Israel, the adversary of the Arabs, was neither automatically nor necessarily the foe of the Africans, even as South Africa, the enemy of the Africans, was neither necessarily nor automatically the foe of the Arabs.

The Lack of a Mutuality Factor in the "Alliance."

It has to be emphasized, for all that, that even within such limited perimeters, the success of the "alliance" depended entirely on a mutuality of commitment to the limited methodological conjectures. And yet the evidence suggests that such a reciprocity was lacking from the beginning. The Africans drew upon, and were buttressed by, assumptions of Third World solidarity — "the shared experience of devastation and humiliation under the boots of an expansionist West..."[39] In Nkrumah's words:

> **The fortunes of the African Revolution...are linked with the world-wide struggle against imperialism. It does not matter where the battle erupts, be it in Africa, Asia or Latin America, the mastermind and master-hand at work are the same. The oppressed and exploited people are striving for their freedom against exploitation and suppression. Ghana must not, Ghana cannot, be neutral in the struggle of the oppressed against the oppressor.**[40]

For their part, the Arabs seem to have conceived of the "alliance" solely in terms of self interest. In particular, there was concern to ensure their continued access to the waters of the Nile which, to Egypt, "is a matter of life or death" in the sense that "if the waters of the river were discontinued or were controlled by a hostile state or a state that could become hostile, Egypt's life is over."[41] In Nasser's words:

> **The Nile which runs from Lake Victoria to Cairo is not merely a route crossing the...African continent to the Mediterranean, but is the path of life in the full sense of the word and with all its dimensions.**[42]

This anxiety over the Nile, as old as the Arabs' incursion and occupation of Egypt from 642 A. D., was a key motivating factor in Muhammed Ali's annexation of the Sudan to the Egyptian empire in the 19th century, and remains as acute as ever, as in Sadat's threat of June 5, 1980 to "retaliate with force" if Ethiopia interfered with the river's flow to Egypt.[43]

And now to sum up the essence of the matter. In the eyes of Arab leaders, Egypt is the most important entity in the Arab Nation. It therefore matters very much that Egypt's lifeline, the Nile, lies in African hands. A united and hostile Africa could strangle Egypt. Among other uses, then, an "alliance" between Africans and Arabs could be exploited to forestall such a unification of black Africa.

Organizationally, the "alliance" was born with the conference of Independent African States (CIAS) which Nkrumah convened in Accra in March 1958, and which assembled Tunisia, Morocco, Egypt, Sudan, Libya, Ethiopia, Liberia and Ghana, and where Nkrumah declared: "If in the past the Sahara divided us, now it unites us. And an injury to one is an injury to all of us."[44] We now proceed to assess the "praxis" of the alliance since its inauguration in 1958, drawing on case illustrations in African-Arab intercourse in the Sudan, Mauritania and the Organization of African Unity (OAU); on the triangular mesh of African-Arab-Israeli relations; and on the effect of Islam on African-Arab connections.

AFRICAN-ARAB RELATIONS

In the Sudan

The backdrop to African-Arab relations in this, Africa's biggest country (sharing borders with 8 countries, including Ethiopia) is provided by the Turko-Egyptian conquest of 1821 and the subsequent rule by a Turko-Egyptian government headed by Muhammed Ali which witnessed, among other things, the traffic of over one million African slaves for the Middle East market.[45]

This was followed, in 1898, by the Anglo-Egyptian colonization and rule, which ended with the granting of independence to a united Arab-dominated Sudan in 1956.[46] By the time of the launching of the "alliance" at the Conference of Independent African States (CIAS) in Accra, the Sudan had been independent for some two years, during which everything had been done to complete the process of the political incapacitation and economic disinheritance of the indigenous African population in the land.[47]

Even though the Sudan attended the conference, it came away from it with no wish whatsoever to achieve any Afro-Arab synthesis in the country in line with the spirit of, if you will, "methodological solidarity" which the "alliance" symbolized. On the contrary, the government continued the tradition of Arab predominance at the expense of the African majority. As a former Prime Minister, Sayed Sadiq el Mahdi, conveyed the point:

> **The dominant feature of our nation is an Islamic one and its overpowering expression is Arab, and this nation will not have its entity identified and its prestige and pride preserved except under an Islamic revival.[48]**

This inner purpose has been echoed over the years by successive governments and remains the guiding principle of the Arabs in the Sudan to this day. Thus, another Sudanese Prime Minister, Mahgoub, proclaimed in 1968:

> **Sudan is geographically in Africa but is Arab in its aspirations and destiny. We consider ourselves the Arab spearhead in Africa, linking the Arab world to the African continent.[49]**

Nor did the "revolutionary rhetoric" spawned by Ja'far al-Nimeiry since coming to power in the aftermath of a May 1969 *coup d'etat* amount to any radicalization of the situation, as some have maintained.[50] "The reality of the political situation", as Wai observed in 1979, "shows that revolutionary change is lacking" in the country.[51] Indeed, following Nimeiry's accession to office, the Pan-Arabists "gained disproportionately high influence", as reflected in his decision in the summer of 1970 to sign the Tripoli Charter which committed the Sudan, Egypt and Libya to a political federation.[52] When some Africans protested the new wave of Pan-Arabist effusion, expressing the fear that a Pan-Arabic federation incorporating the Sudan would convert the Africans into a minority and thereby worsen their plight, they were readily dubbed "racialist conspirators" and then arrested.[53]

Meanwhile, Nimeiry's Prime Minister intoned loud and clear the purpose of his government, for the benefit of those who still might misconstrue its essential character:

> **The revolutionary government, with complete understanding of the bond of destiny and forces of Arab Revolution, will work for the creation of economic, military, and cultural relations with brother Arab nations to strengthen the Arab Nation...[54]**

Not to be outdone, Nimeiry himself let it be known that the Sudan "is the basis of the Arab thrust into the heart of black Africa, the Arab civilizing mission."[55]

Even though the African majority's value systems resisted assimilation into the minority Arab culture, the Arabs insisted on seeing them as a "cultural vacuum" to be filled by Arab culture "by all conceivable means."[56] In consequence, under the Arab heel, a sizable number of Africans Islamized and Arabized themselves, even to the point of "giving themselves Arab genealogies."[57]

The ultimate ambition of the Arabs, however, as the official quotations cited above portray, was to have the Sudan wrenched from Africa and absorbed into the Arab fold — made into an integral part of the Arab world — on the basis of "the unity of blood, language and religion." To this end and, according to Allan Reed, at the further impetus of a desire to create room in the South of the country for settlement of displaced Palestinians,[58] they embarked on a policy of systematic extermination of the African population.[59]

Inevitably, through their own organization, the Sudan African National Union (SANU), the Africans resisted this regime of carnage; inevitably, this resulted in a civil war, pitting the SANU's Pan-Africanist nationalism[60] against the Pan-Arabism of the Arabs. It was a classic conflict between a people's yearning for political self-determination and cultural autonomy and, in the words of the historian Arnold Toynbee, the "flagrant colonialist" ambitions of the Arabs.[61]

Meanwhile, even as the Africans outside the Sudan, (perhaps out of embarrassment) affected ignorance of the strife in the Sudan, or found specious excuses for staying aloof from it,[62] the Arab world, for its part, threw in its collective weight as Syria, Libya and Egypt, among others, took on direct combat involvement against the out-gunned and out-supplied Africans.[63]

The 1972 settlement, which granted the Africans regional autonomy in the South, was a tactical accommodation that changed little.[64] Writing seven years later, D. Wai noted that the only thing that tied the two racial groups together was "a mutually hateful contiguity from which neither could escape."[65] It was an "illusion," he emphasized, to think that the schism that separates the two races had been resolved. For, despite the numerical superiority of the Africans, and despite the settlement, Africans still remained "at the periphery of central decision-making."[66]

Subsequent developments have more decidedly unravelled the expediency behind the settlement, in the thinking of the Arabs. Upon the discovery of oil in the South, Nimeiry moved, in February 1982, to unconstitutionally dissolve the South's ruling bodies, to replace them with a military-led administration of his own choosing, and to pursue a new policy of dividing the region into three sub-regions, the better to reduce the South's political influence and dilute its autonomy. When African politicians voiced opposition to these violations of the 1972 settlement, Nimeiry promptly had them detained.[67]

Not a synthesis, then, but the triumph of Arabism over Africanism is the tale of the Sudan in the era of the "alliance". According to O. Aguda:

> **The greatest achievement of Arabism in the Sudan has been the unquestioned acceptance by the whole world that this is an Arab state, in spite of the fact that only about 30% of the population is Arab. Indeed, the predominance of the Arab Sudanese in the country's culture, politics, administration, commerce and industry makes it *de facto* an Arab state.**[68]

The fact of the matter is that, invariably, the Arabs in the Sudan "have conceived of the universe as rooted fundamentally in Arabism. For them, as Wai writes, there is little disagreement about what national character the Sudan should adopt, and what its national aspirations and loyalties should be."[69]

In Zanzibar

The Arab slave trade and Arab enslavement of Africans in the lands they controlled were interrelated, indeed twin, phenomena. For centuries, African slaves in Arab hands served as domestics, eunuchs,[70] soldiers,[71] agricultural serfs, and as slave-gangs on irrigation works, in sugar and cotton plantations, as well as in gold, salt and copper mines.[72] Nor has the phenomenon evaporated into the thin air of history. Survivals, Bernard Lewis informs us, "can still be met" in Egypt, for instance, where the Nubian servant "remains a familiar figure...to this day."[73]

But our concern is not so much with the remnants of the odious institution in some specific Arab countries as with the parametrical continuities of it in the Arab world as a whole. What we are here addressing is an historical phenomenon which appears to have "continued without interruption" to the present day.[74]

Consider Zanzibar. It is difficult not to remember that the outrage of Arab wholesale enslavement of Africans in that island, which began in 1698 with the Omani Arabs' creation of a plantation economy and a commerical empire in the North-Western Indian Ocean[75] ended only in 1964 with the Pan-Africanist Okello's heroic overthrow of the Sultanate.[76] In the period between 1698 and 1964, Zanzibar attained a dubious distinction as the most important slave market in the Indian Ocean, became a land where being "upper class" meant that one was not only an Arab first and foremost, but also that one could afford a great number of African slaves,[77], and where the convention developed that, once born an African, one was "a slave forever, even in the next world."[78]

Indeed, the Africans were called *washenzi* —"uncivilized beings of a lower order"[79]— and, on this account, were considered to be deserving of every abuse. Thus it was customary according to seventeenth century chronicles to have the wombs of pregnant African women opened so that capricious Arab women could see how babies lay inside them,[80] even as it was fashionable to have Africans kneel for Arab women to step on their backs as they mounted their mules.[81] Slaves suspected of fugitive intentions had their necks "secured into a cleft stick as thick as a man's thigh, and locked by a cross-bar. Sometimes a double cleft stick was used and one man locked at each end of it..."[82] Routinely, men, women and children were killed or left tied to a tree for the scavengers to finish off when they couldn't keep up with the caravan, either through illness and exhaustion, or starvation, or both. Mostly, they were finished off with a blow from a rifle butt, or their skull smashed with a rock, as in the case of the child whose mother complained that she couldn't go on carrying him *and* the heavy ivory tusk. Ammunition was too precious to waste on a slave.[83]

Okello, upon visiting the island, and before singlehandedly planning the coup that overthrew the Arab regime in 1964, learned, to his chagrin, that a phenomenon he assumed to be buried in history was alive and vigorous in that land. He heard an elderly African lament: "My grandfather was a slave, my father was a slave and I too am now an Arab slave,"[84] heard the shrill retort of an Arab: "Whether you like it or not, you niggers and black slaves will forever remain under the flag of our Holy Sultan. We shall deal with you as we please."[85]

Significantly, Nasser gave the unqualified support of the United Arab Republic to the Arab oligarchy in Zanzibar. Like the old British Colonial Office, the Arab leader took the side of the Arab minority against the African majority over the future of the protectorate, prompting this comment from a British newsletter: "Zanzibar is a part of Africa and not the Middle East. The Afro-Shirazi are a more important group than the Arab minority. These facts should be taken into account before the protectorate ends. If not, there will be trouble in the sweet-scented remote islands..."[86] And, once trouble erupted in the form of an African *coup d'etat* which eventually ousted the Arab political order, it became the turn of Mu'amar Qadhafi of Libya to take up the championship of Arabism in Zanzibar:

> **Zanzibar was all Muslim, and almost all the people were Arabs...In 1964, the enemies of Zanzibar plotted and staged a massacre in which they slaughtered over 20,000 Arabs in Zanzibar. It was the most notorious massacre in the world...All the Arabs were annihilated in Zanzibar and African rule developed there..."[87]**

Partly in retaliation for this "massacre" of the Arabs. Qadhafi then set out, by his own admission, to support Idi Amin's Uganda in its war against Tanzania, the political entity that has, since 1964, incorporated Zanzibar.

In Mauritania

But if Zanzibar in East Africa represents an outrage that has only recently been ended, Mauritania in Northwest Africa, occupying as it does another vital zone of interaction between Arabism and black Africa, represents an ongoing and terrible anachronism.

The problem began with the invasion of "white Berber nomads" into the area in the first millenium A. D. An Arab invading force joined them from the 14th century and, in time, out of the fusion of the Berbers and Arabs, came the present ruling elite, "the white Moors."[88] Whatever residual biological differences separate the Moors from pure Arabs, they are now so completely identified with the Arabs linguistically, religiously, culturally and ideologically that, to all intents and purposes, they are indistinguishable from them. That the Arabs have fervently embraced them adds reinforcement to the point. Indeed, a number of historians, Bowdich among them, use "Moors" and "Arabs" interchangeably in their works.[89]

The official designation of this Northwestern portion of Africa is the Islamic Republic of Mauritania. As in the Sudan, the Pan-Arabist outlook of the political system has never been in question. Thus, upon the country's admission into the Arab League in 1973, President Ould Daddah pledged: "Mauritania will make every effort and mobilize all its energies for the Arab cause."[90]

Nor is it any surprise that a Pan-Arab Ministry was created in the country and that Jiddou Ould Salek, as its political head, reaffirmed, in 1979, the country's attachment "in its totality to Arabo-Islamic culture."[91] Again, as in the Sudan, policies of enforced Arabization of the indigenous African population have been the norm. For instance, in 1966, Arabic was declared the official language of the country, in the teeth of African opposition.

Out of a population of 1.5 million, the

Africans constitute approximately 400,000. They are *all* slaves, in varying degrees. As the *Anti-Slavery Reporter* has noted, no other nation has so many slaves.[92] Entry into slavery "is by birth, capture or purchase. The first... is the most common: being born to an existing slave woman...."[93] Purchase is still current: the sale of children, who incidentally, all belong to the mother's master, is the most common.[94] Even those Africans who have managed to purchase their freedom and who are thus legally free, continue to be regarded as property by their former Moorish masters. As *Le Monde* has indicated, whenever these "freed slaves" escape the grip of their former masters, they are hunted down by the police and the administration and quickly restored to bondage, all "in the name of an interpretation of Islamic law."[95]

Slavery is indeed the way of life in Mauritania. A typical sight in Nouakchott, the capital, according to Bernard Nossiter, is that of "slaves working in gardens and vegetable plots... while their Moorish masters sit under trees, sipping mint tea."[96] And the avenues of escape from servitude remain as elusive as ever. As recently as February 1980, demonstrations staged by the African Freedom Movement saw the movement's leaders arrested, held without trial for months, and then tortured to a point where some of them went mad.[97]

On July 5, 1980, as a way of "calming the slaves until the Government (of President Haidala) has had time to work out plans on how to cope with the anti-slavery movement,"[98] and in an effort to improve the country's international image, the Mauritanian government published a decree abolishing slavery. Those who knew that slavery had been formally abolished twice before and that the country's independence constitution itself proclaims that "All men are born free and are equal before the law," could only greet the new announcement with skepticism.

Indeed, when investigators of the Anti-Slavery Society visited Mauritania "to see how far the new decree was being put into effect," they concluded that it had had no practical effect.[99] No wonder, for "the upper and middle officials of the government, the judiciary, the police and the rest of the civil service" for the most part have their own slaves and are determined to keep them.[100]

As it happens, the most dramatic consequence of the decree seems to have been the government's decision to set up a national commission, composed of Muslim jurists, economists and administrators to work out compensation for the enslavers for the loss of slaves they have not yet incurred![101]

When the Anti-Slavery Society proposed that, to demonstrate its sincerity, the Mauritanian government should ratify the international convention on the elimination of all forms of racial discrimination, and the supplementary convention on the abolition of slavery, the slave trade, and institutions and practices similar to slavery,[102] this triggered a revealing rejoinder in August 1981 from the Mauritanian government. Mauritania let it be known that it was not the only country in which Africans were enslaved, and that, in any case, any effort "to wipe out this form of discrimination," no matter how earnest, would founder on the rock of Mauritania's technological under-development, "which makes all talk about human liberty completely derisory."[103]

●

In other words, until the country becomes technologically sophisticated, there is, in the thinking of the Moors in Mauritania, every justification for enslaving the Africans. As for Western critics, given the historical record of the West's own victimization of Africans, it was the Mauritanian government's view that they had no moral authority to hold a brief for the Africans:

> **It is very easy for citizens of certain countries who in the past developed this form of discrimination called slavery to its most debasing degree within a framework of pure Machiavellianism and sheer materialism: it is easy...for these people to try to relieve their consciences by setting themselves up as defenders of victims in countries which have not had the chance to experience technological development.[104]**

AFRICAN-ARAB RELATIONS BEFORE, WITHIN AND BEYOND THE ORGANIZATION OF AFRICAN UNITY

Algeria and Frantz Fanon

If there is any relief from the gloom of an historically victimizing Arab behavior toward Africans, it lies in Ahmed Ben Bella of Algeria's stirring rhetoric at the inaugural meeting of the OAU in 1963, pledging 10,000 Algerian volunteers for a showdown in Southern Africa:

> **A charter will be of no value to us, and speeches will be used against us, if there is not first created a blood bank for those fighting for independence. We must all agree to die a little...[105]**

It was the same Ben Bella impulse which dictated that, having itself only recently achieved its independence, Algeria would proceed to organize special programs of training for African liberation movements in Southern Africa. Among those who trained this way in Algeria was a corps of FRELIMO[106] fighters, including Samora Machel, the current President of Mozambique.

To better understand this Arab aberrancy, it is necessary to explore some background factors. These relate, for our purposes, to the tenacity of support which Algeria received from three "radical" African states (Ghana, Guinea and Mali) operating within the Casablanca bloc alongside two "radical" Arab states (Egypt and Muhammed V's Morocco) and the Algerian government in exile, the GPRA.[107] The three African countries not only gave recognition to the Algerian government in exile, but carried their support to the point where they boycotted the Lagos conference of independent states, held in January 1962, in reaction to the refusal of the organizers of the conference to invite the GPRA.[108]

Beyond such collective efforts, Nkrumah, for one, tirelessly proclaimed the justness, the moral imperatives, of Algerian liberation in international forums,[109] while also giving Frantz Fanon, the GPRA's Ambassador to Africa, a base in Accra from which to solicit support for the Algerian cause among the non-Casablanca African countries, and to work toward the opening of a southern front through the Mali frontier to ease the delivery of arms to the FLN.[110]

Hardly forgettable is also the selfless, even self-sacrificial, contribution of Frantz Fanon to the same Arab cause. A black man, and a native of Martinique, he was soon to discover in his travels that it was not only in Europe that a black person, "regardless of his level of education and culture, was always primarily a Negro- — and therefore inferior"[111], but that, even in the Third World, supposedly united by the struggle against imperialism, racism remained rife against black people. Thus, while he served in the Free French army in North Africa, "the eyes that turned to watch him in the street never let him forget the color of his skin."[112] In Fanon's own testimony, "...I was astonished to learn that the North Africans despised men of color. It was absolutely impossible for me to make any contact with the local population."[113] In all, he concluded, there was no question that the Arab "does not like the Negro."[114]

For all that, Fanon set out to counterpose universalism[115] to this virus of racism, Arab or otherwise, and, after studying medicine and psychiatry in France, and while serving the French government in Algeria in the fifties, formally joined the FLN in 1956.

From that time on until his death, he devoted himself, according to Irene Gendzier, "with the intensity and the enormous talents at his disposal to the many tasks he performed for the FLN and Algeria."[116] On the strength of a conviction that the plight of the oppressed knows no boundaries, he made Algeria, rather than Martinique or France, the focal point of his life. So seriously did he take his adopted cause that in 1958, while pleading the Algerian case at the Accra All-African People's Conference, he was so emotionally overcome that he "appeared almost to break down."[117] All this, even while he continued to encounter what he himself characterized as an "appalling" level of racism against Africans in the Arab world.[118]

Ben Bella, as one of the "historic leaders" of the FLN, was impressed by this multifaceted black support and so moved, after Algerian independence, to show his appreciation in reciprocal gestures both on the African scene, as we have noted, and inside Algeria, in measures commemorating Fanon.[119]

The point that must be stressed, however, is that these efforts at reciprocity, given their transience, are not so remarkable as the fact that anti-African tendencies inherent in the Arab world quickly extinguished them. Thus, within two years after his Addis Ababa oratory, Ben Bella was ousted from office by forces in Algeria which, among other things, deeply resented Ben Bella's "deviation" from Islamic fundamentalism and Arabocentrism, and which, in the post-Bella era, have been concerned to emphasize Algeria's "Arab-Islamic heritage" and to de-emphasize any African orientation in foreign policy.[120]

The ouster of Ben Bella and the reorientation of Algerian foreign policy is not unrelated to the de-Algerianization of Frantz Fanon. Visiting the country following Fanon's death and Ben Bella's ouster, Simone De Beauvoir discovered that "no one in Algeria spoke for Fanon." Similarly, Gendzier noted, writing in 1970, that Algerian officials "consistently avoid any discussion of Fanon's political ideas..."[121] Any suggestion that he contributed significantly to the Algerian struggle was resisted; indeed, there was a "concerted policy" to downgrade him as a theorist of the "Revolution"; to prove "that he was not even Algerian;"[122] to protect the "authenticity" of the "Revolution" as an all-Algerian, all-Arab and all-Muslim phenomenon. In short, as one official put it, the burden of official effort was to "de-Fanonize" Algeria and, in the process, to "de-Algerianize" Fanon.[123]

When all is said and done, then, Fanon's "fatal flaw" as Gendzier notes, was that he was neither Arab nor Muslim.[124] It is significant that, as far back as 1957, he was left out of the political inner circle — the National Council of the Algerian Revolution.[125] In a revealing confession, El Mili, an Algerian official, indicated that, had Fanon been an Arab, he would have been acknowledged as "the major theoretician of the Algerian Revolution."[126] (It is noteworthy that Fanon's exclusion from the inner council of the FLN occurred well before the Algerians achieved a settlement with the French, thereby making any further resort to violence unnecessary. On this account it cannot be said that the disownment of Fanon had anything to do with the philosophy of violence he represented.)

The reality that emerges from all this is that, for today's Algerian officialdom, what is of paramount importance is "blood ties as opposed to commonly held values".[127] Though Fanon helped their cause, he was black, and therefore not one of them, and therefore had to be repudiated.[128]

It is no less noteworthy that, either out of customary Arab contempt for things African, or as a function of the reorientation of national priorities away from African concerns, the Algerians have studiedly kept those of Fanon's writings that touch on the predicament of black people (such as the text of his statement at the AAPC in Accra in 1958 and of his lecture delivered at the Second Congress of Black Writers held in Rome in 1959) out of the limelight of print.[129]

There is no greater evidence ofArab repudiation of any Afro-Arab "common anti-imperialist front" than is offered by this dismal tale of the dispossession of Fanon in Algeria.

The Case of the Congo

Another specious fruit of the Casablanca "radical" coalition was the involvement of Morocco, the UAR and, later, Algeria in the Congo, ostensibly on the side of the pro-independence forces, as the crisis-engulfed country battled against Western neocolonialist penetration and dismemberment.

The Congo, "the heart of Africa", constituted, economically, geographically, strategically and politically "the most vital region in Africa", whose degree of independence, Nkrumah had declared, would substantially determine the ultimate fate of the whole continent of Africa.[130] If the "alliance" was to have a modicum of credibility, it was of the essence that the Arabs should be seen to contribute appreciably to the African effort to wrest the Congo from the neocolonialist web of the West, spearheaded by the Belgians, the Americans and the British.

The point attains special pertinence when it emerges, in retrospect, that the Arabs had, in their own right and in collaboration with the Belgians, played a not inconsiderable role in the rape of the Congo. As Edward Alpers has shown, the violence, degradation and rampage that accompanied the Arab slave trade was "most noticeable in the Congo...where the Arabs...totally devastated the countryside, killing and seizing hundreds of people in order to supply the ivory which was being sought."[131] Henry Stanley, the explorer, also had occasion in 1889 to remark, concerning Arab activities in the eastern Congo, that "slave raiding becomes innocence when compared with ivory raiding."[132]

Later — and significantly — King Leopold of Belgium entered into association with Tippoo Tip, the leader of the Arab slave traders, appointing him governor of his Congo International Association — its trademark was the use of "force of arms" to compel the Africans to exploit the country's wealth in rubber and ivory.[133] Tippoo Tip had earned the status of paramountcy because, more than any other Arab slaver, he knew how to "denude the back country" of the Congo and throughout East Africa "with the gangs of ruthless raiders who marched out every human being, male and female, that could not elude him."[134]

Against this backdrop, let us assess the contribution of the Arabs to the struggle for genuine decolonization in the Congo. In the early stages of the crisis of post-independence disintegration, Morocco and the UAR, in company with the African Casablanca powers, contributed troops to the UN peace-keeping force. Upon the failure of this effort (marked by the assassination of Patrice Lumumba) Moise Tshombe, widely considered the puppet of the West, assumed office as the country's prime minister. From that time, as is pointed out by Ali Mazrui, among those who were "the most forthright" in refusing recognition of Tshombe's accession were the "radical" Arab States.[135] This they did, Mazrui goes on to explain, out of a conviction that to recognize Tshombe was to forgive him for his betrayal of the Congo's independence.[136]

Upon a closer look at the evidence, however, it is not at all clear that the anti-Tshombe exertions of the Arabs in the Congo had anything to do with an altruistic urge to aid the cause of African independence. As part of the evidence, we must recall the brutal and terroristic career of the French *Organization de L'Armee Secrete* (OAS) in Algeria in waging for years, and to the very end, a hideous war in defense of French "civilization". Only Algeria's accession to independence drove the French colons, some 800,000 of them, from Algeria.[137] The connection between all this and the Congo is that Tshombe, in Arab eyes, committed an unpardonable offense when he recruited many of these die-hard former French settlers of Algeria into his army.[138] From all this, it would seem decidedly more plausible to attribute Arab opposition to Tshombe to a concern to settle old scores with the Congolese, rather than to any motivation to minister to African independence.

The interestedness of the Arabs is further underscored by the incident of July 1967, when the plane on which Tshombe was travelling was hijacked over the Mediterranean and brought to Algeria. The Congo government requested his extradition to the Congo to face a death sentence. In response, and quite revealingly, the Algerians made the return of Tshombe conditional on a complete re-alignment of Congolese foreign policy vis-a-vis Israel.[139]

Overall, the cutting edge of our thesis of, at best, Arab self-interest calculus and, at worst, Arab active antipathy to African interests in the Congo, as elsewhere, is provided by the role of the UAR and Morocco, by their contribution of troops and logistical support and, in collaboration with the U.S. and France, in aiding Mobutu to push back radical African insurgents across the Shaba province in 1977 and 1978.

Arab Interests and the OAU

As for the OAU, the organizational expression of the Afro-Arab "alliance" since 1963, its very composition bespeaks the familiar imbalance in African-Arab relations. Nine members of the Arab League — Morocco, Algeria, Tunisia, Libya, Djibouti, Egypt, Sudan, Mauritania and Somalia — are also members of the OAU. While, on this account, Arab interests are well represented in the OAU, African interests, on the other hand, are hardly represented in the Arab League. The membership of Somalia and Djibouti in the Arab League, far from aiding the counter-penetration of the Africans, constitutes the triumph of the Islamization-Arabization efforts of the Arabs. The explanation of Somalia's Arabization lies, firstly, in the age-old conversion of its people to Islam and the susceptibility to Arab influence that this engendered, and, secondly, in the seduction and entrapment of the country by Arab aid.[140] As for Dijbouti, even though its population is made up of the Issas (who are related to the Somali and the Galla of Kenya and Ethiopia) and the Afars (who are relatives of the African people of Ethiopia), its Arab puppet president, Hassan Gouled Aptidon, insists that the people of the country "are 100 percent Arab" and that this justifies his decision to adopt Arabic as the country's official language, as also to make the country the 21st member of the Arab League.[141]

It goes without saying that the Arabs have been doing everything to capture control of the OAU. This was apparent, for instance, at the OAU Summit in Mogadishu in June 1974 when all the Arab members relentlessly pushed for the candidacy of a Somali for the Secretary-Generalship of the organization, as against a Zambian candidate. As Mazrui observed of the incident: "At least among the English-speaking black states there was some bitterness. The behavior of the Arab States in their lobbying for the Somali was interpreted as an attempt to put the OAU under Arab or Muslim control."[142] This scenario was again played out at the eleventh annual meeting of the African Development Bank in Dakar in May 1975 where it became impossible to elect a new president of the bank because the delegates "were bitterly...and almost equally...divided between a Ghanaian and a Libyan candidate."[143]

Arab bid for influence in the organization attained marked success with the accession of President Moktar Ould Daddah of Mauritania to the chairmanship in 1971, of King Hassan of Morocco in 1972, and of the Islamized Idi Amin of Uganda in 1975, upon the holding of an OAU Summit in Kampala in July of that year.

It is significant that in spite of the manifest objectionableness of Kampala as the venue of the Conference in many African eyes[144] (and, on that account, the boycotting of the conference by a number of African countries) the leaders of six of the eight OAU member states which are also members of the Arab League[145] attended the Summit, highlighting, in the view of a Tanzanian daily, "the Arab world's determination to take Africa along with it in its Middle East policy."[146] The well-documented charges by international organizations such as the International Commission of Jurists, the U.N. Commission on Human Rights, Amnesty International, and the European Economic Community that there had developed, under Idi Amin, "a consistent pattern of gross human rights violations"[147] did not bother the Arabs one whit. Indeed, as Qadhafi pointedly told *Newsweek* in a 1979 interview: "That's not our business."[148] Clearly, Arab interests in Uganda were confined to the promotion of Arab interests — the establishment of a beachhead from which to work for the control of the source of the Nile[149] and also to make room for a large number of Palestinians.[150]

For the Arabs, then, the imperatives of the Arab Nation, rather than any concern for solidarity, albeit in a tactical "alliance", account for their membership in the OAU. It is significant, in this regard, that virtually all the Arab members boycotted the 1967 Summit meeting in Kinshasa on the grounds that Middle Eastern questions were absent from the agenda.[151] They were, and have been, interested in the organization only to the extent of holding it captive to their own purposes. That they have been markedly successful in this objective is reflected by the Organization's silence about Arab atrocities in the Sudan, Mauritania, as elsewhere, as also about Qadhafi's aggression in Chad and elsewhere, even as it vociferously condemns Israeli incursions into Arab lands.

The Organization's accommodation and indulgence of Qadhafi is especially revealing. Many African leaders have protested that the Libyan leader has been subverting their countries.[152] Many have denounced Qadhafi's aggression against Chad, manifested, in part, by his seizure of the uranium-rich Aouzou strip since 1973, and in his unconcealed bid to absorb Chad into an Islamic union with Libya.[153] Many have expressed concern about his self proclaimed discipleship of the Nasser doctrine of an Arab civilizing mission in Africa, and his ambition to create an Arab-Islamic empire across Africa into the Middle East.[154] They fear his demonstrated and menacing zeal to acquire sophisticated military capabilities, which would enable him to fulfill his anti-African ambitions,[155] yet he has been allowed to operate within the OAU and even to come close to becoming its chairman in 1982.

In the face of so much African acquiescence, Qadhafi felt at liberty in 1973 to initiate a boycott of the OAU's tenth anniversary celebrations unless the site was either moved to Cairo, or Ethiopia agreed to break relations with Israel.[156] To nobody's surprise, Ethiopia caved in and broke relations with Israel.[157]

It is a fitting tribute to the African self-immolation in the OAU that the issue which has now virtually paralyzed it is an intra-Arab one. The matter in question, the abortion of the August 1982 Tripoli OAU Summit, had nothing to do with African outrage over, for instance, Arab efforts to carve Eritrea out of Ethiopia and make it part of the Arab world,[158] but about which Arab interests, Moroccan or Algerian, should prevail in the phosphate-rich Western Sahara. The decision by the OAU in February 1982 to admit the Polisario Front as its 51st member opened a split that now mortally threatens the Organization. Meanwhile, even as the OAU wallows in the throes of demise, the Arab League is left relatively intact to pursue Arab business.

A second effort to convene a Summit in November 1982 also failed, this time on account of Qadhafi's effort to impose the exiled former leader Goukouni Oueddei on Chad.[159] Qadhafi, the prospective host, simply refused to admit the delegation of President Hissen Habre of Chad, presumably because Habre had proven to be less pliant. The Foreign Minister of Chad then requested "all African countries present in Tripoli not to take their seats at the sides of the enemies of Africa."[160]

THE ROLES OF ISRAEL AND SOUTH AFRICA IN AFRICAN-ARAB RELATIONS

The British offer, at the beginning of this century, to provide an area of land in their protectorate of Uganda for Jewish settlement in place of Palestine was rejected by the Zionist movement, but Theodore Herzl, the founder of modern politicial Zionism, had said, "Our starting point must be in or near Palestine. Later on we could also colonize Uganda; for we have vast numbers of human beings [in pogrom-torn Eastern Europe] who are prepared to emigrate..."[161] This has since jarred on many an African ear, yet it pales into insignificance when compared with the very real Arab atrocities in Africa.

Israeli protestations of solidarity with African causes have been as impressive as any professions made by the Arabs. Golda Meier, for instance, was moved to articulate the common experience and consciousness of oppression, discrimination, and slavery shared by the Africans and the Jews,[162] while Theodore Herzl himself wrote:

> **There is still another question arising out of the disaster of the nations which remains unsolved to this day, and whose profound tragedy only a Jew can comprehend. This is the African question. Just call to mind all those terrible episodes of the slave trade, of human beings who, merely because they were black, were stolen like cattle, taken prisoners, captured and sold. Their children grew up in strange lands, the objects of contempt and hostility because their**

> **complexions were different. I am not ashamed to say...that once I have witnessed the redemption of the Jews, my people, I wish also to assist the redemption of the Africans.**[163]

Upon occasion, it developed that there was more to such declarations than words. Thus in July, September and November of 1961, when the "alliance" between the Africans and the Arabs had already been struck, the Israeli government openly condemned Apartheid and voted at the General Assembly in favor of sanctions against South Africa.[164] Significantly, these efforts evoked reprisals from South Africa in the form of a rescission of the special concessions in foreign-currency regulations which allowed Jewish organizations to transfer money and goods to Israel.[165]

In spite of such travail, and despite the flourishing links that developed via technical assistance and diplomatic representation between Israel and Africa,[166] Africans made a habit of condemning Israel to please the Arabs. Thus, the All-African People's Conference of December 1958 adopted a resolution condemning Israel as one of "the main perpetrators of neocolonialism".[167] Three years later, at a conference in Casablanca, Ghana, Guinea and Mali joined Arab voices in railing at Israel "as an instrument in the service of imperialism and neocolonialism not only in the Middle East but also in Africa and Asia."[168]

In African eyes, Israel has committed a number of political sins against Africa. It maintains a legation in Pretoria and a Consulate General in Johannesburg. It received South African Prime Minister Daniel Malan as a State visitor in 1953 and in the 1960s sustained a flourishing trade with South Africa.[169] South African Jews are "the most ardent Zionists"[170] and their financial contributions to Israel are proportionately the highest of all the Jewish communities. Africans tend to identify Jews with Israel. Therefore the fact that Jews as well as Gentiles in South Africa support the racist system,[171] and that Israel is a direct beneficiary of the financial "blessings" of apartheid is troubling to them. And Israel took an anti-African stand on the equally troubling issue of the Congo, siding with Tshombe,[172] and it supported French nuclear tests in Africa, over spirited African opposition.[173]

It is one thing, however, to condemn Israel on these scores and quite another to castigate that country primarily to please the Arabs.

The Africans can be said to have fulfilled their obligations under the Arab-African "alliance" when they supported the Arabs in the 1967 Middle East war. Guinea, Somalia, Burundi, Zambia, Mali, Tanzania and Senegal were among those who vociferously declared their support. The general African reaction was captured in Senghor's statement: "We cannot...remain indifferent to the struggle which our brother Arabs are undergoing".[174] These gestures earned an Israeli retort: "Israel makes it clear to African countries that it could not provide effort, money and expertise for development if they repaid all this with anti-Israeli demonstrations."[175]

Undaunted, the Africans were even more forthcoming in support of the Arabs in the 1973 war, when almost to the last country, they severed diplomatic relations with Israel. This extraordinary display of solidarity was self-sacrificial in the extreme. As Mazrui elaborates:

> **A suggestion that Africa broke off relations with Israel for the sake of cheaper oil from the Arabs...distorts the sequence of events. By the time the OPEC dramatically raised the price of oil, much of Africa had already sided with the Arabs on the Palestine question...The trend against Israel in black Africa started in 1972, and had converted even Mobutu Sese Seko of Zaire to its side before the outbreak of the October war, while the energy crisis did not hit the world until about the last ten weeks of 1973.**[176]

To better appreciate the altruism in play here, compare this African response to the Middle East situation in 1973 with the African default over the cause of liberation in Rhodesia in 1965, when only a handful of states complied with a unanimous OAU resolution that member states break diplomatic relations with Britain over its foot-dragging policies. Overall, it is fair to say that when Feit declared that he knew "of no historical instance" where a people have "voluntarily invited unknown persecutions and sanctions upon itself for another",[177] he reckoned without the Africans. Inevitably, all these unrestrained demonstrations of Arabophilia triggered an Israeli backlash. "No longer constrained by the necessities of black African friendship", as E. A. Nadelman saw it, "Israel [now] pursued its relationship with South Africa with an element of vindictiveness."[178]

And how did the Arabs repay this extraordinary African gesture?

In the face of the emergency energy crisis that followed the Arab oil boycott, Africans asked for help and received a stingy response.[179] Afro-Arab relations were quickly reduced, in Arab hands, to inter-Islam relations, or at best to small and sporadic aid flows.[180] The so-called Bank for the Economic Development of Africa turned out to be an Arab and not an African-Arab bank, with decisions on all projects under consideration made solely by the Arabs. And as a commercial bank, and not an interest-free loan institution, the bank's objectives proved to be profit rather than aid.[181]

Reduced to supplicants, the Africans alternated between shrill calls for substantial Arab "reciprocity of Solidarity",[182] accusations of Arab ingratitude,[183] and empty threats of economic retaliation — as when, in June 1974, the East African Legislative Assembly at its meeting in Nairobi suggested that the Nile River be diverted by the East African States so that they could then sell its waters to the Arabs in exchange for barrels of oil.[184]

ARAB-SOUTH AFRICAN RELATIONS

At the emergency session of the Council of Ministers of the OAU in Addis Ababa in November 1973, a resolution was adopted calling on the Arabs "to extend the oil embargo to South Africa, Portugal and Southern Rhodesia until they comply with the United National General Assembly and Security Council resolutions on decolonization."[185] Significantly, four years later, in March 1977, at the Summit Conference of African and Arab leaders in Cairo, President Kaunda of Zambia both complained and pleaded that "Our Arab brothers should not be a party" to the aggressive actions of the Southern African racists by keeping up oil supplies to them.[186] The implication, in Kaunda's statement, that the Arabs still had economic ties with South Africa, was soon, if obliquely, confirmed by the South African Foreign Minister, Hilgard Muller, in a claim that South Africa had been neutral in the 1973 war and that it had sought systematically in "recent years" to build up contacts with the Arabs "by means of discreet diplomacy".[187] There were, indeed, reports of substantial deals between the Arabs and the South Africans, involving the exchange of oil for gold.[188]

What emerges then, is the triumph, once again, of the traditional imbalance in the relations between Africans and Arabs. As Thomas Land has reflected:

> **In theory, in exchange for the diplomatic isolation of Israel, black Africa was to enlist the support of the Arab north in unseating the white-minority government of South Africa. But, in practice, South Africa gained in the process by strengthening its ties with an increasingly friendless Israel, while it went on trading with the Arabs as well as the rest of the world.[189]**

These facts make the Africans' singling out of Israel's relationship with South Africa for special condemnation both hypocritical and irrational. Since African states maintain diplomatic relations with France, West Germany, Britain, Japan and the U.S. (all these powers have strong ties with South Africa) this insistence on the ostracism of Israel cannot logically have anything to do with Israel's relations with South Africa, but only with the Africans' compulsion to please the Arabs at the expense of their own best interests. It all fits into the traditional mold of the asymmetrical relationship between the Africans and the Arabs across the centuries.

Cast in this analytic light, the argument that the Arabs owe the Africans no political debts in that "most of the Arab world has treated South Africa as a common enemy for many years"[190] becomes lame. While, on the one hand, the Africans' break with Israel in

1973 had nothing to do with outrage over Israel's relations with South Africa, but was calculated to oblige the Arabs, the Arab sense of antipathy toward the South African regime is, on the other hand, due to such links between Israel and South Africa as the Arabs deem injurious to their cause (as in their furor over the intelligence that South Africa aided the Israeli air force during the 1973 war)[191] and has little to do with any sentiment of solidarity with the Africans.

ISLAM AND AFRICAN-ARAB RELATIONS

From the beginning, Pan-Africanism demonstrated a concern to cater to the spiritual needs of its racial constituency. It was recognized that every enduring race and people who have emerged over the historical expanse have had some concept of Deity and, on this basis, have nourished a religion which gave them strength and pointed them in a direction of positive achievement.[192] Such a religion has had to be autochthonous, in the sense, among other things, of visualizing the Supreme Being in a physical form corresponding to that of the people or race in question. As Garvey reasoned, no race of people ever made any impact on the world who allowed themselves to become enslaved to a religion which derogated and diminished them.[193] Succinctly put, again in the words of Garvey, "it is only the inferior race which worships an alien God".[194]

Islam, for the Arabs, bears the necessary hallmarks of originality and indigenousness. Traditional African religion, based on the intermediacy of dead ancestors, also fulfilled these requisites. That the Asante, for instance, cultivated and practiced it, explains in good part the remarkable durability of the political order they brought to bear in West Africa in the 18th and 19th centuries.[195] In the same vein, Pan-Africanism, at its dawn, sought to create its own religious infrastructure in the form of an African Orthodox Church which Garvey founded in 1920, proclaiming: "Our God must be seen through the spectacles of Ethiopia; our God must make us strong... not slaves to another race and another people... Instead of pictures of white Christs and Madonnas, the Church featured pictures of black Christs and black Madonnas. Instead of the inculcation of meekness and docility into the African congregation (the specialty of "alien" religions) the African Orthodox Church sermonized, "The God we worship and adore is a God of war as well as a God of peace..."[196]

Despite these efforts at an autochthonous religious institutionalization to underpin the movement, and owing to the disjunction, particularly since Garvey's demise, that plagues the doctrine and practice of Pan-Africanism, black people as a whole remain immersed in alien religions and continue to pay heavily in psychological disorientation and servility. Archbishop Emmanuel Milingo of Zambia's tribulations in this latter part of the 20th century, his admission that the African's continuing subordinacy to non-African overlords in spiritual matters is a reflection of "the inferiority complex which haunts Africa", and his plaintive cry that "To convince me that I can only be a full Christian when I shall be well brought up in European civilization and culture is to force me to change my nature,"[197] bear witness to the phenomenon in so far as the Africans' relationship to white Christianity is concerned. Significantly, the Archbishop's efforts to remodel the Catholic Church in Zambia in a manner more suited to Africa's spiritual realities stirred the concern, if not the ire, of the Papacy, leading to his summons to Rome, apparently for disciplinary purposes.[198]

The same continuing negativity has marked the relationship of the Africans to Islam. As we have intimated, Islam, the religious infrastructure of Pan-Arabism, has, from the first, been a source of Arab penetration of non-Arab societies. The fervent commitment of Arabs to the practice of Islam and, on the other hand, the lack of praxis in Pan-Africanism as much in religious as in nonreligious domains has meant that the familiar imbalance in African-Arab relations emerges in the field of religion as well. As far back as 1917, British policy makers expressed awareness, concerning the Africans in East Africa, of "a tendency on the part of the natives to call themselves members of the Mohammedan nation. . . ."[199] The gains of Islam in molding masses of Africans into Arabophiles have been no less spectacular in recent years, thanks to such additional impetuses as Nasser's 1961 pledge, as part of the UAR's drive to win influence in Africa, "to exploit Cairo's considerable resources in Muslim teaching and culture".[200] As Nadelmann has written:

> **The influence of Islam in the continent, where one of every four or five Africans is a Muslim has created a sense of identification and religious brotherhood with the Arabs to the North. Islamic Africans have often encouraged closer ties between the Arab and African states...comprising as they do the majority of the population in the Arab League states of Sudan, Somalia and Mauritania, as well as in Senegal, Mali, Gambia, Guinea, Niger and Chad, about half the population in Nigeria, Ivory Coast, and Ethiopia; and substantial minorities in Tanzania, Kenya, Cameroon, Upper Volta, the Central African Republic, Sierra Leone, Ghana and Benin. Africa contributes close to 50% of the membership of the Islamic Conferences...and its avowedly Muslim countries make up 40% of the total membership of the OAU.**[201]

Nor does Islam's influence stop at such psychological engineering in orienting millions of Africans toward the Arabs and their contra-African purposes. More directly and devastatingly, Islam, in its antithesis to Christianity, has been and remains a source of enfeebling separatism in various African societies. As Mazrui has noted, the spread of Islam through East and West Africa has served "to reinforce separatist tendencies. In Nigeria in the last decade before independence, Muslim Northerners . . . fearful of the political militancy of Christian Southerners. . .talked seriously of secession. The word 'Pakistanism' entered the vocabulary of West African politics."[202] Since then, Islam-induced disturbances have been the norm in the West African country. As recently as October 1982, rioting by Muslims in Northeast Nigeria erupted in Maiduguri, spread to two other northern cities and reaped a death toll of 452.[203]

Similarly, the Eritreans, "primarily Muslim," have been in rebellion against a longstanding Christian theocracy which was only recently taken over by the military government of Mengistu Haile-Mariam. Mazrui calls this a "Muslim bid to pull Eritrea out of Ethiopia. . ."[204] Noticeably, the Arabs, at the Eighth Conference of Islamic Foreign Ministers in Tripoli in May 1977 insisted that the Eritrea issue is essentially a religious problem and one that they reserve the right to resolve in their favor.[205] The secessionist movement in Chad, instigated by Qadhafi is, like that in Eritrea, "a rebellion by defensive Muslims against a supposedly Christian threat or hegemony."[206]

It is to be remembered that one of the conditions attached to the meager aid that the Arabs have given to the Africans has required the promotion of Islam in the recipient African country. Thus, for example, President Bongo of Gabon was compelled to change his name from Albert-Bernard to Omar in October 1973.[207] In Uganda, this took the form of a systematic persecution of Christians, who constitute the overwhelming majority in the land.[208] Visiting Uganda in 1974, Qadhafi demanded of Amin that he Islamize the country "at any price."[209] Amin himself would later admit that his decision to turn Fridays into days of prayer and rest was a price the country had to pay for continued Arab cash, especially Libyan.[210] Not surprisingly, at the Islamic Summit Conference held in Lahore, Pakistan, in February 1974, Uganda was admitted as a Muslim state, even though, according to the 1959 census, little more than 5% of the population of Uganda was Muslim.[211] In all, it has hardly mattered to the Arabs that the 1958 CIAS in Accra, in which all the independent Arab states of the day participated, passed a resolution attacking religious separatism as an evil practice which militates against African liberation and unity.

The emphasis on Arabic as the only vehicle for the comprehension of the Qur'an has added to the Arab edge in the equation. Adherence to the Islamic faith is, almost everywhere, virtually inescapable from knowledge and thought in Arabic. There is an inevitable connection between the faith and the language because, as Aguda has noted, "a translation of the Qur'an into any other language is regarded by orthodox Islamists as an 'interpretation' and not an authentic doctrine."[212] In consequence, the remarkable spread of Islam in Africa has been accompanied by the equally remarkable spread of the Arabic-influenced languages of Swahili in East Africa and Hausa in the West. Swahili has been adopted as a national language by Tanzania, Kenya and Uganda. It is in widespread use in such countries as Zaire, Rwanda and Burundi.[213]

Despite the low opinion of blacks existing in Arab tradition, black American leaders like Edward Blyden and Malcolm X have proclaimed that the Arabs and Islam are free from the infection of prejudice against black people. Yet the leading Middle East scholar, Bernard Lewis, has documented the reality of an association in Arabia of blackness, ugliness and inferiority — of "a very close connotation of inferiority attached to darker and more specifically black skins."[214] The Prophet Muhammad himself was known to refer to Africans as "the distorted of God's creatures".[215] And the Qur'an connects sin, evil, devilry and damnation with blackness, while whiteness has the opposite associations.[216]

At its most basic, the Muslim belief that black people are condemned to a fate of slavery by divine ordinance[217] is at the root of the Arabs' enslavement of Africans. Thus, despite the fact that Muslim law unequivocally forbids the enslavement of free Muslims of whatever race, evidence shows that the law was generally not enforced to protect Muslim captives from Africa.[218] The record shows that African Muslims in the Arab world "were regarded as inferior and subjected to a whole series of fiscal, social, political, military and other disabilities."[219] Nor has time changed these realities. Louis Farrakhan, the leader of the Nation of Islam, a black American Muslim sect, following a recent tour of Arabia, came away vociferously attacking the hypocrisies of classical Islam, especially in regard to race. He writes,

> **I see Muslims taking advantage of Blacks in Arabia and Africa. I will not jump over the black Christian to find brotherhood with a Muslim....The ghettoes in the Holy city where the Sudanese and other black African Muslims live are some of the worst I have seen anywhere...I see racism in the Muslim world...**[220]

Set against these facts, Libya's self-righteous assertions of Islamic beneficence to Africa attain a surreal quality:

> **Christianity equals imperialism, Islam equals freedom and the age of the masses-...Colonialism has exploited the Christian religion for its own interests especially in Africa...Islam did not come to Africa through colonialism but as a humanistic religion for the liberation of man.**[221]

Significantly, this rhetoric was tailored for the consumption of African delegations attending a conference of Islamic Foreign Ministers in Tripoli.

THE PERSISTING IMBALANCE IN THE AFRICAN-ARAB "ALLIANCE"

The grim tale of African-Arab relations that began with the Islamic whirlwind and erupted into the Arab slave trade is hardly buried in antiquity. On the contrary, over the years, it has been recharged and re-enacted, and remains a fixture in contemporary politics, albeit under the guise of an "alliance".

We have sought to establish that in spite of the "alliance", the imbalance has persisted. Arab aggression and penetration has continued, taking such detrimental forms as UAR and Moroccan intervention in Zaire, Saudi Arabian-Libyan machinations in Djibouti, Libya's invasion of Chad and, to this day, its occupation of its rich uranium fields, and Libyan-Palestinian adventurism in Amin's Uganda.

And Arab enslavement of Africans is hardly a thing of the past. It persists to this day, in such places as Mauritania, while colonization and forcible Arabization of Africans survives in such places as the Sudan. The assumed *quid pro quo* of the African-Arab alliance has worked one-sidedly, and to the Arabs' advantage. The very institutional expression of the "coalition" since 1963, the OAU, has become a virtual captive of the Arabs in the service of Arab interests. Despite the organization's injunction against the fomenting of religious separatism, the path of Arab imperialism has been oiled and smoothed by the weapon of Islam, whose spoils include the conversion of untold millions of Africans as well as the dissipation of the dream of black unity through the fostering of religious divisiveness among African populations.

There is a dualistic dimension to the asymmetry of African-Arab relations in the sense of a coincidence of racial and national imbalance in the political exchanges between the two. The sweeping victimization of the Arab slave trade and the examples of collective Arab racial designs and stances in the contemporary era (as in the push for a favored candidate for the post of Secretary-General of the OAU) establishes the racial dimension of the case, while the one-way street of lopsided international relations (as in Morocco's habitual intervention in Zaire's politics, Saudi Arabian and Iraqi penetration of Djibouti, Kuwaiti and Saudi Arabian meddling in Somalia, and Libya's aggression on Chad as well as its adventurism in Amin's Uganda) all underscore the inter-nation dimension of the equation. This duality of race-nation Arab-African superordinate-subordinate relations makes for a doubly asymmetrical model of political relations.

The postulate of an antithesis between Pan-Africanism and Arabism emerges clearly in the history of the past, the events of the present, and the prospects for the future. Should Pan-Africanism, now dormant and languishing, receive a practical boost and become activated and rejuvenated at the hands of some future generation of imaginative and purposeful African leaders bent on the "redignification" of the African people, there is no question that this would trigger a massive defensive or offensive rally not only by the white South African regime but also by the Arabs.

Over the years, the Arabs have been more committed to Pan-Arabism than the Africans have been to Pan-Africanism. While it is true that the Arab ranks have often been torn by disputes over means, it is still the case that even in disarray, the individual Arab states have, more often than not, made strenuous efforts toward the attainment of one objective or another of Pan-Arabism. With the Africans, the story has been different. Since the demise of Nkrumah, Pan-Africanism has fallen into limbo. A memory of the agony of African history, and a mature awareness of the ignoble contemporary realities of African life today should, under normal circumstances, be enough to ignite the movement once more, and give it urgent relevance and application.

But "normal circumstances" require a capacity for discernment, calculation and identification of vital interests. Unfortunately, this capacity appears to be in very short supply in the African world. The African presumption, in the face of the realities, of "solidarity", "alliance", and "brotherhood" with the Arabs is an example of that African eccentricity that makes it impossible for Africans to be Africentric in thought and action. As one African scholar, Chinweizu, has elaborated:

> **Having lost a clear and detailed sense of our identity, we have naturally also lost our ability to create a point of view of the world strictly our own. With our scrambled sense of reality we have forgotten how to see things in terms of our separate crucial interests...We behave as if it were some sort of betrayal to discover and insist on our own point of viewing the world.**[222]

FOOTNOTES

1. *Foreign Policy,* Vol. 28, Fall, 1977, p. 56.
2. *Plain Truth,* Summer, 1981, p. 6.
3. *The New York Times,* October 24, 1982, p. E21.
4. *Plain Truth,* Summer, 1981, p.6.
5. *Business Week,* January 29, 1979.
6. Chancellor Williams, *The Destruction of Black Civilization: Great Issue of a Race from 4500 BC to 2000 AD,* Third World Press, Chicago, 1976, p. 23.
7. Cited in O. Aguda "Arabism and Pan-Arabism in Sudanese Politics", *The Journal of Modern African Studies,* Vol. II, No. 2, 1973, p. 180.
8. C. Williams, *The Destruction of Black Civilization,* p. 24.
9. For the story of the antiquity of black civilization, the amazing heights it reached before recorded history, the foreign invasions that began around 4000 BC with the successive assaults of Western Asians and Europeans, Israelites, Persians, Greeks, Romans and Arabs, the ensuing deAfricanization and Caucasianization of Egypt, the southward migrations of the Africans in "a historic race for survival", and the final collapse of the Ethiopian empire in the 4th century AD see C. Williams, pp. 88, 125, 127, 159, 164, 167, 197; Walter Rodney, *How Europe Underdeveloped Africa,* Tanzanian Publishing House, 1972, pp. 63-64. Williams notes that the conquest of Egypt by the Muslim armies in particular "was not only to change the character of Egyptian civilization radically, but it was to have a disastrous impact on the dignity and destiny of Africans as a people". (C. Williams, *op. cit.,* p. 127).
10. For accounts of the high levels and the similarity of achievement by these successor empires, as well as the Arab role in their liquidation, see C. Williams, pp. 210, 211, 213, 214-217, 219, 223; Chinweizu, *The West and the Rest of Us,* Vintage Books, New York, 1975, p. 193.
11. Allan G. B. Fisher and Humphrey Fisher, among others have conclusively established that the overland Arab slave trade across the Sahara had become a matter of critical importance "centuries before the first slave crossed the Atlantic." (A. G. B. Fisher and H. J. Fisher, *Slavery and Muslim Society in Africa,* Doubleday and Co., New York, 1971, pp. 1-2. See also Bernard Lewis, *Race and Color in Islam,* Harper Torchbooks, Harper & Row, 1970, p. 28). For accounts of the "unbelievable cruelty" entailed in the "trade", of the inhuman essence of slave economics, and of the uses to which African slaves were put in the Arab world, see Leda Farrant, *Tippu Tip and the East African Slave Trade,* St. Martin's Press, New York, 1975; B. Lewis, *Race and Color in Islam, op. cit.,* Reginald Coupland, *East Africa and Its Invaders,* Clarendon Press, Oxford, 1938; R. Coupland, *The Exploitation of East Africa,* Faber and Faber, 1939; J. L. Burckhardt, *Travels in Nubia,* London, 1822, J. F. Buxton, *The African Slave Trade and Its Remedy,* London, 1840; R. N. Colomb, *Slave-catching in the Indian Ocean,* London, 1873; R. Hill, *Egypt in the Sudan 1820-1881,* London, 1959; R. Gray, *A History of The Southern Sudan 1839-1889,* London, 1961; P. H. Holt, *A Modern History of the Sudan,* London, 1936; G. Baer, *Studies in the Social History of Modern Egypt,* Chicago, 1969; A. G. B. Fisher and H. J. Fisher, *Slavery and Muslim Society in Africa,* London, 1970. The contribution of the slave trade to African underdevelopment is well analyzed by Walter Rodney in his *How Europe Underdeveloped Africa,* pp. 103-115, 144-5.
12. Described as "the greatest murderer of Blacks that ever set foot on the African continent", massacring men, women and children "on such a scale that even the white world protested", Muhammed Ali annexed the Sudan to the Arab Egyptian empire. See C. Williams, p. 169.
13. It is on record, in this connection, that the Egypt of the Arabs, regarding the Upper Nile "as her right and proper frontier, a black African backyard to be possessed and imperialized from Cairo in the manner of the European overseas empires", annexed Southern Sudan in 1874 with the assistance of European mercenaries. From this base, the Arabs then organized expeditions against Ethiopia in 1875 and 1876. In the end, however, hampered from achieving lasting success by its shortcomings in requisite resources for sustained imperialism, the Arabs teamed up with the British in an Anglo-Egyptian expedition which eventually overwhelmed the Sudanese nationalists in 1898. The ensuing Anglo-Egyptian colonization of the Sudan, with British and Egyptian officials jointly ruling it, lasted until 1955. (Chinweizu, p. 14).
14. Kwame Nkrumah, *Africa Must Unite,* International Publishers, New York, 1963, Introduction, p. xvii.
15. E. David Cronin, *Black Moses: The Story of Marcus Garvey and the UNIA,* University of Wisconsin Press, 1955, p. 16.
16. *Ibid.,* p. 70.
17. A. Jacques-Garvey, ed., *Philosophy and Opinions of Marcus Garvey,* Atheneum, New York, 1977, p. x.
18. *Ibid.,* p. 52.
19. *Ibid.,* p. 5.
20. *Ibid.,* p. 2.
21. Chinweizu, *The West and the Rest of Us,* p. 399.
22. E. D. Cronin, *Black Moses,* p. 16.
23. See A. Jacques-Garvey, *Philosophy and Opinions....,* Vol. I, pp. 63-64. Sidney Willhelm has expanded on this thesis in his *Who Needs the Negro?,* Anchor Books, New York, 1970, pp. 177, 266, 306, 309, 334.
24. Chinweizu, p. 494.
25. Broadcast over Radio Cairo and Radio Voice of the Arabs, April 18, 1959; cited in W. A. Beling, *PanArabism and Labor,* Harvard Middle Eastern Monographs, Cambridge, 1960, p. 28.
26. Gamel Abdel Nasser, *Egypt's Liberation: The Philosophy of the Revolution,* Public Affairs Press, Washington, DC, 1955, p. 111.
27. W. A. Beling, *PanArabism and Labor,* p. iii.
28. The Prophet Muhammad's French biographer, Maxime Rodinson, makes this point, which is cited in *Time,* April 16, 1979, p. 49.
29. B. K. Narayan, *Mohammed: The Prophet of*

Islam, Lancers Publishers, New Delhi, 1978, pp. 10-11.

30. It bears emphasis that the efficacy of Islam as an instrument of political and social transformation derived from its indigenous quality. To pull the Arabs "out of the deep rut of degradation they were embedded in", it was necessary for a new set of scriptures and a new prophet to emerge, "a man from among themselves, born and living among them, speaking their language and performing all the duties and functions as a member of their society..." (See B. K. Narayan, *Mohammed*, pp. 10-11).

31. The view of Ibn Khaldun, the 14th century Arab historian, cited in W. Rodney, *How Europe Underdeveloped Africa*, pp. 62-3.

32. See C. Williams, *The destruction of Black Civilization*, p. 215-6; W. Rodney, *How Europe Underdeveloped Africa*, p. 63.

33. Ali Mazrui, "Black Africa and the Arabs", *Foreign Affairs*, Vol. 53, No. 4, July 1975, p. 725.

34. C. Williams, *The Destruction of Black Civilization*, p. 223. This is by no means an isolated case. The historical sources are replete with complaints by black Muslim rulers about "holy wars" launched against them to take captives. The enslavement of black Muslims became very much the confirmed pattern. See B. Lewis, *Race and Color in Islam*, p. 68.

35. G. A. Nasser, *Egypt's Liberation*, p. 113.

36. *Ibid.*, pp. 109-110.

37. Chinweizu, *The West and the Rest of Us*, p. 494.

38. This concept of the "alliance" as necessarily expedient received practical affirmation from the beginning. Thus, despite Nkrumah's eloquent invocation at the 1958 Accra Conference of Independent African States of the "continental mystique" binding Africans and Arabs in Africa (see *Speeches of the First Conference of Independent African States*, Government Printer, Accra, 1958, p. 2), he and George Padmore, his Adviser on African Affairs, at the same time did what they could "and very effectively too, to hamper the Egyptians at the first meeting of the All-African People's Conference by reducing their proposed delegation's strength from a hundred to five". (J. R. Hooker, *Black Revolutionary*, F. A. Praeger, New York, 1967, p. 135).

39. Chinweizu, *The West and the Rest of Us*, p. 23.

40. Kwame Nkrumah, Address to the National Assembly, June 12, 1965.

41. The words of an Egyptian army colonel, cited in Fareq Y. Ismael, *The UAR in Africa: Egypt's Policy Under Nasser*, Northwestern University Press, Evanston, 1971, pp. 163-164.

42. Statement on September 22, 1966 during a State visit to Tanzania. See *The Nationalist*, Dar es Salaam, September 23, 1966. While the source of the Blue Nile lies in Ethiopia, the larger White Nile flows out of Uganda through the Sudan, where it joins with the Blue Nile at Khartoum to flow North through Egypt to the Mediterranean. Riparian rights are also shared by Kenya and Tanzania, which border with Uganda on Lake Victoria.

43. This was in retort to Ethiopia's complaint to the OAU that Egypt was abusing its rights to the Nile by diverting it to irrigate stretches of Sinai desert in a million-acre irrigation scheme launched by Anwar Sadat. (see *The New York Times*, June 6, 1980, p. A3).

44. Cited in Ali Mazrui, *Towards a Pax Africana: A Study of Ideology and Ambition*, Weidenfeld and Nicolson, London, 1967, p. 62.

45. Allan Reed, "The Anya-nya: Ten months' Travel with His Forces Inside the Southern Sudan", Munger Africana Library Notes, Issue No. 11, California Institute of Technology, Pasadena, California, February 1972, p. 3.

46. At the insistence of the Egyptians, the British excluded the Africans from the independence talks. Then, a few months before independence, the Equatorial Corps of the Sudanese army based in the South was disarmed and sent to the North, for fear that otherwise the Africans might break away from the imposed unit. (Allan Reed, "The Anya-nya", p. 14).

47. For instance, some 300 African workers on the Nzara Cotton Scheme were arbitrarily replaced by Arabs. As for the new Sudanization policy which transferred posts held by the British to the Sudanese, all the Africans got out of it was 4 posts out of the 800. The remaining 796 jobs went to Arabs. For additional details on the different economic fortunes of Africans and Arabs in the Sudan, see O. Aguda, "Arabism and PanArabism in Sudanese Politics", p. 199.

48. Dunstan M. Wai, "Revolution, Rhetoric, and Reality in the Sudan," *The Journal of Modern African Studies*, 17, 1, 1979, p. 73.

49. Interview with the Cairo weekly, *Al Mussawar*, March 29, 1968.

50. See, for instance, Ali Mazrui, "Is the Nile Valley Turning into a New System?", Makerere University, Kampala, 1971, mimeo, p. 25.

51. D. M. Wai, "Revolution, Rhetoric and Reality in the Sudan", p.93.

52. *Ibid.*, p. 83.

53. O. Aguda, "Arabism and PanArabism in Sudanese Politics", *Journal of Modern African Studies*, Vol. II, No. 2, 1973, pp. 177-8.

54. *Ibid.*, p. 178.

55. See Allan Reed, "The Anya-nya", p. 27.

56. D. M. Wai, "Revolution, Rhetoric and Reality in the Sudan", p. 73.

57. O. Aguda, "Arabism and PanArabism in Sudanese Politics", p. 183. See also D. M. Wai, "Revolution, Rhetoric and Reality in the Sudan", pp. 72-73.

58. See Allan Reed, "The Anya-nya", p. 29; A. Mazrui, "Is the Nile Valley Emerging as a New Political System?", p. 44.

59. By July 1965, as Allan Reed has ably chronicled, the intellectual class among the Africans, in particular, had become the object of a furious extermination campaign. (See "The Anya-nya", p. 12). Nor did this policy of extermination change under successive governments. As late as December 1969, Allan Reed witnessed the bombings of the cattle camps in Upper Nile. As he later wrote: "I passed through villages that were totally levelled, just a few months after Nimeiry had talked about regional autonomy" (*Ibid.*, p. 13). Writing in 1968, *The Daily Nation* lamented that for years "whole villages have been destroyed" and untold atrocities committed by the Sudanese army. (*Daily Nation*,

(Nairobi), Editorial, "The Sudan Question", July 22, 1968).

60. For the essentially PanAfricanist ideology of SANU and its military wing, the "Anya-nya", see Allan Reed, "The Anya-nya", p. 26.

61. Interview in *Playboy*, London, April 1968, cited in D. M. Wai, "Revolution, Rhetoric and Reality in the Sudan," p. 73.

62. Thus, Nyerere, while he volubly took up the cause of Biafra in the Nigerian civil war, at the same time downplayed the tragedy in the Sudan on the grounds that foreign interests were not involved in the conflict. (See Extracts from a Tanzanian Government pamphlet on the Nigerian-Biafran Crisis", issued at the OAU Summit of 1968, in *West Africa*, 2665, June 29, 1968, p. 745). This argument, of course, flew in the face of the facts, as virtually the whole Arab world, the USSR and Israel, were deeply embroiled in it.

63. See Allan Reed, "The Anya-nya", pp. 13, 29, 33; Ali Mazrui, "Is the Nile Valley Turning into a new Political System?", Kampala, 1971, mimeo, p. 41.

64. For the changing configuration of forces within the country which forced Nimeiry's hand and brought about the "settlement", see O. Aguda, "Arabism and PanArabism in Sudanese Politics", pp. 197-8; D. M. Wai, "Revolution, Rhetoric and Reality in the Sudan", p. 84).

65. D. M. Wai, *Ibid.*, p. 88.

66. Only one person from the South was represented in the Cabinet; only one out of the 45 ambassadors was from the South; only 8 out of the more than 200 Sudanese in the diplomatic service were from the South (See D. M. Wai, pp. 88n, 89).

67. *The New York Times*, February 17, 1982, p. A2; and February 22, 1982, p. A7. The petroleum reserves in the South are sizable enough to have caused Standard Oil of California to spend about $300 million on exploration. See *The New York Times*, February 22, 1982, p. A7).

68. O. Aguda, "Arabism and Pan-Arabism...", p. 177.

69. D. M. Wai, p. 73.

70. Known as the "guardians of female virtue", these African eunuchs served in harems throughout Arabia. Thousands of African boys between eight and ten years old were castrated every year and the survivors of the crude and painful operation reared into eunuchs. (See B. Lewis, *Race and Color in Islam*, p. 85; Leda Farrant, *Tippu Tip and the East African Slave Trade*, St. Martin's Press, New York, 1975, p. 2).

71. The tendency was for these African military slaves, once they had outlived their usefulness, to be betrayed into slaughter by those they served self-sacrificially. (B. Lewis, *Race and Color in Islam*, pp. 69, 70, 72, 77).

72. W. Rodney, *How Europe Underdeveloped Africa*, p. 158; B. Lewis, *Race and Color in Islam*, pp. 65-66, 89.

73. B. Lewis, *Race and Color in Islam*, p. 82.

74. B. Lewis, *Ibid.*, p. 81; E. P. Alexandrov, *Political Economy of Capitalism*, Moscow, p. 60.

75. Edward A. Alpers, *The East African Slave Trade*, Historical Association of Tanzania, Paper No. 3, East African Publishing House, Nairobi, 1967, p. 10.

76. See John Okello, *Revolution in Zanzibar*, East African Publishing House, Nairobi, 1967.

77. L. Farrant, *Tippu Tip....*, p. 2.

78. B. Lewis, *Race and Color in Islam*, p. 7.

79. L. Farrant, *Tippu Tip....*, p. 9.

80. J. Okello, *Revolution in Zanzibar*, p. 108.

81. L. Farrant, *Tippu Tip.......*, p. 146.

82. *Ibid.*, p. 16.

83. *Ibid.*, p. 15.

84. J. Okello, *Revolution in Zanzibar*, p. 88.

85. *Ibid.*, p. 95.

86. A Confidential Newsletter, July 15, 1960.

87. Qadhafi, speaking at a rally at the Tripoli Sports Stadium to mark the anniversary of the Italian evacuation from Libya on October 7, 1972; cited in *Daily News*, Dar Es Salaam, November 6, 1972.

88. *Anti-Slavery Reporter: The Anti-Slavery Society for the Protection of Human Rights*, series VII, Vol. 13, No. 1, December 1981, p. 16.

89. See, I. Wilks, *Asante in the Nineteenth Century*, Cambridge University Press, London, 1975, particularly pp. 238-314.

90. *West Africa*, 2947, December 3, 1973, p. 1711.

91. Confidential Newsletter, February 28, 1979.

92. *Anti-Slavery Reporter*, p. 17.

93. *Ibid.*

94. *Ibid.*

95. Cited in *Africa News*, August 4, 1980, pp. 2, 11.

96. B. D. Nossiter, "UN Gets a Report on Slaves", *The New York Times*, August 26, 1981, p. A11.

97. *Anti-Slavery Reporter*, p. 17.

98. *Ibid.*, p. 18.

99. *Ibid.*, p. 16.

100. *Ibid.*, p. 17.

101. *Africa News*, August 4, 1980, pp. 2 and 11.

102. *Anti-Slavery Reporter*, p. 18.

103. Cited in *Ibid.*, p. 20.

104. *Ibid.*, p. 20.

105. *West Africa*, 2743, December 27, 1969.

106. Abbreviation for *Frente de Libertaçao de Moçambique*.

107. Abbreviation for *Le gouvernment provisoire de la republique algerienne*.

108. Kwame Nkrumah, *Africa Must Unite*, International Publishers, New York, 1963, p. 148.

109. See, for instance, Ali Mazrui, *Towards a Pax Africana*, p. 63; K. Nkrumah, *I Speak of Freedom*, Praeger Paperbacks, New York, 1961, p. 272.

110. Irene L. Gendzier, *Frantz Fanon: A Critical Study*, Pantheon Books, New York, 1973, p. 188; F. Fanon, *Toward The African Revolution*, Grove Press, New York, 1967, p. 177.

111. David Caute, *Frantz Fanon*, The Viking Press, New York, 1970, p. 3.

112. Observation by Simone de Beauvoir, cited in David Caute, *ibid.*, p. 4.

113. F. Fanon, *Black Skin, White Masks*, Grove Press, New York, 1967, pp. 102-103.

114. *Ibid.*

115. Fanon defined this in terms of "faith in common values based primarily on the dignity and grandeur of men, of all men". (See I. L. Gendzier, *Frantz Fanon*,

p. 245.)

116. In addition to his medical work in Tunisian hospitals and contributing his services to the *L'Armée de liberation nationale* (ALN) centers for soldiers and refugees, he worked for the FLN press organs, first *Resistance Algerienne* and then *el Moudjahid*. He also, as we have noted, represented Algeria to the Africans. See I. L. Gendzier, *Frantz Fanon*, pp. xii, 188; F. Fanon, *Toward the African Revolution*, p. 177.

117. I. L. Gendzier, *Frantz Fanon*, pp. 190-191.

118. *Ibid*., p. 223.

119. See *ibid*., pp. 214, 239.

120. See, for instance, H. Jackson, *The FLN in Algeria: Party Development in a Revolutionary Society*, Greenwood Press, Westport, Ct., 1977, p. 181.

121. I. L. Gendzier, *Frantz Fanon*, p. 243.

122. Gendzier concludes from the evidence that, had Fanon survived Algerian independence, there was a high likelihood that he would have been denied citizenship and shown the way out of the country. (*Ibid*., p. 257).

123. *Ibid*., 243, 244.

124. *Ibid*., p. 247.

125. *Ibid*., p. 249.

126. Cited in *ibid*., p. 247.

127. *Ibid*., p. 246.

128. *Ibid*., p. 244.

129. The texts of these statements certainly should have been included in such volumes of Fanon's writings as *A Dying Colonialiam* and *Towards the African Revolution*. See Gendzier, *ibid*., pp. 142-3.

130. K. Nkrumah, *Challenge of the Congo*, Thomas Nelson, London, 1967, pp. 235-237.

131. Edward A. Alpers, *The East African Slave Trade*, pp. 23-25.

132. Cited in *Ibid*., p. 25.

133. I. Davies, *African Trade Unions*, Penguin African Library, Marmondsworth, 1966, p. 32.

134. See R. Resh, Ed., *Black America: Accommodation and Confrontation in the Twentieth Century*, D. H. Heath & Co., 1969, p. 259.

135. A. Mazrui, *Violènce and Thought*, p. 237.

136. *Ibid*.

137. See D. Ottaway, *Algeria: The Politics of a Socialist Revolution*, University of California Press, Berkeley, 1970, pp. 10-11.

138. See A. Mazrui, *Violence and Thought*, p. 242.

139. *West Africa*, 2619, August 12, 1967, p. 1064. It is always useful, when dealing with Arab-African relations, to delve beneath the surface of declared Arab intentions. Thus, when the UAR, in particular, took an active military involvement in the Biafran war on the side of the Nigerian Federal government, while the Arab world, in general, also professed sympathies for that government, the ostensible reason given was that secessionism was an invitation to imperialist interference in Africa. A closer look at the facts, however, suggests that the Arabs took the federal side for a religious reason: the concern to support the Muslim north against the Christian south. This is what prompted the Biafran leader Ojukwu's warning in 1968 against Islamic totalitarianism in Africa. The other reason for Arab support of the federal side had to do with a concern to counter the influence of the Israelis who were involved in the war on the side of Biafra. (See A. Mazrui, *Violence and Thought*, p. 251, *The Nationalist*, December 27, 1968).

140. See David Laitin, "Somalia's Military Government and Scientific Socialism" in Carl G. Rosberg and Thomas M. Callaghy, *Socialism in Sub-Saharan Africa*, Institute of International Studies, University of California, Berkeley, 1979, pp. 194-195.

141. See *Daily News* (Dar es Salaam), July 8, 1977 and *The New York Times*, June 12, 1980, p. A14 for details of Arab neocolonization of Djibouti since its independence from France in 1977.

142. A. Mazrui, "Black Africa and the Arabs" *Foreign Affairs*, Vol. 53, No. 4, July 1975, p. 740.

143. See *Ibid*.

144. In a lengthy and strongly worded statement, the Tanzanian government, for instance, indicated that the OAU's acceptance of hospitality of the Amin government was tantamount to acquiescing in crimes against the people of Uganda. (See *The Nationalist*, Dar es Salaam, July 26, 1975).

145. Among these were H. Boumedienne of Algeria, Qadhafi of Libya, Anwar Sadat of the UAR, and Ja'far Nimeiry of the Sudan.

146. *The Nationalist*, July 28, 1975.

147. See, for instance, *The Weekly Review*, Nairobi, August 11, 1978.

148. *Newsweek*, June 12, 1979, p. 39.

149. Significantly, the post-Amin Ugandan authorities charged, in July 1982, that Libya was training and arming anti-government guerilla "bandits" in Uganda in an attempt to gain control of "the head waters of the Nile River", (*The New York Times*, July 9, 1982, p. A5).

150. To this end, the Arabs pushed for the March 1975 agreement on "technical, economic and scientific cooperation" signed between Amin's Uganda and the Palestinian Liberation Organization (PLO). The consequence was the influx of an additional large number of Palestinians into Uganda where, among other things, they took over businesses left by expelled Asians, as well as the training of the Ugandan army. As Obote complained to the OAU: "Cases were known in Uganda in which Palestinians, together with Amin's murder squads, kidnapped and subsequently murdered their victims...all of whom were Ugandan citizens of African stock". (*The Nationalist*, Dar es Salaam, May 28, 1973.) As we know, a large number of Palestinians and over 1,000 Libyan troops were captured by Tanzania during the Uganda-Tanzania war which ended in Amin's expulsion from Uganda and his migration to Libya. (See *The New York Times*, March 5, 1981, p. A23).

151. *West Africa*, September 9, 1967, p. 1162.

152. For a Ugandan accusation, see *The New York Times*, February 25, 1982, p. A9 and February 26, 1982, p. A7; for a similar charge from Ghana, see *Daily News* (Dar es Salaam), October 12, 1977, p. 2; for the accusations of Senegal and Gambia, see *West Africa*, November 10, 1980; and for a more general treatment of the subject, see *West Africa*, January 19, 1981, p. 98. As President Kountche of Niger sums up the case: "Each

country has its internal quarrels and ethnic and national particularisms. It is just these particularisms upon which a certain Libyan called Gaddafi has seized to practice subversion in our country". (*West Africa*, January 19, 1981, p. 98).

153. See *West Africa*, January 19, 1981, p. 97.

154. See *ibid.*, pp. 98-99; *The New York Times*, March 4, 1981, p. A3; December 14, 1981, p. A 27; and January 4, 1982, p. A3.

155. Over the years, Qadhafi has managed to acquire a high-tech military industrial empire that includes Telemit of West Germany. He now also largely controls the Orbital Transport and Rocket Corporation (OTRAG), another West German corporation based in Libya which develops rockets with a range that can blanket Africa, the Middle East and Southern Europe. He is also known to be actively involved in Pakistan's effort to build an "Islamic bomb" through his supply of uranium "stolen" from Niger. With OTRAG developing long-range surface-to-surface missiles, and with Pakistan building a bomb, Qadhafi's dream of Islamic missiles with nuclear warheads seems far from remote. As Leslie Gelb writes, "...With more than 2,000 tanks and 300 combat aircraft, and with a substantial arsenal of missiles of all kinds, Libya is...a storehouse of weapons for a possible war." (See *The New York Times*, January 24, 1982, pp. 1, 16; Also *Africa Research Bulletin*, October 15-November 14, 1981, p. 6207; *The New York Times*, March 5, 1981, p. A23; October 1, 1981, p. A 35).

156. E. A. Nadelmann, "Israel and Black Africa: A Rapprochement?", *The Journal of Modern African Studies*, 19, 2, 1981, p. 207.

157. Because the Africans in Eritrea are Muslims, the Arabs claim that Eritrea is part of their world, and over the years have given every assistance to the secessionist movement in that region of Ethiopia. The Ethiopian leader, Mengistu Haile-Mariam, has suggested that the Arabs' intention is not only to colonize and Arabize Eritrea, but also, thereby, to bring the Red Sea under their control. To this Arab ambition he pledges: "Our Red Sea Rights will be made sacred through our red blood." (*Daily News*, Dar es Salaam, May 3, 1977). The Tanzanian daily's own opinion of the matter bears notice: "...In Ethiopia we see the forces of the new regime fighting secessionist movements that are enjoying the open support of a number of Arab countries...We must be vigilant and denounce imperialism and its agents in the Middle East and Africa." (*Daily News*, Dar es Salaam, July 26, 1977, p. 1).

158. See *The New York Times*, March 14, 1982, p. 8; November 27, 1982, p. 3; December 3, 1981, p. A27.

159. See Alan Cowell, "Africa at Crossroads: Is OAU Dying?", *The New York Times*, November 27, 1982, p. 3.

160. See *The New York Times*, November 26, 1982, p. A4.

161. See Julian Amery, *The Life of Joseph Chamberlain*, MacMillan, London, 1951, pp. 262-265.

162. G. Meier, *My Life*, London, 1975, pp. 263-90.

163. Cited in *Ibid.*, p. 266.

164. E. A. Nadelmann, "Israel and Black Africa", p. 213.

165. *Ibid.*, p. 212.

166. By the mid-1960s, Israel had established diplomatic relations with all but two (Mauritania and Somalia) of the 35 black African states and signed cooperation agreements with 20 of them. (See E. A. Nadelmann, "Israel and Black Africa", pp. 189, 190.)

167. *Ibid.*, p. 195.

168. *Ibid.*

169. *Ibid.*, p. 203, 212.

170. R. G. Weisborg, "The Dilemma of South African Jewry", *The Journal of Modern African Studies*, 5, 2, 1967, pp. 235-6.

171. Edwin Munger asserts, in this regard, that "the overwhelming majority of Jews favor apartheid and would be reluctant to give up its blessings." (Cited in H. Adam, *Modernizing Racial Domination*, University of California Press, Berkeley, 1971, p. 237.

172. A. Mazrui, "Black Africa and the Arabs," p. 729.

173. E. A. Nadelmann, "Israel and Black Africa," p. 202.

174. See *West Africa*, 2610, June 10, 1967; 2612, June 24, 1967; 2614, July 8, 1967; 2618, August 5, 1967; 2614, 2648, March 2, 1968; 2625, September 23, 1967.

175. Cited in *West Africa*, 2648, March 2, 1968, p. 266.

176. A. Mazrui, "Black Africa and the Arabs", p. 736.

177. E. Feit, "Community in a Quandary: The South African Jewish Community and Apartheid", *Race*, April 1967, pp. 398-399.

178. E. A. Nadelmann, "Israel and Black Africa...." p. 212. Contending that "the enemy of my enemy is my friend," Israel now upgraded its mission in Pretoria to full ambassadorial status, even as it broadened cultural and military links with the Apartheid regime. Meanwhile, Mr. Menachem Begin became President of Israel-South African Friendship League, the South African Prime Minister, B. J. Vorster, visited Israel in April 1976; while a number of Israeli officials, Defense Minister Ezer Weizman included, returned the visit in February 1978 and in March 1980. (See *Ibid.*, p. 213.)

179. Nadelmann observed that "the relative paucity and maldistribution of Arab aid in the face of continuously rising oil prices" was soon to fuel disenchantment throughout Africa "with the merits of Third World brotherhood". (*Ibid.*, p. 219).

180. A. Mazrui, "Black Africa and the Arabs," p. 742.

181. Zdeneck Cervenka, "Afro-Arab Relations: Exploitation or Cooperation?", *Africa*, No. 34, June 1974, p. 48.

182. *West Africa*, 2950, December 24/31, 1973, p. 1812.

183. *Ibid.*, 2946, November 26, 1973, p. 1677.

184. See A. Mazrui, "Black Africa and the Arabs", p. 738.

185. See. Z. Cervenka, "The Afro-Arab Alliance", *Africa*, No. 31, March 1974, p. 79.

186. See *The Weekly Review*, Nairobi, March 14, 1977, p. 24.

187. Cited in a confidential newsletter.

188. See, for instance, William Korey, "The Myth of Israel's Collusion with South Africa", *Newsday*, New York, November 19, 1979.

189. Thomas Land, "Black Africa and Israel", *The New York Times*, February 11, 1980, p. A19.

190. See A. Mazrui, "Black Africa and the Arabs", pp. 738-9.

191. See E. A. Nadelmann, "Israel and Black Africa....," p. 204.

192. John Henrik Clarke, ed., *Marcus Garvey and the Vision of Africa*, New York, 1974, p. 381.

193. *Ibid.*

194. *Ibid.*, p. 382.

195. See K. A. Busia, *The Position of the Chief in the Modern Political System of Ashanti*, Frank Cass, London, 1968; W. Tordoff, *Ashanti Under the Prempehs: 1888-1939*, Oxford University Press, London, 1965.

196. A. Jacques-Garvey, *Philosophy and Opinions of Marcus Garvey*, Atheneum, New York, 1977, Vol. I, p. 43. As Garvey elaborated: "The greatest battle ever fought was not between the Kaiser of Germany on the one hand and the Allied Powers on the other, it was between Almighty God on the one hand and Lucifer the Archangel on the other...When anyone transgresses His power He goes to war in defense of His rights...The Creator has bequeathed to Angels and to men the same principles, the same policies that govern Him as God..." (*Ibid.*, p. 43).

197. See Alan Cowell, "Christians Are Torn in the Land of Dr. Livingstone", *The New York Times*, December 28, 1982, p. A2.

198. *Ibid.*

199. Cited in A. R. M. Babu, *African Socialism or Socialist Africa?*, Zed Press, London, 1981, p. 120.

200. Cited in O. Aguda, "Arabism and PanArabism in Sudanese Politics", p. 135. Qadhafi, who has been vigorously carrying on Nasser's crusade, typically announced plans in 1980 to establish a $10 million Islamic Education Center in Accra to cater for Islamic education from kindergarten to secondary levels. Islamic teachers would be sent from Libya to organize the center in Accra. (See *The Mirror*, Accra, June 20, 1980, p. 1).

201. Ethan A. Nadelmann, "Israel and Black Africa: A Rapprochement?", *The Journal of Modern African Studies*, 19, 2, 1981, p. 210. See also Lansine Kaba, "Islam's Advance in Tropical Africa", *Africa Report*, March-April, 1976, p. 39.

202. A. Mazrui, "Black Africa and the Arabs," p. 737.

203. See *The New York Times*, November 1, 1982, p. A5.

204. Ali Mazrui, "Black Africa and the Arabs," p. 737.

205. Confidential Newsletter, June 10, 1977.

206. Ali Mazrui, "Black Africa and the Arabs", p. 737-8.

207. Astonishingly, Bongo let it be known that his reason for converting was "because Islam makes no distinction between men". (See *West Africa*, 2943, November 5, 1973, p. 1556).

208. *The Weekly Review*, Nairobi, September 26, 1977, p. 7; August 11, 1978, pp. 11, 14.

209. *Ibid.*

210. *Ibid.*

211. See A. Mazrui, "Religious Strangers in Uganda: From Emin Pasha to Amin Dada," *African Affairs*, Vol. 76, No. 302, January 1977, p. 21.

212. O. Aguda, "Arabism and Pan-Arabism in Sudanese Politics", *The Journal of Modern African Studies*, Vol. II, No. 2, 1973, p. 180.

213. A. Mazrui, "Black Africa and the Arabs", p. 726.

214. B. Lewis, *Race and Color in Islam*, pp. 9, 14.

215. See *Ibid.*, pp. 91-92. This is only one of the many *Hadiths*, the traditions concerning Muhammed's actions and utterances. Even if spurious in terms of their being the Prophet's own views, it is nonetheless the case, as Lewis indicates, that these traditions remain an "important evidence on the development of attitudes during the period in which they were manufactured". (*Ibid.*, p. 18).

216. See *Ibid.*, p. 101. Thus for instance, a good black slave who lives a life of virtue and piety "will be rewarded by turning white at the moment of death", (See *Ibid.*, p. 5).

217. See *Ibid.*, pp. 66-67.

218. *Ibid.*, pp. 67, 68.

219. *Ibid.*, p. 23.

220. Louis Farrakhan, Speech at "Welcome Home Brother Farrakhan" rally at the Nat Holman Gymnasium, City College of New York, Harlem, New York, May 18, 1980, cited in L. H. Mamiya, "Minister Louis Farrakhan and the Final Call: Schism in the Muslim Movement", Mimeo, 1980, p. 7.

221. Dr. Ali Treiki, Foreign Minister of Libya's address at the Eighth Conference of Islamic Foreign Ministers in Tripoli, May, 1977.

222. Chinweizu, *The West and the Rest of Us*, Vintage Books, 1975, p. 495.

4

The Maghrib and the Middle East Conflict

By Elbaki Hermassi

In studying the relationships between the Maghrib (the west wing of the Middle East) and the Machrik (the Arab east wing), it is important to beware of two temptations. The first is to blur the Maghrib's specificity in the manner of those who speak of the Arabs as if they were an undifferentiated whole rather than a complex world susceptible to the laws of history and society. The second equally prevailing temptation is to accentuate the peculiarities of the Maghrib to the point of dissociating its past from that of its cultural and regional surrounding. While a host of reasons, such as the lack of in-depth research, the pressures of partisanship, and the urgencies of daily politics, make these temptations hard to resist, the overall effect is to deflect attention from the true nature of these relationships and in the process to let faulty judgments lead to political blunder.

The idea of the Middle East as a structured system with laws of its own remains one of the most neglected research efforts. In the Arab world in particular, where almost by definition coalitions are constantly shifting, where commitment is as common as withdrawal, and where every ethnocultural unit acts as a concerned member without ever surrendering its autonomy, this particular dynamic has eluded orientalists, journalists and politicians alike. Yet only in this light can one understand why, on the one hand, every North African country is described by its leaders to be an integrated part of the Maghrib, and the Maghrib itself part of the larger Arab world, and yet, on the other hand, every country acts as if it were a finite community and a self-sufficient nation having to defer to no one outside of its boundaries. We suggest that an adequate grasp of the situation requires an effort to grapple with this paradox of affinity and differentiation, of solidarity and independence, and nothing illustrates better this

---

Dr. Hermassi is Professor of Sociology at the University of California at Berkeley, and has also taught at Tunis University. He is the author of *Leadership and National Development in North Africa* (University of California Press, 1972), and *The Third World Reassessed* (University of California Press, 1980).

paradox of participation and independence than the Maghribi attitude toward the enduring Palestinian tragedy.

It may be said that aside from the highly publicized position of President Bourguiba, the Maghrib had remained detached, for all practical purposes indifferent to the Middle East conflict until the June War of 1967. Then followed a period of active involvement, dramatized by the military participation during the October War of 1973 against Israel and, at present, the pendulum may be swinging the other way once again. To understand the ebb and flow of the Maghrib's involvement in Middle Eastern affairs, one has to take into account North Africa's geographic position, its historical legacy, as well as its modes of interaction with the West. The Maghrib is at the intersection of three central configurations, the Middle East, Africa, and Europe. With the Middle East it shares what Gustave Flaubert aptly calls *l'immensité ténébreuse de l'histoire,* from which it derives its conceptual and cultural categories. With Africa it shares the common battle against colonialism on the Continent, and Europe constitutes its object of resentment as well as its door toward modernity and effectiveness. Out of these various interactions the Maghrib has evolved its present political culture, marked primarily by piety, the cult of unanimity, and its acute sense of independence.

Left to themselves, the countries of the Maghrib tend to concentrate on internal problems. Most of the regimes which came to power after independence concentrated primarily on regime-building and economic development. But this splendid isolation was dramatically interrupted by the 1967 war, which was felt as a humiliation by all—and at least was described as such by a jubilant Western press; the war brought mass demonstrations in every major North African city. As a result of these demonstrations, the Palestinian problem became a major "national" issue.

The shock felt by leaders and intellectuals alike has been quite traumatic. Whether what was triggered by the war was the old Mediterranean mechanism of honor and shame, or whether it was the anti-hegemonic principle peculiar to the region—the equilibrium of co-existence being upset here by the Israeli inclination to expand—we cannot analyze at this point. What is certain is that the Maghribi elites were aware of their position at the margin of the Arab world and thus, precluded from being confrontation states in a conflict into which they were drawn, they awakened to the necessity of designing a role for themselves in this inescapable conflict.

The Maghribi Approach

An outsider is likely to notice the wide difference which separates Qadhafi's commitment to revolutionary pan-Arabism from, say, King Hassan II's art of compromise, and may conclude that the Maghrib lacks any consistent policy in this matter. I would argue that despite the real ideological and situational differences between the various regions, there exists such a thing as an overall Maghribi approach, an approach which can be described by the following characteristics:

1) At the most general level, commitment to the welfare of the Palestinian people is matched by the asserted necessity to find the solution which can be sanctioned by world opinion and international law. Being at the crossroads of the Middle East, the Maghrib is as sensitive to the plight of the oppressed as it is to the norms of international legality. In addition, to the extent that the national liberation movement in the Maghrib sought to enlist world support, ranging from the European Left to the United Nations, it was assumed, especially in view of Western sympathy for the Israeli cause (whether motivated by admiration or guilt), that it was even more indispensable for the Palestinians to bring their cause to the West and to enlist Third World support;
2) The provision of ideas and models of struggle: the most important of these ideas were Bourguiba's gradualist tactics and the Algerian guerrilla warfare precedent;
3) The contribution of critical support in times of war, dramatically illustrated

by the presence of Algerian, Moroccan and, to a lesser extent, Tunisian soldiers in the October 1973 War;

4) The role of mediator in inter-Arab conflicts: the Tunisian, Bahi Ladgham, helped to arbitrate between the Palestinians and Jordan in 1970; Algiers hosted the heads of states' meeting in November, 1973, designed to legitimize the principle of negotiation with Israel and, at all times, Maghribi foreign ministers have played a crucial role in the mapping out of strategy.

There is little doubt that the combined effect of these actions has been of some help to the Palestinians. It was all the more helpful because the effort was deployed at a distance and went on without any interference whatsoever in their internal affairs. The interference of other Arab regimes has always been resented by leaders in the Maghrib with, of course, the exception of Libya, which brings us to the question of how the various countries differ in their attitudes toward the Middle Eastern conflict.

In their attempt to reconcile sentiment and effectiveness, solidarity with embattled brethren and the realities of world politics, the Maghribi elites took the dilemma by the horns, calling at one time or another for the right of revolutionary struggle and for negotiation with Israel, while at the same time pleading with the great powers. While some goverments did all of these simultaneously, a particular country's policy can be located along a political spectrum ranging from pragmatism, like Morocco and Tunisia, to ideological extremism, like Libya and, to a lesser extent, Algeria.

Analytically, the most systematic effort to articulate the Middle East conflict in contemporary terms has been made by President Bourguiba, who was most sensitive to the ambiguous official Arab attitude in the face of international opinion. The Arab cause, Bourguiba argued, has been "jeopardized by wanton threats against Israel and by the spectre of a military solution in the face of a materially stronger enemy." This policy of "make it all or nothing," has, in his eyes, given Israel a considerable propaganda advantage, by allowing it to portray itself as eager for a negotiated settlement while its opponents, in their intransigence, refuse to consider such a solution. To strengthen the Arab position with regard to world opinionn Bourguiba suggested a strategy designed to turn the tables against Israel. He argued that the Palestinian situation should be considered as a colonial situation in which Palestinians are "now living in sort of concentration camps similar to those of the Jews during the Second World War." And since, in his words, "the remedy for Diaspora cannot be to condemn another people to another Diaspora," the conflict has to be treated as a colonial problem which entails the fight of the colonized people for their independence. In the meantime, the threat of armed struggle is stressed in conjunction with the United Nations 1947 decision, the purpose being to secure an acceptable "modus vivendi" on the basis of the original United Nations partition plan, which recognized the "reality" of Israel and the rights of the Palestinians. These views were shared by Tunisians even when they did not agree with their President's economic or political management. But they remained unpopular throughout the Middle East until they appeared, in a relatively changed form, in the aftermath of the 1967 and 1973 wars.

A country in which the gradualist approach was popular was Morocco.* Belief in a political settlement was strong in that country, but due to a combination of factors, such as the weight of political opposition to the regime, foreign policy was tailored to strengthen the monarchy and to close whatever options opponents could use. Thus fund-raising during religious rituals and army contingents to the Syrian front were all destined, like the calls for mobilization to recapture Western Sahara from Spain, to be more acts of realpolitik for the legitimation of the monarchy than an indication of a revolutionary stand on the Middle East.

In contrast to the Tunisian and Moroccan sense of political compromise, Algeria and

*Both Tunisia and Morocco have supported Sadat's peace initiative.

Libya are more ideological in their approach. Tying the fate of their own revolutions to that of the Palestinians, the two countries denounce Israeli aggression, justify resistance in all its forms, and call for a widening of the battle along revolutionary lines. The 1973 war offered the opportunity not only to put this stand to the test but to illustrate the role of internal and external constraints on the two countries. Algeria's participation in the war effort was very substantial. Army contingents and air force units took part in the fighting. Two hundred million dollars (the equivalent of the amount annually transferred by a million Algerian workers in Europe) was donated and Russia was pressured to keep its promise to deliver the weapons. To underline his country's intensity of commitment, Algeria's President Boumediene declared, "not only is our hand in the fire, but our whole body is in Hell—the Hell which our brothers of the Orient are enduring."

Qadhafi of Libya, on the other hand, who based his whole career, as well as that of his regime, on unity and revolution in the Arab world, remained paradoxically marginal during this major confrontation. The fact that he had, all along, considered himself to be a leader without a country, and Egypt as a country without a leader, led Sadat secretly to launch his October offensive, leaving his young competitor entirely out in the cold, and thus condemning him to isolation and bitterness. In the meantime, Algeria was able to temper its support for Third World revolutions, especially when it began to discover that the blank check delivered for guerrilla action could mean, among other things, the embarrassment of having Black Panthers and the Popular Front for the Liberation of Palestine bring the planes they hijacked to Algiers. Sooner or later, commitment to revolutionary strategy came to be balanced against sensitivity to international standards and the growing Algerian interest in its membership in the conservative—if efficient—club of oil-producing nations. This may be the reason why, after all is said and done, the Algerians have ended up endorsing the Tunisian thesis which calls the U.N. partition plan of 1947 a minimum platform for negotiation. It may take Qadhafi longer to bring his position into relative consonance with that of his neighbors.

In sum, for a variety of reasons, cultural affinities, ideological commitment, internal considerations, and i ternational competition, the countries of the Maghrib have found themselves bound to take an active stand on Middle Eastern developments. In every instance, this constellation of factors has helped shape the contours of each country's policy, as well as the overall pattern of involvement. Once again we find that on the whole, the similarities between the countries are more striking than the differences. Being part of many worlds, the peoples of the Maghrib cannot but be influenced by cross-pressures and geopolitics. Even at the height of their solidarity, Maghribis know, in the words of Boumediene, that they "cannot be more Egyptian than the Egyptians, more Syrian than the Syrians, let alone more Palestinian than the Palestinians." To the extent that the Maghrib is precluded from direct confrontation, it must assume the role of a distant brother, emphasizing unity of ranks, rationality of approach, and a sensitivity to world opinion. More than any other thing, the Maghrib's contribution has been to bring the Palestinian issue to world consciousness and to convey the world's views to the Palestinians. By doing so, the peoples of the Maghrib have undeniably played a role, albeit a modest one, in maximizing the chances for the "historical compromise" between Jews and Arabs.

---

5 Policy Implications of Boundary Disputes in the Persian Gulf

By Lenore G. Martin

American policymakers have spent much time and effort in recent years on the challenge of military preparedness in the Persian Gulf. Equally and perhaps even more important for us to develop in the Persian Gulf is what might be termed political preparedness. In that vein we must ask what types of conflicts may arise and between which Gulf states? One answer can be derived from the unsettled nature of many of the boundaries in the area which create the potential for disputes. A number of these potential boundary disputes endanger countries which either sit upon the major waterways used by oil tankers or are important suppliers of oil for the United States and even more so for its allies. For these reasons it seems vital to our self interest to consider the difficulties involved and the policy options available in Persian Gulf boundary disputes.

Why focus on potential boundary conflicts? What makes border disputes *per se* so problematic for the foreign policymaker is the quandary of having to decide if such disputes are really preludes to wholesale takeovers or merely containable conflicts. Prudentially the decision maker might consider first the ultimate risks of border conflicts erupting into larger scale aggression. With the incentive of oil and the motivation of ideological splits at work among the nations of the Gulf the stakes are higher, and accordingly the risks of such eruptions are greater. The focal questions for an investigation of potential border conflict in the Persian Gulf, therefore, become: Which areas of border unrest involve oil exporting states? How could the border disputes affect oil exports to the United States? What roles can the United States play in affecting these disputes?

The Gulf borders in which the potential for conflict is most likely would have to include Iran-Iraq, Iraq-Kuwait, North Yemen-South Yemen, South Yemen-Oman. The reasons for such potential conflicts and their policy implications will be explored below, border by border.

Iran-Iraq

The border between Iran and Iraq has a long history of unrest stretching back to at least 1639 when the Turks and Persians drew the forerunner of their present frontiers and effectively divided the Kurdish tribes of the mountainous areas east and northeast of Baghdad. The Kurds have never accepted this division and have continued to engage in clashes with the authorities at the border regions in their search for the formation of an autonomous Kurdish state. The Shah provided the Iraqi Kurds with enough military help to maintain their rebellion though never quite enough to win autonomy. (No doubt because Iran had no desire to increase the incentives for its own Kurds to achieve autonomy.) This strategy used potential border conflict successfully to divert the Iraqi military from other military activity in the Gulf.

Other parts of the border have erupted in the recent past as well. The area around the Shatt al-Arab, the major shipping way of the two countries, erupted in 1937, 1960 and 1969. Until 1975 Iran was denied equal control of the shipping lanes of the Shatt by Iraq. Clashes also occurred along the central border, though here the major explanation

---

Dr. Martin is chairperson of the Department of Political Science at Emmanuel College in Boston.

The substance of this article is adapted from her book and is reprinted by permission of the publisher from the forthcoming, *The Unstable Gulf: Threats from Within*, Lexington, Mass.: Lexington Books, D.C. Heath and Co., copyright 1983.

given by the U.N. investigator in 1974 was poor demarcation.

In 1975 at an OPEC meeting, the Algerian Premier mediated a comprehensive border agreement (known as the Algiers Agreement) between Iran and Iraq. Both sides obtained agreements on their outstanding issues: Iran for its claim to more equal control of the Shatt, and Iraq for better control over the Kurds. Specifically, Iraq recognized Iran's border at the Shatt to the middle of the main navigation channel of the whole river. Iran in return promised to refrain from aiding the Iraqi Kurdish rebellion. Both sides agreed to a joint commission to demarcate their central border. Final agreement took place in June, 1975.

The Algiers Agreement was denounced by the Iraqis as a prelude to their invasion in September, 1980 of the often contested 90 square miles from Qasr-i-Shirin (in the north) to Badra and Mehran (in the south). They simultaneously reclaimed unilateral control of the Shatt al-Arab, and pushed their invasionary forces deep into the oil-rich Iranian province of Khuzistan.

Iraqi military advances through the Iranian oil depot city of Khorramshashr, into areas populated by Iran's dissident Sunni Arabs, at a time of Khumayni's international isolationism, raised serious questions as to the limitation of Iraqi's border war objectives. Furthermore, without renouncing its ties to the Soviets who have been its major arms supplier, Iraq balanced its support of the revolutionary Gulf States with overtures to the traditional Gulf States, playing on their heightened fears of Khumayni-inspired Shiite revolution. Iraq's military successes at the head of the Gulf further raised the possibility of Iraqi recovery of the Iranian held islands of Abu Musa and the Tunbs.[1] An Iraqi military presence at the Straits of Hormuz, through which over one-third of the world's oil passes, could give Iraq control over the entire Gulf waterway.

Recent Iranian repulsion of the Iraqi invasion has resolved some of these possibilities of an Iraqi predominance for the present. But the disinclination, at time of writing, of Iran to negotiate a settlement of the conflict keeps alive the possibilities of renewed attempts by either Iran or Iraq to assert control over the border regions and from there predominance in the Gulf.

Such predominance would be threatening to the Saudis who do not have the military capability to resist regional takeovers by either Iraq or Iran. The Saudis might then turn to the United States, or, as one option short of direct U.S. action, seek Egyptian involvement. With or without U.S. assistance, Egypt has the military capability and conceivably shares Saudi concern over Iraqi or Iranian predominance over the Gulf.

What are the likely U.S. options in the present situation? The United States clearly has an interest in securing the Gulf waterway for the free flow of Gulf oil. Neither side in the Iraq-Iran conflict is likely to seek either U.S. military assistance or diplomatic intervention. This leaves the U.S. with, if anything, an indirect role in supporting other potential regional or international efforts at diplomatic mediation. There is no lack of forums, but similarly no obvious easy choice: the United Nations has been ignored or unsuccessful in the past; the Arab League has been dominated by Iraq since the expulsion of Egypt — as a result of the Camp David accords with Israel; OPEC through which the Algiers Agreements was enforced still remains a viable possibility.

The Soviets have taken a background role during the Iraq-Iran conflict. Their potential for intervention should not be discounted, however. They remain available to either side for replenishing depleted arsenals. Supplying arms to both sides could invite Soviet peacemaking similar to the U.S. at Camp David, and with it an extension of Soviet influence over the northern Gulf.

Iraq-Kuwait

While the exact outcome of the current Iraq-Iran war is not predictable, the longer term regional international political system remains susceptible to bids for predominance by Iraq. A resurgent Iraq would pose a threat to its more vulnerable neighbor to the south, Kuwait, and endanger Kuwait's supply of high quality oil to the West. Indeed Iraq has made claims on Kuwait three times within the last twenty or so years: 1961, 1973 and 1976. Upon the termination of Kuwait's protectorate treaty with Britain in 1961 Iraq's Prime Minister, Abdul Karim Qasim, claimed Kuwait as a former *qada* (administrative unit) of the Turkish *vilayet* (province) of Basra, now part of Iraq. Kuwait requested British and Arab assistance and both Britain and Saudi Arabia sent forces into Kuwait on July 1, 1961. Later that month Kuwait was accepted as a member of the Arab League and a composite Arab League force (Egypt, Jordan, Sudan and Saudi Arabia) was sent to Kuwait in September. Qasim himself was overthrown early in 1963. In the course of reestablishing relations with other Arab states, which had been ruptured to varying degrees by Qasim's diplomacy, Iraq recognized Kuwait's independence and sovereignty.

Although Qasim's claim was a grand one on the entire oil-rich Kuwait territory, Iraq in 1969, 1973 and 1976 turned its interests to gaining smaller portions of Kuwaiti territory, ostensibly for the protection of the Iraqi port of Umm Qasr. Iraq's only other major port, Basra, was vulnerable to Iranian interference because of its location on the Shatt al-Arab. In 1969 Iraq gained permission to place troops garrisoning Umm Qasr on Kuwaiti soil. But in 1973 the Iraqis pressed further and captured a Kuwaiti border post near Umm Qasr. The Iraqis then laid claim to the Kuwaiti islands which guarded its entrance — Bubiyan and Warba. Again the Arab League played the role of peacemaker and pressured Iraq into withdrawing. In 1976, it was reported that an Iraqi force had again crossed into Kuwait and that once again Egypt was trying to settle the dispute. (All in all, there were three reported border clashes in the mid 1970s.) In 1977 talks between the two governments again ensued and it was agreed that both would withdraw their troops from the area around their mutual land boundary.[2]

If in the future a resurgent Iraq were to reassert claims to Kuwaiti territory, where would Kuwait turn for its protection? The most likely answer is Saudi Arabia with whom Kuwait has historically strong ties and consistently mutual interests. Additional support would be forthcoming from the recently formed Gulf Cooperation Council ("GCC", discussed further below). But neither the Saudis nor the GCC are likely to have the military capability to resist a determined Iraqi move. As a last resort, therefore, Kuwait would be likely to turn to the United States and its allies (the "West") which has often expressed preparedness to aid the conservative Gulf Sheikdoms.

North Yemen-South Yemen

The North Yemen-South Yemen border has long been the scene of tribal skirmishes and larger invasions. Formally only a partial border exists as drawn by the British and Turks in 1905. Intermittent fighting on the frontiers continued until 1934 when a ceasefire was achieved without any further definition of a border. Sporadic clashes resumed again in 1957 and are still persisting today.

The recent border clashes result from a complex mixture of factors. They include ideological issues, questions of unification and the interests and involvement of both regional and major world powers. South Yemen identifies closely with the communist world and its own government is based on a radical Marxist model. The Soviet Union, Cuba, China and Eastern Europe have been involved with the development of South Yemen's military forces, economy and government. North Yemen on the other hand is governed by a military council and pursues a more neutral position between East and West. Since the late seventies the North Yemenis have sought military aid from Saudi Arabia, the conservative Arab States, and the United States, as well as the Soviet Union and Iraq.

Notwithstanding their ideological differences and countervailing international influences, North Yemen and South Yemen have at various times sought to erase their border altogether by unifying both countries. Efforts at the unification process have variously looked hopeful and subsequently broken down in the late 1970s and early 1980s. Thus, for instance, a provisional agreement for unification was arrived at in March, 1979 after a two week border war. No constitution for the unified Yemens could be agreed upon until January, 1982. It is unclear at this point if this constitution will be ratified and a stable integration of the disparate nations will ensue.

Certainly unification is one option for bringing peace to the border — but unification which would create a larger nation, if aligned with the Soviet Union, would be viewed as a threat to the more conservative nations in the area. Oman is already coping with an unresolved border problem with South Yemen and would be concerned about conflict with an even larger and stronger state. Saudi Arabia, whose southern border is shared in part with North and South Yemen, has invested substantial aid in North Yemen. Nevertheless, Saudi policy and recently that of the GCC has been to encourage unification in order to increase political stability in the area.

While the United States has provided military assistance to North Yemen, as have the Saudis, these efforts have not succeeded in eliminating North Yemen's ties with the Soviet Union. There is, accordingly, Saudi reluctance to build up a strong North Yemen, which alone could constitute a threat to Saudi Arabia's west coast.[3] The maritime routes through the Red Sea and Suez Canal are already jeopardized by Soviet alignments with South Yemen and nations across the Bab- al-Mandeb on the Horn of Africa.

South Yemen-Oman

South Yemen has also been involved in conflict on its eastern boundary with Oman. Here the conflict has not so much involved a drawing of a line — as at this point Oman has no defined borders — but South Yemen's aid to the Dhofar rebellion in Oman, which began in 1963. The Dhofar rebels consisted of a group of anti-monarchical leftist insurgents based in Oman's western province of Dhofar. The South Yemen-Oman border has been the scene of military action since South Yemen's independence in 1967. At that time it began to provide sanctuary to the Dhofar insurgents operating in Oman as well as a route for the supplies to the insurgents from the Peoples Republic of China and the Soviet Union. Omani troops have not only had to fight the insurgents but regular South Yemeni forces as well.

The international involvement in the conflict on this border is similar to that of the North Yemen-South Yemen border. In its fight to quell the Dhofar insurgency Oman received aid of forces and material from Great Britain, troops and material from the Shah of Iran, money from Abu Dhabi and Saudi Arabia, some troops from Jordan and the United Arab Emirates, and Omani men were also given military training in schools in Great Britain, Jordan, Saudi Arabia, Egypt and Pakistan. The insurgents on the other hand not only have received arms from China and the Soviet Union, their men received training in these countries as well as in North Korea. Children in the Dhofar region have even been taken over the border into South Yemen to a "Lenin School".

Oman reported eliminating the insurrection by December of 1975. In March of 1976 South Yemen and Oman announced the establishment of diplomatic relations, followed two days later by a ceasefire. Subsequently the bulk of the British and all the Iranian forces aiding Oman were withdrawn. This withdrawal may have encouraged the reactivation of the insurgency, for in June, 1979 it was reported that the Dhofar insurgency groups were beginning to operate again near the South Yemen border.

This dispute is strategically important to the United States from two perspectives. First, Oman shares a long border with Saudi Arabia. If the insurgents, backed by the Soviets and Cubans, were successfully to overthrow the Sultan almost the entire southern border of Saudi Arabia would be shared with radical revolutionary states. The United Arab Emirates, another rich producer of oil, would also be bordered by a radical Omani state. Even more disconcerting is the fact that a radically leftist government in Oman would be in a position to control the Straits of Hormuz. One side of the Straits of Hormuz is located on the tip of the Musandum Peninsula which is owned by Oman. It is not certain that a leftist revolution in Oman would include this geographically separate section of Oman, but if it did, the supply of oil to the West could be threatened.

The U.S. would obviously be concerned over the effects on Gulf shipping by a hostile takeover of Oman. A radical Oman however would present an even more complicated situation, since the recent agreement with Oman giving the U.S. base rights on Masirah island (off Oman's east coast, formerly used by the British) would be jeopardized. Loss of such a strategically located Gulf base would (absent a substitute provided by Kuwait or Saudi Arabia) seriously interfere with U.S. ability to secure oil supplies and tanker routes through the Gulf. From a number of perspectives then the United States has a vital interest in supporting a stable Oman.

Policy Alternatives from the U.S. Perspective

Clearly a potential for more conflict over boundaries in the Persian Gulf exists. In some situations the disputes can actually be seen as forthright claims on land, in others the underlying reasons for the disputes are more politically complex — the tip of an iceberg. Because of the peculiarly Persian Gulf admixture of oil and ideology, the political impact of the disputes will extend beyond the immediate nations involved. U.S. policy must accordingly, become prepared to deal with the possible effects of such Gulf boundary disputes. Presently, U.S. preparedness has been symbolized by the promise of a "Rapid Deployment Force", able to respond to threats to the region from the Soviet Union. From the preceding discussion it is apparent that threats to the security of the Gulf states arise from within the area itself and often involve disputes over or at the boundaries. For these internal problems the Rapid Deployment Force is no deterrent.

What then are the policy alternatives for the U.S.? Five major options can be considered: An international peacekeeping force; a Rapid Deployment Force; a series of bilateral agreements; a regional alliance; and a NATO type alliance of the traditional Gulf states, the U.S., and other Western allies.

International Naval Peacekeeping Force

An international naval peacekeeping force would have as its objective the maintenance of a neutral or demilitarized Straits of Hormuz. Such a force would be akin to land-based peacekeeping forces which have been deployed in other hostile situations in lieu of direct superpower intervention. A successful enactment of such a force would protect the oil routes but it would not be useful in decreasing the possibilities of conflict which exist abundantly on land and which are at least as threatening to the oil supplies of the West.

The Rapid Deployment Force

The Carter Administration chose to deal with the problem of Persian Gulf security through the formation of a Rapid Deployment Force which would ostensibly be able to interject itself into the area if the need arose from a threat from outside of the region. There are a number of problems with this policy. First, when would the U.S. choose to activate a Rapid Deployment Force? Would its use be confined to responding to Soviet military movements? Certainly the possibility of aggression from other quarters is even more likely. The second, and perhaps the most often referred to problem, is that such a Force will not be viable at the very earliest until 1984-85 and would take approximately one week before being able to intervene in the Gulf. Thus, the West by depending on a Rapid Deployment Force, would be vulnerable to a concerted and well executed attack which could cut off a large percentage of the West's oil supply for a reasonably long period of time — simply by disabling the fields quickly at an early point in a conflict. The West must be able to act fast enough with enough power to stop any such interference with the oil flow. In Albert Wohlstetter's paper "Half-Wars and Half-Policies" he suggests the use of a naval fleet in the Gulf able to react to protect key points on the Gulf.[4] Such a fleet would certainly aid in providing security to the region. Wohlstetter reasons that such a naval force would avoid a destabilizing political involvement of the local Gulf nations with the United States. What remains unclear is the degree to which such a naval force can maintain its readiness without port facilities in the Gulf — and therefore the automatic involvement of Gulf nations in providing such facilities. At this point only the island of Masirah has been reported as providing some base facilities, but on what conditions and whether sufficient for the scale of naval deployment proposed is not publicly known.

An essential problem posed by reliance on a strong naval presence and/or a Rapid Deployment Force is the lack of a clear indication to rival powers as to precisely where the U.S. sees its vital interests and under what conditions it would intervene. On the other hand, both a clearer stand and a more flexible military strategy could be created by basing ground forces in the Gulf, particularly if deployed in conjunction with a naval fleet and Rapid Deployment Force.

Admittedly, the stationing of Western ground forces within the traditional nations around the Gulf is problematic. The traditional Gulf states fear that such a move would make them more politically vulnerable to the radical leftists, Muslim fundamentalists and Pan-Arabists.

Bilateral Agreements

A series of bilateral agreements with each of the traditional Gulf states would be a logical extension of the current U.S. policy to undertake separate military arrangements with a number of the Gulf and Southern Arabian Peninsula states. However, such a series of bilateral arrangements would be quickly denounced as American Imperialism, not without historical justification since this was the British strategy between the two World Wars. Besides, for the United States there would be no assurance of the stability of these arrangements. The current Gulf system allows for switching of alignments or neutrality.

This perspective is not shared by all analysts of Persian Gulf politics. Some analysts perceive a switch in alignments by Iraq from the Soviet to the Western bloc and urge the United States to woo the Iraqis on a number of different levels to encourage the switch. This policy suggestion, however, overlooks two problems: First the stability of the Persian Gulf nations is precarious; secondly, bilateral alliances of these same nations have been easily broken in the past. Moreover, alliance switching has serious risks. For example, to envision U.S. security as being based on an alliance with Iraq would be self-deception — especially if such an alliance would require the weakening of a truly long term ally in the region, as one recent commentator, Adeed I. Dawisha, appears to recommend when he suggests that the U.S. encourage Iraqi friendship by pressuring Israel to give in to Palestininan demands.[5] Certainly the Palestinian issue is a source of great discontent in the area, but it is an issue which is no more destabilizing to the area than the other disputes discussed earlier in this paper and as exemplified by the recent Iran-Iraq war. In short, bilateral alliances at this stage would be just too vulnerable to shifts of alignments to provide the security the U.S. needs and seeks.

Regional Alliance

The traditional Gulf states of Saudi Arabia, Kuwait, Bahrain, Qatar, the U.A.E. and Oman have already formed a Gulf Cooperation Council ("GCC") as a forum for discussion and formulation of policy concerning collective security issues.[6] The most apparent problem with the GCC is its military vulnerability to an aggressive Iran or Iraq. Even if such a coalition turned to the U.S. and/or others for weapons assistance, it would still lack the manpower necessary to resist a takeover attempt on any one of them.

NATO Type Alliance: A Gulf States Defense Organization

The fundamental problem of all the prior options is that they have not taken account of the international system of the Persian Gulf region. An analysis of the region today as an international system suggests that it operates most like an unstable balance of power. There are two major regional actors, Iran and Iraq, whose military capabilities surpass those of the other actors in the system. Instability is also created by ideological cross-currents which inhibit coalitions and realignments. The instability is not so great, however, as to transform the system. Neither Iran nor Iraq has been successful in achieving predominance and transforming the system either by aggrandizement or by creating a cohesive bloc. The continued operation of the unstable balance poses the greatest threat to the traditional Gulf states who will remain vulnerable as long as they are unable to militarily resist their stronger neighbors.[7]

The plight of these traditional Gulf states is remarkably similar to that of Western Europe in the aftermath of World War II. The Western Europeans were militarily vulnerable to a preponderant Soviet Union with relatively superior armed forces at their frontiers. The popularity of wartime communist resistance movements created crucibles for internal takeovers. The weakened Western European states did not have the military capabilities for their own security arrangements (for example, the Brussels Pact of 1948). In response to this situation the concept of NATO was developed. At the outset, as is well known, the U.S. committed itself to provide when needed the military wherewithal for European regional security. The actual deployment of U.S. ground forces was not galvanized until the outbreak of the Korean War. Underlying the U.S. commitment to NATO, however, was the clear perception that the Soviet threat to the Western European system was a threat to the security of the U.S. itself.

This same perception of threat to U.S. security animates the U.S. concern for the integrity of the Gulf states. The Soviet threat from a presence in Afghanistan and ties to Iraq and the Yemens cannot be denied. And from a long term perspective there are appreciable threats to the territorial integrity of the Gulf states as outlined above which their own security arrangements cannot withstand.

A NATO type alliance of the U.S. and members of the GCC (hereinafter referred to as a Gulf States Defense Organization) would offer a collective security arrangement of the Gulf states the military assistance, including ground forces, necesary to restore the regional balance. This type of organization would be less vulnerable to bilateral alliance switching, so common today in the area — especially since the defense arrangements would be more widespread. A Gulf States Defense Organization could also include other Western nations whose vital interests are involved in this region, such as Britain, West Germany, France and Japan. Egypt also might be a likely alliance partner. Inclusion of these nations would strengthen the possibility for stabilizing the new organization.

The only other pro-Western state capable of a rapid deployment of significant military forces in the area is Israel. Although Israeli military forces might well substitute for and limit the need for U.S. or European forces, it is unlikely that Israel could even be mentioned in conjunction with a Gulf States Defense Organization. The Gulf States presently have great ideological and political problems dealing with a potential Western alliance. The possibility of such negotiations with Israel — a country still not recognized by the Gulf States — is all but impossible at this point.

A NATO type arrangement in the Persian Gulf would involve a coordination of defense goals and strategies and could in fact adopt some of the principles and procedural mechanisms employed by the Atlantic organization itself. These arrangements involve collective defense along with ultimate independent national control and could well prove to be a workable solution in the Persian Gulf. It would ease Arab fear of U.S./West predominance in the area. And the fear expressed by some in the West of the continual shipment of sophisticated weaponry to this unstable region could also be tempered. There would not be as great a need for large transfers of weapons to ensure security of the Gulf's traditional nations, since for example Western troops stationed in the area would already possess such weaponry. Ground forces of the Organization would be able to respond to crises faster than a Rapid Deployment Force and would provide a more tangible demonstration of the West's commitment to the security of the Gulf nations.

A Gulf States Defense Organization will require a long term commitment to building bridges of trust and coordination among nations whose security would be greatly enhanced with its success. For the Arab nations it could mean political stability; for the nations of the West it could mean more secure energy sources and a firm foothold from which to halt Soviet advances in the region.

FOOTNOTES

1. In 1971 Iran purchased Abu Musa from Sharja, giving Shaja one-half the oil revenues from the island and 3.5 million dollars aid until 1980, so that Iran could build a military post and control internal affairs. Iran in that same year forcibly wrested the Tunbs from Ras al Khayma which would not come to an agreement with the Shah.

2. Richard Nyrop *et al, Iraq a Country Study,* 3d ed. (Wash., D.C.: The American University, 1979), p. 237.

3. James Buxton, *Financial Times,* April 3, 1980.

4. Albert Wohlstetter, "Half-Wars and Half-Policies", *From Weakness to Strength,* ed. W. Scott Thompson, (San Francisco: Institute for Contemporary Studies, 1980), p. 169.

5. Adeed I. Dawisha, "Iraq: The West's Opportunity", 41 *Foreign Policy,* Winter, 1980-81, pp. 150-153.

6. Reportedly, North Yemen has also been considered for membership in the GCC. *The Middle East,* April, 1982, p. 6.

7. According to *The Military Balance 1981-1982* published by the International Institute of Strategic Studies in London, pp. 49-59, the number of men in the armed forces of the Persian Gulf states is as follows: Iran, 195,000; Iraq, 252,250; Bahrain, 2,500; Kuwait, 12,400; Oman, 14,500; (excluding expatriate personnel); Qatar, 9,700; Saudi-Arabia, 51,700; U.A.E., 42,500. Assuming all GCC components could commit their manpower, the total GCC force available would be 90,800.

6

Turkey's Liberal Revolution

By Dankwart A. Rustow

Two years ago Turkey embarked upon a major economic, social, and political transformation which in its sweep is likely to rank with the Atatürk revolution (1919-26) that created the modern Turkish nation-state, and with the decision by Atatürk's successor Ismet Inönü in 1945-46 to move the country toward democracy and into a long-term alliance with the West.

Most striking has been the reversal of Turkey's economic fortunes. As recently as five years ago, Turkey was in the throes of a major foreign debt and payments crisis. The country surmounted the crisis not just by making a series of concessions to the International Monetary Fund, or consortia of international bankers. Rather, Turkey then reoriented its economy fundamentally by abandoning a half century of protectionism and import substitution and initiating a sustained and aggressive export drive. Dismantling the entrenched structures of subsidized government enterprises and of currency controls, she made a major commitment to open competition and market forces. And after decades of tight restrictions on foreign ownership of capital and land, she instituted a two-pronged long-term strategy to attract foreign investment in the country's agricultural and mineral resources and to transform Turkey into a major international banking and trading center midway between Europe and the Middle East. Thus, although five years ago, Turkey was near the top of any international banker's sick list, today she is held up to other Third World countries as a model of rapid and sustained recovery.

The major turning point foı Turkey was the national election of November 6, 1983, which gave a strong popular vote (45.2%) and solid parliamentary majority (211 out of 399) to Turgut Özal's newly-founded Motherland Party. No one symbolized as clearly the changes that were taking place in Turkey as did Prime Minister Özal himself. In the 1983 election he had emerged as an effective organizer, a tireless campaigner, and Turkey's first public figure to use television to full advantage. In private life he was a devout Muslim. By profession he was an engineer trained in Turkey and the United States, who had helped plan a major hydroelectric dam and had risen through the ranks of Turkey's State Planning Organization. Özal had originally drawn up his economic reform program for the last government in Turkey's moribund Second Republic early in 1980, but he had no opportunity to implement it fully until September 1980, when Turkey's military junta promoted him to Deputy Prime Minister for Economic Affairs. Although levered out of office in 1982 by some of the entrenched economic protectionists from the previous era, he was returned to power in 1983 by his election victory which dramatically reconfirmed the country's commitment to Özal's free enterprise policies.

The results have been widely recognized as a model of export-led growth. Inflation, which had hovered around 100% in 1980, subsided to around 25% by mid-1984; the flow of remittances from Turkish workers in Europe reached an alltime high; exports doubled by 1982; and by 1984, the country was wide open to foreign investment. Meanwhile, Turkish firms reconnoitering the Middle East discovered a lucrative market for construction contracts in countries such as Libya and Saudi Arabia. Moreover, by maintaining scrupulous neutrality in the

---

Dr. Rustow is Distinguished Professor of Political Science at the Graduate School of the City University of New York. His most recent book is *Oil and Turmoil: America Faces OPEC and the Middle East* (New York: W. W. Norton, 1982).

Gulf war, Turkey managed to become the leading trade partner of, and a major transit route for, both Iraq and Iran.

Kemal Atatürk, Turkey's first president from 1923 until 1938, had founded the Turkish Republic on a policy of Westernization, including separation of religion and government, mass education, and adoption of the European alphabet, calendar, and dress.[1] In his economic policies, Atatürk had been concerned, above all, to overcome the country's earlier quasi-colonial status, symbolized by the "capitulations" (trade privileges for foreigners) which the European powers had imposed upon the Ottoman Empire over the centuries. Thus, after some hesitation, Atatürk had espoused the policy of *étatisme,* or public enterprise and government economic planning, then prevalent in depression-ridden Europe.

For today's generation in Turkey, Atatürk's cultural reforms have become so well accepted as to have lost their earlier flavor of militancy. The urban population rose from 24 percent in 1927 to 44 percent in 1980. 82 percent of Turkish men and 54 percent of Turkish women are now literate; English has become the second language in education; and Turkish scientists, engineers, and musicians have made their mark internationally. Mosque attendance is probably the lowest in any Islamic country, and successive Islamic-conservative parties, even under the freest of electoral regimes, have typically attracted no more than 8 or 9 percent of the total vote.

In the Turkish economy, there has been a concerted effort since the 1950s to expand the infrastructure of ports, roads, and power lines. Efforts to increase soil productivity through irrigation and fertilization have raised agricultural productivity during the 1970s by nearly 50%, almost double the rate of population growth. In the industrial sphere, however, the *étatisme,* protectionism, and currency controls of the Atatürk period have been continued and even supplemented with a policy of import substitution. The result has been a series of intermittent but increasingly severe economic crises accompanied by extraordinary strains on the political system, which have caused suspension or curtailment of democratic institutions at about 10-year intervals (1960-61, 1971-73, and 1980-83).

Özal's own prescription for Turkey, from a vantage point of sixty years after Atatürk, is patterned on the example of Japan, a country with scarce natural and highly qualified human resources, dedicated to respect for its traditional cultural values, as it exports the products of its advanced technology that produces a huge volume of exports to the world at large.[2] To be sure, Turkey's economy, with a 1981 per capita GDP of $1,260, still lags far behind Japan's $9,600. Yet, Turkey has a highly diversified base of exports, including textiles, chromium, tobacco, cotton, and hazelnuts. Not to be overlooked are its human exports of industrial workers sent to Germany, and the Turkish construction firms operating throughout much of the Middle East.

The political dialectic that brought Turgut Özal to power was just as remarkable as were the economic consequences. After their bloodless coup of 1980, General Kenan Evren and his military colleagues had set as their first task the suppression of organized terrorism and random political violence, which earlier had cost an average of thirty lives a day. A new constitution, adopted by overwhelming popular vote in 1982, did away with the excessive checks and balances of the previous constitution of 1961, and strengthened the powers of both president and cabinet.

Under Turkey's Second Republic (1961-1980), a system of proportional representation not unlike Israel's had had some of the same party-splintering effects. As a result, the mainstream political groups, such as Süleyman Demirel's conservative Justice Party or Bülent Ecevit's social-democratic Republican People's Party, were unable to form responsible governments. Instead, the system lodged decisive power in the hands of two extremist groups, the Islamic-conservative National Salvation Party of Necmettin Erbakan and the quasi-fascist pan-Turkish party of Alparslan Türkeş. For even though these splinter parties were repudiated in election after election by more than 80 percent of the voters, they could make or break the uneasy parliamentary coalitions, or the even uneasier minority governments which Demirel and Ecevit were forced to form.[3] The mounting frustration of those leaders embittered their personal relations, and thus further aggravated the deadlock. Finally, the Ankara parliament, after five months of desultory balloting early in 1980, proved unable to fill a vacancy in the presidency of the Republic. The perennial stalemate in Ankara encouraged extremists of left and right to take the law into their own hands.

It should be noted that the military regime installed by the bloodless coup of September 1980 proceeded with equal vigor against terrorists of left and right. It succeeded in stopping the smuggling of arms from Bulgaria and Syria to the leftists and the leaking of arms from military depots to the rightists. Similarly, in the trials of perpetrators of political violence and other unconstitutional activities, the authorities impartially prosecuted not only the leadership of "revolutionary" trade unions but also Erbakan's Muslim fundamentalists and Türkeş's ultranationalists. In response to sharp criticism by the Council of Europe and by organizations such as Amnesty International, the government instituted measures to prevent further incidents of alleged police brutality and mistreatment of prisoners. The true measure of the military regime's performance is that security of life and of persons from indiscriminate violence has been reestablished, and a new democratic framework instituted. The overwhelming reaction of Turkish citizens to the 1980 coup has been gratitude for the restoration of law, order, and workable government. This gratitude was expressed in the vote that endorsed the 1982 constitution and elected General Evren to a seven-year term for the presidency.

Two other aspects of the military regime's performance, nonetheless, have come under much criticism, perforce muted in Turkey and more vocal abroad in such bodies as the Council of Europe. The regime continued martial law and press censorship, and sought to control not only the institutions but also the personnel of the succeeding democratic regime. Thus, in the fall of 1983, the junta called for an election in which, though the balloting itself was free, the contest among the candidates was carefully restricted by barring all parliamentarians, parties, and party leaders of the pre-1980 period. Indeed, some parties founded by newcomers — such as Professor Erdal Inönü's Social Democratic Party — were also barred at the last minute, presumably for being too close to some of the outgoing former parties.

It was at this point that Özal's entrance upon the political stage caused the junta's overdetailed game plan to go awry: Turkey returned to democracy at a much faster rate than the generals had planned. With the pre-1980 leaders and parties barred from the arena, the generals of the junta expected the vote to be divided between two groups they themselves had encouraged to form. Moreover, they expected the majority of the vote to go to the Nationalist Democracy Party, which was led by a former general, Turgut Sunalp; and the reaminder to Necdet Calp's Populist Party as the loyal opposition. Yet in the actual election, Calp came in second and Sunalp a poor third, with the voters registering their strong preference for Özal's Motherland Party as the group with the broadest appeal and, among those allowed on the ballot, the only one truly independent of the military. This strong lead of Özal's party was dramatically reconfirmed in the local elections of March 1984, in which the previously banned successors to the older parties were for the first time allowed on the ballot.[4] In sum, despite a number of continuing restrictions, the trend in Turkey by the end of 1984, thanks to the maturity of the Turkish electorate and of its current generation of political leaders, was clearly toward political reconciliation and full restoration of democracy.

The same trend toward bold innovation and reconciliation has become evident in Ankara's recent conduct of its foreign policy. The 1970s had been a period not only of mounting economic and political crisis, but of severe strains in the American-Turkish alliance. In 1974, Turkey, claiming her rights under the 1961 Cyprus Treaty of Guarantee, came to the aid of the beleaguered

Turkish minority by landing her troops in Northern Cyprus. The U.S. Congress, highly dissatisfied with Secretary of State Henry Kissinger's handling of the crisis, and facing Greek-American pressures in a post-Watergate atmosphere, suspended American military aid to Turkey from 1975 to 1979. Such a move in many other countries might have provoked a turn toward neutralist or even anti-American policies. Yet, in the event, it was Greece which temporarily withdrew from NATO military operations. Turkey, on the other hand, welcomed continued cooperation with Washington within the wider alliance framework.

The crisis was overcome through the Carter administration rescinding the aid embargo by 1979. Significantly, the Defense and Economic Cooperation Agreement, which early in 1980 fully restored Turkish-American relations, was negotiated by the Carter administration with governments headed successively by Ecevit and Demirel. It came into full implementation under the Reagan and Evren administrations, thus demonstrating the non-partisan nature, on both sides, of America's relationship with her oldest Middle Eastern ally.

A new crisis over Cyprus threatened late in 1983, when the Turkish community of the North, after a decade of sporadic and fruitless negotiation, proclaimed the formation of an Independent Turkish Republic of Northern Cyprus. Nonetheless, the Congressional response this time was comparatively muted. Conversely, Turkish hopes for recognition of the new state by members of the Islamic Conference Organization (which Turkey had joined in 1976) proved vain. President Rauf Denktash of Northern Cyprus had stressed that the unilateral declaration of independence was meant to promote rather than to cut off negotiation, and so-called proximity talks under United Nations auspices were indeed held intermittently throughout 1984. By year's end, a carefully balanced plan for a bi-communal, bi-zonal federal republic had been drafted, and in January 1985, a first meeting was held between Presidents Spiros Kyprianou of Cyprus and Rauf Denktash of the Northern Republic.

During the period of maximum strain in Washington's relationship with Turkey, Ankara had responded constructively by giving its diplomacy a broader outreach. The main elements in this trend toward "diversification" are Turkey's continuing status as a full member of NATO (since 1952) and an associate member of the European Communities (since 1964); her more recent association with the Islamic Conference Organization (1976);[5] the detente in her relations with the Soviet Union; and her thriving trade with the Middle East and scrupulous neutrality as between Iraq and Iran.

Meanwhile, the years of the Congressional embargo on military aid to Turkey (1975-79) coincided with a major transformation of the Middle Eastern diplomatic scene. President Anwar al-Sadat's trip to Jerusalem (1977), the Camp David talks (1978), and the Washington treaty (1979) had brought about peace between Israel and Egypt, but at the cost of alienating Egypt from the remainder of the Arab world. The fall of the Shah's regime early in 1979 opened a wide gap in American plans for defending the Middle East against Soviet expansionism. This happened at a time when the second oil-price shock reminded the West of its continued dependence on Middle Eastern oil, and when the invasion of Afghanistan demonstrated the reality of the Soviet threat. The Carter Doctrine early in 1980 took the logical step of proclaiming the Persian Gulf a region of America's vital interest, to be defended by military force if necessary. Nevertheless, the bungling of the Iran hostage-rescue effort made a mockery of Carter's proclamation, and certainly made Saudi Arabia and other states of the region reluctant to rely on the protection of America's still-hypothetical "Rapid Deployment Force" (RDF). In the meantime, the eruption of the Iraq-Iran war (September 1980) presented an even more acute danger to the Gulf's oil than had the Soviets in Afghanistan. The final step in the transformation was brought about by the Reagan administration's misadventure in Lebanon (August 1982-February 1984), which further mortgaged U.S. prestige and distracted Washington from more serious Middle Eastern concerns.

The conclusion of the Turkish-American Defense and Economic Cooperation Agreement of 1980, by contrast, presaged a more positive turn of American policy. Among the first tasks under the new agreement was the modernization of Turkey's aging military equipment — and also the construction of new airfields in Turkey's East to block any Soviet push through Western Iran toward Iraq or the Gulf. Late in 1982 the American RDF came closer to reality with the establishment of a permanent U.S. Central Command and the preparation of facilities in Egypt and elsewhere. By mid-1984 the Reagan administration, its hands no longer tied in Lebanon, was free to respond positively and effectively when friendly nations called for help — e.g. in dispatching AWACS (Airborne Warning And Control System) planes to Egypt to thwart a possible incursion from Libya, and to Saudi Arabia to repel a possible Iranian air attack on vital oil installations.[6]

In September 1982, President Reagan had suggested a solution involving Jordan in an attempt to deal with the central, Palestinian aspects of the Arab-Israeli conflict. By the end of 1984, relations between Egypt and Jordan had been restored, and a parliamentary meeting of Yasir Arafat's Palestine Liberation Organization had taken place in Amman. The new situation indicated that King Hussein was readying himself for the role envisaged in the Reagan plan. Similarly, the continuation of the Iraq-Iran war and the prospect of Syrian predominance in Lebanon further helped to rally moderate Arab countries including Hussein's Jordan and Mubarak's Egypt. The Soviet Union itself, feeling isolated throughout most of the Middle East and having reason to consider Syria and Libya less than fully reliable partners, pursued its own interest by reestablishing relations with Egypt, providing tanks and airplanes to Iraq, and supplying an air defense system to Jordan.

In short, the Middle East in 1984 and 1985 presented a spectacle of intense diplomatic maneuvering with moderate Arab states such as Egypt and Jordan in the forefront of the action. Yet with the Arab scene thus in constant flux, it was doubly fortunate that cordiality had been restored to U.S.-Turkish relations by the 1980 agreement. Turkey has long served the West as a reliable ally on Russia's Middle Eastern flank, and the Iranian Shah's fall has vastly enhanced the importance of that function. It is only behind this solid Turkish shield on the northern edge of the Middle East that governments in Cairo, Baghdad, or Damascus can afford to play their precarious balancing acts by leaning toward Moscow one year and toward Washington the next without incurring the fate of governments in Warsaw, Prague, or Kabul. Only behind that Turkish shield can Israel effectively cope with the intermittent hostility of the surrounding Arab countries without having to confront Soviet armies on the Golan Heights.

In sharp contrast to this shifting and volatile Middle Eastern scene to the South, Turkey has pursued its policy unwaveringly for forty years, having resolved in 1945 (fully two years before the U.S. rallied to the cause with the Truman Doctrine) to resist the threat of Soviet expansionism.

Nor is there any fear of domestic reversals or upheavals changing that Turkish policy. As noted earlier, Turkey clung steadfastly to NATO through the days of the Congressional embargo and under governments headed by Ecevit, Demirel, Evren, and now Özal. Just as Özal's economic policy constructively adapts Atatürk's demand for Turkish economic independence to the realities of the late twentieth century, so Turkey's recent policy more generally blends external and domestic elements in much the same way as did Atatürk's national revolution of the 1920s, and Inönü's democratic revolution in the late 1940s.

Atatürk's achievement seems all the more remarkable when we realize that a specifically national Turkish consciousness emerged only toward the beginning of this century. The nineteenth-century dissidents who in their exile in Europe became known as "Jeunes Turcs" had called themselves "New Ottomans." When they came to power in 1908, they found themselves embroiled in a vigorous internal debate among the ideological advocates of Ottomanism, Islamism, and Turkism. It was only with the loss of the non-Turkish speaking parts of the Ottoman Empire in the Balkan and First World Wars, and with the military collapse of the Empire in 1918, that Turkish national consciousness became fully crystallized. And it was victory in the Turkish War of Independence (1919-23) and subsequent diplomatic recognition by the Great Powers that gave Kemal Atatürk and his followers the self-assurance necessary for drawing a clear distinction between their Turkish national identity and their Islamic-Ottoman heritage. Only then was Turkey able to embark on a program of radical Westernization.

The newly founded Turkish Republic owed part of its strength to the fact that though it had inherited the vast majority of the Ottoman Empire's military, administrative, and educational elite, it had nevertheless had the courage to abandon the sultan's imperial and caliphal pretensions, as well as the compensatory pan-Turkish dreams that had proved so fatally alluring to Young Turk leaders such as Enver Pasha. In sum, the Atatürk revolution, combining continuity of leadership with radical change of direction, used Turkey's defeat in World War I and its victory in the War of Independence as a grand opportunity to transform a decaying, traditional, dynastic-theocratic empire into a vibrantly modern nation-state.

The foreign policy of Atatürk's republic was based on cautious normalization of relations with each of the major European powers with which it shared borders (Russia in the Caucasus; and Britain, France, and Italy in Iraq, Syria, and the Dodecanese respectively), as well as with Greece, which had been the main antagonist in the Turkish War of Independence. The friendship treaty with Moscow (1921); the population exchange and friendship treaty with Greece (1923, 1930); the peaceful resolution of the Mosul and Alexandrette questions (1925, 1938); the Montreux Convention on the Straits (1937); and the Treaty of Mutual Assistance with Britain and France (October 1939) — all these may be considered landmarks in a policy that Atatürk summed up in his slogan "Peace at home, peace in the world." The Ottoman Empire had been at war for seven out of every ten years of its 500-year existence. Atatürk's republic has never been at war in the six decades since its founding. This long spell of peace has enabled the Turkish people to concentrate on three revolutions in succession: the national, the democratic, and the economic.

Like Atatürk's national revolution a generation earlier, to Turkey's transition after 1945 from a benevolent single-party dictatorship toward freely and competitively elected government had its foreign and domestic antecedents. At home it could build on the principles of civic equality, universal education, and social mobility introduced by Atatürk while providing an outlet for the accumulated economic and political strains of Turkey's precarious neutrality in World War Two. From abroad, there loomed the threat of Soviet postwar expansion, directed in 1945 first and foremost against Turkey, and hence the acute need to secure the backing of Western powers such as Britain and the United States. "Today the nations of the whole world recognize only one sovereignty, national sovereignty," Atatürk had insisted in rallying his countrymen to a desperate defense in 1919.[7] Just so his successor Ismet Inönü in May 1945 informed his listeners that now that the democracies had won their victory in World War II, the time had come for Turkey to implement the democratic principles contained in her constitution and in the program of Atatürk's and Inönü's own Republican People's Party. Just as Atatürk's choice of national identity became irrevocably consolidated in the following decades, so Turkey's commitment to democracy has been reinforced by the process of economic development and social mobility to which democracy itself so markedly contributed.

The emerging pattern of Turkish politics under President Evren and Prime Minister Özal may be seen as a result of a similar convergence of domestic and foreign factors. The commitment to European civilization, made somewhat reluctantly by the pashas and vezirs of the nineteenth century Ottoman Empire, had filtered down, by Atatürk's day, to lieutenants and school teachers. Today, as a result of universal education, rural economic development, and the mass migration of Turkish workers and villagers to jobs in Western Europe, that commitment to Western values including democracy has become the inalienable property of the Turkish masses. It was the purpose of the political intervention of the military in 1980-83 to reform the country's constitutional and political machinery so as to combine democracy and stability in the future. Yet, aside from institutional details, that stability now rests on a solid social basis, just as the Westernization of Turkish villagers and workers reinforces the country's commitment to its traditional military alliance with the Western democracies.

Turkey's recent foreign policy has preserved the country's close ties with the United States and Western Europe while cultivating closer diplomatic and economic relations with regimes as diverse as Iraq, Iran, Libya, Saudi Arabia, and the Soviet Union. This newly diversified foreign policy is bound to weaken even further the demagogic appeal, on the Turkish domestic scene, of such themes as Islamic fundamentalism and neutralism. Thus it will contribute, indirectly but materially, to the country's internal political stability. The resulting combination of political stability at home and constructive neighborly relations abroad (a latter-day application of Atatürk's "Peace at home, peace in the world") is unique in the Middle East, and hence makes Turkey uniquely valuable as America's ally in the late twentieth century.

FOOTNOTES

1. On Atatürk and his achievement, see (Patrick Balfour) Lord Kinross, *Atatürk: A Biography of Mustafa Kemal, Father of Modern Turkey,* New York: Morrow, 1965; Bernard Lewis, *The Emergence of Modern Turkey,* 2nd edn., London: Oxford University Press, 1968.

2. The Japanese model first attracted attention in Turkey in 1905 when Japan, after one generation of intensive Westernizing reforms, militarily defeated Tsarist Russia. For an attempt at systematic comparison see Robert E. Ward and Dankwart A. Rustow, eds. *Political Modernization in Japan and Turkey,* (Princeton: Princeton University Press, 1964).

3. For an analysis of Turkey's mounting political crisis of the 1970's see my article, "Turkey's Travails," *Foreign Affairs,* vol. 58, no. 1, Fall 1979, pp. 82-102.

4. The percentage polled by the Motherland Party candidates in the local elections was almost the same as in the national election of November (44% as against 45%). The main opposition party in the local and municipal assemblies became Inönü's Social Democrats, followed by the True Path Party endorsed by ex-premier Demirel, with the parties favored by the 1980/83 junta once again coming in last.

5. But note that Turkey routinely accepts the resolutions of the I.C.O. only with explicit reservation of her own constitutional provisions on secularism and strict separation of religion and state.

6. For an analysis of the changing Middle Eastern scene and Reagan's success in implementing the Carter Doctrine, see my article, "Middle East Realignments," *Foreign Affairs,* Vol. 63, no. 3 ("America and the World, 1984").

7. The statement is quoted in D. A. Rustow, "The Army and the Founding of the Turkish Republic," *World Politics,* XI (1958/9), 513-552; for Inönü's announcement of 1945, cf. Rustow, "Turkey's Travails," *op. cit.,* p. 87n.

PART II
RELIGIOUS AND ETHNIC FACTORS

7

The Return of Islam

By Bernard Lewis

In the great medieval French epic of the wars between Christians and Saracens in Spain, the *Chanson de Roland,* the Christian poet endeavors to give his readers, or rather listeners, some idea of the Saracen religion. According to this vision, the Saracens worshipped a trinity consisting of three persons, Muhammad, the founder of their religion, and two others, both of them devils, Apollin and Tervagant. To us this seems comic, and we are amused by medieval man unable to conceive of religion or indeed of anything else except in his own image. Since Christendom worshipped its founder in association with two other entities, the Saracens also had to worship their founder, and he too had to be one of a trinity, with two demons co-opted to make up the number. In the same spirit one finds special correspondents of the New York *Times* and of other lesser newspapers describing the . . . conflicts in Lebanon in terms of right-wing and left-wing factions. As medieval Christian man could only conceive of religion in terms of a trinity, so his modern descendant can only conceive of politics in terms of a theology or, as we now say, ideology, of left-wing and right-wing forces and factions.

This recurring unwillingness to recognize the nature of Islam or even the fact of Islam as an independent, different, and autonomous religious phenomenon persists and recurs from medieval to modern times. We see it, for example, in the nomenclature adopted to designate the Muslims. It was a long time before Christendom was even willing to give them a name with a religious meaning. For many centuries both Eastern and Western Christendom called the disciples of the Prophet Saracens, a word of uncertain etymology but clearly of ethnic not religious connotation, since the term is both pre-Islamic and pre-Christian. In the Iberian peninsula, where the Muslims whom they met came from Morocco, they called them Moors, and people of Iberian culture or under Iberian influences continued to call Muslims Moors, even if they met them in Ceylon or in the Philippines. In most of Europe, Muslims were called Turks, after the main Muslim invaders, and a convert to Islam was said to have "turned Turk" even if the conversion took place in Marrakesh or in Delhi. Farther east, Muslims were Tatars, another ethnic name loosely applied to the Islamized steppe peoples who for a while dominated Russia.

Even when Europe began to recognize the fact that Islam was a religious and not an ethnic community, it expressed this realization in a sequence of false analogies beginning with the name given to the religion and its followers, Muhammedanism and Muhammedans. The Muslims do not, and never have, called themselves Muhammedans nor their religion Muhammedanism, since Muhammad does not occupy the same place in Islam as Christ does in Christianity. This misinterpretation of Islam as a sort of mirror image of Christendom found expression in a number of different ways—for example, in the false equation between the Muslim Friday and the Christian Sunday, in the reference to the Qur'an* as the Muslim Bible, in the misleading analogies between the mosque and the church, the ulema and the priests, and, coming more directly to our present concern, in the imposition on Muslim history and institutions of purely West-

Dr. Lewis is Cleveland E. Dodge Professor of Near Eastern Studies at Princeton University. His most recent books are *The Muslim Discovery of Europe* (1982) and *The Jews of Islam (1984).*

*Koran is the more generally used Western transliteration.

ern notions of country and nation and of what goes on within them. Thus, for example, in Gibbon's fascinating account of the career of the Prophet, Muhammad and his contemporaries were inspired by patriotism and love of liberty, two concepts which somehow seem inappropriate to the circumstances of 7th-century Arabia. For many centuries, Europe called the lands of the Ottoman Empire Turkey, a name which the inhabitants of those lands did not apply to their own country until the final triumph among them of European political ideas with the proclamation of the Republic in 1923.

Modern Western man, being unable for the most part to assign a dominant and central place to religion in his own affairs, found himself unable to conceive that any other peoples in any other place could have done so, and was therefore impelled to devise other explanations of what seemed to him only superficially religious phenomena. We find, for example, a great deal of attention given by Western scholarship to the investigation of such meaningless questions as "Was Muhammad Sincere?" or "Was Muhammad an Enthusiast or a Deceiver?" We find lengthy explanations by historians of the "real" underlying significance of the great religious conflicts within Islam between different sects and schools in the past, and a similar determination to penetrate to the "real" meaning of sectarian and communal struggles at the present time. To the modern Western mind, it is not conceivable that men would fight and die in such numbers over mere differences of religion; there have to be some other "genuine" reasons underneath the religious veil. We are prepared to allow religiously defined conflicts to accredited eccentrics like the Northern Irish, but to admit that an entire civilization can have religion as its primary loyalty is too much. Even to suggest such a thing is regarded as offensive by liberal opinion, always ready to take protective umbrage on behalf of those whom it regards as its wards. This is reflected in the present inability, political, journalistic, and scholarly alike, to recognize the importance of the factor of religion in the current affairs of the Muslim world and in the consequent recourse to the language of left-wing and right-wing, progressive and conservative, and the rest of the Western terminology, the use of which in explaining Muslim political phenomena is about as accurate and as enlightening as an account of a cricket match by a baseball correspondent.

•

If, then, we are to understand anything at all about what is happening in the Muslim world at the present time and what has happened in the past, there are two essential points which need to be grasped. One is the universality of religion as a factor in the lives of the Muslim peoples, and the other is its centrality.

"Render unto Caesar the things which are Caesar's; and unto God the things which are God's." That is, of course, Christian doctrine and practice. It is totally alien to Islam. The three major Middle Eastern religions are significantly different in their relations with the state and their attitudes to political power. Judaism was associated with the state and was then disentangled from it; its new encounter with the state at the present time raises problems which are still unresolved. Christianity, during the first formative centuries of its existence, was separate from and indeed antagonistic to the state with which it only later became involved. Islam from the lifetime of its founder *was* the state, and the identity of religion and government is indelibly stamped on the memories and awareness of the faithful from their own sacred writings, history, and experience. The founder of Christianity died on the cross, and his followers endured as a persecuted minority for centuries, forming their own society, their own hierarchy, their own laws in an institution known as the Church—until, with the conversion of the Roman Emperor Constantine, there began the parallel processes of the Christianization of Rome and the Romanization of Christ.

In Islam, the process was quite different. Muhammad did not die on the cross. As well as a Prophet, he was a soldier and a statesman, the head of a state and the founder of an empire, and his followers were sustained by a belief in the manifestation of divine approval through success and victory. Islam was associated with power from the very beginning, from the first formative years of the Prophet and his immediate successors. This association between religion and power, community and polity, can already be seen in the Qur'an itself and in the other early religious texts on which Muslims base their beliefs. One consequence is that in Islam religion is not, as it is in Christendom, one sector or segment of life, regulating some matters while others are excluded; it is concerned with the whole of life—not a limited but a total jurisdiction. In such a society the very idea of the separation of church and state is meaningless, since there are no two entities to be separated. Church and state, religious and political authority, are one and the same. In classical Arabic and in the other classical languages of Islam there are no pairs of terms corresponding to lay and ecclesiastical, spiritual and temporal, secular and religious, because these pairs of words express a Christian dichotomy which has no equivalent in the world of Islam.* It is only in modern times, under Christian influence, that these concepts have begun to appear and that words have been coined to express them. Their meaning is still very imperfectly understood and their relevance to Muslim institutions dubious.

For the Muslim, religion traditionally was not only universal but also central in the sense that it constituted the essential basis and focus of identity and loyalty. It was religion which distinguished those who belonged to the group and marked them off from those outside the group. A Muslim Iraqi would feel far closer bonds with a non-Iraqi Muslim than with a non-Muslim Iraqi. Muslims of different countries, speaking different languages, share the same memories of a common and sacred past, the same awareness of corporate identity, the same sense of a common predicament and destiny. It is not nation or country which, as in the West, forms the historic basis of identity, but the religio-political community, and the imported Western idea of ethnic and territorial nationhood remains, like secularism, alien and incompletely assimilated. The point was made with remarkable force and clarity by a Grand Vizier of the Ottoman Empire who, in reply to the exponents of the new-style patriotism, replied: "The Fatherland of a Muslim is the place where the Holy Law of Islam prevails." And that was in 1917.

In the 18th century, when, under the impact of Austrian and Russian victories against Turkey and British successes in India, Muslims began to be aware that they were no longer the dominant group in the world but were, on the contrary, threatened in their heartlands by a Europe that was expanding at both ends, the only really vital responses were religious reform movements, such as the Wahhabis in Arabia and the reformed Naqshbandi order which spread from India to other Muslim countries. In the early 19th century, when the three major European empires ruling over Muslims, those of Britain, France, and Russia, were advancing in India, North Africa, and Central Asia, the most significant movements of resistance were again religious—the Indian Wahhabis led by Sayyid Ahmad Brelwi from 1826 to 1831, the struggle of Abd al-Qadir in North Africa from 1832-1847, the dogged resistance of Shamil to the Russians in Dagistan and the Northern Caucasus from 1830 to 1859. All of them were crushed, but made a considerable impact at the time.

Then, for a while, Muslims were sufficiently overawed by the power, wealth, and success of Europe to desire to emulate European ways. But from the middle of the 19th century onward came a further wave of European imperial expansion—the suppression of the Indian mutiny followed by the disappearance of the last remnants of the Mogul monarchy in India and the consolidation of the British Empire in that formerly Muslim realm, the rapid advance of the Russians in Central Asia, the expansion of the French into Tunisia and of the British into Egypt, and the growing threat to the Otto-

*The modern Arab word for secular is *alamani*, literally worldly, i.e., pertaining to this world. Probably of Christian Arab origin, it passed into general use in the 19th century.

man Empire itself, all of which brought a response in the form of a series of pan-Islamic movements.

The unification of Germany and Italy was a source of inspiration in Muslim lands, particularly in Turkey where many Turkish leaders thought that their country could play a role similar to that of Prussia or Savoy in the unification of Germany and of Italy by serving as the nucleus for the unification of a much larger entity. But what would that larger entity be? Not a pan-Turkish entity. Such ideas were still far away in the future and were not even discussed at that time. The basic political identity and aspiration were Islamic, and pan-Islamism was the first and natural response to pan-Germanism and pan-Slavism. It was not until much later that pan-Turkism and pan-Arabism appeared on the political horizon and, even then, there is some doubt as to what they really signified.

The end of World War I, the breakup of the Ottoman Empire, the strains and stresses that followed and the opportunities which seemed to be offered by the collapse of Czarism in revolution and civil war also gave rise to a series of religiously inspired movements—Enver Pasha in a last throw formed the ambitiously titled Army of Islam, the objective of which was to liberate the Muslim subject peoples of the fallen Russian Empire. Some of these movements were linked with the Communists or taken over by the Communists at a time when the fundamentally anti-Islamic nature of Communism was not yet understood. Almost all were expressed in religious rather than in national or even social terms. Most significant among these movements was that which has since come to be known as the Turkish Nationalist Movement. Yet the revolt of the Kemalists in Anatolia was in its first inspiration as much Islamic as Turkish. Islamic men of religion formed an impressive proportion of its early leaders and followers. The language used at the time, the rhetoric of the Kemalists in this early stage, speaks of Ottoman Muslims rather than of Turks, and the movement commanded a great deal of support in the Islamic world. It was not until after their victory and after the establishment of the republic that, as a result of many factors, they began to lay the main stress on nationalist and secular aims.

During the 20th century, at least in the earlier decades, such movements of resistance were more commonly expressed in the fashionable form of political parties and in the fashionable language of political, more or less secular, nationalism. But neither the party organization nor the nationalist ideology really corresponded to the deeper instincts of the Muslim masses, which found an outlet in programs and organizations of a different kind—led by religious leaders and formulated in religious language and aspiration.

•

The most important movement of this type in the 20th century is the organization known as the Muslim Brothers, *al-Ikhwan al-Muslimun,* founded in Egypt by a religious teacher named Hasan al-Banna. The early history of the movement is not clearly known, but it appears to have started in the late 20s and early 30s and to have been concerned in the first instance mainly with religious and social activities. The founder, known as the "Supreme Guide," sent missionaries to preach in mosques and other public places all over Egypt. The Brothers undertook large-scale educational, social, charitable, and religious work in town and countryside, and even engaged in some economic enterprises. They began political activity in 1936 after the signature of the Anglo-Egyptian Treaty in that year and, by taking up the cause of the Palestine Arabs against Zionism and British rule, were able to extend the range of the movement to other Arab countries. They sent volunteers to fight with the Arab armies in the war of 1948, and thereafter seem to have controlled an armed force capable of playing some role in affairs. As a result, the Egyptian Prime Minister Noqrashi Pasha dissolved the organization, confiscated its property, and ordered the arrest of many of its members. He was assassinated in 1948 by one of the Brothers and shortly afterward the Supreme Guide himself was assassinated in circumstances which have never been established.

The Brothers, though illegal, continued to function as a clandestine organization. In April 1951, they were again legalized in Egypt, though forbidden to engage in any secret or military activities. They took part in actions against British troops in the Suez Canal zone and seem to have played some role, of what nature is still unknown, in the burning of Cairo on January 26, 1952. They had close links, dating back to the war years, with some members of the secret committee of the "Free Officers" which seized power in Egypt in 1952. Apart from some general similarities in ideology and aspiration, many of the officers who carried out the coup were either members or at least sympathizers of the Muslim Brothers.

At first, relations between the Brothers and the officers were intimate and friendly, and even when, in January 1953, the military regime dissolved all political parties, the Brothers were exempted, on the grounds that they were a non-political organization. Relations between the new Supreme Guide and the Free Officers deteriorated, however, and before long the Brothers were attacking the new regime for its alleged failures to live up to their Islamic ideals. A period of quiet but sharp conflict followed, in the course of which the Brothers were very active, especially among workers and students and even among the security forces. In January 1954, the government again decreed the dissolution of the Order and the arrest of many of its leaders and followers. Later, there was some reconciliation as a result of which the arrested Brothers were released and the organization allowed to function on a nonpolitical basis. The Anglo-Egyptian agreement of October 1954 stirred up trouble again and was bitterly opposed by the Brothers who insisted that only armed struggle could attain the desired objectives. On October 26, 1954, one of the Brothers just failed to assassinate President Nasser, who retaliated by taking severe repressive measures. More than a thousand were arrested and tried, and six, including some of the intellectual leaders of the movement, were sentenced to death and executed. The Brotherhood was now entirely illegal but nevertheless continued to function and seems to have engaged, from time to time, in conspiracies to overthrow the regime. Many arrests were made and in August 1966 three further executions took place, among them Sayyid Qutb, a leading ideologist of the Brothers. The Order continued to be active, albeit illegal, in some, and more openly in other, Arab countries. It remains a powerful if concealed force at the present day and there are recent signs of a return in Egypt.

The Egyptian Free Officers Movement in 1952 is not the only political movement with which the Muslim Brothers were connected. Another is the Fatah, the largest and most important of the Palestinian guerrilla organizations. Here, too, for obvious reasons, there are some uncertainties regarding the earlier history of the movement, but its past links with the Muslim Brothers seem to be clear. The imagery and symbolism of the Fatah is strikingly Islamic. Yasir Arafat's *nom de guerre,* Abu 'Ammar, the father of 'Ammar, is an allusion to the historic figure of 'Ammar ibn Yasir, the son of Yasir, a companion of the Prophet and a valiant fighter in all his battles. The name Fatah is a technical term meaning a conquest for Islam gained in the Holy War.* It is in this sense that Sultan Mehmet II, who conquered Constantinople for Islam, is known as *Fatih,* the Conqueror. The same imagery, incidentally, is carried over into the nomenclature of the Palestine Liberation Army, the brigades of which are named after the great victories won by Muslim arms in the Battles of Qadisiyya, Hattin, and Ayn Jalut. To name military units after victorious battles is by no means unusual. What is remarkable here is that all three battles were won in holy wars for Islam against non-Muslims—Qadisiyya against the Zoroastrian Persians, Hattin against the Crusaders, Ayn Jalut against the Mongols. In the second and third of these, the victorious armies were not even Arab; but they were Muslim, and that is obviously what counts. It is hardly surprising

*Another proffered explanation of the name Fatah is that it represents a reversed acronym for *Harakat Tahrir Falastin,* movement for the liberation of Palestine.

that the military communiqués of the Fatah begin with the Muslim invocation, 'In the name of God, the Merciful and the Compassionate.'

•

The Muslim Brothers and their derivatives were in the main confined to the Arabic-speaking countries. But there were other parallel movements elsewhere. In Iran this trend is represented by an organization called the *Fida'iyan-i Islam,* the Devotees of Islam, a terrorist group which was active mainly in Tehran between 1943 and 1955 and carried out a number of political assassinations, the most important being that of the Prime Minister, General Ali Razmara, in March 1951. For a while they played some part in Persian politics, until another, this time unsuccessful, attempt on the life of a Prime Minister, Hossein Ala, in October 1955 led to their suppression and prosecution and the execution of some of their leaders. The *Fida'iyan* had links with the Muslim Brothers in Egypt and elsewhere and exercised very considerable influence among the masses and, by terror, on politicians. They even seem to have enjoyed some limited support from the semi-official religious leadership.

In addition to these, there were many other religiously inspired movements in various Islamic countries—the Organization of Algerian Ulema, the Tijaniyya Brotherhood, and, more recently, the National Salvation party in Turkey, and one of the most interesting, the Basmachi Movement in Soviet Central Asia. The word Basmachi, which in Uzbek means brigand or marauder, is applied by the Soviet authorities to a succession of religiously inspired revolts against Russian or Soviet rule which began in January 1919 and continued until 1923 when the movement was decisively defeated, though activity by small groups of rebels continued for a number of years after that. The last Basmachi leader, Ibrahim Beg, withdrew to Afghanistan in 1926 and continued to raid into Soviet territory from there. He was captured by Soviet troops and executed in 1931. It is characteristic of Western attitudes that a search of half-a-dozen major encyclopedias failed to disclose any article on the Basmachis—probably the most important movement of opposition to Soviet rule in Central Asia.*

It is not, however, only in radical and militant opposition movements that this kind of religious self-identification and alignment are to be found. Governments—including avowedly secular and radical governments—have responded to the same instincts in times of crisis. After the Treaty of Lausanne, an exchange of population was agreed between Turkey and Greece under the terms of which members of the Greek minority in Turkey were to be repatriated to Greece, and members of the Turkish minority in Greece repatriated to Turkey. Between 1923 and 1930, a million and a quarter 'Greeks' were sent from Turkey to Greece and a somewhat smaller number of 'Turks' from Greece to Turkey.

At first sight, this would seem to be a clear case of the acceptance to the last degree of the European principle of nationality—Greeks and Turks unwilling or unable to live as national minorities among aliens, returned to Greece and to Turkey, to their own homelands and their own people. On closer examination, this exchange proves to have a somewhat different character. The words used were indeed Greeks and Turks—but what precisely did these words mean at that time and in that place? In the deserted Christian churches left by the Greeks of Karaman in southern Turkey, the inscriptions on tombstones are written in Turkish, though in Greek characters; among the families of the so-called repatriates, the great majority had little or no knowledge of Greek but spoke Turkish among themselves, writing it in Greek characters—just as Jews and Christians in Arabic-speaking countries for long wrote the common Arabic language in Hebrew or in Syriac instead of in Arabic characters. Script all over the Middle East is closely associated with religion. In the same way, many of the so-called Turks sent to Turkey from Crete and other

*The *Sovyetskaya Entsiklopediya,* on the other hand, devotes a long article to discrediting them.

places in Greece had little or no knowledge of Turkish, but habitually spoke Greek among themselves, frequently writing their Greek vernacular in the Turco-Arabic script. By any normal Western definition of nationality, the Greeks of Turkey were not Greeks, but Turks of the Christian faith, while the so-called Turks of Greece were for the most part Muslim Greeks. If we take the terms Greek and Turk in their Western and not in their Middle Eastern connotation, then the famous exchange of population between Greece and Turkey was not a repatriation of Greeks to Greece and of Turks to Turkey but a deportation of Christian Turks from Turkey to Greece and a deportation of Muslim Greeks from Greece to Turkey. It was only after their arrival in their putative homelands that most of them began to learn their presumptive mother tongues.

This occurred among two peoples, one of which is Christian though long subject to Muslim influence, and the other, though Muslim, the most advanced in secularization of all the Muslim peoples. Even today, in the secular republic of Turkey, the word Turk is by common convention restricted to Muslims. Non-Muslim citizens of the Republic are called Turkish citizens and enjoy the rights of citizenship, but they do not call themselves Turks nor are they so called by their neighbors. The identification of Turk and Muslim remains virtually total. And here it may be noted that while the non-Muslim resident of the country is not a Turk, the non-Turkish Muslim immigrant, whether from the former provinces of the Ottoman Empire or from elsewhere, very rapidly acquires a Turkish identity.

●

With Arabs the situation is somewhat more complex. In the Arabic-speaking countries there have for long been substantial minorities of Christians and Jews speaking the same Arabic language, though in the past writing it in a different script and often speaking it with a slightly different dialect. When the idea of Arabism as a common nationality was first launched in the late 19th and early 20th centuries, Arabic-speaking Christians played a prominent part in the movement. It was natural that they should be attracted by a national rather than a religious identity, since in the one they could claim the equal citizenship to which they could never aspire in the other. According to this view, the Arabs were a nation divided into various religions, in which Christians and even at times Jews might hope to share in the common Arabism along with the Muslim majority.

From the beginning, Christians played a leading role among the exponents, ideologists, and leaders of secular nationalism. As members of non-Muslim communities in a Muslim state, they occupied a position of stable, privileged, but nevertheless unmistakable inferiority, and in an age of change even the rights which that status gave them were endangered. In a state in which the basis of identity was not religion and community but language and culture, they could claim the full membership and equality which was denied to them under the old dispensation. As Christians, they were more open to Western ideas, and identified themselves more readily in national terms. The superior education to which they had access enabled them to play a leading part in both intellectual and commercial life. Christians, especially Lebanese Christians, had a disproportionately important role in the foundation and development of the newspaper and magazine press in Egypt and in other Arab countries, and Christian names figure very prominently among the outstanding novelists, poets, and publicists in the earlier stages of modern Arabic literature. Even in the nationalist movements, many of the leaders and spokesmen were members of Christian minorities. This prominence in cultural and political life was paralleled by a rapid advance of the Christian minorities in material wealth.

In recent decades, this prominence has ceased to be tolerable. Partly through measures of nationalization adopted by socialist governments, partly through other more direct means, the economic power of the Christian communities has been reduced in one country after another and is now being challenged in its last stronghold, the Lebanon. Christian predominance in intellectual life has long since been ended, and a new generation of writers has arisen, the overwhelming majority of whom are Muslims. There are still Christian politicians and ideologists, but their role is much circumscribed in a society increasingly conscious of its Muslim identity, background, and aspirations. Among the various organizations making up the Palestine Liberation Organization, the Fatah is overwhelmingly though not exclusively Muslim. On the other hand, many of the extremist organizations tend to be Christian, for in the radical extremism which they profess Christians still hope to find the acceptance and equality which eluded them in nationalism.

●

As the nationalist movement has become genuinely popular, so it has become less national and more religious—in other words, less Arab and more Islamic. In moments of crisis—and these have been many in recent decades—it is the instinctive communal loyalty which outweighs all others. A few examples may suffice. On November 2, 1945, demonstrations were held in Egypt on the anniversary of the issue by the British government of the Balfour Declaration. Though this was certainly not the intention of the political leaders who sponsored it, the demonstration soon developed into an anti-Jewish riot and the anti-Jewish riot into a more general outbreak in the course of which several churches, Catholic, Armenian, and Greek Orthodox, were attacked and damaged. A little later, on January 4-5, 1952, demonstrations were held in Suez, this time against the British in connection with continuing occupation of the Canal Zone. The demonstrators looted and fired a Coptic church and killed a number of Copts. Catholic, Armenian, and Greek Christians had nothing whatever to do with the Balfour Declaration, and the Copts are not English; indeed, there is none more Egyptian than they. One may go further and say that no attack or harm to the Copts was sought or desired by the nationalist leaders. Yet, in the moment of truth, the angry mob reacted instinctively to a feeling that the Copts—native Egyptian, Arabic-speaking, yet Christian—were on the other side, and treated them accordingly.

In such incidents there are no doubt local causes which may help to explain the actions of the mob.* But in both cases, and in others which could be quoted, they reflect a more fundamental attitude summed up in the tradition ascribed — probably falsely, but this makes no difference—to the Prophet, *"Al-Kufru millatun wahida"* — unbelief is one nation (or one religio-political community). The world is divided basically into two. One is the community of the Muslims, the other that of the unbelievers, and the subdivisions among the latter are of secondary importance.

The Lebanese civil war in 1958 and the struggle in Iraq between nationalists and Communists in the spring of 1959 also assumed a strongly religious character. On March 17, 1959, a prayer was recited in Egyptian mosques and published on the front pages of the Egyptian papers, for those who had been killed in Mosul:

> God is great! God is great! There is no might and no power save in God! May He strengthen the martyrs with His grace and ordain them everlasting life in His mercy and abase their enemies in shame and ignominy! God is great! God is great! There is no victory save in God! Whoever offends, God will crush him; whoever exalts himself by wrongdoing, God will humble him! Consider not those who are killed in the cause of God as dead, but as living, with their Lord who sustains them.
>
> O God Almighty, All-powerful! Conquer Thine enemy with Thine omnipotence so that he returns to Thee! O God, Almighty, All powerful, strengthen the community of Thy Prophet with Thy favor, and ordain defeat for their enemy . . . . In faith we worship Thee, in sincerity we call upon Thee, the blood of our martyrs we entrust to Thee, O merciful and compassionate One, Who answers the prayers of him who prays—our innocent martyrs and pure victims for the sake of Thy religion. For the

---

*Local official inquiries decided that these actions had been instigated by "foreign agents." If so, the agents knew which themes to evoke, and how to direct the response.

> glory of Thy religion they shed their blood and died as martyrs: believing in Thee, they greeted the day of sacrifice blissfully. Therefore place them, O God, as companions with the upright and the martyrs and the righteous—how good these are as companions! (Qur'an, iv, 69.)

The religious passion and fervor are unmistakable and did not fail to alarm the Christian minorities in Lebanon and elsewhere as indicating a resurgence of Islamic feeling.

Since then the regimes of the various Muslim states have become more, not less, self-consciously Islamic both in the respect they accord to their own religion and in their treatment of others. This is particularly noticeable in the so-called radical and revolutionary states which are intellectually and socially far more conservative than the politically conservative states, and find themselves obliged to show greater deference to popular sentiment. The treatment of Christians, though still falling well short of persecution, has changed for the worse and has led to a growing number of Christian emigrants, some to Lebanon, others to countries abroad. A Christian Arab writer has described the feelings of these emigrants as follows:

> Christians (they say) have no future in a country which is becoming all the time more socialist and totalitarian. Their children are indoctrinated in the schools, where the syllabus is devoted more and more to Islam and their faith is in danger. Debarred increasingly from public office and from nationalized societies (*sic,* the writer presumably means companies or corporations), robbed of the property of their parents and unable to engage in profitable business in a society where almost everything is under state control, how can they survive?*

An interesting side-effect of these changes is the evolution of attitudes among the groups who are now called Arab Americans. These consist overwhelmingly of Christians of Syrian and Lebanese origin. At the time of their arrival in the United States, they were, apart from a very small circle of intellectuals, virtually unaffected by Arab nationalism, which was in any case still in its infancy even in their countries of origin. At the time that they left their homelands and migrated across the ocean, they, like their neighbors, still thought in unequivocally communal terms. They were first and foremost Christians, and their feelings toward their old homelands resembled not those of American Jews toward Israel but rather those of American Jews toward the countries in Central and Eastern Europe from which they had come seeking a better and freer life in America. For a long time the development of the Palestine conflict left the American Arab Christians unmoved. Their recent involvement is a reflection not of their Arabism but of their Americanism, for in this way they are conforming to a common American pattern of ethnic identity, loyalty, and lobbying. Recent developments such as the suppression and expropriation of Christian schools in Syria, the pressure on Christian communities, and, above all, the current struggle in Lebanon seem already to be leading to a reassessment of their position and, among some of them, a return to earlier attitudes.

●

The growth of Islam's political effect can be observed in two respects—in the field of international politics, and in internal affairs. The attempt to exploit the sentiment of Islamic brotherhood for international political purposes dates back to the 1870s, when the Ottoman government under Sultan Abdulaziz, and then more actively under Sultan Abdulhamid, tried to mobilize opinion all over the Muslim world in support of the faltering Ottoman state and to provide it with the alliances which it needed at this time of weakness and impoverishment. This policy came to be known by the name of pan-Islamism — a reflection in Islamic terms, as was noted above, of such European movements as pan-Germanism and pan-Slavism.

From the beginning, pan-Islamism was of two kinds—one official and promoted by one or another Islamic government in pur-

---

*In *Religion in the Middle East,* edited by A.J. Arberry (Cambridge, 1969), Volume 1, p.415.

suit of its own purposes; the other radical, often with revolutionary social doctrines, and led by a more or less charismatic religious figure, with or without the sponsorship of a government. The counterpart of Abdülhamid was the popular activist Jemal al-Din, known as Al-Afghani. Neither Abdülhamid's official pan-Islamism nor Jemal al-Din's radical pan-Islamism produced much by way of political results, though both undoubtedly heightened the common Muslim sense of identity. This was further helped by the rapid improvement of communications—the press, the telegraph, and, in more recent times, radio and television.

Radical pan-Islamism of various types appeared during the interwar period—at first from left-wing and, indeed, frequently Communist, sources, and later from right-wing, nationalist, and sometimes fascist sources. The most noteworthy example of the latter was the Pan-Islamic activities of the Mufti of Jerusalem, Haj Amin al-Husayni, who enjoyed Nazi sponsorship and eventually spent the war years in Hitler's Germany.

The postwar period brought several new forms of pan-Islamic activity. None came to much until the convening of the Islamic Congress of Mecca in 1954. From the first, the most important initiative in the Mecca Congress was that of the Egyptians whose intentions can already be seen in Nasser's booklet, *The Philosophy of the Revolution*.

> There remains the Third Circle (the first two were the Arab and African circles)—the circle encompassing continents and oceans which, as I have said, is the circle of our Brethren-in-Islam who, wherever their place under the sun, turn with us toward the same Qibla, their lips solemnly saying the same prayers.
>
> My faith in the magnitude of the positive effectiveness that could result from strengthening the Islamic tie that binds all Muslims grew stronger when I accompanied the Egyptian mission to Saudi Arabia to offer condolences on the death of its great king.
>
> As I stood before the Kaaba, with my thoughts wandering round every part of the world which Islam has reached, I fully realized the need for a radical change of our conception of the Pilgrimage.
>
> I said to myself: The journey to the Kaaba should no longer be construed as an admission card to Paradise, or as a crude attempt to buy forgiveness of sins after leading a dissipated life.
>
> The Pilgrimage should have a potential political power. The world press should hasten to follow and feature its news not by drawing attractive pen pictures of its rites and rituals for the delectation of readers, but by its representation as a periodical political conference at which the heads of all the Islamic states, leaders of opinion, scientists, eminent industrialists, and prominent businessmen assemble to draw up at this world Islamic Parliament the broad lines of the policies to be adopted by their respective countries and lay down the principles ensuring their close cooperation until they have again gathered together in the following session.
>
> They assemble demure and devout, but mighty strong; unambitious of power, but active and full of energy: submissive to Divine Will, but immutable in difficulties and implacable with their enemies.
>
> They assemble confirmed believers in the Life to Come, but equally convinced that they have a place under the sun which they should occupy in this life.
>
> I remember I expressed some of these views to His Majesty King Saud.
>
> His Majesty assented saying, "Truly this is the real purpose of the Pilgrimage."
>
> Truth to tell, I personally cannot think of any other conception.
>
> As I contemplate the eighty million Muslims in Indonesia, the fifty million in China, the few millions in Malaya, Thailand, and Burma, the hundred million in Pakistan, the well-nigh over a hundred million in the Middle East, the forty million in the Soviet Union, and the millions of others in other remote and far-flung corners of the earth—as I ponder over these hundreds of millions of Muslims, all welded into a homogeneous whole by the same Faith, I come out increasingly conscious of the potential achievements cooperation among all these millions can accomplish—cooperation naturally not going beyond their loyalty to their original countries, but which will ensure for them and their Brethren-in-Islam unlimited power.*

Under the skillful and energetic leadership of Anwar Sadat,who had been appointed Secretary-General, the Islamic Congress, thus conceived, served as a useful adjunct to Egyptian policy, along with such parallel organizations as the Afro-Asian Solidarity Conference and the Arab League. But it was no doubt this kind of use which also led to its failure. Like the previous attempts by other Muslim governments, this new Egyptian-sponsored pan-Islamism was too obviously related to state purposes and failed to arouse the necessary response from elsewhere.

But there is, perhaps, a deeper reason for the persistent weakness of official pan-Islamism. In the first century and a half of the Caliphate, Islam was indeed one single world state. But at that early date, it ceased to be so, and was never reunited again. Thus, while the political experience of Muslims, the shared memories of the past which they cherish, condition them to a sense of common social and cultural identity, they do not bring them any tradition of a single Islamic state, but rather one of political pluralism combined with socio-cultural unity.

●

Attempts at international pan-Islamism have produced limited results. They have, however, already gone very much further than anything comparable within the Christian world, and have occasionally had diplomatic consequences, as for example when the Arab states as a bloc voted for Pakistan against India's candidacy for the Security Council—and this despite India's devoted and selfless service to the Arab cause. Similar choices may be discerned in the support given to Muslims in the Philippines, Eritrea, and some African countries when they find themselves in collision with non-Muslim majorities or governments. But caution has so far prevailed concerning the position of Muslims in the Soviet Union, in Eastern European states, and in China.*

Islam has shown its strength much more clearly in the internal politics of Muslim countries. Here two examples may serve, both of them in countries under autocratic rule. The first case was in Tunisia, where in February 1960 President Bourguiba put forward the interesting idea that the month-long fast of Ramadan with the resultant loss of work and production was a luxury that a poor and developing country could not afford. For a Muslim ruler simply to abolish or disallow a major prescription of the holy law is unthinkable. What President Bourguiba did was to try to justify its abolition in terms of the holy law itself. This law allows a Muslim to break the fast if he is on campaign in a holy war, or *jihad*. Bourguiba argued that a developing country was in a state of *jihad* and that the struggle to obtain economic independence by development was comparable with a defensive war for national independence. In pursuit of this argument he proposed to abolish the rules whereby restaurants, cafés, and other public places remained open at night during the month of Ramadan and to oblige them to keep normal hours. In support of this new interpretation of the law, he tried to obtain a *fatwa,* a ruling, from the Mufti of Tunis and other religious authorities. The religious authorities refused to give him what he wanted. The great mass of the people observed the fast despite the President's dispensation, and Bourguiba was finally compelled to beat a more or less graceful retreat. Even an autocratic socialist head of state, in pursuit of so worthy an end as economic development, could not set aside a clear ruling of the holy law.

A more striking illustration of the religious limits of autocracy occurred in Syria in the spring of 1967. On April 25 of that year, the Syrian official army magazine, *Jaysh al-Sha'b,* the Army of the People, published an article by a young officer

*Gamal Abdel Nasser, *The Philosophy of the Revolution,* Cairo, n.d., pp.67-68.

*A different kind of exception is the refusal of some Arab and some other Muslim countries to support Turkey on the Cyprus question. One element in this is residual resentment against former rulers; another is disapproval of the policies of Westernization and secularization pursued by the Turkish Republic since its inception.

named Ibrahim Khalas entitled "The Means of Creating a New Arab Man." The only way, according to this article, to build Arab society and civilization was to create

> a new Arab socialist man, who believes that God, religion, feudalism, capitalism, and all the values which prevailed in the pre-existing society were no more than mummies in the museums of history. . . . There is only one value; absolute faith in the new man of destiny . . . who relies only on himself and on his own contribution to humanity . . . because he knows that his inescapable end is death and nothing beyond death . . . no heaven and no hell. . . . We have no need of men who kneel and beg for grace and pity.

This was the first time that such ideas had been expressed in print in any of the revolutionary and radical Arab states, and the response was immediate and violent. Until that point an apparently cowed population had passively acquiesced in a whole series of radical political and economic changes. The suppression of free speech, the confiscation of property evoked no response—but a denial of God and religion in an officially sponsored journal revealed the limits of acquiescence, the point at which a Muslim people was willing to stand up and be counted.

In the face of rapidly mounting tension and violence, the government took several kinds of action. One was to arrest a number of religious leaders; another was to confiscate copies of the journal containing the offending article and to arrest its author and the members of the editorial board. On May 5, the author and editors were imprisoned and on the following day the semi-official newspaper, *Al-Thawra*, "The Revolution," proclaimed the respect of the Syrian regime for God and religion. On May 7, Radio Damascus announced that

> the sinful and insidious article published in the magazine *Jaysh al-Sha'b* came as a link in the chain of an American-Israeli reactionary conspiracy. . . . Investigation by the authorities has proved that the article and its author were merely tools of the CIA which has been able to infiltrate most basely and squalidly and to attain its sinful aims of creating confusion among the ranks of the citizens.

The resistance, it was later announced, had been concerted with the Americans, the British, the Jordanians, the Saudis, the Zionists, and Selim Hatum (a Druse opponent of the regime). On May 11, the author and editors were sentenced by a military court to life imprisonment.

●

Even in Nasserist Egypt, Islam continued to provide a main focus of loyalty and morale. Thus, in the manual of orientation of the Supreme Command of the Egyptian forces, issued in 1965, the wars in the Yemen and against Israel are presented in terms of a *jihad* or holy war for God against the unbelievers. In reply to questions from the troops as to whether the classical Islamic obligation of *jihad* has lapsed or is still in force, orientation officers are instructed to reply that the *jihad* for God is still in force at the present time and is to be interpreted in our own day in terms of a striving for social justice and human betterment. The enemies against whom the *jihad* is to be waged are those who oppose or resist the achievement of these aims, that is to say imperialism, Zionism, and the Arab reactionaries.

> In accordance with this interpretation of the mission of Islam and in accordance with this understanding of the *jihad* we must always maintain that our military duty in the Yemen is a *jihad* for God and our military duty against Israel is a *jihad* for God, and for those who fight in this war there is the reward of fighters in the holy war for God. . . . Our duty is the holy war for God. "Kill them wherever you come upon them and drive them from the places from which they drove you." (Qur'an, ii, 191.)

That is to say, the war is a holy war, and the rewards of martyrdom as specified in scripture await those who are killed in it. Similar ideas are found in the manual of orientation issued to Egyptian troops in June 1973, and it is noteworthy that the operational code name for the crossing of the Canal was Badr, the name of one of the battles fought by the Prophet against his infidel opponents. Incidentally, the enemy named in the manual is not Zionism or even Israel but simply "the Jews." One of the major contrasts between Syrian and Egyptian orientation literature is the far greater stress laid by the Egyptians on religion as contrasted with the more ideological approach of the Syrians.

There have been two recent wars in which Muslims fought against non-Muslims—the Turkish landing in Cyprus and the subsequent fighting, and the Syrian and Egyptian war against Israel in October 1973. Both in Egypt and in Turkey, the language, the rhetoric accompanying the offensives, were strikingly religious. Popular legend, of the kind that flourishes in wartime in all societies, also assumed an overwhelmingly religious character, with stories of intervention by the Prophet and the angels of Allah on the side of the Muslims—i.e., the Egyptians against their enemies. A writer who complained of this in the press, pointing out that it devalued the achievement of the Egyptian armed forces, was bitterly denounced. Not all the Egyptians are of course Muslim. An important minority is Christian, and these too fought in the army and, indeed, number several senior officers among them. This fact is recognized in the guidance manual of the army which invokes Christian as well as Muslim religious beliefs. Yet, at the moment when news got through of the Israeli crossing to the west bank of the Canal, a rumor immediately appeared ascribing this penetration to the treachery of a Coptic officer. There was of course no truth whatsoever in this story, and the Egyptian government took immediate steps to discount and deny it. It was probably not entirely coincidental that a Coptic general was promoted to an army command at that moment. Even more striking is the appearance of religious language among the secular Turks who in the fighting in Cyprus used numerous Islamic terms to describe themselves, their adversaries, and the struggle between them.

In recognizing the extent to which communal loyalty remains a significant force in the life of Muslim countries, one should not fall into the opposite error of discounting the degree of effective secularization. Particularly in the more developed countries, changes which are probably irreversible have already taken place, especially in the realms of social and economic life and in the organization of the law and the judiciary. In some countries, such as Turkey, Iran, and Egypt, geography and history have combined to give the inhabitants a special sense of separate identity and destiny, and have advanced them on the path toward secular nationhood. But even in these Islam remains a significant, elsewhere a major, force. In general, the extent of secularization is less than would at first appear. In education, for example, ostensibly secular schools and universities have to an increasing extent been subject to religious influences. Even in radical states like Syria, the net effect of secularization seems to be directed against minority religions much more than against Islam. A Syrian government report published in October 1967 states that private schools, meaning for the most part foreign-based Christian schools, would be obliged to use Ministry of Education textbooks on Christianity and Islam in which the teaching of the two religions was unified "in a manner which would not leave room for confessionalism . . . incompatible with the line of thought in our age."

●

From the foregoing, certain general conclusions emerge. Islam is still the most effective form of consensus in Muslim countries, the basic group identity among the masses. This will be increasingly effective as the regimes become more genuinely popular. One can already see the contrast between the present regimes and those of the small, alienated, Western-educated elite which governed until a few decades ago. As regimes come closer to the populace, even if their verbiage is left-wing and ideological, they become more Islamic. Under the Ba'thist regime in Syria, more mosques were built in the three years after the *Jaysh al-Sha'b* incident than in the previous thirty.

Islam is a very powerful but still an undirected force in politics. As a possible factor in international politics, the present prognosis is not very favorable. There have been many attempts at a pan-Islamic policy, none of which has made much progress. One reason for their lack of success is that those who have made the attempt have been so unconvincing. This still leaves the possibility of a more convincing leadership, and there is ample evidence in virtually all Muslim countries of the deep yearning for such a leadership and a readiness to respond to it. The lack of an educated modern leadership has so far restricted the scope of Islam and inhibited religious movements from being serious contenders for power. But it is already very effective as a limiting factor and may yet become a powerful domestic political force if the right kind of leadership emerges.

In the period immediately preceding the outbreak of the Six-Day War in 1967, an ominous phrase was sometimes heard, "First the Saturday people, then the Sunday people." The Saturday people have proved unexpectedly recalcitrant, and recent events in Lebanon indicate that the priorities may have been reversed. Fundamentally, the same issue arises in both Palestine and Lebanon, though the circumstances that complicate the two situations are very different. The basic question is this: Is a resurgent Islam prepared to tolerate a non-Islamic enclave, whether Jewish in Israel or Christian in Lebanon, in the heart of the Islamic world? The current fascination among Muslims with the history of the Crusades, the vast literature on the subject, both academic and popular, and the repeated inferences drawn from the final extinction of the Crusading principalities throw some light on attitudes in this matter. Islam from its inception is a religion of power, and in the Muslim world view it is right and proper that power should be wielded by Muslims and Muslims alone. Others may receive the tolerance, even the benevolence, of the Muslim state, provided that they clearly recognize Muslim supremacy. That Muslims should rule over non-Muslims is right and normal.* That non-Muslims should rule over Muslims is an offense against the laws of God and nature, and this is true whether in Kashmir, Palestine, Lebanon, or Cyprus. Here again, it must be recalled that Islam is not conceived as a religion in the limited Western sense but as a community, a loyalty, and a way of life—and that the Islamic community is still recovering from the traumatic era when Muslim governments and empires were overthrown and Muslim peoples forcibly subjected to alien, infidel rule. Both the Saturday people and the Sunday people are now suffering the consequences.

---

*The same concept finds expression in the Muslim law of marriage, which allows a Muslim man to marry a non-Muslim woman, but categorically forbids a marriage between a non-Muslim man and a Muslim woman. The rationale is that in a marriage the man is the dominant, the woman the subordinate, partner—and Islam must prevail.

8
Understanding Islam in Politics

By Daniel Pipes

Much of the conventional wisdom about Islam and politics needs to be examined with skepticism.
—*Michael C. Hudson*

Events in recent years have made clear the extraordinary role of Islam in world politics. As fundamentalist Muslims took power and achieved international importance in such states as Pakistan and Iran, understanding Islam became necessary to interpret their goals and ideology. Islam also gave direction to governments in Saudi Arabia and Libya, influenced electoral politics in democracies such as Turkey, India, Malaysia, and Indonesia, and posed important challenges to Communist regimes in Yugoslavia and Afghanistan. Islam heightened domestic tensions in Nigeria, the Sudan, Egypt, Syria, Iraq, and Burma, and it defined rebellions against the central government in Chad, Ethiopia, Cyprus, Lebanon, Thailand, and the Philippines. It fueled international conflicts between Turks and Greeks, Arabs and Israelis, Pakistanis and Indians, and Somalis and Ethiopians. In the Arab-Israeli dispute, for example, Islam helped account for the nature of Arab resistance to Israel's existence, the intense involvement of such distant countries as Iraq and Libya, and the meaning of the call in the Palestine National Covenant for the establishment of a "secular and democratic" state in Palestine.

There has been an increasing need to understand the political impact of Islam. Proposals for solving the Arab-Israeli conflict must consider the special Islamic concern for the control of territory. American or Soviet negotiators seeking military bases in the Middle East must take into account vehement Islamic sensibilities against the presence of non-Muslim troops. NATO strategists must keep abreast of Islamic sentiments among Turkey's population if they want to gauge the likelihood of the alliance's southeast flank holding firm. As Muslims of the Soviet Union increase in number and grow out of their isolation, the Islamic drive for self-rule will probably shape their aspirations; in all likelihood, they will use religious institutions to organize against the regime and they will look to foreign Muslims for support. Even business interests need to watch Islam, for many key oil-exporting states entertain "powerful sentiments of grievance and resentment against the Christian West"[1] which could seriously upset the oil market in coming years.

How Muslims feel and act has enormous international repercussions: they number about 832 million strong and make up roughly one-fifth of mankind; substantial groups of Muslims live in ninety-one countries and in them constitute a population of about 3.6 billion. Muslims control most of the oil available for export and they inhabit many of the globe's most strategic areas. Yet the question of Islam in politics has been given little serious thought until recently and remains a largely obscure topic in the Western world. In my view, this is not so much because of the subject matter's complexity but because of the many blinders that obstruct the vision of observers. For Westerners, the main problems have to do primarily with an historic animosity toward Islam and a disinclination to acknowledge the political force of religion. In the hope of clearing up some of these problems, this

---

Dr. Pipes is Director of the Foreign Policy Research Institute in Philadelphia. He is also the author of *An Arabist's Guide to Egyptian Colloquial* (Foreign Service Institute, 1983) and *Slave Soldiers and Islam* (Yale University Press, 1981).

This article, with minor changes by the author, forms Chapter 1 of *In the Path of God, Islam and Political Power,* by Daniel Pipes, © 1983, by Daniel Pipes. Reprinted by permission of Basic Books.

article discusses some obstacles that face a Westerner interested in understanding Islam and politics.

Recognizing Religion's Impact on Politics

For Westerners of the late twentieth century the notion that Islam — or any religion — acts as an autonomous political force may be a somewhat novel thesis. The influence of religion in the West has diminished so much during the past five hundred years that many persons, especially intellectuals, find it difficult to appreciate the political import of religion in other times and places. Developments such as the Iranian Revolution, the central role of the Catholic church in Poland, and the rise of fundamentalist pressure groups in the United States provoke much discussion, but the deeper, ongoing influence of religion tends to be ignored. Three obstacles are especially important in this: secularism, materialism, and modernization theory.

Secularization is a "process whereby religious thinking, practice and institutions lose social significance" and are increasingly restricted to the domain of private faith.[2] Since the early Renaissance the West has experienced a steady contraction of religion away from politics, ethics, education, and the arts; this process has gone so far that faith retains hardly any importance in the lives of many people. But secularization has not been universal, for some people in the West and many in other regions of the world, especially Muslims, are still deeply swayed by religious concerns. Secularized observers often disbelieve that the faith that they disdain can retain such force. For someone who views religion as a sign of ignorance and backwardness, the passions it arouses can be baffling. "To the modern Western mind, it is not conceivable that men would fight and die ... over mere differences in religion; there have to be some other 'genuine' reasons underneath the religious veil."[3] For someone whose daily life is not touched by faith, understanding the power of religion in politics is difficult and requires an open mind and a willingness to see things from a different vantage point. There is a tendency to discount the power of religion. Khumayni's rise to power is viewed as a result of economic discontent, of social tensions, political disenfranchisement, repression, charismatic leadership — anything but the fact that millions of Iranians believed this man could create a new order which, in fulfilling God's commands, would solve Iran's problems. More generally, "many commentators ... believe that present Islamic activism is primarily nationalist or socialist or economically motivated movements dressed in the garb of religion." Yet, "to ignore religious desires and to concentrate only on the economic drives or secularized political motives is to limit unnecessarily the scope of our understanding."[4]

The philosophical doctrine of materialism impedes comprehension of religion in politics even more than secularism. This doctrine originated in the nineteenth century, when European intellectuals, expressing unlimited confidence in rationality and science, formulated elaborate theories to demonstrate how predictably mankind responds to its environment. One of these theories was Karl Marx's historical materialism which emphasized the importance of changes in economic conditions. According to Marx, the system of labor (slave, serf, capitalist, or socialist) determines all other aspects of society, including its politics, social relations, and culture. Neo-Marxists later modified this theory to allow more flexibility, but Marxist thought continues to emphasize the role of economic relations, while discounting the importance of ideas (scornfully dismissed as "ideology"). Individuals may believe they are motivated by ideals — patriotism, religious fervor, justice, and humanitarianism — but materialists invariably discern hidden economic motives. They believe that a calculus of cost and benefit, often unconscious, determines most actions. For example, abolitionists in the United States thought they were motivated by morality to fight the slave trade, but the materialists would argue that slavery hurt their economic interests. So, too, material concerns spurred American rebels in 1776, French revolutionaries in 1789, and Nazi supporters in the 1930s.

The trouble with this is that the theory of materialism reduces humans to one-dimensional beings, and the truth is not so simple. Economic factors indisputably have a major role (and they had been quite neglected before Marx), but they do not singly determine behavior. One cannot ignore the wide range of emotions that are not tied to material self-interest: loyalties to family, tribe, ethnic group, language group, neighbors, nation, race, class, or religion sometimes overlap with material interests and sometimes run contrary to them. Material factors alone fail to account for the actions of a George III or a Hitler. They cannot explain the endurance of Communist rule so long after its economic deficiencies have become manifest. Nor can they explain why Japan, an island almost barren of natural resources, is so much better off than mineral-rich Zaire. Much less do material factors show why so many people willingly give up their lives for political causes they believe in.

Similar problems arise when economic motives are assigned to actions taken in the name of religion. Materialists dismiss faith as a camouflage for self-interested drives, and they consider it naïve to accept religious impulses at face value. But how do material interests explain the wars of the Reformation that split communities and made family members into one another's enemies? What possible gains could the early Mormons have expected as they left their homes and trekked to Utah? Though the Crusades, the long conflict in Ireland, and the recent proliferation of religious sects in South Korea all had economic dimensions, it is surely mistaken to view them primarily as economic phenomena. The Crusades, for example, were far more than an imaginative method of making work for the unemployed or a way to gain new markets; material factors alone could never have inspired such enormous undertakings, with such risks. And how would material factors explain the suicide massacre at the People's Temple in Guyana?

Islam too must be understood as a potent force. Popular views in the West ascribe almost everything Islamic to "fanaticism," as though this were an independent cause,[5] but serious discussions usually discount the role of Islam in favor of material factors. For example, a collection of essays, published in 1978 under the title *Muslim-Christian Conflicts: Economic, Political and Social Origins,*[6] covers five countries (Lebanon, Egypt, the Sudan, Yugoslavia, and Cyprus), but not once in 245 pages do the authors ascribe clashes between Christians and Muslims to emotions arising from religious allegiance! As the book's subtitle indicates, they interpret every conflict as a symptom of material grievances. But how would such grievances explain, for instance what happened during one week in May 1982 in Lebanon: the explosion of a car bomb outside a mosque under construction, injuring four persons; the bombing of a West Beirut mosque near the house of a former Muslim prime minister; the assassination of a senior Islamic figure; the killing of a Maronite priest; and the suicide mission conducted in a Maronite church in Tripoli, killing three and injuring five? Whatever the economic relations between Muslims and Christians, these acts could have been inspired only by religious sentiments; similar examples can be found in all the other conflicts too. The mere fact of adherence to Islam has profound political consequences. If one-quarter of India's people had not converted to Islam, the subcontinent would not have been split as it was; further, the millions of Muslims who abandoned their homes in India to move to Pakistan neither expected nor received material benefits for this transfer. Islam, like other religions, inspires impractical acts which cannot be ascribed to economic self-interest.

Modernization theory, an explanation of how nations develop, was articulated in the two decades following World War II, during a unique period of prosperity and self-confidence in the West, when science seemed invincible and progress irresistible. Modernization theory postulates that all nations must follow the lines laid down by the first countries to become modern, especially Britain and the United States. In the political sphere, this means rationalization, the civic society, and secularization. Religion is seen as an obstacle to modernization and its hold is expected to weaken as nations advance.

These ideas were already discredited before 1979, but the Iranian Revolution delivered a final blow. Modernization theorists could not account for the emergence of Ayatullah Ruhollah Khumayni as the Iranians' leader against the shah, whose revolt represented the first major political movement *away* from Western political ideals in the twentieth century. Until Khumayni, the leaders of all great social upheavals in modern times espoused objectives deriving at least in part from European thought, whether liberal, Marxist, fascist, or other. Prominent non-Western leaders such as Kemal Atatürk, Gamal Abdul Nasser, Ahmed Ben Bella, Kwame Nkruma, Robert Mugabe, Mahatma Gandhi, Pol Pot, Ho Chi Minh, Mao Tse-tung, Sukarno, and Fidel Castro espoused goals familiar to the West, notwithstanding their local flavor. They conceived of all aspects of public affairs — sovereignty, economics, justice, welfare, and culture — in ways that could be traced to European origins, and this encouraged many observers to assume that peoples everywhere in the world must emulate the West politically.

But Khumayni was different. Although unconsciously influenced by Western notions, he rejected them; his lack of interest in the West was symbolized by his spending four months in the tiny village of Neauphle-le-Chateau and never visiting Paris, a mere twenty miles away. Khumayni's goals existed entirely within an Islamic context; further, he had no Western constituency and was indifferent to his image in Stockholm or Berkeley. Satisfied to live as his ancestors had, unfamiliar with the Western concepts of progress, he wished for nothing more than to return to the Islamic ways he supposed had once prevailed in Iran. Khumayni showed that the force of religion need not wane with the building of an industrial society, that secularism need not accompany modernization. Yet the discrediting of modernization theory did not signal its disappearance; the notion that religion is on the way out has been so widely disseminated that it may take decades before it loses force. Perhaps the time has come to suggest that secularization is a transient process peculiar to the West; not only will it not affect the rest of the world, but it is likely to be reversed even in the Occident: "An historian of the non-Western world can hardly fail to see Western secularism as a sub-facet of specifically Christian history; indeed, of specifically Western Christian history."[7]

Together, secularization, materialism, and modernization theory cause the press and scholarship too often to ignore Islam's role in politics. In recent times, Islam came to the attention of Western analysts in the mid-1950s, as the Soviet Union, threatening Western interests, built up links to Abdul Nasser's government in Egypt and other countries of the Middle East. In response, European and American writers debated the relationship of Islam to communism. One school of thought saw Islam as a "bulwark against communism," on the grounds that its emphatic monotheism precluded Muslims from accepting any ideology based on atheism; the other (and more subtle) view was that structural similarities made the transition from Islam to communism an easy one. As fears that the Middle East would accept Marxism-Leninism abated, however, interest in Islam among political observers subsided, and nationalism became the focus of attention. Discussion of Islam as a political factor then went into dormancy for about twenty years. Views expressed in a 1965 book, *Islam and International Relations*, summed up the attitudes of those times. One writer, Fayez A. Sayegh, stated that "at least with respect to 'neutralism,' ... Islam has had little, if any noticeable influence upon the reasoning, planning, decision-making, or expression of Muslim policy makers." The volume's editor noted that most of the authors "maintained that Islam is actually of quite limited significance in shaping the attitudes and behavior of Muslim states in international relations today."[8] For years, politics in Muslim countries was discussed almost without reference to Islam.

Attention to Islam increased after the 1967 Arab-Israeli war, and even more after the 1973 conflict. In 1976, Bernard Lewis urged in "The Return of Islam" that more attention be paid to the phenomenon of Islam, criticizing "the present inability, political, journalistic, and scholarly alike, to recognize the importance of the factor of religion in the current affairs of the Muslim world."[9] Westerners were increasingly receptive to the role of Islam by the time Khumayni appeared. As he gained power, the Western world watched with amazement; Islam seemed capable of unleashing the most extraordinary forces. Then, overreacting to events in Iran, many in the Occident suddenly thought Islam capable of anything; "in a remarkably brief span of time, Islam has been elevated from a negligible coincidence of human geography, to a political force of global import."[10] Indeed, interest in Islam became excessive, leading one journalist to complain in 1981 that "where before Islam was largely ignored, now it is seen everywhere, even where it has no particular relevance."[11] The war between Iraq and Iran which broke out in September 1980 was almost universally understood in terms of Shi'i-Sunni differences and the threat of Shi'i revolt in Iraq, though the cause of fighting had much more to do with a straightforward dispute over territory.[12]

But if Islam received too much attention in Iran, it remained underestimated elsewhere. In May 1981, the press portrayed disturbances in the Yugoslav province of Kosovo in purely nationalist terms, as Albanians versus Serbs, and stressed the Albanians' economic plight, without making any mention of the underlying Muslim-Christian tension. In other cases, the impulse toward materialistic interpretations prevailed: increased emphasis on religious law in Pakistan was portrayed as a function of economic travails, and the upsurge of the Muslim Brethren in Egypt was seen as a symptom of poverty.[13] Economic factors did have great importance, but they fitted within a cultural context molded by religion. Were Iranians Buddhist, a religious leader would not have vanquished the shah; were Lebanon entirely Christian, the civil war would not have occurred; were Israel Muslim, its neighbors would have accepted its establishment.[14]

Western discussions of the Islamic revival of the 1970s consistently de-emphasized the importance of religious feelings; indeed, some analysts even disputed the significance of Islam in the Iranian Revolution.[15] Others denigrated the role of Islam more generally. In 1977, Michael C. Hudson referred to "the growing irrelevance of Islamic standards and criteria" to Arab politics.[16] Two studies of Islam and politics which appeared in 1982 made even more sweeping and more surprising statements. Thomas W. Lippman asserts that "religion as such had nothing to do, for example with Somalia's decision to end its partnership with the Soviet Union" or the Libyan invasion of Chad, or Arab opposition to the Baghdad Pact, and so forth; Edward Mortimer concludes a book on "the politics of Islam" with the observation that "it is more useful, in politics at any rate, to think about Muslims than to think about Islam."[17] (Why then, one wonders, did he write a book about Islam?)

False Parallels with Christianity

Approaching Islam in politics with the Christian experience in mind is misleading. Because the community of Christians shares almost no political traits, there is a mistaken predisposition to assume that Muslims also do not.

Superficially, there is much in common between the two faiths. Just as devout Christians disagree on their proper role in public life, so do observant Muslims. At one extreme, medieval popes and Imam Khumayni* claimed supreme political authority for the religious leaders; at the other, some Protestant sects and Sufi (mystical) orders encouraged their adherents to total political quiescence. The role of Christianity varied enormously in the Roman Empire, medieval Scandinavia, fifteenth-century Ethiopia, Calvinist Geneva, Spanish Mexico, Mormon Utah, and Soviet Russia; so too did Islam in Muhammad's Medina, Abbasid Baghdad, Almoravid Spain, Mongol Iran, Mataram Java, the Murids' Senegal, the Turkish Republic, and Saudi Arabia.

Catholic, Orthodox, and Protestant Christians spanned the entire ideological spectrum, advocating every form of political authority and economic system, working toward mutually exclusive goals — all in the

*This was the accepted title for Khumayni after his return to Iran in February 1979.

name of the same religion. The Catholic church served as a bulwark against communism in Poland, yet priests led leftist causes in South America. New Protestant movements in South Korea and the United States were identified with conservative causes, while the Zimbabwean clergy had a key role in rebelling against White rule in their country. It is difficult to imagine what a book on "Christianity and political power" could say that would apply to Christians generally; any search for common themes would surely fail.

"Islam and political power" might appear to have as little validity, for pious Muslims had political objectives as diverse as those of their Christian counterparts. In recent years, the three most prominent and self-conscious Islamic states were neatly spread across the political spectrum, Saudi Arabia being aligned with the United States, Libya with the Soviet Union, and Iran rejecting ties to either super-power for as long as it could. Some Islamic movements opposed pro-Western governments (as in Egypt and Turkey) and others conflicted with Soviet-backed regimes (as in Syria and Afghanistan). In the Sudan, Islamic sentiment favored greater state control, in Thailand it inspired a revolt against the central government. Islam had a populist quality in Tunisia but served as an instrument of state in Pakistan. Identification with the religion indicated defiance of the regime in the USSR and solidarity with it in Malaysia. Islam stood behind conservatism and revolution, peace and war, tolerance and bigotry; how does Islam and politics lend itself better to generalizations than Christianity and politics?

The answer is that Islam, unlike Christianity, contains a complete program for ordering society. Whereas Christianity provides grand moral instructions but leaves practical details to the discretion of each community, Islam specifies exact goals for all Muslims to follow as well as the rules by which to enforce them. If Christians eager to act on behalf of their faith have no script for political action, Muslims have one so detailed, so nuanced, it requires a lifetime of study to master. Along with faith in Allah comes a sacred law to guide Muslims in all times and places. That law, called the Shari'a, establishes the context for Islam as a political force; however diverse Muslim public life may be, it always takes place in the framework of Shar'i ideals. Adjusting realities to the Shari'a is the key to Islam's role in human relations. Hence, this analysis emphasizes the role of sacred law, the motor force of Islam in politics.

Emphasis on the law implies that other aspects of Islam require less attention. Topics that can be nearly omitted include: (1) Theology. Whatever its spiritual significance, theology has little bearing on public life. To the extent that disputes about the nature of God, faith, the Qur'an, and the day of judgment do affect politics, it is through their impact on the Shari'a. (2) Sufism. The mystical orientation of Sufi groups often implies a lack of interest in details of the law or in public affairs; those Sufis who do become engaged in politics have concerns which fit into the same Shar'i context as everyone else. (3) Differences in sect and *madhhab*. Mainstream Muslims (that is, Muslims whose faith is acknowledged as valid by a majority of other Muslims) follow legal tenets so similar to each other that their differences can be ignored. Practices of the Sunni, Shi'i, and Khariji sects do vary, but only in minor ways; for example, Shi'i laws differ most dramaticaly from those of the Sunnis in that they permit temporary marriage. Sunni Islam contains four *madhhab*s, or rites of law, whose rulings differ enough to affect crucially a defendant in a courtroom but not so much as to concern us. (4) Fringe groups. Such non-mainstream groups as the Assassins, Druze, 'Alawis, Ahl-i Haqq, Baha'is, and Ahmadis venture far from the Shari'a, and in doing so they step beyond the pale of Islam. (5) Intellectual discourse. Thinkers affect Islam's role in politics only to the extent that they deal with the Shari'a. Philosophical, historical, and moral discussions are ignored here except where they touch on the problems of living in accordance with the sacred law. (6) Personal faith. Islam in politics concerns the implementation of laws more than individual faith. A believer is more likely to try to live by

Islamic precepts, but not always. Non-Muslims or Marxists from a Muslim background occasionally find it useful to apply some of the Islamic laws (this happened in the European colonies and in Soviet-dominated Afghanistan), while devout believers who are mystics or secularists may resist implementing the Shari'a.

Islam as an Identity

There are other sources of confusion between religion as a personal faith and as a factor in social relations. From a political viewpoint, the faith of the individual Muslim eludes analysis; also, it usually has little direct bearing on matters of power. Private feelings need not be related to political actions. Islam is more usefully studied as a source of laws, affiliations, customs, attitudes and traditions, with an emphasis on its influence over behavior in the public sphere.

Examples may help to demonstrate this point. Muhammad Ali Jinnah, the founder of Pakistan, and most of his strongest supporters were Western-educated and not notably pious Muslims, yet it was they who fought to establish a state defined along religious lines. In contrast, the Islamic leaders opposed the creation of Pakistan and preferred to remain citizens of India. (This parallels the Israeli case: Zionism appealed mostly to assimilated Jews.) By all accounts, Muhammad Anwar as-Sadat was a pious man, yet he strenuously resisted the efforts of Islamic fundamentalists in Egypt, he made the country's family law more European, and he was assassinated by Islamic extremists. In contrast, some of the leaders of the Iranian Revolution, notably Abolhassan Bani-Sadr, were suspected of indifference to the Almighty; this did not prevent them, however, from taking an active part in the most rigorous re-assertion of political Islam in the twentieth century. Throughout the 1970s, as Mu'ammar al-Qadhafi developed his own ideology and moved further away from Islam, he placed increased emphasis on Islam as a political bond and identity. In secularizing societies, the notion of a "non-believing Muslim" is widespread; in the Soviet Union, for example, Communists of Muslim origin routinely avow that while they are atheists, they are also Muslims and proud to be so. Perhaps the sharpest distinction comes from Lebanon: a driver, the story goes, was stopped at a checkpoint sometime during the civil war and asked to tell his religion. "Atheist," came the answer. But in the midst of a war fought along religious lines, the guard needed to know the driver's confessional affiliation, not his personal beliefs, so he asked, "Are you a Christian atheist or a Muslim atheist?"

Muslim and Christian Relations

Iranian occupation of the United States Embassy in Tehran in November 1979 did more than prompt a diplomatic crisis between two governments; it also unleashed a flood of passions among Iranians and Americans. Iranians took to the streets by the thousands to blame America for every conceivable ill in Iranian life, "from assassinations and ethnic unrest to traffic jams [and] drug addiction."[18] Imam Khumayni called America the "Great Satan," vilified its culture, and insulted its leaders. Americans responded with uncommon rancor, harassing Iranian students and painting Khumayni's dour features on dart boards and toilet bowls. Iranians provoked more American venom than any other foreign people since World War II; Koreans and Vietnamese, for example, never inspired a fraction of this abuse. The passions on both sides hinted at something more than the usual political difference; they suggested the pinching of a nerve.

Previous tensions between Iran and the United States could hardly explain this outpouring of feeling, for the two states had enjoyed consistently good relations from W. Morgan Shuster's trusty service as Iran's financial advisor in 1911 to Jimmy Carter's exuberant New Year's Eve toast to the shah in 1977, when he described Iran as "an island of stability in one of the more troubled areas of the world" and termed this achievement "a great tribute to you, Your Majesty, and to your leadership and to the respect, admiration and love which your people give to you."[19] The two governments enjoyed a broad cooperation, especially in the two vital areas of oil production and staving off the

Soviet Union. Tens of thousands of Iranians studied in the United States and similar numbers of American technicians worked in Iran without arousing special problems.

If previous relations between Iranians and Americans cannot account for the strength of feeling in 1979, the explanation lies further back, in the long history of hostility between Muslims and Christians. Since A.D. 634, when, only two years after the death of Muhammad, Arabians and Byzantines first went to battle, Muslims and Christians have experienced a uniquely bellicose relationship. Arabians, Turks, Moors, Moros, and Somalis earlier filled the role now taken by the Iranians, while Greeks, Spaniards, Franks, Russians, and Ethiopians had the American part. Even today, Muslims and Christians carry on the long tradition of conflict in such places as Chad, the Sudan, Uganda, Cyprus, Lebanon, and the Philippines. As a diplomat recently observed in reference to the Muslim-Christian rivalry in the Malaysian province of Sabah: "What is happening in Sabah today is only a small reflection of what happened in the Crusades 1,000 years ago."[20]

This hostile legacy still lives, influencing Muslim and Occidental perceptions of each other. On the Muslim side, resentment and envy of the West have seriously impaired attempts to come to terms with the modern world. On the Christian side, biases inherited from medieval times concerning the corruption of the Islamic faith, the licentiousness and violence of its adherents, and the fanaticism of its appeal continue still to shape attitudes. "People who melt at the plight of Asians and Africans are unaffected by that of Arabs and Moslems."[21] Of course, any attempt to see Islam and the Muslims as they really are requires that these prejudices be recognized and set aside. Common images of fatalism, fundamentalism, and fanaticism are simplistic and mean; they do injustice to a full and rich faith which satisfies the spiritual and emotional needs of hundreds of millions of adherents. The old biases are false and gratuitous.

If uncritical hostility has been the historic obstacle to understanding Islam, a new tendency toward uncritical adulation is almost equally unhelpful. In recent years, Islam has won the self-serving support of two types of Westerners. The first group uses it as a vehicle to attack its own society; for people who feel ill at ease in the West, embracing Islam serves as a way to change allegiance and to reject the world they grew up in. Conversion to Islam by the British foreign service officer Harry St. John Philby[22] or the American boxer Cassius Clay symbolized a radical rejection of Western ways precisely because Islam is so widely considered antithetical to the West. Although few go so far as to convert, other people—Jews, anti-Semites, and disaffected intellectuals especially — take up Islamic causes as a way to express their own discontent. Radicals such as Voltaire, Napoleon, and Marx, all known for their antagonism toward religion, had a soft spot for Islam, precisely because it stood for the negation of religion as practiced in the West.

The second group of apologists, more recent but far more influential today, promotes Islam for profit. Praise for Islam and the Muslims often translates into better access to research materials for professors, funds for administrators, visas for journalists, votes at the United Nations for diplomats, and trade opportunities for businessmen. Incentives for Islamphilia have multiplied many times with the coming of the oil boom and the huge increase in disposable income available to some Muslims.

With the exception of the Black Muslim movements in the United States, pro-Islamic sentiments tend to be restricted to the elite in the West, for it is they alone who have enough contact with Islam to become familiar with it or gain from it. Sufi disciples come from the ranks of the affluent no less than do the sponsors of the National Committee to Honor the Fourteenth Centennial of Islam, an American group organized in the late 1970s to promote goodwill toward Islam and funded primarily by businesses with interests in the Arab oil-exporting states. Thus, a dichotomy results: while a few Westerners at the top praise Islam for personal reasons (be it alienation or profit), the masses, still swayed by the old hostility, despise and fear Islam.

Ideal and Reality

Islam calls forth intense reactions. It inspires a powerful loyalty among Muslims which no other faith can rival. Muslims almost never apostacize and they feel particularly strong bonds to their fellow believers. At the same time, Islam provokes an unparalleled animosity from non-believers, thanks to its reputation as an aggressive faith. These contrary opinions of Islam are roughly equal in scope; just as Muslim solidarity has a strong emotional appeal from Morocco to Java, so too does a suspicious, even hostile, reaction prevail among non-Muslims from Spain to Bali.

Accordingly, polarized attitudes dominate almost every discussion of Islam as a social and political force. Muslims and those sympathetic to Islam emphasize the idealism of the faith, while its detractors concentrate on the failings of Muslims. "There is a tendency ... for believing Muslims to use the term [Islam] as an ideal, and for outside observers to use it [to mean] an historical-sociological actuality."[23] Believers speak of Islam's concern with justice, its high moral and political standards, and its cultivation of learning; opponents respond by noting the corruption, political instability, and illiteracy in Muslim countries. Muslims see their society as spiritually superior to the materialistic West; critics call this an excuse for continued poverty. Supporters recall Islam's medieval splendor, denigrators point to its contemporary woes. What Muslims call communal solidarity, foes call facelessness; warm relations for one appear as a lack of privacy for the other. Muslims decry open sexuality in the West and claim that the veil protects the honor of women; for outsiders, Islamic mores are hypocritical, the veil demeans females, and honor merely justifies the double standard for men and women. Promiscuity appalls Muslims, polygamy scandalizes Westerners.

But it is Islam's attitudes toward non-Muslims that provoke the most arguments: Muslims proudly point to their record of tolerance and contrast it with the attacks on their lands by the Crusaders, modern European imperialists, and Zionists. Islam's critics emphasize the lack of equal rights for non-Muslims under Muslim rule and the persecution, insecurity, and humiliation they must endure. They claim also that the Muslim conquests in the Middle East, Europe, Africa, and India were as aggressive as those of the West.

But these polemics do not elucidate the impact of Islam. When one side selects the most attractive ideals of a religion, and when the other chooses only the worst aspects of its history, a disengaged observer lacks balanced information to reach his own conclusion. A lack of non-partisanship severely impedes intelligent discourse about Islam in politics.

A related problem concerns the tendency of Westerners to take Islamic ideals at face value. While those ideals do profoundly influence Muslims, conclusions cannot be drawn directly from them to explain political patterns. For example, one might take the Muslim record in war, and the Western tendency to invoke Islam to explain both success and failure. When Muslims do well, it is explained by their belief that houris in heaven will reward them eternally for death in battle against infidels. This explanation, first heard in early medieval times, still surfaces; as recently as 20 July 1980, a *New York Times* correspondent wrote that the Afghan insurgents do so well against the Soviet Union because they believe that "dying in the name of Islam is a glorious death, one that will insure their place in paradise." When Muslims lose, Islam can be used to explain that too: the Qur'an imbues the Arabs with a love of words, they get caught up in the mists of their own rhetoric, and so their military efforts against Israel are undermined. Thus does Islam spur fanatical resistance in one place and inefficacy in another. Islam is called on to explain other opposites too — fatalism in Malaysia and endemic instability in Syria. Such simplistic characterizations should be discarded.

The real force of Islam in politics lies not in the sparse injunctions of the Qur'an or in the hypothetical unity between religion and politics, but in the complex interaction between Islam's ideals, Muslim historical experience, Western civilization, and current events. To understand these, it is necessary to know something about Islamic law and Muslim history, not just in recent times nor exclusively in the Middle East, but also in previous eras and other regions. In particular, the importance of looking outside the Middle East needs emphasis.

Concentration on the Middle East

"Islam" so vividly conjures up the Middle East that the 612 million Muslims living outside the Middle East receive far less attention than the 220 million within it.[24] Mention of Islam brings to mind Arabs, Persians, and Turks, deserts and camels, baklava and strong coffee, men in flowing robes and veiled women — not Fulanis, Bosnians, and Malays, nor the lush plains of Bangladesh, the gruels of Mali, or the sarongs of Indonesia. Muslims receive attention in rough proportion to their proximity to the eastern Mediterranean. Thus is it easy to miss many facts: that Indonesia has the largest Muslim population of any country; that the Indian subcontinent has more Muslims than does the entire Middle East; that more Muslims are citizens of the Soviet Union than of any Middle Eastern country save Turkey; and that China has a larger Muslim population than the entire Arabian peninsula. Perhaps most surprising, six of the nine countries with the largest Muslim populations are outside the Middle East (Indonesia, Pakistan, Bangladesh, India, the Soviet Union, and Nigeria).

Several reasons account for the prominence of the Middle East. First, it has a special importance and visibility in Islam, being the region where the religion was born, developed, and elaborated; now, as in the past, nearly all the key events take place there. As the core of Muslim life, the Middle East is the location of the most important sites of Islamic pilgrimages (Mecca and Medina as well as others in Israel and Iraq), the key educational institutions (such as Al-Azhar University in Cairo), publishing houses dealing with Islamic topics (Cairo first, followed by Beirut), and leading Islamic movements (the Muslim Brethren, reformist thought, the Iranian Revolution). Arabic and Persian, the two international languages of Islam, are read, spoken, and cherished wherever Muslims live. Languages spoken by Muslims outside the Middle East are unknown inside it, their thinkers unheard of, their political movements without general impact. For these reasons, Muslims in the remoter regions look to the Middle East for spiritual direction, and this situation is seldom reversed. A Syrian would as soon look to Yugoslavia or Indonesia for guidance in Islam as a Frenchman would look to Latvia or New Zealand to learn about European philosophy.

Second, the Middle East is the Muslim area most in contact with Europe. This made it the focal point of Western concern throughout history and the region at the forefront of the Muslim response to modern Europe. Other factors making the Middle East prominent include its location in the heart of the eastern hemisphere (increasing its cultural centrality), the antiquity of its civilization, the presence of Israel, and the oil boom.

Outside the Middle East, only Pakistan can aspire to a role of international importance in an Islamic context, yet even its claim is relatively weak. Pakistan has a very large Muslim population, a sophisticated culture, and strong lines of fundamentalist and reformist thought. It underwent the unique experience of coming into existence as an Islamic state (through the partition from India in 1947). But Pakistanis use primarily Urdu and English, neither of which is widely known by men of religion in the Middle East, so their works remain largely unknown in the core area. Language, however, is not the main obstacle: such writers as Abul Ala Maududi and Abul Hasan Nadwi published in Arabic too, yet even they could not win an influence on Muslims as great as that of Middle Easterners.

The prominence of the Middle East means that most studies of Islam stay within this small portion of the Muslim world and do not touch the full range of Muslim life. Focusing exclusively on the Middle East, however, misses the richness of Muslim experience and the complete picture of Islam's influence. One may legitimately study the Muslims of only the Middle East (or any other region) but it is improper to portray this as a study of Islam in general or as valid for Muslims everywhere, which is so often done. The Muslims of the Middle East are not typical: they have fewer non-Islamic cultural elements to contend with and they fall most thoroughly under the influence of Islam's civilization. No doubt the Middle East is the key Muslim region, but it is far from the only one. Hausas in West Africa are no less inspired than Kurds in Iraq by Islamic goals, and Malays are part of Islamic history as much as Yemenis; an assessment of Islam in politics (or Sufism or the arts) requires that the gamut of Muslim peoples be taken into account.

Muslims live in places rarely associated with Islam. One European country, Albania, has a majority Muslim population, and significant minorities live in Yugoslavia and Bulgaria. Ethiopia, famous as the Christian enclave in Africa, is nearly half Muslim, as is Nigeria. Fiji in the mid-Pacific has an 8 percent Muslim element, and three nations of the Caribbean basin, Trinidad and Tobago, Guyana, and Surinam, have Muslim minorities of, respectively, 6, 9, and 20 percent. Sizeable Muslim communities exist as far north as the Volga River and as far south as South Africa. In the past generation, Islam has acquired a formidable new presence in countries such as the United States, Britain, France, Germany, and South Korea.

Poor Terminology

The study of Islam is complicated by confused and imprecise terms. A brief discussion of usages here may help to reduce these ambiguities.[25]

"Islam" is the faith in one God and in the Qur'an as the literal word of God. A "Muslim" is one who accepts the Islamic faith. These terms derive from the Arabic, closely reproducing its pronunciation, and are acceptable to everyone. "Moslem" and "Mussalman" are older pronunciations of Muslim, reflecting Persian and Turkish influences; while not incorrect, they have an archaic ring and have fallen out of current usage. The term "Muhammadan" (or "Mohammedan" or "Mahometan") also means Muslim, but this is a Western neologism dating from the sixteenth century, which imitates the formation of the word "Christian" by taking the religion's central figure and naming his followers after him. But this term is inaccurate and gratuitously offensive to Muslims, for Muhammad's significance in Islam does not compare to that of Jesus Christ in Christianity (indeed, in Muslim eyes, his stature is hardly greater than that of Jesus; one might as well call them Christians). "Muhammadanism" as a synonym for Islam compounds this error and is even more insulting to Muslims. The confusion that surrounds these terms can be illustrated by the farcical adjective synonyms provided in *The New Roget's Thesaurus* for Mohammedan: "Moslem, Moslemic, Moslemite, Mussulmanic, Islam, Islamic, Islamistic, Islamitic."[26] Ethnic terms have also been used to designate Muslims, including: Saracen, Moor, Arab, Turk, and Tatar. Even today, "Arab" and "Muslim" are often used interchangeably, although five-sixths of the Muslims do not speak Arabic and about five million Arabic-speakers are Christian.

Islam is variously used in English to refer to a place, a people, a faith, and a civilization: "in Islam," "the Islamic community," "the Islamic religion," and "the Islamic world." But this overtaxes a single word and invariably leads to confusion. Marshall G. S. Hodgson suggests referring to the place as Islamdom (patterned on Christendom), to the people as Muslims, to the faith as Islamic, and to the civilization as Islamicate (patterned on Italianate).[27]

"Islamdom" encompasses all Muslims, wherever they form communities (that is, wherever they are more than isolated individuals). It differs from *Dar al-Islam,* which refers to territories under Muslim control, and from *Dar al-Harb,* lands not under Muslim control. Islamdom includes all Muslims, whether living in Dar al-Islam or Dar al-Harb. Like Islamdom, *umma* ("the community of Islam") also refers to the whole body of Muslims, but Islamdom has a geographic quality and the umma has spiritual and emotional connotations. The umma also includes isolated individuals.

Arabic words should be employed where

translations into English conjure up wrong images (such as "holy war" for *jihad*) or cumbersome ones ("the Abode of War" for Dar al-Harb). Although the use of Arabic words may be challenging to read, it is necessary if exact meanings are to be conveyed. In one special case, however, a well-known Arabic word should be translated regularly into English: Allah. Calling the Lord of Islam Allah seems to imply that Muslims direct their prayers to a divinity who differs from that of the Jews and Christians, whereas, in fact, Muslims worship the same Lord; Allah is merely the Arabic translation of God. Note how profoundly this changes our understanding of the Islamic statement of faith, from the bellicose-sounding "There is no God but Allah," to the unthreatening "There is no deity but God."[28]

For an understanding of Islam's role in politics, an outsider must consciously push aside some familiar concepts and tools of analysis. For Westerners, the conventional division of politics into right- and left-wing has little value when categorizing Islamic movements. Nationalism in Islamdom is transformed into something quite distinct from its Western prototype, while law and territory have wholly different meanings. Unless the reader makes efforts to think along new lines, he will probably find comprehension of Islam elusive. When dealing with Islam, first impressions are usually faulty. To take one prominent nonpolitical example: assuming that human relations have the same implications in Islamdom as in the West, Europeans and Americans naturally interpret the harem in light of what it would mean to them—something akin to the Victorian ideal of frail females staying at home, out of harm's way. In fact harems reflect a vision of women as sexually insatiable beings who must be kept away from men, lest they seduce the men from devotion of God and so foment anarchy.

Ironically, it is more difficult to distance oneself from Western notions when dealing with Westernized Muslims; whereas understanding of the Ottoman Empire or Khumayni's Iran obviously requires adjustment of the standard Western tools of political science, Turkey or Tunisia can be seen in more narrowly Western ways, for so much of the tone and style of their politics resembles public life in Europe and America. But this is superficial; despite speaking French fluently or wearing a tie to work, nearly all Muslims live culturally more in a context formed by Islam than in one formed by the West.

FOOTNOTES

1. John B. Kelly, *Arabia, the Gulf and the West* (New York: Basic Books, 1980), p. 494.

2. Ernest Krausz, "Religion and Secularization: A Matter of Definitions," *Social Compass* 18 (1971-72): 212. He defines religion as "an institutional aspect of society based on beliefs in a superhuman or supernatural realm" (p. 211).

3. Bernard Lewis, "The Return of Islam," in *Religion and Politics in the Middle East,* ed. Michael Curtis (Boulder, Colo: Westview, 1981), pp. 10-11.

4. John Olbert Voll, *Islam: Continuity and Change in the Modern World* (Boulder, Colo: Westview, 1982), p. 2.

5. In the words of a veteran Indian administrator, writing in 1901: "All Mussulmans in particular are assumed to have fanaticism, as if it were some separate mental peculiarity, belonging to the Mahomedan faith, which accounted for everything, and especially for any very marked impulse." Meredith Townsend, "Asia and Europe," *Westminster,* 1901; quoted by Norman Daniel, *Islam, Europe and Empire* (Edinburgh: At the University Press, 1966), p. 468.

6. Boulder, Colo.: Westview.

7. Wilfred Cantwell Smith, *On Understanding Islam* (The Hague: Mouton: 1981), p. 252.

8. J. Harris Proctor, ed., *Islam and International Relations* (London: Pall Mall, 1965), pp. 61, vii. In the same book, however, H. A. R. Gibb wrote the following prescient passage:

> The traditional linking of Islam to social and political activity persists, and will continue. I am not prophesying the revival of an overtly militant Islam, but among the unknown range of possibilities now being produced by contemporary stresses in every continent, one that the West would be wise not to discount is the re-emergence of a revived and reconstructed Islam as a world factor (p. 23).

9. Lewis, "Return of Islam," p. 11.

10. Martin Kramer, *Political Islam,* The Washington Papers, no. 73. (Beverly Hills: Sage, 1980), p. 15.

11. Edward Mortimer, "Islam and the Western Journalist," *Middle East Journal* 35 (1981): 502.

12. For an argument making this point, see my article, "A Border Adrift: Origins of the Conflict," in *The Iran-Iraq War: New Weapons, Old Conflicts,* ed. Shirin Tahir-Kheli and Shaheen Ayubi (New York: Praeger, 1983), pp. 3-25.

13. William L. Richter, "The Political Dynamics of Islamic Resurgence in Pakistan," *Asian Survey* 19 (1979): 554-55.

14. This raises the intriguing thought: what would the Arabs have done had the Zionists made Arabic, instead of Hebrew, their national language?

15. For example, note the opening sentence of Mangol Bayat's article, "Islam in Pahlavi and Post-Pahlavi Iran: A Cultural Revolution?": "The 1978-79 Iranian revolution is too often perceived by the superficial observer, the uninformed media representative as well as the religiously inclined Iranian himself, as symbolizing the rise of Islam and the Muslims against its enemies from within and without." In *Islam and Development: Religion and Sociopolitical Change,* ed. John L. Esposito (Syracuse, N.Y.: Syracuse University Press, 1980), p. 87.

16. Michael C. Hudson, *Arab Politics: The Search for Legitimacy* (New Haven, Conn.: Yale University Press, 1977), p. 17.

17. Thomas W. Lippman, *Understanding Islam, an Introduction to the Moslem World* (New York: New American Library, 1982), pp. 182-83; Edward Mortimer, *Faith and Power: The Politics of Islam* (New York: Random House, 1982), p. 406. I am grateful to John Voll for pointing out both these statements.

18. *New York Times,* 6 January 1980.

19. *Ibid.,* 2 January 1978.

20. *Far Eastern Economic Review,* 25 November 1972.

21. Morroe Berger, *The Arab World Today* (Garden City, N.Y.: Anchor, 1964), p. xiv.

22. Who was the father of Kim Philby, the Soviet double agent, a man who turned even more radically against his own society.

23. Smith, *On Understanding Islam,* pp. 43-44.

24. Admirable exceptions include: Clifford Geertz, *Islam Observed: Religious Development in Morocco and Indonesia* (New Haven, Conn.: Yale University Press, 1968); Xavier de Planhol, *Les Fondaments géographiques de l'histoire de l'Islam* (Paris: Flammarion, 1968); and Voll, *Islam.* Almost every other work which deals with more than one region is written by many authors.

25. My article, "Understanding the Middle East: A Guide to Common Terms," *International Insight,* July/August 1981, pp. 33-36, explains usage of Middle East, Arab, Semite, and Islam.

26. *The New Roget's Thesaurus,* ed. Norman Lewis (Garden City, N.Y.: Garden City Books, 1961), p. 399.

27. Marshall G. S. Hodgson, *The Venture of Islam* (Chicago: University of Chicago Press, 1974), 1:56-60.

28. Outside the Arabic-speaking countries, however, "Allah" often acquires a specifically Islamic tone. For example, in late 1981 the Malaysian government banned a Bible translated by Christian missionaries into the Malay language because "some Muslims complained that it translated God as Allah rather than using the generic Malay word for God, which is *tuhan.* Allah, they said, was the name only for the Muslim God" *(Far Eastern Economic Review,* 2 April 1982).

9

Religion and its Role in National Integration in Israel

By Emanuel Gutmann

Religion plays a many-faceted and ambiguous role in the integrative process in the Israeli Jewish community. Very broadly viewed, it has a dual and contradictory function. In one sense it is a source of disaffection, dissension and conflict. But to the extent that it provides a common primordial sentiment, it preserves common attachments and loyalties and thus serves as a fusionary element. Judaism, as one observer put it, has, contrary to many other religions, hardly ever departed from its path as a mono-ethnic religion, and this has strengthened the ethno-national coherence among Jews, both in practice and in purpose.[1] In functional terms it may be said that religion is generally considered to have served as the main integrative factor preserving the unity of the dispersed, pre-emancipation Jewish people,[2] and that if one wishes to speak of a unity of a "community of fate," it is of the fate of co-religionists.

However, in terms of modern national ideology, based on the secular conception of national Jewish identity, one would have to reverse the above formula and say that the Jews have always been a mono-religious people.[3] This may be considered to be the prevailing view in Israel, i.e., a part of the Zionist belief system, and it implies that most Israelis today accept the notion that being Jewish (including Israeli Jewish) has at least something to do with the Jewish religion.[4] Only a tiny minority claim that in the totality of Judaism, religion has — or ought to have — no part at all.

However, this formulation makes it necessary to redefine the role of religious elements in present-day Judaism, and there are widely divergent points of view on this issue, in Israel and in the diaspora. There are those (a few in Israel, and more abroad) who reject outright the major premise of the nationalist formulation, either from a fundamentalist-Orthodox standpoint, which pursues the pre-modern conception of a religious, or ethno-religious congregation; or from a diametrically opposite view: the assimilationist assertion that Jews are members of a "church" (or churches) bound, it may be, by sentiments of solidarity with co-religionists in other countries, but abjuring all ethnic ties.

It is possibly one of the paradoxes of Jewish history that with the advent of emancipation for the Jewish communities in the West in the eighteenth and nineteenth centuries that coincided with the secularization of their host societies and the general decline of religious belief, the Jews were redefined, as a religious congregation in the strict sense of the term. The rise of competing "trends" and movements within Judaism which made for religious diversity produced, in combination with the widespread assimilatory tendencies in the respective countries, a very considerable centrifugal momentum. Consequently, the effectiveness of religion as an integrative factor declined drastically. However, this was at least partly counterbalanced by the anti-assimilatory barriers exercised by their gentile surroundings and, on another level, by the continued cohesiveness of the Jewish communities in most of the Eastern — i.e., Oriental — countries.

With the beginning of the modern Jewish national movement, toward the end of the

---

Dr. Gutmann is Professor of Political Science at the Hebrew University, Jerusalem. His essay (with Jacob M. Landau), "The Political Elite and National Leadership in Israel," appears in *Political Elites in the Middle East,* edited by George Lenczowski (American Enterprise Institute, 1975). He is co-editor of *The Roots of Begin's Success: The 1981 Israeli Elections* (St. Martin's Press, 1983).

nineteenth century, the situation became rather more complex. Zionism, based on the conception of the Jews as a national entity rejected, and was as such rejected, by the assimilationist tendencies prevailing in Western nation-states, and found itself in radical dissension with Jewish orthodoxy and fundamentalism, which repudiated any possibility of a Jewish variant of modern secular nationalism.

Consequently, and as a result of the rather extreme secular and laicist attitudes of a substantial part of the early Zionist leadership, and their often rather clamorous, manipulative adoptions of religious sentiments, rituals and symbols to serve profane purposes and actions — religion became a factor of conflict within Judaism, and with obvious disintegrative effects. Later, and more markedly since Israel's independence, although there has prevailed a widespread consensus about the role of common religious attachments as a sort of all-embracing "umbrella" providing one element of national unity, religion has increasingly become a more contentious subject. The use of state authority by the religious establishment has contributed to formal integration on the legal level, but at the same time has not been able to contain the widening cleavage between the religious and the nonreligious sectors of the population.

•

The single, most important element in the integrative functioning of religion is the "establishment" of the "church" as part of the governmental institutions. The integrative function has thus neither been left to fortuitous, uncontrolled developments nor to fluctuating power relations and the impact of spiritual activities, but has been formally institutionalized. Religious communities (and not only the Jewish) are formally recognized by the State. The rabbinate is a wing of the government, religious courts are part of the judicial system and religious law in matters of "personal status" (i.e., in family and domestic relations) is part of the law of the land. It is this so-called non-separation that is at the heart of church-state relations.[5] However controversial, a substantial majority of Israelis are at least reconciled to this system, precisely because of its reputed integrative effect.

At the cost of possible politicization of religion, in the sense of outside, secular, and at least conceivably even laicist and anti-religious control and interference, religious norms in their orthodox interpretation are being enforced with the sanction of the civil authorities. Rightly or wrongly, the imposition of religious marriage and divorce on all Israelis is generally considered to be the single most effective measure to preserve the unity of the Jewish people in Israel and throughout the world, whereas the introduction of civil marriage (and for that matter, of religious but non-orthodox marriage) would jeopardize this unity irreversibly. How significant this unity is in the eyes of the Israeli public can be gathered from its views, as expressed to pollsters, and by the fact that most Israelis are willing to go along with this situation, even at the price of a feeling of discomfort and uneasiness because of the hardships it can create and what at least some consider as the indignities to which a few unfortunates are exposed by the system.

However, given the prevailing social and ideological cleavages in the Israeli public and, in particular, in its attitudes on religious matters, what can be said about the existing system is that, at best (which is a good deal), it provides the formal premise for national-behavioral unity in a number of small yet crucial ways. One of these is the country-of-origin aspect of this system. Slight differences in ritual, such as in the prayerbook, the conduct of synagogue services and various dietary laws, had developed in the various countries of dispersion over the centuries. When the British Mandatory Government of Palestine gave the rabbinate its first formal status, it was established on a dual basis, i.e., in all its bodies there must be parity between Ashkenazi and Sephardi/Oriental rabbis and also in the case of all other dignitaries. Thus, on the council of the Chief Rabbinate there are two co-equal Chief Rabbis. Attempts to abolish this duality in the name of "national integration" have not been successful; those who resist this change do so, when they feel the need to have recourse to ideological arguments, in the name of pluralism.

In this, as in many of its activities, and because of the very fact of its basis in governmental authority, the religious establishment is hardly conducive to national integration in the sense of promoting consensus or diminishing the effect of cleavages. Moreover, the effectiveness of this system in the wider sense is, to say the least, controversial, and at times may actually be counterproductive from the point of view of its own expectations.

Another example of a practice aiming at behavioral uniformity is the strict surveillance of the rabbinate over the observance of *kashrut* in all public institutions, including the army, and in all organizations and firms open to the public. Even if this aspect of orthodoxy is less weighty from the national-existential viewpoint, it can be more meaningful in everyday life. Here again the Israeli public, in spite of frequent expressions of dissatisfaction, is willing, by and large, to accept the existing arrangements for the sake of unity, even if it actually means adopting the norms of the minority as guidelines for the behavior of the majority. But it is difficult to see in this any substantial integrative achievement and, not surprisingly, many Israelis regard the situation as no more than the result of internal power politics, or more specifically, the outcome of coalition bargaining that puts the votes of the religious parties at a premium.

The same applies to public Sabbath observance and, in particular, to the stoppage of practically all public transportation on the Sabbath. This is the result of coalition agreements alone; it was not a legally established practice, as were some of the laws (on *kashrut*, etc.,) previously mentioned, but its origins are of little importance to that part of the Israeli public that finds it unduly restricting. To the non-religious section of the Israeli public it is seen, above all, as religious coercion, and this feeling is at least partly derived from the belief that this kind of interdiction does not contribute to social integration. And for that matter, it does not even operate effectively in the view of those who do observe the Sabbath.

Quite different kinds of problems are presented by the status of the various non-Orthodox trends in Judaism. Although it would appear at first sight that what is involved here is, perhaps, religious integration, in the Israeli context these problems have very serious connotations for national integration. Partly because of the claim to exclusivity by the "right faith," common to so many religions, but also for the avowed purpose of disallowing what is seen as religious dissension in order to prevent the cleavages and conflicts deriving from it, the "established" Jewish "church" is Orthodoxy, to the exclusion of all others, not only the Conservative, Reform and Progressive movements, but also of such communities as the Karaites, Samaritans and Falashas. Freedom of religion and of worship is, of course, guaranteed, and also operates in practice, and the Supreme Court has actually ruled that freedom of religion and ritual must be allowed and supported by the authorities even if this comes at the price of religious dissension.[6] This is not, however, what is at stake here. The relevant issue is that what must be considered the benefits of establishment, both the material and the legal, are preserved for the orthodox "church" alone, as the only fully recognized Jewish "religious community." Thus the other trends do not receive (unimportant exceptions excepted) any governmental financial support, and their religious dignitaries are prohibited from performing marriages or sitting in religious courts. Moreover, the marriages and divorces performed abroad by rabbis of these trends are not recognized in Israel. The inequity of this treatment can be seen in proper perspective when it is compared with the treatment received by those ultra-orthodox groups and congregations who do not "recognize" the established orthodoxy, but are nonetheless fully supported and recognized by the religious establishment — to the extent that they are interested at all in such support and recognition.

The other, much more salient aspect of this situation from the integrative vantage point is, of course, that as long and so far as the determination of "Who is a Jew?" is in the hands of orthodoxy, all these groups cannot be integrated into the Jewish-Israeli community. This point is yet far from being settled with any finality, and the tug-of-war over it continues. The rabbinate and the religious sector have not had it all their own way by any means, but full social integration into the national community has, to varying degrees, not yet been made possible for members of these non-establishment religious groups.

•

But Man lives not by law and regulations alone, and national integration is not achieved solely by these means. The world of symbols, of ritual and myth has important functions in the lives of individuals and collectives, as creators of group identity, as instigators of group cohesion (and dissensus) and as providers of legitimacy. Because of the peculiarities of Jewish history, there was no symbolism other than religious before secularization began, and all material and spiritual aspects of life were conceived as part of the religious order.[7] The new Israeli state made widespread use of traditional religious symbolism for its own ceremonial and the like purposes, analogous in a way to what Bellah has called "civil religion" in the United States.[8] The reasons for this usage stem both from the feelings of collective filial piety and the appeal these symbols have to the most solid common denominator of the highly heterogeneous Jewish-Israeli population. Zionism, independence and statehood are looked upon (at least by the non-orthodox majority) as the most significant *caesura* in Jewish history, demanding innovative symbols to match a revolutionary ideology. But, at the same time, they are also conceived of as stages in the eternal existence of the Jewish people, a concept which demands the reception of old values and symbols, even if in a new and transformed shape or form. In this process, as often as not, the original or traditional forms have been cast aside and the innate contents or values (which, at least partly, depend on the ideological stand of the people involved), discarded. But at least one observer has seen indications that the traditional religious context or meaning of some of these symbols has recently been reasserting itself, and that other traditional symbols are steadily penetrating into national life without first being secularized.[9] This tendency to make use of religious symbols for non-religious purposes cannot be viewed by intransigently religious people as anything else than a profanation or, at best, as an invalid surrogate, and hence arouses in them uneasiness if not outright repugnance. But among the overwhelming majority of Israelis, religious or otherwise, the integrative effect of these symbols appears to have been quite substantial.

Undoubtedly the most controversial use (or misuse, as some would have it) of religious symbols, feelings and attachments is connected with the ongoing public debate on foreign and security policy, or more specifically, the future of the West Bank and Jerusalem and other areas controlled by Israel since 1967. The special significance of holy places and heavenly promises to the Children of Israel regarding their land are well known, as is the recourse to them as the source for the rightfulness of Jewish settlement in the country. What is new today is the interpretation of the national interest in accordance with what the people who invoke it consider to be Divine guidance (as interpreted by their spiritual leaders), and their insistence that this must take precedence over the rule of law and governmental authority.

But none of this is entirely new. After all, use of symbols for political purposes, even when taken in their full religious context, has been made before. Also, the more orthodox wing in Israeli politics has always accepted the guidance of its Council of Sages for all major political decisions (such as whether to participate in elections, join the cabinet, on important policy decisions, etc.,) and even the less extreme orthodox party, *Mafdal* has, at times, allowed its ministers to receive orders from the rabbinate. Outstanding in the case of *Gush Emunim*, however, is that while the majority of its members and followers are religious, this group also has non-religious participants and adherents, who accept its politics and its activities but apparently disregard the religious aspects involved. Yet the image of *Gush* is that of a highly motivated group of politico-religious zealots who, despite their prominence, remain a small minority in the religious community. And it would be incorrect to view *Gush Emunim* as an extremist group in the religious camp which causes the clash with the non-religious majority. The issues at stake are political, and both the religious and the non-religious in Israel are deeply divided over them.

•

It may be a gross over-simplification to speak of two population sectors, the religious and the non-religious, in Israel (just as it is erroneous to reduce all social problems to the Ashkenazi-Sephardi cleavage), for in both sectors, the religious and the non-religious, there are ample internal divisions, fissions and dissensions. Nevertheless, it is a fact that the religious population is becoming more and more isolated from the non-religious, primarily as a consequence of policies deliberately followed with this aim in mind. As a result, the cleavage between these two separate segments of the population is ever widening.

These developments can readily be shown in many ways. In the first place, there is a growing tendency toward physical segregation, i.e., an increasing percentage of religious people congregate together, so that the phenomenon of strictly religious neighborhoods is on the increase in almost every Israeli city and town. Although the ultra-orthodox have always preferred to live in secluded quarters (in Jerusalm, B'nai Beraq, etc.,) and there is a network of religious kibbutzim (every kibbutz is organizationally affiliated with a specific kibbutz movement in accordance with the ideology of its members), this tendency of the general religious public to herd together is new. Again, though statistics are not available, it appears to be a fact that the percentage of "intermarriages" between religious and non-religious families is comparatively small, and this has not been on the increase recently.

School segregation, from kindergarden through high-school and even to university, is very far advanced. The government school system is divided into two trends, the state (i.e., non-religious) and the state-religious trends, and to these must be added the "independent,"(i.e., non-state) schools controlled by *Agudat Israel,* the ultra-orthodox wing of the religious camp. Some one third of all elementary school children attend religious schools. There has been a slight drop in this percentage, but almost all children from religious homes attend these schools, and the wall-of-separation between the various schools is actually growing. (Ironically, the Zionist Organization too, has a separate department of religious education for the Jewish communities outside Israel.)

In the field of labor, although they collaborate with Histadrut within the framework of their trade union departments and in the provision of social services, there are two separate religious labor federations, each affiliated with a religious political party. A good many religious workers belong to Histadrut and the possible merger of the larger of the religious unions with Histadrut is being mooted, but, so far, the advantages of separate existence appear to be decisive to the religious unions.

The army presents a very special case. Its integrative role has often been described and praised (and in the main, rightly so), for it is the first meeting ground and the provider of a common experience for the diverse elements of the population. Much attention is paid to make army service as compatible with the demands of religious observance as is feasible, so as to obviate any possible argument against army service for religious people alongside everyone else. The chief army chaplain has the rank of general. There is a large staff of rabbis and religious supervisors at all command levels. The army mess is strictly *kosher,* and applicable to all ranks are strict standing orders (in times of non-emergency situations) concerning Sabbath observance.

The exemption (upon request) from military service offered to girls from religious homes (about one third of all girls are thus exempted, not a few on false pretences) as well as to students in the ultra-orthodox *yeshivot* (higher institutions of religious learning) not only actually creates a clear separation between those who serve in the army and those who do not, but also makes for strained relations between the non-religious public and the ultra-orthodox. Most non-extreme orthodox religious people themselves strongly object to this exemption. On a completely different level, the practice has recently begun to become widespread for some *yeshiva* graduates who do not seek exemptions and are reputed to make excellent fighters to form their own sub-units, thus initiating a divisionary practice in the army as well.

Religion plays a major role in nation-building and national integration in Israel, despite all the problems involved. Partly by accident of numbers (electoral strength) and the play of party politics based on it, and partly as a result of ideologically determined and also calculated political conceptions, religion is one of the major elements of everyday politics. Thus, in addition to a process of politicization of religion, very strong tendencies introduce religious matters and interests into politics, thereby levelling religion with other aspects of public life. And, parallel with its integrative function, religion also serves as one more cleavage in Israeli society, with all the political implications of such a situation.

FOOTNOTES

1. Benjamin Akzin, *State and Nation* (London: Hutchinson, 1965), p.48.

2. Ben Halpern, *The Idea of the Jewish State* (Cambridge: Harvard University Press, 1961), pp.4-6. It should perhaps be stressed that in a functional analysis such as this, religion and religious symbols are not simply viewed as manipulative devices or as "an essential piece of equipment." See Kenneth Minogne, *Nationalism* (New York: Basic Books, 1967), p.116. Religious matters are of course constantly being put to political usages, for which neutral terms, such as "cultural engineering" may be more appropriate. See e.g., Ali A. Mazrui, *Cultural Engineering and Nation-Building in East Africa* (Evanstown: Northwestern University Press, 1972). On the use of religious dispositions by African and Asian nationalists, see Elie Kedourie, "Introduction" to *Nationalism in Asia and Africa* (New York; Meridian, 1970); pp. 69-77.

3. There is much truth in the claim that "it becomes impossible to determine the direction of the casual relationship between people and religion. Both possessed each other." Anthony D. Smith, "Nationalism and Religion. The Role of Religious Reform in the Genesis of Arab and Jewish Nationalism," *Archives des Sciences Sociales des Religions*, no. 35, 1973, p.29.

4. Charles S. Liebman, "Religion and Political Integration in Israel," *The Jewish Journal of Sociology*, Vol. 17(1), 1975, p.23.

5. For full details of this situation, see S. Zalman Abramov, *Perpetual Dilemma, Jewish Religion in the Jewish State* (Rutherford, Madison, Teaneck: Farleigh Dickinson University Press, 1976).

6. Israel Peretz and Others vs. The Local Council of the Township of Kfar Shmaryahu, *Supreme Court Judgements* 16 (1962): 21Off.

7. Charles S. Liebman, *op. cit.*, p. 18.

8. R.N. Bellah, "Civil Religion in America," *Daedalus* 96 (1967), pp. 1-21. This is not the place to pursue this topic in detail, but for more reasons than one, the use of the civil religion analogy has to be pursued with care.

9. Charles S. Liebman, *op. cit.*, pp. 19-20.

10

The Role of Minorities In the Modern Middle East Societies

By George Moutafakis

In the nineteenth and twentieth centuries, the role of minorities in the Middle East was shaped by two important forces — imperialism and the rise of the military regimes in the area. During the nineteenth century the minorities were, to a great extent, instrumental in bringing the Middle East into the mainstream of world history; they helped to accelerate the transformation of the Arab societies from subsistence to market-oriented cash crop economies.[1] This factor, and the influence of — particularly Christian — intellectuals who preached nationalism and radical reform had consequences which threatened the very survival of the minorities themselves as viable entities.

The Millet System

At the beginning of the nineteenth century the Ottoman *millet* system (whereby Christian, Jewish and other communities were constituted into distinct entities and structured to live according to their own religious laws and ethnic customs) prevailed throughout most of the Ottoman controlled Middle East. These communities were under the authority of their own religious heads and for all practical purposes of the leading families in their districts, who were responsible to the Ottoman sultan. The *millet* system worked for most minorities in the three hundred years before the effects of the western European industrial revolution and the European powers' intensified commercial expansion began to make serious inroads into the Ottoman empire. During that long period the Greek and Armenian communities, each numbering some 1.5 million and living mainly on the western and eastern fringes of the empire respectively, had the most advanced entrepreneurial elements in the Middle East. The Greeks and Armenians who engaged in agriculture were primarily interested in the production of specialized high profit-earning commodities and preferred to leave cereal crop production to the Turkish Muslim and other communities. The proverb "the Bulgarian tills the soil, the Greek owns the plow" is an allusion to the fact th t the Greeks were more interested in lending for profit than laboring for wages.[2] The Greeks and Armenians advanced credit to the peasants and supplied them with goods at exploitive prices. These minorities were active in the first light industry factories in the empire as owner-entrepreneurs, technicians and engineers. They dominated every form of large and small-scale trade from large-scale shipping, food and liquor (controlled by the Greeks) to the construction, metals and carpet industries (monopolized, essentially, by the Armenians).

Since both the Greek and Armenian minorities were established in the cities as well as in the provinces, they often divided the markets among themselves in order to avoid competition. There was, nevertheless, an intense inter-communal rivalry among them, as was evinced by their struggles to control the administration of the Christian religious sites. On the practical,

Dr. Moutafakis is a member of the Department of History at Queensborough Community College.

everyday level of existence, however, the Greeks and Armenians as government officials, shopkeepers, smiths, bakers, butchers, etc. carried on a lucrative business. Jews (in much smaller numbers) were engaged in such areas as the goldworking, watchmaking, upholstery and haberdashery trades — although the discriminatory nature of the Greek and Armenian business tactics made it difficult for the Jews to expand beyond small enterprises. An example of how the Ottoman government played into the hands of enterprising members of the Greek, Armenian and Jewish communities is demonstrated by the activities of the Galata district brokers and financiers in Istanbul. In order to meet increasing expenditures the Ottoman government frequently resorted to increasing the public debt through the selling of bonds — with often indefinite terms of payment. This led to a vicious cycle of exploitive relationships which benefited the bankers. The bonds would be transferred to the Galata brokers at exorbitant discount rates. The bankers would then exert considerable pressure on the Ottoman authorities to redeem the bonds at their full maturity face value. In order to secure the necessary capital, the government would auction off the tax farming *(iltizam)* revenues for periods of from five to ten years. The *sanjak* (provincial) governors and the Galata bankers were accomplices in bringing about these transactions through fraudulent arrangements. Bankers made advance money payments to the *sanjak* governors, who were often notorious tax farmers, in order to secure the auction, and the governors would proceed to collect the greater part of the revenues for themselves. These transactions and the loans of money to the Ottoman treasury led to the further exploitation of the Muslim population through unbearably high taxation.

Elsewhere in the Ottoman realm, minorities played various special roles. In Syria, the Christians represented by the Melkite and Maronite sects and constituting only fifteen percent of the population, succeeded in securing strong positions in the wholesale trade. They dealt in foreign manufactured and domestic goods, particularly in Damascus where a leading representative house was that of the Hanouris. (One of the wealthiest of the Jewish mercantile houses was that of the Fahris which traded in fine domestic metal crafts as well as imported cheaply manufactured cutlery.) However, as in the case of Ottoman Anatolia, the main commerce of Syria as early as the 1780s was in the hands of the Greeks and Armenians while the Sunni Muslim majority was engaged mostly in agriculture and petty trades. It was noted at the time that it was not the Muslim religion or Arab tradition that prevented the Arab majority from competing with the minorities but rather that it was the Ottoman Turkish government's capitulatory concessions which created the obstacles. By the 1840s the Christian and Jewish merchants in Damascus (the latter, though fewer in number, were far wealthier) controlled the wealth of that city. British trade in Syria was in the hands of Levantine Greeks naturalized and domiciled in London. The Catholic Maronite and local Orthodox churches established religiously-supported schools which educated the minorities to play the role of entrepreneurs, civil servants and professional men. Commercial courts like the one in Damascus, created to protect foreign merchants and local minority agents in their service, usually had a two-to-one advantage in membership favoring the minorities over the Muslim traders. Among the activities of these courts was the protection of minority businessmen who made advances to Muslim peasants to enable them to grow their produce or to pay their taxes. They charged interest rates varying from twenty to twenty-four percent, forcing defaults which enabled them to secure the plots. In Baghdad, where the Jewish community reached a population of over a hundred thousand during the nineteenth century, its members were dominant in finance, trade, medicine and the law. Nevertheless, although a few families like the Sassoons had great wealth, the majority were poor tradesmen and peddlers. This was also the case with the Jews in Yemenite Sa'na where they were important merchants, handicraft workers, silver and goldsmiths. Both communities suffered recurrent episodes of religious pogroms.

Despite the obvious benefits which the *millet* system afforded to the minorities and the guarantees of equality given by the state, there was no assurance of protection from discriminatory attacks. The position of minorities, despite the wealth of some of their members, was precarious because they were not fully accepted into the Islamic state. Whatever sense of nationality existed in the Ottoman empire was either openly or unconsciously identified with status as a Muslim. The non-Muslims were seldom considered quite equal by the Muslim populace or the authorities and subtle social pressures were exerted against them almost everywhere. About the only exception was in the Lebanon, where the balance between the Christian and Muslim Arab population was so nearly equal that by necessity each had to accept the other as fully Lebanese within the Ottoman empire. On the other hand the Sunni Muslims, particularly in Syria, grouped the heterodox Muslim Shiites with the Christians into the category of "imperfect Arabs." This ideological milieu contained a residual deposit of attitudes and reactions from past centuries. There was the Muslim attitude that the community of Islam claimed primacy over the individual. There was the sense that Islam was set against the non-believers from the very beginning of its existence, as reflected in the concept that the Muslim community, as "the place of peace," has been in continuous struggle with the outside western world, regarded as "the place of war." Islam's original expansion was accomplished through the conquest of western territory. The returning tide of the Crusades brought the battle back to the Muslims, but the Muslims were, in the long run, always successful. There was an endemic anti-western feeling; a suspicion which grew out of the religious and political conflicts of the past and which was constantly encouraged by the authorities. This only heightened the suspicions and tensions within the minority communities. Their experience of living in an Arab dominated Middle East had given them a long collective memory of insecurity and uncertainty and an acute susceptibility that made every gesture of one community appear as a menace and a challenge to the other. They sought the protection of foreign powers, particularly those of western Europe, primarily in order to safeguard their own positions within the *millet* system.

The Impact of the West

Western Europeans in search of raw materials, markets for their machine-made goods and bases to protect their political and strategic interests, sought every opportunity to penetrate the Ottoman empire. The minorities, particularly those with Christian religious and western cultural ties, whose activities as agents of economic change gave them a middle class character and whose precarious situation within the Islamic mass required special protection, were the most likely agents to act as intermediaries for the foreign interests. In order to safeguard their arrangements with their local clients, the foreign powers extracted concessions from the Ottoman government in the form of capitulations — one of the earliest occurring in 1673 — and trade agreements, like the 1838 Anglo-Turkish Commercial Convention — whereby they undertook to protect the minorities and give them foreign citizenship upon request even while domiciled in the Ottoman empire.[3] The large foreign mercantile, insurance and banking firms supplied funds directly or through their minority representatives to build an infrastructure for the economic exploitation of the empire. During the nineteenth century they built roads, railways and canals, developed ports and mines, controlled the banks and the greater portion of the productive land and gradually engineered the supply of water, gas and electricity to the urban centers. The minorities found that the capitulations, with their provisions for tax reliefs or exemptions, afforded a further means of safeguarding their wealth. By the end of the nineteenth century, thus, European businessmen and local Christian and Jewish merchants controlled the bulk of the Ottoman trade in textiles, hardware and energy resources.

Gradually, these conditions greatly contributed to the dissolution of a significant part of the Turkish and Arab village communal organization and to its replacement by a system of individual contractual labor. Much of the productive land had been appropriated by a few foreigners, minority group businessmen and local Muslim — mostly absentee — landlords. As a result, that limited security formerly enjoyed by the Muslim peasants was eliminated as the gap between the few wealthy owners and the impoverished masses rapidly widened. In the towns there occurred an even more acute crisis as the minorities dealt mortal blows to the handicraft industries which had traditionally occupied the greater part of the urban populations. The Anatolian town centers as well as Aleppo, Damascus, Baghdad and Cairo greatly felt the disruptive effects of the importation of machine-made goods. As a result, except in a few places like Damascus where such traditional industries as in spices and soap continued, Muslims increasingly played a very minor part in domestic or foreign trade. Consequently, the potential for the development of a Muslim middle class, which could have dramatically altered the course of Arab political life, was severely weakened. In a few cases handicrafts gained a new lease on life through the use of cheaper imported materials, reductions in the earnings of workers or the improvement of processing techniques, but overall the deterioration contributed to the continuous augmentation of the ranks of the unemployed. At times, foreign products even threatened the Greek and Armenian merchants, such as those engaged in the cloth trade. They formed an association in Istanbul to resist the French market but the sultan, under French pressure, destroyed the association by imposing severe restrictions on it.

It is perhaps in Egypt that the cooperation between minority communities and the industrially advanced foreign interests in mutually exploiting local resources was most clearly manifested. Even before the beginning of the nineteenth century when the Turco-Albanian ruler of Egypt, Muhammad Ali, brought more secure conditions to Egypt, removed restrictions on Christian minorities and attracted foreigners to the country (first as petty traders, shopkeepers and skilled workers and eventually as merchants and financiers), minorities like the Copts had begun to exercise a great influence. Constituting, according to general estimates, up to one sixth of the population, the Copts were barely distinguishable from the Muslims for, apart from their Christian faith and traditions — which antedated for centuries the Arab arrival in Egypt — they had integrated themselves into the larger community. Copts had even become members of Islamic institutions like the Cairene *Ashraf,* an organization of privileged Muslim landlords and others claiming descent from the Prophet Muhammad and thereby safeguarding their status, privileges and properties. The Copts had traditionally staffed the bureaucracy in the cities and had served as government accountants and financial inspectors in the provinces, recording agricultural production and calculating taxes. They used their immensely powerful positions to acquire real estate through various legal and illegal means, particularly in the provinces of upper Egypt. Because of their role the Muslim masses of *fellaheen* (peasantry) developed a suspicion of the Copts as profitmongers and identified them with the foreigners.[4] Chronic strife between the two communities and the fear of being submerged into the mass caused the Copts continuously to seek an autonomous relationship in Egypt. They saw an opportunity to bolster their security by strongly allying themselves first with the Turco-Albanian dynasty, then with the newly arriving Greeks and other foreigners with capital connections and, by the end of the century, with the British imperial presence. It was during the nineteenth century that the Copts reached the pinnacle of their power.

The Greeks in Egypt, who came with almost every steamer during the middle of the nineteenth century, rapidly became the providers of seed, supplies and manufactured goods for the *fellaheen* whom they urged to plant cotton everywhere on their small and fragmented plots. Gradually, through profits made in village trade transactions, through the sale of manufactured goods and from capital derived from mercantile and banking houses in London, Istanbul, Izmir and Alexandria, the Greeks began to enter the lucrative loan business at the expense of the *fellaheen*. The money loan rates were extremely usurious, ranging from one to five percent a month. The salinity of the Nile waters in the delta area was high and the Greeks were also in the business of draining away the excess — but the cost added to the indebtedness of the small proprietors, forcing many to mortgage their plots. The lender let the borrower renew his obligations to the limit of his resources and then foreclosed on him. At the turn of the twentieth century, district governors as far south as Wadi Halfa expressed concern about this practice, sought to prevent lands from changing hands and substituted monthly installment payments in place of mortgages. The Greek contractors for agricultural supplies dealt directly with the absentee landlords and in the process starved and defrauded the landless mass of the *fellaheen* making up the corvée labor gangs on the cotton and sugar estates. Enduring great misery and oppression, working from sunrise to sunset for mere subsistence, many of the *fellaheen* fled from the estates. A system of military detachments encamped near the larger estates was developed to deal with this run-away problem. As a result of all these measures cash crops, and particularly sugar and cotton, became very important during the second half of the nineteenth century. Throughout this period the areas of land held by private ownership (called *mulk*) increased rapidly and attracted even more foreign capital.

Not only were the cities of Alexandria and Cairo receiving a new influx of inhabitants but the inland towns and villages were also being overrun. By 1875 Cairo had become the center of the delta's retail trade and railways linked every major delta town with the harbor at Alexandria. The Greeks used the network to develop exclusive monopolies in cotton, sugar and local grains on the international markets. They also engaged in the lucrative business of ginning, which permitted many to recoup their initial investments within a few years. Even the less highly capitalized ventures such as the ownership of village ovens for breadmaking proved profitable. Among the Armenians, who monopolized the tobacco and leather industries, there was strong representation in the professions, administrative positions, sections of the wholesale and retail trades and the skilled crafts in general. As late as the 1950s fewer than five percent were common laborers and not more than two percent were landowning agriculturalists.[5] Socially, the Armenians centered their life around the Armenian Apostolic, and to a lesser degree, the Armenian rite Catholic Uniate church, each of which maintained its own social organization and educational institutions. The Armenians, like the Greeks, rarely mixed with the Muslims and shunned the Coptic Christians, preferring their own closely-knit communities, through which they sought to preserve their linguistic, ethnic and cultural distinctiveness. They stressed their own cultural precedence (if not "cultural superiority") over the practicability of blending into the fabric of the majority culture. The example of the Copts, who had managed to secure positions of economic importance while blending their institutions into the dominant Islamic culture was not attractive to the Greeks and the Armenians. They used French as a working language and had only a superficial acquaintance with Arabic, even after generations of residence in Egypt. They had no particular loyalties to the Egyptian political parties and none to Egypt as a state: the Greeks had strong ties with the City of London's financial interests, the Stock Exchange and the Foreign Office. Some of the leading wealthy Greek families such as the Averoffs and the Rallis made their fortunes in Egyptian cotton. They used portions of these fortunes to make heavy endowments to some of the best elementary and secondary schools in the history of modern Greek education.[6]

During the second half of the nineteenth century there was a great influx of Jewish immigrants into Egypt, adding to the small community that had existed there for centuries. The Jews came from the Ottoman empire, from other areas of the Mediterranean and from western Europe, attracted by Egypt's burgeoning economic development and the existence of the protective capitulations. Gradually, they entered finance, various professions and the administration and by the end of the century, although most of the approximately 65,000 Jews were poor, the community had families of established wealth like the Hararis, Qattawis and Rolos. The Jewish presence in finance was so significant that on the High Holidays the Alexandria customs house, stock exchange and all the banks remained closed. Characteristic of the Jewish community's interest in education, an attitude prevalent throughout the Middle East, are the literacy figures for several communities in Egypt at the beginning of this century. Among the Muslims, eleven percent of the men and less than one percent of the women were considered literate. Among the Copts the figures are twenty-three and two percent respectively and among the Jews fifty and forty-one percent. However, the Jews constantly bore the brunt of Muslim and Christian persecution and the ethnically based Egyptian press regularly published prejudiced articles which sustained the tensions.[7]

Another influx of people, and in greater numbers, occurred in Syria and Lebanon during and immediately after the first world war. As a result of policies set by leaders in the Turkish government in 1915, millions of Armenians were deported from everywhere in Anatolia. A million and a half perished from starvation, the cold, mistreatment and hard labor in the wilderness, mountains and deserts, but thousands, enured to suffering by their history of centuries of adversity, survived. They pressed into the bazaars of Syria, seeking a livelihood, striving to reestablish their communities, churches and private schools. During the French mandatory period between the two world wars, the Armenians built their institutions in Aleppo and Damascus but their ties either in the market, workshop or university, were essentially confined to their own ethnic group. They segregated themselves from the Arab population and resented its rapid growth and its increasing competition for their jobs and its penetration into their neighborhoods — a pressure that became acute by the time of the second world war. On the other hand, they were equally resented by the Muslims because of their different ways, their entry into the already strained job market and their enlistment in the feared Auxiliary Corps organized by the military authorities of the French mandatory government to fight the nationalists. In Lebanon, the Armenians came to dominate the fields of medicine, nursing and engineering and attained important roles in commerce, especially in the clothing apparel and hardware industries. A quarter of the Beirut gold bazaar was owned by Armenian craftsmen and there were more Armenian financial magnates per capita in Lebanon than in any other country by the end of the second world war.

Economic enterprise was not, however, the only characteristic of the minorities' activities in the Middle East. By the late nineteenth century, many families had accumulated enough wealth for education and travel and were drawn to European, and especially French, culture. Many Christian Arabs, particularly in Syria, were instrumental in the dissemination of the views of the western European rational and romantic Enlightenment in the Middle East and certainly of the interpretations of the French Revolution and the mid-nineteenth century positivism and utilitarianism and the concepts of Marx and Darwin.[8] At the turn of the century, several Christian Arab intellectuals like Faris Nimr, Ya'qub Sarruf and Salamah Musa, writing in leading newspapers like *al-Ahram* and *al-Muqattam* and periodicals like *al-Hilal*, *al-Muqtataf* and *al-Jami'a* discussed various progressive reform ideas with Muslim thinkers.[9] Most of these Christian Arab writers were moderates and proponents of the western European power relationships and advanced the concept of reform through some type of secular independence movement.[10] Articles on science, modern industry, laissez-faire economics and the secularization of Arab history inspired many Muslim thinkers to move away from the religious conservatism of

Jamal al-Din al Afghani* and the impractical reformism of Muhammed Abdu.** At the beginning of the twentieth century the Muslim intellectuals Qasim Amin and Abdul Rahman al-Kawakibi*** advocated positive secularism and socialism as a path toward the modernization of Arab life. In the main, however, there was a consensus among the Muslim middle classes in Ottoman Turkey, Syria and Egypt that a laissez-faire economic system, a parliamentary form of government and, for the minority groups, some form of autonomy much like the *millet* system, would constitute the basis for the Muslim nationalist movement. This consensus supported the Young Turks and the *Wafd* (Nationalist) movements in Ottoman Turkey and Egypt but it was doomed to failure because it did not gain the support of the powerful conservative elements; it could not deal with the increasing discontent of the exploited masses, and it could not separate itself from the foreign and minority interests. By the mid-twentieth century it was the more radical ideology of the *Ba'th* (originally formulated by the Syrian Christian Arab Michel 'Aflaq but which quickly became tied to the military and the Muslim bureaucracy) that was to become characteristic of the consensus within the Arab nationalist movement.

The Reaction of Arab Nationalism

As the century wore on, the minorities came into increasing conflict with the nationalist aspirations of the Muslim middle classes, the petty traders, the lower and non-commissioned officers and the religious leaders. When at the turn of the century, the Turkish middle class-led *Committee of Union and Progress* (The Young Turks) proclaimed an ostensibly secular nationalist program to introduce reforms, it only succeeded in expelling the Armenian population from Anatolia. Mustapha Kemal's republican movement defeated the foreign interventionists and abolished the capitulations and exploitive commercial agreements. It also expelled the Greek population from Asia Minor and curtailed or nationalized foreign and minority concerns while granting preferential treatment to the indigenous Turkish firms. In Egypt, between the two world wars, the government was able to secure enough revenue through the accumulation of huge foreign trade balances to buy up the public debt as well as a significant number of the shares and bonds of corporations operating in the country. The Egyptianization of the economy was spearheaded by Bank Misr, assisted by the Muslim-dominated legislature and by administrative pressure. By 1930 Egypt had recovered its tariff autonomy and by 1936 had abolished the capitulations. The percentage of capital invested by Muslims in joint-stock companies rose from nine percent in 1933 to eighty-four percent in 1948 and the number of Muslims serving on the board of directors of companies in Egypt rose from a negligible number in 1920 to thirty-one percent in 1951 and sixty-four percent in 1966. During the same period Greek and Armenian representation was drastically reduced; that of the Copts remained at four percent. It appeared that the minorities were powerless to reverse the diminishing of their roles in face of the rising nationalism everywhere in the Middle East. The Armenians in Syria, like the Greeks in Egypt, refused to associate themselves openly with the existing political forces. The Syrian nationalist congresses and the first Syrian Arab feudal-middle class governments after the second world war even praised the Armenian stand of non-involvement with the French mandatory schemes against Syrian independence. But as is clear from the newspapers and articles of the ethnic press at the time, the minorities understood that the growing movement for independence meant not only the removal of the imperialist powers but also the danger that the state would fall under the control of militant pan-Arab Islamic influences.

* An influential intellectual and writer who advocated Muslim nationalism. His principal aim was to strengthen and reform one of the Islamic states as a trailblazer for the others.

** Regarded as the founder of the modernist movement in Islam, he strove to reconcile religion and science.

*** Molded by Afghani; leaders of the Islamic unity and revivalism movement.

The fear of being submerged into an Arab Islamic community has been experienced by other minority groups, both large and small, during the greater part of this century. The Jews of Baghdad, beginning with the 1920s when the British structured the Iraqi state, suffered repeated acts of violence at the hands of brutal bureaucrats who had been trained by the Ottoman government and who had then become members of the Iraqi civil service. Jewish shops were wrecked and looted, bombs were thrown and members of the community were murdered in the streets. Six hundred Jews were killed in the June 1941 Baghdad massacres. Although the Jews resisted and often closed their shops in protest, they were regularly intimidated, culminating in the April 1950 Iraqi law which obligated them to leave Baghdad within a year. Those who remained had to suffer the continuation of bomb throwing, the wrecking of synagogues, homes and shops and sporadic arrests and executions on charges of espionage. In northern Iraq the Assyrian minority experienced a genocidal massacre when it sought to assert its rights as citizens of the country. To the Iraqi state, dominated by the Arab Muslim majority, the presence of the Assyrians, the Jews and the Kurds was a threat to national unity. A parallel can be drawn between the treatment of the Muslim Kurdish peoples in northern Iraq and the Afro-Nilotic inhabitants of the southern Sudan. The Kurds, who constitute a third of the population, have encountered the chronic opposition of the Baghdad government. They have never been granted autonomous status; they have never been allowed to use their own language or to study their own culture in the schools and they have never been granted the right to exploit their own natural resources, particularly petroleum, for their own local development. The Nilotic peoples constitute a third of the population of the Sudan but the Arab Muslim-dominated Khartoum government has insisted on their adoption of Muslim institutions and on the teaching of Islam in both state and private schools regardless of the fact that the majority of these peoples are either animists or Christians. These campaigns to enforce a different national pattern on both the Kurdish and the Black Sudanese have involved large military operations from time to time.

The coming to power of the military regimes during the last twenty-five years, with their declared radical programs, has constituted the most serious threat to the minorities. Both the Egyptian and the Syr-ian movements during the 1950s and 1960s stressed the fact that the socio-political system which had been introduced into the Middle East by the imperialist powers and which had permitted the minorities to play their modern role had broken down. The military-bureaucratic regimes also declared that the concept of middle class nationalism which the imperialist system had spawned in the Middle East, no longer sufficed to meet the needs of the masses, since much of its energy had been consumed in the drive to monopolize power and distribute privileges within a closed circle in its own ranks. The alleged intent of the new Arab military elites was to organize the masses, which for so long had been outside the system of power, into a class-conscious element and to make them the mainstay of the national community. In 1962 the Egyptian National Charter declared that political democracy could not be separated from social democracy, which was based on guarantees of freedom from exploitation in all its forms, on equal opportunity to share in the national wealth and on a secure future for the individual. The Syrian *Ba'th* party's position was even more explicit when, in the 1960s, it called the Arab middle class accommodation of the minorities an example of opportunism in alliance with imperialism. It condemned the traditional Arab middle class moralistic and intellectual positions, claiming that the Graeco-Christian traditions no longer had any meaning or relevance for the masses. For the starved and illiterate millions the only true values, according to the *Ba'th,* were the revolutionary ones; only the peasants, workers, soldiers and progressive intellectuals could share the power.

The Greeks in Egypt and the Armenians in Syria regarded these countries' military coups with caution and concern. They were aware of the reprisals taken against the

Jewish community in Egypt between 1950 and 1957, when the Jews were barred from citizenship and many were expelled and had their property confiscated. Much of the property belonging to foreigners and minorities, including companies, banks and insurance firms, had been confiscated following the Suez-Sinai war and, in 1956, the special confessional church courts and the rabbinical courts were also abolished.[11] Matters of personal status and domestic relations became subject to state jurisdiction (on the grounds that Egyptian law and custom had to be unified). Even the Copts, whose press had condemned both Israel and also the Iranian government for recognizing Israel's existence as a state, began gradually to be pushed out of the nerve centers of power. Yet the Greek and Armenian press hailed the new regimes and extolled the drive to stamp out bribery and corruption as the concomitant evils that had plagued Egypt and Syria and had kept the Muslim peasantry in an unending cycle of poverty and ignorance. Nevertheless, in 1961, following the dissolution of the United Arab Republic (which the Cairo government attributed to counter-revolutionary elements) large amounts of foreign and minority-owned property and enterprises were expropriated. There followed restrictions on capital investment and private initiative. State monopolies were given greater powers, boards of directors were appointed by the state, employees' profit-sharing plans were imposed and also steep income taxes on large incomes, and particularly those of members of minority groups. Land ownership, which was at first limited to two hundred acres per owner, was further limited to one hundred acres, affecting 2,500 owners possessing a total of one million acres.

As a result of these measures and a certain amount of unofficial harassment which extended even to the indigenous Copts, many members of the minority groups elected to emigrate. The largest emigration was that of the Greeks, who left for Greece, Canada, the United States, South Africa and Australia. In 1965 the Cairo government allowed a large number to leave, provided they took only one-third of their pre-World War II accumulated assets out of Egypt. There followed closings and amalgamations of minority schools and the scaling down of cultural and educational activities. Most members of the minority communities, recalling the vibrant hey-days that had lasted a century, now complained bitterly that the new Egyptian officials were bringing the country to the precipice of disaster. Yet others (a distinct minority and most of them Copts), acknowledged the heavy burdens placed on the minorities but believed that the Cairo government was sincere in its drive to reduce social and economic inequality and to uplift the *fellaheen,* the mainstay of the nation, upon whose backs their ancestors, as Muhammed Heykal, writing in *al-Ahram* in the 1960s reminded them, had accumulated so much wealth.

In Syria the military *Ba'th* regime accused the representatives of the Armenian community, which was larger in Syria, than in any other state, of conspiracy, sedition and espionage. Many leaders were arrested, enterprises were confiscated or restricted and cultural associations were sharply curtailed. By the fall of 1967 Armenian schools were brought under state supervision, special curricula were imposed, informers were placed in the classrooms and the principals were made responsible to the Syrian Ministry of Education. Arabic became the compulsory language of instruction in all matters except religion and Armenian history, but for all practical purposes this minority's language and culture were technically eliminated in the schools. The activities of the Armenian churches were also restricted; their prelates were often forbidden to leave or to enter the country. Many Armenians elected to emigrate.

The old days had come to an end. The protected privileges had ceased to exist. Yet recent developments in both Syria and Egypt indicate that there may still be a future for the remnants of the communities that have remained. In Egypt, President Anwar Sadat, having curtailed the radical wing of the Arab Socialist Union, has said that he would consider returning their confiscated assets to foreigners and members of the minority groups and allowing them to function in the country with certain restrictions. Since General Hafez al-Assad's coup of 1971, the Armenians have been encouraged to remain. Their prelates are moving about more freely and there has been a partial relaxation of the stringent economic and cultural controls. But in neither state can the changes be reversed and the destiny of those who remain is shrouded in uncertainty.

The interests of the Arab Muslim middle classes, government officials, military officers and religious leaders have been served by the Arab nationalist movement. As these levels of the population, long deprived of power, have achieved ascendancy, the role of the minorities has decreased. Many of the members of the minority groups who have remained are willing to accept their national identity as Egyptians or Syrians, etc. But they need to have their rights as citizens of these states guaranteed and they need to have the protection of the law. They cannot accept cultural domination as reflected in the many Islamic religious references incorporated into the national structures of the modern Arab states. Their future remains just as uncertain as does the future course and the attitudes of the Muslim Arab states in which they live.

FOOTNOTES

1. Charles Issawi, Ed. *The Economic History of the Middle East 1800-1914* (Chicago, 1966), p. 226.
2. *Ibid.*, p. 116.
3. *Ibid.*, p. 38.
4. Edward Wakin, *A Lonely Minority: The Story of Egypt's Copts,* (New York, 1963), pp. 18, 55.
5. Richard G. Hovannisian, "The Ebb and Flow of the Armenian Minority in the Arab Middle East", *Middle East Journal,* XXXVIII (Winter, 1974), p. 22.
6. Athanase G. Politis, *L'hellenime et l'egypte moderne,* (Paris, 1930), p. 525.
7. Jacob M. Landau, *Jews in Nineteenth Century Egypt,* (New York, 1969), p. 215.
8. Hisham Sharabi, *Arab Intellectuals and the West: The Formative Years 1875-1914,* (Baltimore, 1970), p.20.
9. P. J. Vatikiotis, *The Modern History of Egypt,* (New York, 1969), p. 171.
10. Sharabi, *op. cit.*, p. 58.
11. Landau, *op. cit.*, p. 254.

11 A Perspective on the Shiites and the Lebanese Tragedy

by Stuart E. Colie

Islam's Sunni-Shiite schism started only thirty years after the death of Muhammad—almost nine centuries before western Christianity's Catholic-Protestant split.[1] Shiism and Protestantism both originated as protest movements, but whereas the latter was highly successful, the former was not. Self-confidence marked the "Protestant ethic." The Shiites present a sharp contrast. Theirs has been mainly a history of defeat and subordination; consequently, the "Shiite character" has been stamped by resignation and submissiveness, broken at times by outbursts of revolt.

A second Shiite-Protestant difference is that the original Shiite protest had far less to do with theology and more to do with plain power politics. The Prophet Muhammad left no clear procedures to contain the inevitable rivalries over his succession. Uthman, the third Caliph (successor), was overthrown and murdered by partisans of Ali, Muhammad's son-in-law, who assumed the Caliphate and moved it to Iraq where his main support lay. Uthman's family, the Syrian-based Ummayads, refused to accept Ali's rule. Civil war followed. Ali was killed and the Caliphate passed to the Ummayads in Damascus. Ali's son, Hussein, in turn raised the banner of revolt in Iraq where he was defeated and slain at the battle of Karbala in 680. The partisans of Ali, the *Shi'at Ali,* continued to recognize him and his descendents as the true leaders, or Imams, of Islam. They refused to recognize the Ummayad Caliphs.

Power in the Ummayad Caliphate lay in the hands of an Arab warrior aristocracy, which lorded it over the expanding empire's many non-Arab converts to Islam. As their wealth and power grew, the Ummayads departed from the equalitarian ways of early Islam and began also to oppress and exploit the poorer among their fellow Arabs. Many non-Arabs, above all the Persians, as well as other Arabs, especially in Iraq where traditional hostility toward Syria and sympathy for Ali were strong, turned to Shiism. The Shiites joined forces with a powerful Iraqi Sunni family, the Abbasids, in a successful revolt. The Abbasids moved the Caliphate to Baghdad. There they were soon as corrupted by power as the Ummayads had been in Damascus.[2] The poor and the Shiites suffered, Arab as well as non-Arab.

The Shiites have remained subordinate in most of the Arab world, although during the Arab empire's disintegration they were at times dominant in many of its lands from Morocco to Iraq. Today the Yemen is the only Arab state in which Shiites dominate.[3] They are also dominant in non-Arab Iran and are numerous and powerful in Pakistan and among the some seventy million Muslims of India.

* * *

Certain common doctrines are shared by most Shiite sects. Those relevant to the role of the Shia in today's Middle East require discussion.[4] The core doctrine is that the legitimate spiritual and temporal leader, or

Dr. Colie is Professor of Political Science at Central Connecticut State College. He taught Political Studies at the American University of Beirut in the 1960s.

Imam, of Islam must be a direct descendent of Ali. The Caliphs recognized by the Sunnis, from the Ummayads to the last of the Ottoman sultan-Caliphs, were therefore considered illegitimate. For the Shiites, Islam can only be redeemed when an Imam descended from Ali holds supreme power.

Every substantial Shiite community has an imam whose authority comes from that of the Imam, the sole legitimate leader of all Islam.[5] There is a powerful mystical aspect to the concept of the Imam. He is considered infallible and his authority absolute. This authority extends to all religious and political leaders who are in effect the Imam's delegates.

The Sunnis are less absolutist. In the words of Sir Hamilton Gibb:

> In orthodox [Sunni] Islam the Caliph . . . cannot define dogma; he is simply the political and religious leader of the Community. But for . . . [the Shia] . . . the only authoritative source of doctrine was the Imam himself. Thus . . . their religion was centered on a principle of absolute personal authority, foreign both in politics and religion to the orthodox theory.[6]

This absolutist-authoritarian side of Shiism is not incompatible with a social revolutionary tradition. As often happens in history, the two tendencies can fuse. Thus in one medieval Shiite sect, the Karmatians, "socialistic demands were heightened to the point of communism which however . . . in view of the authoritarian attachment to an imam or his representative was only a mask for a despotic oligarchy."[7] Fanaticism combined with authoritarianism can produce formidable military-terrorist organizations. Medieval Shiism produced one of the most formidable; the Assassins of northern Iraq and Syria.

Although Shiism has spawned movements of violent social revolt, its broader tradition has been one of resignation and a mystique of Martyrdom. The anniversary of Hussein's death at Karbala is a holy day, during which many celebrants flagellate themselves. Such behavior, hardly unusual in groups that have known defeat and subordination, encourages social passivity and apathy. In the Shiites these traits, together with the notion that communal leaders derived infallibility from the Iman, served to foster a blind obedience to those leaders, which often endured no matter how corrupt and exploitive they might be. Yet long-suffering passivity can give way to violent revolt, as history has often shown. Such revolts come easiest when the oppressor is perceived as alien in any way, including most definitely in religion. Then the group's traditional and religious leaders ·m y head the revolt. Yet the revolt can turn against the traditional leadership, or even the religion itself.

* * *

Like most religions, Shiism has divided and sub-divided into a bewildering complexity of sects. Only a few can be discussed here. Members of the most numerous sect are called Twelvers (Ithna'asharis in Arabic) or Imamis.[8] The unmodified term, Shiite, usually refers to them. In non-Arab Iran theirs is the state religion. In neighboring Arab Iraq they make up most of the Shiite 50 percent, which must play second fiddle to the Sunni 40 percent. This is one among many factors contributing to Iraqi-Iranian frictions. Most of Lebanon's Shiites are Twelvers, but there they are often called Matawila; in this article they will simply be called Shiites. In Syria and among the Palestinians their role, like their portion of the population, is minimal.

The Ismaili Shiites are also known as Seveners (Sabiyah in Arabic).[9] Once all-powerful in Egypt, they retain some following there and elsewhere in the Arab world, but more in Pakistan and India.[10] The Ismailis have departed far from Twelver Shiism and some commentators refer to "Shiites and Ismailis" as if they were unrelated. An offshoot of Ismaili Shiism has departed so far as to be often considered no longer Muslim. These are the Druze. After breaking with the Ismailis, they established strongholds in the mountains of Lebanon and Syria where they maintained their independence by their fierce martial skills.[11] They have had an important role in Lebanese and Syrian politics.

Another Shiite offshoot plays a critical

role in today's Syrian politics. These are the Alawites (or Alawis) also known as the Nusairis.[12] They glorify Ali as divine and view Muhammad as merely his forerunner. This is heresy to both Sunni and Shia and, coupled with the Alawis' adoption of various Christian rituals, inevitably brought persecution. The Alawis eked out a marginal existence in Syria until the French mandate enabled many to rise through the ranks of the military. Today General Hafez al-Assad, the country's president, and many key men in Ba'thist Syria are Alawites. But the Alawites are a 10 percent minority in a country with a Sunni majority, a fact that has added to the riskiness of President Assad's venture into Lebanon's confessional complexities.

* * *

Under the Ottoman Empire, Lebanon was treated as a province of Syria. Most non-Muslim religious communities enjoyed considerable rights and self-rule. Not so the Shiites, who were viewed as Muslim backsliders by the staunchly Sunni Ottomans. They were placed under Sunni control, chiefly emanating from Damascus. Frequently victims of Sunni persecutions, they were at the bottom of the economic scale.

In the mid-nineteenth century, the Ottoman regime, responding in part to western pressures, adopted reforms that established semi-legislative regional assemblies and theoretically secularized the state and its citizens' rights. The Shiites could only benefit from such changes, but the chief beneficiaries were a few feudal, landed families. Assured of the tradition-bound support of their peasantry, they monopolized Shiite representation in the assemblies. Their wealth and power grew significantly, but that of the Shiite masses did not.

In 1860, a Druze-Maronite conflict in Lebanon turned into a massacre of thousands of the latter, in which the Sunnis soon joined. The Shia, despite their hostility to the Maronite Christians, shared with them a common fear of the Sunni and of the Druze. Shiites gave shelter to Maronite refugees and often intervened to prevent their extermination.[13]

Out of the crisis of 1860 came a political system in Lebanon under which the Shiites enjoyed securely guaranteed rights. Under pressure from the European powers an autonomous district was established in the mainly Maronite and Druze Mount Lebanon region. Sectarian peace was maintained by a great power guarantee and on the basis of the following balance in a legislative council: 4 Maronite, 3 Druze, 2 Greek Orthodox, and one each Sunni, Shiite and Greek Catholic. This was the prototype of the confessional balancing system that was extended under the French and brought to its ultimate conclusion in independent Lebanon.

Although the Shiites of Mount Lebanon benefited under this system, the vast majority of Lebanese Shiites lived outside it, mainly in the Bekaa area of the east and northeast and in the southern mountains. With the exception of a few feudal families, they remained religiously subordinate, economically depressed and politically powerless.

Like their Sunni, Druze, and Maronite counterparts, Shiite family leaders used the loyalty of their tradition-bound constituencies to build political machines of which they were the bosses. Such a political boss was and is known in Lebanon as a *zaim*. This pattern of family-based bossism is an almost universal phenomenon wherever rural traditionalist influences are strong.[14] In Shiite communities, however, the habit of obedience to imam-like leadership provides especially fertile soil for it.

The first stirrings of Arab nationalism among the intelligentsia of late nineteenth century Syria-Lebanon cut across sectarian lines. Younger members of notable families who were exposed to modern education were often infected. Shiites joined Sunnis and Maronites in anti-Turkish activities; and a prominent Shiite family, the Khalils of Tyre, provided one of many multi-religious martyrs hung by the Turks in 1915. The circumstances of Abdul Karim al-Khalil's death tell us something about power politics among the zaims. Young Khalil was betrayed to the Ottoman authorities by an older established zaim of the rival Shiite Assad family: ". . . Kamel al-Assad could not forgive him for having presented himself for the elections of the Ottoman Parliament in Nabatiah. 'Kamel Bek was of the opinion that representing the Shiis of Jebel Amil was his prerogative precluded to anyone else . . .' "[15]

Under the French mandate the Shiite rite was given official recognition for the first time:

> This meant a right of community jurisdiction in personal status matters, which heretofore had been within the jurisdiction of the Sunni courts. The measure . . . gave them the opportunity to work for the much needed social and material progress of their community.
>
> From then on, Shii leaders were encouraged by the French . . . as well as by shrewd Maronite politicians to play a wider role in government . . . as a means of bringing greater benefits to their community. The mandatory was careful, however, to back only those feudal leaders who were willing to cooperate with it. Still, support from both the French and the Maronites eventually helped the Shii leaders to become independent of Sunni influence and to come into their own politically.[16]

Among the Shiite zaims who were willing to cooperate was Ahmad al-Assad, nephew of Kamel al-Assad, who had betrayed young al-Khalil to the Turks. Ahmad al-Assad became the major power in south Lebanon during the latter years of the mandate. Yet few of the favors to cooperative Shiite zaims from the French and their Maronite protegés trickled down to the Shiite masses. Furthermore, despite memories of Sunni oppression, the pull of Arab nationalism was strong for many Shiites, particularly among the younger and better educated. To them the new French-made, Maronite-led Lebanese state was suspect, as were collaborators such as the Assads. In 1926, a Druze-Sunni revolt against the French in Syria spread into Lebanon where Shiites joined in attacks on Maronite villages.[17]

This Shiite ambiguity worked to the advantage of their zaims: "With the power he exercised over his followers, any tribal lord could easily make trouble for the state if he chose to. Thus it was wise to keep the Shii leaders friendly and content, which would help keep their followers friendly and content too."[18]

After independence from France, the Shiite notables retained their power to make trouble for the state. In the National Pact of 1943, the Shiites were guaranteed the speakership of the Chamber of Deputies. For most of the first eight years this position alternated between Ahmad al-Assad, still the most powerful boss in South Lebanon, and Sabri Hamadeh, his counterpart in the Bekaa. Through their control of the Shiite bloc in the Parliament these men wielded power comparable to the President's and, in the view of one observer, for a while "actually ruled Lebanon."[19] Such personal power did not, however, improve the social-educational-economic position of the Shiite community. Without such improvements the Shiites remained underrepresented in the key positions of a modernizing state. Some figures can illustrate the point. During the 1950's the Shiites constituted some 18 percent of Lebanon's population, compared to the following for four other major sects: Maronites 30, Sunnis 20, Greek Orthodox 10, Druze 6.[20] The Shiites' parliamentary representation was comparable to their population percentage (so were those of the others); their ministerial representation was slightly below it (the others were above). In the higher administrative and diplomatic posts, however, a gross disparity appears: Shiites 3.6, Maronites 40, Sunnis 27, Greek Orthodox 11.7, Druze 7.2.[21]

In 1952, a reformist alliance led by the Maronite Camille Chamoun and the leftist Druze zaim, Kamel Jumblat, forced President Khoury to resign. Chamoun became President and set about to create his own political organization to undercut the power of the traditional zaims and provide a reliable parliamentary majority. In the Shiite south, Chamoun helped the rival Khalil and Osseiran families cut into the power of Ahmad al-Assad and his son Kamel. Parliamentary electoral "reforms" increased the representation of pro-Chamounists, and in 1953 the Assad-Hamadeh monopoly of the speakership was broken when parliament elected Adel Osseiran to that post. Yet the blind loyalty of their followers still enabled the Hamadehs and Assads to make trouble for the state. In a 1954 parliamentary debate Chamoun's Sunni Prime Minister charged that Ahmad al-Assad and his son Kamel had "ruined the country." On the next day a life was lost when a thousand protesting Assad partisans rioted before the Parliament.[22]

Chamoun's coming to power coincided closely with Nasser's in Egypt and soon the Maronite President was buffeted by rising winds of Arab nationalism. He responded by appealing to Maronite fears of Islam, linking his foreign policy to the Maronites' traditional western protectors, and further tightening his control of the electoral and parliamentary systems at the expense of non-cooperative zaims.

Lebanon's Shiites, more rural and apathetic than the Sunnis and more suspicious of appeals from Sunni sources, responded less fervently to Nasserism. Yet the Assads and Hamadehs, with Chamoun undercutting their power bases, were ready to turn to any allies against him. The allies were there, for Chamoun's electoral manipulations also threatened wealthy Sunni zaims like Tripoli's Rashid Karami.[23] These Sunni notables found it necessary to play up to the Nasserist sentiments of their urban followers. Thus they and such traditionalist Shiite zaims as the Assads and Hamadehs found themselves allied in an anti-Chamoun front increasingly committed to the rhetoric of leftist Arab nationalism. They also found themselves allied with one other leader whose leftist nationalism was more than rhetoric. The feudal Druze zaim, Kamel Jumblat, had been Chamoun's ally in 1952 — and a bitter foe of Ahmad al-Assad. But Chamoun's increasingly rightist and pro-western policies were anathema to him, and Jumblat was one of the established zaims, whose power Chamoun was trying to undercut.

In 1958, these tensions flared into civil war. Most of the Shiite south took up arms against Chamoun under the leadership of Ahmad al-Assad and his son Kamel. The Shiite tribesmen of the Bekaa-Hermel mountain area went into oppositon behind Sabri Hamadeh. It is worth noting that among Hamadeh's temporary allies were the Maronite Frangiehs of Zhgarta, including the future President Suleiman Frangieh. Their reason for joining the opposition forces was simple: Hamid Frangieh was a frustrated presidential rival of Chamoun. The pro-Chamoun Shiite leaders were unable or unwilling to raise any significant forces on his behalf, as were Chamoun's dwindling Sunni supporters. The Muslim front against Chamoun was almost solid. Both the Sunni Mufti and the Shiite Imam of Lebanon, joined by the Druze religious leadership, issued joint anti-Chamoun statements. There never was, however, a corresponding Christian solidarity behind Chamoun. The Maronite Patriarch, Paul Meouchy, even before the civil war had charged Chamoun with hardening sectarian divisions and had drawn praise from the Assads.[24]

Meouchy and other Maronite moderates were instrumental in bringing about the settlement by which Chamoun was replaced by General Fuad Chehab. As President (1958-1964), Chehab made a genuine effort at reform and to overcome, in the words of Professor Leonard Binder, "the alienation of the proletarian Sunni and the apathy of the Shii tribesman-peasant."[25] Yet Chehab tried to achieve reforms through the existing cabinet-parliamentary system and to reconcile all sides of the civil war by giving them full access to the system. Consequently, the reforms got lost in the maneuvers of shifting coalitions of zaims.

Most of the pro- and anti-Chamoun Shiite zaims managed to find places in the parliament and often in the cabinet, but the latter fared better. The veteran Sabri Hamadeh regained the speakership from the pro-Chamounist Adel Osseiran. On the death of his father Ahmad, Kamel al-Assad became leader of his family's forces. In 1964, he challenged the much older Hamadeh for the speakership. Assad lost by a close vote followed by a chair-throwing brawl between parliamentary partisans of the two former civil war allies.

Kamel al-Assad had presented himself as spokesman for the younger generation in challenging Hamadeh. This was clearly part of what Professor Michael Hudson described as the strategy by which "some of the younger notables like Kamel al-Assad . . . have tried, though with little apparent success, to establish organizations distinct from their traditonal power base."[26]

Assad needed to create a more broadly based organization, for in Hudson's words, new leaders were springing up among a generation of highly educated Shiites. Similar trends were at work in the Hamadehs' fiefdom "where pluralism has blossomed and traditonal seigneurs find it increasingly difficult to maintain their dominance." A "decline in the traditional feudal spirit" cut into Sabri Hamadeh's power. The margin by which he had been returned to Parliament since 1925, during the French mandate, dropped dramatically in 1953, rose again in 1957 "based less on his feudal position than his . . . oppositon to President Chamoun," and declined again in the 1960s.[27]

* * *

In the 1970s, three developments have accelerated the erosion of traditional Shiite leadership patterns. As the poverty of the rural Shiite areas remained relatively untouched by reform, Shiite peasants flocked to economically booming Beirut. Yet as this migration increased in the 1970s the boom began to lose steam. The Shiite newcomers swelled the slum "belt of misery" surrounding the new high-rises of Beirut. A vicious circle was at work; for one of the many factors deflating the boom was political instability, to which the growing restlessness in the "belt of misery" contributed.

The second development was the growth of the Palestinian guerrilla organizations in Lebanon. The bulk of the Palestinian commando forces concentrated in the heavily Shiite south. At first there was suspicion between the Shiite peasant-villagers and the Palestinians. For one thing, the Palestinians were overwhelmingly Sunni; there were more Christians than Shiites in their minority. Yet Palestinian radicalism got some response from the Shiite poor, and more among the younger Shiite intelligentsia. Many Shiites have joined the Communist Party and the para-military Lebanese Communist Action Organization. The L.C.A.O.'s main training base was set up in the southern Shiite town of Nabatiah.[28]

These two developments were intensified by a third. Palestinian raids drew Israeli reprisals, which took their toll of Shiite villages. Much the same happened in neighboring Maronite villages, but the two communities' reactions differed significantly. The Maronites tended to blame the Palestinians for their woes and to demand Lebanese government and military action against them. The Shiites, long the stepchildren of the Lebanese state, tended to join in the Palestinians' denunciation of the state's failure to resist the Israelis. As the level of violence mounted, more Shiites became more radicalized and more fled to swell the "belt of misery" pressing in on Beirut.[29] Here they fused with the population of the Palestinian camps, at least one of which was recently reported to contain more Shiites than Palestinians.[30]

Such pressures not only undermined the control of traditonalist Shiite leaders over their followers, but forced them toward the militant left in order to retain such control as they could — rather as many Sunni zaims had been forced toward Nasserism in the 1950s. The declining authority of the Shiite zaims was partly replaced by the resultant rise in that of the community's religious leader, Musa Sadr, the Imam of Lebanon. But Sadr's growing power depended largely on his own militancy. He organized his followers into a social-political Movement of the Disinherited. In response to an Israeli raid in January, 1975, Sadr demanded that Lebanon "mobilize a force to protect the south from Israeli occupation" and promised to be "the first to sign up for military service."[31] In July of 1975, some forty members of the para-military wing of Sadr's movement were killed in a land mine accident while being trained by Palestinian commandos.[32]

Yet the Imam Sadr has the responsibilities of trying to lead a community. He has been in the forefront of many efforts to make peace and patch together government coalitions during Lebanon's present agony. At one point he was described in a *New York Times* report as "a political moderate trusted by both the Palestinian guerrilla leadership and the Lebanese Christians."[33] Such a role is difficult to play and was almost certain to stir suspicion among leftist militants whose weight constantly increased in the Shiite community. After Syria's turn against the Lebanese Left and the Palestinians, Sadr's frequent contacts with and public praise for President Assad could only have the same effect. Small wonder then, that it is reported that the Shiite Superior Council now has a leftist majority and that the Imam has lost control of it.[34]

The most prominent of the remaining Shiite zaims has played a comparable, but more cautious role. In 1971, Kamel al-Assad became Speaker of the Parliament when the ancient Sabri Hamadeh finally yielded the post.[35] In response to Israeli air strikes in 1974, he called for "a joint Arab plan of action," adding that it would be "unfair for Lebanon alone to make all the sacrifices."[36] In December, 1975 he "issued reform proposals to 'reestablish factional balance and rebuild tranquility among the citizens.' "[37] Assad personally presented to President Frangieh the parliamentary resolution calling for his resignation. These modest gestures were hardly enough to win the trust of the Left, and his continued efforts to stay in Syria's good graces after her move against the Left sufficed to earn its active distrust. With his Speaker's chair in effect shot out from under him, Assad is no longer able to play a strong zaim role in a radicalized Shia community. Perhaps only a Shiite Jumblat could do that.

* * *

The heyday of the traditional Shiite religious and political leaders seems beyond recall in Lebanon. Should Syria be able to impose an effective control over Lebanon, it is possible that traditional leaders such as the Imam Sadr and Kamel al-Assad could prove useful instruments in keeping the Shiite community passive. But after the changes the community has undergone, that is doubtful. It seems likely that, among such traditional Shiite traits as do survive, social revolt will prove stronger than passive obedience.

The alliance of radicalized Shiites with the Palestinians and with Jumblat's Druze and other Lebanese leftists is apt to be strong enough to prevent the Syrians from achieving secure control over Lebanon.[38] Indeed the religious complexities of Hafez al-Assad's intervention in Lebanon could threaten his regime. He is an Alawite, a spin-off of Shiism considered far further removed from orthodox Islam than its source by the Sunni Syrian majority. Anti-Alawi tensions have risen in Syria as Assad presses his intervention in Lebanon on behalf of Christians and against Sunni — and Shiite — Muslims.[39] Syria's rejectionist Sunnite-Shiite neighbor, Iraq, stands ready to exploit such tensions. Should religious and ideological passions combine to topple Assad, the consequences for peace in the Middle East would be incalculable.

In a June 1976 interview Zbigniew Brzezinski worried that the "small-steps" approach to peace in the Middle East might be overtaken by "certain dangerous processes at work in the region." He explained, "By dangerous trends I mean, in particular, the underlying processes of the radicalization of the Arab masses . . ."[40] He cited recent events on the West Bank as an example. The Shiites of Lebanon provide another.

FOOTNOTES

1. Footnotes are used in this article for clarification and to cite the sources of data or direct quotations that are significant and not more or less common knowledge. The simplest and most common American newspaper transliterations of Arabic terms are used. Direct quotations are accordingly modified for consistency.

2. The depths of the roots of Syrian-Iraqi rivalry, which remains very much alive between the two countries' Ba'thist regimes, should be evident in this short account.

3. This is the Yemen Arab Republic, politically centrist and presently on good terms with Saudi Arabia. In the leftist People's Democratic Republic of Yemen, i.e., South Yemen, the Shafais, a Sunni sect, are dominant.

4. Shia is the collective term for the community of Shiites i.e., the individuals who constitute it. Save perhaps by strict purists, the terms can be used interchangeably.

5. There is no Imam of all the Shiites. He is a Messiah-like concept, differing from sect to sect, whose ultimate materialization is awaited.

6. H.A.R. Gibbe, *Mohammedanism*, Galaxy Book, Oxford University Press, 1962, p. 123. To be sure, Gibb is here mainly referring to the more esoteric Shiite sects which carried the doctrine of the Imam's infallibility to extremes. He feels that the difference is less pronounced between Sunnis and the more moderate Shiite sects, but that it definitely exists, see p. 125.

7. *Shorter Encyclopedia of Islam*, E. J. Brill Publishers, Leiden, 1953, p. 536. The value judgement passed on the Karmatians may or may not be too harsh, but there seems little question about their authoritarianism.

8. They exalt an historic-mythic line of Imams, above all, the twelfth and last, who lived in the ninth century and, the Twelver-Imamis believe, never died and will yet return to unite Islam.

9. Where the Twelvers hold that there were twelve Imams and revere the twelfth, the Seveners hold that there were seven and exalt Ismail, whom they claim to have been the seventh. The Twelvers deny that Ismail was an Imam.

10. Their spiritual leader, Aga Khan and his son Ali, gained celebrity status in the West.

11. There are also some 35,000 Druze in Israel.

12. Any Arabic group name ending in "i" usually can also take an English ending of "ite," i.e., Alawi or Alawite, Nusairi or Nusairite, Shii or Shiite.

13. Leila Meo, *Lebanon: Improbable Nation,* Indiana University Press, 1965, pp. 30-31. Meo mentions that in some cases Sunnis protected Christians from the Druze. Actually, the relations of religious groups varied greatly over time and between regions depending on such factors as how neighboring groups habitually got along, or the personal interests and relations of their leaders. Alliances and enmities changed: Druze and Maronites had been pre-1860 allies.

14. For example, British squires, especially in the Tory countryside, Prussian Junkers, and French and Mediterranean notables. Zaim-like figures have been common in Latin America and not uncommon in the U.S., especially in the South. On Lebanon, see Arnold Hottinger's "Zu'ama' in Historical Perspective" in *Politics in Lebanon* ed. by Leonard Binder. John Wiley & Sons, 1966. Zuama is the Arabic plural of zaim.

15. *Ibid.*, Hottinger, p. 93. The passage quoted by Hottinger is from a Lebanese historian, Muhammed Jabir.

16. *Op. cit.*, Meo, pp. 60-61.

17. *Ibid.*, p. 51.

18. *Ibid.*, p. 62.

19. Michael C. Hudson, *The Precarious Republic: Political Modernization in Lebanon*. Random House, 1968, p. 132.

20. Lebanon has not had a census since the 1930s; the results might have been too controversial. All figures are, therefore, estimates. Demographic trends, e.g., higher birth rates among the poor, have apparently made the Shiites the largest single sect today. See, for example, *The New York Times,* September 15, 1975.

21. These figures are from Michael W. Suleiman's, *Political Parties in Lebanon*, Cornell University Press, 1967, p. 49. See also Ralph E. Crow's "Confessionalism, Public Administration and Efficiency" in Binder *op. cit.*, p. 172. Crow is Suleiman's original source.

22. Op. cit., Hudson, p. 133. Any self-respecting family of Shiite zaims could inspire such devotion. When I was at the American University of Beirut, a Maronite instructor flunked a Khalil family member on an economics exam. A day or two later, two young toughs from the student's home town came on campus and beat up the instructor. The University was reluctant to have charges pressed and apparently agreed to have the family discipline the offenders.

23. Prime Minister throughout much of the 60s and 70s, including most of the present civil war.

24. Fahim I. Qubain, *Crisis in Lebanon*, The Middle East Institute, 1961, p. 60.

25. "Political Change in Lebanon" in Binder, *op. cit.*, p. 309.

26. *Op. cit.*, Hudson, p. 146.

27. *Ibid.*, p. 229.

28. See Eric Rouleau in *Le Monde*, September 20, 1975.

29. The belt of misery is a term commonly used in Beirut and in the reports of correspondents there. For example, see Rouleau *op. cit.* in *Le Monde*, also James Markham, *The New York Times*, July 19, 1975.

30. *Ibid.*, *The New York Times*.

31 *The New York Times*, January 22, 1975.

32. *The New York Times*, July 7, 1975.

33. *The New York Times*, April 17, 1975, Juan de Onis.

FOOTNOTES, cont.

34. So it was reported to me in June by a very well-informed source, whose permission for attribution I did not ask at the time.

35. The Shiite Assads of Lebanon are not related to the Alawite Hafez al-Assad, President of Syria.

36. *The New York Times*, June 23, 1974.

37. *The New York Times*, December 20, 1975.

38. Should Syrian military intervention, aided perhaps by Greater Power diplomatic intervention, create a balance of power, from which the Maronite-Right and the Palestinian-Muslim-Left could reach a settlement, then Sadr, Assad, and other traditional leaders might play a role in keeping the settlement glued together.

39. See Eric Rouleau, *Le Monde*, June 4, 1976. It may be added that the Syrian Druze also have cause for resentment against Assad's regime. See ''The Dilemma of the Druze'' by Arnold Sherman, *Hadassah Magazine*, Vol. 56, No. 2, October, 1974.

40. *Bulletin of the American Professors for Peace in the Middle East,* June, 1976.

12 The Kurdish Struggle For Independence

By Omran Yahya Feili and Arlene R. Fromchuck

The Kurdish people have lived in the Middle East for some five thousand years. Their history began when, during the third millenium B.C., a semi-nomadic people who spoke a primitive Indo-European language began to migrate from southern Russia toward Anatolia. They conquered the existing states of Asia Minor, formed the Hittite Empire and became the first Iranian-speaking Kurds.[1] With the collapse of the Hittite Empire (*circa* 1200 B.C.) there is evidence of the migration of the Hittites into Luristan, an area inhabited by Kassites who were also Kurds.[2] At about the same time another Aryan group from southern Russia moved into what is the Iranian plateau, first settling in the Caucasus and then spreading west and south to the peripheries of contemporary Luristan and Kermanshah. These tribes, known as Medes, are the best known among the ancestors of the Kurdish people. They have been described by the classical authors from Herodotus and Xenophon to Horace and Tacitus. Tacitus, for example, relates a story of the Mede, Aryo-Barzanes (whose name is the ancient forebear of Mulla Mustafa Barzani), whom the Emperor Tiberius installed as king of Armenia. Although the Armeniasre not Kurds, Aryo-Barzanes was, according to Tacitus, nevertheless willingly accepted because of his "singularly handsome person and noble spirit."[3]

Fortune has played a negative role in the history of the Kurdish people. It was the misfortune of the Medes that their last king, Astyages, did not have a son of his own but only a daughter, Mandane, whom he gave in marriage to one of his Persian generals, Cambyses. Astyages made Cambyses satrap of Persia. The offspring of this marriage was a son, Cyrus, who became heir to Astyagas. When, in 550 B.C. Cyrus took over the affairs of the Mede Empire from his grandfather, the emergent Achaemenid dynasty began to be known as the Mede-Persian Empire, although it was still also known as the Mede Empire.[4] The alliance was ended by the crushing defeat of the Achaemenes by Alexander (who was married to a Kurdish woman.)*

Yet another group of Kurds whose existence can be traced to the mid-third millenium B.C. were the Guti, whose kingdom corresponds with the part of Kurdistan currently held by Iraq and who were one of the oldest independent kingdoms of the ancient civilized East.[5] This group conquered

---

Because they are not represented in any international organization and, within their own country, Kurdistan, have not been permitted to create a national organization, nearly all the available information about the Kurds derives from persons and governments whose interests collide with the Kurdish national interest. In the case of Iraq, Turkey, Iran and Syria the objectives have always been the same, namely, to present the Kurdish people first as a non-people and second, as undeserving of human rights, principally the rights of cultural development and national self-determination.

Because Kurdish territorial claims have a basic historical legitimacy, it has been in the interests of the governments under whose rule Kurdistan falls to attempt to discount Kurdish history. This paper seeks to reverse this trend of historical annihilation and to bring into focus the place of Kurdistan in the contemporary Middle East. (the authors)

Mr. Feili is a Ph.D. candidate in Economics at New York University. Prof. Fromchuck is Associate Professor of Classics at Brooklyn College, CUNY.

---

* During Iran's 1972 celebration of the 'founding of the Persian Empire by Cyrus the Great' 2,5000 years earlier, the official Persian government press, radio and television stations minutely described the life of Cyrus but avoided any mention of his Mede (Kurdish) origins.

KURDISTAN

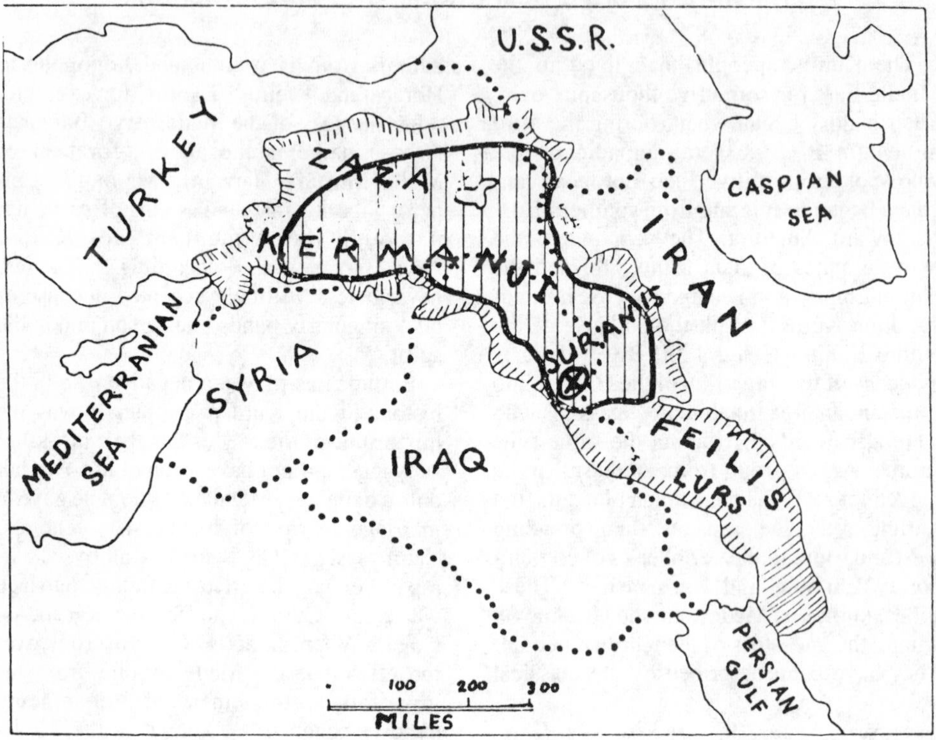

International territories

An approximation of Kurdistan as generally accepted by Kurdish nationalists. Similar boundaries were drawn by the British office in India for their own guidance.

Foreigners, when pressed, view Kurdistan within these boundaries.

Kirkuk oil fields

Source: Based on map taken from *El Kadhiyah el Kurdiey,* by Mahmoud el Dorah, (Beirut, 1968).

Babylonia and was responsible for ending the Jewish captivity there.[6] In fact, the probable reason for the emergence of the word *Kurd* as the national appelation for all these Aryan groups is that Gutium (Kardochium to Xenophon) was the largest and oldest of the tribes. The name is recalled in the second capital of the Medes, built in 580 B.C., which was called Kurtansha, "the city where Kurdish kings reside" (modern Kermanshah).[7]

"Political scholars" have, for their own purposes, claimed that the Kurds are not a nation since the Kurdish ancestry is made up of four groups, i.e., Hittites, Kassites, Medes and Guti. Yet Persia itself is made up of Persians, Parthians and Elamites, and Turkey is made up of Mongols, Uzbeks, Tatars, Black Sheep, White Sheep and a host of other nations. Turkish morphology bears absolutely no resemblance to any one of these groups. The geneology of the Arabs reveals that one half of the Arabian peninsula, before the rise of Muhammad, was inhabited by Yemenites who were not Arabs and did not speak an Arab language;[8] many of the northern tribes were considered *musta 'arriba* or "arabized Arabs."[9] Even at the peak of their supposed "racial purity" (prior to the mass migration from the Arabian peninsula) the Arabs were made up of Hamites, Yoqtanites and many other peoples. "Arab," in fact, has no meaning as a common noun in Arabic but derives from the ancient Semitic *'arabha* and is akin to *'aribu* in Assyrian and *'arabhi* in Hebrew, all meaning "steppe." Thus, "arab" is the precise equivalent of *bedu* in Arabic: i.e., a man of the steppe.[10]

It is a fact, moreover, that the Kurdish people have been a united nation throughout most of their history. They were not only united among themselves, but they also brought unity to the rest of the Iranian nations of which they are part. One of the earliest of the political forces, the Medes had such extraordinary discipline and cooperation that they impressed both the Greeks and the Romans. Media also produced Zoroaster, the prophet whose religion of vitalism and activism was responsible for the rise of one of the world's most powerful societies: the Mede-Persian Empire of the 6th century B.C.[11] Only since the Kurdish people were forced to submit to the inconsistent and contradictory Muslim principles have they failed to remain unified. Most damaging to Kurdish unity has been the Sunni sect of Islam, the religion of the Arab establishment and of what became the Ottoman Empire. While a discussion of the damages which this Islamic ideology has brought to the Kurdish people is not within the scope of this paper, suffice it to say that the Kurdish people have never been unified from the time of the victory of Islam over the Kurdish people in the 9th century A.D.

In addition to the deliberate attempts to discredit and distort their history, investigation of the Kurdish question is further hindered, not by the lack of books about the Kurdish people[12] but rather by the lack of any objective and serious analytical approach to the problem. Most of the books written by American and English scholars have generally been apologias for unpopular policies. For example, Eagleton's book, *The Kurdish Republic of 1946,** was basically written to convince the reader that the United States had nothing to do with the destruction of the Kurdish autonomous movement in Mehabad in 1946. He asserts that the U.S. was sympathetic toward the Kurds but that the Shah of Iran, then a 23-year old playboy, simply rejected the ambassador's request not to execute Qazi Mohamed, the president of the republic. Iran in 1946 was merely a buffer zone between Russia and the West. Its army was financed, trained and managed by the United States. Its kings were installed by Britain. Yet Eagleton alleges that it was within the king's power to say no to the United States. Oddly enough, the very same Shah who today rules a powerful country with an economy of "super-abundance" and an army of "awesome fire-power" found himself unable to say no to the CIA directive to seal off the Iranian border against the Kurds in 1975!

On the serious issues of population, geography and national origin, most English-

---

* See bibliography, p. 59.

language publications reiterate the position of the Middle East governments, although in a somewhat more sophisticated manner. They too obscure the origins of the Kurdish people. They carve a map of Kurdistan that excludes all the fertile and the mineral-rich lands and with these lands also the history of the Kurds inhabiting them. A recent and typical example is the map in E. O'Ballance's book on the Kurdish revolution, *The Kurdish Revolt: 1961-70*.* Westwards, this map excludes (by a fraction of an inch) the Tigris and Euphrates rivers, which actually flow through the middle of Kurdistan for two hundred miles,[13] and also the oil fields of Kirkuk which are in the heart of Kurdish land. Southwards, most of the province of Kermanshah and all of Luristan, whose inhabitants, as we have noted, are the direct descendants of the Medes, ancient ancestors of the Kurdish people, are conveniently excluded. This type of cartography appears to suggest that the Kurdish people must eventually be granted self-determination but seems to envision a Kurdistan much as a native reservation on the order of Botswana or Zululand.

* See bibliography, p. 59.

Turkey and the Kurds

The distortion of Kurdish history, the gerrymandering of Kurdish lands and the misrepresentation of Kurdish political aims have contributed immeasurably to the West's misunderstanding and antipathy toward the Kurdish people. In their modern history only twice, and for short periods of time, have they experienced some relative freedom and peace. The first came in the early 1940s when the Russian army expelled the pro-Nazi government of Iran from some parts of Iranian Kurdistan, and the second was during the 1958-60 revolutionary period in Iraq when the Iraqi army expelled the British-sponsored regime. Ironically, the Kurdish people have gained independence when, as on both occasions, western influence was absent. It would appear that where the western powers have more influence the Kurdish people in these countries have less rights. In Turkey, where NATO's influence has been immense, no Kurdish rights exist and there is not even an opportunity to discuss them. As a member, Turkey has attempted and still attempts to influence NATO's attitude on the Kurdish question. Turkey was the pioneer in waging a cultural war against the Kurdish people. An eight volume "scholarly" history of the Ottoman Empire by Enver Ziya Karal mentions only a single Kurd. He is Çeteci Kurt Mustafa, "the gangster Mustafa the Kurd," who was killed by the Turkish security forces "and, with his execution, peace and prosperity was brought to Anatolia."[14]

During the Iraqi war against the Kurdish people, Turkey seized the opportunity to wage its own secret war. This began with the enactment of Law Number 105 in 1960 which authorized the *gendarmerie* to deport any Kurd from Anatolia without court consent. The attitude of the Turkish establishment can best be shown in the following illustration: In 1960 General Jemal Gursel (who removed the civilian government and appointed himself president) standing on an American tank in the city of Diarbeker, the capital of Kurdistan occupied by Turkey declared, in a long speech; "There are no Kurds in this country. Whoever says he is a Kurd, I will spit in his face."[15] In addition to its own economic embargo on the millions of Kurds in Turkey, that country imposed an economic embargo on Iraqi-held Kurdistan; an act of war in itself. Its propaganda machine spread misinformation against the Kurds throughout Europe.[16] There have been mass assassinations of the Kurdish intelligentsia, the latest occurring in January 1974. Turkey has made its services available to both Iraq and Iran and was instrumental in bringing about the Iranian embargo of the Kurds in March of 1975. Istanbul was the seat of the negotiations of the so-called Algiers Accord.* Turkey's Kurdophobia appears to be limitless.**

* The Treaty between Iraq and Iran of March, 1975.

** Some 700,000 Turks live in Iraq. There is no constitutional recognition of their existence and they have no cultural rights, yet Turkey has never protested against this state of affairs — although it was ready to go to war on behalf of the 80,000 Turks in Cyprus who in fact had these rights. Similarly, it is the basic pre-

Iraq and the Kurds

In Iraq, the beginnings of the Kurdish renaissance can be traced to the abolition of the monarchy by Abdul Karim Kassem in 1958. It brought about what the Kurdish people regarded as an undreamt of miracle. Saluting the people of Iraq, Kassem hailed the end of British imperialism and handed down a constitution acknowledging that Iraq was made up of two nations, Arabs and Kurds, partners in the ownership of the country.[17] Iraq's insignia was an intertwining sword and dagger; the dagger symbolizing the Kurds and the sword the Arabs. It was the first time in their modern history that a country ruling over the Kurdish people acknowledged their existence and showed them respect. But it placed Iraq in direct conflict with the Syria of Nasser's United Arab Republic, with Iran and with Turkey. Its recognition of the existence of the Kurds within its borders was, according to Nasser, tantamount to the partitioning of Iraq itself, which, he said, was a purely Arab land. He regarded this as an unpardonable act of treason. Radio Cairo and Radio Tehran, which up to that point had possessed absolutely nothing in common found, in Kassem, a common enemy. It is ironic that one of the major reasons for the conflict between Iraq and Iran in 1958 was Iraq's consent to the return of the Kurdish leader, General Barzani, and its recognition of the Democratic Party of Kurdistan.[18] Not surprisingly, this fact has been obscured by many writers, who have described the Iraq-Iran conflict as based on a border dispute over the Shatt-el-Arab river.[19]

But Kassem, the strongman of the Iraqi revolution of July 14, 1958 was a loner. He did not belong to any party or tribe and his national origin is unknown. His mass execution of Arab nationalists, mostly Nasserists and members of the Ba'th party, and his willingness to allow the Kurds to regroup and organize raised suspicions about his racial origins; there was speculation that he was a Feili Kurd*—asked by a foreign journalist whether he was a Kurd or an Arab, he replied that he was the "son of the people."

In 1959, the Iraqi first division stationed in Mosul and commanded by an Arab pro-Nasserist, Abdul Wahab el-Shawaff revolted with Nasser's encouragement, raised the flag of the United Arab Republic over Mosul and declared Iraq to be a part of the U.A.R. Kassem, at this stage, had no confidence in his Arab officers or soldiers. Accordingly, he dispatched General Barzani to the north, supplying him with all the weapons he needed. Barzani rounded up the rebels in less than twenty-four hours. In the ensuing combat 10,000 Arab nationalists were killed, most of them Nasserists and Ba'thists. Barzani all at once became a hero, not to his Kurdish followers alone but to all the anti-Nasserists and anti-Ba'thists, mainly the Shiites of Iraq who constitute the majority Muslim sect in the country. He also became a threat to Kassem, who began plotting to curb his influence and that of the KDP. Kassem demanded the immediate return of all the weapons he had given to Barzani. Mulla Mustafa[20] (Barzani) replied that his service to Kassem had made him more enemies among the Arabs than at any other time and that he therefore needed even more weapons and also a greater voice in Iraqi government policy-making. Neither one of these men was politically mature enough to work out a solution to their conflict. Kassem, a good conspirator, was a bad politician. Harassed by the incessant conspiracies of the Arab nationalist officers, he finally forced Barzani into a direct confrontation.

---

mise of Iraq and the rest of the Arab world that the creation of the State of Israel has made several hundred thousand Arab refugees homeless, yet Iraq has a surplus of land and is importing two million Egyptians to settle it. (See Letter to the Editor by Mohammed Abdul Wahab, Press Adviser, Iraq Mission to the U.N. [*New York Times,* June 8, 1976].)

---

* There are four branches of Kurds: Kermanji, Zaza, Surani and Feili. The Feili Kurds inhabit the states of Kermanshah and Lursitan in Iran; in Iraq they inhabit all states adjacent to these two states. Their total population in Iran is approximately two and a half million and in Iraq close to 600,000. The Lurs are the largest group within the Feili Kurds. The most famous of the Feili Kurds in modern times was Karim Khan Zand, Emperor of Iran from 1757 to 1779, noted for his "probity, his tolerant views and his kindliness." (Britannica, *Persian History*)

Neither Kassem nor Barzani had any friends outside Iraq. Both men had only enemies. Kassem was overthrown in February 1963 by a coalition of right wing forces consisting of Nasserists, Ba'thists and the Muslim Brotherhood and the leftovers of the Nuri Sai'd bureaucrats. He was brutally murdered, together with several thousand of his followers. Western press accounts at the time testified to the inhumane nature of the Ba'th Nasserist onslaught.[21] In the ensuing chaos the Arab nationalists seized the opportunity to kill several hundred Kurdish intellectuals who, for the most part, had opposed Kassem and worked against him.

By early March the Iraqi army had become exhaused by the internal and the Kurdish war. Its arms were depleted and its manpower severely reduced. It had aroused the anger of both the West and the East. There was an international outcry against it. Instead of seizing the opportunity to push his military operations against the Ba'thists, Barzani had offered a truce on February 10. His unilateral gesture was opposed by the Central Committee and the political bureau of the KDP, both of which were under the leadership of the veteran of Kurdish nationalism, Abrahim Ahmed.[22] The Central Committee's attitude proved to have been the more farsighted: by June 1963 Iraq's new leader, Aref, without warning unleashed 90% of his armed forces against the unprepared and defenseless cities, towns and villages of Kurdistan. The following February, although it was obvious that he had no intention of recognizing Kurdish rights, Aref now offered a truce — following the defeat of his forces on every front. Mulla Mustafa (Barzani) agreed, without consulting the KDP's Central Committee, and his acceptance of the truce was regarded as a coup by the Kurdish leftists.

It must be explained, at this point, that the Kurdish army at the time consisted of two divisions. One was under the direct command of Barzani and consisted of rural Kurds operating around Mosul in the northeast corner of Iraq and constituting approximately 80% of the total Kurdish armed forces. The other, which was responsible for the operations in the southern front, i.e., around Kirkuk and Khanaqin, was under the direct command of Abrahim Ahmed. Its leadership consisted of lawyers, engineers, journalists and teachers and its troops were mostly urban Kurds. This group carried out the major military operations since it was closer to Baghdad and to the oil fields of Kirkuk, which it succeeded in sabotaging on many occasions, thus preventing the operation of oil extraction from the wells. Barzani's region served as a position of retreat for Abrahim Ahmed's front line; his forces would not have been able to operate without this hinterland.

The division between the two factions never healed,[23] and a struggle surfaced between the right wing and the left wing for control of the Kurdish revolution. The year 1964 began with the receipt, by Iraq, of massive arms supplies from Britain, France and Pakistan (which Iran regarded as its territory), while the Kurds received supplies of food and medicine from Iran[24] and several organizations in the United States. The British government supplied Iraq with Hawker Hunter aircraft, tanks, armored troop transports and artillery. In times of emergency they also airlifted weapons and this British policy continued into 1975.[25] The Russian high speed, high altitude MIGs which Iraq also received proved ineffective in guerrilla warfare — the British Hawker Hunter aircraft are specifically designed for this purpose. In aiding the Kurds, Iran's chief interest was to acquire influence; an objective that has remained constant although the manner in which it has been pursued has varied from time to time.

The Kurdish revolution posed a very great threat to all the Muslims and the Middle East establishments. For the first time, civilians had organized and formed an army of their own and had successfully defeated an established army equipped with modern weapons.

•

There have been many political upheavals in the Middle East — the western press has often carelessly called them revolutions — and real power has changed hands, but this has always taken place from within the establishment itself, with the army as the final arbiter. The Kurdish revolution on the other hand involved, from its inception, peasants and wage earners and rarely included anyone connected to an established government. This may well be the reason why the American press, which often echoes government policy in foreign affairs, has almost always been negative in its reporting of the Kurdish struggle. Thus *Time Magazine* (July 14, 1967) called the Kurdish nation a "troublesome minority." The *New York Times* has referred to "Kurdish tribes" and has termed General Barzani a "chieftain" and a "red Mullah"[26] but has never described him as the chairman of the KDP, which is his proper title. In 1965 the *Columbia Journal of International Affairs* unprofessionally allowed its pages to be used in a vicious slander against the Kurds.[27] Western interest in the Kurdish revolution only actually began in 1962, when Kassem decided to nationalize Iraq's oil. The Kurdish revolution was already in its second year and had waged its fiercest battles. When Kassem retreated from his threat to nationalize Iraq's oil, the West retreated from its coverage of the Kurdish revolution. It was at this point that the Iranian government reversed its stance and permitted limited cooperation between the Kurds in Iran and Iraq. It was rumored that this policy change was the result of British pressure in order to keep Kassem at bay and to secure a Kurdish promise not to hinder oil production operations. This sort of cooperation between the Iranian government and the KDP continued in varying degrees depending on the political climate; uncertainty regarding the aims of Iraq's rulers made cooperation between Iran and the Kurds a kind of insurance policy against any radical change within Iraq. By 1966 the Iranian army had even engaged, on some occasions, in actual combat against the Iraqis. These clashes were provoked by Iraq in order to gain the support of the Arab world and to give the impression that Iran was the cause of the unrest in Kurdistan.

The Rise of the Kurdish Middle Class

As the cooperation between the KDP and Iran increased, the position and role of the Kurdish leftists declined. It is reasonable to assume that the decline in influence in the KDP of men like Abrahim Ahmed and Jalal Talabani was the result of the conditions for cooperation set by the Iranian government. By 1970 the old guard was completely isolated from the decision-making process in the KDP, and a new class of Kurds with no previous affiliation with the revolution or with the KDP in general suddenly assumed the vacant positions of power. Most of them had once been members of the police apparatus of the old Nuri Sai'd regime. They prided themselves on the fact that they or their parents had, at one time or another, served in some bureaucratic capacity in the Ministry of Interior under Nuri Sai'd, and the honors they bestowed upon one another were tied to the rank to which each had risen during this regime. Since this class of bureaucrats makes up the bulk of the Kurdish middle class, a description of the Kurdish class structure will facilitate an understanding of the behavior of the factions within the KDP.

The majority of Kurds are peasants, making the Kurdish people not only a distinct nationality in the Middle East but also a distinct class, with its own social and economic aims. The Kurdish people are, however, much like any other mountain people. They are generally courageous, generous and self-reliant: they prefer to live and let live. In its modern history, Kurdistan has been ruled by feudal kings; a very proud breed of leaders with very limited desire for change. As long as their provinces were not challenged or interfered with, they remained peaceful and cooperative. But their kingdoms were, one by one, subdued by the central authorities of the Persian and Ottoman Empires, who feared that this class of Kurdish nobility might form internal or external alliances. The last of these kingdoms to be subdued was Luristan (also known as Pusht-e-Kuh) which came under the complete control of the Iranian government by 1938.[28] As a result of the twenty-five-year war which Iran waged against the Feili Kurds, nearly a half million of them took refuge in Iraq, which became a not always secure haven for them.[29] The Kurdish nobility did not want their subjects to share their power and were typical oriental despots but their pride would not permit them to accept an external ruler. In political if not always economic matters, their own interests in the main coincided with those of the Kurdish people and ran counter to those of the Turks and Persians, and most of them fell in defense of their national pride and freedom. Those who did not die fighting the enemy left the Middle East. Mulla Mustafa Barzani, who is a descendant of a several hundred year old dynasty of princes of the Kermanj tribe, is the last of this breed of nobility.

With the destruction of the feudal kings and the complete conquest of Kurdistan the administration of the provinces was assumed by the conquering governments. Because efficient control of the provinces required native expertise, the new foreign rulers managed to recruit a class of Kurds who were willing and even eager to cooperate with them and to share in the booty. This group was trained to function as the Kurdish branch of the civil service and was taught the art of government. Like all other government servants the upper echelon was well paid and took large bribes; some accumulating substantial wealth and "honors." The emergent Kurdish middle class was thus peculiar; it was the offspring of the efficiency and the administrative requirements of the conquering forces and not of advancing Kurdish industrialization and commercial enterprise.[30] To prove their loyalty these Kurdish officials often displayed an over-zealous efficiency in controlling the Kurdish masses; their cruelty shocked even the conquerors in its excesses. Typical of these was Said Kazaz who achieved the rank of Minister of the Interior in Iraq in 1950 and held it until his execution by Kassem in 1958. Among his innovations to the existing catalogue of torture was sexual abuse of both men and women in the process of interrogation.[31]

This Kurdish middle class has brought to Kurdistan a system of agricultural feudalism that had never existed there, even during the Dark Ages. Its major contribution to its "employers" has been to lower the cost of the occupation of Kurdistan. On the propaganda level, the Iraqi government has been able to use these peoples' participation in the civil service as evidence that equality of opportunity exists in Iraq — and thus has led to empty hopes among many Kurds, and to an undermining of the Kurdish independence of spirit. Since they are Muslims this class of Kurdish administrators, taking their claim from the Koran, advocates Muslim solidarity yet overlooks the slaughter of Kurds by Muslim Turks and Muslim Arabs. Patriotism is defined by them as loyalty to the existing government. As "communist internationalists" (this group only surfaces when the ruling regime is pro-communist) its members are quick to abandon the "unprofitable" cause of national liberation in favor of "class struggle" and dependence on the Moscow line. As "infiltrators" it claims that its members' climb to high ranking positions in government will help the Kurdish cause. But, to achieve power in the "enemy" government they must prove themselves to the authorities. The Kurd — inevitably a suspect — can only prove his loyalty through a display of cruelty toward his own people. By the time he has reached a high position in government, thus, his hands are stained with blood. Or he has reached retirement age, he claims, or he has too many family responsibilities to be able to become involved in the struggle for Kurdish independence.

Offering pretexts for their attitudes, shifting overnight from Islamic fundamentalism to Communism, this class is so numerous that any occupying power would have no difficulty in forming a cabinet from among its ranks which would still carry on the ruling anti-Kurdish racial policy in all its present force.[32]

In 1958, Kassem expelled this class from his government so as to win the support of the Kurdish people. It disappeared for some ten years and then quietly surfaced around Mulla Mustafa Barzani in 1969-70, when CIA-SAVAK* money began to find its way to the Kurdish struggle. An independent Kurdistan became their goal — until the CIA-SAVAK money was cut off.

---

* *Sazimani Anniyet Ve Intizamati Kishwar* (Committee for National Security)

Kassem's 1958 revolution gave the Kurdish leadership an opportunity to organize peasant organizations, workers' unions, students' unions, youth organizations, women's organizations, and, above all, the Kurdish Democratic Party. By the late 1960s the struggle for power between Abrahim Ahmed and General Barzani, as we have noted, resulted in an obvious rift in Kurdish unity as each faction conspired to expel the other. Since Abrahim Ahmed's faction consisted of the professionals (whom Barzani needed for the party machinery and the administration of the rebel-held land) he could not easily dispose of them without a substantial loss in power and effectiveness. He began, therefore, to look for alternatives. The revolution had at that stage almost succeeded, both militarily and politically. Militarily, the Kurdish army had mastered the techniques of warfare from a mobile position. Politically, the Kurds called for the overthrow of the Iraqi government and for a democratic election in Iraq. This helped to arouse sympathy and respect among Arab intellectuals, particularly the Shi'ites, who constitute the majority of Iraq's population and who stood to benefit from a free election. It strengthened the Kurdish military position by undermining the fighting spirit of the Arab soldiers and officers, since it appeared to contend that the Kurds were fighting for all the people of Iraq. Though its army did not outfight the Iraqi regime, the KDP began to out-legitimize it. Its central objective was not simply to achieve the moral isolation of the Iraqi government but also to confirm, perpetuate and institutionalize its own government by providing an alternative to the discredited Ba'th regime with its promise to create a parliamentary democratic regime in Iraq. It had already held elections in the north, where it created a bicameral legislature. Foreign aid during this period was not of crucial importance.

In 1970, at the height of the Iraq-Iran conflict, Barzani accepted a truce offer from Iraq without consulting his friends in Tehran. He did so in order to create his own machinery. But it gave the old Nuri Sai'd bureaucrats an opportunity to move in. They were mistrusted by the Kurdish people and by General Barzani himself — a considerable number of his relatives had been killed by the very government these people had worked for. But they had the price of entry: the administrative skills which could, once and for all, replace Abrahim Ahmed and his group. And they had connections with the West, which Barzani thought would increase American and Iranian confidence in the Kurdish struggle. Barzani, who was eager to obtain heavy artillery and to get rid of Abrahim Ahmed, accepted these newcomers — composed mainly of junior politicians — and their promises at face value. The leftists made no effort to stop their entry and did not try to create their own organization. They disliked these foreign agents but liked the arms supply their presence brought in.

The newcomers filled the Kurdish bureaucracy but failed to penetrate the army — the army's distrust of even its own agents abroad cannot be overstated. The tough and resourceful *pesh merga** commanders and troops who had to face the enemy every day were not easily to be controlled by the noncombatant political arm. The army was a suspicious and hard to please ally. Its commanders were virtual monarchs of all they surveyed, soldier-politicians accustomed to command and to making swift decisions. Each had his own constituents, each his own dreams of power and of the type of community he wanted and his own commitment to expressed goals. United by shared experience and a common sentiment, defiant and insular, they shared a suspicion of politicians and diplomats who had always, in the past, "sold them out" and forced them into settlements which were not necessarily in their interest.

Yet, if the new leadership was to achieve complete control it had to control the army. To this end it developed a game plan that entailed the transformation of the economy and technology of the war from self-sufficient mobile warfare to fixed position

* "Ready To Die": Beginning as guerrilla groups the pesh merga became the official appellation of the Kurdish army.

warfare; a tactic facilitated by the introduction of heavy artillery and armament. The result was to make the army, while still insulated, nevertheless technically and economically dependent upon the new leadership. For its logistics the *pesh merga* found itself at the mercy of the bureaucrats and their masters in Tehran. During the four years of truce, from 1970-1974, the *pesh merga* had abandoned its training in guerrilla warfare and had concentrated on conventional training instead. Mulla Mustafa himself became caught between these two contradictory and opposing forces.

Toward Betrayal

In the Spring of 1974 the Iraqi Ba'th government defaulted on its promise of Kurdish autonomy (especially as applied to the oil region of Kirkuk). Preparations started for war. The Soviet Minister of Defense, Grechko, who visited Iraq and travelled to Kurdistan to meet with Barzani,[33] made two requests: first, that Barzani curtail his relations with the U.S. and Iran and second, that he forego, for the time being, Kurdish claims over the Kirkuk oil regions in exchange for some guarantee that a form of autonomy for Kurdistan would be worked out minus the state of Kirkuk. Barzani's advisers persuaded him to stick to his demand for the total autonomy of Kurdistan, as had been agreed upon in March 1970, and that he could expect substantial arms including aircraft as well as economic aid from the United States. Grechko failed in his attempt to avert the war. Barzani did not know of Kissinger's decision that it was in the U.S. interest to "drop the Kurds." The aid which subsequently came from across the Iranian border was nominal, consisting mostly of World War II artillery; the light weapons consisted of a potpourri of Chinese, Russian, American and British arms. The *pesh merga* was forced to retreat to the high mountain areas where the range of their artillery could be increased, yet even in retreat they inflicted heavy casualties on the Iraqis (in fact, the number of Iraqis killed from the summer of 1974 through February 1975 far exceeded the total number of Iraqi casualties since 1961). Forced to give up a large amount of real estate in its retreat to the mountains, the army received no more than empty promises of modern arms to come — and these when they finally arrived consisted of several anti-aircraft rockets so old that their thrust was 50 percent lower than the flying altitude of the Iraqi war planes.

Yet, ironically, these weapons and the many statements by the Kurdish leadership about the Kurd's newly acquired allies — Iran, Israel and the United States —aroused the displeasure of the Arab masses and led to a consolidation of the Ba'th's position. The Iraqi army's will and desire for combat increased while the Soviet Union looked upon the Kurdish struggle as a challenge to its prestige in Iraq. Massive Soviet arms shipments began arriving, accompanied by a large number of Soviet instructors. The Soviet political machine began rallying world-wide support for Iraq. The Iraqi army grew to 180,000 men, 90 percent of whom were deployed against the Kurds. The Kurdish revolution had become, in the eyes of the ordinary Iraqis, no longer a popular struggle for democracy in Iraq but a CIA-SAVAK affair. Iraq had to crush it as a national necessity!

As Iraqi morale, armament and manpower increased, the promises of aid to the Kurdish people dwindled daily. This time, the Iraqi government did not even trouble to offer to negotiate with Barzani since it was aware that the die-hard leftists like Abrahim Ahmed, Jalal Talabani and Omar Debabeh were out of power and that the new group in power were getting their orders from Tehran and Washington. They therefore moved to negotiate directly with Tehran and Washington, which they did successfully. In March 1975, one year after the State Department's request that it do so, the Iranian government notified Barzani's command that it was closing its border and was prohibiting the delivery of any aid, no matter what the source. The Shah expressed his wish that the struggle be discontinued. He said that it had cost him $200 million a year and that he simply could not afford that. (Here one might note that the non-productive Iranian economy has, for the last several decades, drawn its main strength from oil extracted from the heart of Kurdish land in Iran.)

The new Kurdish leadership accepted the Shah's order immediately, and mainly because Barzani and his inner circle had, for some time, been aware of the U.S. decision to abandon them. A breakdown of command ensued. Kurds streamed across the border into Iran on such a scale that chaos broke out in the rank and file, creating a greater panic among the Kurdish masses than had ever been created by the massive Iraqi attacks. The blow to the Kurdish struggle for independence had come from the most unexpected quarter of all. Kissinger's statement, that "covert action should not be confused with missionary work"[34] was only seen as revealing the bankruptcy of United States policy in the Middle East.

This was not the first time that Iran's Pahlavi regime had joined forces with the enemy of the Kurds. In 1928, during the Ararat revolution in the section of Kurdistan occupied by Turkey commanded by the Kurdish general, Ihsan Nuri Pasha, Mustafa Kemal Ataturk had been so severely defeated that he called on Iran (through the British) for military assistance, and the armies of Ataturk and Reza Pahlavi had forced the rebels to surrender. Mohammed Reza Pahlavi, the son of Reza Pahlavi, did precisely the same thing in March 1975. This time, however, the Pahlavi army joined forces with the Iraqi Arabs and their orders originated not from London but from Washington.[35] In 1975 the U.S. interest was served by sealing the fate of a struggle which was felt to constitute a potential danger to the U.S. allies. In addition a host of concessions were exacted from Iraq, such as the granting of huge contracts to American corporations to operate in Iraq, the cessation of leftist activities from Iraq against Saudi Arabia, Kuwait and Iran and the silencing of Iraqi criticism of Sadat.

The modern borders of Iraq[36] — and of most of the states in the Middle East — were not defined by the states themselves but by France, Britain and Germany, to suit their imperialist interests. In the process, Kurdistan lost much of its territory, wrested from the Muslim Kurds by Muslim Arabs, Turks and Iranians. The tragedy of the Kurdish people is the loss of their land as well as their independence. What has never been lost, in all the bloody history of the Kurdish struggle, is their will to survive, to maintain their own unique and distinctive identity and their hope of achieving self determination in a Middle East mosaic of many peoples living peacefully in their own independent entities.

FOOTNOTES

1. A.T. Olmstead, *History of the Persian Empire* (Chicago 1948) p. 11.

2. See André Godard, trans. M. Heron, *The Art of Iran* (Praeger 1965) 82ff; also, Arshak Safrastian, *Kurds and Kurdistan* (London 1948) p.22.

3. Tacitus, *Annals* 2.4.

4. Olmstead, *op. cit.* , p. 37.

5. *Ibid.*, p. 7.

6. Safrastian, pp. 17-21.

7. *Pahlavi Encyclopedia* (Pahlavi Foundation 1346 [Iranian Calendar]).

8. E.A. Belyaev, trans. A. Gourevitch, *Arabs, Islam and the Arab Caliphate* (Praeger 1969) p. 53.

9. *Ibid.*, p.59.

10. *Ibid.*, p. 48.

11. According to the commentary by Professor Poor Dawood in his annotated edition of the *Yasna,* the sacred book of Zoroastrianism contained in the *Avesta* (Avicenna Publishers, Tehran 1954 p. 108) Zoroaster was born in 595 B.C. in the time of the Mede emperor Kai-Gheşthasp, son of Kai-Lurhaspan, the forebear of the Lurs.

12. See, for example, Dana Adams Schmidt, *Journey Among Brave Men* (Little Brown and Co. 1964); Hassan Arfa, *The Kurds* (Oxford 1966); William Eagleton, Jr., *The Kurdish Republic of 1946* (London 1963); and E. O'Ballance, *The Kurdish Revolt: 1961-70* (Archon 1973).

13. *Frahat,* the word from which Euphrates derives, is Kurdish and means "abundance".

14. Enver Ziya Karal, *Osmanli Tarihi,* Volume 8 (Ankara 1962) p. 330.

15. Mustafa Remzi Buçak, "Memorandum to Ismet Inonu, Prime Minister of Turkey" (New York 1965) p. 6. Representative Buçak's memorandum was designed to advise Inonu on the creation of a federal republic of Turks and Kurds.

(continued on next page)

FOOTNOTES, cont.

16. See, "Ankara Concern over Kurdish Claims." *The Times* (London), November 22, 1967.

17. In its obituary on Kassem *The Times* (London), February 11, 1963 noted: "A similar failure marked his policy in Kurdistan. The republic he brought into being was declared a brotherhood of Kurds and Arabs. By the end almost the whole Kurdish north was disaffected and the Iraq army had suffered severe defeats."

18. Subsequent references to the Democratic Party of Kurdistan will be noted by the abbreviation KDP.

19. The Shatt-el-Arab dispute basically has to do with the problem of sovereignty over the river. Iraq has insisted that ships entering the river must fly the Iraqi flag. Iran has insisted that ships headed toward Iranian ports must fly the Iranian flag. There has never been any dispute over other aspects of the use of the river. For a detailed discussion of the question see Lauterpacht, "River Boundaries: Legal Aspects of the Shatt-el-Arab Frontier" *International and Comparative Law Quarterly,* Vol. 9, April 1960, pp. 208-235.

20. *Mulla* is an Iranian title which is the equivalent of "Professor." It is not, as is commonly thought, a religious title. In this case, however, it is also Barzani's first name.

21. For an account of the press reports see *The British Committee for the Defence of Human Rights in Iraq, Report From Iraq* (London 1964).

22. *The New York Times,* Monday, March 2, 1964 reported that Jalal Talabani, commander of the southern front, accepted the cease-fire under protest. *Time Magazine,* May 31, 1963 reported the following: "The very day of the revolt against Kassem," said an angry Kurdish rebel, "the new Iraqi Revolutionary Command called for Kurdish support. With the revolution, the Iraqi armed forces were totally disorganized, and we could easily have struck deep into Iraq. Instead we accepted their promises and held our fire."

23. The intensity of the conflict surfaced in *Chabat,* the organ of the KDP, especially in issue no. 494, January 1967.

24. Abrahim Ahmed had in the past tried to enlist the aid of the Iranians but had failed because of lack of trust.

25. The following substantiation is offered in chronological order beginning with a press report of June 19, 1963: "Iraq has concluded an agreement for 250 British Saracens, ideal as troop-transporters in mountain warfare and for more Hawker Hunter aircrafts." (*Daily Telegraph,* June 19, 1963); "...if the Iraqis place a large order for French aircraft and insist on rapid delivery (they are believed to want their first Mirage at the Beginning of 1970), this could mean that the French Air Force will have to wait for delivery of some of its own orders." (*The Times* [London], Feb. 8, 1968); "Is it not incredible that on a humanitarian issue such as this involving up to half a million refugees the Government are not prepared to make a diplomatic move? Is the right Hon. Gentleman aware that the British voluntary agencies, including War on Want, have made an on-the-spot investigation and are appalled at the extent of the human suffering? Is it a fact that the Government are making arms available to Iraq? If that is so, will the Government reconsider the position and try to induce a change in a situation which has appalled all those who have had the opportunity of witnessing what has happened?" (Sir Bernard Braine, *Hansard* of the House of Commons, in *Oral Answers Section,* January 29, 1975).

26. It is an interesting epithet, supposedly referring to the red headdress of the Barzan tribe but it has, needless to say, served to confuse, by associating Barzani and the Communists.

27. *Columbia Journal of International Affairs,* Volume 19, number 2 (Columbia U. P. 1965) pp. 320-321.

28. Reza Shah has entered into an alliance with the Iraqis and their British allies and jointly parcelled out the kingdom. The portion received by Iraq consisted of most of today's Lewaa el Diyalah, Lewaa el Kut and Lewaa el Amara. Even at the peak of the Ottoman Empire these territories never belonged to Iraq, but Reza Shah has now made this possible. See Stephen H. Longrigg, *Iraq, 1900 to 1950* (Oxford 1953) p. 13.

29. William O. Douglas, *Strange Lands and Friendly People* (Harper and Row 1951) pp. 104ff.

30. It should be noted that an environment has for the first time been created for the growth of the real middle class in the Kurdish regions of Iran, as witnessed by the growth of the city of Kermanshah from 50,000 in 1956 to a quarter of a million today. This is because the Iranian economy is a free enterprise system and has a heavy influx of multinational corporations which primarily employ cost-benefit analysis as against a reliance solely on military-strategic interests.

31. Iraqi government publication, *Mehkamat el Shaab,* Volume 1 (Baghdad 1958).

32. For example, both the Prime Minister of Syria, Mahmud al-Ayubi (a descendent of the Kurdish Sultan Salahedin Ayubi) and the Minister of Interior, General Ali Zaza, are Kurds. Yet Syrian policy toward the Kurds is one of the most vicious.

33. See "Son of 'Secret Sellout' " by William Safire, *The New York Times,* February 12, 1976.

34. *Ibid.*

35. In 1975 the atmosphere in Washington where the CIA came under intense pressure and investigation by the House Select Sub-Committee on Intelligence permitted a few leaks to be made public through Daniel Schorr and William Safire. The Sub-Committee report, however, was and still remains top-secret.

36. The region which is today called Iraq was not intended, originally, as an Arab state and would not have been one if the British had not put their trust in Prince Feisal and his Sunni Arabs. The people's candidates for king of Iraq were Gholam Reza Khan, Lord of Luristan and Pusht-e-Kuh (a Kurdish prince), Agha Khan and Prince Burhan al-Din (a Turkish prince). See Longrigg, p. 130; also Dr. Ahmed Hamed el Seraaf, *el Waqaaeh el Iraqieh* (Baghdad 1955).

PART III
ECONOMIC FACTORS

13

Energy: The Short View and the Long

By Kenneth J. Arrow

The foreshadowing of the coming crisis in the supply of energy has been common over the last few years. Indeed, it has long antecedents; the economist, W. Stanley Jevons, wrote a book on *The Coal Question* as long ago as 1865, and the Annual Report of the Secretary of the Interior of the United States, Carl Schurz, for 1870 predicted the exhaustion of the United States' coal reserves in thirty years. But the last years have seen a steady increase in the tempo of pessimistic prognostications. Scientific journals discussed the possibilities of alternative energy sources; the continuing work on nuclear energy has been justified on the basis of the coming exhaustion of fossil fuel sources; and the well-known studies of Jay Forrester, Dennis Meadows, and their collaborators under the auspices of the Club of Rome have gloomily foreseen the extinction of civilization as mineral resources, including energy, have become exhausted (the last group, however, thoughtfully supplied some alternative forms of extinction, such as death by pollution or starvation). In New England, there have been fears of a shortage of fuel oil every winter, and there even have been genuine temporary interruptions of delivery. In the Spring and Summer of 1973, gasoline was temporarily unavailable at some stations, and some oil companies took to advertising their fears about an energy crisis. Finally, of course, the embargo of oil to the United States by some Arab oil exporting countries as the result of the Arab Israeli war of October, 1973, was followed in the United States, Western Europe and Japan by shortages of gasoline an dother forms of oil, and the energy crisis becme the center of attention, overshadowing even Watergate.

I

It is important to realize that the energy problems of this country and of the world are really compounded out of several distinct issues, relating to different time perspectives. It is very important to distinguish them but at the same time not disregard any of them. Different policies are appropriate to different perspectives, but if anything effective is to be done, the policies should be designed to reinforce each other, not to conflict. At the same time, it is important that the policies adopted impose the minimum cost as measured in terms of other values among society. In general, of course, we wish to be efficient in terms of diverting as little capital and labor from other needs to the production of energy. But, in particular, I have in mind that policies designed to meet shortages of energy not be at the expense of the newly recognized needs of our society for a decent and habitable environment.

Let me turn first to the shortage situation in the shortest run. Energy, at the present moment, both in the United States and in the rest of the world, is largely synonymous with oil and its byproduct, natural gas. When shortage of energy is perceived, it is essentially a question of these two products. They

---

Prof. Arrow is Professor of Economics at Harvard University. He was awarded the John Bates Clark Medal of the American Economic Association in 1957 and the Nobel Memorial Prize in Economic Science for 1972. He is also the past President of the American Economic Association.

are the source of some 75% of the energy used in the United States today. From the viewpoint of the United States at least, in the new situation that has arisen, we have begun to import oil, formerly a substance of which we were an exporter. Further, the trends are adverse to self-sufficiency. The domestic supply has been largely explored and there is relatively little chance of large increases in output. Today our self-sufficiency of energy is about 88%. With rising demands and stationary supplies, it is expected to fall to about 70% by 1985. The immediate problem is that at the present moment not enough oil and natural gas are available to meet the demand in all its forms, including gasoline, heating oil for homes and residual fuel oil for industries, at prices comparable to those which have prevailed in the past. Precise information is lacking; the exact flows and inventories of oil are kept relatively secret by the oil companies, and published estimates from presumably informed sources have varied considerably. The most authoritative estimate I know of suggests that the shortfall for the first quarter of 1974 is about 11%, certainly below previous estimates; and even this forecast has certain conservative features in it.

As an economist, I approach the word "shortage" with some trepidation. As we all know, a shortage is defined relative to a price or set of prices. If prices rise, demand and supply shift. No matter how much of a necessity something appears to be it is surprising how one can do with somewhat less. Prices of oil products have of course risen, and this price rise will have an effect in reducing demand. Actually, the effect of price rises will be greater over a period of time when individuals have had a chance to adjust to them. For example, high gasoline prices are inducing a shift to smaller cars, with more miles per gallon. Obviously, such shifts cannot take place in a short period of time but require turnover of the stock of automobiles.

It is of course also true, however, that the very fact of shortages in some sense is self-correcting. What I have in mind is that the fear of being caught short of gasoline inhibits long distance trips; similarly, a fear of shortage of heating oil causes conservation.

The immediate causes of the current shortfall are of course well-known. Domestic refining capacity has not risen *pari passu* with demand for the last few years. On top of this the Arab oil embargo against the United States has restricted the supply of crude oil and therefore added to the shortfall. With regard to the first it may be asked why it happened and why it is so important?

Refining capacity is indeed being expanded, but the new refineries are located abroad. There are a combination of circumstances which explains this. Perhaps most important are the tax advantages created by our present system. The royalties charged by the producing countries for crude oil extraction are regarded by the United States government as taxes on corporate income, with no apparent justification. As such they are regarded as a credit to be deducted from taxes on profits earned abroad. Since, in fact, the royalties greatly exceed any possible taxes on such profits, there is in effect no tax on profits for refinery operations abroad.

The tax incentives were added to historically by the way the import quotas were used. It must be remembered that, under pressure from domestic oil companies, the United States until last year imposed quotas on the importation of oil. Since the quotas were under attack, however, oil companies may have felt sufficiently uncertain about their sources of supply to go slow about building domestic refining capacity. Fnally, the demand for oil abroad has been increasing even more rapidly than in the United States. It was more profitable to locate refineries elsewhere.

One must also ask whether the location of refineries makes any difference. After all, it is always possible to import refined oil as well as crude. Transportation is not irrelevant in this context, as the fuel oil shortages in New England have already shown. However, the more important point is that locating refineries overseas and making them dependent on foreign sources of crude turned out, in the event, to make them more vulnerable to politically-motivated interruption.

II

The immediate cause of the Arab oil embargo was to put pressure on the United States to cease aiding Israel. As these lines are being written, it is announced that the embargo is being lifted, though with a commitment to review the situation in June, 1974, presumably to see if United States policy remains acceptable to the Arab position. However, there are several economically interesting aspects about the embargo and its background in recent history. (1) By no means all of the Arab countries have participated; it is primarily Saudi Arabia and the small sheikdoms on the Persian Gulf. There have been reports that even some of the latter have violated the embargo to some extent. These countries have one rather remarkable distinctive feature; they are virtually empty. This situation is quite abnormal in usual international trade bargaining. A country may have a strong supply position in a valuable commodity, and this monopoly position may be exploited. But ultimately the selling country has an interest in continuing the trade, though at prices as advantageous as possible for itself. The situation is analoguous to collective bargaining; the union and the employers are both anxious to get the best bargain for themselves. But both have a strong stake in arriving at a bargain. Saudi Arabia, Kuwait, Abu Dhabi, and Qatar have very few people in them indeed. The population of Abu Dhabi, to take an extreme case, is 50,000; before any of the recent oil price rises, the per capita income was about $50,000. The population of Saudi Arabia is not of sufficient concern to its rulers even to number them properly; estimates range from 4 million to 8 million. As the government of Kuwait correctly pointed out in its advertisement, these governments have nothing useful to do with the receipts from the oil royalties. In fact, these countries are simply investing these vast and growing receipts in Europe and the United States. Some relatively small amounts are being doled out to their less pecunious fellow-Arab countries. The empty oil-rich countries can easily afford the luxury of embargoing the United States for political purposes. In fact, as the events show, the price rises are such that they can have their embargoes free of charge. A populous country, such as Iran or even such a determinedly anti-Israeli country as Iraq, cannot afford such luxuries. Iran needs the income for its development plans and has strongly opposed the oil embargo. Even Libya has been very irregular in observing the embargo, though its motives are, as usual, obscure.

(2) As King Feisal has said, it is impossible to impose an embargo in the United States without cutting back on oil production and therefore sales to all countries; otherwise the oil would simply reach the United States through indirect channels. But the United States is much less dependent on Arab oil than any of the countries of Western Europe, and above all, Japan. As a result, the chief threat fell in the first instance on those countries. Their first reaction was surrender to the political demands of the Arab countries. But in fact it appears that considerable political pressure has been put by them on the Arab countries, and this may have been instrumental first in reducing the cutbacks and finally in raising the embargo.

(3) Perhaps still more significant is the historical background of price and behavior. In 1971, for the first time, all the petroleum exporting countries (other than the United States and the Soviet Union) united to negotiate for higher

prices. The Organization of Petroleum Exporting Countries (OPEC) embraces non-Arab countries such as Venezuela and Iran. The international oil companies, who were the other side of the negotiations and who were given exemption from anti-trust laws to engage in them, offered little resistance to higher prices; whether it was because they could not or because they realized the profitability of cooperation cannot be judged. As the Chairman of British Petroleum Corporation has stated, they have now become essentially tax collectors for the exporting countries. As a result, crude oil prices have risen by leaps and bounds. From 1971 to 1973 they went up about 150%. Since October they have tripled again. The oil exporting countries have recognized their monopoly position and have exploited it successfully. Much a part of their strength and bargaining is, again, the emptiness of Saudi Arabia and the small shiekdoms, which supply more than half the total sales in international trade; they can afford not to worry about temporary sales losses if need be.

III

With regard to the immediate effects on the United States economy, policy has caused the impact to fall primarily on gasoline. Fuel oil usage for industry has been maintained, so that employment has been largely preserved except to some extent in energy production itself and in the transportation industries. There has been some downward shift in aggregate demand. The forced reduction in purchases of gasoline and heating oil has not been fully compensated by shifts to other expenditures, and there is also a very considerable fall in the demand for automobiles, pending a transition to smaller automobiles. Various forecasters have anticipated that the real gross national product will be reduced by about one half of one per cent as a result of this downshift in demand. Later in the year the automobile industry may be expected to revive as the shift to small cars takes place, but the shift to smaller cars does mean that the output of the automobile industry is, in effect, reduced.

The effect of the energy crisis on the domestic price level is straightforward. It is essentially a question of passing through the cost increases. It must be kept in mind, however, that the effect cannot be very large. Roughly speaking, the effect of a price increase in any sector is proportional to the size of that sector of the economy. Despite its crucial importance from certain points of view, the expenditures on the primary sources of energy are less than 5% of the gross national product. As a result, the typical economic forecast which had previously expected prices rises of 7.3% during 1974 has shifted to 7.5%.

Looking ahead a bit it is hard to see that oil prices can rise much above the present level. Some writers have emphasized that both supply and demand are responsive to price, and the more so as the period of time lengthens. For example, the elasticity demand for gasoline has been estimated at about .075 over a period of one quarter but reaching up to .24 in a long run. The demand for electricity is even more price elastic. However, even without going to any fuel other than oil itself, domestic oil production may be expected to react significantly to price increases, in the form of secondary and tertiary recovery from the existing oil wells. In addition, Alaskan supplies will be available in any case, and we may expect intensified exploration of oil in the outer continental shelf. Hence it seems very reasonable to infer that the cartel cannot successfully raise the price much beyond its present level without considerable damage to itself.

IV

Looking a little into the future, there are two possible developments for the persistence of the cartel, and no one can know which will prevail. One is that the cartel will eventually break down, as most cartels have done, because of the division of interests of its members. If some of the countries find the lure of high profits irresistible, they will expand output. Venezuela, Iran and Indonesia will be especially tempted to do so. If this happens, the Arab countries will find themselves losing markets and may be impelled to restore all cutbacks and even increase production over its previous level. Some close observers expect this development, possibly aided by the interests of the oil companies themselves. Another possibility is that the consuming countries will bargain with the producers on a united basis. It seems clear that the combined economic and political power of Western Europe and Japan should be capable of keeping the oil producing countries from unreasonable price behavior and, above all, from the use of oil as a political weapon.

However, the spontaneous effects of the market in reducing demand can and should be assisted by deliberate government action. Conservation of usage is the policy of first importance. In transportation we need a shift to smaller cars, the greater use of rapid transit, and improvement of railroad services, especially for freight. To give an idea of the energy savings involved, an automobile, as typically used, supplies 32 passenger-miles per gallon, an airplane only 22, but a double decked suburban train 200 passenger-miles per gallon of fuel.

Another potential source of economy is in space heating of homes and commercial buildings. Immediately, we can do with less heating in the winter and less cooling in the summer time (air conditioning is a great consumer of electricity and therefore ultimately of primary energy sources). In the longer run, particularly with new buildings, improved insulation will make a great deal of difference. What may not be economical or convenient with low oil prices becomes very profitable at higher oil prices. It is estimated, indeed, that a reduction of 30% in total space heating requirements is feasible, with no significant change in the way of life. While a great deal of this may be expected to occur as a reaction to price increases, particularly if they are permanent, it is clear that the revision of building codes will be very helpful.

In talking about government direction we need a word about the profits of oil companies and the taxes on them. I am not sympathetic at all with the idea of price controls, as has been frequently proposed. We need to produce more primary energy, and above all we need prices to curtail demand. I am more concerned about the windfall profits that are being earned by the large oil companies. However, what seems to be the best case for taxation is that in fact the tax system on oil companies is both inefficient and unjust to begin with. A reduction or even an abolition of the depletion allowances is clearly called for; at present they amount to a subsidy of oil. Further, as a subsidy, it cannot be justified on security grounds, for it encourages the consumption of oil, not its retention, against an emergency. Quantitatively even more important would be the change in the treatment of royalties abroad. It is clear that they have to be regarded as an expense of doing business, not as a credit against profits taxes. This would not only reduce a vast source of enrichment, but encourage a shift in refining operations to domestic locations, a change which would conduce both greater overall efficiency and the improvement of self-sufficiency.

V

At this point the problems we are discussing merge into issues of a still longer run. Clearly, in some sense oil is an exhaustible resource which sooner or later will be used up. The present high prices are an artificial scarcity, a creation of a monopoly. But sooner or later the real scarcity of oil would have driven up prices to these levels anyway, though perhaps not for another twenty or thirty years. All that has been done is to accelerate the recognition of an impending drying up of oil sources. We will have to shift to alternative sources and we may, in fact, be thankful to the present situation and to the Arabs for making us anticipate what will have to come about in any case. We should be able, therefore, to plan much more effectively.

Some of the shift to new kinds of energy will take place under the impetus of the market and the desire of companies to make money. For example, the tar sands of Canada yield a product very close to ordinary oil; production has not hitherto been profitable because the extraction process is costly, but at present prices, tar sands are beginning to be exploited. However, the capital requirements are so vast that it is not expected that supply will be considerable until 1990. Since the supplies of oil from tar sands are potentially as great as that of all underground petroleum in the United States, it is clear we have a very considerable damper on any further rise in the price of oil. In real terms we have an extension of supply for another thirty to forty years. A similar form of oil can be obtained from shale in Colorado and other Western states, apparently at costs which are reasonable in relation to present prices. However, there are considerable environmental problems, though they are probably solvable with sufficient research. Essentially, vast amounts of rock have to be crushed in order to extract the bitumen from it. Ways of rehabilitating the environment after mining are needed.

There is one delicate problem that must be mentioned here, because I am afraid it will give rise to considerable difficulties. All forms of oil extraction are very capital intensive, but extraction from tar sands and shale involves even more of a capital commitment per unit output. There is nothing wrong with high capital intensity provided that there is an adequate payoff, as there would be under present prices. But any capital expenditures do impose a great rigidity on the system. If conditions should change in the future and oil becomes cheaper or some other source of energy becomes economic, this capital may be wasted. Indeed the Arab countries, if they can remain united enough, could play a very clever game of keeping the price hovering just about the break even point for tar sands or shale oil. Private industry would be inhibited from investing, so that the present oil monopoly could be perpetuated. Unfortunately, it will probably be necessary to give guarantees of assured markets to those engaged in the production of oil fram tar sands and shale. I see no way out of this, unpleasant as it is.

The development of new sources of energy, more radical than tar sands or shale oil, will require extensive research and development. Indeed even the shale oil development, as we have seen, requires some research to solve the environmental problems as well as detailed development of equipment. I think it unlikely that private industry will be capable of accomplishing the necessary research nor will it have the motivation. If one company develops a suitable new source of energy, others will benefit. A company might well be willing to take chances of this type for sufficient benefits relative to research costs, but the costs are likely to be so vast here as to inhibit this form of risk taking.

Coal is at the present time by far the largest energy source, much greater in potential magnitude than oil. Oil has had its place because of its great convenience in use and in transportation, but this era cannot last very long. However, it will be very desirable to convert coal to forms in which it is more useful. Also, we have developed, quite properly, an increasing concern over the environmental implications of energy usage; in particular, coal typically has a high sulphur content. The simplest solution is the development of cleansing apparatus in the smoke stacks. The cost of energy derived from coal burned this way, taking into account the costs of cleaning, would probably be equivalent to something like $4 to $8 per barrel for oil producing the same energy, a price certainly below present prices and probably future ones too. More significant, however, is the possibility of turning coal into other forms, liquid or gaseous. The principles are well enough known though there are a great many technical problems in their solution. It has of course been long possible to turn coal into a gas with relatively low energy content, but this gas has a lot of sulphur in it and requires large pipelines for transmission. What is desired is turning the coal into a high energy gas from which the sulphur has been removed. While there is no question of principle, the practical execution of design would require a great deal of research. It is important to stress a wide variety of research efforts, going from coal gasification to more far-reaching improvements of our knowledge. The overall effect is comparable to the magnitude of the atomic bomb and would require the same kind of intense effort. The government's emphasis so far has been exclusively on nuclear fission and especially the breeder reactor. The technical problems there have turned out to be more difficult than contemplated, though no doubt solutions are possible. There is also the problem of insuring safety from runaway reactors and providing safe disposal of nuclear wastes. Whether or not these problems are adequately solved at the present time is a matter of dispute among experts, and it is imperative that a publicly convincing demonstration of safety be made before expensive use is made of the new reactors. There is also need for extensive research on economizing the use of energy in industrial and electricity-generating plants and in the home. Here there is even less motivation for any work to be done, however, since any individual firm will benefit so little, and the need for government supported efforts is even more considerable.

Efforts at conservation have an especial importance, because an important byproduct is a reduction in air pollution. Basically, the problems of air pollution arise from combustion of fuels, and therefore conservation will have a double function. From this point of view I want to emphasize that, in general, a properly planned energy policy will work with, rather than against, our needs for improvement of the environment. It is important to plan ahead precisely to avoid the kind of last minute pressures and hysteria which led, for example, to authorization of the Alaskan pipeline without adequate safeguards against severe damage to the last great unspoiled wilderness area of the United States.

Conservation and planning for alternative energy uses together work to reduce our dependence on Arab oil. The policies themselves cannot yield significant output for many years, but planning for them immediately signals that we cannot seriously be held to political and economic blackmail, even in the near future. Further, it removes the economic incentive to withhold oil from current production in anticipation of still higher prices in the future.

My recommendations for action can be summed up as follows:

(1) First, maintenance of our position that we will in no way let our foreign policy in the Middle East be affected by any oil embargo. So far our policy has remained firm, and there is every indication that it will continue to do so.

(2) We need to introduce rational and effective taxes on profits of oil companies. Depletion allowances should be reduced and gradually phased out; royalties paid abroad should be treated as expenses rather than as credits against corporate income taxes.

(3) We should seek to coordinate the consuming countries for effective bar-

gaining with the oil producers. This bargaining should not necessarily be a totally antagonistic relation; many of the oil producing countries are poor and can make effective use of their revenues, but the aim should be tocreat a stable supply situation. The Arab oil-rich countries should be encouraged to provide funds for the development of their poorer Arab brethren. The aim should be, basically, to create a stable supply situation and, in particular, to bar the political use of oil.

(4) The environmental implications of shale oil and strip mining should be given high priority of research, so that when development does take place, we neither destroy the environment nor do we inhibit the development of needed energy as the only way of maintaining a habitable environment.

(5) A large investment should be made in research on the gasification of coal, on geo-thermal and solar energy, on increased efficiency of the use of energy, particularly in the production of electricity, and on the use of hydrogen as a way of distributing energy.

(6) In nuclear research, more effort must be made in assuring the adequacy of emergency cooling systems for preventing danger from runaway reactors and in the study of nuclear waste disposal. It should be made clear that installation of breeder reactors will not start until and unless such safety measures are reliable.

(7) Finally, and most important, measures to insure the conservation of energy, such as changes in building codes, subsidies and planning for the use of railways, rapid transit and other forms of mass transportation, and possibly taxes on energy use, should be studied and undertaken on a large scale.

14 Oil and the Middle East: The Impact of Ideology on Performance and Policy

By Fred M. Gottheil

The Nature of the Problem

Identifying the problem is, perhaps, the most difficult problem we confront on the question of energy. No one has too much difficulty identifying a six fold increase in the real price of oil in one decade as a problem of some seriousness. But why the increase?

Are we running out of oil? Is that the core of the problem? Or, is the increase in the price of oil a result of something else? Could it instead reflect OPEC's overly aggressive market manipulations? And what about the oil multinationals? Are they part of the problem or, as some have suggested, an answer to it? And is the problem strictly a matter of geology and finances? Is geography an issue? Just where does our Middle East policy fit into the oil question? Is what we do in the Middle East parenthetical to OPEC objectives or is it instead a central concern? In short, what is the nature of the oil problem?

Conventional Wisdom is not of one voice on this issue although the range of views is remarkably narrow. We can conclude before we start: Conventional Wisdom believes that the energy problem is the very real scarcity of oil. Fundamentally, it is a matter of nature's niggardliness. OPEC's manipulations of price and output are dutifully noted, but these are generally assigned a minor role in explaining cause or in pointing to directions that policy should take. The oil companies? Companies are price-takers, not price-makers; innocent bystanders, so to speak, not culprits.

Dr. Gottheil is Professor of Economics at the University of Illinois-Urbana. His articles have appeared in many journals and anthologies.

But Conventional Wisdom has discovered a villain. We are the villain. As an oil consuming people, we are described as gluttons, and our oil policy generating government, is described as incompetent and interfering. Conventional Wisdom's solution to the oil problem focuses upon both these attributes in our character.

To Conventional Wisdom, the energy problem would never have arisen had it not been for government interference in the marketplace. The market is a self adjusting institution. Left unfettered, it always clears. Supply equates demand. There can be no excess demand or excess supply at the right price. And the right price will always obtain if only the forces of supply and demand were permitted to operate freely.

Based upon this belief in the efficacy of the market, the solutions proposed by Conventional Wisdom are as simple as they are comprehensive. Consuming nations must adjust to the new reality of oil scarcity. Such an adjustment requires on our part (1) acknowledging the legitimacy of higher oil prices, (2) acknowledging the legitimacy of higher gross profits for the oil multinationals, (3) dismantling government control on prices, and (4) *the need to be more responsive to the non-economic interests of the Middle East OPEC nations*.

Because the locus of power now resides in OPEC, policies of cooperation rather than confrontation appear to be more rewarding for the oil consuming nations. For this reason, the fourth imperative takes on considerable importance. Whatever may be the priority assigned to this fourth imperative in OPEC's set of objectives, it is perceived by OPEC to be a virtually costless item. By insisting upon some response to these non-economic interests, it creates a rationale in the oil consuming world for a "reassessment" of policy concerning those interests in question.

But this fourth imperative, mentioned only *passim* by Conventional Wisdom remains essentially a non-issue in the extensive political, economic, and technical literature on the problem. And that is a problem. For how do you question the validity of the imperative when the imperative is said not to exist? How do you respond to policy prescriptions concerning the Middle East when the prescriptions are not designed to address the substance of policy, but rather to contribute to the stabilization of oil prices and production?

For this reason, critical analysis of Western Middle East policy — however honest an enterprise — becomes, by the very nature of the oil circumstances, a most unproductive exercise. For example, to argue the merits of the European Economic Community's Venice resolution on the Middle East is to miss the point of the resolution entirely. If there is a lesson to be learned from a reading of Conventional Wisdom, it is that to insist on evaluating the Middle East policy of oil consuming nations as if Middle East content were an issue accomplishes little apart from sheer frustration.

The Conventional Wisdom

There is no want of "wisdom" from any perspective on the subject of energy. Never, it seems, has so much been written on energy by so many. As if on cue, academic research, both theoretical and applied, has shifted to the question of non-augmentable resources (a 19th century concern, by the way) and specifically to energy. In government, departments of energy were created where none had existed before, adding their own set of oil experts and data collectors. Energy "czars" took their place alongside traditional ministries of government. In industry, oil experts and independent consultants added to the swelling stock of oil information and misinformation.

This wealth of talent divides into two branches of thought: the Conventional Wisdom and the Others. The Others' expert opinion, found in industry as well as in the academic world, describes the oil condition in a variety of ways but points essentially to an arrogance of power. It regards OPEC, the oil multinationals, and industry's disproportionate influence on government as the principal perpetrators of rising oil prices and profits. It discounts real scarcity as an issue. It advocates economic confrontation rather than cooperation.

But this view, distinguished by its many distinguished contributors, remains largely benign. In the few instances where the view is considered by Conventional Wisdom, it is treated disdainfully. For example, James Akins, private oil consultant, former head of the State Department's Office of Fuels and Energy, and later Ambassador to Saudi Arabia in the Nixon Administration, argued in a 1976 *Joint Economic Committee* testimony:

> ...our present difficulty in energy matters has been made worse by our own gullibility and our willingness to swallow the tasty but nutritionless pap fed to us by fools and charlatans.[1]

His view is shared by another member of Conventional Wisdom, Paul McCracken, Professor of Business Administration at Michigan, former chairman of Nixon's Council of Economic Advisors, and member of *The Wall Street Journal*'s board of contributors, who writes in the *Journal* (1973): "...suggestions that the problem is nothing more than the cabal of oil companies sounds like an intellectual retrogression back to witch doctors, demons, and evil spirits."[2]

The assumption held by Conventional Wisdom on the issue of cause is most articulately expressed by James Schlesinger, formerly of Nixon's Bureau of the Budget, chairman of the Atomic Energy Commission, head of the Central Intelligence Agency, Secretary of Defense, and later under President Carter, Secretary of Energy:

> We face in the energy area a standard Malthusian case of exponential growth against a finite resource... There is no amount of expertise that is going to create supplies of fossil fuels. It is not a government matter of laissez faire. It is not a matter of government planning or regulation. It is not a matter of Marxist economic planning. We are just running out.[3]

James Akins says the same thing in the same

way: "The world is going to run out of conventional hydrocarbons some time soon, almost certainly before the end of the century."[4]

William Simon, former Secretary of the Treasury and Nixon's first energy "czar" adopts, too, this basic assumption about the world we live in: "The biggest job was to persuade the public that the crisis was real—not an exaggeration manufactured by government and oil companies."[5] Conventional Wisdom footnotes each other as evidence of fact. Vermont Royster, contributing editor of *The Wall Street Journal* writes: "Of course there have been a few voices saying yes, Virginia, there is really an oil shortage. Including the voice of William Simon, the energy czar, who by now ought to know as much as anybody about it."[6]

This common belief in the real scarcity of oil is at the heart of Conventional Wisdom thinking. Frank Zarb, successor to William Simon at the Federal Energy Administration inherits as well its ideology:

> [The Others] simply entertains the public with the idea that the era of cheap energy will return and ignores the *truth* which must be confronted...if we allow price to reflect the economic facts of energy — that it is a scarçe and valuable commodity, then consumers, both industry and individuals will begin to react to reality.[7]

This belief is repeated over and over, year in and year out in *The Wall Street Journal*.

Paul McCracken, a frequent contributor on this issue echoes the theme: "The first requirement for government is to recognize that there is a bona fide problem."[8] Ralph Lapp, energy consultant and member of the WW2 Manhattan Project adds his distinguished voice: "The United States is entering a disquieting new era in its economic history. We are moving out of an era when energy was easy to find and easy to exploit — a fundamental development whose implication will reach well into the 21st century."[9] Bertram Wolfe, of GE's Fuel Recovery and Irradiation Products, says of future prospects: "But even the Mid East oil fields are finite and some time around the end of the century, the world faces the prospects of competing for an ever-diminishing supply of petroleum products."[10]

The marshalling of citations is not meant to be an exhaustive expression of Conventional Wisdom. It is simply meant to reflect a belief system that has made a significant imprint on the way we view oil.

Having pronounced on the validity of the oil scarcity argument, Conventional Wisdom can proceed to explain the oil crisis in the conventional terms of market imperfections. Of course, such an explanation implies that non-crisis oil prices were themselves outcomes of a functioning competitive market. This, Edward Mitchell, Professor of Business Administration at Michigan and Director of Energy Policy Studies for American Enterprise Institute assures us is so, citing as supporting evidence the collected wisdom of his profession: "A recent survey of university economists who have studied the petroleum industry showed that 78 percent believed it to be competitive at every level."[11]

Hendrik Houthakker, economist at Harvard and member of Nixon's Council of Economic Advisors, would count himself among the 78 percent: "All this talk about energy being 'essential' should not blind us to the fact that it is subject to the laws of supply and demand."[12] Philip Gramm, Professor of Economics at Texas A&M and consultant to Canada's Ministry of Natural Resources, too, is impressed with the applicability of economic laws in the case of oil: "Economic science teaches us that shortages cannot exist in free markets."[13] And specifically on the question of fuel taxes, he writes: "Until the forces of the marketplace can once again achieve equilibrium, it is proposed that the high fuel tax would serve to trim some of the excess demand..."[14] Note the "once again," as if the impersonal operations of marketplace forces dictated at any time the level of oil prices.

The call for an overhaul in policy and thinking is sounded by Paul McCracken: "The time has come when we can no longer delay primary reliance on market forces and the pricing system to extricate us from energy problems we have created for ourselves with our national policies."[15]

The villain is uncovered. Market imperfections in the case of oil are man-made, designed and executed by government to obtain objectives that are both unwarranted and unobtainable. It is here, perhaps more than anyplace else, that Conventional Wisdom ideology is unmistakable. Government is the villain in the piece. In a free world economy, it must be.

William Simon, Nixon's first energy czar interprets history: "History has shown that the more the government has tinkered with the intricate marketplace machinery, the worse things have become."[16] Simon's successor Frank Zarb continues the ideology: "Where in the history of our Republic have we seen that government controls as a means of achieving a national goal has been anything but counterproductive?"[17] In case the point was missed, Simon makes it abundantly clear: "It is folly to believe that the same people who have created this mess can now improve the situation by tightening their grip over every single energy source."[18]

Not only has the villain been identified, but Conventional Wisdom is careful to dismiss charges against OPEC and the oil companies. Paul McCracken writes:

> It should be clear now [after 6 years] that our energy agonies are not fundamentally caused by OPEC or bureaucratic mediocrity or the Energy Secretary or oil companies or other "villains." Our policies are the logical consequences of having chosen a strategy of detailed government management — and even the worse form of government cannot avoid having this result in the inevitable morass of economic distortions.[19]

Randell Olsen, economist at Yale, concurs: "The oil companies are only a pawn in this game."[20] Harvard's Robert Stobaugh writes: "It is discouraging how many otherwise intelligent people think the whole thing is just a plot by the oil companies or the failure of our federal government."[21] And James Akins adds to this stock: "Many Americans still believe that the oil shortages and the price increases of 1973-1974 were caused by the oil companies."[22]

Conventional Wisdom's confidence in the efficacy of the market allows many to predict future prices of oil. Its performance here is a matter of historical record.

In 1973, James Akins offered what he thought was a somewhat radical forecast for oil costs and prices. Based on cost estimates for oil substitutes he predicted: "I now suggest that this figure is around $5 per barrel in 1970 dollars and roughly $7.50 in 1980 dollars."[23] Gramm concurs: "The free market oil price in constant dollars would be below $8 per barrel. At $8, a vast amount of energy from other sources would cut deeply into the conventional oil market."[24]

William Simon, as early as 1974, explained why a price beyond $10 per barrel would be unobtainable for OPEC: "If a barrel of oil brings a producer $10 now, and can be invested at 8 percent, a barrel of oil in the ground until 1984 would have to bring them a price of $21.59..."[25] To Simon, this seemed beyond reach. Houthakker, too, in 1974 saw $10 per barrel as approaching an upper limit: "At a domestic price of $3 per barrel these sources were not worth looking at...Today we are up to $10."[26]

Still, in 1974 John Sawhill, FED Administrator, unfolded a White House blueprint for oil independence by 1985. The projections were based on a set of prices — $11 per barrel representing the upper range."[27] Critics of the blueprint viewed the $11 as too low citing instead $15 per barrel.[28]

In 1977, MIT's Robert Pindyck predicted prices (in constant dollars) to rise no more than 2 percent per year over the next decade.[29] A year later, shortly before the onslaught of the second oil price shock, Pindyck explained why his computer model generated an $11 to $15 per barrel optimum price range:

> If production cutbacks are distributed roughly as they are today, the cartel price would be about $15 a barrel. But if only Saudi Arabia, Kuwait, the Emirates and Qatar are willing to absorb cutbacks and other OPEC members produce at capacity...OPEC production would rise about 3 million barrels and the price would be about $11 a barrel — some 25 percent lower than it would be otherwise.[30]

Just a year later, when these forecasts were already shown to be quite useless, W. W. Rostow, Professor of Economics at Texas, reported that the Department of Energy forecasted oil prices to rise to $30 per barrel by 1990.[31]

These and other estimates of future oil prices clearly marked in the records of *The Wall Street Journal* are, upon reflection, somewhat surprising. It would be difficult to find another set of predictions that were so divorced from the reality of the oil world. And yet, although the predictions of Conventional Wisdom lay buried and forgotten, the set of assumptions and accompanying ideology that generated them remains alive and well.

Oil and The Middle East

The connection between the market ideology of Conventional Wisdom and Middle East policy is not unrelated to the issue of international and intranational income redistributions promoted by oil — who gains and who loses in this new oil world. The deliberate policy of non-confrontation between oil producing and oil consuming nations adopted by Conventional Wisdom assumes, as we have seen, that high and increasing prices as well as reductions in supplies are both inevitable and justifiable. Confrontation, therefore, according to this view, would be pointless. Rather than confronting OPEC, as the economic logic of bilateral monopoly would dictate, Conventional Wisdom has chosen to "live with the problem".

Living with the problem is not an unreasonable strategy so long as the consequences generated by the problem are tolerable. But for much of the oil consuming population, this non-confrontation policy has produced serious detrimental effects on its well-being. It is unclear, however, whether oil-related economic interests — oil, banking, military, construction — have been so affected.

For these vested interests, Conventional Wisdom's policy makes good sense. The new oil world for them is a tolerable one. Accommodating the supplier is a workable strategy. One arena of accommodation is Middle East policy.

As early as 1974, Walter J. Levy, private oil consultant, observed: "The immediate reaction [to the 1973 embargo] of practically every importing country was to engage in a competitive scramble for oil supplies, coupled with offers to adapt its Middle East policies to Arab demands..."[32] That the Saudis tied Middle East policy to oil was considered by James Akins (a former U.S. Ambassador to Saudi Arabia) as a fact of life:

> When Saudi Minister of Oil Yamani said in March, 1973 that if there were no changes in the US Middle East policy, if there were no move toward peace, the Arab might not be able to increase production to the point needed by the West, he was not believed.[33]

The implications were unmistakably put: "If there is a war, it could cause us enormous problems. Therefore, if we want to be assured of oil supplies at reasonable, stable prices, our first effort must be made toward achieving peace in the Middle East."[34] How to achieve this peace was not overlooked by Akins. According to *The New York Times*: "He advised companies in October 1973 to approach American officials at highest levels to press for softening of Washington's Israeli policies."[35]

The *Congressional Quarterly*'s account of Western Europe's change of heart on Middle East policy points to oil:

> The embargo was immensely effective to the Arabs from a political standpoint as well. On November 6, 1973, representatives of the European Economic Community (EEC), meeting in Brussels, adopted a statement calling on Israel and Egypt to return to the Oct. 22 cease-fire lines that had been drawn before Israeli troops completed the encirclement of Egypt's III corps. They called on Israel to 'end the territorial occupation which it had maintained since the conflict of 1969...' ...Later that month, Japan followed suit.[36]

Robert Stobaugh, too, noted the connection between oil's economic power and Middle East policy:

> The result would be increased support in the US for the Arab position...an inevitable shift of political power to the Arabs. The UN invitation to the Palestine Liberation Organization is but an early example....Because this shift in economic and political power to the Arabs will be followed by a shift in military power, Israel's position becomes weaker each day-....The most that would be expected would be a modest drop and even then there would be continuing pressure on the Saudi leadership to raise prices and to demand additional concessions from Israel.[37]

Although William Simon firmly believed that the oil shortage was a result of growing scarcity, he also believed that day-to-day availability still depended on Middle East policy. Commenting on the 1973 embargo, he wrote: "The shipments were cut off to protest US support for Israel."[38] The implications are obvious. A. Gary Shillings, economist and first Vice-President of White, Weld and Co., reviewed possible events that could lead to price relaxation: "Further weakness in oil demand...should make the Arabs more conciliatory [on price] as could some sort of workable settlement of the Palestinian question."[39]

Paul McCracken, too, forged the connection by linking our economic health to Middle East policy: "The Middle East war has now made peering at the economic future like the problem of a man with cataracts looking into a fog."[40] The point could not be missed.

Michael Blumenthal, Secretary of the Treasury in the Carter Administration, made the connection by attempting to downplay the political impact of oil economics:

> I believe that the Gulf States are sincere when they say they will not use oil as a political weapon again...The Arab members of OPEC have great hope and faith in President Carter's peace initiative. It's a factor. [Arabs holding the line] would be a friendly gesture. It also helps President Carter's standing in his efforts to bring peace in the Middle East by showing that he has some influence with Arab countries.[41]

James Schlesinger summed up the connection in as succinct and comprehensive a statement as one could make on the issue: "We have become more vulnerable, not only in the physical and economic sense, but in a geopolitical sense as well."[42]

Vulnerability and Saudi Moderation

This geopolitical vulnerability is not entirely unrelated to Conventional Wisdom's predisposition to create unwarranted distinctions — moderates and immoderates — in the Arab world. The incentive to create these illusory distinctions is understandable. After all, if a new special relationship is to be established between the Arab oil producing countries and the oil multinationals, then it is simply more politic to portray the Arab States as both reasonable and reliable.

The stamp of moderation so applied to Saudi Arabia refers both to its oil pricing policy and to its position on the political economy of the region. In both cases the stamp of moderation is misapplied.

The factors contributing to the oil price increases from 1973 to 1982 — from about $3 to over $30 — are, at best, unclear. The specific role played by any one participant in this price history is difficult to assess except, perhaps, to argue that no oil pricing country — Saudi Arabia included — exercised much economic muscle in moderating prices. The fact is that Conventional Wisdom's promotion of Saudi Arabia as a moderate centers not on the actual level of prices obtained but, rather, upon the narrow range that separates the pricing policies of the Arab hawks and doves. This separation, however, seldom exceeded 5 percent of price. For example, James Tanner, reporting on an OPEC pricing conference in 1977, described the issue thus:

> As previously reported, the new Saudi prices are $12.32 a barrel for its medium grade and $12.02 a barrel for its heavy oil. That is five cents to 17 cents a barrel less than the prices charged by other Persian Gulf producers of comparable grades.[43]

That is to say, in this case, Saudi Arabia is moderate to the extent of a less than 2 percent spread. Hardly worth the label. But the label was applied.

Admittedly, *The Wall Street Journal*'s reporting of Saudi pricing is a mixed one in the sense that its inclination to refer to Saudi Arabia as a pricing moderate confronts head on its more analytic day-to-day reporting of Saudi pricing behavior. For example, as early as July 1974, the *Journal* noted:

> The U.S. and other Western industrial nations view Sheikh Ahmed Zaki Yamani of Saudi Arabia as the "good guy" in the oil producers' cartel.... But a different picture emerges from conversations with sources close to the cartel and with key OPEC insiders. The cartel is banking on Saudi Arabia to prop up petroleum prices, not bring them down.[44]

The New York Times, too, quickly distinguished rhetoric from reality:

"and it must be remembered that they masterminded the original oil embargo that opened the way to the quadrupling of the world price."[45]

Three years later, and with another doubling of price, the December 15, 1977 *Journal* article repeats its assessment of Saudi immoderation in terms not dissimilar from those of the *Times*:

> But OPEC insiders have long maintained that they depend on Saudi Arabia to provide a floor for OPEC pricing when necessary in some cases, although it is often overlooked Saudi Arabia has even been in the forefront of a price increase for the cartel. It was Saudi Arabia, for example, which in effect underwrote the quadrupling of prices by OPEC in 1973-74.[46]

Saudi complicity and leadership in the rapid escalation of oil prices notwithstanding, the image of Saudi Arabia as a pricing moderate prevailed.

Indeed, oil price increases and Saudi moderation were combined in a strange logic by Saudi's Sheik, Yamani which was reported without critical comment in the *Journal* by Karen Elliott House:

> Because the Saudis have been the U.S.'s best ally in holding down oil prices, Mr. Yamani [believes] that gradual price increases are good for the Western economies... "The U.S.'s short-term interests may be better served by another price freeze next year," he said, "But if you look at the U.S.'s long-term interests, you are better off with price increases."[47]

The image of Saudi moderation extended to include Saudi concern for the health of all Western economies. Ray Vicker, for example, states: "The Saudi approach was due in part to concern about the world's economies."[48] Three months later, James Tanner, too, reports without comment Yamani's views that Saudi attempts to hold the line on prices was "intended to protect the world's economies."[49]

Even in December of 1979, after the Saudis led OPEC in the single-most price increase in five years — 33 percent — it seemed impossible to dispel the moderate image. Steven Rattner of the *Journal* wrote about the increase:

> The development has already raised questions about why the U.S. should continue to offer a wide range of support to Saudi Arabia — from nultibillion arms sales to the hundreds of Americans providing technical assistance — when the Saudis choose to lead a huge oil price increase by the so-called moderate producers.[50]

Yet the article concludes: "And despite yesterday's price increase, the Saudis remain among the most moderate oil producers."

This Saudi image, portrayed so carefully in the world of oil-pricing, is applied as well on the related issues of Middle East politics and political economy. Here, too, the image is questionable. Putting aside the Saudi refusal to follow Sadat in recognition of Israel — the one clear criterion that distinguishes moderates from immoderates in the Middle East — the Saudi threat of exercising the oil-weapon against the U.S. when compliance to Saudi policy is not forthcoming points to anything but moderation.

Saudi Arabia, for example, was instrumental in creating the Arab boycott of firms dealing with Israel. The Saudis insisted on U.S. compliance on the boycott issue even though such compliance violated traditional U.S. principles of free and fair trade.[51] However understandable the compliance was from the point of view of the threatened U.S. firms, this forced departure from our traditional principles highlights the extent to which the character of our economic system can be so easily manipulated. President Carter, as candidate in 1975, regarded the post-1973 Saudi behavior as contributing to our "moral bankruptcy" and accused the Ford Administration of "bowing down to foreign blackmail."[52] The image of blackmail stands in sharp contrast to the image of moderation and yet, when President Carter succeeded to the White House, he, more than his predecessor, referred to the Saudis as our moderate ally.

U.S. tolerance of Saudi immoderation extended to our compliance in Saudi religious discrimination against certain U.S. citizens: viz., Jews. *The New York Times* reported on such discrimination as early as 1976:

> It is understood...that the Saudis routinely turn down visa requests from American Jews

> with certain exceptions such as if a local businessman sponsors the person, or if the person is connected with the joint Saudi-United States Economic Commission that was set up in 1974 to provide some technical aid....[53]

Such moderation in the Camp David issue is virtually non-existent. Steven Rattner, in *The New York Times* reported:

> The Saudis have apparently moved from a position of nonintervention and perhaps even tacit support at the time of Egyptian President Anwar el-Sadat's trip to Jerusalem to a more vocal unhappiness. A year ago, they refused to attend a radical Arab, anti-Sadat summit in Tripoli. Last month, they not only attended a similar session in Baghdad, but also agreed to contribute to a $3.5 billion anti-Sadat fund.[54]

The *Journal* made a similar observation.[55] Yet, in spite of the distance Saudi Arabia created between itself and Egypt on this vital issue of peace, Conventional Wisdom still insisted on referring to the Saudi position as moderate in the Middle East.

Ironically, the moderate misnomer used by Conventional Wisdom became, itself, an instrument of Saudi threat against the U.S. on the issue of the F-15 sale to Saudi Arabia. Robert Keatly and Karen Elliott House would uncritically argue in the *Journal*:

> The Saudis consider the sale promised since 1975 by two Presidents as a basic test of whether their friendship with the U.S. and their policy of Mideast moderation is worth anything.[56]

Two years earlier, the same parade of moderation was used as a threat to expedite the U.S. sale of 650 air-to-ground Maverick missiles to Saudi Arabia. John Finney reported in *The New York Times*:

> Another State Department witness, Alfred L. Atherton, Assistant Secretary of State for Near Eastern and South Asian Affairs, warned that disapproval of the missile sale could do serious damage by "undermining moderation and stability in the Middle East and jeopardizing our own economic well-being."[57]

The idea is clear enough. Saudi Arabia is moderate regardless of Saudi behavior because the issue in question isn't moderation at all — it is oil. Oil interests are real. Moreover, it is the only real interest.

Under these conditions, analyzing Middle East policy as if it reflects the substance of Middle East events can be, as we have noted above, a highly unproductive enterprise.

FOOTNOTES

1. *Multinational Oil Companies and OPEC: Implications for U.S. Policy,* Hearings before the Subcommittee on Energy of the Joint Economic Committee of the United States, 94th Congress, 2nd Session, June, 1976, p. 179.
2. *The Wall Street Journal [WSJ]*, December 20, 1973.
3. *Business Week*, April 25, 1977, p. 71.
4. *op. cit.*, p. 176.
5. *The New York Times*, December 17, 1973.
6. *WSJ*, January 23, 1974.
7. *WSJ*, September 10, 1975.
8. *WSJ*, May 23, 1979.
9. *WSJ*, April 23, 1974.
10. *WSJ*, March 1, 1977.
11. *Los Angeles Times*, May 27, 1979.
12. *WSJ*, January 22, 1974.
13. *WSJ*, November 30, 1973.
14. *WSJ*, December 26, 1973.
15. *WSJ*, February 26, 1979.
16. *WSJ*, June 10, 1976.
17. *WSJ*, September 10, 1975.
18. *WSJ*, June 10, 1976.
19. *WSJ*, May 23, 1979.
20. *WSJ*, January 4, 1980
21. *WSJ*, October 15, 1979.
22. *Joint Economic Committee*, June 1976, p. 179.
23. *American Academy of Political and Social Sciences*, November, 1973, p. 80.
24. *WSJ*, December 26, 1973.
25. *The New York Times* May 13, 1974.
26. *WSJ*, January 22, 1974.
27. *The New York Times*, May 13, 1974.
28. *The New York Times*, May 13, 1974.
29. *WSJ*, December 20, 1977.
30. *WSJ*, December 13, 1978.
31. *WSJ*, June 1, 1979.
32. "World Oil Cooperation or International Class," *Foreign Affairs*, July, 1974, p. 696.
33. *Joint Economic Committee*, 1976, p. 173.

FOOTNOTES

1. An exception is the usual denunciation of "obscene profits" allegedly earned by the oil industry because of supply disruptions.

2. Such confusion may serve a valuable political purpose, as arguments (for controls) that have a surface plausibility but that analytically are incorrect nonetheless may serve to reduce effective political opposition. See C. M. Lindsay, "Pork Barrel Politics and the Fog Factor," unpublished manuscript.

3. For a discussion of the income distribution dimensions of the emergency management policy issue, see Benjamin Zycher, "Emergency Management," in S. Fred Singer, ed., *Energy Policy In A Free Market Environment*, forthcoming.

---

34. *Ibid.*, p. 186.

35. *The New York Times*, August 7, 1974.

36. *The Middle East*, The Congressional Quarterly, Fifth Edition, 1981, p. 91.

37. *WSJ*, December 9, 1974.

38. *The New York Times*, December 17, 1973.

39. *WSJ*, April 10, 1975.

40. *WSJ*, December 20, 1973.

41. *Newsweek*, November 14, 1977, p. 92.

42. *WSJ*, January 18, 1979.

43. *WSJ*, July 13, 1977.

44. *WSJ*, July 8, 1974.

45. *The New York Times*, June 20, 1974.

46. *WSJ*, December, 1977.

47. *WSJ*, June 5, 1978.

48. *WSJ*, February 16, 1977.

49. *WSJ*, May 11, 1977.

50. *The New York Times*, December 24, 1978.

51. *WSJ*, April 12, 1977.

52. *The New York Times*, October 1, 1976.

53. *The New York Times*, April 12, 1976.

54. *The New York Times*, December 24, 1978.

55. *WSJ*, December 14, 1978.

56. *WSJ*, May 4, 1978.

57. *The New York Times*, September 28, 1976.

15

The Rise and Fall of Arab Oil Power

By Eliyahu Kanovsky

Since the "oil shock" of 1973-74 the policies and actions of governments, both in and outside of the Middle East, have been greatly influenced by their perceptions of "Arab oil power." These perceptions were based on the analyses and prognoses of the overwhelming majority of "experts" in government, in academia, in research institutes, in the oil companies, in the banks, private consultants, and so on. There were a handful of specialists who reached conclusions diametrically opposed to those of the large majority, but, until recently, their views were largely ignored. The projections of a very well-known American oil consultant, published in the prestigious journal *Foreign Affairs* in 1974, were rather typical: "Most of the nations of the world will, at least for the foreseeable future, depend almost entirely on (oil) imports from a handful of oil exporting countries . . . in . . . the Middle East (of whom) Saudi Arabia is predominant . . . the financial drainage (i.e., the huge and growing accumulation of financial assets mainly on the part of the major oil exporters) is *not* (italics in original) only a short-term and passing issue. It will be with us for many, many years."[1]

Echoing these views, Alfred Atherton, the Assistant Secretary of State for Near Eastern and South Asian Affairs, made the following statement to a congressional committee in 1974: "A small group of countries in the (Persian) Gulf are well on their way to becoming financial giants, since the world must continue to depend on the oil resources of the region."[2]

The prophecies of gloom and doom were based on analyses on two levels. (1) With respect to oil and energy markets the prevalent view was that the escalation in oil prices would hardly dent world oil consumption, and since the Arab oil producers, and particularly Saudi Arabia, had a dominant position with respect to the world's known oil reserves, the demand for their oil would continue to grow, and prices would inexorably rise. (2) These small-population countries could not possibly spend more than a fraction of their huge and growing flood of oil revenues. Thus, their financial surpluses, popularly referred to as "petrodollars," would reach massive dimensions, affording those countries overwhelming financial power, in addition to their oil power. The latter view was clearly expressed by an eminent American economist serving in a major capacity in the World Bank: "It will take several OPEC countries (i.e. the small-population Arab oil exporters) from five to twenty years to develop their economies sufficiently to absorb their foreign exchange earnings."[3] This led to the dire conclusion that the Arab oil exporters had the ability to manipulate the market, and thereby force prices to rise, or at least, prevent them from falling.

And yet, within a few short years reality proved to be different. Measured in constant dollars, oil prices fell by about one fourth between 1974 and 1978, and much more steeply when measured in German marks or Japanese yen. More important, Saudi Arabia's huge budgetary surpluses had turned into deficits in 1977-78, and this was the pattern in a number of other oil-exporting countries as well. The oil sellers

Dr. Eliyahu Kanovsky, chairman of the Department of Economics and Business Administration at Bar Ilan University , Israel, and Senior Researcher at its Dayan Center for Middle Eastern Studies, is Visiting Professor of Economics at Queens College, City University of New York.

This article is adapted from a paper which he presented at the Institute for Advanced Political and Strategic Studies, Jerusalem, June 1985.

were beginning to compete for markets, and price discounting became increasingly prevalent. The Iranian revolution was fortuitous for the (other) oil sellers. It eliminated the world's second largest oil exporter — following Saudi Arabia — thereby stimulating a speculative binge probably unprecedented in recent history. Oil prices skyrocketed from $12-13 per barrel in 1978 to $30-40 per barrel in 1980-81. For reasons rather difficult to understand, the "experts" attributed the oil price escalation to the power of OPEC, and especially of Saudi Arabia. The doomsday predictions of that period were even more frightening than the earlier ones. The usually cautious Morgan Guaranty bank projected that prices would rise by 8-21% per annum between 1980 and 1985, reaching $44 to $78 per barrel by the latter year. Inevitably, according to this view, the financial surpluses of the Saudis and of the other small-population Arab oil exporters would reach unheard-of dimensions.[4]

In the eyes of political leaders in the U.S. and elsewhere, the Saudis had joined the great powers of the modern world. Every utterance of the Saudi oil minister or of other Saudi leaders made the headlines, and was scrutinized by governments, the media, oil specialists, and political analysts. In 1979 Yamani was confidently predicting that OPEC output would rise from 30 million barrels per day (mbd) in 1980 to 35 mbd by 1985. He warned that "existing world oil and gas reserves, in a few years, will be depleted at alarming rates . . . (and) prices will reach levels three or four times the current ones." The implications were obvious: the world would have to pay obeisance to Saudi Arabia which alone possesses about one fourth of the world's known oil reserves.[5]

Yamani might be accused of wishful thinking, but, regrettably, similar views were expressed by U.S. "experts" and echoed by government leaders. Two American oil specialists, in an article published in *Foreign Affairs* in 1979, stated that: "Saudi Arabia is favored by a unique conjunction of huge (oil) reserves, extraordinary ease of exploitation, and a population so tiny that domestic revenue needs . . . have no practical effect on the (Saudi) level of (oil) production."[6] In other words, the Saudi level of oil exports is determined more by political than economic considerations. Israel would have to pay a heavy political price, or be compelled to do so by the U.S., in order to induce the Saudis to increase their oil supplies. Researchers at the American Enterprise Institute concluded in 1980 that "if Saudi Arabia . . . cut its production in half, the economic after-shocks caused by the Iranian revolution would pale by comparison."[7] The impact of these views was powerful both in economic and political terms. Based on testimony of a host of "experts" a U.S. Senate Committee concluded in 1980 that "the industrialized world will remain heavily dependent on imported oil (mainly from the Middle East) for the rest of this century or well into the next . . . the world is likely to witness increasing competition . . . for privileged access to foreign sources of oil. Such competition will lead to higher (oil) prices, and greater political and military concessions in return for oil . . . (oil) has become a source of political leverage." James Schlesinger, formerly U.S. Secretary of Defense and subsequently Secretary of Energy, concluded ominously, that "Whoever controls the oil tap in the Middle East will possess sufficient leverage to dominate the world."[8]

Events have shown that any relationship between these predictions and reality is purely coincidental. Saudi output has been cut by more than half, and the oil glut persists. As a result of the Iran-Iraq war, Iraqi oil exports are but one third of their prewar level — and the oil glut persists. The Saudis have run balance of payments (current account) deficits, for three years in a row, and their financial reserves accumulated in the "years of plenty" are steadily dwindling — and no end is in sight. To paraphrase a famous Churchillian statement: "Never, in recent memory, have so many been misled by so few for so long."

Let me briefly outline the factors accounting for the many errors of projection and prediction. Broadly speaking, there were *two* revolutionary changes: (1) in the energy and oil markets; and (2) in the economies of the major oil-exporting countries. What transpired was that the elasticity (or responsiveness) to the oil price changes, both with respect to demand and supply, was far greater than had been projected by almost all analysts. This includes the improvement in energy efficiency, the substitution of other sources of energy for oil, and the growth in non-OPEC production. In the non-Communist world, oil consumption dropped by about 11 percent from its peak in 1979 to 1984. This was due, in part, to the recession, but was mainly due to improved energy efficiency and fuel-switching away from oil. At the same time non-OPEC output (outside the Communist countries) which had been stagnant between 1970 and 1976 (16-17mbd) has been rising steadily and strongly since 1977 (over 24 mbd in 1984). In other words, the sharp oil price increases set into motion powerful economic forces which, in a relatively short time, began to undermine prices. OPEC production which had peaked in 1979 at 31 mbd (about the same as in 1973) fell very sharply to 18 mbd in 1984. For the Arab members of OPEC the decline was steep: from 21 mbd in 1979 to 11 mbd in 1984 — i.e., back to their level in the mid-1960s. Saudi output was cut by more than half — and the oil glut persists.

The second revolutionary change is at least as dramatic and important. While the world was adjusting rather quickly to far lower levels of OPEC, and particularly Arab, oil, the oil-exporting countries were "adjusting" their spending plans to huge and rising oil revenues. This behavior was perfectly understandable in view of the almost unanimous projections of the oil "experts" that oil revenues would continue to rise rapidly. Why worry?

It is almost a truism that readjusting to far lower incomes and expenditures presents *any* government with very critical problems. Saudi Arabia is a case in point. Government revenues — largely from oil — rose dramatically from $38 billion per annum in 1976-78 to $106 billion per annum in 1980-82, and then plummeted to half that level in 1983-84. The 1980-85 Development Plan had been based on higher income levels expected to finance housing, electricity, water, health and educational services, huge military outlays, and the development of industry and agriculture. When the Saudi authorities were faced, unexpectedly, with far lower revenues, they were unable to cut back spending significantly, and have been utilizing their financial reserves to cover deficits. But these are rapidly dwindling. The Saudis have, more recently, joined other oil exporters in barter deals and other actions which effectively undermine prices set by OPEC. The Saudis are at or near their "red line" with respect to restraints on expenditures. There are severe social, political and other constraints with respect to spending cutbacks. In democratic countries dissatisfaction would lead to expulsion of the existing leadership; in autocratic regimes heads roll — and not only in the figurative sense. In short, the Saudi ability to regulate the oil market has vanished, for all practical purposes.

•

What we are witnessing today is the initial stages in the long-term decline of those countries overwhelmingly dependent on oil exporting, and that includes the small-population oil countries in the Gulf and Libya. I believe that the U.S. and other Western countries have begun to alter their perceptions of Arab oil and financial power. I would conclude that we are in the midst of a longer term decline in oil prices, at least in real terms, with all its implications.

The ramifications of this trend are far-reaching, not only for the major Arab oil exporters, but also for Egypt, Syria, Jordan, Israel, and others. In 1975 Egypt again became a net oil exporter, but the rise in oil prices, especially in 1979-81, gave a powerful boost to Egypt's revenues. In 1981 its oil exports — over $3 billion — were worth three times all its other commodity exports combined, including cotton. The reopening of the Suez Canal in 1975 gave an additional boost to its economy. The oil boom in the rich countries also stimulated a large increase in tourism as well as private Arab investment in Egypt, especially in real estate. But of far greater importance were the millions of jobs opened up for Egyptians, and others, in the booming Arab oil states. One out of every six, (or even, possibly, one out of every five) Egyptian workers was employed in the oil states in the early 1980s. They sent home some three to four billion dollars a year through official channels and probably an equal sum through unofficial (black market) channels. For an economy with a gross domestic product of $25-30 billion, these remittances add up to enormous sums. The end of the oil boom, the sharp drop in oil prices from their early-1981 peak and the beginning of large-scale dismissals of foreign workers in the oil states all add up to trouble for Egypt, and others. The faltering Egyptian economy cannot cope with the existing growth in domestic job seekers, let alone also provide for those disemployed workers returning from the Gulf countries and Libya.

There are important differences, but Syria has also been suffering from economic stagnation during the past few years, due, in addition to similar reasons, to the decline in Arab financial aid. Jordan, possibly the strongest of the Arab economies, is also feeling the pinch. North Yemen, with possibly one third of its labor force in Saudi Arabia, will necessarily feel the impact in terms not only of lost job opportunities, but also the decline in Arab aid which has already taken place. In short, the end of oil boom spells trouble not only for the major oil-exporting countries, but for many of the others which, in various ways, benefited from the boom while it lasted.

•

While all the oil-importing countries benefit from lower prices, Israel will probably gain most, in the same manner that Israel was amongst the hardest hit by the oil shocks, both economically and politically. Israel paid over two billion dollars annually for oil imports in 1980 and 1981. To put this figure into perspective it was equal to total U.S. net aid, or, if you will, it equalled or exceeded Israel's huge arms imports. Back in 1972 Israel had paid less than $100 million for its oil purchases. The huge increment was due both to skyrocketing oil prices, and the withdrawal from the Sinai oil fields in 1975 and 1979. Israel's fuel imports in 1984 were down by about one half billion dollars from their peak, but were still a severe drain on its economy. The end of the oil boom should help stimulate the economies of the Western countries, thereby aiding Israel's drive to increase exports. During the heyday of the oil boom Saudi Arabia was on a binge of weapons purchases, and it was also financing the arms purchases of a number of Arab countries. The arms race was, and is, a terrible economic burden for Israel. But declining oil revenues have already had their effect. The recently-announced Saudi military budget for the year beginning March 1985 is $17.8 billion — far lower than in the previous year, $22.7 billion, though still over three times Israel's military budget. There is also reason to believe that the persistent and growing Saudi deficits have reduced their willingness to finance the arms purchases of other Arab countries.

Recent months have seen a flurry of predictions that an oil crisis will overtake the oil-importing nations in the 1990s. Although their previous predictions of an oil crisis in the mid — or late — 1980s were never realized, some forecasters are unable to resist the temptation to climb out on a new limb. Apparently they choose to ignore probabilities in making their predictions. For the probability is far greater that an oil crisis will affect not the oil importers but rather the exporters. The crisis for the oil exporters will be precipitated by a continuing downward pressure on oil prices in response to a number of factors:

(1) Geologists have *consistently* grossly underestimated the magnitude of new oil and gas discoveries (outside the Middle East).

(2) Long-term projections must take account not only of technological changes which tend to improve energy efficiency but also of further development of non-oil sources of energy.

(3) Eventually Iran and Iraq will terminate hostilities. In that event both countries are likely to seek great increases in their oil exports in order to finance reconstruction, to pay off some of their huge and growing foreign debt (especially in the case of Iraq), to spur economic development, and, possibly, to rebuild their armed forces. In the relatively recent past, the combined oil production of these two countries approached that of Saudi Arabia at its peak. Even now, as hostilities continue, each is seeking to augment its oil-export capacity. Iraq, about to complete an oil pipeline through Saudi Arabia, is already planning additional pipelines. Iran is negotiating with Turkey for a pipeline through that country.

(4) Governments in the oil-importing countries will, in many cases, raise taxes on crude oil imports or on refined oil products in order to reduce the impact on consumption of lower international oil prices.

(5) Almost all the oil-exporting countries, including Saudi Arabia, are eager to increase their oil revenues, thereby stepping up competition for markets. All these factors will continue to exert inexorable downward pressure on oil prices.

Oil prices will therefore continue to decline, at least when measured in constant prices, and the decline is likely to be long-term. This should benefit the oil-importing countries by lowering inflation and raising their rates of real economic growth. On the other hand, for the major Middle Eastern oil exporters, the consequences are likely to be destabilizing. Sharp declines in income can have catastrophic effects on these countries regardless of their absolute level of income. Aside from the major Middle Eastern oil exporters, the other countries in the region which had benefited greatly from the oil boom through high-paying jobs for (and huge remittances from) their nationals in the booming oil countries as well as through financial aid, trade and tourism, are already feeling the impact of the end of the oil boom. The decline in financial aid, and in trade and tourism, coupled with the oil exporters' wholesale dismissals of the nationals of the poorer Arab countries, is already weighing heavily on Egypt, Syria, Jordan, and others. These trends are likely to continue. Thus, the end of the oil boom, and the resulting sharp decline in Arab oil power, will have profound economic consequences for the Middle East, not to mention far-reaching political and strategic repercussions.[9]

FOOTNOTES

1. Walter J. Levy, "World Oil Cooperation or International Chaos," *Foreign Affairs,* July 1974, pp. 690-697.

2. *The Persian Gulf, 1974: Money, Politics, Arms and Power.* Hearings before the Subcommittee on the Near East and South Asia of the Committee on Foreign Affairs, House of Representatives, July 30, August 5, 7, and 12, 1974. Washington, D.C. 1975, p. 65.

3. H. B. Chennery, "Restructuring the World Economy," *Foreign Affairs,* January 1975, p. 247.

4. *World Financial Markets,* Dec. 1979, pp. 4-5.

5. A. Z. Yamani, "Energy Outlook: The Year 2000," *The Journal of Energy and Development,* Autumn 1979, pp. 1-8.

6. R. Stobaugh and D. Yergin, "After the Second Oil Shock: Pragmatic Energy Strategies," *Foreign Affairs,* Spring 1979, p. 838.

7. American Enterprise Institute, *Foreign Policy and Defense Review,* Vol. 2, nos. 3 and 4, 1980, p. 13.

8. *The Geopolitics of Oil,* Committee on Energy and Natural Resources, U.S. Senate, December 1980, pp. 2, 3, 69.

9. For sources and details the following studies are suggested. "Deficits in Saudi Arabia" *Middle East Contemporary Survey,* Vol. II, Holmes and Meier, New York 1979. "An Economic Analysis of Middle East Oil," *Middle East Contemporary Survey,* Vol. IV, Holmes and Meier, N.Y. 1981. "The Diminishing Importance of Middle East Oil," *Middle East Contemporary Survey,* Vol. V, Holmes and Meier, N.Y. 1982. "Mubarak's Inheritance: Egypt's Troubled Economy," *Middle East Contemporary Survey,* Vol. VI, Holmes and Meier, N.Y. 1984. "Jordan's Decade of Prosperity: Will It Persist?" *Middle East Contemporary Survey,* Vol. VII, Holmes and Meier, N.Y. 1985. "Migration from the Poor to the Rich Arab Countries," Occasional Paper, Shiloah Center for Middle Eastern Studies, May 1984. "What's Behind Syria's Economic Problems?" Occasional Paper, Shiloah Center for Middle Eastern Studies, March 1985. (Scheduled for publication in *Middle East Contemporary Survey,* Vol. VIII, due to appear in 1986.) "The Iran-Iraq War: Its Economic Consequences." Paper presented at Symposium of Jaffee Center for Strategic Studies of Tel Aviv University, April 1985.

PART IV
THE ARAB WORLD

16 The Arab World in the 1980s: Have the Predicates of Politics Changed?

By Victor T. Le Vine

Introduction

Ibn Khaldun, who understood the Mediterranean and Middle Eastern worlds of his time better than anyone, argued that both qualitative and quantitative social — and in particular, cultural — change necessarily occur gradually, subject, however, to the possibility of chance *(itifaq)* and fortune *(bakht)*, or unintended results.[1] His observations remain as valid for the same region during the latter decades of the twentieth century as they were in the fourteenth century. The underlying social and cultural patterns of the Arab world still change with glacial slowness: after nearly a hundred "modern" years, the lot of most peasants is still poverty and victimization by the rich and powerful; social relations, even in the so-called "revolutionary" states, remain largely subject to the ancient servitudes of kinship, gender, rank, status, and position; and everywhere, the old dialectic between Islamic verities and secular values continues to be played out in a variety of inconclusive confrontations. On the other hand, it requires little or no proof that the Arab world's material, quantitative landscape has altered a great deal under the impact of Western technology and goods. Much less visible, however, and hence more difficult to prove, is the extent of qualitative change, particularly in the political realm, where language, ideology, strutting regimes, and the fireworks of charisma and patriotism tend to occlude and distort, where they do not conceal, political realities. Yet, and it is the argument of this paper, despite the general persistence of older social patterns, a series of critical events — of chance, of fortune, of unintended result — during the past five years have in fact altered some of the basic predicates of Arab political life, both locally and in the region as a whole.

The premises, and the rules, have changed radically in at least five connected general political arenas: in the relationship between secular and religious values, whose current epiphenomenon is the much-discussed Islamic fundamentalist revival; in the Arab-Israeli conflict and its related Palestinian problem; in the contexts and dimensions of inter-Arab relations; in the political economy of Middle Eastern oil and its correlative dimensions of power and influence; and in the role and effect of super-power involvement in the region. Each will be considered in turn.

It should be added that the purpose of this exercise is polemical: to paint with broad rather than detailed strokes, to suggest the outlines of change rather than aggregate its particulars. In short, it is to provoke argument, not end it.

I.

A recent article by Patrick Arfi in *Le Monde Diplomatique* advanced the provocative argument that Israel, by seeking to crush the PLO establishment in Lebanon, may have effectively undermined the last viable secular (Arab) bastion *(garde-fou)* against

Dr. LeVine is Professor of Political Science at Washington University, St. Louis. His most recent book (with Timothy Luke) is *The Arab-African Connection* (Westview, 1979). He is currently working on a study of energy policy in Cameroon, Gabon, and Congo.

This paper was presented at a panel of the American Academic Association for Peace in the Middle East on "Political Changes in the Arab World" at the Annual Meeting of the American Political Science Association, Chicago, September 1-4, 1983.

the rising tide of anti-Western, Islamic fundamentalist fervor.[2] It may seem passing strange to represent Yassir Arafat and the PLO as the champions of Western values and virtues, but Arfi claims that given the patent failure of the various Arab attempts to promote both modernization and nationalism *à l'européenne,* large numbers of educated Arabs embraced the Palestinians' vision of a "secular-democratic" state precisely because it spoke to their deepest but frustrated political aspirations.

There is no way of knowing how much there is to Arfi's paradoxical thesis; at best his evidence is inconclusive. At least, however, Arfi's argument has the virtue of focussing on what may be one of the most important recent political trends in the Arab-Muslim world: what is widely perceived as the failure of the Sadats, Mubaraks, Sadam Husseins, Assads, Nimerys and Bourguibas to deliver the promised benefits of Western-style developmental policies, be they launched under the banners of "Arab Socialism," "Ba'thism," "Arab democracy," or some other ideological device. Jamal al-din al-Afghani, Mohammed Abduh, and Rashid Rida, all of whom sought a syncretic but sympathetic Islamic response to the Western challenge, have few credible heirs today, and those heirs have fewer disciples still. It is the words and/or writings of those with the harshest religious indictments of modernism and the West — such as Hasan al-Bánna, Sayyid Qutb, Abdul Ala Maududi, Sadiq al-Mahdi, the Ayatullah Khumayni — that today resonate in the Arab-Muslim world.[3]

It is not argued here that the strong reflex toward Islamic fundamentalism so evident during the past ten years is anything new. In times of political, or social, or economic crisis; during war, dynastic collapse, or natural or man-made calamity, there was always the mosque — at once often the fortress of the most conservative, retrogressive, and xenophobic elements of society, *and* the guardian of the only true vision of the just society, one that offered, and still appears to offer, hope and guidance to the poor, the disenfranchised, and the disillusioned. What must be stressed is the reflex's political-reactive character: in the past, direct challenges to the political and social status quo frequently took the form of movements for fundamentalist Islamic reform, and the same is evident today.[4] The assassins of Anwar Sadat in 1981 explicitly combined their demands for a thorough moral cleansing of Egyptian (and by implication, Arab) society and a return to Islamic first principles with an attack on the corrupting influences of the West, for whose dissemination they blamed Sadat. The same message was explicit in the seizure of the Grand Mosque of Mecca, on 20 November 1979, save that in that instance the target was the rulers of the Saudi state, accused of (Western) degeneracies and therefore, judged to have forfeited the right to guard the Holy Cities.[5] In general, it hardly needs demonstration that the "partisans of God" have been extraordinarily active during the past several years: in addition to the assassination of Sadat and the seizure of the Great Mosque, noted above, a very incomplete list would include the Islamic revolution in Iran, religious riots in Egypt, near-civil war in Syria, plots in the Gulf emirates, the executions of politically intractable religious dignitaries in Iraq, agitation and demonstrations by religiously-inspired students in Moroccan, Tunisian, and Egyptian universities, public trials of religio-political dissidents in Algeria, the reinforcement of religious law covering all aspects of civil life in Kuwait and Pakistan, an unprecedented rush to the mosques in Turkey, and various, often bloody, incidents of civil disorder from Nigeria to Indonesia to Bangladesh. Again, what all these cases have in common is not only the catalyzing presence of some variety of fundamentalist Islamic impulse, but the fact of an explicit or implicit attack on "Western" or "modern" or "European" ways, ideas, institutions, or policies.

Revolutions, riots, assassinations — these are the headline events of the change. Yet it could not be labelled as change if there were not also overwhelming evidence of more prosaic, mundane acts and deeds at the broader social levels — the village, the street, the *suq,* the *salariat.* Part of that evidence is the notable increase in mosque attendance, even in Turkey, where the Middle East's secular tradition — the legacy of Mustafa Kemal — is supposed to be strongest. Another part is the fact of the multiplication of religious newspapers and journals, as well as the skyrocketing sales of religious and political-religious books, pamphlets, and tracts. For example, the Egyptian weekly, *al-Liwa al-Islami* (The Islamic Standard), an "independent" (though officially-sponsored) journal of popular Islamic criticism and commentary, now has a circulation of over 750,000, "not far," notes Emmanuel Sivan, "from that of established dailies such as *al-Ahram* and *Al-Akhbar*."[6] *Al-Liwa* goes in heavily for discussion of occult matters, offers advice and *fatwas* (rulings) by religious authorities, execrates *afkar mustawrada* (imported ideas, particularly on TV and radio), and excoriates what is called the "new *jahiliyya*" (pagan barbarism) of contemporary society.[7]

It may well be true, as Albert Hourani contends, that "with the exception of Iran, all (Arab) regimes, having first acquired legitimacy by creating the state (as in Sa'udi Arabia) or leading the struggle for independence (as in Algeria), now try to claim it in new terms, those of development, of a concerted national effort, directed and led by the government, in order to create a modern society, one which is directly administered, literate, and predominantly urban and industrial."[8] It is also true that the modern Arab state (and its modernizing elite) has recently entered many more spectacular failures than successes on the historical record. The cumulative effect of these failures — some of them traumatic indeed — incontestably underlies much of the current fundamentalist attack on the secular state. Arab socialism — in its Algerian, Egyptian, Iraqi, or Syrian mutations — has patently failed to deliver the good life to the Arab masses. Five wars with Israel, including the latest in Lebanon, have succeeded only in demonstrating the military and political impotence of the Arab states involved. The 1967 war, in particular, brutally shattered many Arabs' illusions about themselves,[9] and not even the 1973 war, ostensibly "won" by Egypt and in whose aftermath the Sinai was returned to Arab hands, failed to deliver the expected economic and social benefits to the Egyptian masses. (Nor, it must be added, did Sadat's peace with Israel.) Besides, only Egypt "won" anything from that war, and in less than ten years Israel had heaped further humiliation on the Palestinians, the Syrians, and the hapless Lebanese. The unexpected failure of Arab Iraq, ostensibly militarily and economically stronger, to defeat an Iran said to have been weakened from its recent revolution, remains both visible and frustrating.

And finally, of course, the political collapse of an Iran once considered the strongest military power in the region and whose ruler had committed himself to transforming the country into the "West Germany of the Middle East," is a lesson whose repercussions need no further comment.

Chance, fortune, unintended results have created a new, possibly more unstable set of political premises in almost all the states of the Middle East. What is now emerging, as much through the efforts of rulers frightened by what they see from their palace windows as through the ferment from below, is quite possibly a new form of the Arab state, much more explicitly committed to "Islamic morality," much less willing to embark on secular reform, even less tolerant of its opponents and more brutal toward its enemies, increasingly xenophobic — particularly as regards relations with the West, and one that self-consciously masks developmental efforts with the sanctions of religious legitimacy. It may well be, for example, that the Saudi model — in which Western corporate capitalist forms have been disguised in Islamic cloth and reinterpreted as a new "Islamic developmentalism" — will prove persuasive for rulers elsewhere in the region.[10]

II.

In 1948, each of the Arab governments involved in the first Arab-Israeli war sought not only to liquidate the new Jewish state, but to seize as much territory as possible before the war ended (as they were confident it would), in the inevitable Arab victory. Arguably, the war of 1967, before the Israelis preempted it, was to have had the same first objective and that instead of further partition among the victorious Arab states (it's safe to assume that had the Arabs won, the Egyptians would not have surrendered the Gaza Strip, nor the Jordanians the West Bank and East Jerusalem), what was left of Palestine would somehow become the charge of the Palestinian Arabs, whose cause the Arab states had by then explicitly espoused. In 1973, Arab rhetoric again insisted that the twin goals of an Israeli defeat and the political repatriation of the Palestinians still obtained. However, as subsequent events demonstrated, while the Arab allies on the northern front still held to these objectives, the Egyptians were willing to settle for a much more limited set of aims: to recapture the Suez Canal by seizing a narrow strip along its east bank. In the end, the northern allies were soundly defeated, but the Egyptians, with Kissinger's help, not only regained the Canal and their honor, but managed to inflict incalculable damage to both Israel's self-esteem and its image abroad.

Egypt has always been the key to any hope the Arabs may have had of ultimately defeating Israel in the field; yet the evidence suggests that by 1972, when he began to prepare for the October war, Sadat had decided to hedge his bets. If Israel could not be defeated by the joint Arab forces, he could at least reclaim the Canal and declare a victory.[11] He turned out to be right, so right in fact, that by a series of audacious moves culminating in the peace treaty with Israel, he recovered the Sinai as well. Of course, in the process, by removing Egypt from the ranks of the confrontation states, he also made realization of the first objective — the destruction of Israel — a practical impossibility. And if Israel could not be destroyed by military means, so also did it now become impossible for the Arabs to think of simply handing over the rest of Palestine to the Palestinians. At any event, by the time Sadat took his historic trip to Israel in November 1977, it had become clear that official Egyptian rhetoric to the contrary notwithstanding, Sadat had pretty much dumped the Palestinian problem into the laps of his erstwhile allies and the United States. To the latter was assigned the unpleasant role of trying to pressure the Begin régime into concessions on behalf of the Palestinians, and to the former (especially the Syrians), the even more unrewarding task of trying to cope with a restless, unhappy, and unassimilable population.

For a time, between 1975 and the Spring of 1978, it looked as if the Arab governments had made the best of a bad situation — to be sure, at the expense of the Lebanese — by sponsoring the creation of an unofficial Palestinian "state-within-a-state" in south-central Lebanon and west Beirut. Here the several Palestinian factions could create protected enclaves for their civilian populations, train their fighters, stock as much weaponry and munitions as they liked, and set up the economy, institutions, and structures of an embryonic Palestinian state. However, what seemed a rational, if cynical, expedient, turned out to be a serious miscalculation. Setting up what amounted to a dumping ground for Palestinians had the unfortunate, unintended consequences of provoking first the March 1978 Israeli incursion into Southern Lebanon, and then, in 1982, a full scale invasion resulting in dismemberment of the Palestinian military and political apparatus, the occupation of Beirut, and the *de facto* partition of Lebanon into Israeli and Syrian spheres of influence.

It is clear that despite all of Arafat's brave talk and the carefully staged withdrawal of the *fedayeen* fighters from Beirut, the Lebanese war turned out to be an unmitigated disaster for the Palestinians. Not only did they lose the only relatively autonomous base of operations they had ever had, but they were forced to the realization that in the crunch all their friends — the Syrians, the Russians, the other Arab states — had been unable (or unwilling) to help them. Scattered to a half dozen Arab countries or forced to flee to the Syrian lines the Palestinians have quite literally returned to square one: they are once again the unwilling, unwelcome guests of various surly Arab regimes, dependent upon them for survival and subject to the vagaries of their internal politics. Nor did Arafat emerge unscathed from the debacle; currently under attack from the Syrians and elements of his own Fatah, who accuse him of various acts of "treason" and "betrayal," he may yet witness his own loss of power and the collapse of the PLO itself.

In short, as a result of the Lebanese war, the Palestinians lost their capacity for organized independent action, that is, their power to affect directly those aspects of the Arab-Israeli conflict of most concern to them. At least for the time being, what happens to them will be largely decided by others — by host Arab governments, by Israel, by the United States and the Soviet Union.

If the Lebanese war resulted in the military and political emasculation of the Palestinian movement and confirmed basic changes in the Arab side of the Arab-Israel equation, it also marked the emergence of Israel as a regional mini-superpower, able and willing to take whatever initiatives are dictated by its leaders' perceptions of the Israeli national interest. There was no secret about Israel's readiness to invade Lebanon; the Begin government had made its intentions public many months before the actual invasion by massing its forces along the Lebanese border and by declaring that further acts of terrorism against Israeli citizens would force its hand. The trigger, of course, was the attempt on the life of Ambassador Shlomo Argov in London, and neither the United States, nor the U.N., nor the Syrians, nor any other power was able to prevent the Israeli move. It took the Israelis only a week to reach Beirut, and in the process the Palestinian forces were crushed and the Syrian army severely mauled. Backed by a new, assertive Sephardic majority, animated by what Ofira Seliktar calls "the new Zionism,"[12] the present Israeli government appears determined to pursue a set of policies designed to ensure that the country will maintain both its new power position in the region and the initiative in dealings with its neighbors. It may be added that the depth of popular support for the regime was amply demonstrated by events following the publication of the Kahane Commission Report, which had condemned Defense Minister Ariel Sharon and several other military and official figures for various acts of official irresponsibility in connection with the Shetila and Sabra massacres of September, 1982.[13] Though Chief of Staff Rafael Eitan was replaced and Sharon removed from the Defense Ministry, Begin defiantly retained Sharon in the Cabinet with ministerial rank in the face of cries of outrage from the opposition, attacks by the press, and massive anti-government demonstrations in Tel Aviv. Begin was on safe ground: at the time, the most reputable Israeli polls indicated that Begin and the Likud would win any national electoral test of strength, and the politicians of the opposition, twice easily defeated on votes of non-confidence in the Knesset, conceded the point.[14]

Further, it is also clear Israel has seized the initiative with respect to the West Bank and Gaza, not to speak of the Golan Heights, which were to all intents and purposes annexed in 1981. New settlements in the West Bank are being set up at a rate which will bring the Israeli population of the area up to around 100,000 by 1985, despite admonitions from the U.S., protest from the United Nations, angry words from the Arab states, and demonstrations and violence by West Bank Arabs. It is difficult to avoid the conclusion that Begin was trying for a *fait accompli* in the occupied territories; the more settlers in the West Bank, the more politically costly would become any attempt by a post-Begin government even to consider negotiating a territorial solution to the Palestinian problem. Israel may not, in fact, formally annex the West Bank and Gaza, and for obvious reasons, but no one can now question the depth of the Begin government's feelings about what it claims are the Biblical and historic rights to "Judea and Samaria," nor its resolve to prevent the creation of a Palestinian state on the West Bank of the Jordan.* (At least on the latter goal, there was a harmony of views between Begin and King Hussein.) The point is that all this has effectively stymied (perhaps a more apt description is "anaesthetized") the autonomy negotiations, made the Reagan Plan redundant, and radically constricted the

*Begin's departure did not change this situation. His successor, former foreign minister Shamir, gives no indication that there will be substantial departures from the broad policy lines laid down by the Begin government.

range of future options available to the Palestinians and their supporters. Whether the new situation, including the near-disintegration of the PLO establishment, will make the West Bank and Gaza Palestinians more politically pliable and/or amenable to the Begin version of "autonomy" remains to be seen — at the moment at least that does not seem to be the case. (Amos Perlmutter, among others, has argued that *that* was the true objective of the Israeli invasion of Lebanon.[15]) At any event, it is now clear that the present combination of Arab disarray, Western (and Eastern) political ineffectiveness, and Israeli initiative has a least for now, and perhaps indefinitely, precluded the possibility of a *territorial* solution to the Palestinian problem which includes the West Bank and Gaza. A Palestinian community now even more fragmented than before (1982), reduced again to the status of client and unable to bring effective pressure to bear either on the Arab states or the international community, shorn of its larger military capability, with its leadership ranks in shambles, may have to wait a very long time before it can again mount a credible campaign on its own behalf — and by then it may be too late. In the meantime, and barring some sort of (improbable) Palestinian resurgence, the Palestinians are pretty much left to their own local devices and the mercies of their neighbors, patrons, "friends," and enemies.

Without recapitulating the facts, and if the analysis presented here is at all credible, the conclusion is inescapable that the predicates of the Arab-Israeli conflict have indeed changed, and changed radically. In the light of the Egyptian-Israeli peace treaty, and given the hesitations, backings and fillings of most other Arab states, the once solid front against Israel appears to have crumbled, and with it, the resolve (if not the means), to destroy the Israeli state. With the destruction of the Palestinians' military capacity by Israelis and the recrudescence of violent internecine conflict within the PLO and among the armed Palestinian groups, the once fervent Arab champions of the Palestinian cause seem already to have cooled their ardor. It may be too early to tell, but there does not appear to be any Arab (or Russian) haste to re-arm the Palestinians with heavy weapons, and even the Syrians, most recently the PLO's best friends, now seem most concerned with bringing to heel what is left of the autonomous armed Palestinian groups still operating in their sector of Lebanon. Perhaps the most telling indicator of the change on the Arab side of the conflict is the unhappy lot of the 300,000 or so civilian Palestinians left in the wake of the Lebanese war: the Lebanese government has made it brutally clear that it doesn't want them in the areas under its control, and no Arab government has thus far stepped forward to offer them sanctuary. And finally, there is the dramatic metamorphosis of Israel from beleaguered victim to regional overdog.

Just how these developments will affect inter-Arab politics is still unclear, but it may be the case, for example, that the conflict can no longer serve as one of the principal bases for what there is of inter-Arab political consensus. At minimum, henceforth it will probably be much more difficult for the regimes of the confrontation states to use the Israeli threat to rally support for themselves, or to divert attention from pressing domestic problems. For Egypt, certainly, that has been one of the unpleasant, unintended consequences of its peace with Israel. It can also be argued that these changes could exacerbate interstate disputes and rivalries partially or largely submerged by the thirty-five years' war with Israel. It is to this latter aspect of the changed Arab political scene that we now turn.

III.

It may be conceded at once that there is nothing very unusual about the current spate of interstate hostilities in North Africa and the Middle East. The word "endemic" is often used to describe the frequency and scope of such disputes, and it is easily demonstrated that every state in the region is in more or less active confrontation with another or others of its proximate or distant neighbors. Some of these conflicts are of relatively recent vintage, but others such as the Iranian-Iraqi dispute, have political roots reaching back centuries. There is not much new in the stakes of the conflicts, either:

territory, military or political supremacy, an economic prize, the imperial vision of some leader, the suppression of a transterritorial ethnic revolt, control of a strategic land or water passage, or some variety of real or artificial irredentism.

Yet, if the current crop of conflicts is closely examined in its regional contexts, there do emerge a number of significant differences generated by some radical qualitative changes in the underlying political predicates of inter-Arab relations. Five sets of these changes are worth noting.

There is, first of all, the transformation of the Arab-Israeli conflict, discussed above, two of whose major consequences have been on the one hand, to force an introversion of national political attention and on the other, exacerbation of interstate disputes, particularly among the "confrontation" states.

Second, the recent Islamic resurgence, catalyzed by the Iranian revolution, has introduced what are often highly disruptive religio-ideological elements into *both* domestic politics and interstate relations. The case of Saudi Arabia, mentioned briefly earlier in relation to the 1979 attack and seizure of Mecca's Great Mosque, is more than instructive in this connection. According to Bernard Schechterman, the seizure of the Great Mosque was but one, albeit the most spectacular, of a number of acts of rebellion by organized Hejazi, al-Hasa, and Shammar tribesmen seeking the fall of the Saudi monarchy and independence for their regions. The perpetrators of the earlier incidents, who probably benefitted from Libyan, Iraqi, and (South) Yemeni aid, seem to have acted largely without religious sanction. However, the Great Mosque Insurrection differed from the rest in that those involved deliberately invoked religious themes to cover and justify their actions and chose a day fraught with religious meaning for their attack. Moreover, the Insurrection (during which fighting continued to the end of November in Mecca, and to mid-December in Taif and Medina) also included attempts by Khumayni supporters on the *hajj* to demonstrate, and apparently triggered widespread anti-regime and pro-Iran demonstrations by Shi'i oil workers in the Al Qatif (Eastern Province) area.[16]

It comes as no surprise, therefore that Saudi Arabia, Kuwait (where pro-Khumayni-Shi'a elements attempted a coup), Bahrein, the United Arab Emirates, and Oman (plus Jordan) would not only side with Iraq but give it continuing active financial and logistical support in its war with Iran.[17] For Saudi Arabia and the oil kingdoms of the Gulf the threat from revolutionary Iran is far greater than any posed by Ba'thist Iraq, with whom some Gulf states have long-standing boundary disputes, and which was often implicated in various plots, incidents of violence, rebellions, and civil disturbances that took place in their territories during the 'sixties and 'seventies. The threat lies not so much in incidental acts of disorder inspired by pro-Iranian partisans, as in one of the most easily understood and exportable lessons of the Iranian revolution: that a morally rearmed Muslim people can prevail against hated rulers, whatever the latter's Islamic pretensions. Put another way, the Iranian revolution pointed a loaded ideological pistol at the heads of the hereditary princes, sheikhs, and kings of the Muslim world, and in the interest of their own survival they were willing to support any agent (even one as distasteful as Iraq) that could serve to disarm that weapon.

It should be added that the Middle East's dynasts are not the only rulers in the area threatened by the Iranian revolution. A credible case can be made for the proposition that one of the reasons why Sadam Hussein went to war against Iran was to put an end to the increasingly dangerous pro-Khumayni (and by definition, anti-regime) agitation among Iraq's very large Shi'a population.[18] And finally, as Iran is considered by many of its neighbors to be the *mashreq*'s most dangerous source of religio-political infection, so Libya plays the same role in the *maghreb*. This is not because the Libyan political model is particularly Islamic, or that Qadhafi has exceptional religious credentials, but because, in the pursuit of his aims in the region, he is prepared to help (with money, sanctuary, and if need be, arms) Islamic fundamentalist leaders and groups that can either cause political trouble for, or are in fact opponents of, regimes in neighboring countries.[19]

The third set of changes, highlighted by the tragic Lebanese example, admittedly lies more in the realm of probability than of established fact. The reality, however, is the fact of the events in Lebanon since 1975, which, by vividly demonstrating the fragility of contemporary Middle Eastern state structures, may have opened the way for the use of forms of intervention and conflict hitherto held in abeyance or reserve. Perhaps the Republic of Lebanon, jerry-built by the French and at independence already burdened with a long history of bloody intercommunal and inter-confessional strife, was more intrinsically fragile than its similarly artificial neighbors. Yet, for a time, under the extraordinary compromises embodied in the informal National Pact of 1943, the Lebanese state prospered and the Lebanese themselves could take pride in being citizens of what was often referred to as "the Switzerland of the Middle East." The point remains, however, that Lebanon's factional strife could not be contained once the political-demographic premises on which the National Pact rested had ceased to be tenable, and that Lebanon's leaders, by calling on their external friends for assistance against their internal enemies, contributed to the country's dismemberment. Again, there is little new in the fact that warring or dissident groups in one country seek support next door or in their neighborhood, or that regimes like Libya's actively pursue opportunities for intervention abroad. What is new is the increased scale of that intervention and the higher levels of confrontation which opposing regimes in both *mashreq* and *maghreb* are now willing to countenance. The goals of conflict and intervention now not only openly include the downfall of governments (e.g., Libya in Chad, Iraq and its allies vs. Iran and its allies), but it is apparently no longer unthinkable to seek the collapse or disintegration of another state (besides Israel). Admittedly, in any one case the stakes of conflict, or its intensity, may be raised to the point where either or both of these goals become attractive, but it is not unreasonable to suggest that both the Lebanese example and the transformed predicates of the Arab-Israeli conflict may have helped create the conditions for an important qualitative change in the levels and goals of the region's interstate conflicts.

Fourth, a quantitative and qualitative improvement in the military capability of Middle Eastern states, including nuclear weaponry (epitomized by the so-called "Islamic bomb") has made the region as a whole much more potentially dangerous than it has been since the end of the 1973 Arab-Israeli war. All the available evidence indicates that since 1973 not only have the confrontation states replenished and markedly improved their armories, but so has almost every other state in the region. From 1973 to 1982, some $112 billion worth of arms were delivered to or ordered by the Arab group of states including Syria, Iraq, Libya, Saudi Arabia, Kuwait, Morocco, the United Arab Emirates (UAE), Oman, and Egypt; of this amount, more than $70 billion is accounted for by Saudi Arabia alone.[20] (The larger figure does not, of course, include the more than $20 billion in arms purchased by Iran between 1973 and 1977, nor the approximately $20 billion worth of Israeli purchases to 1982.[21]) The annual lists published by London's Institute of Strategic Studies show that some of the most sophisticated weapons produced by or in the arsenals of the United States, the Soviet Union and its allies, France, Britain, Canada, Italy, Brazil, Switzerland, and West Germany have been sold, given, or have otherwise found their way to the Middle East. Even the Chinese have successfully entered the lucrative Middle East arms trade: in 1982 they sold two of their R-class submarines to Egypt, and they provide infantry weapons to North Yemen and Sudan. Though many of the major arms deals with Middle East states take place under bilateral and security assistance agreements involving the United States, the Soviet Union, Britain, and France, there is also evidence of a good deal of inter-Arab movement of arms, and in 1979 a consortium of states operating under the Gulf Cooperative Council (GCC), agreed to set up an $8 billion arms industry in the United Arab Emirates.[22]

Certainly, and with the exceptions of Iran and Iraq (who are using up their arms and munitions faster then they can be replaced), the states of the Middle East have weaponry enough for any purpose, including a major war with Israel, though that exigency — as suggested above — seems largely out of the question for now. What remains is dangerous enough: the possibility that the Iran-Iraq war may expand in scope, rather than wind down from its present stalemate, or that other points of continuing confrontation (notably Syria vs. Iraq, or Libya vs. Egypt and/or Sudan, or Morocco vs. Algeria) could erupt into open, full-scale warfare. It should be recalled that Libya and Egypt fought a short but intense five-day armored confrontation in July 1977, that Libya has been on the verge of war with Sudan several times and is in fact at war in Chad, that Syria and Iraq periodically exchange bellicose threats (more frequently these days, in view of Syria's support for Iran against Iraq), and that Algeria and Morocco could easily go to war if the Western Sahara issue is not resolved between them. Given the growing lack of restraint in interstate relations, the tempting availability of sophisticated weapons, and the continuing irritation of unresolved interstate conflicts and problems, the resort to large-scale military adventure could — at least in the cases suggested above — become irresistible. And finally, if nuclear weapons are added to this mixture, the prospects become even more unsettling.

This is not the place for yet another extended discussion of the question of nuclear weapons in the Middle East. Suffice it for our purposes to point out that Israel almost certainly has a nuclear weapons capability, that the development of the so-called "Islamic bomb" undoubtedly proceeds apace (notwithstanding the denials of Pakistan, the next most likely candidate for the the nuclear weapons club) and that the technological base for nuclear weapons development already exists in Egypt, Iraq, and Libya.[23] And if Libya in fact now mines exploitable quantities of uranium ore in Chad's Aozou strip (which it has occupied since 1973), the possibilities become even more disturbing.[24] The danger lies not so much in a potential nuclear exchange involving Israel, or between other countries in the region, but in the very appearance of new nuclear actors on the Middle East stage: their entrance will automatically raise the stakes and increase the range of risks attending any serious interstate confrontation.

Fifth, and finally, because the superpowers are finding their local clients and allies much less manageable than they were, say, in the 'fifties and 'sixties, the scale and violence of interstate conflicts have become proportionately less manageable and, hence, the conflicts themselves much more dangerous and unpredictable. In this connection, one needs only to be reminded that as the United States could not prevent the Israeli invasion of Lebanon, so the Soviet Union could neither restrain nor limit the Iraqi war against Iran. Moreover, it is difficult to conclude that the Soviet Union has much control over Colonel Qadhafi's often quixotic international ventures, despite the military patron-client relationship between Libya and the USSR. Arguably, with few exceptions, states in the Middle East have never made particularly reliable allies of the Soviet Union, the U.S., or European powers; recent events suggest they are now even less so.

IV.

For about eight years, during the period roughly between October, 1973 and mid-1981, when the per barrel price of crude petroleum increased some 1300 percent, the Middle East's oil producing states appeared to have become the nexus of a new, extraordinary political-economic power configuration. Their leaders were hated, feared, and courted by a world seemingly at their mercy, and every word uttered publicly by Sheik Zaki Yamani, or Jamshid Amuzegar, or King Faisal was breathlessly received and minutely scrutinized for hidden portents. J. B. Kelly, in a vivid description of a triumphant European tour by two Arab oil ministers acidly catches the sense of their moment:

> **Everywhere ministers and functionaries scurried to attend upon them, to court their favor and seek their approbation. The press and the luminaries of**

> **television and radio hung upon their slightest word... It was a spectacle worthy to be captured on a vast and crowded canvas in the style of Tiepolo, depicting a throng of gorgeously attired dignitaries all pressing forward with beseeching gestures toward two proud figures standing sternly aloof, the whole tableau perhaps to be grandly entitled 'The Plenipotentiaries of Arabia and Mauretania receiving the submission of Britain and Gaul'.[25]**

Kelly did not exaggerate by much. For several years OPEC meetings received more media coverage than all other international meetings and conferences combined, and as the petrodollars began accumulating in the oil producers' accounts, so also did their influence increase in the region and the world. That story is too well known to need retelling here and besides, there is a very substantial literature on the subject.[26] The point is that purchasing power was quickly translated into political influence. For example, Iran was able to parlay its new wealth into an American-backed role as the West's bulwark against possible expansion of Soviet power in the Gulf; Saudi Arabia became the Palestinians' principal financial angel and the instrument with which new European and Third World champions of the Palestinians' and other Arab causes could be rounded up; Col. Qadhafi was able to launch his various idiosyncratic political and economic campaigns; vast new stockpiles of arms could now be acquired and nuclear programs begun in earnest; and the United States was persuaded to play a more "evenhanded" role in Middle East politics, to the point where (particularly after 1978) the military defense of Middle East oil supplies became a principal preoccupation of American decision-makers.

The reversal of the Arab oil producers' good fortune, when it occurred, came relatively swiftly; again, its causes and circumstances are less important for our purposes than its shape and consequences for Middle East politics. Most visible are a set of new facts about the international oil market: non OPEC sources now account for well over half of the world's oil production; this shift in the sources of supply, along with the success of energy conservation, substitution, and replacement measures in the industrialized countries, has resulted in a world oil glut; the price of oil now tends to hover well below OPEC floors, given the inability of OPEC to police its pricing agreements and the willingness of both OPEC and non-OPEC producers (particularly those in serious financial difficulties, such as Iran, Iraq, Nigeria, Indonesia, and Mexico) to undersell each other. The political consequences of these changes are equally patent. For one thing, the ability of OPEC, especially of the Arab producers, to command political attention has sharply diminished as that organization lost its cohesiveness. For another, with Iran (after 1978) effectively lost as a major petrodollar recycling platform, and with petrodollar surpluses elsewhere shrinking rapidly after 1981, there was a commensurate decline in the ability of the Arab producers not only to finance their own ambitious development programs, but to use the international oil market for political purposes. For example, and though the connection is neither direct nor straightforward, a case can be made for the proposition that the recent noticeable rise in Israel's political stock in Black Africa is related to the Arabs' inability (or unwillingness) to maintain the economic incentives which largely underwrote African support for Arab causes.[27] Above all, these changes signaled a marked decline in the power and influence of Saudi Arabia, hitherto OPEC's economic anchor. The "oil weapon" no longer exists (if it ever did), and "Saudi Arabia's ability to persuade or coerce other countries to follow its lead in setting oil prices or determining foreign policy has diminished along with the oil revenues."[28]

All this is not to deny the continuing importance of Middle East oil to the economy of the industrialized world, or to belittle the strategic significance of the Gulf oil-producing area, or to minimize the importance of petrodollars in international finance and investment. Yet there is no doubt that in the remaining years of the 1980s the Middle East's oil producers will no longer be able to wield the kind of economic and political power that was theirs in the eight fat years following the 1973-74 oil crisis.

At the very least, it is already evident that they no longer have much leverage over their non-oil producing Arab neighbors (not to speak of Israel, whom they could hope to affect through pressure on the United States), and that (especially in the cases of Saudi Arabia and the Gulf emirates) petrodollars can no longer buy exemption or respite from accumulated domestic tensions. Above all, the loss of the Arab oil producers' power means that they have become increasingly vulnerable — to their neighbors' political, social, and economic problems, to the infections borne by the region's interstate conflicts, and to the ambitions, maneuvers, and influences of the superpowers.

V.

When the changes discussed above are considered together, a paradox emerges. On the one hand, the Arab states (and Israel) have become, and will probably remain for some time, intensely preoccupied with their own and their neighbors' problems. As they attempt to deal with the new sets of political premises, they have also become much less reliable allies, much less predictable in their interstate dealings, and consequently, much less easily influenced and manipulated by powers outside the region. On the other hand, as Arab states became increasingly insecure and unstable, so did they also become much more vulnerable not only to pressures generated in and by their regional neighbors, but to the maneuvers of the superpowers — including those of the new regional mini-superpower, Israel.

One reaction to this situation has been the *ad hoc* creation of a number of regional, defensive/offensive coalitions, e.g. Libya, Syria, and South Yemen with Iran against Iraq; Jordan, Saudi Arabia, and the Gulf emirates with Iraq against Iran; Egypt and Sudan against Libya; Sudan, Morocco, and Oman (plus informally, Israel) with Egypt against Syria and Iraq; and the Gulf Cooperative Council (Bahrain, Kuwait, Oman, Qatar, Saudi Arabia and the UAE) against real and potential threats to the security of the Gulf area, notably those posed by Iran and the Soviet Union. Another reaction has been to seek security in pragmatic alliances with the superpowers; usually embodied in bilateral agreements ("Treaties of Friendship and Cooperation," security and strategic cooperation pacts, security assistance programs, arms purchase and transfer arrangements, etc.), these alliances function both to help Arab states in their conflicts against one another, and to offer the superpowers strategic and political footholds in their continuing confrontation in the region.[29]

It can be argued that such alliances with the superpowers sometimes benefit the superpowers more than they do the Arab states involved, but since they are often accompanied by economic assistance, and since their military components can and frequently do make a difference in local conflicts as well as ward off the unwelcome attentions of the other superpower, they are either eagerly sought or difficult to turn down when offered. For example, had not the U.S. provided the wherewithal to permit Morocco to fight the Polisario (and Algeria) to a draw in the Western Sahara, the phosphate mines at Bu Craa could not have been reopened or the possibility of a negotiated settlement of the dispute become a reality in 1984. The American agreement with Oman to provide military and economic aid in exchange for permission to use Salalah and Masirah as staging bases not only gives the U.S. a military presence on the strategic south shores of the Straits of Hormuz, the Gulf of Oman, and the Arabian Sea, but it (in effect) allowed Oman to replace friendly Iranian forces with American planes (and if need be, troops) in its off-and-on war with South Yemen in the Dhofar region. A similar agreement exists between the U.S. and Somalia where, in exchange for harbor and staging rights at Berbera, the U.S. replaced the Soviet Union in supplying Somalia with "defensive" weapons against its Ethiopian foe. And certainly, the Soviet Union's alliances with Libya, Iraq, Syria, South Yemen, and Ethiopia serve similar sets of multiple, reciprocal purposes.

What has changed? Some partners, to be sure — Egypt traded the USSR for the U.S., Algeria has become catholic in its choice of friends, Ethiopia and Somalia exchanged ties with the Soviet Union, Iran now embraces "progressive" Arab and Islamic friends instead of the U.S. (and the USSR), and Egypt, by force of circumstances, has become an uncomfortable ally of Israel. However, other ties remain solid — Turkey with the U.S. and NATO, Israel with the U.S., Morocco with the U.S., Libya and South Yemen with the USSR, Syria and Iraq with the USSR (though there are indications that the latter is seeking to broaden its contacts with the West, and to establish its credentials as a major non-aligned country). In fact, most of the latter and some of the former alliances considerably predate the five year period set initially as a framework for our discussion. Moreover, there is nothing very new about inter-Arab or great power-Arab alliances, whatever their duration or reasons for being. The change, then — as far as the superpowers are concerned — is not quantitative (in Ibn Khaldun's sense), but again, qualitative, situated in the altered contexts of Arab and Middle Eastern politics.

If, as this essay argues, the Middle East has entered an indeterminate period of regional and local instability, and if the region's political actors have become less predictable in their affections and obediences, then the superpowers may have to tread much more warily in the area. Admittedly, much of what each superpower will do is already biased, if not determined, by its past commitments, alliances, policy lines, as well as by its apparent need to prevent the other from gaining an overwhelming strategic and/or political presence in the region. Nevertheless, it is clear that in dealings with the region's governments, pragmatism and cold calculation of costs and benefits are more likely to guide the superpowers' behavior than considerations of ideology, friendship or philanthropy. The Soviet Union, who once saw ideological compatibilities with and socialist hope in the PLO, Algeria, Libya, Egypt, Iraq, Syria, Somalia, Ethiopia, and (even) Khumayni's Iran, now makes only perfunctory obeisance to such sentiments. Nor, given Lebanon and the realities elsewhere in the region, can the U.S. and the West harbor any illusions about what was once euphemistically called "the prospects for democracy in the Arab world." The Soviet Union has had the uncomfortable experience of being burned by its overcommitment to Egypt, of watching its clients being militarily mauled by the Israelis, and of seeing local communists trooped in and out of prison as Russian relations with such countries as Egypt, Sudan, Iraq, Syria, Jordan, and Morocco fluctuated unpredictably between "undying friendship" and irritated rejection. And as for the United States, given the present Administration's failure to rally support for the Reagan Peace Plan, its inability to deter or limit Israel's 1982 Lebanese venture, and the unexpected lack of applause for its campaign against Col. Qadhafi, an appreciation has undoubtedly developed about the limits of leverage on close and trusted Middle Eastern allies.

Indisputably, the Egyptian-Israeli peace treaty, the Iranian revolution, the 1982 Lebanese war, the Iraq-Iran war, the near-collapse of OPEC, have all been events of extraordinary consequence for the politics of the Middle East. In each, elements of chance, of fortune, of unintended result have served to give their effects regional (and international) rather than simply local, meaning. Chance and good fortune permitted the 1973 Arab-Israeli war to lead to the Egyptian-Israeli peace treaty; its unintended result was to split the Arab world and fundamentally alter the character of the Arab-Israeli conflict. The Iranian Revolution was hardly the result of chance; however, it had the effect of galvanizing the current Islamic revival and the unintended result of unleashing the Iraq-Iran war. The 1982 Lebanese war, like the Iranian revolution, was not the product of chance, yet it radically affected the fortunes of the Palestinian movement and of the Palestinians themselves, as well as providing the painful unintended consequence of demonstrating the fragility of many (if not most) of the region's states. Clearly, the Iraqis would never have attacked Iran had they not read the auguries of the Iranian revolution in their favor. Unquestionably, the Iraqis intended a quick victory but what they got was a costly stalemate, having to face an informal enemy alliance of what should have been ideologically compatible states, and the destabilization of the whole Gulf area. And finally, it goes without saying that the OPEC states (in particular the Arab oil producers and Iran) never intended that the edifice of political and economic influence they constructed after 1973 should begin to crumble at its OPEC base. Chance — the outbreak of the October 1973 war — and extraordinary good fortune — a combination of Western oil dependence and the West's inability (or unwillingness) to resist — gave them the opportunity they needed to amass unprecedented wealth and the political clout that came with it. How a combination of greed and miscalculation resulted in a drastic reversal of their once pre-eminent position is another story, but it is sufficient here to note that their fall from grace has radically changed the Middle East's patterns of power and influence, further split the Arab world, and given new play to the maneuvers of the superpowers in the region.

The combined effects of these and other critical events has been to alter, and alter substantially, the political landscape of the Middle East region. Though that change has had important quantitative aspects, it is the base of politics, its qualitative predicates, that has been most affected.

FOOTNOTES

1. Muhsin Mahdi, *Ibn Khaldun's Philosophy of History* (Chicago: University of Chicago Press/Phoenix, 1964), pp. 254-260, *passim*.

2. "Islam et modernisme au Proche-Orient," *Le Monde Diplomatique*, May 1983, p. 28.

3. Hasan al-Banna (1906-1949) was the founder and "Supreme Guide" of the Muslim Brotherhood *(Al-Ikhwan al-Muslimum)*, whose members are today found not only in Egypt, but also in Syria, Iraq, Lebanon, Sudan, and Algeria. Sadiq al-Mahdi, the grandson of the "Sudanese Mahdi" (Mohammad Ahmad Ibn Abballah, 1844-85), is the leader of Sudan's *Ansar* party. The Ayatollah Khomeini needs no introduction. Abdul ala Maududi (1903-1979) was an Indian-Pakistani sage and political leader whose writings and speeches have been translated from their original Urdu into Arabic, English, Turkish, and other languages. According to Flora Lewis *(The New York Times*, 28 Dec. 1979), the Tunisian magazine *El Moujtamaa* named the trio of Maududi, al-Banna, and Khumayni as the inspiration for the Islamic upsurge. Sayyid Qutb, who was executed in 1966 for complicity in a plot to assassinate President Nasser, was the *Ikhwan's* leader at the time. His book, *Ma'alim fi'l-tariq* (Signposts on the Road), is "probably the Brotherhood's most sustained and inspiring book," and his testimony at his trial, are together possibly the Brotherhood's most widely-read literature. (Fouad Ajami, "In the Pharaoh's Shadow: Religion and Authority in Egypt," in James S. Piscatori, *Islam in the Political Process*. New York: Cambridge University Press, 1983, pp. 22-28.)

4. This view is expressed by Maxime Rodinson, "Islam Resurgent?" *Gazelle Review of Literature on the Middle East*, no. 6 (1979) pp. 2-18; Detlev H. Khalid, "The Phenomenon of Re-Islamization," *Aussenpolitik* (English ed.) 29 (1978) pp. 433-453; and Martin Kramer, *Political Islam* (Beverly Hills, Calif.: Sage, 1980).

5. The day of the attack was deliberately chosen: November 20, 1979 was also the first day of the 14th century of the Islamic era (1 Muharram 1400). A universal Islamic tradition is that at the beginning of each Islamic century, a "renewer of religion" *(mujaddid)* will appear. Other Islamic traditions have it that on the first day of a century great, often supernatural things, occur, such as earthquakes, floods, miracles, the martyrdom of saints, and the fall of mighty dynasties. See the discussion by Edward Mortimer in his *Faith and Power: the Politics of Islam* (New York: Random House/Vintage, 1982) pp. 180-185; also, Youssef Ibrahim, "New Data Link Mecca Takeover With Islamic Political Discontent," *New York Times*, 25 February 1980, p. A-1; and Bernard Schechterman, "Political Instability in Saudi Arabia and Its Implications," *Middle East Review*, Vol. XIV, Nos. 1 and 2 (Fall-Winter, 1981-82), pp. 15-25.

6. Emmanuel Sivan, "The Two Faces of Islamic Fundamentalism," *The Jerusalem Quarterly* 27 (Spring 1983), p. 127.

7. *Ibid.*, pp. 132-133, 141-143.

8. Albert Hourani, "Conclusion" in Piscatori, *Islam in the Political Process, op. cit.*, p. 229.

9. In particular, see Fouad Ajami's brilliant discussion on this theme in his *The Arab Predicament* (New York: Cambridge University Press, 1981.

10. Timothy W. Luke and I argued this point in our *The Arab-African Connection* (Boulder, Colo.: Westview Press, 1979), pp. 73-96. See also Tim Niblock, ed., *State, Society, and Economy in Saudi Arabia* (New York: St. Martin's Press, 1982), and Muhammad Abdu-Rauf, *The Islamic Doctrine of Economic and Contemporary Economic Thought* (Washington, D. C.: American Enterprise Institute, 1979).

11. That, at least, is one of the conclusions that can be drawn from a close reading of Sadat's own account of

the October War in his autobiography, *In Search of Destiny* (New York: Harper & Row, 1977), pp. 232-270. See also Louis Williams, ed., *Military Aspects of the Israeli-Arab Conflict* (Tel Aviv: University Publishing Projects, 1975), pp. 225-265.

12. Ofira Seliktar, "Israel: The New Zionism," *Foreign Policy* 51 (Summer 1983), pp. 118-138.

13. "Report on Officials' Responsibility in Beirut Killings," as issued in translation by the Government Press Office and published in *The New York Times*, Feb. 9, 1983, pp. 6-8.

14. See "Israeli Coalition in Disarray: Election Seen Helping Begin," *New York Times*, Feb. 9, 1983, p. 9.

15. Amos Perlmutter, "Begin's Rhetoric and Sharon's Tactics," *Foreign Affairs* 61, 1 (Fall 1982), pp. 67-83.

16. Schechterman, *op. cit.*, p. 19.

17. See, for example, the report by Karen Elliott House, "U.S. Apparently Dissuades Iraq's Allies from Widening Iran War; Oil Flow Cited," *Wall Street Journal*, Oct. 3, 1980, p. 2.

18. For details, see Joe Stork, "Iraq and the War in the Gulf," *Merip Reports* 97 (June 1981), pp. 4, 7, 8; and Mortimer, *Faith and Power, op. cit.*, pp. 361-372.

19. Among the beneficiaries of Libyan assistance have been, apparently, Sadeq al-Mahdi, the *Ansar*, and the Muslim Brotherhood in Egypt and Sudan; the Muslim *al-Takfir wa al-Hijrah* in Egypt, and various religious groups in Saudi Arabia such as those described by Schechterman, above.

20. "Arms Sales to Arab States," AIPAC Memorandum in House of Representatives, Committee on Foreign Affairs, Subcommittee on Europe and the Middle East, *Foreign Assistance Legislation for Fiscal Year 1983, Hearings and Markup* (Washington, D.C.: Government Printing Office, 1983).

21. See Barry Rubin, *Paved With Good Intentions* (New York: Oxford University Press, 1980), pp. 158-189. The estimate for Israel derives from *World Military Expenditures and Transfers*, published annually by the U.S. Arms Control and Disarmament Agency.

22. International Institute for Strategic Studies, *The Military Balance 1981-82* (London: 1983), p. 52.

23. Robert E. Harkavy, *Spectre of a Middle Eastern Holocaust: The Strategic and Diplomatic Implications of the Israeli Nuclear Weapons Program* (Denver, Colo.: University of Denver, Monograph Series in World Affairs, vol. 14, book 4), pp. 53-56; for a discussion of the long-range prospects, see Steven J. Rosen, "A Stable System of Mutual Nuclear Deterrence in the Arab-Israeli Conflict," *American Political Science Review* 71, 4 (December 1977), pp. 1367-83.

24. The Aozou strip, named after a town near the Libyan border and as defined by the Libyan claim, runs along the entire length of the Chadian border with Libya and ranges between 105 and about 60 miles in width. Within it is much of the Tibesti mountain range. There is little documentation on the region, but former French officials who served in Chad, during conversations with me, insisted that there are sizeable uranium deposits in the strip. French documentation refers to uraniam ore in the Aozou as a fact, but offers little detail. Oddly enough, all discussions about the Aozou strip before U.S. Congressional committees have been conducted in executive session and are hence unreported in detail. For a full discussion of the Chad-Libya boundary dispute, see Bernard Lanne, *Tchad-Libye, la querelle des frontières* (Paris; Karthala, 1982).

25. J. B. Kelly, *Arabia, The Gulf, and The West* (New York: Basic Books, 1980), p. 411.

26. In addition to Kelly's lively book, one may note (among others) the following: Jamers A. Bill and Robert W. Stookey, *Politics and Petroleum* (Brunswick, O: King's Court Communications, 1975); Charles F. Doran, *Myth, Oil and Politics* (New York: Free Press, 1977); J. C. Hurewitz, ed., *Oil, the Arab-Israeli Dispute, and the Industrial World* (Boulder, Colo: Westview Press, 1976); Leonard Mosely, *Power Play* (Baltimore, Md.: Penguin, 1974); Peter R. Odell, *Oil and World Power* (New York: Penguin/Pelican, 1979); Naiem A. Sherbiny and Mark A. Tessler, eds., *Arab Oil* (New York: Praeger, 1976); Benjamin Schwadran, *Middle East Oil* (Cambridge, MA: Schenkman, 1977); Dankwart A. Rustow, *Oil and Turmoil* (New York: W. W. Norton, 1982); and Raymond Vernon, ed., *The Oil Crisis* (New York: W. W. Norton, 1976).

27. Le Vine and Luke, *The Arab-African Connection, op. cit., p. 51.* See also Robert Anton Mertz and Pamela MacDonald Mertz, *Arab Aid to Sub-Saharan Africa*, (Boulder, Colo.: Westview Press, 1983).

28. Lois Gottesman, "Saudi Arabia: OPEC Giant with Feet of Clay," *Middle East Review* XV: 3 & 4 (Spring/Summer 1983), p. 72.

29. *The Military Balance 1981-82, op. cit.*, p. 53.

17 Islamic Political Movements

By Bernard Lewis

At first sight, the political role of Islam in the world today appears to be something of an anomaly. The heads of state or ministers of foreign affairs of the Scandinavian countries and West Germany do not from time to time foregather in a Lutheran summit conference. Nor do the rulers of Greece, Yugoslavia, Bulgaria and some other countries, temporarily forgetting their political and ideological differences, hold regular meetings on the basis of their current or previous adherence to the Orthodox Church. Similarly, the Buddhist states of east and southeast Asia do not constitute a Buddhist bloc at the United Nations, nor for that matter in any other of their political activities.

The very idea of such a grouping, based on religion, in the modern world, may seem to some observers absurd or even comic. However, it is neither absurd nor comic in relation to Islam. More than forty Muslim governments, including monarchies and republics, conservatives and radicals, exponents of capitalism or socialism, supporters of the Western bloc, the Eastern bloc, and of a whole spectrum of shades of neutrality, have built up an elaborate apparatus of international consultation and, on many issues, cooperation. They hold regular, high-level conferences and despite differences of structure, ideology and policy have achieved a significant measure of agreement and common action.

If we turn from international to internal politics, the difference between the Islamic countries and the rest of the world, though less total, is still substantial. In that minority of countries which practices multi-party, open democracy, there are political parties which call themselves Christian or Buddhist. These are, however, very few, and religious themes play little or no part in their appeals to the electorate. In most Islamic countries, in contrast, religion is even more powerful in internal than international affairs.

Why this difference? Some might give the simple and obvious answer that Muslim countries are still profoundly Muslim in a way that most Christian countries are no longer Christian. Such an answer would not in itself be adequate. Christian beliefs and the Christian clergy who uphold them are still a powerful force in many Christian countries, and although their role is no longer what it was in past centuries, it is by no means insignificant. But in no Christian country at the present time can religious leaders command the degree of religious belief and the extent of religious participation by their followers that remain common in Muslim lands; more to the point, they do not exercise, or even claim, the kind of political role that in Muslim lands is not only normal but is widely seen as natural.

The far higher level of religious faith and practice in Muslim lands, as compared with those of other religions, is no doubt an element in the situation, but it is not in itself a sufficient explanation. The difference must rather be traced back to the very beginnings of these various religions, and to an intimate and essential relationship between religion and politics, creed and power, that has no parallel in any major religion besides Islam. The founder of Christianity is quoted as saying: "Render unto Caesar the things which are Caesar's and unto God the things which are God's." In this familiar

---

Dr. Lewis is Cleveland E. Dodge Professor of Near Eastern Studies at Princeton University. His most recent books are *The Muslim Discovery of Europe* (1982) and *The Jews of Islam (1984)*.

and much quoted dictum, a principle is laid down, at the very beginning of Christianity, which remained fundamental to Christian thought and practice, and which is discernible throughout Christian history. Always, there were two authorities, God and Caesar, dealing with different matters, exercising different jurisdictions; each with its own laws and its own courts for enforcing them, each with its own institutions and its own hierarchy for administering them.

These two different authorities we normally term church and state. In the Christian world they have always been there, sometimes in association, sometimes in conflict; sometimes one predominating, sometimes the other — but always two and not one. The doctrine of the separation of church and state is now accepted in much although not all of the Christian or post-Christian world. In historic Islam such a doctrine was not only non-existent but would have been meaningless. One can separate two things; one can hardly separate one. For a Muslim, church and state are one and the same. They are not separate or separable institutions, and there is no way of cutting through the tangled web of human activities and allocating certain things to religion, others to politics, some to the state and some to a specifically religious authority. Such familiar pairs of words as lay and ecclesiastical, sacred and profane, spiritual and temporal, and the like, have no equivalent in classical Arabic and other Islamic languages, since the dichotomy which they express, deeply rooted in Christendom, was unknown in Islam until comparatively modern times, when its introduction was the result of external influences. In recent years those external influences have been discredited and weakened, and the ideas which they brought, never accepted by more than a relatively small and alienated elite, have begun to weaken. And as external influences weaken, there is an inevitable return to older, more deep-rooted perceptions.

The distinction between Islam, Christianity and Judaism can be seen very clearly in the narratives of events which constitute the sacred foundation history of the three religions, and in which each of them perceives the very core of its religious message and historic identity. Moses led his people out of the house of bondage and through the wilderness, but was not permitted to enter the promised land. Christ died on the cross. Muhammad, the Prophet of Islam, suffered neither of these fates but on the contrary achieved worldly success during his lifetime, becoming a sovereign head of state. As the Ayatollah Khomeini has recently reminded us, the Prophet Muhammad founded not only a community but also a polity, a society and a state, of which he was sovereign. And as sovereign, he commanded armies, made war and peace, collected taxes, dispensed justice, and did all those things which a ruler in power normally does. This means that from the very beginning of Islam, from the lifetime of its founder, in the formative memories which are the sacred classical and scriptural history of all Muslims, religion and the state are one and the same. This intimate connection between faith and power has remained characteristic of Islam in contrast to the other two religions.

There are some further differences. Christianity arose amid the fall of an empire. The rise of Christianity parallels the decline of Rome, and the church created its own structures to survive in this period. During the centuries when Christianity was a persecuted faith of the downtrodden, God was seen as subjecting his followers to suffering and tribulation to test and purify their faith. When Christianity finally became a state religion, the Christians tried to take over and refashion the institutions and even the language of Rome to their own needs. Islam in contrast arose amid the birth of an empire and became the creed of a vast, prosperous and flourishing realm, created under the aegis of the new faith and expressed in the language of the new revelation. While for St. Augustine and other early Christian thinkers the state was a lesser evil, for Muslims the state — that is, the Islamic state — was a necessity obtained by divine law to maintain, defend and promulgate God's faith and to maintain and enforce God's law. In this perception of the universe, God is seen as helping rather than testing the believers, as desiring their success in this world, and manifesting his divine approval by victory and dominance. Muslims of minority and opposition sects form a partial exception to this; in Shi'ism an almost Christian-style conception of suffering and passion combines with Muslim triumphalism to produce an explosively powerful social force.

These perceptions from the remoter Islamic past have certain important consequences for the present time, notably their effects on the shaping of Muslim self-awareness. Perhaps the most important and far-reaching of these effects is that for most Muslims Islam rather than any other element is the ultimate basis for identity, loyalty and authority. In most parts of the modern world we are accustomed, at different times for different purposes, to define ourselves collectively in a number of ways; by country, by nation, by race, by class, by language, and by various other criteria. All of these have their place in Islamic self-perceptions as reflected in historical writings; sometimes that place is an important one. But overall they are seen as secondary. For most of the recorded history of most of the Muslim world, the primary and basic definition, both adoptive and ascriptive, is not country or nation, not race or class, but religion, and for Muslims that of course means Islam. In their view, it is religion that marks the distinction between insider and outsider, between brother and stranger. Whatever other factors may have been at work, in order to become effective they had to assume a religious or at least a sectarian form.

Since Islam is perceived as the main basis of identity, it necessarily constitutes the main claim to loyalty or allegiance. In most Muslim societies the essential test by which one distinguishes between loyalty and disloyalty is once again religion. What matters here is not so much religious belief or theological conviction, though these are not unimportant; what matters is communal loyalty and conformity. And since religious conformity is the outward sign of loyalty, it follows that heresy is disloyalty and apostasy is treason. This insistence on conformity has meant, throughout history, a great stress on consensus, both as a source of guidance and as a basis for legitimacy. Despite the vast changes of the last century or two, Islam has clearly remained the most accepted form of consensus in Muslim countries, far more potent than political programs or slogans; Islamic symbols and appeals are still the most effective for the mobilization of society, whether behind a government or against it.

Along with identity and loyalty, authority too is determined by Islam. In most Western systems of political thought or symbolism, sovereignty comes by inheritance and tradition, or in more modern times, from the people. In the traditional Muslim view, the source of a ruler's authority is neither his predecessors nor the people but God. Since God is the sole source of authority, it is he who delegates and empowers the head of state, he too who is the sole source of law and indeed of legislation. If the ruler is God's ruler and the law which he enforces is God's law, then obedience to him is a religious obligation, and disobedience is a sin as well as a crime, to be punished in the next world as well as this one. If the ruler does not draw his power from God, and the law he administers is not God's law, then he is a usurper. The duty of obedience lapses and is replaced by a duty of disobedience. In the course of the centuries Muslim jurists and theologians have produced a considerable literature discussing the questions of legitimacy and usurpation. How does a ruler become legitimate? When does he cease to be legitimate? In what circumstances does the subject have the right or even the duty to disobey him — and ultimately to remove him? Islam has its own corpus of revolutionary doctrine, its own record and memory of revolutionary actions, which still have a powerful evocative appeal. Recent events in Iran and in some other countries have given them a new relevance.

Since early days there have been two major religious traditions in Islamic states, one which might be called official, the other popular. One is the kind of religion which is concerned with dogma and law, and which generally enjoys the sponsorship of the state. In many ways it is remote, having limited contact with the people and looking with disapproval on some of the more emotional forms of religion. These latter constitute the other Islam, that of the brotherhoods and of other popular movements. These tend to play down the significance of dogma, even at times of law, and instead stress the intuitive and mystical aspect, the direct personal relationship between the believer and his pastoral guide, between the believer and God. These two strains in Islam have always been present, sometimes associated in greater or lesser harmony, sometimes in conflict, but always mistrustful of each other. The latter, the popular tradition, has usually, with some reason, been regarded with suspicion by the state authorities, who recognized — and feared — the ability of popular leaders to control or release powerful, pent-up religious emotions. We have seen examples of this in recent years.

For some time past — more than two centuries in some areas, considerably less in others — the heartlands of Islam have been subject to the influence, at times the rule, of Europe. During this period of European impact and domination, there was a series of different Islamic responses; acceptance and imitation, rejection and revolt. What is surely significant is that whenever there was a genuine popular outbreak, involving the masses and going beyond a small educated leading elite, the movement expressed itself not in nationalist, not in patriotic, not in social or economic, but in Islamic terms. During the first major phase of European expansion into Islamic lands in the 19th century, when the British Empire was absorbing the Muslim northwest of India, when the French were invading North Africa, when the Russians were conquering the Caucasian lands, in all three places the most effective and persistent resistance was Islamic — organized in Muslim brotherhoods, led by Muslim religious leaders. The careers of Ahmad Brelwi in India, of Shami in Daghistan and of Abd al-Qadir in Algeria all express the markedly religious character of this first major resistance of the Islamic world to the advance of imperial Europe into all three places.

In due course all three were crushed, and a period of acceptance and accommodation followed. Muslim subjects of the three major empires began, despite some opposition, to learn the languages of their imperial masters, and even to adapt some of their cultural patterns. A second phase in Islamic resistance came towards the end of the 19th century, when for the first time we hear the word "pan-Islam" to denote an explicitly political movement aiming at a greater unity of the Islamic world against European encroachment. Already at this time we see what became a characteristic feature of such movements — the distinction between two types, one state-sponsored and used mainly diplomatically, the other more popular and with more than a tinge of social radicalism.

The constitutional revolutions in Iran and in the Ottoman Empire in the early 20th century brought a phase of liberal constitutionalism, which was reinforced by the victory of the Western Allies, the main standard-bearers of this form of government, in 1918. For a while there were some stirrings of a new Islamic militancy, notably in Anatolia and in Central Asia, but with the consolidation of the secularist Kemalist Republic in Turkey and of the Soviet Union in Transcaucasia and Central Asia, this phase of Islamic activity ended and a period of secular movements began — in some areas nationalist, in others socialist, in many both at the same time.

By the late thirties this process was under attack, and the first stirrings of a new kind of militant Islam could be discerned. This phase seemed to have come to a halt in the early fifties with the consolidation of powerful rulers in Iran and in Egypt, which had been the main centers of militant Islamic activity at that time. Though the Shah and President Nasser differed in many significant respects, they seem to have agreed in seeing militant Islamic movements as a threat to the kind of regime they were each trying to establish, and in using whatever means were feasible to keep them under control. But there were still many signs of active militancy under the surface, sometimes breaking out into the open, as for example in the Lebanese civil wars and the internal struggles in Iraq.

For a long time the importance of Islam as a political force was consistently underrated by the outside world. Indeed, until the upheaval in Iran, there was a general refusal to take cognizance of the fact that Islam was still a force in the Muslim world. Since then there has been a tendency in some circles to move to the opposite extreme, and those who previously could not see Islam at all now sometimes seem to have difficulty in seeing anything else. Both views are exaggerated; both are misleading. Islam is a reality, and its importance as a political factor is immense. But having accepted Islam as a fact, we should remember that there are still other facts. Muslims, like other people, seek ways to protest and rebel against political oppression and economic privation; Muslims, like other people, will react and respond in ways that are familiar to them. Whatever the cause — political, social, economic — the form of expression which Muslims most naturally find to voice their criticism and their aspirations is Islamic. The slogans, the programs, and to a very large extent the leadership are Islamic. Through the centuries, Muslim opposition has expressed itself in terms of theology as naturally and as spontaneously as its European equivalents in terms of ideology. The one is no more a "mask" or "disguise" than the other.

At the present time we can still see many of the characteristic features of the classical Islamic situation. One is the dichotomy between official Islam and popular Islam. The first kind is expressed in governmental and diplomatic pan-Islamism, manifesting itself through summit conferences, inter-Islamic banks and development organizations, regional cooperation projects and the like.

The second produces more radical forms of pan-Islamic activity, operating through underground movements, sometimes also supported by a radical Islamic government. These movements seek to achieve a renewal of society by ending the rule of alien infidels and domestic apostates, and returning to what they see as a pure and authentic Islamic order.

The philosophy and program of these radical movements is well formulated in the name given to one of the religious opposition groups in Egypt — *al-takfir wa'l-hijra. Takfir* means to recognize and denounce an infidel, even if he claims to be a Muslim; its political implication is the rejection of allegiance to such a ruler. *Hijra* evokes the decision of the Prophet to migrate from Mecca to Medina — that is, to abandon a pagan society and create one that is truly Islamic. By present-day militant Islamic groups this migration is of course interpreted in a spiritual, social and political, not a territorial sense. To denounce, reject and, if possible, overthrow impious rulers, and to withdraw from a pagan and corrupt society, are seen as essential prerequisites to the establishment of God's kingdom on earth. At a time when imported institutions are breaking down and imported panaceas are failing to produce the promised and expected results, such doctrines have a powerful appeal.

18

Khumayni's Islamic Republic

By Raymond N. Habiby and Fariborz Ghavidel

The victory in Iran of the Ayatollah Al Ozma Agha Sayed Ruhallah Khumayni[1] is but a dramatic development in a movement which, differing in intensity, can be seen in motion throughout the Muslim world, from North Africa to South East Asia. This movement of Islamic revival and renaissance affects a total of 600 million Muslims. It professes to offer a political, economic and social system that provides a "better" alternative to both the Western and the Communist systems; one that Muslims can call their own, with the hope that it will bring the Islamic nations a new vitality, a stronger sense of identity and renewed pride in being Muslims. The West views this revival as a return to the "archaic 7th century A.D." Its Muslim proponents believe it will propel the Islamic states into the twentieth century.

Muslim thinkers have been examining the Islamic way of life ever since the power of the Muslim states began to decline, first in India and later in the Ottoman Empire, in an effort to determine whether this decline and the relative weakness of the Islamic world came about as the result of religious, as opposed to economic or political, fragility. This examination, which began in India in the 17th and 18th centuries, spread to the rest of the Islamic world and is still going on. In his book, *The Middle East and the West,* Bernard Lewis traces the history of this movement which began in India in the early 17th century with the militant revivalism of the reformed Naqshbandi order. In the Middle East,the militant puritanical Islamic revivalism of the Wahhabis of Arabia began when "the Ottoman Empire was suffering defeat and humiliation at the hands of Christian enemies . . . [Wahhabism showed] the way to an activist, militant attack on the religious and political order which, so they believed, had brought Islam to its present parlous condition."[2]

In those formative years, Muslims did not regard the encroachments of the West on the Islamic domains as imperialist. They saw it as an attack by the Christian nations aimed at the destruction of Islam. Thus, whenever the West pointed to Islam as the cause of the weakness of the Islamic World, the only reaction this produced was a Muslim upsurge in Islam's defense.* The idea of pan-Islamism, in the sense of Muslims uniting against the common threat posed by the Christian empires appears to have been born among the Young Turks in the 1860s and '70s, when intellectuals like Namik Kemal and Ali Suavi advocated a more militant brand of pan-Islamism as the way to save the Ottoman Empire.[3] This doctrine found its fieriest advocate in Jamal al-Din, also known as al-Afghani or al-Asadabadi (1838/39-1899), who electrified the Muslim world with his writings and who is still the idol of every movement of Islamic revival. It is not known whether al-Afghani came from Afghanistan or from Persia and thus was a Sunni or a Shi'ite.[4] He wrote in both Arabic and Persian, and his writings have produced a great deal of intellectual ferment and debate in the Muslim world. In Egypt, his disciple, Muhammad Abdu (1849-1905) preached that a Muslim's first concern must be with Islam, which educates, civilizes and

---

Dr. Habiby is Associate Professor of Political Science at Oklahoma State University.

*Voices like those of Sir Sayyed Ahmad Khan (1817-1898) in India and Abd al Qayyum Nasiri (1825-1902) in Russia were raised advocating that Muslims had to model their societies on those of Britain and Russia if they wanted to modernize them, but this movement of Westernization made little impact.

identifies him and makes him what he is. Muslims, Abdu wrote, had to cast off the accretions of the post-classical Islamic age and return to the pure, unadulterated and uncorrupted faith and practices of the early Islam of the great *salaf* (ancestors) if Islam was successfully to withstand the attacks of the West.

The Islamic revival took an openly militant turn with the rise of the Senussi order in Libya, the Mehdi uprising in the Sudan, the *Ma al-Aynaym* in Mauretania and the so-called "Mad Mullah" of Somaliland. It played a leading role in the Persian Constitutional Revolution of 1905-6, which was led by the Shi'a mullahs and, with the demise of the Ottoman Empire after World War I and the division of the Islamic world into colonies of the West, give rise to movements seeking to drive out the Western Christian imperialist forces. *Al Ikhwan Al Muslimun* (The Muslim Brotherhood) developed in Egypt. In India, a movement arose that led to the creation of Pakistan, and in Iran the rise of the *Fidai-yan-i-Islam* (Devotees of Islam) opened the way for the Mussadeq regime of 1951-53. (Iran's prime minister, Mehdi Bazargan and many of his colleagues either served in the Mussadeq cabinet or were very close to him).

Khumayni can thus be seen as in the direct line of succession in this movement of Islamic revival. Like Jamal al-Din al-Afghani (presumably a Shi'ite) Khumayni, a senior Shi'ite leader,[5] advocates pan-Islamism, i.e., not simply the revival of Islam in Iran but the revival of Islam in the whole Muslim world. Iran had been evolving as a Shi'ite Iranian state rooted in traditional Persian culture ever since its Safavid dynasty (1501-1736). The same policy had been pursued by the Shah and was symbolized by Iran's national flag, which was the ancient Safavid flag. Khumayni has cast himself in the role of healer of the centuries-old and bloody rift between the Sunni and Shi'ite divisions of Islam. He has already announced that the national flag will now become the flag of Islam.

Iran, a country morbidly fascinated by martyrdom, is the perfect setting for Khumayni, whose personal suffering has won him great respect and the unofficial title of *Imam* (a title borne by the first twelve Shi'ite leaders, most of whom met with violent deaths).[6] Iran also had two well-established and well organized systems of authority, one headed by the Shah and comprising the army, the police, and the notorious SAVAK (secret police), the other comprising the religious establishment of mosques and mullahs (the religious order). Khumayni managed to assume control of the religious establishment early in the battle. He was able to summon thousands of young mullahs and theological students, who made telephone calls, ran duplicating machines, organized meetings in mosques and prepared banners, and who "were more radical and far more attuned to reborn Islamic militancy than were the ayatollahs."[7] The Shah's governmental structure collapsed, but the religious establishment continued to function, and became the sole government of Iran. This helps to explain how an exiled Iranian, living first in Iraq and then in France, managed to wield such immense power and achieve victory.

In the Muslim view, Islam is the universal religion of God on earth and an Islamic government can only represent the direct government of God. The state is God's state. He commands and Muslims submit to His will. Thus a Muslim's central political obligation is based on the religious dicta of the Qur'an. Present-day Muslim reformists present an idyllic portrait of the early Islamic state and insist that it can be resuscitated in the modern world under the law of the Qur'an, which was given by God and which contains all the principles needed to govern the Muslim *Umma* (community). So long as Muslims abide by the law, they are with God and in God's care. He will grant them power, freedom, happiness and success. Those who are not with God are punished on earth as in heaven. On earth, this punishment may take the form of having to endure foreign rule, decadence and poverty. However, they speak of the Islamic state and the *shari'a*, but fail to provide adequate details about the nature, structure and political processes and function of the state. Many appear content merely to use the vocabulary of Islamic political theory, like *biat* (contract of investiture), *ijma al Umma* (community consensus), *mashwara* (consultation), *adalat* (justice) and *hurriat* (freedom) in place of providing practical applications of these concepts.

Nevertheless, Khumayni does deal with some of these features of the Islamic state, although he tends to slur over the details about its political processes and functions. In fact, he appears more to be responding to criticism of the Islamic state system than to be tackling the subject of government. His perceptions of this Islamic state are expounded in a book written in Persian entitled *Hukumate Islami* (The Islamic State), published in the *Nahzate Islami* series in 1971 (it first appeared in *Najaf al Ashraf,* published in Iraq, where he was exiled, in 1969).[8]

Primarily, he does not recognize the separation of church and state. They were not separate in the days of the Imam 'Ali,* he declares — this concept of separation was placed in the minds of the Muslims by the agents of colonialism to prevent them from struggling for freedom and independence (p.23). The colonialists want to "prevent you from industrializing and will continue to provide you with dependent industries like assembly plants," he tells his Muslim readers (p.25). "This is why they call us political mullahs, but was not our Prophet also political?" (p.25).

He defends Islam against the "colonialist propaganda" that claims Islam fails to provide for a system of government. "We believe in a state, and we know that the Messenger of God had selected a Caliph," he maintains (p. 21). The form of government he advocates, however, does not resemble any contemporary system (p. 52). It will not be an autocracy, for it will not have a self-appointed or self-proclaimed autocrat at its head. It will be a constitutional government in the sense that government officials will be bound to carry out and implement the law (*shari'a*) and decisions will be taken in accordance with the precepts of the *sunna* (tradition) and the Holy Qur'an. "Administrators and executives as such will act in accordance with the provisions of the Qur'an, and the Islamic government will, thus, be called the rule of the Almighty" (pp. 52-53).

The government and administration of the Umayyad (661-750) and Abbasid (750-1258) caliphates are dismissed as anti-Islamic (p. 39) because they altered the early Islamic system of government and adopted a monarchical system similar to that of Rome, the Persian Kingdoms and the Pharoahs of Egypt. "This anti-Islamic form of government has continued to the present day," he asserts (p. 39). "Islam does not recognize the Institution of the monarchy and the concept of princely rule" (pp. 13 and 55). "Our only basis of reference is the time of the Prophet and the Imam 'Ali."[9]

Khumayni does not speak of an Islamic state, but of an Islamic republic. The word "republic" was not used in the early days (*sadr*) of Islam. Since he is a Shi'ite, he is probably referring to the state created by the first four Orthodox Caliphs, who were selected for life by the *biat*. Translated into modern terminology, this means that the first four Caliphs were elected presidents for life. Yet, in a press interview with *Le Monde* (May 6, 1978) Khumayni showed a willingness to accept the Iranian constitution of 1906 — if and when it was amended "to serve the cause of Islam." "We will choose qualified persons from among those who are well acquainted with Islamic ideas and concepts of government," he declared in this interview.[10] These ideas are elaborated in his book, *Hukumate Islami*. The Islamic *umma* needs a government that is honest, not corrupt, and powerful and competent," he writes (p. 50). Government is necessary in order to guard against moral corruption and the disintegration of the Islamic ways of life and Islamic principles (p. 51) and because of the needs of national defense and the permanent protection of the Islamic state (p. 37). "We need to develop institutions of government and a bureaucratic organization

---

*A cousin of the Prophet Muhammad and the husband of his daughter Fatima. 'Ali is regarded by Shi'ites as the Prophet's legitimate successor. Those claimed as successors of the Prophet were called Imams. 'Ali was succeeded by his sons al-Hasan and al-Husayn.

to enforce Islamic law. They are essential in perpetuating Islamic law and in maintaining social order'' (p. 30). ''Without them one can expect anarchy'' (p. 29).

The government he appears to be advocating is one that will comprise an executive, a legislature, a judiciary, a bureaucracy, a political party and the Islamic law. In Islam, he writes, the *Amir al-Mu'mineen* (Commander of the Faithful) heads the executive branch (p. 28). Khumayni also refers to him as Caliph (p. 21). As the executive, the Caliph, he maintains, ''is selected to enforce the laws that were handed down by God to the Messenger'' (p. 22). ''He is not selected to create laws, as this has already been done by the Prophet and is collected in books'' (p. 21). ''He is to carry out and enforce the Islamic laws and to ensure their fullest implementation. It is the execution and the implementation of the law, not the creation of law which will advance the cause of man and guarantee him justice, happiness and prosperity'' (pp. 21 and 27).

The need for an executive branch is also stressed, for without one it is impossible to carry out all the provisions of the *Shari'a,* he declares (p. 33). The essence of the executive system is the *vilayet* (trusteeship) system (p. 22). Islamic government equates leadership with duty and service rather than privilege. It entails the duty to carry out the administrative tasks set forth in the holy *shari'a* (p. 64). The ruler must therefore possess superior knowledge of the laws pertaining to social justice; he must be familiar with the Islamic concepts of the administration of the state and the science of management (p. 60); he should also know how to perform his functions lawfully, no matter how small these may be (p. 59); he should disassociate himself from the luxuries of life and lead a humble existence (p. 55) and he should have good moral and ethical qualities and must not be touched by sin, since he will be responsible for the collection and expenditure of state revenues and will be dealing with all budgetary affairs (pp. 60 and 61).

The head of the government must also meet two fundamental requirements: he must have a thorough knowledge of Islamic law and he must be just and well versed in Islamic jurisprudence (p. 58).

Khumayni rejects the idea of social superiority or status for those in special positions. This idea, he writes, does not exist in Islam. Superiority must be expressed in superior intellect and morality (p. 64). For this reason government should lead to social justice and not to social privilege or social prominence and wealth (p. 85). He advocates a system of succession based on the competence of the leader and the service he has rendered to the people and not on a system of favoritism or a self-imposed autocracy (p. 55).

Regarding the legislative branch, ''the main difference between the Islamic republic and a constitutional monarchy or a republic is that the representatives of the people do not assemble to pass laws or to make laws. Such power in Islam is in the hands of the Almighty. No other law is legitimate. The Almighty is the sole legislative power. Therefore, in Islam legislative assemblies and law-making bodies are replaced by consultative assemblies which shall meet to plan social service projects, with Islamic law as the determining source'' (p. 53). The law is the Qur'an and the *sunna* and in Islamic society absolute *ijma* (consensus) exists in this respect. That is why the Islamic government will prevent passage of anti-Islamic laws by sham and illegitimate so-called ''national assemblies'' (p. 53). In the judicial branch, ''in order to maintain Islamic laws and perpetuate the essence of law, it is essential that an Islamic government have a judicial arm as prescribed by the *shari'a*. It will, together with the executive, protect Islam against anarchy and abuse'' (p. 62). As to political parties, he declares, ''all factions should become one and develop a united front. One Front. One Party. The Party of God'' (*hizb Allah*).[11]

The Islamic laws of the state are to be applicable at all times and are not limited by either time or space. They are basic to all forms of social organization (p. 28). The Qur'an and the *sunna* embody all the laws and systems required for the well-being and the prosperity of human beings (p. 33). The ''law'' provides for all of a human being's needs (p. 33). It provides the rules governing social relationships, such as with neighbors, children, fellow citizens and also marital relations. It provides the laws of war and of peace, of relations with other nations, of commerce, industry, agriculture and a penal code (p. 32).

According to Khumayni, the difference between the laws of Islam and the laws of Western society are these: Islamic law does not regulate the sale of liquor, of interest-bearing bank loans, or of prostitution. This is not because Islamic law is incomplete, as some claim, but because these activities were declared illegal (*haram*) in Islam, and therefore they are not subject to regulation (p. 13). Imported laws have been the source of the problems of Islamic society, he maintains. "I am shocked to read about those who claim that the laws of Islam are crude and harsh, and that they reflect the violent nature of Arab society. The imported laws provide that a person be shot by a firing squad if he smuggles in heroin, but this violent punishment is necessitated by the permissiveness of the imported laws. They claim that the firing squad is not a violent punishment in heroin smuggling cases, yet to them eighty lashes administered for drunkeness is regarded as violent" (p. 15). He cannot, he writes, see how the sale of liquor to corrupt the mind and the maintenance of prostitution can be regarded as acceptable while the smuggling of drugs, an activity that can be traced to drink, is regarded as evil. "It is acceptable and non-violent for the 'powerful boss' to shed the blood of thousands in Vietnam, yet Islamic law, which sets guidelines for the fight against corruption and defends freedom is not acceptable" (p. 17).

The sources of revenue in Islam, he writes, are the *khoms* (a tithe of one-fifth of income) and the *zakat* (alms giving), which are paid into the *bait mal al muslimun* (state treasury). These are collected for the administration of the Islamic society and the well being of its citizens, and are sufficient for the administration of a large government apparatus (p. 34). The state budget must be spent on social services such as health, education and development, and also on defense. However, no member of the ruling class should acquire an advantage over other citizens by securing special benefits from the state revenues (pp. 35-6).

In a November 1978 speech[12] Khumayni declared that the Islamic Republic, and the kind of laws it would have, "will be up to the people of Iran." The referendum on the Islamic Republic was held March 31-April 1. Khumayni has made it clear, however, that what he plans is a step-by-step procedure. ". . . the ideal is the creation of the Islamic state," he has declared, but the first concern was the destruction of the Shah's regime, to be followed by the creation of a regime which "answers the essential needs of the people."[13] The government of Mehdi Bazargan thus appears to be a provisional government whose task is to prepare the groundwork for the Islamic Republic.

It would be wrong to dismiss the wave of Islamic revival now sweeping through the Islamic world as a reactionary religious movement. Rather, it should be seen as an effort, on the part of an important segment of mankind, to deal with its world on its own terms. Unfortunately, however, because there are so many Muslim states, this Islamic revival may become a game played by these states to prove which is the most Islamic.

If there is going to be a conflict of ideologies in the Islamic world, it will be between the forces of Islam, Marxism and nationalism. And the West appears to have no ideology, at this stage, to offer in their place.

•

KHUMAYNI ON THE SHAH

The Shah could not head an Islamic state because he was the very essence of obscurantism, was oriented toward the past and carried out the policy of the imperialists in order to keep Iran a backward state.[14] His subjugation to foreign powers compromised the progress of the Iranian people and his claim that he was leading Iran to the "frontier of a great civilization" was a lie and only an excuse to undermine the country's independence.[15]

Khumayni's movement also gave other reasons for the uprising. These were spelled out in a *Statement* issued in March 1977:[16]

1. The Shah is a King, and of kings the Qur'an says: "Kings when they enter a country despoil it and make the noblest of its people the meanest." (S. XXVII v. 34), (p.1).

2. Shah-in-Shah (King of Kings), the title given to himself by the Shah, is an Islamic title belonging to God alone. According to the Prophet Muhammad: "The curse of Allah will be upon one who calls himself King of Kings and upon one who calls another man by such a title" (p.ii).

3. The Shah uses the title *Khodayagan Aryamehr,* which means 'God-like.' Can a real Muslim call himself God-like? (p. 3).

4. The Shah, and his father before him, plotted to destroy the anti-colonialist and revolutionary ideals of Islam. Like his father, the Shah is a loyal follower of Muawiya and Yazid[17] (p.3).

5. The Shah follows in the footsteps of Muawiya and Yazid, his ancestral teachers. He proclaims Islam yet he donated petroleum to the Israeli aggressor, so that Zionist phantom jets are free to drop bombs on Muslim Arabs (p.4).

6. The Shah exiled the Ayatollah Khumayni (p.4).

7. He granted the development contract for Dasht Ghazvin (an agricultural area) to Israel. The food produced is shipped to Israel to feed Israeli soldiers so that they can slaughter homeless Palestinian revolutionaries and Muslim Arabs (p.4).

8. He placed the fate of the people in the hands of American and Zionist spies and military advisors (p.6).

9. He spent money on his coronation, goes on skiing trips to Switzerland, changes his clothes every day, buys fur coats; he and his wife take milk baths to soften their skins while many Iranians are freezing, starving and destitute (p.14).

10. He purchased arms from the U.S. to "blow up the innocent hearts of revolutionaries in Zofar and Palestine" (p.16) and thousands of Iranians (p.15).

The *Statement* also quotes from a speech delivered by the Imam 'Ali at the Battle of Saffain. (From *Nahgul Balaghah*):

Aim at the center . . . Satan is hidden there. He is hidden deep inside the enemy's chief and his clowns, who claim to be Muslims (p.iv).

WHY MUSLIMS MUST BE REVOLUTIONARIES

The *Statement* issued in March 1977 also gives the reasons why Iranians who believe in Islam have to be revolutionaries. These are:

1. The Islam of the Prophet Muhammad is the only true Islam. The true Islam is a revolutionary Islam . . . The Islam which the Prophet Muhammad brought is revolutionary; the Iranian Muslims are joining this revolution precisely for this reason (p.5).

2. A true Muslim can be nothing else but a revolutionary. A Muslim is either a revolutionary or he is not a Muslim (p.6).

3. This war (against the Shah) is a sacred war, and in response to God's commandment (p.7).

4. This is a battle between truth (*hagh*) and falsehood (*batil*), (p.12).

5. Allah has given the Muslims assurance of victory (p.5), and Islam is providing, again, light and warmth to the spirits of every free and dignified man and woman; is giving them hope and encouragement (p.10).

6. The Islam of the colonialists — those who claim that Islam is for the next world — allows the colonialists to loot all the wealth, resources and productivity of the Muslim nations (pp.4 and 5).

VIEWS ON MARXISM

On Iranian Marxists and communists, Khumayni is quoted in the May 6, 1978 *Le Monde* interview as having this to say: ". . . the Islamic concept based on the unity (oneness) of God is the antithesis of Marxism," and therefore the term "Islamic Marxist"* is an absurdity. He denied that an alliance between the Muslim masses and the communist elements ever existed, and averred that he had instructed his followers to "shun any organic collaboration" with them and had commanded them not to cooperate with Marxists even in the overthrow of the Shah, since "we are opposed to their ideology and know they will stab us in the back if they come to power, and will establish a dictatorial regime which is contrary to the spirit of Islam."

In his Islamic society, nevertheless, "the Marxists will be free to express themselves, because Islam answers the need of the people and is capable of counteracting the Marxist ideology." Marxists will not, however, "be free to conspire." (According to *Newsweek,* the Tudeh communist party is to be banned).[18]

The question was also dealt with in the *Statement* of March, 1977. Here, the "great unity between the Muslim revolutionaries and the Marxist revolutionaries in the common struggle against the criminal enemy" was cited. While the Shah termed the Islamic movement (*Mujahidin-e-Khalgh*) "black revolutionary and Islamic Marxist," it stated, a person can only be either a Marxist or a Muslim. He cannot be both simultaneously," it declared (p.2). "There is no doubt that Islam and Marxism differ in many areas . . . yet a Marxist who is slaughtered for the cause of the people . . . is following precisely the advice 'Ali gave to his two sons: *Be the enemy of the oppressor, and the supporter of the oppressed*" (p.10).

*The Shah labelled the opposition "Islamic Marxists."

ON INTERNATIONAL RELATIONS

During the Second World War, Khumayni developed a program of action on three issues: Liberty, Independence and Resistance to Foreign Domination.[19] It now appears that he envisages a pan-Islamic nationalist policy for Iran, whereby the country will ally itself with the neutralist states and gradually normalize relations with the U.S., the Soviet Union and Britain. Iran has already announced that it will no longer act as the policeman of the Persian Gulf and that it would withdraw its forces from Oman and Zofar and its contingent now serving with the U.N. forces in southern Lebanon. It will probably withdraw its garrisons from the islands of the Hormuz Straits at the entrance to the Persian Gulf and leave the Central Treaty Organization (CENTO).

In its new Muslim role Iran's relations with Israel come to an end. Iran gave as its reason for its decision to pull its U.N. contingent out of southern Lebanon the fact that it has now become a confrontation state against Israel, and as already announced, no longer sells its oil to Israel (and South Africa). Khumayni is particularly embittered against Israel which, he has declared, "usurped the land of a Muslim people and committed innumerable crimes. The Shah, by maintaining diplomatic relations with Israel and extending economic aid to it was acting against the interests of Islam and Muslims."[20] He called on all Muslims to join in the fight against all their enemies, including Israel and vowed to persist in the same path. Concerning the Israeli action of March, 1978 in Southern Lebanon, where the population is mainly Shi'ite, he declared that he wanted the people of Iran and all the Shi'is of the world to help their southern Lebanese brothers, but that only governments have the means at their disposal to put pressure on Israel in order to compel it to withdraw.[21] One of Khumayni's first acts was to recall the Iranian mission in Israel. His followers ransacked the Israeli Mission in Tehran and proclaimed it the Embassy of the PLO. Iran's first foreign visitor was Yasser Arafat, who was given a hero's welcome. In Khumayni's announced path of pan-Islamism, closer cooperation between Iran and the PLO can be expected, and Iran may join the Arabs in the event of a new Arab-Israeli war.

OIL POLICY

Iran needs its oil and must sell oil in order to acquire foreign exchange. Oil is to be sold to all countries except Israel and South Africa, it has been announced, but oil, and gas, will be developed primarily to fill Iran's own needs and not necessarily those of the rest of the world.[22] It is not likely that production will be permitted to reach the pre-revolutionary level, but it will be sold to the highest bidder at the highest possible prices, and the present oil consortium of foreign companies will be phased out.

POLITICAL, SOCIAL AND ECONOMIC ISSUES

Political and religious freedom is promised to all (so long as no one attempts to undermine the Islamic Republic) except the Tudeh party. In Iran's present transitional stage, however, it is difficult to see how this promise will be effected. Khumayni had, also, criticized the Shah for "granting freedom." Freedom, he declared, "is not something to be awarded . . . Freedom is an inalienable right which belongs to the people. The law (*shari'a*) has given the people freedom."[23]

ON THE STATUS OF WOMEN

Personal status for Muslims is to be ruled by Islamic law.[24] "Islam has always been opposed to the concept of women as (an) object and has restored her dignity. Women are equal to men and like (man) is free to choose her destiny and her activities . . . we wish to liberate women from the corruption that is menacing them."[25]

ON INDUSTRIALIZATION

Khumayni has said that he does not oppose the industrialization of Iran, but its industries must be nationalized and integrated into the economy, in a harmonious balance with agriculture. Industry should not consist of assembly plants that are dependent on the foreigner.[26] His three-point program for reform was presented in a 1978 speech:[27]

> 1. *In the Agricultural Sector:* "We will create the conditions to enable the Iranian farmers to live on a par with their fellow countrymen."
>
> 2. *In the Industrial Sector:* "We will take steps to enable us to respond to domestic needs independent of assistance from abroad and the colonialist nations, so that we will not need their assistance. We will improve the life of our workers to enable them to enjoy a better standard of living."
>
> 3. *On Mineral Resources:* "We will adopt a policy that will take into consideration the needs of the world but will also protect an independent Iran and the way in which the people benefit from these resources."

Khumayni appears to be in full agreement with al-Afghani on the issue of Islam and industrialization. According to al-Afghani, it was Islam that inspired a philosophic spirit and science among the Muslims:

> Those who forbid science and knowledge in the belief that they are safeguarding the Islamic religion are really the enemies of that religion . . . there is no incompatability between science and knowledge and the foundation of Islamic faith.[28]

In his book, *Hukumate Islami*, Khumayni is critical of those nations that have achieved such great technological advancement that they have conquered outer space, and yet these so-called advanced nations have failed to cope with their social problems. This is because they lack the ethical and moral power to do so, despite their immense material power. Technological advancement should be balanced by the moral and ethical values of the Holy Qur'an; this advancement must serve mankind, not produce destruction, he declares.

FOOTNOTES

1. This spelling is used in all the English translations of the publications of the Liberation Movement of Iran.

2. Bernard Lewis, *The Middle East and the West*, (University of Indiana Press, 1965), p. 99. See also, Fazlur Rahman, *Islam*, (Anchor Books, 1968), among others.

3. The best study of this period is by Sarif Mardin, *The Genesis of Young Ottoman Thought: A Study in the Modernization of Turkish Political Ideas*, (Princeton University Press, 1962).

4. Nikki R. Keddie insists, in *An Islamic Response to Imperialism: Political and Religious Writings of Sayyid Jamal-al-Din "Al Afghani,"* (University of California Press, 1968), that al-Afghani was born in Iran and was a Shi'ite.

5. Khumayni is one of the four senior Ayatollahs in the Shi'ite Imami sect of Iran. The other three are: Kazim Shariatmadary of Qum; Hazarat Shirazi of Mashad; Mahmoud Taleghani of Tehran. Khumayni was attached to the holy city of Qum, to which he has returned, leaving Taleghani in charge of Tehran.

6. From an article by R. W. Apple Jr., in *The New York Times, Week in Review*, Section 4, p. 1E, January 28, 1979. Shi'ism highly values the *shehada* (martyrdom) and the Shi'ites punish themselves ritually for their ancient failure to help al-Husayn at Karbala.

7. *Ibid.*

8. Ayatollah Khumayni, *Hukumate Islami* (The Islamic State), (*Nahzate Islami* Series No. 2, No place of publication, 1971). The quotations in this article were translated by the authors from the Persian text, and the relevant pages are given in parenthesis.

9. From a press interview with the correspondent of *Le Monde*, translated into English and published as a pamphlet by The Liberation Movement of Iran Abroad, P.O. Box A, Belleville, Ill. The interview appeared in *Le Monde* on May 6, 1978.

10. *Ibid.* , p.12.

11. *Kamnimeh Khabarnameh* (speech delivered by the Ayatollah Khumayni on the occasion of the death of the martyrs of Yazd and other cities in Iran), published by the National Front of Iran (*Jabha Melli Iran*), *Najaf*, No. 17, June 1978, p.13.

12. *Iran Times*, No. 37, Friday, November 24, 1978, p.6.

13. *Ibid.*, p. 11.

14. *Ibid.*, p. 7.

15. *Ibid.*

16. *The Statement of O.M.K.I., in Response to the Recent Accusations of the Iranian Regime*, (Liberation Movement of Iran Abroad, Belleville, Ill., March 1977); henceforth referred to as the *Statement*.

17. *Ibid.* Muawiya and Yazid, founders of the Umayyad dynasty, cursed by Shi'ites for being responsible for the deaths of 'Ali and al-Husayn.

18. *Newsweek*, February 12, 1979.

19. *Newsweek, op cit.*

20. *Le Monde, op cit.*

21. *Ibid.*

22. *Newsweek, op cit.*

23. *Zamimeh Khabarnameh, op cit.*, p.18.

24. *Ibid.*

25. *Le Monde, op cit.*

26. *Ibid.*

27. *Iran Times, op cit.*, p.6.

28. Quoted in Nikki R. Keddie, *An Islamic Response* . . . p. 107.

19

Nationalism in Twentieth Century Egypt

By James P. Jankowski

Perhaps more than other areas of the world, the Middle East demonstrates the variability of modern nationalism. It has its dead nationalisms as well as its unrealized ones, and the existing states of the region differ tremendously in the nature and strength of the nationalist sentiment found animating their emergence and buttressing their continued existence. In general terms, however, three main variants of nationalism have, over the last century, been the main competitors for the allegiance of most of the population of the Middle East. These are a sense of religious nationalism, in which one's religious community was perceived to be the object of ultimate loyalty; territorial nationalism, based on a land and on a sense of the uniqueness of its people because of their geographical and consequent historical distinctiveness, and linguistic nationalism, derived from a people's sharing of a common language and the common heritage that goes with language. Loyalty to the religious community or *umma*; to a local homeland or *watan*; or to ethnic groups or *qawm*: these are the three great alternatives between which the nationalist thought of the Arab population of the Middle East in particular has revolved. Each of these variants has had its adherants in Egypt over the past century.

•

Modern nationalist concepts first found expression in Egypt in the 1860s and 1870s. By then the *de facto* autonomous state created earlier in the century by Muhammad 'Ali, its precocious socio-economic growth which was eroding old loyalties and making necessary new ones, and contact with European ideas by the educated elite all had developed sufficiently to generate new ideas of political community. The half-century from the 1860s to World War I was a fairly unitary period in Egypt's history in terms of nationalism. While traditional sentiments of allegiance to one's religious community or more immediate feelings of loyalty to one's kinship group, village or quarter are presumed to have been still predominant among the bulk of Egyptians, among leaders of Egyptian public life and opinion it was doctrines of Egyptian territorial nationalism or patriotism, of devotion to the geographically-defined Egyptian *watan*, which were most frequently expressed over this half century. Also widespread through much of the elite were sentiments of Islamic loyalty, specifically a sense of allegiance to Egypt's technical sovereign, the Ottoman Empire. Ideas of linguistic Arab nationalism were virtually non-existent among articulate Egyptians prior to World War I.[1]

Together with the first intellectuals writing in partially-nationalist terms in the 1860s and 1870s and with the impact of the political leaders of the 'Urabi revolt against Khedival despotism and European encroachment in the late 1870s and early 1880s, it was orientations towards Egypt, considered as a separate historical and political unit, which dominated the public expression of articulate Egyptians. The most prominent political speculators of this period, such as Rifa'a Rafi' al-Tahtawi or Shaykh Husayn al-Marsafi demonstrate, in their writings, an awareness of the contemporary European terminology of nationalism, a focus upon Egypt as a distinct land with a distinct history stretching back in time beyond the Islamic-Arab epoch to that of Pharaonic Egypt, and a definite tendency

---

Dr. Jankowski is Professor of History at the University of Colorado at Boulder. He is the author of *Egypt's Young Rebels; Young Egypt, 1933-1952*, (Hoover Institution Press, 1975).

to think of this *watan* of Egypt as a national entity analogous to the *patrie* of early European nationalism. Similarly, the 'Urabi revolt was, in many respects, an Egyptian patriotic movement directed against the existing foreign (both Ottoman and European) domination of Egypt and striving for at least the autonomy, if not the independence, of Egypt considered as a separate political unit. The most graphic expression of this primary orientation towards Egypt found in this first generation which thought in nationalist terms is the unambiguous slogan of the 'Urabi movement; *Misr lil-Misriyin*, 'Egypt for the Egyptians.''

The same primacy of Egyptian territorial nationalist conceptions continued to be found in the decades between the British Occupation of Egypt in 1882 and World War I, if anything being reinforced by that Occupation. The classic statements of Egyptian territorial nationalism indeed date from the period between 1900 and 1914, in the speeches and writings of the two great tribunes of prewar Egyptian nationalism, Mustafa Kamil and Ahmad Lutfi al-Sayyid. Opposed as the ideas of these two were in several respects, particularly in regard to Egypt's relationship with the Ottoman Empire, both men were, nevertheless, indisputably Egyptian territorial nationalists.

References to Egypt as ''the world's paradise,'' ''the flower of Islam,'' ''God's heaven on earth'' dot the speeches and writings of Mustafa Kamil. His views show a consistent if somewhat simplistic emphasis on the themes of the uniqueness of Egypt, the unity of its population, the majesty of its history. He also expressed a messianic sense of mission parallel to that found in some European nationalisms, a call for Egypt to ''become, as she once was, the cradle of moral and cultural greatness, the dispenser of civilization throughout the lands of the East.''[2] Both the emotional basis and the almost-mystical tone of the Egyptian nationalism of Mustafa Kamil appear clearly in the following excerpt from a speech of 1907:

> **Oh you critics, look at it [Egypt]), contemplate it, acquaint yourselves with it. Read the pages of its past, and ask visitors to it from the ends of the earth: has God created any *watan* higher of station, finer of nature, more beautiful of character, more splendid in antiquities, richer in soil, clearer in sky, sweeter in water, more deserving in love and ardor than this glorious homeland?**
>
> **The whole world answers you with one voice: Egypt is the world's paradise. . . . If I had not been born an Egyptian, I would have wished to become one.[3]**

The nationalism of Ahmad Lutfi al-Sayyid was more rationalist and pragmatic in its basis, but equally (if not more) Egypt-oriented. Perhaps the most prominent feature of Lutfi's territorial nationalist views was his belief in a distinct Egyptian national character. Basing himself on the belief that ''Our nation today does not exist independent of our nation in the past,'' Lutfi expounded the concept of a unified, homogeneous Egyptian people possessing their own unique characteristics:

> **No one has any doubt that we are a nation distinct from any other by virtue of qualities peculiar to us, and which possibly no other nation shares with us. We have our own peculiar color, our own peculiar tastes, and a single, universal language. And we possess a religion which most of us share, ways of performing our activities, and a blood which is virtually one flowing in our veins, while our fatherland has clearly defined natural boundaries which separate us from everyone else.[4]**

Thus Egyptian territorial nationalists like Lutfi al-Sayyid, while recognizing language and religion as powerful bonds uniting a people, still elevated neither to the position of sole determinant of national identity. Rather, language and religion were seen as only part of a complex of factors which in their totality produced not a Muslim nation nor yet an Arab one, but the Egyptian nation ''distinct from any other.''

But Egyptian territorial nationalism was not the only doctrine of nationalism voiced by articulate Egyptians in the late nineteenth and early twentieth centuries. Also widespread was a sense of Islamic political loyalty, more precisely, allegiance to the main independent Islamic state in the Middle East and also the state formally sovereign over Egypt until 1914, The Ottoman Empire. There were various and frequent expressions of Ottomanism, as the sentiment is called, in prewar Egypt; it was found in the verse of Egypt's leading poets, in the prose of Mustafa Kamil and his followers as well as in the writing of several other political leaders, and also in considerable Egyptian support for the Ottoman Empire at times of international crisis, such as the Ottoman-Greek War of 1897, the dispute between the Ottomans and the British over their respective jurisdictions in Sinai in 1906, or the Italo-Ottoman War over Libya in 1911-1912.

There are several qualifications which need to be made in regard to pre-World War I sentiments of Ottoman loyalty in Egypt, however. First, for most articulate Egyptians it was not a case of Islamic/Ottoman loyalties instead of Egyptian patriotism. Rather, allegiance to the Ottoman Empire usually coexisted alongside loyalty to Egypt, with no incompatibility between the two being seen. "For every living nation there are two great obligations; the obligation towards its religion and its creed, and the obligation towards its *watan* and the homeland of its fathers," said Mustafa Kamil, adding that "adherence to religion demands adherence to the *watan*. . . ."[5] Secondly, in this blending of nationalist sentiments it was Egyptian territorial nationalism which was the deeper and more primary with most leaders of articulate Egyptian opinion. Politicians from Ahmad 'Urabi to Mustafa Kamil who had contacts with the Ottoman regime by no means desired the restoration of direct Ottoman rule over Egypt. Rather, the sense of loyalty to the Ottoman Empire expressed by many Egyptians seems to have been a sentiment auxiliary to their Egyptian nationalism, a perception articulated in particular after the British Occupation of 1882, that a strengthened *partial* tie with the Ottoman state would be of instrumental value in their more fundamental goal of liberating Egypt from European domination. Again, as Mustafa Kamil wrote: ". . . our love for Egypt takes precedence over everything else. . . . We wish that Egypt be for the Egyptians."[6] For many of the leaders of Egyptian opinion in this period it is indeed debatable whether their orientation to the Ottoman Empire should be termed nationalism; perhaps the contemporary sense of Third World solidarity against a common enemy would be a closer analogue. Finally, there were prominent Egyptian leaders who explicitly opposed an Ottoman allegiance by Egyptians. The most important of these was Ahmad Lutfi al-Sayyid. A secularly-oriented thinker who believed that there was "no common bond among the Islamic nations," Lutfi's position was simply that "we absolutely reject any attachment to any other homeland but Egypt;" he thus enjoined his countrymen to "repudiate today as they have in the past, any accusation of religious bigotry, i.e., "pan-Islamism and fanaticism."[7]

In comparison to the primary sense of Egyptian territorial nationalism and the secondary, more instrumental, attitude of Muslim solidarity with the Ottoman Empire, ideas of Arab linguistic nationalism had virtually no impact in Egypt prior to World War I. An articulate Arab nationalist movement only emerged in the Fertile Crescent just before the war and its doctrines overwhelmingly date from after that conflict; thus there was very little Arab nationalism for Egyptians to interact with up to 1914. But even in relation to what Arab nationalism there was, Egyptian opinion was at best benignly aloof, and at worst suspicious or hostile. As early as 1898, Mustafa Kamil denounced the idea of an Arab Caliphate, with its implicitly anti-Ottoman connotations, as a British plot to sow dissension within the Ottoman Empire, and more than a decade later, after his death, the party he had founded is reported to have rejected a suggestion for cooperation between Egyptian and Arab nationalists.[8] Similarly, Ahmad Lutfi al-Sayyid in 1911 denied the very existence of an Arab problem in the Ottoman Empire, and in 1912 termed both pan-Islamism and "Arab unity" mere "delusions" and "fancies."[9] The only Egyptian leader for whom ideological involvement in pre-World War I Arab nationalism has been documented is the Ottoman Army officer 'Aziz 'Ali al-Misri, the founder of one of the main Arab nationalist societies just before the war. But there seem to have been no other Egyptians connected with early Arab nationalism, and Misri was hardly representative of most Egyptian elite opinion; it was his appeal for cooperation which was rejected by the leaders of Mustafa Kamil's party.[10]

•

In regard to the development of nationalism in Egypt, the four decades from the outbreak of World War I in 1914 to the consolidation of power of Jamal 'Abd al-Nasir in 1954 divide, without undue strain, into two periods of roughly equal length.[11] In the first of these, from World War I to the mid-1930s, Egyptian territorial nationalism reigned supreme within articulate Egyptian opinion, indeed becoming enshrined in the political institutions of the country as well as in the cultural expression of educated Egyptians. In relation to the other potential foci of national loyalty, this period was marked by the eclipse of sentiments of Islamic political solidarity among the leading segments of Egyptian opinion and by the continued insignificance of Arab linguistic nationalism. The major development of the second period, from the mid-1930s through the early 1950s, concerns this last possible nationalist alternative. Beginning in the 1930s and accelerating thereafter, a sense of national identity with the surrounding Arab world developed among significant numbers of Egyptians. Although in retrospect it appears not to have challenged the emotional primacy of territorial nationalism among most articulate Egyptians, it laid the basis for the official ascendancy of the Arab nationalism in Egypt which was to occur from 1954 onwards.

In politics and also in cultural life, sentiments of Egyptian territorial nationalism were dominant in Egyptian public life between the two world wars. The Revolution of 1919 against the British Occupation was explicitly and solely Egyptian nationalist, uniting Egyptians of different religions in an impressively secular movement, aiming at the "complete independence" of Egypt and its nineteenth-century annex, the Sudan, and its leaders eschewed cooperation with other "Easterners" waging parallel struggles for independence. When Egyptian independence was formally attained in the early 1920s, the wording of the Constitution of the new state began with the ringing sentiment "Egypt is a sovereign state, free and independent" (Article 1) and, while citing Islam as the religion of the state and Arabic as its official language (but only in Article 149), made no mention of political ties or obligations extending beyond the Nile Valley. The political parties established during and immediately after the Revolution of 1919 were equally Egypt-oriented, their programs speaking in terms of Egypt alone. The pre-eminent party of the period of the parliamentary monarchy, the Wafd, followed a line best summarized as "little-Egyptism" through most of the interwar period, its publicists maintaining that Arab problems such as the war between King Husayn and ibn Sa'ud in the Arabian peninsula in 1924 were "no affair of Egypt," or that an Islamic issue such as the possibility of the Caliphate being reinstituted in Egypt would be only "a new lasso around the neck of Egypt."[12] The policies followed by Egyptian governments prior to the late 1930s similarly avoided any official Egyptian involvement in Islamic or Arab questions.

The supremacy of Egyptian territorial nationalism through most of the interwar period was expressed in realms besides the political. The 1920s were the heyday of "Pharaonicism;" academic, literary, and artistic schools of expression which emphasized ancient Egypt's influence upon contemporary Egypt and which correspondingly denigrated Egyptian links to peoples and cultures outside the Nile Valley. In literature, creative artists such as Tawfiq al-Hakim wrote dramas expounding on the continuity of the "Egyptian mind" between ancient and modern Egypt, while literary critics issued manifestos calling for the birth of a genuinely Egyptian "national literature" emancipated from what they perceived to be alien Arab-Islamic canons of poetry and prose. In the visual arts a school of Pharaonic sculpture flourished in the 1920s, giving rise to monumental statuary inspired by Pharaonic models, such as "The Revival of Egypt" which today stands in front of Cairo University and buildings festooned with lotus and papyrus (the tomb of Sa'd Zaghlul of the Wafd is a prime example). In journalistic and academic circles commentators such as the Copt, Salama Musa, in the 1920s and the Muslim, Taha Husayn, in the 1930s propounded the radical (and admittedly much-disputed) thesis that the land and people of Egypt were not essentially part of the "Eastern" world but rather part of the "Western" universe of discourse which had begun with Egypt and Greece; Egyptians therefore should orient themselves towards Europe, not towards Asia.

A good example of the spirit of Egyptian territorial nationalism of the interwar period is found in the essay *The Policy of Tomorrow* written by the Wafdist leader Mirrit Boutros Ghali in 1937.[13] Few passages state the geo-historical bases of interwar Egyptianism more clearly than the following:

> **If we look upon the geographical contour of Egypt, we find that its frontiers are perfectly defined and that these have remained unchanged for some sixty centuries. Nature has so arranged, by surrounding Egypt with a desert on all sides — East, West and South — that the country has grown independently and by itself since the earliest times. A unique, permanent form has developed in it, and it has preserved its peculiar characteristics up to the present day.**

Ghali did not go as far as Egyptian nationalists like Musa or Husayn. He readily admitted that "Egypt was in fact part of the Islamic world, marked by Oriental characteristics which were conferred upon her by the Arabic language and the Arabian culture." But what marked the interwar thinking of Ghali and many other Egyptian territorial nationalists was that these horizontal influences were trifling in comparison with the more profound vertical links of Egyptians with their land and their past. While external influences, and even external obligations, were accepted — the need for Egypt to be "*what it has always been, namely a connecting link and a mixing ground for the civilizations of the Mediterranean world*" — these came nowhere near the emotional commitment which an Egyptian should have for Egypt itself:

> **. . . the vortex of Egyptian patriotism and test of Egyptian nationalism is nothing but the name of "Egypt" and of "Egyptians." In the heart of our national consciousness, we recognize that we belong to neither East nor West. We admit no doctrine except that of our nationalism. . . .**

The main change in relation to nationalist concepts in Egypt between 1914 and the mid-1930s was the fading of visible Islamic political loyalties which occurred from World War I onwards. Externally, World War I and the subsequent emergence of the new Turkish state was accompanied by the abolition of the Ottoman Empire and its Sultan in 1922, the elimination of the Caliphate in1924, and the sentiment of Ottomanism found in prewar Egypt was thus abruptly deprived of its central focus. Internally, the gradual secularization of the Egyptian elite which had been occurring since the mid-nineteenth century and the even partial success of Egyptian territorial nationalism in the creation of the formally-independent parliamentary monarchy were perhaps the most important factors sapping an Islamic political orientation by the interwar years. As already mentioned, the political structure, parties and policies found in interwar Egypt, at least up to the late 1930s, all demonstrated a general aloofness from Islamic issues. The main apparent exception — the dabbling of Egypt's King Fuad in Islamic politics in the mid-1920s in the hope of obtaining the Caliphate for himself — indeed confirms the generalization, for Fuad's ambitions and maneuvers were opposed, on both political and ideological grounds, by the Wafd and the bulk of Egypt's civilian political establishment. Identification by Egyptians with Arab nationalism in particular between 1914 and the 1930s continued to be insignificant. The oft-quoted remark made by the Wafdist leader Sa'd Zaghlul in 1925 when asked about the possibility of cooperation with Arab nationalism — "If you add a zero to a zero, then another zero, what is the result?" — accurately captures the dominant attitude towards Arab nationalism found within the Wafd prior to the late 1930s.[14] While anti-imperialist uprisings in the Arab world, or what were perceived as Western assaults upon the integrity of Islam could generate Egyptian protests and limited financial assistance, they produced no major Egyptian involvement in these issues until the very end of the interwar years.

•

The collapse of an active Islamic political orientation in Egypt after World War I should not be taken to mean that sentiments of Islamic identity were dead in Egypt, however. Rather, it seems more accurate to say that a certain segment of the Egyptian elite — the Western-educated, heavily-Europeanized segment, those who wore frock-coats and fezzes and who, by upbringing, had little that was still "Muslim" about them — was temporarily dominant in Egyptian public life. It was they who drafted the Constitution, formed and led the political parties and staffed the ministries running the country in the interwar period, and they followed their largely-secular inclinations in thinking and working in terms of Egypt (and their own interests) alone.

Parallel with this group, however, was another Egypt, a less-Europeanized, more genuinely Muslim — and Arab — one, represented by the *'ulama* on one level,and on another by the burgeoning lower middle class of government functionaries and teachers, educated but less thoroughly Westernized, closer in thought and lifestyle to the traditional Muslim and Arab dimensions of Egyptian life. The existence of this "other Egypt" is seen in various ways in the interwar period: in protests and demonstrations at the time of external religious crises such as the Turkish abolition of the Caliphate in 1924; in periodic agitation over perceived Christian proselytizing in Egypt; in Sa'd Zaghlul's confession of 1926 that the issue of the Caliphate was still "a sensitive one with the masses."[15] Initially co-opted and controlled by the Westernized elite, by the middle of the interwar period this segment of Egyptian opinion was forming its own ostensibly religious or social, but in actuality inherently political, organizations: the *Young Men's Muslim Association* in 1927, the *Muslim Brotherhood* in 1928, the *Young Egypt Society* in 1933. In brief, it was this Egypt which from the 1930s onwards was to challenge the Westernized elite for ascendancy over Egyptian public life, with one of the major issues being precisely the insufficient attention paid by the establishment under the parliamentary monarchy to Islamic customs internally and to Arab solidarities externally.

Islamic customs internally, Arab solidarity externally: why the dichotomy? Two factors seem largely responsible for Arabism's replacement of Islam as the main external focus of allegiance for part of Egyptian opinion in the interwar period. The first is the frequently-noted symbiosis between Islam and Arabism in the thinking of many Arab Muslims. Islam as an historic religion and the Arabs as an historic people were born together, and ever since their birth there has been a considerable overlap between being Muslim and being Arab to Arabic-speaking Muslims. The other factor is that an Islamic allegiance lost its central focus in the early 1920s with the end of the Ottoman Empire and that the fiascos surrounding the attempts to resurrect the Caliphate in the mid-1920s made meaningful Islamic solidarity appear to be impossible, or at best very remote (as well as somewhat disreputable, due to King Fuad's involvement in the issue) to many Egyptians. On the other hand, at almost the same time a potentially-promising movement for Arab cooperation/unity was developing in Western Asia, beginning with the negotiations for an "Arab alliance," under Iraqi initiative, from the early 1930s. Thus, with being Muslim and being Arab as overlapping identities in the first place, and with the prospects of Islamic unity perceived as highly unlikely while Arab unity seemed to be entering the realm of the possible, Egyptians of a Muslim-Arab orientation began to make an almost unconscious transfer of their outward vision from Islam to

Arabism. The switch in emphasis was greatly facilitated by Arabism and Islam being seen by many not as alternatives but as stages, the former being merely a phase along the road to the latter: "we believe that, when we work for Arabism, we work for Islam and for the good of all the world."[16] To use an optical analogy, for many Egyptians the movement from Islam to Arabism was not a change of focus: it was to continue to look in the same place but to see something new there.

But the Islamic-Arabic symbiosis was only one aspect of the growth of a sense of Arab nationalism in Egypt. Another, and perhaps equally important factor, was the growing Egyptian connection with the Arab world, and the corresponding perception by Egyptians that it was in Egypt's interest to associate with, or even assume the leadership of, the neighboring Arabs. A perceived economic interest probably ranked highest; the belief that the natural markets of an Egypt desirous of industrialization lay in Arab Asia and beyond. Political interests were not far behind economic ones; the attitude that Egypt's Eastern "first line of defense" lay in Arab Asia,[17] or that the hopes which Egyptians had of becoming a regional power (particularly pronounced after the signing of the Anglo-Egyptian Treaty of Alliance of 1936) would be threatened by the creation of an Arab alliance *sans* Egypt — or by the establishment of a modern Jewish state in Palestine. Cultural factors also figured, although less prominently — the combination of Egyptian pride and sense of *mission civilisatrice* which had developed out of the leading cultural role in the Arab world that Egypt had attained by the interwar years. Thus the sense of Arab identification which began to develop in Egypt from the 1930s onwards drew from two powerful sources; the primarily cultural one of the relationship between the Arabs and Islam, and the largely pragmatic economically and politically rooted one of perceived Egyptian interests in the Arab world. It seems not unreasonable to speculate that much of Arabism's power in Egypt came from the combining of these two streams of inspiration.

Whatever its causes, a considerable growth in Egyptian identification with and involvement in Arab nationalism is apparent after 1930. It began in the early 1930s, when *pourparlers* over the possibility of an Arab pact or an alliance among Western Asian Arab states prompted a new phenomenon in Egypt; press debate over Egypt's relationship to such plans, and even considerable controversy over the Egyptian-versus the Arab component of the Egyptian "personality." However, the major surge in Arabist sentiment in Egypt dates from the later 1930s.

For nationalist sentiment to become manifest and tangible a referent is often useful: an issue or institution about which opinion can find expression and, in the process of expression, feed itself and grow. The Ottoman Empire had been such a referent for Islamic sentiment prior to World War I, and its postwar elimination goes a long way to explaining the eclipse of that sentiment in interwar Egypt. A similar referent for Arabism in the 1930s and after was the Palestine issue. The Palestinian Arab Revolt of 1936-1939 raised, in a pressing way, several questions which reached across the spectrum of Egyptian opinion and prodded it to consider Egypt's relationship to developments in Palestine and, by extension, also to Egypt's connections with the Arab world in general. For many Muslim Egyptians the Palestine problem raised the primarily religious issue of the fate of the Muslim Holy Places in that land; for more secular Egyptians the disorders in Palestine and the plans for the partition of Palestine which these engendered posed questions of a now-independent and industrializing Egypt's political and economic interests; and for Egyptians of both inclinations there was the emotional factor of sympathy with what was the longest and most intense anti-European revolt in the Arab east in the interwar period. With these several factors fueling it, Egyptian involvement in the Palestine problem and, with it, in the emerging movement for Arab cooperation/unity increased greatly in the later 1930s. Popular organizations like the *Young Men's Muslim Association* or the *Muslim Brotherhood* took the lead in issuing declarations, in fundraising, in organizing meetings and demonstrations in support of the Palestinian Arabs. Within a few years, the leadership of the established political parties were compelled to make public statements expressing their solidarity with other Arabs over the Palestine issue. Nor did Egyptian politicians limit themselves to platitudes: the later 1930s also saw the first Egyptian governmental involvement in Arab affairs, first with confidential representations to the British about the situation, then by 1939 with the public participation of the Egyptian government along with other Arab (and only Arab) governments in the St. James Conference concerning the Palestine Mandate.[18]

If the 1930s was the decade of the beginnings of significant Egyptian involvement in Arab affairs, the 1940s was the decade when that involvement became institutionalized. Between 1942 and 1944, a Wafdist ministry headed by Mustafa al-Nahhas took the lead in putting together the League of Arab States. The League constituted much less than full Arab unity, indeed in good part being the result of an Egyptian attempt to forestall the creation of a tighter Arab union in the Fertile Crescent which might have been a threat to Egypt's position as the leading state of the Arab world. Yet Egyptian initiative in its establishment was a step which would have been inconceivable to Nahhas' predecessor, Zaghlul, a generation earlier. In the late 1940s Egypt and the other states of the League bumbled their way into the first Arab-Israeli war. Thus, within a decade of the surfacing of significant Arabist sentiment in Egypt, the country's leaders felt their interests and ambitions sufficiently engaged in the Fertile Crescent to go to war there. The defeat of the Arab states in 1948-1949 produced a partial reaction against an Arab orientation in the early 1950s, with powerful voices reasserting a sense of Egyptian separateness and isolation as well as questioning the utility of Egypt's involvement in the Arab world. This proved to be only a temporary phase, however. By 1954, with the consolidation of power by Jamal 'Abd al-Nasir, Egypt resumed that march towards Arab leadership and unity which was to be one of the most prominent features of its public life through the 1950s and 1960s.

As with the pre-World War I Islamic/Ottoman orientation found in Egypt, several qualifications need to be made about the sense of Arab identification and involvement which developed in Egypt between the 1930s and the 1950s. Obviously, Egyptian involvement in Arab affairs was, in part, prompted by political rather than ideological motives. The rivalry between Nahhas and King Faruq, and the desire of each to enhance his domestic position by becoming a regional leader, certainly had a great deal to do with Egyptian sponsorship of the Arab League, and similar instances of political motivation underlying Arabist policies could be adduced both before and after World War II. But issues do not become "political" ones if they are not, to some degree, popular ones as well. It seems questionable whether Egyptian ministries of the 1930s and 1940s, mainly composed of men of the older generation who held Egyptian territorial nationalist views, would have become as involved in Arab affairs if not for considerable popular sentiment prodding them to adopt Arabist policies. This is certainly what these leaders repeatedly told the British in their confidential representations from the 1930s on.

Yet there were also influential Egyptians who never bought Arabism (at least prior to its becoming an official — and enforced — ideology under Nasir). Perhaps the most notable of these was Isma'il Sidqi, Prime Minister of Egypt from 1930 to 1933 and again in 1946 who, as late as 1950, was publicly questioning the value of Egypt's involvement in Arab affairs and writing of the potential benefits of peace and cooperation with Israel. Other prominent Egyptians who wrote in anti-Arabist terms in the partial reaction against Arabism of the early 1950s included Ahmad Lutfi al-Sayyid, still a believer in exclusive Egyptian nationalism, and (a figure of some importance in contemporary Egypt) the journalist Mustafa Amin.[19] Arabism in Egypt before the mid-1950s may have grown a great deal, but it was still a fragile growth.

Finally, the sense of Arab identification which did develop in Egypt between the 1930s and the 1950s did not challenge the deeper sentiment of Egyptian identity felt by many articulate Egyptians. As with prewar Ottomanism, the feeling of Arab identity was not a replacement for their Egyptian identity: it was, rather, a supplement. Like other supplements, it had a heavily-instrumental aspect: the promotion of Egyptian self-defense or aggrandizement, economic advantage, cultural leadership. In this convergence of two loyalties, the Egyptian often continued to be the more central. There is no better example than the views expressed by the Secretary-General of the Arab League, 'Abd al-Rahman 'Azzam, in a famous debate explicitly concerning Egyptian national identity in 1953.[20] While arguing strongly for continued Egyptian involvement in and leadership of the Arab world ("We cannot under any circumstances isolate ourselves from the Arabism of which we are the heart and the center"), 'Azzam justified this Arabism primarily on the combined grounds of Egypt's civilizing mission and its economic-political imperatives. "Egypt is the first school of humanity, Egypt is God's gift to the world," he asserted, and asked his audience how Egyptians could possibly forget their millenial mission; in his view they could not. Beyond that, Egypt had vital interests in the Arab world. Terming the Arab area "our living-space," 'Azzam offered arguments both for the political importance of the Arabs to Egypt ("We cannot leave Syria to do what it wants by itself") and its economic importance to Egypt ("industrial development demands that we have a living-space, and this living-space is our brothers who understand us"). Thus, even for 'Azzam, the Arab world was not the center of his national consciousness: it was, rather, closer to an arena, a "circle" in Nasir's terminology of a year later, in which everlasting Egypt would find its destiny.

●

The complex details of Egypt's championship of Arab nationalism under Jamal 'Abd al-Nasir have been the subject of several detailed studies.[21] A brief consideration of terminology alone is sufficient to indicate the scale of the formal change in national orientation which occurred in Egypt in the 1950s and 1960s. The Egyptian Constitution of 1956 refers to Egypt as "a sovereign independent Arab state" and to the people of Egypt as "part of the Arab nation" (Article 1). The country's change of name from Egypt to the United Arab Republic in 1958, was maintained throughout the 1960s in spite of the collapse of union with Syria in 1961. The 1962 Charter of National Action (probably the most authoritative statement of Nasir's orientation and goals) early makes references to the "Arab people of Egypt" and ends with the affirmation that "Ours is an Arab people and its destiny is tied to the destiny of the unity of the Arab Nation."[22] All are indicative of an attempt to reorient Egyptian national allegiances from the narrow confines of the Nile Valley to the broader linguistic unit of the Arab world.

But some of the limitation of Arabism as it developed in Nasir's Egypt need to be pointed out. The first is that, certainly with Nasir himself, Arabism was an acquired taste arising out of circumstances rather than an ingrained conviction carried since childhood. As Nasir's *The Philosophy of the Revolution* recounts the evolution of his views, it took him some time to become an Arab nationalist. What began with participation in demonstrations over Palestine inspired by "the echoes of sentiment" in the late 1930s only a decade later grew into the intellectual conviction that "the whole region" was "one complete whole."[23] Secondly, as the above references imply, even Nasir's Arabism was not totally devoid of elements of Egyptian separateness. As perhaps the best known passage in his *Philosophy* puts it, the Arab world was only the closest and most important of three "circles" (Africa and the Islamic World being the other two) with which Egypt, by geography and history, was intimately linked.[24] Although Nasir's tendency to dissolve Egypt into the "Arab Nation" seems to have developed over time, it was never complete: even the National Charter of the early 1960s had, in addition to phrases like the "Arab people of Egypt," references to "the Egyptian people, the creator of civilization."[25] On the level of action, the long-debated question of whether Nasir's Arabist policies were designed primarily to promote Arab nationalism or primarily to serve Egyptian national interests is probably a moot point, given the ambiguity of the evidence about Nasir (many public statements, but no private papers) and the fact that the blending of ideology and interest to the point where they become inextricable in an individual's mind is not unknown in Egypt, as elsewhere. It does seem fair to say, however, that the sense of Arab nationalism found in Nasir was "far from the urgency of unity, the Fichtean vocation to national fusion" found in Arab lands like Syria.[26]

But the most important qualification about Arabism in Egypt under Nasir is that it may have been much more idiosyncratic than it appeared to be at the time. It certainly became *de rigueur* to voice sentiments of Arab nationalism in Egypt in the 1950s and 1960s. Given the rigorous censorship of public expression in Egypt at the time, however, that in itself is not sufficient to indicate a thoroughgoing commitment by Egyptians to Arab nationalism. While an Egyptian sense of identity with the Arabs had been growing since the 1930s and, in all probability, increased under Nasir, there is reason to question how many articulate Egyptians really shared their leader's orientation towards the Arab world. The most important indication comes from what has occurred in Egypt since Nasir's death; the reversion of Egyptian policy and opinion to a more Egyptianist stance under Anwar al-Sadat.

The drift away from Arab nationalism in the Egypt of the 1970s is too well-known to need elaboration. The change of name from the "United Arab Republic" to the "Arab Republic of Egypt" in the 1971 Constitution was but an early indication of things to come. A retreat from Arabism was certainly apparent in Egypt's policies in the years which followed; Sadat's non-pursuance of Nasir's efforts to forge Arab unity, his emphasis upon Egyptian internal development, his *de facto* withdrawal of Egypt from the cause of Palestine, perceived as so vital by other Arabs. In the Egyptian media, discussions of Arab unity have been replaced by analyses of "Arab solidarity," with leading publicists taking the position that Arab unity is "impossible" given contemporary Arab and world conditions.[27] The converse of this public withdrawal from Arab unity is the resurfacing of themes of unadulterated Egyptian territorial nationalism. To read President Sadat's recent autobiography and his addresses of the late 1970s is to be thrust back into the mental universe of Mustafa Kamil or the Wafd. There is the opening invocation of the land of Egypt, its beauty and its perdurance; the ritual glorification of Egypt's 7000 year-old history and its role as teacher of the world; the repetitive use of phrases like "Egypt before anything else."[28] Sadat's autobiography concludes by emphasizing that "the Egyptian people differ from many other peoples, even within the Arab world." Its final sentence refers to Egyptians as "a people who are working for a modern civilization comparable to the one they erected thousands of years ago in freedom and peace."[29] For President Sadat at least, Egyptian patriotism seems to be fully as powerful an emotion as it had been for pre-1952 Egyptian leaders.

It also appears that President Sadat's sense of Egyptian territorial nationalism is not unique to himself. Previously quiescent Egyptian intellectuals have launched full-scale attacks on Nasir's Arabism and his attempt to lead the Arab world, criticizing not only the failure of Nasir's Arab policies and their ruinous effects upon Egypt, but also questioning the very desirability of his Arabist vision which "atrophied the Egyptians politically and undermined their patriotism to the point where the word 'patriotism' disappeared. . . ."[30] One has only to visit Egypt to sense and to be told of a considerable Egyptian resentment (which has definitely been encouraged by official spokesmen) against other Arabs because of their ingratitude to Egypt after her expenditure of "the blood of 100,000 Egyptian martyrs and forty billion Egyptian pounds" for the sake of the Arab cause over the past thirty years.[31]

But it is important to note that while there has been a definite swing away from Arab nationalism in Egypt, it has not resulted in turning the clock back to the 1920s or earlier in regard to nationalist alternatives. The criticisms of Nasir's Arabism by some intellectuals have not gone unchallenged. Other writers defend Nasir and his Arab policies. What seems to be occurring is a genuine debate rather than the cloying surface unanimity of the 1960s, a debate in which an Arab orientation for Egypt still has proponents. Nor has Egypt's leadership completely withdrawn from a commitment to interaction with other Arabs. "Arab solidarity" is still asserted to be a desirable goal for Egypt to pursue, and President Sadat's utterances continue to refer to Egypt's "Arab character," to the "Egyptian Arab people," and to "the great Arab nation" of which Egypt is a part.[32] As in the Egypt of the recent past, thus, nationalist alternatives in contemporary Egypt are not mutually exclusive; "In real life dilemmas need not be resolved, they can be lived . . ."[33] While Egyptian territorial nationalism has been the strongest and most permanent variant of national identity found among articulate Egyptians in the twentieth century, a new dimension has nonetheless been added to Egyptian nationalist thought over the past forty years, that of Egypt as part of the Arab nation, with which it shares both characteristics and interests. Although this position is not now being expressed as strongly as it was under Nasir, Arabism has not been eliminated from Egyptian public life.

FOOTNOTES

1. The ideological dimensions of nationalism in pre-World War I Egypt are dealt with in detail in the following: Jamal M. Ahmed, *The Intellectual Origins of Egyptian Nationalism* (London, 1960); Jacques Berque, *Egypt: Imperialism and Revolution* (translated by Jean Stewart: London, 1972); Albert Hourani, *Arabic Thought in the Liberal Age, 1798-1939* (London, 1962); Mounah A. Khouri, *Poetry and the Making of Modern Egypt, 1882-1922* (Leiden, 1971); Nadav Safran, *Egypt in Search of Political Community* (Cambridge, 1961); Charles Wendell, *The Evolution of the Egyptian National Image: From Its Origins to Ahmad Lutfi al-Sayyid* (Berkeley, 1972).

2. Cited in Wendell, *op. cit.*, 267.

3. Quoted in Muhammad Muhammad Husayn, *al-Ittijahat al-Wataniyya fi al-Adab al-Mu'asir* (two volumes: Cairo, 1954), I, 67.

4. Quoted in Wendell, *op. cit.*, 237-239.

5. Cited in Faruq Abu Zayd, *Azmat al-Fikr al-Qawmi fi al-Sihafa al-Misriyya* (Cairo, 1976), 58-60.

6. Cited in *ibid.*, p. 60.

7. Quotes from Wendell, *op. cit.*, 229, 233, 259.

8. Reported in the memoirs of Kamil's successor as head of the *Watani* Party, Muhammad Farid, as excerpted in Muhammad Subayh, *al-Yaqaza* (Cairo, 1964), 257.

9. Quoted in Wendell, *op. cit.*, 230.

10. There were also political and financial contacts between Egypt's *de jure* ruler, Khedive 'Abbas Hilmi, and Arab notables and nationalists all the way from the 1890's to World War I; but these involved desires for personal and dynastic aggrandizement which can hardly be termed "nationalist."

11. Of the many works on Egypt from World War I to the Revolution of 1952, perhaps the most valuable for nationalist trends are the following: Berque, *op. cit.;* Leonard Binder, *The Ideological Revolution in the Middle East* (New York, 1964); Marcel Colombe, *L'*Évolution de l'Égypte (Paris, 1951); Sylvia G. Haim, *Arab Nationalism: An Anthology* (Berkeley, 1961); Hourani, *op. cit.;* Safran, *op. cit.;* Afaf Lutfi al-Sayyid Marsot, *Egypt's Liberal Experiment, 1922-1936* (Berkeley, 1977); and David Semah, *Four Egyptian Literary Critics* (Leiden, 1974).

12. 'Abbas Mahmud al-'Aqqad writing in *al-Balagh*, October 19, 1924, and *ibid.*, May 11, 1926.

13. Mirrit Boutros Ghali, *The Policy of Tomorrow* (translated by Isma'il R. el Faruqi: Washington, 1953). The following quotations are taken from pp. 105-111 of this work. (Italics in the original.)

14. Cited in Abu Khaldun Sati' al-Husri, *al-'Uruba Awwalan* (Beirut, 1961), 60.

15. As related by Muhammad Husayn Haykal in his *Mudhakkirat fi al-Siyasa al-Misriyya* (two volumes: Cairo, 1951, 1953), I, 258-259.

16. From a pamphlet of 1942 by Hasan al-Banna of the Muslim Brotherhood as given in his *Majmu'at Rasail al-Imam al-Shahid Hasan al-Banna* (Beirut, 1965), 71.

17. 'Abd al-Qadir al-Mazni writing in *al-Shabab*, Sept. 16, 1936.

18. For further material on the effects of the Palestine issue in interwar Egypt, see my "Egyptian Responses to the Palestine Problem in the Interwar

Period," *International Journal of Middle East Studies*, forthcoming.

19. This reaction is discussed in Anis Sayigh, *al-Fikra al-'Arabiyya fi Misr* (Beirut, 1959), 254-261.

20. Quoted extensively in Husri, *op. cit.*, 116-126, from which the following passages are taken.

21. In addition to their autobiographical statements and biographies, the following works should be consulted on nationalist trends in Egypt under Nasir and Sadat: Anouar Abdel-Malek, *Egypt: Military Society* (Translated by Charles Lam Markmann: New York, 1968); A. I. Dawisha, *Egypt in the Arab World: The Elements of Foreign Policy* (New York, 1976); Malcolm Kerr, *The Arab Cold War: Gamal 'Abd al-Nasir and His Rivals* (third edition: New York, 1971); Nissim Rejwan, *Nasserist Ideology: Its Exponents and Critics* (New York, 1974); Patrick Seale, *The Struggle for Syria: A Study of Post-War Arab Politics, 1945-1958* (London, 1965); P. J. Vatikiotis, *Nasser and His Generation* (London, 1978).

22. State Information Service, United Arab Republic, *The Charter* (Cairo, n.d.), 3, 9, 103.

23. Gamal Abdel Nasser, *The Philosophy of the Revolution* (Buffalo, 1959), 62-66.

24. *Ibid.*, 58-62.

25. State Information Service, *op. cit.*, 32.

26. Abdel-Malek, *op. cit.*, 249.

27. See 'Ali Hamdi al-Jamal, "Nahnu wa al-Tadamun al-'Arabi" ("We and Arab Solidarity"), *al-Ahram*, Oct. 13, 1978.

28. A speech by President Sadat to the Egyptian National Assembly, April 5, 1979, as given in *al-Ahram*, April 6, 1979.

29. Anwar el-Sadat, *In Search of Identity: An Autobiography* (New York, 1978), 312-313.

30. Louis 'Awad as quoted in Vatikiotis, *op. cit.*, 332.

31. Prime Minister Mustafa Khalil as quoted in *al-Ahram*, April 6, 1979.

32. President Sadat before the National Assembly as quoted in *al-Ahram*, April 6, 1979.

33. Hourani, *op. cit.*, 297.

20

The Forces Behind Syrian Politics

By Adam M. Garfinkle

The knowledge I muster about the forces shaping Syrian politics derives mainly from historical records, a deeper familiarity with some neighboring Arab countries, and a close attention paid over the years to the reports, analyses, and speculations of journalists, academics, and diplomats. While none of these founts of wisdom (or error) substitute fully for the absence of personal experience, they nevertheless correspond more or less to the raw materials on which high-level decision makers in the U.S. and other governments rely in their most practical assessments of Syrian politics and policies.

One can make the best or the worst of such sources. The Reagan Administration might have avoided some of the errors it has made over the past few years in misconstruing Syrian interests and intentions had it read the political roadmap more carefully. Still, it must be granted that the perpetual difficulty of predicting the actions of other governments is made harder when policymaking is the domain of a few willful men — as it is in Syria today. Since, in any case, the future is in no simple way an extrapolation of the past, even the best scholarship is little insurance against intellectual ataxia such as might befall us in the future.

All political cultures nevertheless display certain stabilities. Things do change, of course, but not in erratic ways. This is because many aspects of political culture derive from a mix of more or less fixed demographical and geographical conditions and from deeply rooted historical endowments. A grasp of contemporary Syrian politics should start with a sketch of these natural conditions and historical endowments, and suggest some of their implications for the development of Syrian politics. It will then be possible to gain some perspective on the politically relevant changes that have taken place in Syria over the last few decades.

I

The Arab Republic of Syria, as it exists today in about 73,000 square miles, is geographically diverse. There is a narrow western littoral on the Mediterranean, but it is arid and sandy save for where mountain streams — notably the Kabir in the north — run to the sea. The greater eastern part of the country is a gradually sloping desert plateau descending toward the Iraqi border. Between the coast and the desert is a north-south line of relatively low but fairly rugged mountains. On the western side of this range is much of Syria's farmland; on the eastern side, in a valley graced by three rivers, are still more agrarian villages as well as Syria's major cities. In these cities and villages live roughly 80 percent of Syria's 9.3 million people.

The more sparsely populated areas of the country are less germane to the development of Syria's political life, but they are not irrelevant. The desert has operated historically as a kind of filter. On the one hand, it has limited Syria's military vulnerability; only nomadic peoples — the Arabs and later the Mongols — have used the desert successfully as an invasion route. Syria has more often been captured from its west, south and north and its early history was thus domi-

Dr. Garfinkle is Research Associate and Coordinator of the Political Studies Program at the Foreign Policy Research Institute and a Lecturer in Political Science at the University of Pennsylvania. He is the author of numerous articles on Middle Eastern and U.S. defense policies.

nated by contact with peoples of Indo-European origin — Hittites, Macedonian and Selucid Greeks, and Romans. Syria was a Christian nation for hundreds of years before the Muslim conquest of the 7th century and remained a predominantly non-Islamic society until the reconquest of the Levant from the Crusaders in the 12th century.

But the desert is not dead. It has for centuries been populated by nomadic Semitic-speaking peoples, and still holds perhaps three quarters of a million people today. These peoples have over the centuries settled themselves in Syria and given the country a decidedly non-Indo-European population. The desert has also allowed a significant commerce. The cities that lie astride the desert — Aleppo in the north, Damascus in the south, Hama and Homs in between — have long been outposts for trade and conduit points for passage from the east to the Mediterranean. Each of these four cities developed over the centuries close ties with a seaport city. For Aleppo, that city was Alexandretta, now in Turkish possession and called Iskenderun. For Hama, that city was Banias and, to a lesser degree, Tartus. For Homs, it was Tripoli (now in Lebanon), and for Damascus, it was Beirut and, secondarily, Haifa (now in Israel). These four cities also sit astride major north-south trade routes leading from Asia Minor southward to Palestine, Egypt, and the Red Sea coast to the Yemen. It is not surprising therefore that Syria's inland cities developed mercantile habits and traditions.

At various times in history, trade has made the cities of Syria quite prosperous. Over many decades, the wealthy of the cities reached out to the adjoining countryside with a mind to both economic acquisition and political control. Throughout Syrian history, the rural population — well over 70 percent in most periods — has been dominated, even owned, by urban elites. Modern political divisions have not wholly effaced these patterns; as recently as twenty years ago, Damascene businessmen owned more than a third of Lebanon's Beka'a valley. Even when modern changes have altered these relations, memory of them remains an important factor in contemporary life.

Syria's more densely populated western sector has been blessed with both rivers and usually ample, though erratic, seasonal rainfall. The mountains trap moisture from the west and block out the dry desert winds from the east, rendering Syria a traditional breadbasket of the Middle East. The variable altitudes on the western slopes have also enabled Syrian agriculture to become quite diverse and self-contained. Syria's good fortune in land and water has enabled the sustaining of relatively large sedentary populations, and both its abundance and urban ownership early on instilled the concept of the "cash crop." One consequence of this was the nurturing of a sophisticated and specialized economy at a relatively early date.

Nevertheless, Syria has rarely been a great political power. Its agricultural self-sufficiency and commercial sophistication did not translate into a successful imperium. For much of its history, Syria has been a hinterland of other empires — and often a poor one. It has been ruled at various times from Baghdad, Cairo, Constantinople and Istanbul, and even Paris, and its cities, though rarely destitute, have been provincial in nature, featuring neither great technical, administrative, cultural, nor educational achievement. One can only speculate as to why this is. The vulnerability of Syria to invasion has been noted. But there is also the fact that Syria's agricultural good fortune has not rested on the use of rivers but on rainfall. Both in the Nile valley and the Tigris-Euphrates delta, the organization required to finance, control, and maintain complex systems of irrigation bred a degree of administrative centralization and proto-authoritarianism which may well have been the seeds of expansion and the martial spirit. The upper Euphrates river and two main tributaries run across northeastern Syria for over 400 miles, but its banks have forever been dry and sparsely inhabited. The Qoenig river serves Aleppo, but it is a modest affair and soon disappears into the desert. Hama and Homs are served by the Orontes river, but they are not served particularly well. The Orontes tends to flood during the rainy season, to produce a malarial swamp in the spring,[1] and to virtually dry-up by mid-summer. For this reason, and also because it flows from south to north across the Turkish border, it is called by local Arabs *al-Asi* — the rebel. Damascus' river is the brief but brilliant Barada, which seems to rush full blown from the southwestern spur of the Anti-Lebanon mountains. It has produced the Ghuta oasis of roughly twenty miles square, and the Ghuta has produced Damascus. Just to the east of the city, the Barada and four lesser streams disappear into the desert.

The point is that until very recently, none of Syria's major rivers have been cultivated to maximize the utility of their waters — no canals, no dams, no irrigation, no reservoirs. Even in the middle of this century, the most sophisticated waterworks operating in Syria were those built by the Romans 1,800 years earlier.

Syria's relative political weakness may also be due in part to the regional cleavages that have afflicted Syrian society throughout its history. Ironically, these cleavages have been enabled by Syria's agricultural prosperity.[2] The abundance of food, the large sedentary population it nurtured, and the particularist ties formed by Syria's urban traders created self-contained political units — like city-states — one each orbitting Aleppo, Hama, Homs, and Damascus. Over the years a sense of rivalry grew up, especially between Aleppo and Damascus. Each city developed a different character and attracted a different mix of people. Damascus, being closer to northern Arabia, Palestine, and Egypt, developed a more cosmopolitan culture. Its people today are diverse, the city's quarters holding large numbers of Orthodox Christians, Kurds, Armenians, and others. Hama, on the other hand, has been less colorful and more religiously orthodox Sunni Islamic, yet its surrounding agricultural districts are a mosaic of minoritarian communities. Homs, though primarily a Sunni city, lies on a main east-west trade route through a prominent break in the mountains. It has therefore been less isolated than Hama, and near Homs lies the Wadi al-Nasara, or, the Valley of the Christians, where live a large concentration of Greek Orthodox. Aleppo, due to its proximity both to Anatolia and to the upper Euphrates with its caravan routes, has had greater intercourse with Asia Minor, central Asia, and Iraq, and through Iraq with Persia. Also, many Kurds reside near Aleppo, as do Christians who are a remnant of pre-Islamic times when Aleppo (and Antioch) were Hellenic Christian cities far greater and more prosperous than Damascus.

It is difficult to overstate the severity and debilitating political effects of Syria's regional cleavages. For all the references one hears about the political integrity of "greater Syria," it is only a geographical concept (like "Scandinavia") not a political one. Geographical, or "greater," Syria embraces an area stretching from the Mediterranean coast eastward to the hinterland of Mesopotamia, and from the Tarsus mountains in the north to the Sinai desert in the south, embracing both sides of the Jordan river. But this area has rarely been administered or ruled together and it was ruled as one from Damascus only once, and that was for but nine decades over 1200 years ago. What stands out about independent Arab rule in Syria today is that it is uncharacteristic historically within any borders whatsoever.

While Syria's regional cleavages, many of which persist today, owe much to geography and climate, the vicissitudes of history are as much to blame for Syria's traditional political divisions and also for its general backwardness. It is to this history that we now briefly turn.

II

History is an inseparable blending of information and images, the former residing mainly in books, the latter also resting in people's heads. From the former, historians derive some capacity for establishing empirical knowledge about the past. From the latter, the living construct identities in the present and direct their progeny into the future. The empirical side suggests that Syrian history has tended to reinforce social and political fragmentation, and to encourage a backwardness born of cultural stagnation. This in turn seems to have produced an historical consciousness that stresses parochial political loyalties and a propensity to believe that war and conflict is more the norm than the exception in relations between nations.

In ancient times, geographic Syria was the site of successive waves of migration from Asia Minor, from both the Syrian and north Arabian deserts, and from Egypt and the Red Sea coast. Groups of people settled in Syria in layer after layer, attracted by the verdant oasis of Damascus and the rainfall of the western mountain valleys. A succession of invasions (Hittite, Egyptian, Aramaean, Assyrian, Babylonian, Persian) all left a mark on the area, but none effaced the basic semitic character of the country or had a major effect on the racial and cultural stabilities of those living in outlying rural districts. The most consequential of these migrations was the Aramaean influx at the end of the second millenium B.C.E., which bequeathed to the region the Aramaic language, which became the lingua franca of the Levant for nearly a thousand years.

In 333 B.C.E. Syria was conquered by the armies of Alexander the Great, commencing an era of Greco-Roman influence that was not overturned until the rise of Islam nearly a thousand years later. Particularly after the Romans arrived in 64 B.C.E., northern Syria around Aleppo and Antioch developed as more important centers than Damascus. Roman rule was briefly interrupted in the first century C.E. by the Nabateans. In later times, an occasional regional Syrian vassal state, drawing strength from nomadic migrations, arose on the periphery of Roman power. In the 6th century, the local state of Ghassan served the Byzantine Empire as a buffer against other desert tribes in league with Sassanid power in Persia. As it turned out, these tribesmen were the first to face the Arab invasion of the 7th century — unsuccessfully

In the four centuries before the Arab conquest during which Syria was predominantly Christian, independent religious practices and theological proclivities emerged. Syrian Christianity was Monophysite and the rejection of Byzantine orthodoxy caused trouble between Constantinople and Syria. Moreover, Byzantium had long been locked in a debilitating struggle with Sassanid Persia, sapping Syria of its wealth and breaking its peace. Thus, when the Muslim Arabs swept into Syria, capturing it in 634-35 C.E., the local inhabitants were grateful, expecting fuller religious autonomy and a less burdensome rule. Initially, they got the former, but not the latter. The early Umayyad court was filled with Christians of various kinds and little effort was made to convert the multitudes to Islam. Even one of Muawiyah's wives was a Christian and it was this wife who mothered his successor, Yazid.[3] At the same time, however, Muslim coffers were filled by a heavy tax (jizya) imposed upon the majority non-Muslim population. In other words, the Arab Umayyad dynasty, though it chose to rule from Damascus, lorded over Syria as a warrior caste, taxing its people to finance further imperial successes and caring little about their souls.

Within a few generations this situation changed considerably. Non-Muslims came to play a lesser role in the Umayyad court and much of the local population found it prudent to become Muslims, thus impoverishing the empire. Although new converts (mawali) were in theory equal to "original" Arab Muslims, the older Arabian elite clung to its special privileges. This led to conflict and not only in Syria, for as Muslim conquests grew, the numerical preponderance of non-Arab Muslims eroded the power of the Arab elite. These conflicts often took on a pre-existent tribal organization and frequently spawned heterodox religious expression.[4] Ultimately, these conflicts paved the way for the defeat of the Umayyad house in 750 at the hands of abu-al-Abbas, a descendant of the prophet's uncle. The new Abbasid dynasty shifted the capital from Damascus to Baghdad reflecting both the empire's concentration on eastward military campaigns and greater Persian cultural and religious influences. From that time forth, well into the 19th century, Syria was for the most part economically stagnant, politically dependent, and internally fractured in both ethnographic and administrative realms. Wars both large and small were endemic and for long periods disease was epidemic.

This sad saga began with the crushing of numerous pro-Umayyad revolts during the first century of Abbasid rule. In the 9th century, Syria fell under Egyptian domination for a time, commencing a new phase of Egyptian-Iraqi rivalry — fought mainly at Syrian expense. In the 10th century, a local dynasty arose, the Hamidanid, with its capital at Aleppo. But the Hamidanids unwisely provoked the Byzantine reconquest of northern Syria. At the start of the 11th century, northern Syria was again subject to Christian influence; Damascus and Palestine were held loosely by the Shi'ite Fatimid dynasty of Egypt. Both Fatimid and Byzantine rule proved fragile and by mid-century much of the area was governed (also loosely) by a Seljuk Turkish dynasty. This succession of weak rulers fostered local self-reliance and nurtured a tradition of self governance, a development allowed by self-sufficiency in food. So while conquerors came and went from the cities and traversed the well worn paths of invasion and retreat, village life off the beaten path remained a good deal more stable than one might suspect.

Political division and military weakness proved favorable for the success of the first crusade at the end of the 11th century. The Crusaders took Jerusalem, Antioch, Edessa, Tripoli, Acre, and the Syrian coast under control, but the interior cities they never held. A Muslim counterattack began under a Turkish family but passed in the 12th century to the famous Saladin who reunified Muslim Syria and turned the tide against the Crusader states. But his passing and the limited success of the third crusade (1189-92) delayed the full triumph of the Muslim reconquest for a century; the final Christian stronghold in Acre fell in 1291 to the Mamluk sultanate of Egypt.

It was during the Muslim reconquest of Syria that the majority of the population became Muslim for the first time. Some Syrian Christians had cooperated with the crusaders and their fate was sealed by the reconquest. Other groups in rural areas that had never become fully Christian, but had clung to their ancient traditions, were also affected by the chaos of this period and first adopted both offshoots of Islam and the Arabic language. It was during the final phase of the reconquest under the Mamluks, for example, that the Persian al-Darazi spread into Syria the cult of al-Hakim, a mad Fatimid caliph of the early 11th century who had proclaimed himself the deity. Only in Syria, however, the religious/political shatterbelt of the time, did al-Hakim's claims win a permanent following — the Druze.

With far greater consequences for contemporary Syrian politics, it was also during this period that another pre-existent tribe adopted a syncretic variant of Isma'ili Shi'ite Islam — the Alawis. Isma'ili Islam was strong in central Syria near Hama during the period of the Crusades.[5] It was during the 11th century that ibn-Nusyr preached a mystical blend of Islam, Christianity, and local animistic beliefs. Alawis worship a trinity of Muhammad, his son-in-law Ali, and a companion of the prophet, Salman al-Farisi (the Persian). Like the Isma'ilis, the Alawis believe in a system of progressive divine incarnations but, unlike Isma'ilis, Alawis regard Ali as the incarnation of the Deity in the Divine Triad. Ali is referred to as "the meaning." Muhammad — who was created by Ali — is called "the name." Salman is called "the gate." Alawis express the following formula: "I turn to the gate, I bow to the name, I adore the meaning." Although Alawis are secretive about their beliefs and religious texts, it is known that Alawi myth holds that all were stars in a world of light until disobedience to the meaning caused life to fall to earth. Each person must be transformed seven times before rejoining Ali, who is prince of the stars. Blameworthy people are reborn as Christians, with whom they must stay until atonement is complete. Infidels are said to be reborn as animals. Some Alawi festivals are Muslim, some are Christian, some are solar and predate both Christianity and Islam. Alawis recognize the Qur'an as a holy book, but have secret interpretations of its meaning. Their liturgy is found in a book called Kitab al-Majmu, probably derived from Isma'ili writings. Much of their ritual is influenced by Christian practice. Wine is used, for example, something unthinkable for an orthodox Muslim. Alawis are organized tribally into four groups and there are religious variations among modern Alawis which tend to correspond to tribal groupings. One such variation derives from followers of Sulaiman al-Murshid, who claimed prophetic powers in 1923. His adherents are mainly from the Khaiyatin tribe.[6]

Even with the defeat of the crusaders there was no peace for Syria. Mamluk rule was challenged even before it was consolidated by the Mongols. For more than 40 years, disastrous warfare plagued Syria before the Mongols were defeated in 1303. There then ensued a series of outbreaks of bubonic plague in the next 120 years, reducing the population by perhaps 30 to 40 per cent. When Ottoman rule commenced in 1517, the population of geographical Syria was perhaps one third of what it had been at the height of Umayyad power more than eight centuries earlier.

Ottoman rule lasted 400 years, from 1517 to 1918. Though "foreign" in the conventional sense, Ottoman rule was relatively stable, predictable, peaceful, and Sunni orthodox in orientation. The main exception was the seizure of Syria in 1831 by Mohammed Ali of Egypt, which lasted until 1840. Nevertheless, the rule of Mohammed Ali's son, Ibrahim Pasha, greatly modernized and centralized Syrian administration. Since the Ottomans, on their return, thought nothing special of Syria, local administration grew still stronger. On the other hand, the Ottomans refined the millet system, deepening the various divisions in Syrian society and emphasizing religion as the source of political identification. Moreover, the Turks did not administer geographical or even modern Syria as a single unit. For the most part, Damascus grew larger than Aleppo during this period, sometimes adjoined to the administration of both Beirut and Jerusalem (both of which are nearer to Damascus than is Aleppo).[7] Northern Syria was treated separately as a district adjacent to Anatolia proper.

III

With the demise of the Ottoman Empire came the French, whose influence in Syria during the 19th century was the most extensive of the European powers. The French turned Syria's ethnographic and regional diversity, and its tradition of separatist and communitarian rule from a fact of political life into an imperial asset. French policy was consciously one of *divide et impera,* as Paris divided Syria into various administrative districts, created greater Lebanon out of the Syrian mandate, bartered away Alexandretta to Turkey, and utilized minorities disproportionally in the administration of the country. The latter tactic sharpened intercommunal tensions, but it also eroded gradually the political hierarchy of the foregoing centuries. Together with the penetration of European political ideas and culture, starting in later Ottoman times but accelerated greatly under the French, the disruption of traditional politics in Syria set the stage for the modern politicization of Syria's minority communities. Unlike Syria's Sunni Muslim population, for whom being a Muslim and being an Arab and being a Syrian were all mutually compatible labels, the minority groups — Alawis, Christians, Kurds, Circassians, Druze — were driven to redefine their political identities. It was their inability to apply easily the traditional Muslim formula of political loyalty, which did not separate faith and citizenship into components, that attracted them to Western notions in which citizenship was a "non-tribal" and non-religiously bound concept, and yet did not require the dissolution of inward looking community ties.

By the end of the French Mandate with World War II, regional, sectarian, and ideological cleavages were rife in Syria. Newly independent Syria was governed by the Sunni Muslim urban elite which had been galvanized into unified action by French colonial policies. But with the departure of the French, this group redivided and strove with itself. Other fissures in Syrian life were also still present. Independence seemed only to magnify the problems of the status of the newly aware minority communities, the artificiality of Syria's borders, the conflict between more concrete and parochial Syrian interests and those of Pan-Arabism which attracted the Sunni majority, and the tension between the traditional Islamic worldview and that of secularist Western ideologies.

These cleavages in turn worsened long-standing rural/urban cleavages in both obvious and more subtle ways. The penetration of Western ideas was uneven; while the minority groups to which they most naturally appealed were rural people, intellectual ferment is more usually an urban affair. Independent Syria quickly centralized its administration, centered on Damascus, and enlarged the role of the public sector. So, on the one hand, the enhanced role of the cities, ruled by Sunnis, overlapped with traditional urban/rural cleavages and even seemed to presage a reversal of trends toward sectarian equality in the Mandate period. But the enhanced role of the cities also drew minority peoples to urban areas where they were more easily politicized. As is the case in other developing countries, a ring of recently arrived folk of rural origin gradually surrounded the central urban areas, and it was on the boundaries of these urban "rings" that conflict was most evident.[8]

Thus, it is fair to say that in the early independence period the raw materials for the launching of modern Syrian nationalism were scarce indeed. Syria was a political entity but not a political community; it was a state, but not a nation. Its ruling political elite was divided by interest, personality, and ideology. The People's Party, representing the merchant-aristocracy of Aleppo, vied constantly with the more powerful National Party, made up of the Damascene merchant-aristocracy and a group of industrialists and professionals.[9] In this divided elite alone was there any development of a national attachment for "Syria," and even here it was weak, diluted by Pan-Arab and Pan-Islamic elements. Meanwhile, the numerous and socially significant minority communities defined their loyalties more parochially. Instead of being tempted by political identifications that were larger than Syria, they were bound instead to tribe and sect.[10] The Druze cared more for their kinsmen in Lebanon and Palestine than for their fellow Syrian "citizens"; the Kurds more for their fellows in Iraq, Turkey, and Iran. For the Alawis, Latakia province was home; the rest of Syria was as strange to them as any other foreign place. Three levels of identity — religious community, tribe, family — were dominant and, as before, this parochialism was reinforced by local economic autarky. In such circumstances, modern Syrian nationalism generated little loyalty or enthusiasm. Political platforms organized by Sunnis around Western ideologies, or Pan-Arabism, or combinations of the two, similarly failed to garner legitimacy for the government. Even rural Sunni Muslims who could have been expected to respond to Pan-Islamic sentiment, were largely unmoved by the old urban Sunni elite and, like their more heterodox neighbors, were not as "detribalized" as their secularized urban counterparts.[11] If it is true that in the Arab world borders are in the hearts of men, then postwar Syria was a case where many hearts beat to different rhythms, none of them in time with a national Syrian anthem.

The failure of the traditional elites to unify in order to develop a national consensus presaged their downfall. This downfall was speeded by Syria's ignominious role in the 1948 Palestine War, a conflict that, among other things, bequeathed a more prominent political role to the Syrian military. Within a half dozen years after the 1948 war, the dominance of the Sunni elite had been greatly eroded. The first of many *coups d'état* took place in 1949 when Colonel Husni Zaim established a military dictatorship. Zaim was himself anti-establishment but was also a Sunni. This was important because the sectarian divisions in the country were vividly reflected within the army, which had been a main means of social mobility for Syria's disenfranchised minorities. Zaim lasted only 18 weeks; he was displaced by a proponent of the old order, Colonel Sami Hinawi. Hinawi's tenure was even shorter than Zaim's, however. He was overthrown by Colonel Adib Shishakli, whose power also resided in a connection to the old order, namely, Akran Hourani's Republican bloc, a faction of the old elitist National bloc. Shishakli's checkered tenure lasted until 1954, when a coalition of old time politicians, including Hourani, and newer ideological parties threw him out.[12] Among the latter was the Communist Party, the Syrian Nationalist Party, and the Ba'th, or Renaissance Party. The Syrian Ba'th was formed in 1953 by a merger between Hourani's party (now the Arab Socialist Party, formed in 1950) and the original Ba'th, led by Michel Aflaq and Salah Bitar (founded in the early 1940s). All three of these parties tended to seek recruits among minority groups. What Sunnis there were among them tended to be rural in origin and far from the circle of the urban elite. The Ba'th sought particularly to proselytize among members of minority groups within the armed forces.

Between 1954 and 1958, Syrian politics was a strange and tempestuous amalgam of opposing forces. Even though they were a numerical minority, the Ba'th tended to dominate the government through discipline and tight party cohesion, especially after 1956. But pressure from the left led by the Communists — the most powerful Middle Eastern communist party of that era — forced the Ba'th to look for allies, lest the left seize power. Both the Ba'th and more traditional political elements in Syria found an ally in Nasser's Egypt — or so they thought. It was out of exhaustion and fear that the Ba'th and the Syrian army led Syria into union with Egypt in 1958, creating the shortlived United Arab Republic.[13]

The experiment of the UAR was a bitter one. Ba'th members found their activities curtailed in their own country by Egyptian political "commissars." The traditionalists, however, had the most to lose; their already dwindling position was about to be dealt a fatal blow by an ambitious land reform program. By 1961, the traditional Sunni elite had engineered Syria's exit from the UAR, though they were unable to prevent some land reform measures in the doing. The traditionalists did not last long. By 1963, the process of politicization of Syria's minorities and the infiltration of the military by the Ba'th was well advanced. In 1963, a Ba'thi oriented military junta seized the government and Syrian politics have never been the same since.

IV

The rise of the Ba'th and the army in 1963 commenced at least three major longlasting changes in Syria. First, the rise of the Ba'th and the military was the channel through which peoples of rural origins and often sectarian minorities gained a large, disproportionate share of political power. This represented a real social revolution in Syrian history; it was the first time that formerly poor and oppressed peoples dominated the public sphere in Syria. In general, the redistribution of wealth and the restructuring of the system of patronage according to new tribal/family affiliation has had more impact on Syrian society than any ideology. This is well illustrated by the comments of Sami al-Jundi, a founder of the Syrian Ba'th and a minister in the revolutionary government:

> Three days after my entering the Ministry, the comrades asked me for an extensive purge operation.... Success was determined by the list of dismissals, since party members as well as their relatives and the members of their tribes came to demand their kinship rights.... Caravans of villagers started to leave the villages of the plains and mountains for Damascus. And while the alarming *qaf* started to predominate in the streets, coffee houses and the waiting rooms of the ministries, dismissals became a duty so that the new arrivals could be appointed.[14]

Minority rule by the Alawis has not been particularly stable, although by the standards of 1948-1958 it may appear so. A minority government does not build legitimacy for "Syria" as a national entity when it turns the apparatus of government to the advantage of its own community. The Asad regime has not been brazen in this, but the trends are clear. Especially since the second Ba'thi coup of February 1966, Syria has exchanged an elite instability which consisted of intra-Sunni cleavages for one that consists of intra-minority, and even intra-Alawi cleavages. The urban/rural dichotomy still exists, but in a sense it has been turned upside down, with rural people ruling city people from Damascus.

A second major change has been the centralization and modernization of administrative functions under the military, and the concomitant rise in the importance of Damascus over all other cities and regions. Syria is no longer "thoroughly ugly, and cramped, squalid, uncomfortable and filthy," as Mark Twain described it in the 19th century.[15] Thanks to the military bureaucracy, whatever its sins, Syria has creditable educational and health systems, some industry, and a fairly well diversified economy. But while the army has helped modernize and unify the country, the exacerbation of regional tensions caused by the position of Damascus has been troublesome. Indeed, the Asad regime's greatest challenges have come from Aleppo, Homs, and Hama.

A third consequence of the 1963 revolution has been the utter dominance of the military in all walks of Syrian life. Before 1963, the military was an important actor in politics, but it required and sought out coalitions with businessmen, civilian politicians, ideologues, and even clerics. But since the 1966 and 1970 *coups d'état* the position of the military has been virtually hegemonic. This is only partly a function of protracted struggle with Israel and probably a minor part. In many new states with a paucity of political legitimacy to undergird civilian authority, government is a military affair. In a sense, military governments are Praetorian guards for their own elite. In Syria, it just so happens that both the guard and the elite are overwhelmingly Alawi, a group which makes up less than 12 per cent of the population.

We have alluded to the foreignness of the Western concepts of borders and citizenship in the Arab world. But the lawful, constitutional organization of power in Western countries is just as foreign in societies that have known historically only the alternating dominance of some religious/tribal groups over others. The Middle East is perhaps best described as a series of cores, made up of dominant groups that organize political life on the peripheries within their own spheres.[16] When these cores clash with one another, it is the allegiance and expansion of their respective peripheries (in their own countries and in others) that are at issue. If a core should disintegrate (as has the Maronite core in Lebanon) its peripheries become the prey of other cores. The implicit Western insistence on seeing Syria as a Western-type state rather than as a core and periphery system among other such systems may be the root of much of our trouble. If this is so, then perhaps the center of contemporary Syria life is not Damascus but Qardaha, a village in Latakia province that is the center of the Numailatiyah section of the Matawirah Alawi tribe and the birthplace of Hafiz al-Asad.

FOOTNOTES

1. Thanks to the Ghab Project, this problem has been reduced.

2. On this point — and many others — see Albert Hourani, *Lebanon and Syria: A Political Essay* (London: Oxford University Press, 1946), chap. 1.

3. See the lyrical narrative of Philip Hitti, *Capital Cities of Arab Islam* (Minneapolis: University of Minnesota Press, 1973), pp. 66-67.

4. For an illuminating discussion of this period, see Bernard Lewis, *The Arabs in History* (New York: Harper & Row, 1966), chap. 3. Note, too, that it is inaccurate to refer to the residents of Syria as "Arabs" in the period before the Muslim conquest. See Lewis' expansive definition of "Arab," pp. 9-17.

5. See John F. Devlin, *Syria,* (Boulder: Westview, 1983), p. 27.

6. This is noted, along with other interesting details, in Hanna Batatu, "Some Observations on the Social Roots of Syria's Ruling, Military Group and the Causes for Its Dominance," *Middle East Journal,* Summer 1981, p. 335.

7. For a brief discussion, see Moshe Maoz, "Attempts at Creating a Political Community in Modern Syria," *Middle East Journal,* Autumn 1972.

8. See the essay by Michael H. Van Dusen, "Political Integration and Regionalism in Syria," *Middle East Journal,* Spring 1972.

9. For a brief discussion, see M. Graeme Bannerman, "The Syrian Arab Republic," in David E. Long and Bernard Reich, eds., *The Government and Politics of the Middle East and North Africa* (Boulder: Westview, 1980), pp. 244-245.

10. See especially the discussion by Nikolaos van Dam, *The Struggle for Power in Syria* (New York: St. Martin's, 1979), pp. 15-27.

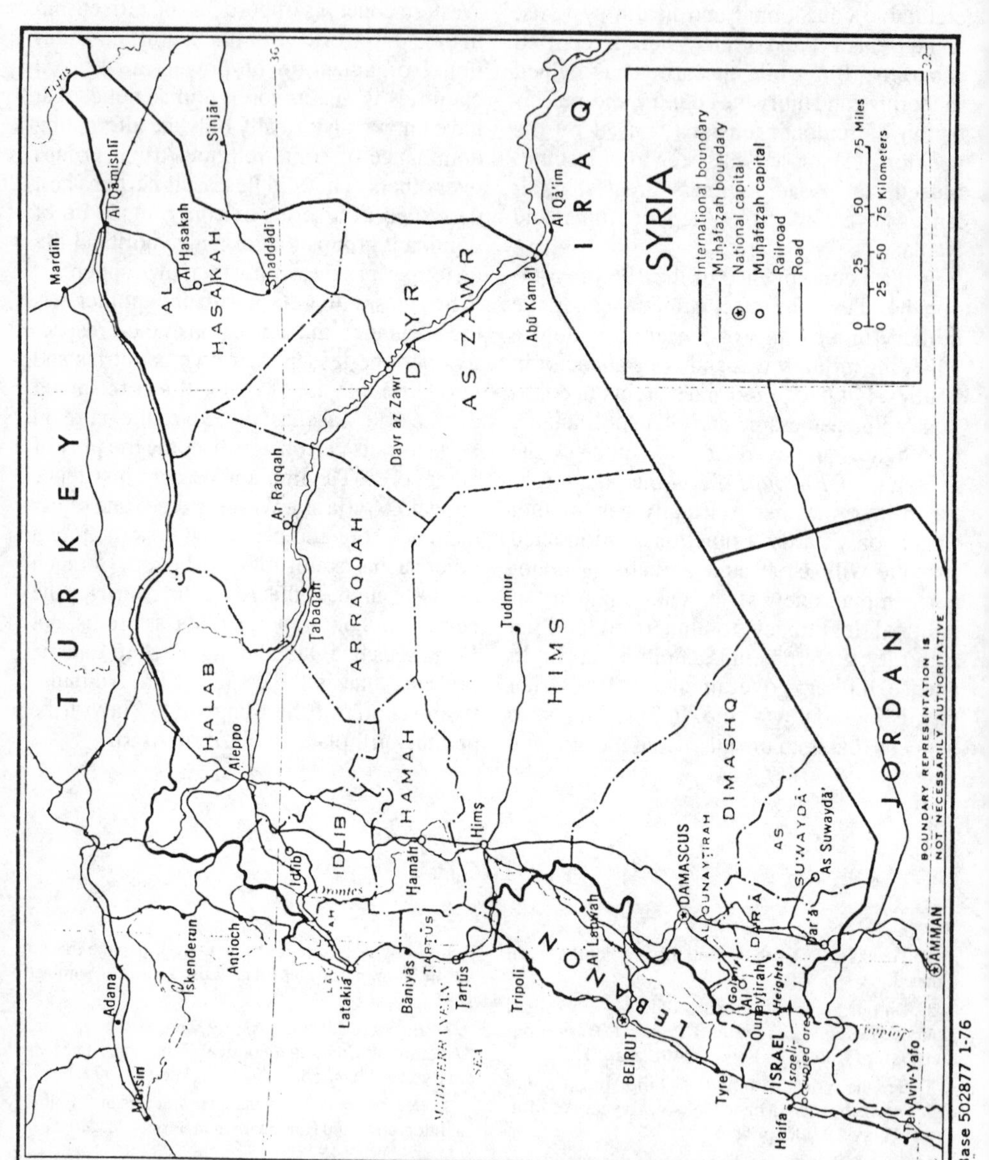

UN Map Collection

FOOTNOTES

11. On this point see the essays by Van Dusen and Batatu cited above.

12. For a discussion of this period, see Don Peretz, *The Middle East Today* (New York: Praeger, 1984), pp. 407-409.

13. For a discussion of this period, see Malcolm Kerr, *The Arab Cold War* (London: Oxford University Press, 1971), chap. 1.

14. Quoted in van Dam, p. 99. As van Dam explains, the *qaf* refers to an Arabic guttural sound which is pronounced prominently in many rural Syrian districts, but not in the cities. Thus, the *qaf* when used by urban people to describe rural people is a term roughly equivalent to the American "hillbilly."

15. Mark Twain, *The Innocents Abroad,* Volume 2, chapter XXI, lines 3 and 4.

16. See James R. Kurth, "U.S.-Israeli Relations: U.S. Policy and the Disputed Territories," in Steven L. Spiegel, ed., *American Policy in the Middle East: Where Do We Go From Here?* (New York: The Josephson Foundation, 1983), pp. 24-26.

21

The Iran-Iraq War

By Sheikh R. Ali

At least six factors precipitated the Iran-Iraq War: territorial irredentism, ethnic dissensions, linguistic chauvinism, religious cleavages, ideological contests and personal arrogance. When the war broke out in September 1980, adding new dimensions to the already turbulent Middle East, many analysts predicted a short campaign that would be ended by mutual exhaustion, economic difficulty, and lack of ammunition. It did not prove correct. The end of the war, now four years old, is nowhere in sight.

In 1975, Iraqi President Saddam Hussein and the late Shah of Iran had signed the Algiers Agreement, whereby the two countries had established the navigable channel on the Shatt al-Arab River as the official border between them.[1] Iraq had long considered the entire river as falling within its territorial jurisdiction, and the agreement granting Iran rights on the estuary was reached only after considerable pressure by the Shah. President Hussein agreed to settle the border dispute on the Shatt and in return the Shah agreed to stop aiding the Iraqi Kurds in their struggle against the Iraqi regime. With the overthrow of the Shah and the rise of Khomeini to power, the historical enmity between Iranians and Iraqis flared up into war when Iraq moved its forces across the Shatt al-Arab border.

Antecedents of the Conflict

To further appreciate the antecedents, one has to look into the first spread of Islam and Arab culture into Iran and other areas of the world, which began from the time of the Ummayyad dynasty (661-750 A.D.). This purely Arab dynasty succumbed to the Abbasids, a Persianized dynasty. In the meantime, the Prophet Muhammad's son-in-law, Ali, who was the fourth caliph of Islam, met with a violent death. Ali's son Husain, who was to succeed him was also killed (680 A.D.). Out of this succession battle emerged a sect in Islam known as the Shi'ite Muslim. Martyrdom is at the core of the Shi'ite creed, and Shi'ites seek ever to avenge the martyrdom of Husain, whom Sunnis trampled to death at Karbala in Iraq.

The Sunnis emphasize consensus in formulating law. Shi'ites have developed the concept of the awaited *mahdi*, or messianic leader who is empowered constantly to reinterpret the Qur'an.

Still, the rift between the two major sects in Islam was incomplete until the emergence of the Ottoman empire in the fourteenth century and the rise of the Safawid dynasty in Iran. The Safawids backed the Shi'ites, while the Ottomans took over responsibility for the predominant Sunnis. It is this Shi'ite-Sunnite schism that is at the heart of the religious and sectarian dispute between Iraq and Iran.[2] None of the warring nations would like to admit it, because Islam forbids "Muslims killing Muslims," yet both countries are creating a holy war zeal in order to inspire and galvanize the masses in support of their war policy.

Second, the Ottoman-Iranian rivalry created instability and tension in the Middle East which resulted in the political autonomy of many tribes on the frontiers between the two countries. A ferocious struggle continued between the two empires for control over tribes and ethnic populations in Iranian Khuzistan, which the Arabs call Arabistan.

This local dispute between the Arabs and Persians became international once the out-

---

Dr. Ali is Associate Professor of Political Science at North Carolina Central University, Durham. He has written numerous articles and books on Middle Eastern affairs and his latest book is *Oil, Turmoil, and Islam in the Middle East* (Praeger, 1985).

This paper was prepared for presentation at a panel of the *American Professors for Peace in the Middle East* at the meeting of the American Political Science Association in Washington, D.C., on August 30, 1984.

side powers had taken the offensive in the Persian Gulf. In 1546, the Ottomans attacked Basra, an Iraqi port, in order to defeat the Portuguese and break their alliance with the Persians. Despite Ottoman expansion, Portugal maintained its control over Arabistan. When Spain annexed Portugal in 1640, England and Holland made their entry into the Gulf. Although France negotiated a treaty of friendship with Persia, the former was not able to establish a foothold in the area. As the Persian empire weakened, enmity between the British and the Russians developed in the Gulf region. The basic principle of Anglo-Russian policy in the Middle East was to maintain the area as a buffer zone in order to stop further rival imperialist expansion. "This common interest," Tareq Ismail notes, "brought them into cooperation and collusion in settling Ottoman-Persian disputes, even while they competed and conspired against each other."[3]

Third, underlying the rivalry between Iran and Iraq is a clash of linguistic and cultural differences — of a sense of superiority on the one side and an inferiority complex on the other. Iran is inhabited by Farsi (Persian)-speaking Indo-European people. Iraq is primarily composed of Arabic-speaking Semitic people. The Muslims in general and Arabs in particular revere and respect the Arabic language — the language of the Holy Book (the Qur'an). No such reverence could be claimed for Farsi. Iraq has repeatedly renewed its claim to Arabistan, an Arabic-speaking Iranian province, as its own territory. Iran, on the other hand, has accused Iraq of cultural chauvinism. The Iraqi feeling of superiority, which emanates from the seventh century Arab conquest of Iran still lingers on. Because Islam originated in Arabia and the language of the Qur'an is Arabic, many Arabs, including Iraqis, consider Iranians and other non-Arab Muslims as inferior and second-class Muslims. The Persian-Iranians, who inherit an ancient civilization and culture, resent this attitude of the Arab-Iraqis.

Holier Than Thou

As a fourth factor, Islam, the religion of the two countries, instead of uniting them, has divided them. As discussed earlier, Iran's population is predominantly Shi'ite, which contrasts with the orthodox and doctrinal Sunni Islam of other Muslim countries in the world. The Iraqi population is split between Sunni and Shi'ite Muslims, but the Shi'ites are more numerous. Khomeini's followers regard him as a mahdi. Therefore, they say, he was entitled to call Iraqi President Hussein anti-Islamic and to declare a holy war against Iraq. The ruling elites in Iraq, including Hussein, are mostly of the Sunni persuasion, and therefore strive to orient Iraq toward Sunni Islam. The Shi'ites periodically demonstrate their dissatisfaction with the Hussein regime. This religious division has created a "holier-than-thou" attitude between the ruler and the ruled in Iraq, between the elites and also between the masses of the two countries. The superiority/inferiority complex which dominates the socio-political scene is described by Stephen R. Grummon as follows:

> Moreover, both Arabs and Persians remember that it was the Arabs who conquered Iran and gave Islam to the Persians, but that it was Persian civilization that took raw, desert Islam and refined and tempered it.[4]

A fifth factor is this: Ayatollah Khomeini, long in exile in Iraq, was expelled by the Iraqi regime in 1978 at the behest of the Shah. From his second exile in France, Khomeini began to urge his Shi'ite followers in Iraq to overthrow Hussein who was preaching a secular ideology of Ba'thism.[5] On returning home in 1979, Khomeini called upon the Iraqi Shi'ites to join him in revolution and to struggle against the anti-Islamic policies of Hussein and his Ba'thist followers. Iraq viewed the success of the Iranian revolution as yet another attempt to destabilize the region and bring about the downfall of the Ba'thist regime and disgrace to Iraq. As Hussein himself said in a speech:

> They [the Ottoman empire] took turns on Iraq; Turkey goes, Iran comes. All this is done in the name of Islam. Enough; no more Turkey, no more Iran... We will not accept anybody coming everyday with a new path that aims at dividing Iraq and dividing the Arab nation.[6]

Iraq sees its war with Iran as Arab nationalism facing a tough conflict with Iranian imperialism. The Ba'th, as a secular political party, views Islam as the cultural and spiritual source of inspiration for Arab nationalism.

Iran's humiliation is the sixth factor, and this was considered to be Iraq's call to greatness. The Iraqi leader's ambition envisions leading the Arab world in the suppression of Iran. Hussein dreams of resurrecting the glorious days of the Arab empire, and of Iraq as the regional great power.

Iran's chaotic state in the aftermath of the revolution was considered an appropriate time to strike the death knell against the dictatorship of the clerics in that country. The Shah's Iran had been seen as essentially a conservative power that sought to expand Iranian influence mainly by strengthening Iran's ability to preserve the stability in the region. By contrast, the new revolutionary regime is seen as a revisionist power fomenting revolution and unrest. Khomeini's Iran has used the instrument of foreign policy to challenge the domestic order of its neighbors, and has been far more persistent in the use of propaganda, subversion, and force than the Shah's regime ever was. (In this respect, the xenophobic dictatorship of the clerics and Khomeini's personal rule has led to even greater repression than existed under the Shah's rule.)

The Gathering Storm

We have proffered six explanations for the gradual outbreak of hostility between Iran and Iraq. Iraq's dissatisfaction with the Algiers agreement of June 13, 1975, which had settled long-standing territorial and boundary disputes, its involvement in the ethnic uprising in Iran, the build-up of political tension and frequent border skirmishes between the two nations, and Khomeini's call for the overthrow of Hussein all indicated increasing tension in the region. As tension heightened, the Iraqi government asked Iran, in November 1979, to abrogate the Algiers treaty, and to return the border areas and the Shatt al-Arab river basin to Iraq. It also demanded autonomy for Iran's minorities — the Kurds and the Baluchis.

Faced with growing pressure from Iraq, the new Iranian regime sought to restore ties with the United States. However, Iranian Prime Minister Mehdi Bazargan's meeting with high American officials aroused suspicion among the radicals in Iran that the Americans were conspiring to mount another 1953-style coup (which had brought the Shah back to power), and they struck back by occupying the United States embassy in Tehran and, with the support of the Iranian government, taking American diplomats hostage. Iran's confused and chaotic regime, playing directly into the hands of the radicals, now mobilized a crusade against "foreign enemies" in order to divert attention from domestic troubles.[7].

The hostage crisis, and the ensuing confrontation with the U.S., temporarily united those political forces in Iran which advocated the export of the Iranian revolution to the neighboring states — including conservative Saudi Arabia. Thus the Mecca Mosque takeover of November 1979 was inspired by Khomeini, who encouraged the radical elements all over the Gulf states to believe that the time was ripe for revolution in the Middle East and throughout the Muslim world. And in pursuit of this policy, in January 1980, Iran organized a conference of revolutionary Islamic organizations and initiated a campaign to stimulate revolutionary zeal in the region.

The hostage crisis isolated Iran from its traditional friend — the U.S. — and antagonized many nations in the region who were fearful of further revolutions in the area. Although Iran's new President, Bani Sadr, sought to resolve the hostage crisis in order to remove U.S. misgivings and so reduce Iran's isolation, the militant Iranians prevailed upon him not to do so until the Americans had been thoroughly punished. Inevitably, Iran's provocative policy not only created internal chaos, ethnic unrest, and plots by the army to overthrow the regime, but also served to isolate the nation and weaken its military capabilities.

With time seemingly in its favor, Iraq chose to strike, calculating that since that country was diplomatically isolated, politically fragmented, militarily weakened, and without access to American arms and spare parts, it would immediately fall to the Iraqis. But Iraq had grossly miscalculated Iran's resourcefulness, and Hussein failed to achieve a quick victory.

Several other facts have clearly emerged from this war, now in its fourth year. The superpowers have shown great reluctance to intervene directly in the war. The U.N., the Organization of Islamic Conferences (OIC) and the non-Alignment Movement have all failed to bring about a cease-fire. The Gulf Cooperation Council (GCC) has also attempted to serve as a mediator — the foreign ministers of Kuwait and the United Arab Emirates (UAE) traveled to Baghdad and Tehran seeking to initiate a dialogue between the two disputants — but they, too, were unsuccessful.

All such efforts have foundered because of Iran's insistence that any resolution of the dispute must include identification of Iraq as the aggressor and that Iraq pay substantial reparations to Iran. Unable to induce Iran to accept a cease-fire and negotiations, Iraq, for its part, has intimated that it would step up attacks on Iranian oil facilities as well as tankers transporting Iranian oil through the Gulf in order to force Iran to the negotiating table. In response, Iran has repeatedly claimed that if its oil exports are substantially reduced it will seek to prevent any other country from exporting oil via the Persian Gulf by closing the Straits of Hormuz.

The Oil War

The Iran-Iraq war has sparked renewed concern about an Iranian long-standing but ambiguous threat to close the Strait of Hormuz, the 26-mile vital waterway used by tankers carrying about 20 percent, or approximately 8 million barrels of oil, of the non-Communist world's daily supply. Iran has repeatedly warned that it will block the Strait (which lies at the mouth of the Gulf) if foreign powers get involved in the war, or if Iraq tries to cut off Iran's oil exports. The possibility of Iran's closing the Strait cannot be ruled out, and this could precipitate another global energy crisis, and may also provide the opportunity for other OPEC members to raise oil prices yet again.

The six Arab nations that make up the GCC sit on one-third of the world's proven oil reserves.[8] Recent attacks on oil tankers have not only increased the cost of insurance, but have also made its availability more difficult. Air attacks on commercial shipping have prompted the group to seek better security through diplomacy, but as yet with no results. If the crisis continues, there might be pressure in the U.S. for American military intervention to prevent Iran from closing the Strait. President Reagan has already declared (at a press conference on February 22, 1984) that there was "no way that we [the U.S.] could allow that channel to be closed."

Even if the fighting were to end soon, it would take about a year to repair the damage caused to oil producing, pumping, and shipping installations in both countries, and the restoration of refineries will take longer. The effects are sure to be felt economically. The soaring oil price would renew inflation and increase the prices of other commodities, goods, and services. While this would hit both the industrialized nations and the Less Developed Countries (LDC), the latter would suffer more, as they have in the past.

For it is a sad fact that those burdened with heavy debt would be most vulnerable. Although the Third World debt problem is a result of many factors: of imprudent borrowing practices and flawed internal policies, the more fundamental explanation of the indebtedness of many of these Third World countries lies in the energy crises of the 1970s and in the unexpectedly rapid disinflationary process which was triggered by the anti-inflationary measures adopted by the industrialized nations.[9] A third energy crisis would be disastrous for most of the non-oil Third World countries, precipitating widespread discord and leading to change of governments and other developments such as authoritarianism. Should another oil crisis occur, Third World leaders are sure to adopt aggressive foreign policies as a means of laying the blame for their internal problems on foreign scapegoats, and a rising level of tension will be the certain outcome of such policies.

Superpower Strategy

In itself, the war presents a puzzle, and appears to be self-contradictory, chaotic and ambiguous to the superpowers. The U.S. does not have formal relations with either Iraq or Iran. (Iraq broke off diplomatic relations with the U.S. during the 1967 Arab-Israeli war, and because of the 1979 seizure of the American Embassy and its occupants, the U.S. broke off relations with Iran in April 1980.) However, the U.S. has professed neutrality since the beginning of the war, and does not supply arms either directly or indirectly to Iran or Iraq. While the two sides slug it out amidst minefields and trenches, however, the U.S. is committed to freedom of navigation in the Gulf, a matter of vital importance to the world community.

An occasional ally of Iraq, the Soviet Union has also maintained neutrality (while facilitating the supply of arms to both sides). If, however, it is Soviet strategy to seize control of the warm water ports in the Indian Ocean, thus attempting to control the Strait of Hormuz, or the oil fields, this is a riskier game than the Soviets can afford to play. As Joshua Epstein, in an article entitled, "Soviet Vulnerabilities in Iran and the RDF Deterrent," maintains, "the Soviets themselves seem to have appreciated these difficulties in a battle assessment of the region as long ago as 1941."[10]

Where the U.S. was concerned, however, despite its proclaimed neutrality, certain elements of U.S. policy toward the war and the region quickly emerged. These consisted of attempts at containment, calls for cessation of hostilities, continued access to oil fields and efforts to avoid a U.S.-Soviet confrontation. For the U.S., the war could not have come at a more opportune moment. It was in the midst of the Iranian hostage crisis. Although the war interrupted the sequence of the secret negotiations going on between the U.S. and Iran, U.S. Deputy Secretary of State Warren Christopher met in Bonn with Sadegh Tabatabai, who had connections with Khomeini, and Tabatabai apparently gave a favorable report to Khomeini on the prospects for a negotiated settlement of the hostage crisis. Taking advantage of the difficult situation in which Iran was involved, the Americans were able to negotiate the release of the hostages from a position of strength: the Iranian demands of $24 billion to cover their frozen assets and the property taken by the Shah and his family was cut to $9.5 billion. Iran paid $3.67 billion in outstanding loans with Western banks.[11]

The war came as welcome news to Americans, who had helplessly watched the terrible hostage drama. Washington, however, remained uncommitted, because of the hostage crisis and also its desire to avoid Soviet intervention. It agreed, however, to supply AWACS and Stinger missiles to Saudi Arabia, along with the military personnel to operate them. This was considered by Iran as favoring the Arab side of the war, although by procuring these sophisticated weapons, Saudi Arabia was attempting to prevent Iran from attacking its oil fields. What had prompted the United States government to deliver the AWACS and the Stingers to Saudi Arabia, however, was the imminent danger, as events showed, of an expanding war in the Gulf. Iraq had reportedly moved some of its commandos and helicopters to Saudi Arabia, the United Arab Emirates, Oman, Kuwait, Jordan, and North Yemen — all friendly Arab countries — in order to attack the Iranian port of Bandar Khomeini. U.S. pressure on Saudi Arabia and the other Arab states forced Iraq to withdraw them.[12]

Linked to this U.S. policy was its desire to secure the Western and Japanese oil supply, and to protect the oil supply route against any perceived Soviet threat. With this objective, the U.S. has reinforced its naval presence in the region, and this reinforced position appears to aim at a possible — but unlikely — blockade.

In addition, the U.S. has acquired military facilities in Oman, Somalia, Kenya — and possibly Egypt and Saudi Arabia — for deployment of CENTCOM, and has conducted training and joint exercises. (Few analysts, nevertheless, believe that CENTCOM would be able to stop a major military move into the Gulf region: in spite of geographical and logistical problems, the Soviets could probably sweep aside any resistance should they decide to move into the region. A major deterrent to such an action would be the economic costs involved in keeping the military operation there in the face of local resistance and guerrilla actions, and this, taken in conjunction with their occupation of Afghanistan, would be a great financial burden. The political costs would also be heavy, for this would further alienate the Muslims of the Middle East and other areas of the world.)

For its part, the Soviet response to the Iran-Iraq war was anticipated by President Leonid Brezhnev in a declaration made in India. The principles of this declaration are:

> (1) Not to set up military bases in the Persian Gulf and on contiguous islands, and not to deploy nuclear or any other weapons of mass destruction there;
>
> (2) Not to use or threaten to use force against the Persian Gulf countries, and not to interfere in their internal affairs;
>
> (3) To respect the status of nonalignment chosen by the Persian Gulf states, and not to draw them into military groupings of which nuclear powers are members;
>
> (4) To respect the inalienable right of the region's states to their natural resources; and
>
> (5) Not to create any impediments or threats to normal trade exchange and the use of maritime communications connecting the states of this region with other countries.[13]

Like the U.S., the Soviet Union can hardly be considered neutral, in view of its readiness to offer arms to Iran and its supply of weapons to Iraq (although it is likely that the Soviet offer of arms to Iran reveals its fear that Tehran might lean toward the West under the pressure of its need for weapons). In addition, the proximity of the Soviet Union to the Middle East leads to important security considerations for Moscow. According to Stephen R. Grummon:

> A ring of states closely tied to the United States to the south of the Soviet Union could force Moscow to divert resources, particularly military resources, to its southern borders. On the other hand, weak and pliant states on the southern border mean that military resources can be channeled to other areas such as Western Europe and China.[14]

Also, the Soviet Union has "taken an unexpected interest in Middle Eastern oil.[15] As far back as 1921, it attempted to establish its claim to northern Iranian oil. During the interwar period, it joined the Western powers in obtaining oil concessions in the Middle East. In 1947 Stalin extracted the promise of oil allotments from Iran as a condition for withdrawing Soviet troops from Azerbaijan, but this fell through mainly because of American and British interference.

Recently, the Soviet Union, unable to meet the growing demands of Eastern Europe, has allowed the Communist bloc to import oil from the Middle East. Eastern European countries have thus made oil deals with the Arab countries as well as with Iran.

Should the U.S. engage in major military operations, the Soviets might provide support to Moscow's clients and take other actions which could lead to a dangerous superpower confrontation. Such an eventuality would spur opposition in Europe and the U.S. itself. (Some European critics of the U.S. say that the U.S. relies on military approaches to the problems of the Gulf and the Middle East because, as Gregory Treverton writes, "...those are easier in domestic politics than, for example, an attempt to move forward on the Palestinian issue.")[16]

The War's Impact on the Combatants

The war is now four years old. What are the combatants doing, and where are they going? Nobody knows. Both Iraq and Iran have given widely conflicting reports of the fighting, which sometimes follows months of relative inactivity. In the interlude, both sides prepare for further onslaughts, and when they return to battlegrounds launch massive air and missile attacks on towns and airfields across their borders.

The war has already been incredibly bloody. (Some estimates put the number of dead to date as high as 500,000, many of them the result of human wave attacks by Iran's *Pasderan* — Khomeini's Revolutionary Guards. Iraq alone has suffered the loss of 50,000 dead and another 50,000 wounded, with another 50,000 taken prisoner).[17] It is possible that Iran, richer, bigger, and more populous, is gradually wearing

Iraq down in this war of attrition, but since Spring 1983, neither side has been able to make progress on the battleground. For its part, Iraq has been in an increasingly difficult financial position, and its major option is to escalate the war in the hope that Iran will be forced to the negotiating table. Its oil route through the Gulf has been blocked, cutting its revenues and forcing the Baghdad government to rely on monetary support from Saudi Arabia and other Arab states in the region. It has received Super Etendard fighter bombers from France, and aims at destroying Iran's Kharg Island oil terminal complex, and has warned foreign tankers not to load oil there.

Iraq's fear of Iran seems, also, to have exacerbated the Arab cold war and the divisions among the Arab states. The six Arab Gulf states, and Morocco, Jordan, and North Yemen have supported Iraq. A pro-Iranian camp, composed of the radical pro-Soviet regimes of Syria, Libya, Algeria and South Yemen has also emerged. This leaves the Arab world in total disarray, lacking purpose, cohesion and a sense of direction. Equally shattering are the effects of the war on Islamic solidarity. The Organization of Islamic Conferences, which had emerged as a force in international politics, has failed to end the conflict.

It is ironic that pro-Soviet Iraq is being backed by its pro-Western Arab brethren, while fundamentalist-theocratic Iran is strongly supported by the pro-Soviet Arab nations. Iraq had expected that its ties with Arabism would prove stronger for the Arabs than other considerations, but the war has proved that this was not to be the case, and even its relations with the Soviet Union seem to be fading.

Some Conclusions

• The Iran-Iraq war ostensibly involves discreet issues on which well-meaning leaders can compromise. These issues are based on religious differences older than the two nations; they are fighting with the passions of a Crusade.

• The war has exposed the prevailing insecurity in the Persian Gulf region. Although the war is not about to end, the prospect of an Iranian victory would give Iran an edge over other states in the region, thereby establishing its supremacy.

• Since Saddam Hussein chose his own time to strike at Iran, he was expected to show some positive results. Instead, what is at stake now is his survival, and Iraq's image in the world. This failure to accomplish declared objectives could unleash an internal uprising in Iraq. In the wake of internal and external criticism of Iraq's ill-conceived war policy, Hussein cannot afford to prolong the war. Nor can he stop fighting. Unless Iran accepts a cease-fire on Iraq's terms, there are no face-saving measures he can take. On the other hand, the longer the war lasts, the weaker will be his position.

• In Iran, the war has had a profound effect on the revolution: it has helped to dissipate opposition to the Khomeini regime and to consolidate the dictatorship of the clerics. Internally, there emerged a curious balance between Iran's different ethnic and ideological groups. Externally, Iran came out of its isolation in the comity of nations. And, against all odds — isolation, non-relations with major powers, a U.S. arms embargo, domestic unrest — Iran has courageously faced up to Iraq's challenge.

• Even when the war ends, Iraq-Iran irredentism will continue to be an important regional flashpoint — unless a Shi'ite administration takes over in Iraq.

• The Iran-Iraq war has shown, beyond any shadow of a doubt, that weak and insecure nations in the Third World, despite their possession of vital resources such as oil, may *not* succeed in involving the superpowers in their conflicts. Despite the strategic importance of the Gulf, both superpowers reacted to the conflict with restraint, if "imperfect neutrality." Each was careful not to intervene, or to get trapped in a war between two countries.

• The Iran-Iraq war has proved that an aggressor may lose international prestige if he does not achieve a quick victory. Although Iraq denies any territorial ambitions regarding Iran's oil province of Khuzistan, the Iraqi offensive has curbed oil production facilities there. (Iraq has also used chemical warfare.)

• The war has demonstrated that the oil-consuming nations *can* absorb the loss of oil from selected countries. Unless combined efforts are made by OPEC, little or no oil supply crises and consequent price escalations can take place. Indeed, contrary to the predictions, the war has encouraged many OPEC and non-OPEC nations to overproduce oil, causing a surprising drop in prices.[18]

• The war, on the other hand, has offered the U.S. and its allies in the International Energy Agency further reason to cooperate in building up more strategic reserves. A sense of healthy competition for exploration, production and procurement of oil has developed in the world.

• Given their basic objectives in the region, both superpowers will try to forge closer ties with their client states. Washington will spare no efforts to obtain more military facilities in Saudi Arabia and other Gulf states, while Moscow will leave no stone unturned to develop strongholds in the region.

• The Palestinian cause has suffered a further setback because of the war. Neither Iraq nor Iran could provide assistance to the beleaguered Palestinians. The war has pushed the Arab-Israeli conflict off center stage.

• Finally, the war is bound to initiate policy changes in the two belligerents. Whatever directions this policy reappraisal takes, because of the long-standing nature of each country's claims and counterclaims, the prospect for a permanent resolution of the conflict in the region appears bleak.

FOOTNOTES

1. See the text of this and other related treaties in Tareq Y. Ismail, *Iraq and Iran: Roots of Conflict* (Syracuse: Syracuse University Press, 1982), pp. 60-68.

2. For further discussion on the Shiite-Sunnite dispute, see Lawrence Ziring, *The Middle East Political Dictionary* (Santa Barbara: ABC-Clio Information Services, 1984), pp. 74-77, 79-83.

3. Ismail, *op. cit.*, p. 5.

4. Stephen R. Grummon, *The Iran-Iraq War: Islam Embattled* (New York: Praeger Publishers, 1982), p. 2.

5. The ideological foundation of the Ba'th party is based on unity, freedom and socialism. When the party came to power in Iraq in 1968, the Ba'th ideology became the foundation of Iraq's foreign policy.

6. Quoted in Shirin Tahir-Kheli and Shaheen Ayubi, *The Iran-Iraq War: New Weapons, Old Conflicts* (New York: Praeger Publishers, 1983), p. 121.

7. See Adda B. Bozeman, "Iran: U.S. FOreign Policy and the Tradition of Persian Statecraft," *Orbis*, Summer 1979, pp. 387-402.

8. The six countries are: Saudi Arabia, Kuwait, United Arab Emirates, Oman, Qatar and Bahrein.

9. Sylvia Ostry "The Economy in 1983: Making Time," *Foreign Affairs*, Vol. 62. No. 3, 1984, p. 536.

10. Joshua Epstein, "Soviet Vulnerabilities in Iran and the RDF Deterrent," *International Security*, No. 6, Fall 1981, pp. 126-158.

11. Sepehr Zabih, *Iran Since the Revolution* (Baltimore: Johns Hopkins University Press, 1982,), p. 60.

12. *Newsweek*, October 13, 1980.

13. A. Alexeyev and A. Fialkovsky, "For a Peaceful Indian Ocean," *International Affairs* (Moscow), February 1981, p. 87.

14. Grummon, *op. cit.*, p. 63.

15. John A. Berry, "Oil and Soviet Policy in the Middle East," *The Middle East Journal*, Spring 1972, p. 149.

16. Gregory F. Treverton, "Defense Beyond Europe," *Survival*, September 1983, p. 220.

17. *Plain Truth*, March 1984.

18. *Durham Morning Herald*, May 28, 1984.

22
Mu'amar Qadhafi's New Islamic Scientific Socialist Society

By Raymond N. Habiby

Al Fateh is an Islamic Revolution.[1]

The Glorious Qur'an is the *Shari'a* [law] of Our New Socialist Society.

These are but two of the many billboards displayed on walls in Libya. The billboards carry either direct quotations from the two *Green Books*[2] authored by Col. Mu'amar Qadhafi, the leader of Libya, or statements offering explanations or expressing support for the two books. No wall in Libya is spared the brush, or the glue, or the paper. Some of these billboards are even floodlit, permanent fixtures.[3]

In green lettering on a white background, the two billboards quoted above best represent the Libyan leader's attempt to convince the Libyans and the outside world that what he is after is the redevelopment of Libya on the basis of the teachings and dogma of Islam or, better still, how he has interpreted the Islamic teachings and dogma. Since his second *Green Book,* entitled, *The Solution of the Problem of the Economy, Socialism,*[4] hit the stands in late 1977, Col. Qadhafi has lost no time in initiating the implementation of its provisions. Because of its radical approach, it has generated a good deal of criticism among a segment of Libyans, and Col. Qadhafi, in his address in Green Square, Tripoli, on November 19, 1978, on the occasion of the Muslim *Curban Bairam,* took this time to respond to his critics. His socialism, he said, was an Islamic scientific socialism. In this most revealing speech, Qadhafi fully developed his ideas about Islam and his interpretation of Islamic teachings and dogma. He ridiculed those who entertain a feeling of guilt whenever they stage a revolution just because they are Muslims: "The truth is that Islam is a great revolution, nay, it is a world revolution," he declared[5] (p. 13). "The voice of truth and the Islamic revolution must echo in every part of the world" (p. 18). As to the part he and Libya would play, "We, here in Libya, are not ashamed to see a progressive revolution start from the extreme left, yet we will never give up Islam, and we will prove to the world that what has become of the Muslims has nothing to do with Islam . . . Precisely on the contrary, Islam calls for progress" (pp. 17-18).

He recognized the "backwardness of the Islamic nation from Indonesia to Mauritania," but "this has nothing to do with Islam" (p. 21). It is the result of a number of factors, not least of them, the wrath of God. "God is angry with those who forsake Islam. His wrath manifests itself in backwardness, hunger, disease, imperialism, reactionary style of life, and a dictatorship installed over them from within" (p. 20). "God subjects them to any of these evils from within or from without" (p. 21).

He was quick, however, to give glad tidings to the Muslims of the world. "The Muslims of North Africa, and of Libya in particular, have awakened, and have raised the banner of the Islamic revolution. Socialism is being realized in Libya. The chains of exploitation are now broken . . . the chains of slavery . . . the chains of humiliation . . . equality is being achieved and we hear again the name of God. True Islam is being revealed, Islam, the religion of freedom, the religion of progress, the religion of equality, the religion of justice . . . " (pp. 21-22).

In this Islamic revolution, which will, in the end, reach the whole world, because Islam is a universal religion, "You Libyans are to play a big role in leading the new revolution," he declared, "the revolution of

---

Dr. Habiby is Associate Professor of Political Science at Oklahoma State University.

the emancipation of Islam, the emancipation of the subjugated masses . . . You are to play a leading role in preaching the Islamic revolt, the new socialism. This is the *jihad* (Holy War). Now there is hope. Now the Islamic revolt has begun. There is hope that Islam will again emerge in its true form'' (pp. 22-3).

Islamic Socialism

In his two *Green Books* and in his speeches, Col. Qadhafi preaches what he calls Islamic socialism. He is a devout practicing Muslim who believes in the universality of Islam — Islam which is both religion and state. He is a ''thinker''[6] who feels he has succeeded in unlocking the truth of God's word as it was revealed in the Qur'an for the benefit of mankind as a whole and the world at large. In his view, he is doing the world a service. Having already solved the problem of democracy in his first *Green Book,* he has now, in his second, solved the problem of the economy — two problems which have defied man's ingenuity over the centuries. To Qadhafi, political democracy and social and economic justice lie in the teachings of true Islam — that is why the early Muslims were progressive: because they understood Islam (p. 23). ''Islam had opened the minds of Muslims in order to enable them to harness the powers of the universe, air, space, the sun, the moon, the stars, oceans, seas, the sky and the earth, and place them in the service of man, for God has said that they are placed in the service of man'' (p. 23). ''It is our duty to show the world that algebra, arithmetic, geometry, astronomy, medicine, watchmaking, are all the products of Islamic thought. Without them, the world would never have arrived at those thresholds of knowledge'' (p.23). Answering his own question as to why the early Muslims had attained all this knowledge, he declared, ''The Qur'an directed their thinking . . . The Qur'an told them: ''Think . . . think'' (p. 23). ''There are secrets in the Qur'an and verses you do not understand so far. There are truths you have not fathomed, truths which made the Muslims who knew the Qur'an attain all the knowledge I have told you about. Now we do not understand the Qur'an, so we do not understand anything . . . This is why we say that artificial rain is wrong and going to the moon is wrong. Muslims should have been the first to do all this'' (p. 24). ''The fact that we do not possess the know-how in atomic energy or technology has nothing to do with Islam'' (p. 10).

Return to Islam, and all the problems of the world will be resolved. This, in essence, is what Qadhafi teaches in his two *Green Books*. As he told his audience in November 1978, ''Why did we say that the Qur'an is the *shari'a* of society? Read the Qur'an and you will find in it all knowledge. It explains everything'' (p. 24). He ridiculed those Muslims who know so much about so many books yet do not know the Qur'an. ''When you leave here,'' he exhorted his listeners, ''read the Qur'an. You will feel as if you are reading a new book, as if you had never heard of it before . . . as if you are reading it for the first time'' (p. 22).

He was also critical of those who claim that socialism leads to underdevelopment. These people are not true Muslims, as were the ''early enlightened Muslims who understood Islam'' (p. 23). He was also critical of those Libyans who, when they have the benefit of the *Green Book,* still yearn for French, Roman, Italian or other law, ''yet claim to be Muslims'' (p. 23). ''Now that the Islamic revolt has begun . . . There is hope that Islam will emerge in its real form'' (p. 23). ''This is great news to the Muslims . . . the rise of the new Islamic scientific socialist revolution in Libya'' (p. 24). Iran, he claimed, would be next in line to embark on this world-wide revolution. ''The Muslim masses in Iran are on the move . . . Perhaps the Muslims of Iran will emerge victorious and a new peoples' revolt will emerge and another Muslim people will be liberated . . . Thus the revolt will spread, the new revolt, the revolt of Islam will spread'' (p. 24).

For his Muslim audience, and Muslim skeptics, he had this note of warning: if the ''revolt of Islam, the revolt of truth, socialism and knowledge fails, the world will say that Islam is a synonym for backwardness, and is a class system. The people will leave Islam — your sons, grandsons — in the future . . . in one hundred years, five hundred years, or a thousand years, none of them will be Muslims'' (p. 24). To those who still insisted that not what the *Green Book* contains but what they preach is Islam, he said, ''Whenever you say this (i.e., their own preaching) is Islam, you are actually driving your children to give up Islam. They will embrace any doctrine which advocates equality'' (p. 19).

Qadhafi was stressing Islam in Libya, a devout Muslim country. And not surprisingly, at the last meeting of the Fourth General Peoples' Congress, Libya's supreme legislative council, in Tripoli in December 1978, a resolution was passed stating that one of the grounds for the abrogation of Libyan citizenship is a person's abandonment of Islam for another religion.[7] Qadhafi's efforts to combine Islam with modernization are not new in the Islamic world. They began when leaders like Jamal al Din al-Afghani and Imam Muhammad Abdu, in the days of the ailing Ottoman state, sought for reasons for the stagnation of the Islamic empire. Those who followed them, to modern times, either advocated a complete separation of state and religion in order to produce a modern state, or the reinterpretation of the Qur'an and the *Hadith* (sayings) to produce a modern Islamic state, which would match or surpass the viability and development of the states of the West and ward off the inroads of imported doctrines like communism, fascism, etc. Col. Qadhafi, who belongs to the latter school of Islamic thought, believes that he has the answer. The Qur'an and Islam, which are universal, are valid for all time and can serve the modern state and society. These are his ''glad tidings to Muslims.''

God and Economics

Col. Qadhafi sees his *Green Books* as the guides to a total Muslim universal emancipatory system. Any similarities with other systems are only incidental. Thus, as bill-boards in Libya proclaim:

The Green Book Provides for the Final Emancipation of Man.

The Green Book is the Guide for the Whole of Humanity on its Ultimate Journey toward Emancipation.

The Green Book is the Hope of the Toiling Masses.

And, stressing the role of Libya, a billboard reads:

Our Nation Heralds to Other Nations the Beginning of the Age of the Masses.

In his November 1978 speech, Qadhafi made full use of the Qur'an and the *Hadith* to answer his critics and to warn them of God's wrath. The Qur'an, he attempted to demonstrate, supports his economic theories and the role of the Muslims. According to *Sura Imran,* III:110, ''You are the best people given to other peoples.'' As in *The Heifer,* V:143, ''You are selected for the mission . . . Muslims have a knowledge of religion and are given a message to the world.''[8] Quoting from *The Bee,* XVI:89, ''For we have sent down to thee a book explaining clearly everything, and a guidance, and a mercy, and glad tidings to the believers,'' he added, for emphasis, ''This book is the Qur'an. This is Islam . . . It is not misery. It is not evil. It heralds prosperity and happiness. To whom? To the Muslims who embraced it'' (p. 8).

He was also critical of those who interpret Islam to mean ''palaces, money, gold, silver, concubines, wives and children,'' yet who claim it is wrong to reach the moon, that heart surgery is wrong and that progress is wrong, and he reminded them of the words of the Qur'an (quoting from *The Covered,* LXXIV:11-17) ''Leave me alone with him I have created, and for whom I have made extensive wealth, and sons that he may look upon, and for whom I have smoothed things down. Then he desires that I should increase! nay, verily, he is hostile to our signs! I will drive him up a hill'' (p. 11).

Then he reminded his audience of what the Prophet Muhammad had said about a society of masters and slaves, of hungry and overfed, and quoted the *Hadith,* ''He who goes to bed with a full stomach and his neighbor is hungry is not one of us'' (pp. 23-4).

To those who see Islam as capitalism, he

said that capitalism stood for hoarding gold and silver and quoted from the Qur'an (*Night Journey,* XVII:16), "And when we desired to destroy a city we bade the opulent ones thereof (i.e., the capitalists) and they wrought abomination therein (the consequence of corrupt capitalism) and its due sentence was pronounced, and we destroyed it with utter destruction" (p. 11).[9] What they had just heard, he reminded his listeners, was the word of God and not that of Mu'amar Qadhafi (p. 12). Then he asked, "But what does the Qur'an say of the rich, of the capitalists, and those who oppose socialism? Socialism is equality, joint participation of the citizens in the wealth of the country. This is socialism. What does the Qur'an say? 'And leave me and those who say it is a lie, who are possessed of comfort, and let them abide for a while. Verily, with us are heavy fetters and hell-fire, and food that chokes, and mighty woe!' (*The Enwrapped,* LXXIII:11-13). This is for those capitalists who deny Islam, and who reject Muhammad . . . This is what God has prepared for them on the day of resurrection . . . They are the capitalists who reject equality with their slaves, with their women, with the poor, and reject equality among the sons of the Islamic nation" (p. 12).

The capitalists "desire to be God on earth, with slaves prostrating themselves before them . . . If you rise against a capitalist and seek equality he replies 'God in Islam forbids this.' He denies you your money and the product of your sweat. The capitalist acquires the money of the poor. He is rich with their money. Isn't this what God meant when he said in the Qur'an: 'Do not devour your wealth among yourselves in vain'? They reverse this verse and then claim that socialism is against religion" (pp. 13-14). At this point, Col. Qadhafi draws a parable: "What," he asks, "was the relationship between the Prophet Muhammad and his uncle, Abu Lahab, or Abu Jahl? It was one of armed struggle. What did God say about Abu Lahab? 'Abu Lahab's two hands shall perish, and he shall perish' (*Abu Lahab,* CXI:1-4). Why? Because 'His wealth will not avail him, nor what he has earned! He shall broil in a fire that flames.' Why did God curse him? Because he was a nonbeliever. He refused to accept the call of justice. Why? Because he was rich. Who said that? God! It is clear that Abu Lahab was rich and because he was rich his eyes, ears and mind were shut. He could not hear the word of truth" (p. 18).

The rich are doomed. Even in Libya, "They enslave the workers, the farmers and everyone of you. Their religion is the dollar. They smuggle out money, gold and foreign exchange. They do not worship God or serve their country or make good the agricultural land they had laid to waste. One owns a building with one hundred apartments, yet another lives in a shack. One has concubines, yet another is unable to secure a loan from a bank to marry one wife. One owns a luxury car which he replaces every month (as in the other rich Arab countries), yet another has to go barefoot. Is the Islam that they want palaces, gold and silver? Didn't God say, 'But those who store up gold and silver and expend it not in God's way — give them glad tidings of grievous woe!' (*Repentence,* IX:34). And what did the Prophet say in the *Hadith?* 'People are equal like the teeth of a comb.' If one lives in a shack, and another in a palace, are they equal? One has so much money, he does not know what to do with it and smuggles it out to Europe, and another does not have the money to feed his children, so he works twenty-four hours a day. Are they like the teeth of the comb? Isn't this a clear departure from the *Hadith"?* (p. 22).

Qadhafi's second *Green Book*[10] presents, again, as his "solution" to the world's ills, his Third Universal Doctrine, which, he claims, is based on natural law and which will replace and supercede all other doctrines and resolve all the global economic problems once and for all, on the basis of "a new socialist society, which is a happy society, because it is free. Happiness will be achieved by satisfying the spiritual and material needs of man" (p. 19). He specifically points out that "The *Green Book* not only solves the problem of material production but also provides a comprehensive solution to the problem of human society, so that the individual may be both materially and spiritually liberated . . . This is the final solution, that will produce happiness" (pp. 26-7). It is to be achieved by "satisfying (man's) needs, eliminating exploitation by others, ending tyranny and finding the way toward a just distribution of society's wealth" (p. 31). "It is the theory of liberating man's needs to emancipate him" (p. 32). "It is the new socialist society, the culmination of man's struggle to attain his freedom and achieve happiness by satisfying his needs" (p. 31). And this "should be done without exploiting or enslaving others" (p. 32).

All previous attempts to resolve this problem have been either cosmetic in nature or merely acts of charity (p. 4). "Even in those cases where ownership is now public ownership, this is not a solution. Here, assuming that the authority which monopolizes ownership is the authority of the people, public ownership is acquired in the interest of society at large and not that of the workers . . . In both public and privately owned establishments, the workers are wage earners" (pp. 5-6). "The solution lies in the abolition of the wage system . . . and a return to the law of nature . . . which provides for equality among the factors of production . . . namely: raw materials, the instrument of production, and the producers . . . Each factor must receive an equal share in production" (pp. 7-8). "The failure of all attempts so far, in so far as they disregarded the law of nature, makes it imperative to return to it" (p. 11).

All previous attempts failed to resolve the problem because of their concentration on the problem of ownership, while the real problem is that of the producers, who have remained wage earners. The lot of the wage earners has improved over the years as a result of the benefits they have secured, but this has not solved the basic problem (pp. 2, 3).

Qadhafi appears to differentiate between three types of economic activity: domestic help, industrial production involving raw materials, machinery and workers and agricultural production involving the utilization of land by man — and now with the help of machinery.

Regarding industrial production, or manufacturing, Qadhafi sees that, in the days of manual production, the process involved two factors: raw materials and man the producer (p. 9). Animals were soon added, to be replaced later by the machine. "Although the factors of production have, over the years, changed quantitatively and qualitatively, the essential role of each factor has not changed (p. 10). This is why it is still necessary for production to be divided into three equal shares: a share for each factor of production. This is so basic to the solution of the problem of the economy because the producers become partners instead of wage earners.

An exception, however, is agriculture as an economic activity. It involves land and man — unless a machine is used. In this case, three factors exist, and production is then split into three equal shares (pp. 13-14).

The same rule does not apply to domestic help, and therefore Qadhafi proposes that domestics be granted the status of public employees (pp. 37-9).

Forms of Ownership

In his new, socialist society, Qadhafi delineates two forms of ownership as being a natural solution. One is a system of private ownership, to satisfy an individual's needs without an exploitation by others. The other is socialist ownership, with the producers becoming partners in production. This socialist ownership replaces the type of private ownership which produced a class of wage earners who had no rights to what they produced (p. 32). What they produced belonged to private ownership. He holds that "the attainment of freedom depends on the extent of man's ownership of what he needs . . . ownership which is personal and is sacredly guaranteed" (p. 33). "Otherwise you will live in a state of anxiety which will do away with your happiness and freedom" (p. 35).

While the *Green Book* does not explicitly say so, it nevertheless appears that all productive or manufacturing industries will come under the socialist type ownership, with the workers (who are to be called producers) as partners and receiving a share of the production. Agricultural land will be "used," that is, possessed by the farmers, but not owned by them. There will be two types of homes, private and socialist-owned. Private ownership will include an individual's house, means of transportation, clothing, food, a livelihood and the like.

Qadhafi desires a happy society; happy because it is free. Freedom lies in liberating man's basic needs. If these needs are controlled, man can be exploited and enslaved. He lists four basic human needs: (1) Food; (2) A dwelling place; (3) Clothing; (4) Transportation (p. 33), but discusses them under three headings, namely, (1) A dwelling place; (2) A livelihood; (3) Means of transportation (pp. 16-18).

An individual should own his own dwelling, but the house he owns should be for his own use and not to rent out. To build and own a house to rent out would be an attempt to control a need for another person (p. 16). Some means of transportation is also a necessity for a man and his family. "You own it, for in a socialist society, no man or authority can possess means of transportation for hire, as this would lead to controlling the needs of others" (p. 18). As to income, or a livelihood, in a socialist society, Qadhafi points out that this should never be a wage or an act of charity, but that it can be owned as private property. "There are no wage earners in a socialist society. There are partners" (p. 17). Your livelihood comes from a partnership in a production unit, or the use of agricultural land, or the performance of a public service."

In this new society, man will have three alternatives. (1) He can be self-employed in order to guarantee his material needs; (2) He can work for a socialist corporation and be a partner in production; (3) He can perform a public service to society, which would then provide him with his material needs (pp. 19-20). In all this, however, "man's legitimate economic activity is solely the satisfaction of his needs. No person has the right to economic activity that provides him with more than is necessary to satisfy his needs, as any amount he acquires in excess of his needs is actually taken from the needs of others" (pp. 20-21).

A society's wealth must be equally distributed, each citizen receiving one unit. "The disabled and the insane have the same share as the healthy" (p. 30). If this system is not followed, there will be rich and poor, and exploitation will prevail (p. 29). Individuals can save as much as they want for their own needs (p. 30) but "what is left beyond the satisfaction of individual needs shall remain the property of the members of society" (p. 29). "There is still room for the skillful and the industrious. While they do not have the right to acquire the share of others, they can utilize their skill in managing what they receive to satisfy their needs and benefit from that. (pp. 20-30). Individual differences in wealth, in the new socialist society, are "only permissable for those who perform a public service. Society will allocate for them a share of wealth commensurate with that service" (p. 31). He does not clarify, however, whether this distribution of society's wealth will take into consideration and include what a person will acquire as income from permissable economic pursuits.

Qadhafi also answers two anticipated criticisms of his system. One might say, he writes: The present system is producing, so why change it? And one might ask, also, whether his system provides an incentive to produce. A level of production is attainable even under a bad system, he responds, because it is a matter of survival. A person has to work in order to obtain some income to live on. "The best proof is that in capitalist societies production accumulates and expands in the hands of a few owners who do not work but exploit the efforts of others who are obliged to produce in order to survive" (p. 26). Nevertheless, he claims, a system of no wages, in which the producer is a partner in production and, as such, receives an equal share with the other two factors of production provides a system of better incentives. In the present system, he points out, working for wages has failed to solve the problem of increasing and developing production (p. 26).

In a special section on agricultural land, Qadhafi claims that this land "is no one's property. Everyone can use it by working, farming or using it as pasture for their flocks. A man can use this land so long as he does not employ others, and to the extent that he satisfies his needs. His heirs can inherit the use of the land, and can use it in the same manner to satisfy their needs. In all this, man has possession, but not ownership, of the land (pp. 18-19).

Another section deals with domestic workers, or help, paid or unpaid. He calls them the slaves of our modern age. In a socialist society of partnership in production, the natural, socialist law does not apply to them. The solution is, therefore, that "the house shall be serviced by its occupants." Necessary services are to be provided "not by servants, but by employees, who can receive promotion as house workers and can enjoy social and material safeguards like any public service employee" (p. 39).

With all these changes, workers will cease to be called "workers" and will be referred to instead as "producers." In Qadhafi's modern society, the masses of ignorant, illiterate workers will be replaced by a limited number of technicians, engineers and scientists. This will mean the gradual disappearance of trade unions, which will be replaced by professional and technical syndicates (p. 15).

Qadhafi sees, in the growing power of the trade unions in capitalist societies, the means of transforming these capitalist societies of wage earners into societies of partners (p. 35). And, "sooner or later, under the guidance of the *Green Book,* a revolution to achieve socialism will begin, with the producers (the former workers) seeking to acquire a share in what they produce. They will "change their demands, and instead of asking for increased wages, will demand a share in production" (p. 36).

The final step will arrive in a socialist society when profit and money disappear. With full production, the material needs of society will be satisfied. In the final stage, profit will disappear automatically, and there will be no need for money (p. 36). Qadhafi does not explain, however, how his society will function without the institution of money as a means of exchange. And as to profit, he cautions that this is still the driving economic force in pre-socialist societies, so its abolition should not be a step lightly taken. "It must be the result of the development of socialist production. The endeavor to increase profit will ultimately lead to its disappearance" (p. 37).

Turning Theory Into Practice

At best, the *Green Book* is a theoretical discussion of selected aspects of the problem of the economy. It lacks precise detail as to how these theories will be applied; how necessity is to be measured; how the redisposition of land, houses and work will take place in a real situation, both today and in the future, in an ever-changing society. Yet, in Libya, steps have already been taken to implement Qadhafi's second *Green Book.* All persons living in rented homes have become the owners of these homes. Persons owning more than one house or apartment have had to choose which one they wished to retain for themselves and their children. In a major speech on September 1, 1978[11] Qadhafi called on the workers of Libya to begin the implementation of the *Green Book's* guidelines by taking over their factories, and thus becoming partners in them. The Libyan newspapers have, since then, and on a daily basis, devoted special sections to reports of these take overs. Plans are in progress for the reassignment of agricultural land and the implementation of the *Green Book's* guidelines dealing with the communications system.

All this explains the flood of billboards one sees in Libya, proclaiming:

Partners, Not Wage Earners.

The House Belongs to its Occupant.

Equality, Equality.

Victory for the Workers Over the Capitalists.

Freedom for the Toilers — Freedom for the Masses.

Authority in the Lands of Al Fateh Resides in the People, and No One Else.

On December 23, 1978, *Al Fajr Al Jadid,* Libya's leading newspaper, carried this front page, four column headline:

Textile Workers in France's Department of the Loire Occupy Factory in Response to the

Workers' Revolution in *Al Jamahiriya* (Libya).

The story began: "The revolution of the workers in the land of the great *Al Fateh* has had a response in France, where the textile workers in France's Department of the Loire occupied the factory." Following a lengthy report of the incident, *Al Fajr Al Jadid* concluded:

The action of the French workers was a decisive rejection of the oppressive relationship between workers and capitalists in exploitative capitalist society. These are the relationships that the workers in *Al Jamahiriya* have trampled underfoot and destroyed forever, and that are now replaced by the relationship of partners, not wage earners!

FOOTNOTES

1. Literally, *Al Fateh* means "the beginning," in Arabic. *Al Fateh* of any given month is the first of the month. The Libyan Revolution was started on September 1, 1969, so it is regularly referred to as *Al Fateh*.

2. For a discussion of the first *Green Book,* see R. Habiby, "Qadhafi's Thoughts on True Democracy," *Middle East Review,* Vol. X, No. 4, Summer, 1978, pp. 29-35.

3. I saw so many billboards in Libya during my short visit there, December 17-23, 1978. They were in Tripoli International Airport, in my hotel, added to the names of stores, and everywhere.

4. The first edition in Arabic is dated November 1977 and is published by The General Printing, Distribution and Advertising Co., *Jamahiriya* (Libya).

5. This and other quotations from the speech are from the Arabic text of Col. Qadhafi's November 10, 1978 speech in Green Square, Tripoli, as published and distributed by the Libyan Government.

6. The back cover of the Arabic text of the Second *Green Book* says, "The Thinker, Mu'amar Qadhafi, having given us the final solution to the problem of democracy in the first chapter of the *Green Book,* will, in the second chapter . . . " etc.

7. *Al Fajr Al Jadid* (Libya's main Arabic Daily), December 21, 1972, p. 2.

8. All the translations of the Qur'an are from *The Koran,* translated by E. H. Palmer, Oxford University Press, London, 1960. (First published in 1900).

9. Words added to the Qur'anic verse in parenthesis are Qadhafi's.

10. I have compared the Arabic and the English texts published by the Libyan Government. The many mistakes in the English text made me turn to the Arabic. All references in this article from this point on are to the Arabic edition, dated November, 1977 and published by the General Printing, Distribution and Advertising Co., *Jamahiriya* (Libya).

11. *Al Fajr Al Jadid,* September 2, 1978. "The revolution is workers taking over all the production positions in the country. They should advance as of today to free themselves from wages, the chains of bondage and the domination of others."

23

Political Instability in Saudi Arabia and Its Implications

By Bernard Schechterman

Whether one employs a Brintonian, Johnsonian, or Marxian model for an analysis of the stability vs. destabilization dynamics[1] in Saudi Arabia, the expectation points towards "a revolutionary ferment" in the foreseeable future for that society. This paper examines the extent to which destabilization tendencies have evolved.

A major caveat that needs to be emphasized is the existing controversy over this very issue in some sophisticated circles. In *Adelphi Paper No. 158,* Adeed Dawisha[2] confronts this issue in terms of the degree of instability in Saudi Arabia and the prospective implications. On balance, after acknowledging considerable specifics of destabilization, his analysis and conclusions support stability as a more likely outcome. In fairness to Dawisha, it should be understood that he leaves many concerns open-ended and the prospects for an opposite conclusion remain ever-present.

On the other hand, the Daniel Southerland, "Spy War" series in the *Christian Science Monitor*[3] refers to a CIA study prepared by a former Foreign Service officer which greatly offended the Saudi regime and which saw to it that this study was suppressed. The CIA study is still unavailable.[4]

Malcolm Peck notes that Saudi Arabia has been an overlooked (or under-analyzed) society in the Western social science literature.[5] This, he says, has been a shortcoming of the West and therein lies the blame for the misperceptions that have ensued. My contention is diametrically the opposite — the Saudis have deliberately chosen to avoid study and analysis of their system. This has been accomplished by their insistence on the dissemination of information about themselves via their own controlled media, precluding outsiders from news coverage, or allowing only confirmed admirers to observe and comment about their society.[6] Of course, outsiders, including Westerners, have made their own errors, especially in failing to perceive "the elliptical reasoning process" employed by Saudi officials in reaching, enunciating, and implementing policies of importance to themselves as well as others.[7] My own analysis rests its case on research, data and interpretation, using such sources as *Afro-Asian Affairs* and *Middle East Intelligence Survey,*[8] which Dawisha also used — and sometimes neglected to use.

The Inefficiency of the Regime

Very few people remember that Saudi Arabia is a state that takes its name from an indigenous tribal family from the Riyadh region (and the Saudis did not originate in this city — if one traces their genealogy far back enough). In this light, the Royal Family has some presumptuous views about itself and others, and attention should be directed to the issue of why and how one particular family came into prominence in a geographic area populated by a multiplicity of other tribal groupings and principalities. These various groupings existed long before the Saudi regime came into being, and the success of the House of Saud was the result of both conquest (Abd al-Aziz, 1902-1953, was the main architect of the Saudi state) and British policy in the area.[9] The pattern of conquest and consolidation had to overcome historical, demographic, geographic and cultural differences, especially in the major Arabian Provinces of Hejaz, Asir and al-Hasa. The use of force, alliances, family

---

Dr. Schechterman is Professor of Political Science at the University of Miami, Coral Gables. He has published articles in numerous academic journals.

This paper is based on a paper presented at the Third Annual Meeting of the Third World Conference at Omaha, Neb., in October 1980.

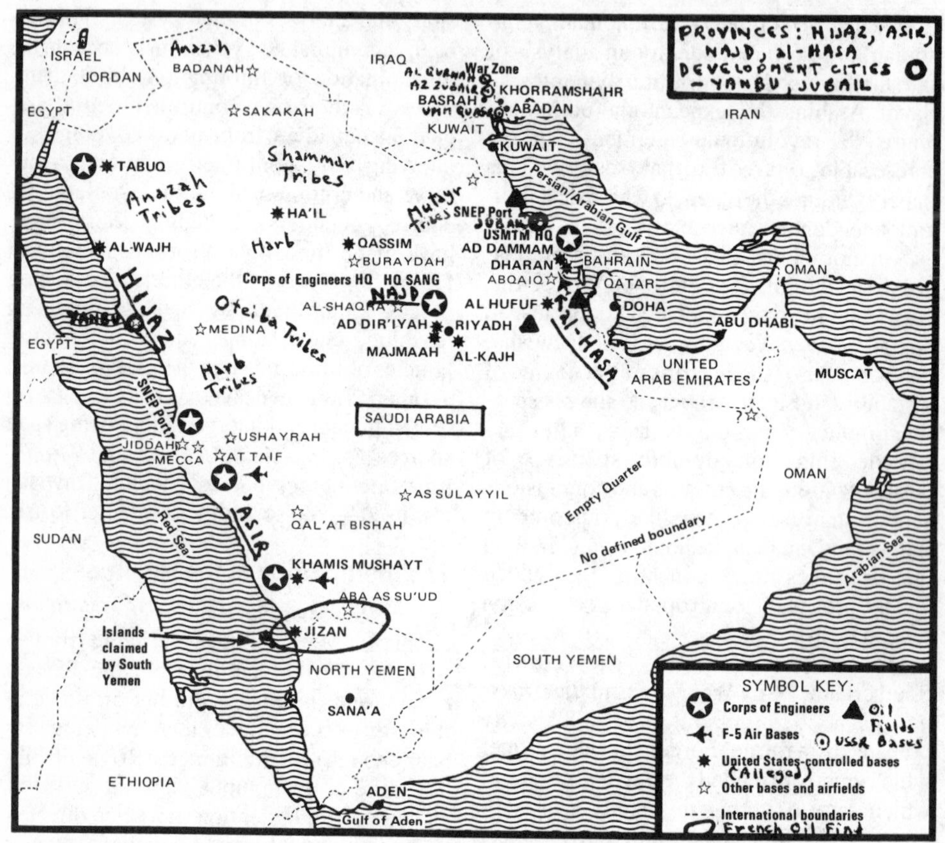
PROVINCES: HIJAZ, 'ASIR, NAJD, al-HASA
DEVELOPMENT CITIES — YANBU, JUBAIL
ISRAEL
JORDAN
EGYPT
IRAQ
IRAN
KUWAIT
BADANAH
SAKAKAH
TABUQ
HA'IL
AL-WAJH
QASSIM
BURAYDAH
Corps of Engineers HQ
HQ SANG
AL-SHAQRA
AD DIR'IYAH
RIYADH
MAJMAAH
AL-KAJH
MEDINA
JIDDAH
MECCA
USHAYRAH
AT TAIF
AS SULAYYIL
QAL'AT BISHAH
KHAMIS MUSHAYT
ABA AS SU'UD
JIZAN
Islands claimed by South Yemen
NORTH YEMEN
SANA'A
SOUTH YEMEN
ADEN
Gulf of Aden
ETHIOPIA
SUDAN
Red Sea
SAUDI ARABIA
Empty Quarter
No defined boundary
War Zone
KHORRAMSHAHR
BASRAH
ABADAN
Persian/Arabian Gulf
SNEP Port
USMTM HQ
AD DAMMAM
DHARAN
BAHRAIN
ABQAIQ
QATAR
AL HUFUF
DOHA
OMAN
ABU DHABI
UNITED ARAB EMIRATES
MUSCAT
Arabian Sea
Anazah Tribes
Shammar Tribes
Harb
Oteiba Tribes
Harb Tribes
Mutayr Tribes
HIJAZ
NAJD
'ASIR
al-HASA
SNEP Port
SYMBOL KEY:
Corps of Engineers
F-5 Air Bases
United States-controlled bases (Alleged)
Other bases and airfields
International boundaries
Oil Fields
USSR Bases
French Oil Find

inter-marriages and vassalage-loyalty arrangements produced the modern version of Saudi rule in the peninsula.[10]

The Saudi Royal Family's perception of its own indisputable leadership and the same perception by outsiders seemed warranted because of the long-term isolation of Saudi Arabia and the sustainment of its "traditional society."[11] Once the impact of a petroleum (Westernization and modernization) revolution overtook Saudi society in the post-World War Two period, the prevailing balance in tribal relations came under severe stress. A most obvious source of tension was the internal distribution of the accrued wealth (in fact, largesse) by the central Riyadh regime in such areas as Asir, Hejaz, and al-Hasa. In the old traditional society, a new awareness and a new set of expectations might not have risen, but between economic development planning and security concerns, the Saudis simultaneously introduced or withheld accumulated surpluses, each policy producing destabilizing tendencies in these Provinces. The military base structure and the concentrated economic development in cities like Yanbu and Al-Jubayl challenged traditional value systems or raised the issue of discriminatory patterns in the use of petro-dollars.[12] Al-Hasa had been one of the earliest impacted Provinces by virtue of the great oil fields that opened in the vicinity. The two major development cities of Yanbu and Al-Jubayl affected al-Hasa and the Hejaz. Asir, more recently, has been opened up to newer economic and political forces that have produced destabilizing tendencies, such as the dispute with the Yemen Arab Republic, and the French discovery of an oil field in the region. Added to these situations is the extended growth of military installations, drawing in new indigenous elements and external populations, particularly from the United States. This normally static society is being subjected to considerable pressure, as well as increasing demands directed toward the central regime.

Combined with these developments is the continued or reemergent ethnocentrism of the past in the form of "liberation movements," supported in some instances by the Iraqis since 1958, which threaten to subvert the Saudi monarchy and the affiliation system. Externally supported efforts are often undertaken as part of the "progressive versus conservative regimes" struggle throughout the Middle East.

Closely related to the problem of economic planning and distribution of the regime's largesse has been the degree of corruption among the members of the Royal Family and others associated with them in the ruling enterprise. The issue is not one of whether such behavior has occurred, but how extensive it has been and its implications for the stability of the system. Basic data reflecting petro-dollar surpluses versus the Treasury shortfalls for economic development plans, investments, and distribution of largesse have been extremely revealing for the years 1977 and 1978.[13] Given the understanding and expectations that surpluses would either grow or consistently be available in the near future,[14] the negation of these facts has had dire repercussions in Saudi society. There had been little dispute that surpluses, among various economic stratagems, would be invested abroad in secure investments once indigenous needs had been met. There was a realistic appreciation that the "absorptive capacity" of Saudi Arabia militated against the use of all surplus capital. However, the scale of "embezzlement" came to public view when the fulfillment of the (second) Economic Development Plan of 1975-1980 appeared unlikely.[15] Insufficient attention has been paid to the corruption factor—the siphoning off of petro-dollars, which are cached abroad. Internal investigations of the scandal in the ranks of the Saudi leadership has led to considerable infighting and disunity in the Royal Family, and this in addition to the challenges in the Provinces and in other spheres.

The most sympathetic observers have had to acknowledge the widespread corruption among the ruling elites and the behavior of princes abroad has produced negative reactions within the government and outside the country. In Saudi Arabia the Great Mosque Insurrection of November 1979 included, in the allegations made by the insurrectionists, charges of corruption and the perversion of Islamic values by those in power,[16] though the insurrectionists have been characterized as religious zealots, despite the fact that there was evidence of politically motivated zealousness as well.[17] The full implication of the "religious thesis" has been overlooked in all the reports and analyses. Religious dissent in this major incident challenges the widely accepted thesis that the Saudi regime's stability is different from the Iranian case, where the struggle was primarily between the religious and the secular. What has been overlooked by those who stress the proximity, if not interdependence of the Royal Family and the religious leadership in Saudi Arabia, is a common political dynamic for all ideological views and movements. People are always available who are prepared to "outradicalize" the in-group or established ideological representatives. Islamic "purists" can always find a basis for criticism, out-promising the "ins," and insisting the established religious-political leadership has strayed from the "true path" (i.e., they have become corrupt). Contrary to the consoling thesis of its inherent religious values, the Saudi regime is always vulnerable to those who present themselves as the "true believers." "Unfaithfulness" will be determined by Islamic fundamentalists who choose to employ their own criteria and not that of the Royal Family and the Islamic establishment,[18] especially when a frightening transition is faced by tradition-oriented (and thus resistant) segments of the society.

Persistent repetition of allegations of corruption, some soundly based, and acts that flow from them, may ultimately force the religious leadership to disassociate itself from the regime and become a truly independent and questioning force in Saudi society for the sake of its own survival. What has begun to emerge seems to be a "no win" situation for the current regime since it needs the legitimizing support of the religious hierarchy but seeks certain contrary secular developments within the social order. The political dynamics of destabilization are built into the predicament, regardless of the rationalizations and interpretations provided by the regime or outside observers.[19]

In the narrowest sense of a specialized civilian bureaucracy there is no reliable evidence of singular disobedience by middle or lower echelons. The basic problem is a manpower problem and the inefficiency of policy implementation that flows from it. Saudi Arabia has some very well educated top echelon bureaucrats but is grossly deficient in middle and lower managerial personnel, both in numbers and quality. The restrictions on female employment dictated by Islam diminishes the manpower pool even further.

Yet, failure to achieve development projects is only partially explained by the manpower problem. Rule by a monarch (currently King Khalid), a Crown Prince (Fahd), and a Royal Family (some 4,000 Princes), has not always been conducive to homogeneity of interest perception and policy responses. Under an assertive and capable monarch such as the late King Faisal, the unity and direction of the Royal Family was usually beyond dispute. What has gone unheeded is the significance of the loss Saudi Arabia suffered when King Faisal was assassinated, in view of the confusion, factionalism and disunity that have emerged since 1975. The centrality of an outstanding "patrimonial leader" in both a traditional and transitional society is well illustrated in James Bill and Carl Leiden's *Politics in the Middle East*. It is very arguable that a major decline of the Saudi regime may have begun with the loss of this outstanding leader. However, the fact that he was assassinated by one of the younger princes, even if internecine vengeance is the accepted motive, supports the existence of discontent even under that venerated King, and demonstrates that historicity and conflictual family relations have never been completely resolved amongst the Royal Family.[20]

The successor monarch, King Khalid, is in poor health and has lacked the talent, assertiveness, or unifying impetus of his predecessor or other great monarchs in the history of the Saudi state. Given a weak central figure, the struggle between the "key princes," especially in the light of the Crown Prince's personal ambition, has led to a variety of contradictory decisions on a multiplicity of vital issues confronting the regime. Ministerial departments have been used in these fratricidal struggles.[21] The princely conflicts, coalitions, shifting alliances, contradictory promulgations, have left the regime uninformed or virtually paralyzed at some critical moments threatening the regime and has reduced its credibility among sections of the population and other Arab states.

The military forces in Saudi Arabia have been relatively small, but this fact only tends to heighten the importance of any section of the military that has revolted against the regime, or that opposes some specific policies. In July 1977, 1,300 army personnel were arrested out of a total force structure of 61,500.[22] Not all those arrested were army officers, thus indicating the presence of civilian bureaucratic allies and local elements of popular dissent who express their opposition through these new elites. The discontent in al-Hasa and the Hejaz Provinces has already been mentioned. The common denominator has consistently been discontent with the regime and its economic policies. Military personnel trained in the United States, or by American personnel in Saudi Arabia, or because of contacts with other American civilians under contract[23] have developed the perspective to question and challenge the Saudi system. This pattern of behavior is consistent with political development dynamics elsewhere among less developed nations. Roughly 40,000 American personnel are involved in training programs and other projects in Saudi Arabia, and the number is alleged to have been as high as 100,000.[24] The ramifications may best be summarized by the Saudi assertion that the Americans may be the greatest threat to their society.[25] They are undoubtedly correct in assuming that the new educated military (and civilian) elites could not readily acquiesce to the old system and would become destabilizing advocates of change.[26] The fact that traditional tribal elements loyal to the regime, the Oteiba and the Kharb, who form part of the support base for the National (White) Guard which protects the Royal Family were among the Great Mosque Insurrectionists indicates the deteriorating situation in Saudi society.[27]

Aside from military insurgency in recent years, other dissenting groups have also been active. The Hejaz and al-Hasa "liberation movements" are active groups among the indigenous population and exiles living in nearby Iraq.[28] In 1975, a formal Communist Party emerged.[29] Foreign workers, because of their poor working conditions and bad treatment have also engaged in some forceful demonstrations, some verging on revolt.[30] The regime has been able to defuse some of this tension and conflict by deporting and replacing the dissidents with other workers,[31] but Saudi Arabia's dependency on foreign workers cannot be overcome. Worse still, in the Eastern Province oil fields, the workers are 45 percent Shi'ites with strong Iranian attachments and are usually Saudi citizens. During the Great Mosque Insurrection, which involved attempts by Khumayni supporters in Haj to demonstrate, the oil workers in the Al Qatif (Eastern Province) area erupted in support of Iran and against the Saudi regime.[32]

Identifying and delineating the challenges to the regime reveals only half the Saudi problem. Equally important has been the regime's responses to the explosions and the undertow of dissent. The inefficiency or ineffectiveness of the Saudi internal security capability was pointed up by the need to reorganize the entire security system under Prince Turki during the 1977-1980 strife.[33] This was attributed to the information gaps and ineffectiveness of the Saudi regime's reactions. The information gaps reflected Saudi geography and demography (East-West population concentrations, and separation by desert and steppe terrain) and the inadequacy of a national communications network to serve the government.[34]

The refusal of military personnel in some instances to put down brother officers, as in the al-Hasa revolts, only exacerbated the disobedience and loss of credibility of the regime. The need to call in outside Arab advice at the highest levels[35] and the use of Jordanian troops in the Hejaz Province to quell military revolt,[36] demonstrated both the pervasiveness and significance of the disaffection and the vulnerability of the regime. The use of French personnel to complete the reconquest of the Great Mosque after the National Guard had failed to do so again highlighted the incompetence of the internal security system and the desperation that permitted this sacrilege —

the presence of non-Muslim French troops — to be committed on holy ground. The displeasure of the *ulama* was predictable, despite their close ties with the regime. What might be labelled as an overreaction (if one discounts the desperation that forced the regime to call in French troops) was carried out in full view of 50,000 pilgrims, who were virtual hostages of the zealots.[37] Calculate the irreparable harm done to the Saudi regime by the awareness of the local population and the foreign pilgrims of the events, and the derogatory reports about the National Guard that were later disseminated everywhere.

Aside from the reorganization of the internal security system, the regime also reacted by introducing liberalization measures. One of these was the deliberate extension of government beyond the traditional *Majlis,* in order to facilitate contact with the views and feelings of the people. What was clearly evident was a "concessional pattern" in the form of an announcement that a Consultative Council and Assemblies were to be established to broaden representation and improve channels of communication. In the subsequent factional infighting between the key princes and the monarch, the Council became a casualty and today remains but a promise of the future. Confusion reigned after the shock of the assault on the Great Mosque, and there is little evidence that the leadership has since clarified itself and its policies.

Another critical fallout from the internal dissent was the major effort by Crown Prince Fahd, appointed successor to the King, to replace him by forcing the latter's early retirement. The public rationale was the illness of the monarch; the greater truth was the King's weaker capabilities. The turbulence of alliance-building, position-jockeying, criticism and countercriticism among the key Princes (Sultan, Saud, Turki, Naif, Ahmed, Abdullah, Muhammad, etc.) has tended to play into the Crown Prince's hands, but the struggle still remains unresolved. What is pertinent, however, is the continuous disarray of the leadership and its weakened responses to internal, external, and fraternal issues and tensions.

External Threats

The most publicized threats to the Saudi regime have been external. From a Saudi public rhetoric perspective, the primary threat has been equated with radicalism associated directly or indirectly with Communist (and atheist) USSR. Indirect but more immediate threats have revolved around the Peoples Democratic Republic of Yemen (South Yemen hereafter) vis-a-vis the Yemen Arab Republic (Sana) and Oman, both allies and/or client states of Saudi Arabia. Up to and including mid-1970 the South Yemenis sponsored and supported the Popular Front for the Liberation of the Gulf (PFLOAG) in the Dhofar War against Oman and Muscat. Incursions and intimidations by South Yemen against the Sana regime of North Yemen were intended to detach it from Saudi influence and achieve a unification with the radical South in a position of preeminence. The Saudi-sponsored version of the unification process, in recent years, coupled with considerable Saudi largesse, was intended to cause a defection of the Marxist state from USSR influence. The loss of North Yemen to South Yemen control would, of course, be a tremendous defeat for Saudi Arabia and its regional buffer state policies.[38]

Other indirect but very immediate threats to the Saudis include Ethiopia's activities as a Soviet client state in the Horn of Africa. The Saudis, in conjunction with the Egyptians, Sudanese, Somalians and the new government of Djibouti, all Islamic states, have sought to stress that the adjacent Red Sea must be viewed as an Arab lake. Ethiopia's threats against some of these states tend to negate the concept and its realization. The Ba'thist radicalism of Syria and Iraq, plus their connections over the years with the USSR, have been of serious concern to Saudi Arabia on its northern frontier, especially in its client states of Jordan, Kuwait, and the various Gulf Principalities. This radical threat pattern is in keeping with Nasser's earlier intervention in Yemen and the Arabian Peninsula which in its time threatened the Saudi regime.[39] Terrorist radicalism has also been of great concern to the Saudis whether sponsored by the Iraqis, Libyans, or the PLO. All have made their influence felt at one time or another in activities directed against the Saudi regime. The 125,000 Palestinian workers in Saudi Arabia have been of particular concern to the government. Drawing on the Kuwaiti experience, the Saudis have much to fear from them, especially the subversion of their society.[40]

The overall perspective and concern of the Saudi regime about the radical tendencies connected in some manner or form with the Soviet Union is not solely based on religious principles. Recognizing the geopolitical and strategic vulnerability of their oil-based economy and society, they see the USSR as the most dangerous threat to their regional role and to the very survival of their regime.

The range of external threats goes beyond communist-influenced radicalism, or even the long-standing "progressives vs. conservatives" (or radical vs. moderate) struggle in the Middle East. Iraq in recent years has evidenced hegemonic aspirations among the Arabs, placing itself on a direct collision course with the Saudis, the keepers of the Islamic faith and the leading power in the Arabian Peninsula.[41] And in the course of post-war politics, Egypt, Iraq, and the PLO have viewed the takeover of Saudi oil facilities as a solution to their dire economic development needs and/or fulfillment of a variety of political aspirations.[42]

The most significant threat to the Saudi regime has come from the Iranian crisis. During the Shah's rule the Saudis often felt uncomfortable with his hegemonic aspirations and activities in the Gulf Region (especially in the Straits of Hormuz, and the seizure of three islands there). Little seems to have changed under the Khumayni regime, except that the basis of the Iranian threat has grown more diverse. Using the Islamic Shi'ite faith as a legitimizing factor, geo-political claims by the Iranian regime have been directed against Bahrain and other Gulf Principalities with substantial Persian and Shi'ite populations.[43] The entire buffer-clientele system set up by the Saudis in the Gulf is being threatened, let alone Saudi Arabia's Eastern Provinces' oil fields.

The greatest paradox is that the fall of the Shah, whose regime caused concern to the Saudis and the Gulf states, has produced an additional threat to their stability. As a powerful pro-Western state Iran, under the Shah, served as something of a protector against Soviet activities in the area. The manner in which the regime was toppled and the inferred loss of United States credibility in failing to support an ally, has been viewed as an intensification of the Soviet threat. The invasion of Afghanistan, Iraqi assertiveness, the Yemeni Crisis, the crisis in the Horn of Africa, etc., have made the Saudis overly concerned about the reliability of the United States as a dependable partner. The subsequent opening of talks, for the first time, with the Soviet Union was the first evidence of a possible self-Finlandization, (i.e., neutralization) of Saudi policy.[44] Even the Saudi willingness to draw rhetorically closer to Iraq, a Soviet client state, was part of a multiple strategy for dealing with these external threats and enhancing the regime's ability to survive.

Certainly, none of these activities were intended to discard or undercut the more traditional United States option and relationship as providing a critical means of political survival. The Saudis have used a variety of policies to continue, sustain, or enhance the United States card for their own stability and survival. In addition to pumping more oil, they have purchased more military hardware than ever before, and asked for a greater American presence in their country,[45] and allowed an American military infrastructure to evolve secretly throughout the country.

By deliberately focussing on the Palestinian problem, the Saudis hope to deflect attention from themselves, but their use of this issue as a unifying force for the Arab and Islamic worlds has consistently run aground on the shoals of national interests and inter-Arab clashes — Iraq vs. Iran, Morocco vs. Algeria, Egypt vs. Libya, Syria vs. Iraq, etc. Contrary to expectations, the unification thrust and the Palestinian issue have intensified the pressure on the Saudi regime, since greater commitments and choices between rivals have been demanded of them. Over the course of Saudi history, such developments and situations have increasingly drawn that country out of its sought-after isolation. They have grown in importance as a destabilizing factor for the Saudi regime and system, and their impact is likely to increase rather than to abate.

Economic Pressures

On the surface, the Saudis have the distinct advantage of being a surplus capital society. This idyllic circumstance has been jeopardized by the population variable and the intensity of security concerns. Deficient in an adequate labor force, undercut even further by the Wahhabi strictures against the employment of women, the qualitative skills shortages have made the Saudis dependent on outsiders, especially Americans and Europeans. They are unable to isolate their own trained personnel and public from infectious outside ideas, and have opted for a time-worn policy of neo-Islamism[46] as the solution to this dilemma of reconciling Islamic values and controlled economic and military modernization. Past precedents seem to doom this policy to failure and an ultimate choice between a retreat into Islam or a predominant secularization of the society. Both options are fraught with danger because of the resistance to change on the one hand and the power struggle inherent in a pluralistic, secularist society on the other. On balance, given the extensiveness and intensity of the Saudi activities in their modernization efforts, the expectations unleashed seem irreversible without immense repression.

Of course, the Saudi regime insists that the dilemma has been faced and that its policies have succeeded, and offers examples of how opposition was defused and mobility provided by coopting dissidents into the regime and the system.[47] Royalists and non-royalists stress their ability to function in schizoid fashion, Westernized when abroad, Islamic at home. Yet while the formal data on cooptation until the early 1970s seems to uphold this interpretation, the number and type of leadership of the revolts in the 1977-1980 period refutes this contention.

Class Conflicts

The autocratic system of a "patrimonial leader" in Saudi Arabia has always been tempered by the accessibility of the regime to tribes and individuals with grievances. However, the era of simple problems associated with a traditional society is gone. A multiplicity of decision-makers for an increasingly complex social order have taken over, and various members of the Royal Family have been appointed to Provincial Governorships and key ministerial positions as guarantees of loyalty to the autocracy. The single, "patrimonial leader" — the King — has given way to a decentralized bureaucracy or oligarchy of the Royal Family, and the efficiency of this decentralized bureaucracy or oligarchy has unfortunately served as the basis for separately emerging power centers for the key princes and has intensified the contradictions in policies and views. Less — or, very little — of this existed under the rule of King Faisal.

Most Saudi citizens have not been impacted by, or have not benefitted from the modernization revolution. The unrest in the Asir Province, joined together with the agitation and claims of elements in al-Hasa and the Hejaz, points up the great discrepancy between the urban (including those in the newly created cities) and the rural populations.[48] The decentralized nature of the Saudi society provides an additional advantage to the discontented. A lot of wishful thinking and flight from reality pervades the Saudi leadership and postpones realistic responses that might enhance its chances of survival.

The Psychological Dimension

Saudi Arabia is confronted by a combination of developments that threaten the survival of its regime. The unleashing of economic and social expectations based on capital accumulation and disbursement is widespread in the urban sectors of the society and is expanding its impact on the hitherto dormant rural sectors. The number and geographic distribution of flare-ups has made most of the society aware of the general discontent. The inefficiency of the regime's response has only encouraged further incidents and increasing contempt for the royal autocracy. The regime's anticipation that the newly educated elites would uniformly support it has been punctured by the challenges of these very people. Traditional values have also become the basis of opposition, placing the Saudi regime in a squeeze from polar positions at each end of a political value continuum.

FOOTNOTES

1. Crane Brinton, *Anatomy of Revolution* (Englewood Cliffs, N.J.: Prentice-Hall, 1938); Chalmers Johnson, *Revolutionary Change* (Boston: Little, Brown & Co., 1966); R. H. Carew Hunt, *The Theory and Practice of Communism* (London: G. Bles, 1950)

2. Adeed Dawisha, "Saudi Arabia's Search for Security," *Adelphi Papers* ;158 (London: International Institute for Strategic Studies, 1979-1980).

3. Daniel Southerland, "The Mideast — How the West was wrong," Spy War Series, *Christian Science Monitor,* Sept. 26, 1980, 13.

4. The *University Press of America* announced in 1980 that it would be publishing material on the Middle East from U.S. Government sources and referred to a 1978 study on Saudi Arabia which may be included. If it is, this will be the first time this study sees the light of day.

5. Malcolm C. Peck, "The Saudi-American Relationship and King Faisal," in Willard A. Beling (ed.), *King Faisal and the Modernisation of Saudi Arabia* (London: Croom Helm Ltd., 1980), 230-247.

6. Beling, *loc. cit.;* this book was a product of a conference organized by the Middle East Center at the University of Southern California, a Center financed by the Saudi Government. They officially funded and co-sponsored this conference as well. This Center has been the subject of considerable public controversy.

7. David Long "King Faisal's World View," in Beling, *loc. cit.,* 181.

8. *Afro-Asian Affairs* (renamed *Arab-Asian Affairs* as of Jan., 1980), published in London by Christopher Story (hereafter AAA); *Middle East Intelligence Survey* (Tel Aviv) (hereafter MEIS).

9. Elizabeth Monroe, *Britain's Moment in the Middle East, 1914-1956* (Baltimore: Johns Hopkins University Press, 1963), 80, 119; Don Peretz, *The Middle East Today* (ed.) (N. Y.: Holt Reinhart Winston, 1978) 430-433; Congressional Quarterly, *The Middle East* (4th ed.) (Washington: Congressional Quarterly Inc., 1979), 155; Emile A. Nakleh, *The United States and Saudi Arabia* (Washington: American Enterprise Institute, 1975) 32-34.

10. *Ibid.;* also Robert Azzi, "Saudi Arabia: The Kingdom and Its Power," *National Geographic,* September, 1980, 301. Peretz, *loc. cit.,* 439; Nakleh, *loc. cit.,* 31; Walter Gunthardt, "Arabia Greets the Future," *Swiss Review of World Affairs*, May, 1977, 6.

11. Peretz, *loc. cit.,* 440; Dawisha, *loc. cit.,* 7.

12. C. L. Cranford, "Bedouin Life," *Christian Science Monitor,* Aug. 26, 1980, B 12-14. For a description of how little input has been made in Asir Province in the economic plans; The Second Economic Development Plan itself is the best indicator of how much infrastructure building is ahead for most areas of the country.

13. Eliyahu Kanovsky, "Saudi Arabia in the Red," *Jerusalem Quarterly,* 16, Summer, 1980, 136-144; *AAA,* April 27, 1977, Nov. 9, 1977, March 29, 1978, June 15, 1978, Sept 1, 1978, Oct. 30, 1978, Jan. 22, 1979, July, 1979, Aug., 1979, June, 1980; Dawisha, *loc. cit.,* 33.

14. Nakleh, *loc. cit.,* 17-18, Gunthardt, *loc. cit.,* 7; Dawisha, *loc. cit.,* 10, 12, 31.

15. Timothy Sisley "Saudi Arabia," Five-Part Series, *London Times,* May 19, 1980; *AAA* under Item #20; Kanovsky, *op. cit.,* 139; Dawisha, *loc. cit.,* 10, 12; Peretz, *loc. cit.,* 440-441.

16. Azzi, *loc. cit.,* 297-298, 313; Eilts, *loc. cit.,* 98. Herman F. Eilts, "Security Considerations in the Gulf," in *International Security,* Fall, 1980.

17. Sisley, *loc. cit.,* May 23, 1980; *AAA,* Dec., 1979, May, 1980.

18. Sisley, *loc. cit.,* May 19, 1980.

19. Gunthardt, *loc. cit.,* 6, 11; Dawisha, *loc. cit.,* 14.

20. *AAA,* Dec. 9, 1976, Nov. 28, 1978, Jan. 22, 1979, March 1979, April 1979, May 1979, Feb. 1980, March 1980.

21. *Ibid.*

22. James A. Bill and Carl Leiden, *Politics of the Middle East* (Boston: Little, Brown & Co., 1979); *AAA,* Aug. 24, 1977; A. H. Riad, "Are the Saudis Combat Ready?" *Neue Zurcher Zeitung, June 10, 1980.*

23. *Wolf Blitzer "U.S.-Saudi Relations Burgeon," London Chronicle,* Aug. 1, 1980; Congressional Quarterly, *loc. cit.,* 154-155; Nakleh, *loc. cit.,* 41; see *AAA* under Item #15.

24. See *AAA* under item #38; Azzi, *loc. cit.,* 319.

25. Southerland, *loc. cit.,* 13.

26. See footnote 19. Gunthardt, *et al.*

27. Azzi *loc. cit.,* 297; *AAA,* Dec. 1979, May, 1980; Mordechai Abir, *Persian Gulf Oil in Middle East Conflicts,* Jerusalem Papers on Peace Problems, 20, 1976, 16. Sisley, *loc. cit.,* May 23, 1980.

28. *AAA,* Nov. 17, 1976, July 14, 1977, July 28, 1977, Aug. 24 1977, June 22, 1977, Sept. 22, 1977, Oct. 14, 1977, Nov. 9, 1977, Sept. 1, 1978, Oct. 30, 1978, Nov. 28, 1978, Jan 1, 1979, April, 1979, May, 1979, June, 1979, Aug., 1979, Oct., 1979, Jan., 1980; *MEIS,* 16-30 Nov. 1979, 123-125.

29. *MEIS,* 16-31 March 1980, 189.

30. Dawisha, *loc. cit.,* 11, 32-33; *AAA,* April, 1979.

31. Dawisha, *loc. cit.,* 33.

32. Azzi, *loc. cit.,* 298, 313; *AAA,* Dec., 1979, May 1980; Sisley, *loc. cit.,* May 19, 1980; *Near East Report,* Dec. 5, 12, 19, 1979.

33. *AAA,* Sept. 22, 1977; See Item #43 for the response to the coups.

Major Incidents in Saudi Arabia: 1970-1980

May 17, 1970: An uprising of Air Force officers, reported to be Nasserites, took place at Bahran air base.

Feb. 11, 1972: An uprising of National Guard officers and 3 sons of deposed King Saud was reported.

— 1974: An uprising of university graduates in collusion with King Saud's associates, backed by Iraq, was reported.

An uprising of Arab communists led by Bassam al-Imari of Iraq was reported.

Late 1974: An uprising of university graduates, air force and armored corps officers, supported by members of King Saud's family, was reported.

Nov. 1976: The arrest and deportation of 16 PFLP activists was reported.

July 17, 1977: 1,500 conspirators (1,300 of them military officers and men) attempted a coup at Tabuk and Taif air bases, declaring they wanted to set up a republican, non-aligned regime. The conspiracy was backed by Libya, Iraq, and the Hejazi Brotherhood (led by Hamid Hassoun). It was suppressed by 3,000 Jordanian troops at Tabuk.

Aug. 9, 1977: The Hejazi National Movement, with Libyan support and seeking self-rule for Hejaz bombed public and private facilities in Riyadh and Jeddah.

Aug. 27, 1977: An uprising occurred of officers and men against the air force commanders at Hail and Hufaf military bases, with Iraqi support. Two leaders of the Arabian Gulf National Liberation Front escaped to Iraq on an Iraqi plane via Kuwait. The coup was put down by armored columns led by Prince Turki.

Sept. 23, 1977: The fact that the Saudi National Liberation Front and the Hejazi National Movement (H.Q. in Mecca) are one and the same was verified. It is led by Saudis of Iraqi and Hejazi backgrounds.

Oct. 30, 1977: Officers at King Saud base attempted to subvert the garrison.

Oct. 30, 1977: A PFLP "hit team" including Iraqis was intercepted. Its mission was to kill King Khalid and his six Sudairi brothers. The hit team admitted that the PFLP had established itself in Saudi Arabia in 1975 to await orders.

June, 1978: Three Iraqis officially working for Iraqi Airways, but in fact working for the Iraqi Communist Party, were arrested. 5 more at the Iraqi Mission in Jeddah were arrested and 3 working as engineers at the Hail military installation. All were in Saudi Arabia on missions of subversion.

June, 1978: The al-Hasa National Liberation Front was formed.

Sept., 1978: Sunni Hejazis demonstrated against the bulldozing near the Holy Shrine in Mecca. Their violence led to the murder of the Governor of Medina by Hejazis. The Chief Engineer was killed the next day.

Oct., 1978: Resistance led by foreign workers, especially from India and South Korea, some of it very serious, was admitted.

Oct., 29, 1978: Brigadier Mahmoud, Commanding Officer of the Kharj military complex (French-built) defected to Iraq with 37 officers. He had refused to liquidate a six-weeks old al-Hasa tribal rebellion. The rebels had occupied a key oil and transport junction. The al-Hasa National Liberation Movement, backed by Iraq, had demanded autonomy.

May, Oct., Nov., 1978: Troops guarding the oil installations at Ras Tanurah, Daman, and Dharan defected to Iraq, Kuwait and Qatar. The number of defections since 1976 was thought to total 4,175.

Oct. 27, 1978: 5 sons of the late King Saud (Abdullah, Rashid, Abdul Aziz, Said, Turki) were deported. They were in collusion with 24 senior officers at the Hufaf, Shegra, 5th Armored Brigade. Shegra's commander escaped, with air force officers, to Libya.

Dec., 1978: 1,100 officers threatened to resign because of the surveillance system instituted over their activities.

Dec., 1978: 3 Iraqi diplomats were deported for aiding and abetting the al-Hasa and Hejazi dissidents. Iraq indicated that 2,500 Saudi military personnel had defected to Iraq since 1975

Dec. 21, 1978: Al-Sadi Sheik Muhammad Said Nawaf, senior Sunni divine in Mecca, denounced the Wahhabi interpretation of Islam as alien to the true belief. He denounced the Royal Family for using force to gain power and ruling against the wishes of the Sunni majorities in al-Hasa, Hejaz and Shammar Regions. He said they would seek peaceful redress, but take up arms if they were not heeded.

Jan. 5, 1979: The Grand Mufti of Mecca called on the Hejazis to oppose Wahhabi domination. The existence of continued unrest among the military forces and the population in Hejazi and al-Hasa Provinces was admitted.

Mar. 24, 1979: The existence of an Arab International Communist Party was discovered among foreign employees. It worked with Hassawi and Hejazi dissidents and its objective was to overthrow the Saudi monarchy and establish an Arab People's Republic of Arabia. The discovery led to the exposure of a list of Saudi Communist Party members and its leader, Ibrahim al-Mamoud.

April, 1979: Prince Fawaz, son of late King Saud, and his brothers, in absentia, plotted a coup in collusion with 100 air force officers and the armored forces commander at Diriyah military base. Saudi Air Force Deputy Commander and 17 co-conspirators defected to Iraq. South Yemen and Iraq were implicated in the conspiracy.

May 11, 1979: 10 air force officers at Jubayl used planes to attack Damman and Dharan bases in coordination with army and armored forces. News of the uprising was leaked ahead of time and nipped in the bud. It was sponsored and backed by Iran at Khari and Harad.

July 3, 1979: A report by Prince Turki accused 43 princes of plotting against King Khalid. 21 were formerly charged. Reportedly implicated were air force and army officers, civilian counsellors to the Royal Family and friends of the King.

Aug. 3, 1979: Attempts at simultaneous take-overs of the Sharga and Tabuk Kharj air bases and a plan to kill the Royal Family, backed by Libya, failed. The defection of the National Guard was scheduled to start with the murder of superiors at Hail, Gassim and Medina City Camps on Aug. 1. 118 persons were arrested, exposing infiltration and perversion of the National Guard.

Sept., 1979: Prince Sultan acknowledged that 3,000 air force personnel had been replaced by Americans.

Nov. 20, 1979: The Great Mosque take-over involved Oteiba, Kharb and Shammar tribesmen. Egyptians, Yemenis, Kuwaitis, Moroccans and Pakistanis were also killed in the Saudi counter-attack. 3,000 dissidents, representing the Hejazi NLF, which demands full autonomy for Hejaz, were involved.

Nov. 22, 1979: Forces of the Hejazi NLF, some occupying the Great Mosque, also attacked the Taif air base and military complex. (There were some 4,000 NLF adherents in Taif itself.) The fighting continued to the end of November in Mecca and to mid-December in Medina and Taif.

Anazah tribesmen and other Hejazi tribes also rebelled.

Jan. 3, 1980: 3 army and air force bases were raided by Public Security forces. The commanding officers and 93 other officers in the Huhuf, Abqaiq and Mubarraz Garrisons were arrested. The National Guard moved into the bases to facilitate the takeover by Public Security forces.

Feb., 1980: 45 percent of Saudis sent abroad for military training in France and the U.S. reportedly refused to return home. The number of new cadets at the Saudi Military academy reportedly declined from 250 in 1971 to 37 in 1979.

May, 1980: 17 officers of Huhuf Garrison defected to Kuwait, including the commanding officer. Iraqi influence along Saudi Arabia's eastern coast still caused concern to the government.

Oct., 1980: 50 Air Force officers were executed following an attempted coup.

Dec., 198(An Arab student reported that he had witnessed demonstrations by Shi'ites in the Eastern Province oil fields.

Prepared by Bernard Schechterman

Sources: *Afro-Asian Affairs* (as of 1980 *Arab-Asian Affairs*); *International Currency Review: Middle East Intelligence Survey* (monthly & bi-weekly, 1976-1980).

FOOTNOTES

34. Gunthardt, *loc. cit.*, 3, 7, 9-10; "Saudi Arabia," The Link, Vol. 8, No. 3, Summer, 1975, 8. Nakleh, *loc. cit.,; Eilts, loc. cit.*, 98-99; *AAA*, Sept. 22, 1977 shows information gaps.

35. *AAA*, Oct. 14, 1977.

36. *Ibid.*, Aug. 24, 1977.

37. *Ibid.*, May, 1980.

38. Dawisha, *loc. cit.*, 22; Eilts, *loc. cit.*, 97; Shahran Chubrin "Soviet Policy Towards Iran and the Persian Gulf," *Adelphi Papers* # 157 (London: Institute for Strategic Studies, 1980) 13-14, 23-24, 28-29; Sisley, *loc. cit.*, May 20, 1980; *AAA*, July 14, 1977, Feb., 1980.

39. Dawisha, *loc. cit.*, 21-22, 33-34.

40. Ibid., 24; Abir, *loc. cit.*, 13-14; *AAA*, Nov. 9, 1977.

41. *AAA*, Feb., 1980; *MEIS*, 1-15 Feb. 1980, 168.

42. See footnote 39, Dawisha, *et al.*

43. *AAA*, May, 1979; *MEIS*, 1-15 May 1980, 21.

44. Abir, *loc. cit.*, 17; *AAA* June, 1979, Feb., 1980.

45. Abir, *loc. cit.*, 16; See *AAA*, under Item # 15.

46. This phenomenon was best exemplified by the Wafd Party in Egypt as described in Peretz, *loc. cit.*, 209-212.

47. Dawisha, *loc. cit.*, 31; Azzi, *loc. cit.*, 297; Nakleh, *loc. cit.*, 40.

48. Peretz, *loc. cit.*, 433-436 for basic life style at the tribal level in Saudi Arabia; see Item # 17.

PART V
THE PALESTINIANS AND THE TERRITORIES

24 Land Ownership in Palestine 1880 — 1948

By Moshe Aumann

A great deal has been spoken and written over the years on the subject of land ownership in Israel—or, before 1948, Palestine. Arab propaganda, in particular, has been at pains to convince the world, with the aid of copious statistics, that the Arabs "own" Palestine, morally and legally, and that whatever Jewish land ownership there may be is negligible. From this conclusions have been drawn (or implied) with regard to the sovereign rights of the State of Israel and the problem of the Arab refugees.

The Arab case against Israel, in the matter of Jewish land purchases, rests mainly on two claims: (1) that the Palestinian Arab farmer was peacefully and contentedly working his land in the latter part of the 19th century and the early part of the 20th when along came the European Jewish immigrant, drove him off his land, disrupted the normal development of the country and created a vast class of landless, dispossessed Arabs; (2) that a small Jewish minority, owning an even smaller proportion of Palestinian lands (5 percent as against the Arabs' 95 percent) illegally made itself master of Palestine in 1948.

Our purpose in this pamphlet is to set the record straight by marshalling the facts and figures pertaining to this very complex subject, on the basis of the most reliable and authoritative information available, and to trace the history of modern Jewish resettlement purely from the point of view of the sale and purchase of land.

Pre-1948 Conditions in Palestine

A study of Palestine under Turkish rule reveals that already at the beginning of the 18th century, long before Jewish land purchases and large-scale Jewish immigration started, the position of the Palestinian fellah (peasant) had begun to deteriorate. The heavy burden of taxation, coming on top of chronic indebtedness to money-lenders, drove a growing number of farmers to place themselves under the protection of men of wealth or of the Moslem religious endowment fund (*Waqf*), with the result that they were eventually compelled to give up their title to the land, if not their actual residence upon and cultivation of it.

Until the passage of the Turkish Land Registry Law in 1858, there were no official deeds to attest to a man's legal title to a parcel of land; tradition alone had to suffice to establish such title—and usually it did. And yet, the position of Palestine's farmers was a precarious one, for there were constant blood-feuds between families, clans and entire villages, as well as periodic incursions by rapacious Bedouin tribes, such as the notorious Beni Sakk'r, of whom H. B. Tristram (*The Land of Israel: A Journal of Travels in Palestine,* Society for Promoting Christian Knowledge, London, 1865) wrote that they "can muster 1,000 cavalry and always join their brethren when a raid or war is on the move. They have obtained their present possessions gradually and, in great mea-

---

Dr. Aumann is a Middle East specialist in Jerusalem.

sure, by driving out the fellahin (peasants), destroying their villages and reducing their rich corn-fields to pasturage." (p. 488)

Tristram goes on to present a remarkable and highly revealing description of conditions in Palestine on both sides of the Jordan River in the middle of the 19th century—a description that belies the Arab claim of a tranquil, normally developing Palestinian rural economy allegedly disrupted by Jewish immigration and settlement.

> A few years ago, the whole Ghor was in the hands of the fellahin, and much of it cultivated for corn. Now the whole of it is in the hands of the Bedouin, who eschew all agriculture, except in a few spots cultivated here and there by their slaves; and with the Bedouin come lawlessness and the uprooting of all Turkish authority. No government is now acknowledged on the east side; and unless the Porte acts with greater firmness and caution than is his wont . . . Palestine will be desolated and given up to the nomads.
>
> The same thing is now going on over the plain of Sharon, where, both in the north and south, land is going out of cultivation, and whole villages rapidly disappearing from the face of the earth. Since the year 1838, no less than 20 villages have been thus erased from the map and the stationary population extirpated. Very rapidly the Bedouin are encroaching wherever horse can be ridden; and the Government is utterly powerless to resist them or to defend its subjects. (p. 490)

For descriptions of other parts of the country, we are indebted to the 1937 Report of the Palestine Royal Commission—though, for lack of space, we can quote but the briefest passages. In Chapter 9, para. 43 the Report quotes an eye-witness account of the condition of the Maritime Plain in 1913:

> The road leading from Gaza to the north was only a summer track suitable for transport by camels and carts . . . no orange groves, orchards or vineyards were to be seen until one reached Yabna village. . . . Not in a single village in all this area was water used for irrigation. . . . Houses were all of mud. No windows were anywhere to be seen. . . . The ploughs used were of wood. . . . The yields were very poor. . . . The sanitary conditions in the village were horrible. Schools did not exist. . . . The rate of infant mortality was very high. . . .
>
> The area north of Jaffa . . . consisted of two distinctive parts. . . . The eastern part, in the direction of the hills, resembled in culture that of the Gaza-Jaffa area. . . . The western part, towards the sea, was almost a desert. . . . The villages in this area were few and thinly populated. Many ruins of villages were scattered over the area, as owing to the prevalence of malaria, many villages were deserted by their inhabitants.

The Huleh basin, below the Syrian border, is described as "including a number of Arab villages and a large papyrus swamp draining south into Lake Huleh . . . a triangular strip of land some 44 sq. miles in area . . . This tract is irrigated in a very haphazard manner by a network of small, primitive canals. It is, owing to over-irrigation, now the most malarious tract in all Palestine. It might become one of the most fertile."

With regard to yet another region in Palestine—the Beisan (Beit Shean) area —we quote from the report of Mr. Lewis French, Director of Development appointed by the British Government in 1931:

> We found it inhabited by fellahin who lived in mud hovels and suffered severely from the prevalent malaria. . . . Large areas of their lands were uncultivated and covered with weeds. There were no trees, no vegetables. The fellahin, if not themselves cattle thieves, were always ready to harbour these and other criminals. The individual plots of cultivation changed hands annually. There was little public security, and the fellahin's lot was an alternation of pillage and blackmail by their neighbours the Bedouin.

This, then, was the picture of Palestine in the closing decades of the 19th century and up to the First World War:

a land that was overwhelmingly desert, with nomads continually encroaching on the settled areas and its farmers; a lack of elementary facilities and equipment; peasants wallowing in poverty, ignorance and disease, saddled with debts (interest rates at times were as high as 60 per cent) and threatened by warlike nomads or neighboring clans. The result was a growing neglect of the soil and a flight from the villages, with a mounting concentration of lands in the hands of a small number of large landowners, frequently residing in such distant Arab capitals as Beirut and Damascus, Cairo and Kuwait. Here, in other words, was a social and economic order that had all the earmarks of a medieval feudal society.

Who Dispossessed the Palestinian Peasant?

The Palestinian peasant was indeed being dispossessed, but by his fellow-Arabs: the local sheikh and village elders, the Government tax-collector, the merchants and money-lenders; and, when he was a tenant-farmer (as was usually the case), by the absentee-owner. By the time the season's crop had been distributed among all these, little if anything remained for him and his family, and new debts generally had to be incurred to pay off the old. Then the Bedouin came along and took their "cut," or drove the hapless fellah off the land altogether.

This was the "normal" course of events in 19th century Palestine. It was disrupted by the advent of the Jewish pioneering enterprise, which sounded the death-knell of this medieval feudal system. In this way the Jews played an objective revolutionary role. Small wonder that it aroused the ire and active opposition of the Arab sheikhs, absentee landowners, money-lenders and Bedouin bandits.

Jewish Land Purchases

It is important to note that the first enduring Jewish agricultural settlement in modern Palestine was founded not by European refugees, but by a group of old-time families leaving the overcrowded Jewish Quarter of the Old City of Jerusalem. (According to the Turkish census of 1875, by that time Jews already constituted a majority of the population of Jerusalem and by 1905 comprised two-thirds of its citizens. The *Encyclopedia Britannica* of 1910 gives the population figure as 60,000, of whom 40,000 were Jews.)

In 1878 they founded the village of Petah Tikva in the Sharon Plain—a village that was to become known as the "Mother of Jewish Settlements" in Palestine. Four years later a group of pioneering immigrants from Russia settled in Rishon le-Zion. Other farming villages followed in rapid succession.

When considering Jewish land purchases and settlement, four factors should be borne in mind:

1. Most of the land purchases involved large tracts belonging to absentee owners. (Virtually all of the Jezreel Valley, for example, belonged in 1897 to only two persons: the eastern portion to the Turkish Sultan, and the western part to the richest banker in Syria, Sursuk "the Greek.")
2. Most of the land purchased had not been cultivated previously because it was swampy, rocky, sandy or, for some other reason, regarded as uncultivable. This is supported by the findings of the Peel Commission Report (p. 242): "The Arab charge that the Jews have obtained too large a proportion of good land cannot be maintained. Much of the land now carrying orange groves was sand dunes or swamp and uncultivated when it was purchased . . . there was at the time at least of the earlier sales little evidence that the owners possessed either the resources or training needed to develop the land."
3. While, for this reason, the early transactions did not involve unduly large sums of money, the price of land began to rise as Arab landowners took

advantage of the growing demand for rural tracts. The resulting infusion of capital into the Palestinian economy had noticeable beneficial effects on the standard of living of all the inhabitants.

4. The Jewish pioneers introduced new farming methods which improved the soil and crop cultivation and were soon emulated by Arab farmers.

The following figures show land purchases by the three leading Jewish land-buying organizations and by individual Jews between 1880 and 1935.

From the table below it will be seen that the proportion of land purchased from large (usually absentee) owners ranged from about 50 to 90 percent.

"The total area of land in Jewish possession at the end of June 1947," writes A. Granott in *The Land System in Palestine* (Eyre and Spottiswoode, London, 1952, p. 278), "amounted to 1,850,000 dunams; of this, 181,100 dunams had been obtained through concessions from the Palestine Government, and about 120,000 dunams had been acquired from Churches, from foreign companies, from the Government otherwise than by concessions, and so forth. It was estimated that 1,000,000 dunams and more, or 57 percent, had been acquired from large Arab landowners, and if to this we add the lands acquired from the Government, Churches, and foreign companies, the percentage will amount to seventy-three. From the fellaheen there had been purchased about 500,000 dunams, or 27 percent, of the total area acquired. The result of Jewish land acquisitions, at least to a considerable part, was that properties which had been in the hands of large and medium owners were converted into holdings of small peasants."

JEWISH LAND PURCHASES, 1880-1935

(in dunams*)

Organization	Total land acquired	Government conces-sions	From private owners	Large tracts**	
				Dunams	Percent (approx.)
PICA (Palestine Jewish Colonization Assoc.)	469,408	39,520	429,887	293,545	70
Palestine Land Development Co.	579,492	66,513***	512,979	455,169	90
Jewish National Fund****					
Until 1930			270,084	239,170	90
1931-1947			566,312		50
Individual Jews			432,100		50

* 4 dunams = 1 acre.

** The large tracts often belonged to absentee landlords.

*** Land situated in the sandy Beersheba and marshy Huleh districts.

**** ". . . created on December 25, 1901, to ensure that land would be purchased for the Jewish workers who were to be personally responsible for its cultivation.

"Since the J.N.F. was as concerned with conforming to socialist ideals as with intensive economic exploitation of land, its Charter was opposed to the use of lands purchased by it as private property. The J.N.F. retained the freehold of the lands, while the people working it are only life tenants. . . .

"The capital of the Jewish National Fund was essentially raised from small regular donations from millions of Jewish craftsmen, labourers, shop-owners and intellectuals in Central and Eastern Europe where the shadow of genocide was already apparent, who felt concerned about the return of Jews to Zion. . . .

"Contrary to colonialist enterprises, which were seeking an exorbitant profit from land extorted from the colonized peoples, Zionist settlement discouraged private capital as its enterprise was of a socialist nature based on the refusal to exploit the worker." (Kurt Niedermaier, *Colonisation Without Colonialism,* Youth and Hechalutz Dept., Jewish Agency, Jerusalem, 1969).

The League of Nations Mandate

When the League of Nations conferred the Mandate for Palestine upon Great Britain in 1922, it expressly stipulated that "The Administration of Palestine . . . shall encourage, in cooperation with the Jewish Agency . . . close settlement by Jews on the land, including State lands and waste lands not acquired for public purposes" (Article 6), and that it "shall introduce a land system appropriate to the needs of the country, having regard, among other things, to the desirability of promoting the close settlement and intensive cultivation of the land." (Article 11)

British policy, however, followed a different course, deferring to the extremist Arab opposition to the above-mentioned provision of the Mandate. Of some 750,000 dunams of cultivable State lands, 350,000, or nearly half, had been allotted by 1949 to Arabs and only 17,000 dunams to Jews. This was in clear violation of the terms of the Mandate. Nor, ironically enough, did it help the Arab peasants for whose benefit these transactions were ostensibly carried out. The glaring examples of this policy are the case of the Beisan lands and that of the Huleh Concession.

Beisan Lands

Under the Ghor-Mudawwarra Agreement of 1921, some 225,000 dunams of potentially fertile wasteland in the Beisan (Beit Shean) area were handed over to Arab farmers on terms severely condemned not only by Jews but also by such British experts as Lewis French and Sir John Hope-Simpson. More than half of the land was irrigable, and, according to the British experts, eight dunams of irrigated land per capita (or 50-60 dunams per family) were sufficient to enable a family to maintain itself on the land. Yet many farmers received far more than that: six families, of whom two lived in Syria, received a combined area of about 7,000 dunams; four families (some living in Egypt) received a combined area of 3,496 dunams; another received 3,450 and yet another, 1,350.

Thus the Ghor-Mudawwarra Agreement was instrumental in creating a new group of large landowners. Possessing huge tracts, most of which they were unable to till, these owners began to sell the surplus lands at speculative prices. In his 1930 Report, Sir Hope-Simpson wrote of the Agreement that it had deprived the Government of "the control of a large area of fertile land eminently suited for development and for which there is ample water available for irrigation," and that "the grant of the land has led to speculation on a considerable scale."

Huleh Area

For twenty years (from 1914 to 1934) the Huleh Concession—some 57,000 dunams of partly swamp-infested but potentially highly fertile land in north-eastern Palestine—was in Arab hands. The Arab concessionaires were to drain and develop the land so as to make additional tracts available for cultivation, under very attractive terms offered by the Government (first Turkish, then British). However, this was never done, and in 1934 the concession was sold to a Jewish concern, the Palestine Land Development Company, at a huge profit. The Government added several onerous conditions concerning the amount of land (from the drained and newly developed tracts) that had to be handed over—without reimbursement for drainage and irrigation costs—to Arab tenant-farmers in the area.

All told, hundreds of millions of dollars were paid by Jewish buyers to Arab landowners. Official records show that in 1933 £854,796 was paid by Jewish individuals and organizations for Arab land, mostly large estates; in 1934 the figure was £1,647,836 and in 1935, £1,699,488. Thus, in the course of only three years £4,202,180 (more than 20 million dollars at the prevailing rate of exchange) was paid out to Arab landowners (Palestine Royal Commission Report, 1937).

To understand the magnitude of the prices paid for these lands, we need only look at some comparative figures. In 1944, Jews paid between $1,000 and $1,100 per acre in Palestine, mostly for arid or semi-arid land; in the same year rich black soil in the state of Iowa was selling for about $110 per acre (U.S. Department of Agriculture).

Effects on Arab Population

In those instances where as a result of such transactions Arab tenant-farmers were displaced (on one year's notice), compensation in cash or other land was paid, as required by the 1922 Protection of Cultivators Ordinance; the Jewish land-buying associations often paid more than the law required (Pollack and Boehm, *The Keren Kayemeth Le-Israel*). Of 688 such tenants between 1920 and 1930, 526 remained in agricultural occupations, some 400 of them finding other land (Palestine Royal Commission Report, 1937, Chapter 9, para. 61).

Investigations initiated in 1931 by Mr. Lewis French disposed of the charge that a large class of landless or dispossessed Arab farmers was created as a result of Jewish land purchases. According to the British Government report (Memoranda prepared by the Government of Palestine, London 1937, Colonia No. 133, p. 37), the total number of applications for registration as landless Arabs was 3,271. Of these, 2,607 were rejected on the ground that they did not come within the category of landless Arabs. Valid claims were recognized in the case of 664 heads of families, of whom 347 accepted the offer of resettlement by the Government. The remainder refused either because they had found satisfactory employment elsewhere or because they were not accustomed to irrigated cultivation or the climate of the new areas (Peel Report, Chapter 9, para. 60).

Purchases of land by Jews in the hill country had always been very small and, according to the investigations by Mr. French, of 71 applications by Arabs claiming to be landless, 68 were turned down.

Arab Population Changes Due to Jewish Settlement

Another Arab claim disproved by the facts is that Zionist "colonialism" led to the disruption and ruin of the Arab Palestinian society and economy.

Statistics published in the Palestine Royal Commission Report (p. 279) indicate a remarkable phenomenon: Palestine, traditionally a country of Arab emigration, became after World War I a country of Arab immigration. In addition to recorded figures for 1920-36, the Report devotes a special section to illegal Arab immigration. While there are no precise totals on the extent of Arab immigration between the two World Wars, estimates vary between 60,000 and 100,000. The principal cause of the change of direction was Jewish development, which created new and attractive work opportunities and, in general, a standard of living previously unknown in the Middle East.

Another major factor in the rapid growth of the Arab population was, of course, the rate of natural increase, among the highest in the world. This was accentuated by the steady reduction of the previously high infant mortality rate as a result of the improved health and sanitary conditions introduced by the Jews.

Altogether, the non-Jewish element in Palestine's population (not including Bedouin) expanded between 1922 and 1929 alone by more than 75 percent. The Royal Commission Report makes these interesting observations:

> The shortage of land is, we consider, due less to the amount of land acquired by Jews than to the increase in the Arab population. (p. 242)
>
> We are also of the opinion that up till now the Arab cultivator has benefited, on the whole, both from the work of the British administration and from the presence of Jews in the country. Wages have gone up; the standard of living

> has improved; work on roads and buildings has been plentiful. In the Maritime Plains some Arabs have adopted improved methods of cultivation. (p. 241)

Jewish development served as an incentive not only to Arab entry into Palestine from Lebanon, Egypt, Syria and other neighboring countries, but also to Arab population movements within the country—to cities and areas where there was a large Jewish concentration. Some idea of this phenomenon may be gained from the following official figures:

Changes in towns: The Arab population in predominantly Arab towns rose only slightly (if at all) between the two World Wars: in Hebron—from 16,650 in 1922 to 22,800 in 1943; Nablus—from 15,931 to 23,300; Jenin—from 2,737 to 3,900; Bethlehem—from 6,658 to 8,800. Gaza's population actually decreased from 17,426 in 1922 to 17,045 in 1931.

On the other hand, in the three major Jewish cities the Arab population shot up during this period, far beyond the rate of natural increase: Jerusalem—from 28,571 in 1922 to 56,400 (97 percent); Jaffa—from 27,437 to 62,600 (134 percent); Haifa—from 18,404 to 58,200 (216 percent).

Changes in rural areas: The population of the predominantly Arab Beersheba district dropped between 1922 and 1939 from 71,000 to 49,000 (the rate of natural increase should have resulted in a rise to 89,000). In the Bethlehem district the figure increased from 24,613 to about 26,000 (after falling to 23,725 in 1929). In the Hebron area it went up from 51,345 to 59,000 (the natural increase rate dictated a rise to 72,000).

In contrast to these declines or comparatively slight increases in exclusively Arab-inhabited areas, in the Nazareth, Beit Shean, Tiberias and Acre districts—where large-scale Jewish settlement and rural development was underway—the figure rose from 89,600 in 1922 to some 151,000 in 1938 (by about 4.5 percent per annum, compared with a natural increase rate of 2.5-3 percent).

In the largely Jewish Haifa area the number of Arab peasants increased by 8 percent a year during the same period. In the Jaffa and Ramla districts (heavily Jewish populated), the Arab rural population grew from 42,300 to some 126,000—an annual increase of 12 percent, or more than four times as much as can be attributed to natural increase (L. Shimony, *The Arabs of Palestine,* Tel-Aviv, 1947, pp. 422-23).

One reason for the Arab gravitation toward Jewish-inhabited areas, and from neighboring countries to Palestine, was the incomparably higher wage scales paid there, as may be seen from the table below.

The capital received by Arab landowners for their surplus holdings was used for improved and intensive cultivation or invested in other enterprises. Turning again to the Report of the Palestine Royal Commission (p. 93), we find the following conclusions: "The large import of Jewish capital into Palestine has had a general fructifying effect on the economic life of the whole country. . . . The expansion of Arab industry and citriculture has been largely financed by

DAILY WAGE SCALES, 1943
(in mils)

	Unskilled labor	**Skilled labor**
Palestine	220—250	350—600
Egypt	30— 50	70—200
Syria	80—100	150—300
Iraq	50	70—200

Source: A. Khoushy, *Brit, Poalei Eretz-Israel,* 1943, p. 25.

have gone up; the standard of living the capital thus obtained. . . . Jewish example has done much to improve Arab cultivation. . . . The increase in Arab population is most marked in areas affected by Jewish development."

During World War II, the Arab population influx mounted apace, as is attested by the *UNRWA Review,* Information Paper No. 6 (September 1962):

> A considerable movement of people is known to have occurred, particularly during the Second World War, years when new opportunities of employment opened up in the towns and on military works in Palestine. These wartime prospects and, generally, the higher rate of industrialization in Palestine attracted many new immigrants from the neighboring countries, and many of them entered Palestine without their presence being officially recorded.

Land Ownership in 1948

The claim is often made that in 1948 a Jewish minority owning only 5 percent of the land of Palestine made itself master of the Arab majority, which owned 95 percent of the land.

In May 1948 the State of Israel was established in only part of the area alloted by the original League of Nations Mandate. 8.6 percent of the land was owned by Jews and 3.3 percent by Israeli Arabs, while 16.9 percent had been abandoned by Arab owners who imprudently heeded the call from neighboring countries to "get out of the way" while the invading Arab armies make short shrift of Israel. The rest of the land—over 70 percent—had been vested in the Mandatory Power, and accordingly reverted to the State of Israel as its legal heir. (Government of Palestine, *Survey of Palestine, 1946,* British Government Printer, p. 257.)

The greater part of this 70 percent consisted of the Negev, some 3,144,250 acres all told, or close to 50 percent of the 6,580,000 acres in all of Mandatory Palestine. Known as Crown or State Lands, this was mostly uninhabited arid or semi-arid territory, inherited originally by the Mandatory Government from Turkey. In 1948 it passed to the Government of Israel.

These lands had not been owned by Arab farmers—neither under the British Mandate nor under the preceding regime. Thus it is obvious that the contention that 95 percent of the land—whether of Mandatory Palestine or of the State of Israel—had belonged to Arabs has absolutely no foundation in fact.

* * *

There is perhaps no better way of concluding and summing up this study than to quote from an article entitled *Is Israel a Thorn or a Flower in the Near East?* by Abdul Razak Kader, the Algerian political writer, now living in exile in Paris (*Jerusalem Post,* Aug. 1, 1969):

"The nationalists of the states neighboring on Israel, whether they are in the government or in business, whether Palestinian, Syrian or Lebanese, or town dwellers of tribal origin, all know that at the beginning of the century and during the British Mandate the marshy plains and stony hills were sold to the Zionists by their fathers or uncles for gold, the very gold which is often the origin of their own political or commercial careers. The nomadic or semi-nomadic peasants who inhabited the frontier regions know full well what the green plains, the afforested hills and the flowering fields of today's Israel were like before.

"The Palestinians who are today refugees in the neighboring countries and who were adults at the time of their flight know all this, and no anti-Zionist propaganda—pan-Arab or pan-Moslem—can make them forget that their present nationalist exploiters are the worthy sons of their feudal exploiters of yesterday and that the thorns of their life are of Arab, not Jewish, origin."

* * *

25 Arab Immigration into Pre-State Israel: 1922-1931

By Fred M. Gottheil

As an historical event of major consequence, it is not surprising that there are at least two conflicting accounts concerning immigration into Palestine prior to the formation of the State of Israel. One account, for example, depicts Jewish immigration into Palestine primarily in terms of filling up vast empty spaces of sparsely populated land.[1] Much of this description centers upon the drainage of the northern marshes and the reclamation of the desert. Essentially, it is an account of man versus nature. Only parenthetically does it consider Arab immigration or the impact of Jewish immigration on the resident Arab population.

By contrast, a second version shifts the focus of discussion to population displacement. It describes the same Jewish immigration as creating in Palestine a demographic overcapacity situation with the indigenous Arab population being forced off the settled land.[2] In this case, it is account of man versus man for control and ownership of extremely limited natural resources.[3] Both descriptions survive today as historical summaries of pre-Israel Palestine.

Although there is substantial disagreement in the two accounts concerning the *impact* of immigration, there is no disagreement as to its *source*. Both emphasize its Jewish origins. Almost completely lost in these accounts is an analysis of concurrent Arab immigration. References to such immigration are made only *in passim* and the conclusion reached is that for purposes of permanent settlement, Arab immigration was insignificant.[4]

This conclusion, however, has not gone completely unchallenged. The Royal Institute for International Affairs, for example, commenting on the growth of the Palestinian population prior to World War II, states: "The Number of Arabs who entered Palestine illegally from Syria and Transjordan is unknown. But probably considerable."[5] Professor Harold Laski makes a similar observation: "There has been large-scale and both assisted and unassisted Jewish emigration to Palestine; but it is important also to note that there has been large-scale Arab emigration from the surrounding countries."[6] Underscoring the point, C. S. Jarvis, Governor of the Sinai from 1923-1936, noted: "This illegal immigration was not only going on from the Sinai, but also from Transjordan and Syria and it is very difficult to make a case out for the misery of the Arabs if at the same time their compatriots from adjoining States could not be kept from going in to share that misery."[7] Even the Simpson Report acknowledged Arab immigration in this form:

> Another serious feature of immigration is the number of persons who evade the frontier control and enter Palestine without formality of any kind. It is exceedingly difficult to maintain any effective control of the various fron-

Dr. Gottheil is Professor of Economics at the University of Illinois-Urbana. His articles have appeared in many journals and anthologies.

> tiers of Palestine. At the present time such controls as exists is carried out at police posts on the roads. The immigrant who wishes to evade the control naturally leaves the road before reaching the frontier and takes to the footpaths over the Hills . . . The Chief Immigration Officer has brought to the notice that illicit immigration through Syria and across the northern frontier of Palestine is material.[8]

Other writers make this same point.[9] Although Arab immigration has been described as "considerable," "large-scale," and "material," such descriptions are nonetheless lacking in precision.[10]

This paper presents some statistical evidence concerning Arab immigration into Palestine. The following issues will be considered: What was the Arab population size in Israel in 1922 and how rapidly did this population grow? What percent of this growth can be attributed to natural increase and what percent to immigration? How do the demographic patterns in pre-State Israel compare with those in non-Israel Palestine during the 1922-1931 period, and what explanations can be offered to explain divergent patterns? Although data will be presented for all of Palestine, a distinction will be drawn between Arab immigration into the part of Palestine that later becomes Israel and the non-Israel sector of Palestine. The analysis will emphasize the former.

The Application of Palestine Census Data to Pre-State Israel: 1922-1931

Census data for Palestine is available only for the years 1922 and 1931. Prior to 1922, there existed, at best, educated guesses.[11] Since 1931, population estimates were derived by applying natural rates of growth and *registered* immigration to the 1931 numbers.[12] Because these population estimates make no attempt to measure unrecorded immigration, the reliability of these numbers is considerably less than those of the census years.[13] For this reason, the analysis here is restricted to the census period 1922-1931.

The transfer of this census data to pre-State Israel is complicated by the character of the Israel borders which were not entirely aligned with the administrative subdistricts of Palestine upon which the statistical reporting of population was made. In 1922, population data for Palestine was arranged by the British Mandatory Government in 18 subdistricts according to urban or rural location and according to religion. The relationship between these subdistricts and the State of Israel is illustrated in Table 1.

The problem of identifying the 1922 Arab population as pre-State Israel or non-Israel Palestine is thus reduced to an intra-subdistrict analysis of population allocation in the 6 subdistricts that are only partially included in the State

Table 1

PALESTINE AND ISRAEL

(by subdistrict)

Subdistricts entirely within Israel	Subdistricts partially within Israel	Subdistricts entirely outside Israel
Safad	Jenin	Nablus
Acre	Tulkarm	Ramallah
Nazareth	Jerusalem	Jericho
Haifa	Hebron	
Beisan	Gaza	
Jaffa	Bethlehem	
Ramle		
Beersheba		
Tiberias		

SOURCE: *Survey of Palestine,* Vol. I, 1946, p. 145.

of Israel. A disaggregation of the census data from the subdistrict level to the village level for those subdistricts whose domain includes the Israel border permits a reclassification of the Palestine census data into Israeli Arab and non-Israeli Arab population. The results are seen in Table 2.[14]

Arab Population in Pre-State Israel: 1922-1931

Total Arab settled population in the pre-State Israel sector of Palestine increased during the 1922-1931 period from 321,866 to 463,288, or by 141,-422. This population increase reflects both natural increases and increases

Table 2

Arab Settled Population 1922 and 1931 in Pre-State Israel and Non-Israel Palestine (by subdistricts)

Subdistrict	Pre-State Israel		Non-Israel Palestine	
	1922	1931	1922	1931
Safad	18,720	35,751		
Acre	34,276	43,465		
Nazareth	20,713	24,090		
Haifa	45,712	69,136		
Beisan	9,925	13,087		
Jaffa	39,866	73,927		
Ramle	44,465	61,329		
Beersheba	2,258	2,948		
Tiberias	14,245	18,877		
Jenin	5,430	7,014	27,978	34,239
Tulkarm	13,424	17,016	21,477	28,581
Jerusalem	18,799	29,201	35,272	45,266
Hebron	11,246	14,359	41,881	53,114
Gaza	42,563	52,763	29,055	42,288
Bethlehem	224	325	22,554	21,444
Nablus			56,482	68,477
Ramallah			28,948	37,771
Jericho			1,888	3,192
Totals	321,866	463,288	265,535	334,372

SOURCE: Barron, J. B., *Report and General Abstracts of the Census of 1922,* Jerusalem, Government Printer, m.d. Mills, E., *Census of Palestine 1931, Population of Villages, Towns, and Administrative Areas,* Jerusalem, 1932.

Table 3

Annual Rates of Natural Increase of Moslem, Christian, and Other Non-Jewish Settled Population (1922-1931)

	Moslem	Christian	Others		Moslem	Christian	Others
1922	2.49	1.91	2.48	1927	2.10	1.84	2.20
1923	2.15	1.98	2.15	1928	2.34	2.10	2.38
1924	2.47	2.34	2.03	1929	2.34	1.96	1.63
1925	2.18	1.81	2.63	1930	2.81	2.21	2.47
1926	2.90	2.16	1.84	1931	2.74	2.28	3.35

SOURCE: *Survey of Palestine,* Government of Palestine, Government Printer, Palestine, 1946, Vol. III, p. 1176. These rates, averaged, for 1922-1925 and 1926-1930, appear in *Palestine Blue Book,* 1938, Government Printer, Jerusalem, p. 144 and Palestine, Office of Statistics, *General Monthly Bulletin of Current Statistics of Palestine,* Jerusalem, January, 1937, p. 4.

through immigration. Since natural rates of growth for the Arab population of Palestine are available for the 1922-1931 period (Table 3), the relative contributions of natural increase and immigration can be measured.

Applying these rates to the 1922 population, we derive, for 1931, a population size of 398,498. Other estimates of rates of natural increase for the Moslem population have been made:

The 1931 Arab population that would obtain using the substantially higher estimates of the *Reports* modifies our results only slightly. The 11.8 percent of Arab immigration to 1931 actual Arab population is reduced to 9.2 percent; the 38.7 percent of total population growth 1922-1931 that is immigration is reduced to 30.2 percent; and the 36.8 percent of total immigration for 1922-1931 that is Arab is reduced to 31.1 percent. This compares with Horowitz and Hinden's estimate of 23 percent for 1922-1936 non-Jewish immigration as a percent of total non-Jewish population growth 1922-1936. *Economic Survey of Palestine,* Hapoel Hazair Co-operative Press. Tel-Aviv, 1938, p. 22.

Table 3 would obtain if natural increase were the only source of population growth. The actual 1931 population, derived from the 1931 census data however, is 463,288 or 64,790 more than can be explained by the natural increase. Since 10,000 represents simply a transfer of territory from Syria to the subdistrict of Safad, the 54,790 residual

	Palestine and Trans-Jordan Reports	Survey of Palestine "true-rate"		Palestine and Trans-Jordan Reports	Survey of Palestine "true-rate"
1922		na	1927	2.85	1.44
1923	2.18	na	1928	2.50	1.32
1924	3.37	na	1929		1.77
1925	2.97	na	1930	2.90	2.12
1926	3.48	1.67	1931		2.02

SOURCE: *Report: Palestine and Trans-Jordan,* His Majesty's Stationery Office, London: *Reports* 1922 through 1931. *Survey of Palestine,* Vol. III, Government of Palestine, Government Printer, Palestine, 1946, p. 1177.

Table 4

ARAB SETTLED POPULATION IN PRE-STATE AND NON-ISRAEL PALESTINE (1922-1931)

	Population Measure	Pre-State Israel	Non-Israel Palestine
1922	actual	321,866	265,535
1931	actual	463,288	334,372
1931	natural	397,728	329,695
1931	immigration 1922-1931	54,790	4,677

is imputed to the Arab immigration from the non-Israel sector of Palestine and from the surrounding Arab countries.[15]

Arab immigration thus appears to be substantial, as Laski, Jarvis, Simpson and others suggested. The 1922-1931 Arab immigration alone represents 11.8 percent of the total Arab settled population of 1931 and as much as 38.7 percent of the total 1922-1931 Arab population growth. This immigration size is no less impressive when compared to the 94,162 Jewish immigration during the same period.[16] The Arab immigration accounts for 36.8 percent of total immigration into pre-State Israel.

Pre-State Israel and Non-Israel Palestine Immigration: A Comparison

The demographic character of the pre-State Israel 1922-1931 period contrasts sharply with that of non-Israel Palestine. This is shown in Table 4.

The population increase for non-Israel Palestine was 4,677 greater than what would have been obtained through natural increase alone. This number compares with the 54,790 immigration for pre-State Israel. The 1922-1931 immigration to non-Israel Palestine constitutes only 1.4 percent of its 1931 population size and 6.8 percent of the total increase for the period. The conclusion derived from the comparative analysis is that while immigration was an important contributor to population growth in pre-State Israel, it was of minor consequence in the non-Israel sector of Palestine.

Although the contrast between the two sectors of Palestine is clear, still, both sectors record for the period a net inflow of population. This outcome contrasts with the experience of the surrounding Arab countries, where, for the 1922-1931 period, emigration in some cases of substantial numbers, are reported.

ESTIMATES OF SYRIAN AND LEBANESE EMIGRATION (1921-1939)

	Origin	Gross emigration
1921-28a	Syria	89,407
1922-27b	Syria	46,500
1925-38c	Syria	38,302
1925-38c	Lebanon	49,586
1920-39d	Syria	54,000
1923-31e	Syria and Lebanon	97,892

SOURCE: (a) Hurwitz, D., "The Agrarian Problem of the Fellahin," *Jews and Arabs in Palestine,* Ed., Sereni and Ashery, Hechalutz Press, New York, 1936, p. 54; (b) *The Jewish Plan for Palestine*: *Memoranda and Statements Presented to the United Nations Special Committee on Palestine,* Jerusalem, 1947, p. 115; (c) Granott, A., *The Land System in Palestine,* Byre and Spottiswoode, London, 1952, p. 47; (d) Helbaoui, Y., *L'Economie Syrienne et les Problemes de son Developpement,* BOSC Freres, Lyon, 1955. (e) Widmer, R., "Population," *Economic Organization of Syria,* Ed., Himadeh, S., American Press, Beirut, 1936, p. 16.

Immigration and Economic Development

The explanation for these diverging patterns of population growth and immigration can be found in the growing disparities of economic performance in pre-State Israel, non-Israel Palestine, and the Arab States.

That migration is highly synchronized with international investment and with disparities in the rates of economic growth in different regions has been well established.[17] Although the statistical record of economic activity in the Middle East is severely limited for the period 1922-1931, a consensus of economic reporting does appear to suggest that an Arab migration of 54,790 to pre-State Israel and 4,677 to non-Israel Palestine should be considered as something less than a total surprise.[18]

In contrast to the "economic paralysis" that seems to have characterized the Arab economies,[19] Palestine had been undergoing substantial economic growth. Capital stock, largely imported, increased by 327 percent while net domestic product rose, at constant prices, by 410 percent.[20] The importance of Jewish-owned enterprises, located primarily in pre-State Israel, can hardly be overstated. Their number increased during 1922-1937 from 1,850 to 6,007.[21] Moreover, 75 percent of the entire industrial work-force in 1927 was employed by such firms and 60 percent of the force was Arab.[22]

The rapid economic development in Palestine was not the exclusive property of the Jewish sector. The extent of Arab participation in the industrialization process is reflected in the growth, from 1918-1928, of 1,373 new Arab-owned enterprises.[23] Although clearly of a smaller scale than the Jewish enterprise, these nonetheless represented over 60 percent of the total enterprises established during the 1918-1928 period.[24]

Economic conditions in Syria, Iraq, Lebanon, and Trans-Jordan appear to have been substantially different. In Syria, for example, the growth of new industry and the conversion of handicraft production to mechanization had been insufficient to absorb the surplus labor generated by the decline in overall industrial and handicraft production.[25] In the agricultural sector, progress appeared to have been equally unattractive. The persistence of agricultural backwardness is attributed to the continuation of primitive technology, excessive peasant indebtedness, climatic conditions, and the skewed distribution of land holdings.[26]

Similar descriptions are offered for Iraq[27] and Trans-Jordan; the latter described as "a parasite existing on the permanent subsidy of Britain and the civil administration of Palestine" with no attempts being made toward industrialization of the modernization of agriculture.[28] Industrial activity in Egypt appeared to have been hardly more successful. Capital in corporate enterprise increased by two percent annually between 1920-1930 and although investment in agriculture did increase, per capita agricultural output actually declined.[29]

Although comparative statistics for the Middle East for 1922-1931 is virtually impossible to construct because of limited comparable data, some regional estimates for 1932-1936 can serve at least as an indicator of comparative economic performance for the few preceding years. Such a comparison is offered in Tables 5 and 6.

The economic portrait shown in Tables 5 and 6 seem clear enough. Consumption of foodstuffs in Palestine among Arabs was 143 percent of the Egyptian, 121 percent of the Syrian, and 166 percent of the Iraqi consumption. Net agricultural productivity was 207 percent of both the Egyptian and Trans-Jordanian, 191 percent of the Syrian and 200 percent of the Iraqi.

Since a capital goods industry was virtually non-existent in the Middle East, the value of machine imports indicates, to some degree, the rate of increase in industrialization and mechanization of

Per Capita Income, Relative Wages, Consumption of Foodstuffs, Net Productivity Per Male Earner in Agriculture, and the Value of Agricultural and Industrial Machinery Imports in Selected Middle East Economics (1932-1936)

	Per capita income (£) 1936 [a]	Industrial daily wages 1933-1935 (mils) [b]	Per capita Consumption of foodstuff (I.U.) 1934-1936 [a]	Net productivity per male earner in agriculture (I.U.) 1934-1936 [a]	Machinery imports (Palestine = 100) [c] 1932-1934 agricultural	industrial
Egypt	12	na	16.0	90.1	10	16
Syria	13	50-310	19.0	97.6	23	17
Iraq	10	40-60	13.8	93.2	10	16
TransJordan	na	na	na	90.1	na	na
Palestine:	19				100	100
Arabs		70-500	22.9	186.3		

SOURCE: (a) Alfred Bonne, *Economic Development of the Middle East,* Kegan Paul, Trench, Truber & Co., London, 1943, pp. 21, 47, 62. The International Unit (I.U.) is defined as the amount of goods and services that could be purchased for one dollar in the USA over the average of the decade 1925-1934. (b) David Horowitz and Rita Hinden, *Economic Survey of Palestine, Hapoel-Hazair Co-operative Press,* Tel-Aviv, 1938, p. 207. 1933 for Syria and Iraq; 1934 for Palestine and 1935 for Lebanon. (c) David Horowitz, "Palestine and the Middle East: An Essay in Regional Economy," *Palestine and the Middle East Magazine,* Tel-Aviv, October/November, 1943, p. 8. 1935-1938 for Iraq.

Table 6

AVERAGE PER CAPITA GOVERNMENT EXPENDITURE (1929)
(in Palestine Mils)

Item	Palestine	Iraq	Syria	Transjordan
General Adm.	608	377	537	400
Army and Police	610	525	460	410
Total Unproductive	1290	902	997	810
Education	150	80	80	70
Health	110	70	40	40
Economy	80	115	30	57
Survey	80	14	63	30
Public Works	330	142	283	110
Total Productive	750	421	496	307

SOURCE: Grunwald, K., *The Government Finances of the Mandated Territories in the Near East,* Palestine Economic Society, May 1932, p. 100.

agriculture. Syrian, Egyptian and Iraqi agricultural machinery imports were 23, 10 and 10 percent of the Palestine imports; industrial machinery imports were 17, 16 and 16 percent.

Disparities between Palestine and the Arab States appear also in the investment outlays in the public sector.

On almost every budget item, and particularly on items of industrial and social overhead capital, per capita expenditures in Palestine were higher than in any of the Arab States. Productive expenditures were, in 1929, for Palestine, 151 percent of the Syrian, 178 percent of the Iraqi and 244 percent of the Trans-Jordanian expenditures. In terms of government revenues, Palestine's per capita tax was 156 percent of Syria's, 167 percent of Iraq's and 295 percent of Trans-Jordan's.[32]

While the comparative evidence offered above is admittedly incomplete, the simple observation that significant disparities in economic activity between Palestine and the Arab States existed is clearly not without substance.

Conclusions:

Arab immigration into Palestine, and specifically into pre-State Israel during the census period 1922-1931 reflects, to some degree, the different levels of economic activity within Palestine and between it and the contiguous Arab States. Arab immigration accounted for 38.7 percent of the total increase in Arab settled population in pre-State Israel, and constituted 11.8 percent of its 1931 population. Although less numerically than the Jewish immigration during the period, the significance of Arab immigration is nonetheless emphasized by its comparison with the Jewish population inflow. Arab immigration composed 36.8 percent of the total immigration into pre-State Israel. The situation in non-Israel Palestine was somewhat different. There, Arab migration was positive, but inconsequential.

FOOTNOTES

1. "Regions that but a few years ago were barren sand dunes, bare hills or pestilential swamps, have been converted into fertile agricultural land dotted with pleasing villages, and where people can live in the faith of their fathers and the children grew up happily. The labour was arduous, but it was cheerfully, even joyfully undertaken and it was lightened by the generous help given by Jews all over the world." Sir John Russell in forward to Lowdermilk, W. C., *Palestine: Land of Promise,* London, Gollancz, 1945.

2. "The increase in Jewish immigration was accompanied by large scale acquisition of land and large-scale dispossession of Arabs. Thousands of Arab farm families, driven from the land which they and their ancestors had lived, were forced to go to the towns. The Jews aimed at controlling the economic life of the country. A landless and distorted class was created." Rousan, Mahmoud, *Palestine and the Internationalization of Jerusalem,* The Ministry of Culture and Guidance, Government of Iraq, Baghdad, 1965, p. 31.

3. It is this second version that is reflected in the Shaw (*Palestine Commission on the Disturbances of August, 1929,* Cmd. 3530, London, 1930) and Simpson (*Palestine Report on Immigration, Land Settlement, and Development,* Cmd. 3686, London 1930) Commission Reports which subsequently formed the basis of British policy restricting Jewish immigration into Palestine during the 1930s and 1940s.

4. It is noteworthy that this conclusion is represented in Arab, Jewish, and British writing alike. See, for example, Hopkins, L., "Population," *Economic Organization of Palestine,* edited by Himadeh, Sa'id, American Press, Beirut, 1938, p. 19; Ruppin, A., "Population of Palestine," *Palestine and Near East Economic Magazine,* Nos. 5 and 6, 1927, p. 130; and *Survey of Palestine,* Vol. I, Government of Palestine, Government Printer, 1946, p. 212.

5. *Great Britain and Palestine,* 1915-1945, Royal Institute for International Affairs, Information Papers no. 20, London, p. 64.

6. "Palestine: The Economic Aspect," *Palestine's Economic Future,* Ed., J. B. Brown, P. L. Humphries and Company Limited, London, 1946, p. 34.

7. United Empire, Vol. 28, p. 633.

8. *Palestine Report on Immigration, Land Settlement and Development,* London, 1930, pp. 126 and 138.

9. See Horowitz, D., "Arab Economy in Palestine," *Palestine's Economic Future,* P. L. Humphries Co., London, 1946, p. 65; Gervasi, F., *To Whom Palestine?* D. Appleton-Century, New York 1946, p. 79; Nemirovsky, M., "Jewish Immigration and Arab Population," *Jews and Arabs in Palestine,* Ed., Sereni, E., and Ashery, R., Hehalutz Press, New York, 1936, p. 81; Jewish Agency for Palestine, *Memorandum submitted to the Palestine Royal Commission,* London, 1936, p. 109.

10. The few estimates offered simply mention numbers. No documentation is presented. Nonetheless, the numbers are of interest: Gervasi mentions 60,000-80,000 for 1926-1946, *op. cit.,* p. 79, 20,000-30,000 is recorded for 1922-1927 by the *Jewish Plan for Palestine: Memoranda and Statements presented by The Jewish Agency for Palestine to the United Nations Special Committee on Palestine,* Jerusalem, 1947, p. 115. 40,000 for 1919-1944 is mentioned in Nathan, R., Gass, O., and Creamer, D., *Palestine: Problems and Promise,* Public Affairs Press, Washington, 1946, p. 136. David Horowitz and Rita Hinden write: "The official net immigration figures are obviously an underestimate, as they include neither illegal Jewish immigrants nor the steady influx of Arabs from the surrounding countries. The official net immigration for 1922-1936 is about 250,000, whereas the figure we arrive at . . . was 322,000—a difference of nearly 30 percent." *Economic Survey of Palestine,* Hapoel-Hazair Co-operative Press, Tel-Aviv, 1938, p. 28.

11. A. M. Carr-Saunders, for example, estimates Arab population in Palestine in 1919 at 642,000. *World Population,* Carendon Press, 1936, p. 307.

12. See *Survey of Palestine,* Government of Palestine, Government Printer, Palestine, 1946, Vol. I, p. 140; Hovne, A., *Labor Force in Israel,* The Maurice Falk Institute for Economic Research in Israel, Jerusalem, 1961, p. 29.

13. "There has been unrecorded illegal immigration both of Jews and of Arabs in the period since the census of 1931, but no estimate of its volume will be possible until the next census is taken." *Report by His Majesty's Government on Palestine and Transjordan.* London, 1937, p. 221. No census was taken.

14. The transformation of population data in the form of Moslems, Christians and other non-Jews to Arab population was made according to the equation: Arab Population = 0.82 Christian + 1.00 Moslem + 0.90 other non-Jews. *Palestine Blue Book 1938,* Government Printer, Jerusalem, n.d., p. 328. The distinction between settled and total population is made by excluding the nomadic tribes

Footnotes (Cont'd.)

of the Beersheba subdistrict. Mills, E., *op. cit.*, Preface to the Census of Palestine 1931.

15. Although no analysis was made of such a residual, it was nonetheless recognized in the Royal Commission Report of 1937. The Report states: "A discrepancy arose at the census of 1931 between the expected and enumerated population due to incomplete recording of births and deaths and of migration, and possibly to faulty enumeration of suspicious and primitive people." *Memoranda prepared by the Government of Palestine for the use of the Palestine Royal Commission,* His Majesty's Stationery Office, London, 1937, Colonial no. 133, p. 2.

16. *Ibid.,* p. 8.

17. See, for example, Thomas, B. "Migration and International Investment," *Economics of International Migration,* Ed., Thomas, B., McMillan, London, 1958; and Kuznets, S., and Dorothy S. Thomas, "Internal Migration and Economic Growth," *Selected Studies of Migration Since World War II,* Milbank Memorial Fund, New York, 1958, p. 199.

18. There is no way of separating out the migration from non-Israel Palestine to pre-State Israel although it is clear that such migration did take place. The *Survey of Palestine,* for example, comments: "Internal migrations have probably operated in the same way, the coastal plain and other regions *of more rapid economic development* attracting immigration from the hill regions," Vol. III., *op. cit.,* p. 1150. *My italics.*

19. The term "economic paralysis" belongs to Z. Y. Herschlag, *Introduction to the Modern Economic History of the Middle East,* E. J. Brill, Leiden, 1964, p. 231. Herschlag's is perhaps the best analysis of Middle East economic development for the pre-World War II period, but here too, the scarcity of statistical evidence is apparent. See his section "The Economy of the Mandated Territories—Syria, Lebanon, Iraq and Trans-Jordan—Between the Two World Wars," pp. 225-275.

20. Szereszewski, Robert, *Essays on the Structure of the Jewish Economy in Palestine and Israel,* The Maurice Falk Institute for Economic Research in Israel, Jerusalem, 1968, p. 82.

21. Gervasi, F., *op. cit.,* p. 104.

22. Grunwald, K., "The Industrialization of the Near East," *Bulletin of the Palestine Economic Society,* February, 1934, Volume 6, Number 3, pp. 78-79.

23. Horowitz, D., and Hinden, R., *op. cit.,* p. 208.

24. Himadeh, S., "Industry," *Economic Organization of Palestine,* Ed., Himadeh, S., American Press, Beirut, 1938, p. 230.

25. Himadeh, S., "Industry," *Economic Organization of Syria,* Ed., Himadeh, S., American Press, Beirut, 1936, p. 172.

26. *Ibid.,* p. 115.

27. *Progress of Iraq 1920-1931: Special Report,* Colonial no. 58, His Majesty's Stationery Office, London, 1931, pp. 205-217, 235-240. See also, Young, E. H., *Reports on Economic Conditions and Policy and Loan Policy,* Government Press, June 1930, Baghdad, p. 4. Young, lamenting the lack of statistical data, "surmises" a process of slow accumulation of wealth.

28. Herschlag, Z. Y., *op. cit.,* p. 237.

29. O'Brien, P., *The Revolution in Egypt's Economic System,* Oxford University Press, 1966, p. 210.

30. Grunwald, K., *The Government Finances of the Mandated Territories in the Near East,* Palestine Economic Society, May 1932, Volume 6, Number 1, p. 97.

26 The Palestinian-Arab Nationalist Movement

By Yehoshua Porat

Arab nationalism is a relatively recent phenomenon which originated in the first and second decade of this century. In the beginning, this nationalism had two foci: the desire to protect the achievements of the Arab cultural and literary renaissance of the previous fifty years and the effort to obtain political rights for the Arab citizens of the Ottoman Empire. This latter effort was based on the Arabs' own awareness that they constituted a separate ethnic community—an awareness as old as the existence of the Arabs themselves.[1]

This movement encompassed the Fertile Crescent, including the numerically small educated elite of Damascus, Baghdad, Basra, Tripoli and Beirut. Palestine, at that time, was a relatively backward area; it hardly played any role in the movement. What is more, the leadership of Jerusalem enjoyed a considerable degree of autonomy and influence, consequently tending to support the Arab element that professed Ottoman patriotism.

During World War I, however, and primarily when the Ottoman Empire broke up at the end of that war, the nationalist trend among the Arabs overcame its two competitors, the Ottoman and the traditional Muslim, and gained widespread public support. In Palestine, the Arab political public was aware of an important change that was taking place among the Jews, beginning in the 1880s: Jews newly arrived in the country (*Hovevei Zion*—"Lovers of Zion") were trying to bring about fundamental changes in the Jewish community and in the country as a whole. The leaders of the Arab community quickly came to suspect that this change among the Jews had political purposes, aiming to restore Israel's ancient status. The heads of the Muslim and Christian communities in Jerusalem petitioned the Sultan as early as 1891 to prohibit Jewish immigration to Palestine and the purchase of land by Jews.[2] As the *Second Aliyah* ("wave of immigration") developed, the newly established local Arab press (*al-Karmil,* and *Filastin*) came to express the Palestinian political public's opposition to Zionism, beginning in 1908. The election campaigns for the Ottoman Parliament which took place in 1908, 1912 and 1914, also offered many opportunities for the expression of this public's anti-Zionist position. In this manner, the nationalist movement of the Palestinian Arabs possessed, from its very beginnings, a specific characteristic: the struggle against a concrete enemy—Zionism.

This Zionist danger became much more important after the British conquest of Palestine, between December 1917 (when Jerusalem was taken) and September 1918. Arabs and Jews alike took the Balfour Declaration to mean a promise that a Jewish state would immediately be set up in Palestine. This resulted in very great enthusiasm on the part of the Jews—and in equally great concern on the part of the Arabs. In the course of 1918, the Arabs expressed this concern by founding various societies, all of which had the purpose of opposing the Zionist danger.

At the end of 1918, the Palestinian Arabs faced a serious dilemma, the likes

---

Dr. Porat is Professor of Islamic and Middle East Studies at the Hebrew University, Jerusalem.

of which they were to face many more times in the course of their history. In Damascus a semi-independent Arab regime was being formed by Feisal, the son of Hussein, king of Hedjaz: This the Arabs considered the seed of inclusive Arab independence. In addition (on November 8, 1918) the governments of Great Britain and France declared their recognition of the right of self-determination for the inhabitants of Syria and Iraq.

Things were different in Palestine however. Here the Jews let their aspirations be known. Far-reaching political demands were submitted to the Versailles Peace Conference. In Palestine, the recently arrived official delegation of the World Zionist Organization (The Zionist Commission) began to work for the realization of the Jewish National Home and was even granted official recognition by the British military occupation authorities. The combination of these circumstances caused the Palestinian Arabs to resolve, at the first congress, held in Jerusalem in January 1919,[3] that Palestine was nothing but "Southern Syria," and that the only way to repel Zionism lay in unity with Damascus. True, the Jerusalem leadership was not excessively enthusiastic about this decision, but the political considerations were held to be the decisive ones.

Until the summer of 1920, the Palestinian-Arab nationalist movement thus supported the slogan of unification with Syria. However, nothing was left of this dream of unity when Feisal was thrown out of Damascus in July 1920 and his regime collapsed: "Southern Syria" disappeared, both as slogan and as the appellation for the country, and "Filastin" was returned to the political scene. From this point on the Palestinians' effort concentrated on the attempt to get the British government's pro-Zionist policy revoked. They were prepared to accept the British Mandate on condition that its Zionist elements be abrogated. They were willing, in other words, to accept a regime that resembled what was coming into existence in Iraq and Transjordan. This tendency found its expression at their December 1920 Congress in Haifa, where an Executive Committee was elected to serve as the organ of struggle against the British government's Zionist policy.[4]

Not only did the slogans of Arab unity disappear, but, during the 1920s, the Palestinian Arabs actually refused to cooperate, to any significant degree, with the Syrian-Arab nationalist movement, which then attempted to continue its activity for Syrian independence and general unification with Lebanon, Palestine and Transjordan. That movement called its organization the "Syrian-Palestinian Congress," but it remained exclusively Syrian in composition — the Palestinians refused to participate in it —also, to a considerable extent, because of the Syrian leadership's moderate attitudes towards Zionism.[5]

However, the steadfast support of the essentials of Zionist policy on the part of the various British governments of that period left the Palestinian-Arabs with their frustration. The delegations they sent to London, the petitions they submitted and the demonstrations they organized all remained ineffective. Because of this, they refused to participate in any activity directed at the establishment of organs of self-government, and they rejected all the proposals made by the British to this effect in 1922 and 1923.

This failure resulted in the decline and split of the nationalist movement. Family rivalries again made their appearance. Some of them, headed by the Nashashibis, favored close cooperation with the Mandatory government. Others, led by the el-Husseini family, entrenched themselves in the Supreme Muslim Council, of which al-Hajj Amin el-Husseini, the Grand Mufti of Jerusalem, was president. The Supreme Muslim Council reinforced its president's status through its control over the Waqf properties and its supervision of the Muslim Shar'i courts.

From the very beginning, the Supreme Muslim Council tried to endow the anti-Zionist struggle with religious content. To this end, the two most important mosques of Jerusalem—el-Aqsa and the Dome of the Rock—were systematically developed. Contributions were collected throughout the Muslim world to finance restoration work, and Muslims everywhere were called upon to assist Palestine's Arabs in preserving Islam's holy places in Jerusalem. This policy inevitably came into conflict with the Jews' desire to obtain the right to pray at the Western Wall, which is part of *al-Haram al-Sharif,* the retaining wall that surrounds the mosque compound. The result was the outbreak of riots in August 1929.

The 1929 riots marked the radicalization of the Arabs' struggle against Zionism. The former leadership, which had limited itself to legal methods, was replaced by the leadership of al-Hajj Amin el-Husseini. The latter found support among a group of young radical leaders, who proposed that Zionism, and later also Britain, be opposed by violent means. They directly and indirectly criticized the Arab Executive Committee in their periodical, *al-Jami'a al-Arabiyya,* contributing to its ultimate dissolution in 1934, after the death of its aged president, Musa Kazim al-Husayni.

The Palestinian Arabs' movement's radicalization during the 1930s was part of more general processes which occurred in Palestine and throughout the Middle East. At that time it appeared that the Arab world was approaching independence, or even that it was about to achieve it. Ibn Saud established his United Kingdom in the Arab peninsula in 1927. Iraq became independent in 1930 and was admitted to the League of Nations in 1932; the Anglo-Egyptian Treaty was signed in 1936, while both Syria and Lebanon initialled similar agreements on their independence that same year.

In contrast to all this, the establishment of the Jewish National Home in Palestine gained momentum at a rate previously unknown. Nothing could represent this process better than the statistics on Jewish immigration during that period.[6]

Year	Number of Jewish immigrants arriving in Palestine
1931	4,075
1932	12,553
1933	37,337
1934	45,267
1935	66,472
1936	29,595
1937	10,629
1938	14,675
1939	31,195

By 1939, the Jewish community already numbered about 450,000—some 30% of the country's entire population.

Under these circumstances, the Palestinian Arabs found themselves in a situation that resembled that of 1919: the Fertile Crescent appeared to be approaching independence while Zionism appeared to be approaching its realization in Palestine. This was the major factor that enabled al-Hajj Amin el-Husseini to push the Palestinian Arabs to an increasingly extremist position, and it constituted the background of the armed Arab revolt in Palestine during 1936-1939. This revolt, for the first time ever, involved the participation of broader population groups, including the peasantry, Bedouin and villagers who had moved to the cities and become laborers. This explains the revolt's strength and persistence.

In military terms, the revolt was defeated, but politically it was quite successful. The Palestinian Arab leadership did manage to exploit the impact that this revolt made in other Arab countries so as to make the Palestine problem the central political issue in nationalist circles in all the Arab countries. The Arab kings' intervention, in October 1936, in favor of ending the general strike, was the direct result of an appeal to them by the Palestinian-Arab leadership.[7] This successful precedent had its impact on the British, who then also invited the participation of the representatives of the independent Arab states when they attempted, in the fall of 1938, to find a political solution to the revolt in addition to its military suppression. This involvement of the Arab states, and the British recognition thereof, finally led to the turning point in Britain's Palestine policy. A new policy was proclaimed by them in May 1939, after the London Conference.

The British considered the friendship of the Arab states to be of vital importance at a time when the world was approaching the brink of war. This belief led to the realization that this friendship could not be maintained while the Palestinian Arabs were in revolt and had to be suppressed and a change in British policy in Palestine became inevitable. This change did not satisfy the Arabs' demands, but it nevertheless constituted a real achievement for them. Jewish immigration and land acquisition were greatly reduced (although Palestinian independence was made conditional upon agreement between the Arabs and the Jews—a requirement that appeared bound to postpone that promised independence to the end of time).

Pan-Arab intervention in Palestinian affairs, which had its beginning at that time, was intensified after the end of World War II. Their revolt had left the Arabs of Palestine divided and in conflict with each other, and they consequently thought it best to let the Arab League—Britain's own creation—manage their struggle for them. With the massive support of the independent Arab states they would be able to oppose the growing Zionist pressure, the result of the Second World War's terrifying consequences for the Jews.

This dependence on the Arab states did not yield the results that the Palestinian Arabs had hoped for. It failed militarily in 1948, and it may even have weakened the Palestinian Arabs' will for self-sufficiency. The effect was to enable the half million Jews in Palestine to show that they had to struggle against the entire Arab world—against independent states with tens of millions of inhabitants and organized armies — a presentation that helped to gain a great deal of international sympathy for the Jewish cause. The 1948 war became a pan-Arab effort against the Jews of Palestine.

The process of "pan-Arabization" of the Arab struggle in Palestine was only intensified by the defeat of 1948 and the consequent fragmentation of the Palestinian Arab population into refugees in the Gaza Strip, into citizens of Israel, into refugees and permanent residents of the Kingdom of Jordan and refugees in Syria and Lebanon, etc.

The first independent Palestinian effort, made during the 1950s, to carry on with the struggle was also pan-Arab in character. This refers to the Movement of Arab Nationalists (*al-Qawmiyyumi al-Arab*), which Dr. George Habash organized in Beirut at that time,[8] in order to achieve Arab unity at all costs, so that all the Arabs' resources could be used for the liberation of Palestine. This organization's slogan was "Unity, Freedom, Revenge"—a formula typical of its general approach. The *Fida'iyyun* (terrorists) of the mid 1950s were no more than one of the instruments used by the Egyptian army to strike at Israel.

During the early 1960s, however, the first indications of a turn towards self-dependence began to appear. In 1959, a small newspaper began to come out in Beirut under the name *Filastinana* ("Our Palestine"), preaching the liberation of Palestine by the effort of the Palestinians themselves. This paper claimed that the lesson of Algeria's struggle for national liberation must be learned. Its appearance was the first harbinger of *al-Fatah* on the political scene. The dissolution of the United Arab Republic in 1961—and, in particular, the failure of pan-Arab Nasserism during the 1960s—only strengthened the trends proposed by *al-Fatah*. *Al-Fatah* began troubling Israel in 1965 by sending terrorists across her borders on missions of sabotage and murder.

The same change also began to make its appearance in George Habash's own party. His organization, originally outspokenly Rightist, gradually came to adopt maximalist Leftist attitudes, stressing the need for "popular," rather than conventional, warfare. The order of priorities also came to be changed. Unity was no longer considered an essential precondition for the liberation of *Filastin* (Palestine); now a popular war for the liberation of *Filastin* was thought to be the way by which Arab unity would be realized. Taking its departure from this change, the Movement of Arab Nationalists established its own terrorist organization, which also began to cross Israel's borders in 1966 and to engage in sabotage and slaughter.[9]

This wave of terrorism—one of the important causal factors of the Six-Day War—intensified after June 1967, and the tendency toward Palestinian-Arab self-sufficiency appeared to be victorious. But this was only a temporary impression. In the first place, many Palestinian-Arabs came to doubt whether they were strong enough to act alone—after the defeats they suffered in Jordan in September 1970 and July 1971—and whether the first step, before the decisive battle with Israel, did not have to be a fundamental change in the Arab world itself. Secondly, even during the heyday of Palestinian independent action, these organizations still remained true to the ideology of all-inclusive Arab unity. The Palestinian National Charter (first formulated in 1964, amended in 1968 and since then ratified by all the national Congresses) defines *Filastin* as an integral part of the Arab homeland, while the people of *Filastin* constitutes an inseparable part of the Arab nation. Even *al-Fatah*, the most Palestine-oriented organization of them all, remained true to the ideology that proclaimed Arab unity. This is even more valid for the Popular Front for the Liberation of Palestine, founded by the Movement of Arab Nationalists, and for the Arab Liberation Front, a creation of the *Ba'ath*.

As in the past, the cultural and linguistic factor now also continues to be the most important element in the definition of the Arabs' national identity, including that of the Palestinians. It is true that political realities and practical considerations led to behavior at variance with such ideological beliefs—but in the ideological sphere, loyalty to the pan-Arab conception reigns supreme. This differentiation between ideology and reality is not the result of deceit. Quite the contrary: it reflects the basic fact that the process crystallizing the national identity of the Arabs, including that of the Palestinians, has not yet reached its conclusion. Common culture and language stand in conflict with factors of territory and local interest, and it is much too early to predict which will ultimately turn out to be decisive.

The Arab nationalist movement's radicalization has brought it to believe that the complete social revolution, as defined along Marxist-Leninist lines, constitutes an inseparable part of the struggle for national liberation. This the Palestinian-Arabs were not the first to advocate: the *Ba'ath* had preceded them in making Socialism an essential part of its nationalist concept. However, when the Movement of Arab Nationalists and the Popular Front for the Liberation of Palestine (the Movement's affiliate) made this turn, the door was opened wide for the penetration of radical Leftist opinion into the Palestinian-Arab movement. In fact, such opinions also reached the other organizations through this opening. Until 1970 *al-Fatah* had considered itself as neutral with regard to the Arab world's different regimes, but since 1971 it too has begun to take a social stand in favor of the "progressive" Arab regimes and of the "Arab working class' struggle against the bourgeoisie and the reactionaries."

The Popular Front's drift to the Left did not satisfy its own Left-wing, which wanted complete identification with the international revolutionary movement. In February 1969 they split from the original organization to form the Democratic Front for the Liberation of Palestine, under the leadership of Na'if Hawatme and Muhassan Ibrahim. At first this move was successful. Most of the members of the Popular Front's central committee joined the new organization, as did its organ "al-Hurriyya." However, this was soon followed by failure and weakness. This was, undoubtedly, due to their attitude to Israel.

Of all the terrorist organizations, it seems that the DFLP was the only one that accepted, with any degree of seriousness, the slogan of a "Democratic Filastin." Certainly, they also registered their reservations, explaining that they did not mean a "bourgeois democracy" of "one man—one vote," but rather, a "popuar democracy," but nevertheless, one cannot ignore the fact that they were the only ones who proposed to amend the National Charter in the spirit of a "Democratic Filastin." What is more, the Democratic Front's platform recognized that the Israelis constitute not a religious community but rather one with a cultural identity of its own. In an article in *Le Monde* and *al-Hurriyya,* Na'if Hawatme even dared to propose that the solution to the Palestine problem might lie in a federative arrangement such as is to be found in Yugoslavia or in Czechoslovakia.

This organization also shows signs of deviation on the subject of Arab unity. In this context, they call for an Arab federation—a concept much less far-reaching than the call for complete unity. This has aroused many of their previous supporters against them, and these supporters have abandoned them in favor of the original Popular Front.

This development indicates that the general concept of unity on the basis of culture and language is accepted in the nationalist Palestinian-Arab camp while any suggestion that certain rights of Israel's Jews can be recognized is regarded by them as anathema.

FOOTNOTES

1. A Hourani, *Arabic Thought in the Liberal Age,* London, 1962.

2. This petition is quoted in *Ha'or.* 27 Nissan 5651.

3. Material on this Congress may be found in the Israel State Archives, Chief Secretary Files No. 156, and also in the Central Zionist Archives, L/4, File 276 IIB. For a description by an Arab eye witness, see Hala al-Sakakini (ed.) *Kadha Ana ya Dunya, Yamiyyat Khalil al Sakakini,* Jerusalem 1955, pp. 164-66.

4. A report on this meeting appeared in the newspaper *al-Karmil,* on December 16, 1920.

5. This problem is discussed at length in my book *The Emergence of the Palestinian-Arab National Movement,* London, 1973, Chapter 2.

6. *Statistical Abstract of Israel 1972,* No. 23, p. 127; these figures are somewhat higher than the official ones reported by the Mandate authorities, since they also include "illegal" immigrants.

7. Public Record Office, Colonial Office, 733/314/75528, parts II and III.

8. For further information on the Movement of Arab Nationalists, see also M. Suleiman, *Political Parties in Lebanon,* New York 1967, pp. 155-172.

9. The development of this organization is analyzed from the Marxist-Leninist point of view in the book *Liladha Munazzamat al-Ishtirakiyin* al-Lubnaniyin, Beirut, 1970.

27

The Nature of the PLO: Some International Implications

By Yonah Alexander

The Palestinian Arab guerrilla movements had their beginning in the early 1950s, when Palestinian students in the Arab countries, particularly in Syria and Lebanon, formed para-military youth movements and became active in the Arab refugee camps. Although they sought to restore "Arab Palestine" to its "rightful owners," they failed to translate their theories into action. In fact, the proliferation of some 50 organizations in the next decade demonstrated their inability to unite against the common enemy. Currently, the PLO consists of a configuration of forces reflecting the painful process in which various groups sprang into existence, merged with other groups under different names, split and regrouped again.

History, Leadership and Structure

Officially, the PLO and its military arm, the Palestine Liberation Army (PLA) were created by the Arab Summit Conference in Cairo in January 1964. This umbrella framework, with headquarters in Cairo, was intended by the Arab League to serve as a military weapon in its attempt to destroy Israel. Ahmed Shukairy, who headed the group, believed in a long-term formation of a regular "Liberation" force that would attack the Jewish state when it was properly ready. His political mentor was President Nasser of Egypt, and his base of operations against the Jewish State was the Egyptian-ruled Gaza Strip.[1] On June 10, 1967, several days after the debacle of the Six-Day War, Nasser stated, on *Radio Cairo:* "The dedicated campaign conducted by our Arab nation has not yet ended. It will continue until the final victory," and in a later broadcast, "The duty of the Arab nation is not only to liquidate the consequences of the aggression but to eradicate the basic danger. We hope the entire Arab nation will develop a fighting stand: the struggle for the liberation of Palestine."[2]

Several months later, Shukairy, who was bitterly accused of failure by other Palestinian groups, was forced to resign as Secretary General of the PLO. With his departure, the PLO became plagued by internal strife and lost much of its former power. Since that event, the history of the Palestinian movements has been characterized by an endless process of separatism and amalgamation.[3] The most important guerrilla organization to survive the test of time and, in fact, to provide considerable leadership, particularly in the role of a unifying force, is *Harakat Tahrir Falastin* (Movement for the Liberation of Palestine), better known as *Fatah* (Conquest). Formed in 1956 under Egyptian sponsorship, this body is led by Yasir Arafat, who developed the movement's ideology and strategy and later became head of the PLO. Under his leadership, *Fatah* was able to appeal to the majority of the Palestinians (who have, however, never been given the right to choose their representation). Since 1970, *Fatah* has become the major power center and the dominant group within the PLO.

With his November 13, 1974 appearance before the United Nations General Assembly, Arafat both consolidated his position as PLO leader and added a degree of legitimacy to *Fatah's* position within the Palestinian movement. Since then, Arafat and *Fatah* have been forced to deal with several crises

---

Dr. Alexander is Professor of International Studies and Director of the Institute for Studies on International Terrorism, S.U.N.Y., and currently Research Associate at the Center for Strategic and International Studies at Georgetown University. He is the Editor-in-Chief of *Terrorism: An International Journal*, co-editor with Robert A. Kilmarx of *Political Terrorism and Business: The Threat and Response* (Praeger Press, New York, 1979), and co-editor with Robert A. Friedlander of *Self Determination: National, Regional and Global Dimensions* (Westview Press, 1980).

that severely tested his own and his group's leadership. The Lebanese Civil War, Sadat's diplomatic initiative, Egypt's peace treaty with Israel and inter-terrorist rivalries have constituted the gravest of these challenges. But both Arafat and *Fatah* have apparently survived these crises.

Fatah's second in command is Saleh Khalef (alias Abu Iyad) who directed the operations of the *Black September* group and now heads the PLO's Security and Intelligence Department. Another major figure, the head of *Fatah's* military arm, Khalil el-Wazer (also known as Abu Jihad) is responsible for coordinating all of *Fatah's* attacks inside Israel. Also prominent is Farouk Kaddoumi (Abu Lutf) in charge of the PLO's Political Department. Kaddoumi and Arafat represent *Fatah* on the PLO's Executive Committee.

Arafat's position in *Fatah* has been weakened by recent internal rivalries. Abu Iyad has emerged as an open opponent to his leadership. Although Arafat has tried to reinforce his position by playing Abu Iyad off against Abu Jihad, the latter harbors his own ambition to become *Fatah's* chief.

Other organizations belonging to the PLO structure are *El Saiqa* (also known as "The Vanguards of the Popular Liberation Army") formerly headed by Zuhir Muhsin, (assassinated in 1979); the *Popular Front for the Liberation of Palestine* (PFLP) headed by George Habash; the *Popular Front for the Liberation of Palestine-General Command* (PFLP-GC) headed by Ahmed Jabril; the *Arab Liberation Front* (ALF) led by Abdel Rahim Ahmed; the *Democratic Front for the Liberation of Palestine* (DFLP) led by Nayef Hawatmeh; the *Palestine Liberation Front* (PLF) directed by Abul Abbas; and the *Palestinian Popular Front* (PPF) headed by Samir Ghosheh.

The "Palestinian Revolution," which is regarded as an integral part of the International Liberation Movement, is not an ideologically monolithic body. Although the defeat of Egypt, Jordan and Syria in the Six-Day War made the loosely organized guerrilla groups realize that the success of their revolution will, in the final analysis, depend on their own efforts, they have been unable, thus far, to create a common ideological base for the confrontation with the Jewish State. On the contrary, with the involvement of a younger, predominantly leftist, Palestinian leadership, ideological differences between the resistance groups have deepened, contributing to sharpened inter-group conflicts. For instance, *Fatah's* only political ideology is the recovery of Palestine through armed struggle, while the *Popular Democratic Front for the Liberation of Palestine* is a Trotskyist group committed to total revolution against Zionism, imperialism and "Arab reactionaries."[4] These differences have resulted in bitter internal rivalries between the two major guerrilla groups and have weakened the growth and effectiveness of all the Palestinian groups.[5]

The PLO's headquarters is currently based in Damascus and its center of operations is in Beirut. Its main administrative agency is a 15-member Executive Committee, consisting of six representatives of the guerrilla groups (2 from *Fatah* and 4 from other organizations) while the rest are unaffiliated intellectuals and members of various professions. Most of these support Arafat. The Executive Committee, whose chairman is Arafat, is served by a 43-member consultative Central Council. The committee is elected by the National Council, a 172-member Parliament which generally meets twice a year. *Fatah* holds one-third of the National Council seats and is supported by one-third of the unaffiliated members. Various coalitions have attempted, over the years, to alter the leadership structure, but none has yet succeeded.

Although Arafat is also the commander of the Palestine Liberation Army, its day-to-day affairs are supervised by its chief of Staff, General Misbah Bueiri, a Syrian-trained Palestinian officer. Conflicts between the military command and the PLO's political leadership have constantly beset the army. The army's five brigades have a total strength of 17,000 men, equipped with 4,000 tanks and 2,000 armored cars and track vehicles. The PLA has no air force, but many officers have been trained as pilots and aircraft maintenance specialists in Syria, Egypt and Iraq. The army has served alongside the Egyptian, Syrian and Jordanian armies, and fought in the Lebanese Civil War.

Apart from its organizations inside the Middle East, the PLO also has an extensive network of offices world-wide. These exist in most communist countries, including the Soviet Union, and in many Western European countries, as well as in England and in several U.S. cities, including New York and Washington. Southern California, in particular, has been an area of concentrated PLO activity. These offices serve several purposes. Countries supporting the PLO are able to have direct contact with PLO officials stationed in the local PLO offices. Through its offices, the PLO's intelligence organization, *Razd*, can collect information, coordinate PLO activities, and disseminate military and political information vital to the Palestinian cause. The PLO is also able to use its network of offices to collect money and recruit manpower from among the Palestinians living outside the Middle East.

The Palestine National Covenant

Fatah's aims are articulated in the PLO's *Palestine National Covenant*, originally promulgated by a Palestinian Congress held in Jerusalem in May 1964, reaffirmed and amended in Cairo in June, 1968, and confirmed at every subsequent meeting of the PLO's governing bodies. Nearly half of its 33 articles state or imply that the Jewish state has no right to exist, and therefore should be eliminated. These major twin themes are clearly set forth in the first three articles of the Covenant and are reiterated throughout the document. Briefly, it demands "the liberation of Palestine," and asserts that it is the Palestinians' "national duty to repulse the Zionist, imperialist invasion . . . and to push the Zionist presence out of 'Palestine'," (Article 15), and that "the existence of Israel is fundamentally null and void, whatever time has elapsed" (Article 19). It "rejects every solution that is a substitute for a complete liberation of Palestine and rejects all plans that aim at the settlement of the Palestine issue or its internationalization."

The most recent demonstration of the PLO's adherence to the Covenant occurred at the meeting of the PLO's Central Committee in Damascus in August 1979, in which the PFLP participated (it had suspended its membership in the Committee in 1974 in protest against the PLO's "moderation"). In Damascus, the radical mood was evident. Khaled al-Fahoum, the Committee's Chairman and Syria's candidate to succeed Arafat, asserted that the "national Palestinian rights, as determined in the Political Platform of the PLO (i.e., the Covenant) must be preserved . . . and any resolution that does not include these rights, or attempts to impair them, must be rejected." A similar statement was made by Farouk Kaddoumi. In an interview on German television on August 12, he declared: "The PLO will never recognize Israel, even if Israel recognizes the PLO." Yet, in September, Arafat said that he "did not remember" any clause in the Charter calling for the elimination of Israel. In an interview with Barbara Walters on ABC T.V.'s *Issues and Answers* he insisted that "the Charter says that we have the right to establish our democratic state."[6]

Fatah spokesmen have always claimed, particularly in communications outside the Middle East, that the PLO's goal is the establishment of "a democratic, secular, Palestinian state" in which Muslims, Christians, and Jews would live side by side in peace. Yet the true interpretation of the "democratic Palestinian slogan" was reported in Beirut's *An-Anwar* of March 8 and 15, 1970, when in an "informal chat," Shafiq Al-Hut, Beirut's *Fatah* representative asserted:

> There is no merit in talking at length about the slogan of a 'democratic state.' It is not possible for such a state, devoid of affiliation, to come into being. If the slogan of a Democratic State is only intended as an answer to the charge that we aim at throwing the Jews into the sea, then it is a successful slogan and an effective political and propaganda act. But if we regard it as a matter of ultimate strategy of the national Palestinian and Arab liberation movements, then I think that it calls for thorough examination.

This view has not changed. In an interview with *Alutan al-Arabi* (a Paris-based weekly) on April 24, 1979, Al-Hut again expressed the ideological rigidity of the PLO position, namely, its unwillingness to coexist with Israel; its acceptance of political means to resolve the conflict as only complementing military means (which, in turn, is the only way to establish a state in the whole of Arab Palestine) and a justification of terrorism as a legitimate weapon in the struggle for Palestinian self-determination.

PLO Terrorist Operations

In light of this consistent disposition, it is not surprising that the PLO is prepared to fight as long as necessary in order to liquidate the Zionist enemy, to liberate all the "usurped" land and to achieve its final victory.

Perceiving revolutionary violence as a sanctified instrument, *Fatah's* military arm, *Al-Assifah* (Storm), which currently consists of approximately 6,000 active members, has been engaged in guerrilla activities, such as border raids, since the pre-1967 period, and aimed at escalating Arab-Israeli tension in order to force a war with Israel on the Arab countries. After Israel's June 1967 victory, however, *Fatah* reorganized, and intensified its terrorist activities inside Israel, declaring that these attacks constituted military operations. Since the signing of the Egyptian-Israeli peace treaty, this group has once again stepped up operations in both Israel proper and the administered territories. In part, the intensification of activities was in response to pressure by the Iraqi-backed *Abu Nidal* (also known as *Sabriel-Banna*) group, which is outside the PLO umbrella. In pursuit of its objective, in addition to its Beirut base, *Fatah* has established new headquarters in Damascus, run by Abu Ziyyad, which has expanded its operations, particularly in the West Bank, with a view to blocking the implementation of the autonomy plans as envisioned in the peace treaty.

According to available data, between January 1965 and September 1979, a total of 1,207 people were killed and 2,950 wounded in all PLO operations, including arson, bombings, kidnappings, assassinations, shootings, hijackings, and miscellaneous incidents. During 1978 alone, a total of 250 PLO terrorist attacks were directed against Jewish and non-Jewish targets outside Israel, with a toll of 245 killed and 334 wounded. Since Israel and Israeli interests were the major targets, approximately half of the dead and injured were Israeli Jews.[7] *Fatah* claimed responsibility for the most spectacular of these attacks and attempted attacks.

Terrorism is in the Arab political tradition. Arafat himself began his career with political murder — when leaders of the Palestinian Student Federation opposed him in December, 1955 they were immediately eliminated. The targets of PLO terrorist attacks include not only Israeli Jews, but also Arabs prepared to co-exist with Israel. From June 1967 to September 1979, more than 350 Arabs were killed and some 2,000 were injured. In addition, hundreds of Gaza residents were killed between 1968 and 1970. When the PLO Executive Committee earmarked 15 "collaborators with Israel" for assassination, Sheik Hashem Khozander, the Imam of Gaza, who was known for his moderate views on the Palestinian question and his support of the Egyptian-Israeli peace treaty, was killed the very next day on his way home from evening prayer. A PLO spokesman claimed responsibility for the attack and announced that his organization would continue to assassinate Arab leaders of whose political views it disapproved.

The PLO, and *Fatah* as its strongest member, were also engaged in operations elsewhere in the Middle East and beyond that region. Faced with the decisive defeat in Jordan in September 1970 and July 1971, *Fatah* established the *Black September* terrorist group in order to demonstrate to the Palestinians and the Arab States that it still remained the major force within the resistance. *Black September*, which began its activities in November 1971, has been responsible for a multitude of operations including political assassinations, sabotage in Europe, skyjackings, the Munich Olympics attack, and attacks on Israeli, European, U.S. and Saudi embassies and diplomats.[8]

Attempting to preserve its image as a "moderate" organization, *Fatah* has not officially acknowledged its connection with *Black September* and has even disassociated itself from this group's deeds, although, as reported in Beirut's *The Daily Star* of March 15, 1973, Arafat asserted that the acts of

Black September "were loud expressions of despair," driving them "increasingly toward the adoption of a policy of consuming the world's tranquility," and suggesting that it was virtually impossible to stop these revolutionary activities. However, the connection between *Fatah* and *Black September* was unexpectedly revealed by Abu Daud, leader of a *Fatah* mission sent to assassinate King Hussein of Jordan. When arrested by the Jordanian security police, he admitted, on Amman's television and radio, and also in an interview with British commercial television, that "*Black September* is not an organization separate from *Fatah*, it is a group of people from *Fatah* itself." This revelation was a contributing factor leading to *Fatah's* decision to halt *Black September's* activities. As announced by Abu Iyad on July 16, 1973,

> We understand the meaning of *Black September* as a phenomenon. We understand the motives which prompt these youths to carry out such acts . . . but this does not mean that we are the planners or the financiers.[9]

After this shift, *Fatah* returned to its earlier policy of simultaneously praising violence in "Arab Palestine" and disclaiming or denouncing terrorism elsewhere. Thus, commenting on the PLFP-GC attack on Qiryat Shemona in Israel, when 8 children, 8 civilians and 2 soldiers were killed, a PLO broadcast from Sana (North Yemen) on April 13, 1975 stated:

> The action proves that the guerrillas can continue the armed struggle to defend their right of representation. International recognition of the PLO will increase only by means of armed struggle, which must expand daily so that it may attain various revolutionary forms in the land of battle.

In December 1975, however, the PLO denied any responsibility for the terrorist raid on OPEC headquarters in Vienna by the *Arm of Arab Liberation*, when 3 persons were killed, 9 wounded, and several taken hostage — including 11 oil ministers of OPEC nations, most of them Arab. The terrorists' demands included the negation of the Egypt-Israel interim agreement and a call to the Arab world for a "total liberation war" against Israel.

The PLO has continued this dual policy. Shaken by the Egyptian-Israeli treaty, it has sought to appear as a moderate force willing to use its influence in a respectable way. (Thus, for example, it disassociated itself from the Palestinian terrorist attack on the Egyptian embassy in Ankara in July 1979, and used its "good offices" to release the hostages involved.) But it has also continued its terrorist activities.

The Impact of the PLO

The Palestinian cause is unquestionably more widely known in the Middle East and beyond as a result of the publicity it has received in the media. This was one of the major propaganda goals of the Arab states and the Palestinian movements.

On the diplomatic level, recognition of the PLO as worthy of international legal status is gaining momentum. On October 28, 1974, the 20 Arab heads of government meeting at Rabat recognized the PLO as "the sole legitimate representative of the Palestinian people." They also endowed the PLO with the right to assert "national authority" and committed the Arab states to support this authority "in all respects and at all levels."[10] The international community endorsed this policy during a reception given to Arafat at the U.N. — a reception of the type reserved for a chief of state.[11] Since that event, the PLO voice in the chambers of the U.N. has been heard repeatedly. The PLO has, indeed, taken a place as a prominent and active national liberation movement not accorded to any other terrorist or guerrilla group in the world organization and its specialized agencies. Moreover, a series of diplomatic moves was undertaken by the Arab states, the PLO, and their supporters, particularly in the Third World nations, to isolate Israel and reject it from international organizations. The reasons for these efforts were articulated by the Lebanese representative at the UNESCO General Conference meeting in Paris on November 14, 1974: "Israel is a state which belongs nowhere because it comes from nowhere." This attitude, coupled with a built-in majority at the meeting, led to the passage of several resolutions discriminating against Israel.[12] In July 1975, the International Women's Year World Conference in

Mexico, held under U.N. auspices included "Zionism" in its final declaration as one of the ideologies — along with colonialism, foreign occupation, Apartheid, and racial discrimination — which must be "eliminated."[13] In August, a Conference of forty Muslim countries, meeting in Jeddah, adopted a resolution calling for the expulsion of Israel from the U.N. and for states participating in the meeting to sever relations with Israel. Another anti-Israel resolution was passed at the Kampala meeting of the Organization of African Unity Summit. On October 17, 1975, the Third Committee of the U.N. decided, by a vote of 70 to 29 with 29 abstentions, to recommend the full General Assembly passage of a resolution depicting Israel as "the racist regime in occupied Palestine," stigmatizing Zionism as "a form of racialism and racial discrimination," asserting that "Zionism is a threat to world peace and security," and calling upon "all countries to oppose this racist and imperialist ideology."[14] On November 10, 1975, some twenty-eight years after voting to establish a Jewish State, the U.N. General Assembly endorsed this resolution, and also passed two other resolutions, the first calling for PLO participation in the Geneva Conference, the second establishing a committee (modeled on the U.N. Committee Against Apartheid) for "the exercise of the inalienable rights of the Palestinian people." This committee is authorized "to receive and consider suggestions and proposals from any State and intergovernmental regional organization and the Palestine Liberation Organization."[15]

On April 21, 1976, the 59-nation gathering of Arab and African ministers in Dakar, Senegal, adopted a resolution condemning "imperialism, colonialism, neo-colonialism, Zionism, Apartheid and all other forms of racial and religious segregation and discrimination, notably in Africa, Palestine and the occupied Arab territories."[16] Similar attempts were made at the U.N. Economic and social Council debate on the *Decade for Action to Combat Racism and Racial Discrimination*, and at the international anti-Apartheid seminar, sponsored by the U.N. Special Committee Against Apartheid, in collaboration with the Organization of African Unity.[17] The seventh annual meeting of the Islamic Conference of Foreign Ministers from 42 countries in Istanbul in May 1976, reiterated demands that Israel withdraw from all occupied Arab land and the Palestinians be allowed to establish an independent state and called for Israel's expulsion from the U.N.[18]

Other actions have been taken in the aftermath of Sadat's initiative and the Egyptian-Israeli treaty. The Summit Meeting of the Organization of African Unity (OAU) in Monrovia, Liberia, July 17-20, 1979, and the Conference of Heads of State or Governments of Non-Aligned Countries in Havana, Cuba, September 3-7, 1979, strongly supported the Palestinian cause. At the U.N., the Committee on the Exercise of the Inalienable Rights of the Palestinian People, during its forty-third meeting on October 1, 1979 recommended to the General Assembly that it be guided constantly by the following principles:

> (a) The question of Palestine is at the heart of the Middle East and consequently no solution to the Middle East problem could be envisaged without taking into account the rights of the Palestinian people;
>
> (b) The realization of the inalienable rights of the Palestinian people to return to their homes and to self-determination, independence and national sovereignty would contribute to a solution of the crisis in the Middle East;
>
> (c) The participation of the Palestinian Liberation Organization, the representative of the Palestinian people, on an equal footing with all other parties on the basis of General Assembly resolutions 3236 (XXIX) and 3375 (XXX) is indispensable in all efforts, deliberations and conferences on the Middle East undertaken under the auspices of the United Nations; and,
>
> (d) The inadmissibility of the acquisition of territory by force and the obligation which devolved on Israel to withdraw completely and quickly from all territory so occupied."[19]

The most prominent European leader to participate in the effort to mobilize support for the PLO is Austrian Chancellor Bruno Kreisky, who met with Arafat in July 1979 and advised him on ways to improve the PLO's international image and facilitate increased formal recognition of the organization, and called for recognition of the PLO as the representative of the Palestinian people during his U.N. General Assembly speech in October. Turkey granted the PLO an informal diplomatic status that same month. Portugal is expected to become the second NATO country to grant the PLO quasi-official recognition.[20]

What is even more remarkable is that even the U.S., which has long refused to recognize the PLO, is expected eventually to negotiate with this organization. In 1976, President Sadat, in interviews in Cairo's *Al-Ahram*[21] and Beirut's *Al-Hawadess*[22] said that he had an agreement with then Secretary of State Kissinger that the U.S. would start a dialogue with the PLO. President Ford, on April 19, 1976, implied a shift in U.S. policy in an interview with Dallas newspaper editors.

The Camp David Accords and the Egypt-Israel Peace Treaty paved the way for the autonomy talks, yet the question regarding whether, or to what extent, the PLO is a terrorist group, and whether it should play a role in any negotiations, remains unresolved. The State Department regards the PLO as an umbrella group, some of whose factions advocate and use terrorism while others do not, a characterization leaving a door open in case the PLO decides to moderate its position on Israel. Presumably, it is also the rationale behind the implicit recognition of the PLO on two other occasions. At a reception in Algiers, Zbigniew Brzezinski shook hands with Arafat; the U.S. indirectly accepted the PLO's suggestion that it act as mediators in efforts to obtain the release of the hostages at the American embassy in Tehran.

Congress too is slowly changing its attitude towards the PLO. As Senator Adlai E. Stevenson (D-Ill.), who met Arafat during a recent trip to the Middle East, has stated, the PLO

> may be distrusted, disowned and despised, but it is a reality, if for no other reason than that it has no rival organization among Palestinians. As long as this reality persists, it will have to be reckoned with in any future multilateral negotiating process.[23]

Senator Stevenson also said that Arab public utterances are distorted by the "exaggeration and hyperbole which mark Arab cultures" and that these only strengthen Israeli "hardliners." The U.S., he said, could not expect Arafat to say in public what he tells visiting officials in private, because he has to watch out for extremists in his organization.[24]

The most forceful advocate of a dialogue between the U.S. and the PLO is Rep. Paul Findley (R-Ill.), who wanted the State Department officially to request that Arafat provide his "good offices" to free the American hostages in Tehran. When Findlay's efforts failed he telephoned PLO officials in Beirut and asked them to mediate in order to improve their public relations image in the U.S. In his interview with the media he explained: "They are considered international bandits and a humanitarian action like this . . would give Americans a better feeling about them."[25]

Ambassador Andrew Young's resignation as the U.S. Permanent Representative to the U.N., coupled with the Middle East mission of several Black American leaders, has also opened a public debate on recognition of the PLO as a full partner in the peace process. The U.S. is widely expected soon to support such a move. In a recent *Los Angeles Times* poll on future U.S. relations with the PLO, 59 percent agreed that the U.S. should negotiate with them, while 29 percent were opposed and 12 percent had no opinion.[26]

FOOTNOTES

1. For an excellent survey see Y. Harkabi, *Fedayeen Action and Arab Strategy* (London: Institute for Strategic Studies, December, 1968).

2. *Radio Cairo*, July 31, 1967.

3. See Fouad M. Moughrabi, "The Palestine Resistance Movement: Evolution of a Strategy," (paper delivered at the XVII Annual Convention of the International Studies Association, Toronto, Canada, February 25-29, 1976).

4. For a description of the organizational development of the Palestinian movements together with an examination of the political ideologies of the various groups see, for example, Leila S. Kadi, *Basic Political Documents of the Armed Palestinian Resistance Move-*

ment (Beirut: Fifth of June Society, n.d.). This report by Gerard Chaliand, was originally published in *Le Monde Diplomatique*, March, 1969. For a briefer discussion of the subject see, for example, *Al-Nahar* (Beirut), March 18, 1969.

5. For a sampling of recriprocal recriminations see, for instance, *As Siyad* (Kuwait), March 11, 1969; *Nida al Watan* (Beirut), July 24, 1969; *Free Palestine* (London), June, 1970; *Akher Sa'a* (Cairo), December 16, 1970; and *An-Nahar* (Beirut), September 23, 1971.

6. Reported in the *Jerusalem Post*, September 10, 1979.

7. See, for example, *Facts* (January 1979), Vol. 25, No. 1. All the data are derived from Israeli sources.

8. For an account of Black September see Christopher Dobson, *Black September: Its Short Violent History* (New York: MacMillan Publishing Co., 1974).

9. *Arab Report and Record* (February 15-28, 1973), p. 83.

10. *Ibid*, No. 20 (1974), p. 465.

11. See Hatem I. Hussaini, ed. *Toward Peace in Palestine* (Washington D.C.: The Arab Information Center, n.d.).

12. *Palestine and Zionism: The Palestinian Perspective at the U.N.* (New York: Office of the Permanent Observer of the Palestine Liberation Organization to the U.N., 1975).

13. "PLO's International Victories," *Palestine* (Beirut), II, No. 10 (March, 1976), pp. 28-32.

14. See *The Jerusalem Post*, October 24, 1975, and *Brief* No. 116 (October 16-31, 1975).

15. "PLO's International Victories," *Palestine* (Beirut), *op. cit.*

16. *Jerusalem Post*, April 23, 1976.

17. *Free Palestine* (London), IX, No. 5 (May, 1976).

18. *The New York Times*, May 16, 1976.

19. *U.N. Press Release* GA/Pal/51, October 1, 1979.

20. *The New York Times*, November 4, 1979.

21. Reported by *The Washington Post*, April 2, 1976.

22. Reported by the *BBC*, January 17, 1976.

23. Quoted in *Near East Report*, XX No. 18 (May 5, 1976).

24. *Near East Report*, XX, No. 21 (May 26, 1976).

25. *The Washington Post*, November 7, 1979.

26. *The Los Angeles Times*, October 21, 1979.

PLO TERRORISM: 1976-1979

1 Jan., 1976. Time bomb explodes in a Jerusalem supermarket, injuring 7.

13 Jan., 1976. Israeli troops kill 4 terrorists attempting to cross into Israel from Lebanon.

7 April, 1976. Terrorists wound 2 passengers on a Tel Aviv bus.

7 April, 1976. Rocket explodes in a Jerusalem suburb.

28 April, 1976. A time bomb explodes in Jerusalem, killing 2 and injuring 4.

3 May, 1976. An explosion in Zion Square, Jerusalem, injures 30.

11 May, 1976. Bomb explodes in a Tel Aviv movie theater, injuring 3.

18 May, 1976. 3 terrorists are killed as they attempt to infiltrate from Jordan.

25 May, 1976. 2 suitcase bombs explode at Ben Gurion Airport. 7 are wounded.

16 June, 1976. U.S. Ambassador to Lebanon, Francis Meloy, and Economic Advisor, Robert Waring are kidnapped and subsequently murdered in Beirut while traveling to meet with Lebanese President Sarkis. (The Scripps-Howard newspaper chain, quoting "senior U.S. diplomats" on July 22 report that Fatah's second-in-command, Salah Khalaf (Abu Iyad) directed the murder of the U.S. Embassy officials in order to provoke the U.S. into intervening in Lebanon with the aim of uniting the factions in Lebanon.

27 June, 1976. PFLP hijacks an Air France jet over Greece in a flight from Tel Aviv to Paris. The 256 passengers are flown to Entebbe Airport, Uganda after refueling in Libya.

4 July, 1976. Israeli airborne commandos successfully rescue 103 Jewish (mostly Israeli) and French hostages held at Entebbe Airport, Uganda. 7 PFLP terrorists are killed, 1 Israeli commando is killed, and 1 elderly woman retained in Uganda by the local authorities.

18 July, 1976. Bomb explodes in a Tel Aviv suburb. 10 injured.

11 August, 1976. 4 are killed (including Harold Rosenthal, an aide to Senator Jacob Javits) and more than 30 are injured when terrorists throw grenades into an Istanbul International Airport building after failing to hijack an El Al plane.

4 Sep., 1976. 3 terrorists hijack a Dutch airliner with 78 passengers aboard and attempt to fly to Tel Aviv to force the release of 7 terrorists in Israeli jails.

11 Jan., 1977. Abu Daoud, accused of planning

the 1972 massacre of 11 Israeli athletes in Munich is freed by a French court, which rejects West German and Israeli requests for extradition hearings.

28 April, 1977. Bomb explodes on a bus traveling to Beersheba, injuring 28.

28 May, 1977. Bomb explodes in Jerusalem's Old City, injuring 5.

6 July, 1977. Pipe bomb explodes in an open air market in suburban Tel Aviv killing 1 and injuring 20.

28 July, 1977. Bomb in Tel Aviv outdoor market injures 9.

28 July, 1977. Bomb in Jerusalem injures 2.

29 July, 1977. Bomb in vegetable market in Beersheba injures 29.

16 Aug., 1977. 9 injured in a bombing incident in the Jezreel Valley.

25 Aug., 1977. Bomb explodes in the town of Natanya.

25 Aug., 1977. Bomb found in Rehovot is disarmed before exploding.

27 Aug., 1977. Explosion at the Jaffa Gate, Jerusalem.

11 Sep., 1977. 10 are injured in a Beersheba bus station explosion.

2 Oct., 1977. Bomb explodes in Jerusalem's Central Bus Station. 3 are injured.

15 Oct., 1977. 2 bombs explode in the Old City of Jerusalem.

15 Oct., 1977. Bombing in the city of Natanya.

6 Nov., 1977. Israel releases Syrian-born Greek Catholic Archbishop Hilarion Capucci from prison following a personal appeal from Pope Paul VI to President Katzir. (Capucci had served 3 years of a 12 year sentence for smuggling arms and explosives into Israel for the PLO.)

7 Nov., 1977. Small bomb explodes in Petakh Tikva's Central Bus Station.

8 Nov., 1977. Rocket attacks on Israeli border settlement. 3 are killed.

3 Dec., 1977. Bomb explodes in the Old City of Jerusalem.

26 Dec., 1977. PLO announces that its terrorists have assassinated Abd al-Khalil Janho in Ramallah for having "collaborated with the occupying authorities."

29 Dec., 1977. Bombing in Natanya kills 2.

8 Jan., 1978. Bomb blast at Damascus Gate Bus Station in Jerusalem injures 3.

13 Jan., 1978. Bomb blast in Jaffa parking lot kills 2.

15 Jan., 1978. Bomb blast in Jerusalem bus. No casualties.

15 Jan., 1978. Bomb blast in Kfar Saba. No casualties.

25 Jan., 1978. Bomb blast in Shmuel Hanavi, Jerusalem. No casualties.

3 Feb., 1978. Bomb blast in downtown Jerusalem. No casualties.

10 Feb., 1978. Bomb blast in Jerusalem supermarket. No casualties.

14 Feb., 1978. Bomb blast in Jerusalem kills 2, injures 46. PLO claims responsibility.

16 Feb., 1978. Bomb blast in Jerusalem. No casualties.

16 Feb., 1978. Gunmen kill a prominent Palestinian merchant, the third Arab known to have Israeli connections to be assassinated in the past 2 months.

19 Feb., 1978. Bomb blast on Hebrew University campus, Jerusalem. 1 Arab killed, 1 Arab woman injured.

11 Mar., 1978. Gail Rubin, (Sen. Ribicoff's cousin) is killed by Palestinian commandos landing on a beach in Israel.

11 Mar., 1978. 11 commandos land on the Israeli coast north of Tel Aviv, seize 2 buses filled with passengers on the Haifa-Tel Aviv road. 44 killed, including 9 terrorists, 72 are injured. Al Fatah claims responsibility.

1 May, 1978. 2 PFLP terrorists are killed attempting to cross into Israel.

22 May, 1978. French police kill 3 terrorists who open fire on passengers waiting for an E1 A1 plane in Orly Airport, Paris. 1 policeman is killed, 3 passengers and a stewardess are injured.

29 June, 1978. Bomb blast in Machane Yehuda, Jerusalem kills 2, injures 47. PLO claims responsibility.

17 July, 1978. Bomb blast in Paris home of French journalist accused of supporting the Jewish Press.

3 Aug., 1978. Bomb blast in Carmel market, Tel Aviv. 1 killed, 40 injured, 4 critically. PLO claims responsibility.

20 Aug., 1978. Attack on E1 A1 bus in London. 1 Israeli stewardess killed, 9 wounded. 1 terrorist killed. PFLP claims responsibility.

23 Aug., 1978. Bomb blast in Gaza. 2 killed.

25 Aug., 1978. Bomb blast in empty bus at Jaffa Gate, Jerusalem. 2 injured.

25 Aug., 1978. Bomb blast at a Jerusalem gas station. An Israeli-American police sapper killed. 1 injured.

17 Sep., 1978. Bomb blast at Jaffa Gate, Jerusalem. 4 Jews and 3 Arabs injured.

30 Sep., 1978. Israeli patrol off Eilat coast foils large-scale A1 Fatah attack.

18 Nov., 1978. Bomb blast in Natanya. 2 killed, 50 injured.

19 Nov., 1978. Bomb blast in Tel Aviv movie theater. 2 wounded.

19 Nov., 1978. Bomb blast in tourist bus on West Bank. 4 killed, 40 injured. Al Fatah claims responsibility.

30 Nov., 1978. Bomb blast on Mount of Olives, Jerusalem. 1 Arab killed.

21 Dec., 1978. Rocket attack on Kiryat Shemona. 1 killed, many injured.

13 Jan., 1979. Attack by 3 PDFLP members on Maalot hotel. All killed. 1 Israeli woman killed in effort to escape. 5 Israelis injured.

18 Jan., 1979. Bomb blast in Jerusalem (Machane Yehuda). 21 injured. PLO claims responsibility.

29 Jan., 1979. Bomb explodes in Natanya. 2 killed. 43 wounded. PLO claims credit.

3 Feb., 1979. Bomb blast at Western Wall. 1 killed, several injured.

27 Feb., 1979. Bomb explodes in Jerusalem's Machane Yehuda market. 5 injured.

7 Mar., 1979. Bombs explode in 3 Arab tourist buses. 12 injured. 2 seriously. PDFLP claims responsibility.

23 Mar., 1979. Bomb explodes near Zion Square. 1 killed. 14 wounded. PLO claims credit. The blast occurred shortly after Prime Minister Begin left for Washington to sign Egypt-Israel peace treaty.

27 Mar., 1979. Bomb attacks in Israel and Paris in reaction to peace treaty. In Israeli town of Lod explosion kills 1, injures 21. In Paris bomb thrown into hostel for Jewish students injures 2. PLO denounces the Paris Bombing.

5 April, 1979. Bomb blasts at Israeli and Egyptian Airlines Office in Cyprus. No casualties.

5 April, 1979. Bomb blast wounds 10 Arabs and 3 Jews in East Jerusalem.

10 April, 1979. Bomb blast in Tel Aviv market. 1 killed. 22 injured. PLO claims credit.

10 April, 1979. Bomb hurled by terrorists at El Al office in Istanbul, Turkey. Several casualties.

10 April, 1979. Premature explosion in Frankfurt Airport of booby-trapped suitcase before loading onto Israeli aircraft.

14 April, 1979. Israelis kill 4 PLO guerrillas crossing into Israel via Jordan.

17 April, 1979. Bomb blast on bus in Tel Aviv. No casualties.

17 April, 1979. Attempted attack on Israeli airliner in Brussels. 12 locals wounded. *Black March* claims responsibility.

17 April, 1979. PLO guerrillas cross into Israel from Lebanon. 1 Israeli soldier killed. 6 wounded. 65 Palestinians killed.

22 April, 1979. Attack on apartment house in Nahariya. 3 Israeli civilians and 1 soldier killed. 2 Palestinians killed. 2 wounded.

15 May, 1979. Bomb blast in Tiberias. 2 students killed, 32 wounded. PLO claims responsibility.

24 May, 1979. Bomb blast at Petakh Tikva bus stop. 3 killed. 13 wounded. Several other explosives found and deactivated in area. In Hebron 3 bombs go off during the night in civil administration offices. Damage to building. No injuries.

Compiled by Dr. Yonah Alexander.

For a list of terrorist acts, 1968-1973, see *The Palestinians. People, History, Politics,* edited by Michael Curtis, Joseph Neyer, Chaim I. Waxman, Allen Pollack, (Transaction Books, 1975).

28 Academic Freedom and the West Bank

By Michael Curtis

On February 3, 1983 *Le Monde,* France's most influential newspaper, published an article by two doctors describing their visit to an Israeli prisoner of war camp in Lebanon. The doctors not only praise "Israel's democratic gesture" in allowing them to visit the camp without imposing any restrictions but also wistfully conclude they still await authorization to visit Israeli prisoners held in Syria.

Their experience points up yet again the asymmetry between the opportunities for inquiry into conditions in a democratic country and the situation in other Middle East countries whose lack of standards of free enquiry are taken for granted, yet about which criticism is rarely mounted.

This difference of attitude and expectation has been shown again and again in the continual attacks on Israel's purported infringements of academic freedom in the higher educational institutions of the occupied territories of the West Bank and Gaza, especially in the best known of them, Bir Zeit University. Yet most of the criticism of Israel on this issue results not from an objective analysis of the state of academic freedom as such but from dislike of or opposition to Israeli policy in the West Bank in general or from differences about attitudes to the Palestine Liberation Organization. Members of the academic profession in the Western world are always rightly troubled by violations of academic freedom and are concerned to denounce such actions. But the differences about Israeli actions in the West Bank are essentially political in character rather than about imperfections in the universities.

The Expansion of Higher Education

To put the issue of West Bank universities in true perspective two crucial factors are pertinent. The first is that private and public educational institutions of university status have existed only since 1967 when Israel began administering the area. Bir Zeit, near Ramallah, obtained university status with a four year study program in 1973. It is now able to grant not only a B.A. degree after 4 years of instruction in its Faculties of Arts and Science, Business and Engineering, but also an M.A. degree in Education. An-Najah National University, in Nablus, became an institute of higher learning in 1975, with a 4-year program leading to a B.A.; Frères University, in Bethlehem, supported by Christian institutions abroad, was founded in 1973. Many of its students major in business or education. The Ash-Shara'iye College and Islamic Center, in Hebron, which offers a B.A. degree was founded in 1971. These four institutions now have over 6200 students and 400 faculty members. A fifth institution, the Al-Azhar Seminary in Gaza, offers two years of college level studies in the Islamic religion. All the institutions have been free to raise funds from any part of the world, and to accept grants from individuals and foreign governments. A particularly significant example of this is the new campus at Bir Zeit, including the fine engineering school, built as a result of a $6 million gift from a Saudi Arabian. A new campus has also been planned, and money raised, for An-Najah University, although its construction has been delayed because of difficulties in getting building permits. Collectively, these Arab universities constitute an important addition to the Arab intellectual fold. The academic level of students is generally regarded as high. One significant feature of the student body is the high proportion of women students, now numbering nearly half the total number of students in the West Bank universities.

In introducing and administering higher education in the West Bank, Israel had three options. The first was to apply to the new institutions the same regulations that Jordan did in 1964 in setting up the University of Amman, which is under state ownership and strict supervision and regulation by governmental authorities. The second possibility was to apply new Israeli law to the area which is still administered on the basis of Jordanian law. It is ironic that some Arab critics complain that the regulations pertinent to universities in Israel itself were not applied in the West Bank. The third option was to apply to the new institutions the Jordanian laws which were pertinent to the licensing and appointment of teachers in the primary and secondary school system when it

Dr. Curtis is Professor of Political Science at Rutgers University, New Brunswick.

was under Jordanian control from 1949 to 1967, and measures to ensure public order and safety. Since Israel has maintained Jordanian law in West Bank affairs if possible rather than introduce its own legislation, this option was accepted. The Jordanian law for schools was applied to universities and the power to issue licenses for establishing private institutions of learning, formerly administered by the Jordanian Minister of Education, is now in the hands of "the competent authority" appointed by the Area Commander. In practice the authority is the representative of the Israeli Ministry of Education working in the Area.

Academic Freedom

The second pertinent factor is that greater intellectual freedom exists in the West Bank institutions than in comparable universities in the Middle East, other than Israel itself. In the West Bank universities, programs of studies have been decided internally and teachers have been chosen without Israeli intervention. Neither has Israel imposed administrative restrictions.

Evidence of academic freedom has come from critics, Arab and Israeli alike. In October 1976 Hanan Ashrawi, lecturer in English literature at Bir Zeit, talked of the intellectual activity at the University and of the paper *Al-Bayader* as "a landmark in the intellectual and cultural life of the occupied territories." In 1981, a committee of Hebrew University professors inquiring into criticisms made about the West Bank universities reported it had found no evidence of interference by the Israeli military authorities in matters of curriculum, budget or admissions, and praised the authorities for allowing the universities to plan their own courses of study and to hire faculty members from Arab countries.

Indeed, restrictions on academic freedom have been imposed by the universities themselves. The Arab press reported that the Bethlehem faculty turned down an opportunity to engage in a dialogue with "democratically minded" Hebrew University professors. Sari Nuseibeh, professor of philosophy at Bir Zeit, who had taught a course at the Hebrew University, was obliged to withdraw from it under pressure.

Nevertheless, some books, papers and journals in Arabic requested by the universities have not been approved. There have also been instances of overzealous censorship. In Israel itself the presence of surrounding enemy countries has necessitated a certain minimum degree of censorship in the school system. Political reality in the West Bank has required some precaution about the universities, as in the territories as a whole. Many of the forbidden works in the West Bank appear to fall in the category of anti-Semitic or racist publications or are considered likely to endanger security.

In the primary school system one of these works was allegedly an edition of *The Merchant of Venice* but was in reality a blood-libel story featuring illustrations of the kind familiar in the Nazi paper *Der Stürmer*. Another book, used in elementary school, was a mathematics textbook which included extracts from the *Protocols of the Elders of Zion*.

What is more pertinent is the intellectual freedom in the West Bank especially when compared with the severe censorship to be found in Arab educational institutions. Probably the most divisive serious political issue in the Arab intellectual world is that between supporters of secular nationalism and proponents of Islamic fundamentalism. In almost all universities in the Arab world only one side of this debate is officially permitted, except in those institutions where neither side is allowed free expression. What is distinctive about the West Bank institutions is that both sides in this debate can be heard and that these institutions are the only universities in the Arab or Muslim world of which this can be said.

Order and Security

In essence, the Israeli authorities have to face two interrelated charges: interference through controls imposed to maintain security and order and the system of entry permits required for non-residents.

Students and faculty in the West Bank engage in free discussion and action on campus. But, following the international obligations laid down by the 1907 Hague regulations for administered territories, they are required to refrain, in the same way as other residents, from activity that might endanger public order and safety. Assessment of such activity is always open to controversy, but on a number of occasions the Israeli authorities have determined that subversive political behavior has occurred or been encouraged in the West Bank institutions. Dr. Hana Nasser, former President of Bir Zeit, who was deported from the West Bank in 1974 for what was termed subversive political activities, but who still has an active university role *in absentia*, has been a member of the PLO Executive, of the Palestine National Council, the PLO-Jordan Joint Commission, and the PLO Actions Committee. It is apparent that some faculty and students are more interested in political activity than in education.

Bir Zeit University, in particular, has been for some years not only a center for demonstrations in support of the PLO but also an environment in which teaching has sometimes been highly politicized. Students at Bir Zeit have incited both their fellow students and students at other universities and in high schools and also citizens in neighboring localities to engage in political action and sometimes violence outside as well as inside the campus. Occasional brutalities have occurred; in the case in 1982 of Anne Scott, a lecturer at Bir Zeit, the perpetrators were punished. Some students, genuinely interested in educational matters, have complained that they have been forced to participate in political demonstrations by student militants. On one occasion buildings at Bir Zeit were used by students to house fire bombs.

Disturbances in these institutions have followed significant political events rather than any matters of academic concern. West Bank students must have been one of the few student bodies in the world to have demonstrated against peace, as they did after the signing of the Egyptian-Israeli peace treaty in 1979. In May 1979, in 1980, in November 1981 and twice in 1982 Bir Zeit was closed after students set up roadblocks, burned tires, and damaged property in the streets of Ramallah, several miles away from the campus. A particularly flagrant action occurred in January 1982 when Sion Gabi, Israeli director of education for the territories, needed hospitalization after being beaten by students at Bir Zeit en route to a meeting with the acting head of the university. In January 1983, An-Najah University was closed after students had incited others to stage an anti-Israeli and pro-PLO demonstration celebrating the 18th anniversary of the founding of *el Fatah,* the main PLO faction, headed by Yassir Arafat. On all occasions Israeli authorities acted to restore order after violence had occurred or actions had provoked retaliation.

The periodic closures of West Bank campuses, even after violent demonstrations, cause concern. But such closures need to be put in the context of the continuing political and military struggle in which faculty and students engage in action in support of the PLO while the PLO, adhering to the principles of its National Charter, has remained intransigent in its hostility to the existence of Israel.

Work Permits

Much criticism has focused on the system by which a West Bank institution must obtain approval from Israeli authorities before hiring an instructor from outside the area. Such approval generally involves the granting of a one-year resident permit to the foreign instructor. Difficulties have occurred in some cases as a result of delays in granting approval to the outsiders, who now number about a third of the total faculty. Yet generally work permits have been granted as a matter of course to non-resident teachers and students unless they are thought to be security risks. In the same way as universities are free to import academic literature and journals appropriate to their needs, non-resident faculty are free to come and go as they please, subject only to those security precautions that apply to the West Bank population.

These precautions have been criticized as a kind of restraint on academic freedom. But logically the statement required since August 1982 of all non-residents, including potential instructors, agreeing not to engage in political activity or to support or assist the PLO while they are in the

support of the PLO but also an environment in which teaching has sometimes been highly politicized. Students at Bir Zeit have incited both their fellow students and students at other universities and in high schools and also citizens in neighboring localities to engage in political action and sometimes violence outside as well as inside the campus. Occasional brutalities have occurred; in the case in 1982 of Anne Scott, a lecturer at Bir Zeit, the perpetrators were punished. Some students, genuinely interested in educational matters, have complained that they have been forced to participate in political demonstrations by student militants. On one occasion buildings at Bir Zeit were used by students to house fire bombs.

Disturbances in these institutions have followed significant political events rather than any matters of academic concern. West Bank students must have been one of the few student bodies in the world to have demonstrated against peace, as they did after the signing of the Egyptian-Israeli peace treaty in 1979. In May 1979, in 1980, in November 1981 and twice in 1982 Bir Zeit was closed after students set up roadblocks, burned tires, and damaged property in the streets of Ramallah, several miles away from the campus. A particularly flagrant action occurred in January 1982 when Sion Gabi, Israeli director of education for the territories, needed hospitalization after being beaten by students at Bir Zeit en route to a meeting with the acting head of the university. In January 1983, An-Najah University was closed after students had incited others to stage an anti-Israeli and pro-PLO demonstration celebrating the 18th anniversary of the founding of *el Fatah,* the main PLO faction, headed by Yassir Arafat. On all occasions Israeli authorities acted

with an organization, 1) opposition to organized government, 2) the overthrow of government by force and violence, 3) the assaulting or killing of government officials because of their official character, 4) the unlawful destruction of property, 5) sabotage, or 6) the doctrine of world communism." It is possible that some hardship has been caused by this policy, especially to those academics who were originally natives of the West Bank area but who, for one reason or another, do not hold identity cards conferring the right of permanent residency. The demand that people seeking employment in a country in which they lack the proper credentials refrain from activities or associations regarded, rightly or wrongly, as hostile cannot in itself be equated with a policy that is undemocratic or a threat to academic freedom. Israeli political policies can be subject to legitimate discussion and criticism. But such discussion is irrelevant to the question of the educational functioning and the academic integrity of the West Bank institutions. Academic freedom is not to be equated with opportunity for political incitement or underground activity in the West Bank or anywhere else in the world.

PART VI
ISRAEL

29

The U.N. Partition Resolution of November 1947

By Joseph Neyer

When the Palestine Arab Higher Committee notified the U.N. Secretary-General in June 1947 that it would not cooperate with the United Nations Special Committee on Palestine (UNSCOP), its negation may have been the consequence not only of its principled stand but also of a weariness with the many commissions of inquiry that Arab and Jewish leaders had to endure under the Mandate. The Shaw Commission of Inquiry, appointed by the British Government in 1929 to investigate the causes of an outbreak of Arab riots, had written a report that was a harbinger of the developing reluctance of the Government to pursue the aims of the Jewish National Home as directed by the Mandate of the League of Nations. The Peel Commission of 1936-37, which refuted the legend that Jewish land purchases and land development had led to the displacement of Arabs and which developed the theme of the benevolent effects of Jewish immigration upon the Arab people, was the first to suggest the partition of Palestine (west of the Jordan River) as a possible solution. And after World War II there was the Anglo-American Committee of Inquiry in the beginning of 1946, which submitted a unanimous report that was in effect rejected by the British Government; in part, it recommended the immediate admission of 100,000 Jewish immigrants from the Europe ravaged by Hitler.

But UNSCOP represented a new kind of effort to deal with the problem of Palestine. For now the attention of the whole politically organized world was directed upon this moral and political issue of considerable complexity, and the Special Committee was aware that the outcome of its labors would serve to dampen or to heighten the optimism with which the prospects of the new world organization were regarded. Further, after all has been said that needs to be said about the "pressures" exercised by the interested parties (including Great Britain, the Soviet Union, and the United States) upon the final deliberations of the U.N. General Assembly, the fact remains that the membership of the Special Committee—representatives of Australia, Canada, Czechoslovakia, Guatemala, India, Iran, Netherlands, Peru, Sweden, Uruguay, and Yugoslavia—consisted, *in the main,* of persons and nations who were as neutral and as relatively free of bias as one can find in this imperfect world. They were ready to apply their industry, their intelligence, and their moral zeal in the pursuit of equity. The Committee came into existence on May 15, 1947, and its report was published on August 31. In the interim, it had studied the records of the past, heard testimony in various parts of the world, including Palestine and Lebanon, and some of its members had visited the Jewish Displaced Persons camps in Germany and Austria.

The majority report, supported by seven members of the Committee, called for political partition with "economic union"; there would be independent Arab and Jewish states, with an internationalized zone of Jerusalem. The minority report, supported by the delegates of India, Iran, and Yugoslavia, proposed a federal solution with the central government (in effect, Arab controlled) responsible for immigration, foreign affairs, and national defense.

Prof. Neyer is Professor Emeritus of Philosophy at Rutgers University, New Brunswick, N.J.

On November 29, 1947, the plenary General Assembly endorsed an amended version of the Special Committee's partition plan as developed in the majority report by a vote of thirty-three to thirteen, with ten abstentions. The Soviet Union and the United States voted affirmatively. The negative votes included those of the six Arab States in the U.N.

It should be noted that among the points of agreement, shared by both majority and minority Committee members, there was the proposition that the Mandate for Palestine, entrusted to Great Britain by the League of Nations in 1922, should be terminated at the earliest practicable date. The Mandate, which provided the only legal basis for Great Britain's governance of Palestine, stated that the primary purpose of that trust was that of "placing the country under such political, administrative, and economic conditions as will secure the establishment of the Jewish National Home . . ."

Now it was not for the purpose of relinquishing its power over Palestine that the British Government had decided, according to its announcement of February 14, 1947, to refer the Palestine Problem to the United Nations, the heir to the League. As Colonial Secretary Creech-Jones put the position, "We are not going to the United Nations to surrender the Mandate. We are . . . setting out the problem and asking for their advice as to how the Mandate can be administered. If the Mandate cannot be administered in its present form, we are asking how it can be administered."

To put the matter more simply, the British Government was asking to have legally sanctioned its design to retain the political authority mandated to it by the League after World War I, while being relieved of the conditions laid upon it relating to the facilitating of Jewish immigration and settlement. The British White Paper of 1939, which had sharply curtailed Jewish immigration, had been presented for review to the Permanent Mandates Commission of the League; and the Commission then reported to the Council of the League "that the policy set out in the White Paper was not in accordance with the interpretation which . . . the Commission had placed upon the Palestine Mandate." In referring the Palestine Problem to the U.N., then, the British were hoping to get a fresh start in developing their post-World War II imperial designs for the Middle East, which called for ridding themselves of any encumbrances that might stand in the way of friendship with the Arabs. The British withdrawal from Egypt and Iraq accentuated the strategic importance of Palestine, which, together with British military privileges in Transjordan, could serve as the base for the future.

There had been the nervous competition of the British with the axis powers during World War II for Arab friendship. The late thirties was the period of England's "appeasement" of the fascist powers, and this political style led in Palestine to courting the bully in the situation—the one most likely to go over to the axis if he were not adequately appeased. It is not surprising, therefore, that when the time came to deal with the Palestine Problem after World War II, the party prepared to represent the Palestine Arabs was the most extreme and intransigent. The leadership of those sectors of the Arab population that were prepared to look for modes of accommodation with the Palestine Jews had been assassinated or intimidated to the point of flight from the country during the "disturbances" of 1936-39, when the number of Arabs murdered by Arabs exceeded the number of Jewish fatalities. Thus, an early precedent appears to have been set for the associates of terrorism to be invited to the halls of the United Nations. The party which was selected to represent the Palestine Arabs was not only the most intransigent with regard to the struggle with the Jews, it also represented the most socially reactionary elements within Arab society. Its "revolt" of 1936-39 had been supported materially by Germany and Italy, and, during World War II, it managed to lay its bets on both sides so as to have a claim to the spoils of whatever victory might ensue.

But these complexities for the British were in the past with the end of the war. The Grand Mufti of Jerusalem, who had taken sanctuary in Germany during the war, was now in Cairo as Chairman of the new Palestine Higher Executive (established by the Arab League), and his Vice-Chairman and cousin, Jamal al-Husayni, was presented to the United Nations as the spokesman for the Palestine Arabs.* The British took the position that they would not assist in the establishment of any plan for Palestine that was not acceptable to both parties to the dispute. And they waited for the ensuing chaos, after which they reckoned their assistance would be called upon to introduce order on their own terms. Their reckoning failed to take account of three factors: the seriousness with which UNSCOP and the General Assembly would undertake their work, the role of the Soviet Union, and, finally, the capability of the Jewish community to withstand the armed incursion of the surrounding Arab states.

A discussion of the last mentioned factor is outside the scope of this essay, but it should be recalled that when the test came, the extent to which British support was nourishing the Arab military position became more and more clear. The British Government declined to cooperate with any of the U. N. machinery for the projected transition in administration, but it simply announced that the Mandate would be terminated on May 15, 1948, months in advance of the date set by the U. N. The Palestine Commission, consisting of five nations appointed to supervise the carrying out of the Partition Resolution, was not permitted by the government to enter Palestine before May 1. Soon after its arrival, the Commission reported that the Arabs alone "were being armed in part with the arms of the Palestine government." On January 12 the Foreign Office had announced that, in accordance with treaty obligations, Egypt, Iraq, and Transjordan were being supplied with arms by Great Britain. Faced with a "neutral" arms embargo on the part of the United States, the Jews succeeded in buying arms from Czechoslovakia (with the negotiated approval of Moscow); and the British sent notes of vain protest to the Czech authorities.

Forces of armed Arab "irregulars" were permitted to enter the country from the neighboring states long before the departure of the British and the official invasion of the regular armies of Egypt, Syria, Iraq, and Jordan on May 15. The Arab Legion, the military force of Jordan, was funded mainly by Great Britain; British officers, including the Commander-in-Chief, occupied the key positions of command. At least until February 1948, British soldiers of various ranks were invited by Army Circular to enroll in the Arab Legion. For reasons always ambiguously explained, the Legion itself was to be found on the west of the Jordan River long before the British departure, and it took part in military operations related to the siege of Jewish Jerusalem before that departure.

A British Communist pamphlet authored by Bert Ramelson and printed after the Six Day War of 1967 stated the following: "It is wrong to describe the war for the establishment of Israel (in 1948) as the first war between the Jews and the Arabs . . . It was a war of liberation waged by the Jewish people in Palestine against British imperialism, which used Arab armies commanded by British officers taking their instructions from Whitehall." The British, the pamphlet goes on to explain, wanted to retain all of Palestine, "and by parcelling it up among Arab stooge rulers, retain indirectly what Britain held directly as the mandatory power." The statement is perhaps an exaggeration.

The role of the Soviet Union during this period was at first ambiguous, and the Man in the Kremlin may have relished keeping on tenterhooks the other parties concerned as they nervously looked for signs of the probable direction of Soviet policy with regard to Palestine. Russian pressures on Iran and Turkey appeared to indicate that she would become a competitor with Great Britain for ties with the Arabs and, indeed, with the world of Islam. During and after World War II, when the Soviet attitude toward religion had become more relaxed, Russian relations with Orthodox Christian authorities in Palestine were reestablished for the first time since the Revolution, and in 1944 Soviet Muslims were permitted to

*Six alleged political opponents of the Mufti's following were murdered between November 1946 and February 1947.

make the pilgrimage to Mecca for the first time in twenty years. At the same time, since the mid-twenties, Zionism was outlawed as a petty bourgeois excrescence and the use of Hebrew forbidden in the Soviet Union. The Jewish community in Palestine had reason to be wary of Soviet intentions in 1947.

On the other hand, the Jews could take encouragement from the fact that the Russians appeared less ready than the British and the French to forget the recent blemishing associations of the Arabs with the German and Italian fascists during World War II, and less ready to forget the recent holocaustal experiences of the Jews. In July 1945 the Yugoslav government placed the name of the Mufti on the United Nations' list of war criminals "for initiating brutalities and for pro-German activities among the Bosnian Muslims." The Mufti had managed, at about the time of the Nazi surrender, to reach France where, in the language of the French authorities, he received the "privileged treatment" that "custom demands . . . for the head of a great Arab community." With the collusion of the British, he eventually reached Cairo, and international pressure on the Yugoslavs got his name removed from the list of war criminals.

In July 1946, when the British government increased its efforts to prevent "illegal" Jewish immigration to Palestine and it called upon European Governments to halt the travel of Jews without appropriate credentials, positive and cooperative responses came from France and Italy. No response came from the Soviet Union or from the countries of Eastern Europe—a silence significant for the Jews.

During the special session of the U.N. General Assembly in April-May 1947, which was called at the request of the British Government and which created UNSCOP, the British, the Americans, and the Russians spent most of the time on questions of procedure. Finally, before the close of the session, only one of the big-powers dared to express its views on the substance of the question, and that was the Soviet Union. Delegate Gromyko declared that the mandate system was "bankrupt." He then made the following statement: "The fact that no western European state has been able to ensure the defense of the elementary rights of the Jewish people, and to safeguard it against the violence of the Fascist executioners, explains the aspirations of the Jews to establish their own state. It would be unjust not to take this into consideration and to deny the right of the Jewish people to realize this aspiration . . . In analyzing the various plans for the future of Palestine, it is essential . . . to bear in mind the indisputable fact that the population of Palestine consists of two peoples, the Arabs and the Jews. Both have historical roots in Palestine."

This speech awakened the Assembly from its procedural slumber. It was the first indication that the Soviet Union was abandoning its traditional anti-Zionist position. And it was made while the Arab delegates were promising, to quote the Iraqi delegate, "that supporting the national aspirations of the Jews means very clearly a declaration of war, and nothing else."

This initiative of the Soviet Union at the special session, as well as its support of the majority report of UNSCOP at the regular session in November,* seemed to many observers to represent a turnabout in Soviet strategy calling for explanation. The fact is that for the Russians, getting the British completely out of Palestine was the first right step in the right direction. As J. C. Hurewitz put the matter, "The Kremlin must have believed that the creation of a Jewish state with its vigorous nationalism would lead more certainly to the elimination of the British than would a unitary Arab state." And, despite the "theoreti-

*At the special session, the U.S.S.R. suggested two possible solutions: (1) a form of bi-nationalism not adequately delineated by the Russians and (2) "partition of Palestine into two independent autonomous states, one Jewish and one Arab". The binational solution is not to be confused with the "federal" recommendation of the UNSCOP minority report, which would have led to Arab control over Jewish immigration. The binationalist alternative would have been the preferred solution, said Gromyko, were it not for the fact that relations between Arabs and Jews had too far deteriorated. The partition alternative, it turned out, was the recommendation of the UNSCOP majority report, which of course went far beyond it in the elaboration of detail.

cal'' objections of Marxism to Zionism, the Russians could appreciate the social achievements of the Jewish community and the effects these could have in stimulating the movement of the Middle East in a progressive direction. As is made clear in the passage from Gromyko's speech quoted above, the Russians could take the position that the creation of a Jewish state under a partition plan followed from their consistent advocacy of the principle of self-determination and from their battle against imperialism.

And the Soviet Union remained firm on the original partition resolution during the spring of 1948 amidst the development of violence and the fears of chaos, as the Palestine Commission reported its inability to carry out its mission without military support. As early as February 24, the United States delegate Warren Austin stated in the U.N. Security Council, ''The Council . . . is directed to keeping the peace and not to enforcing partition.'' On March 19, Austin made the recommendation to the Council that the General Assembly be convened to consider the suspension of partition and the establishment of a temporary trusteeship. Gromyko rose in the Council to defend the authority of the U.N. against the ''special interests'' of the powers. He replied to Austin that the American government was sacrificing the interests of the United Nations to its concerns about oil and its strategic interests. The Russians rightly suspected the collusion of the American and British governments.

The wobbling of the United States government in the spring of 1948, despite its affirmative vote on partition, was a continuation of its hesitant position during the previous period. As J. C. Hurewitz puts the matter, ''The hesitant unfolding of United States' support of partition suggested that Washington was experiencing difficulty in reconciling the traditional pressures.'' On the one hand, the case of Zionism was supported by public opinion more than ever. On the other hand, the Department of State Near East experts and the Joint Chiefs of Staff were concerned about the peril to American strategic interests and to American oil investments that would be the consequence of losing Arab friendship. *(Plus ça change plus c'est la même chose.)* Before the vote on the Partition Resolution, Arab delegates met with Secretary of State Marshall and explained to him how a U. S. affirmative vote would have extremely harmful consequences for American economic interests, including American oil investments. Soon after the U.N. decision on partition, American oil company agents were contacting Arab League leaders, assuring them that partition would not be implemented, and undertaking to convey proposals to the State Department. On January 21, Vice-Admiral Robert B. Carney (Deputy Chief of Naval Operations for Logistics) testified as follows to the House Armed Services Committee: ''In the event of serious disturbance in the Middle East, there is cause for grave concern for the fortunes of American oil facilities throughout that area, and to those who might desire to deny the oil of the Middle East to us [the Soviet Union?], such disturbance could afford nice opportunities for interference.''

The Cold War had begun. An oil company agent reported to his State Department contacts that side by side with the Star of David in Palestine the Red Flag was flying. Non-communist Jews were leaving, he said, and Israel would become a satellite of Russia. As Christopher Sykes describes the situation in the spring of 1948, ''American policy on Palestine was becoming almost as complicated and self-contradictory as that of the erratic mandatory. In March it became incomprehensible.''

Events in Palestine were soon to render discussions in the United Nations irrelevant. On the fourteenth of May the last British High Commissioner left Palestine by the Port of Haifa, and, a few hours later, Ben-Gurion proclaimed the State of Israel. Eleven minutes after independence was effective, midnight (Israel time) on May 14-15, the announcement of President Truman's recognition of Israel was handed to the press. The American delegation at the General Assembly, still advocating all sorts of proposals other than statehood, was taken by surprise on the public floor of the General Assembly. Unknown to them,

Harry Truman had declared his independence of the State Department and of the oil interests.

On that same date of May 15, five Arab states invaded Palestine. This was the first—and perhaps the fatal—serious challenge to the authority of the United Nations, creating the devastating precedent of negation. Or perhaps that negation had already taken place when the Arabs began their guerrilla warfare on the day after the Partition Resolution was announced. On April 16, 1948, Jamal Husayni, spokesman for the Higher Committee of Palestine, told the U.N. Security Council, "The representative of the Jewish Agency told us yesterday that they were not the attackers. We did not deny this. We told the whole world that we were going to fight."

It is sometimes maintained that in challenging by resort to arms the Partition Resolution, the Arabs were merely declining to accept a proposition that had no stronger legal status than a "recommendation." There can be no intention in the present discussion of entering upon the very nice legal questions raised by this position.* However, it may be useful to recall a few historical data in order that the response of the common moral sense be rendered more relevant.

From 1517 to 1917, Palestine was part of a vast under-populated and largely undifferentiated area under Turkish rule—the area from which has since emerged the states of Saudi Arabia, Jordan, Syria, Iraq, Lebanon, and Israel. By the Treaty of Lausanne of 1923, Turkey, defeated in the First World War, renounced its rights over this area. A year earlier, the League of Nations, with the assent of the allied powers, granted the Palestine Mandate to Great Britain under the conditions (indicated above) concerning the development of the Jewish National Home. At this point in time, the non-Jewish population of undivided Palestine numbered less than 600,000; and, as historian James Parkes says, it "had no real feeling of belonging to any wider unit than their village, their clan or possibly confederation of clans."

When the League of Nations dissolved in 1946, it formally took note of the fact that certain provisions of the U.N. Charter corresponded to sections of the Covenant of the League dealing with the mandate system. And Great Britain informed the U.N. that it was ready to conclude Trusteeship Agreements for territories previously administered under Mandate, with the exception of Palestine. Then came Britain's request that the General Assembly "make recommendations under Article 10 of the Charter concerning the future government of Palestine." And, as Lauterpacht puts the matter, "Although there was nothing in the Charter which expressly conferred upon the Assembly the Power to consider the future of a mandated territory, the Assembly nonetheless accepted the competence thus attributed to it by appointing the U.N. Special Committee on Palestine . . ." The very least that can be said for the Resolution finally arrived at is that it was a fair expression of international judgment—after all due deliberation and study—that a Jewish state should be established in a part of Palestine in which the Jews had already become the majority of the population.

Although Arab writers refer to the Resolution of 1947 as a "mere recommendation" when they wish to challenge the legitimacy of Israel's existence, they often depend upon the Resolution when they wish to maintain that Israel's borders should be the vulnerable lines "recommended" in the Resolution, as opposed to the armistice lines established under the mediation of Ralph Bunche at Rhodes in 1949. (These armistice lines lasted until the war of 1967.) The map of the areas designated for the Jewish and Arab states, as depicted in the Resolution, was often referred to as a checkerboard. For, very roughly speaking, the Jewish state was assigned areas in the northeast, west central, and southeast; the Arab state was assigned areas in the northwest, east central, and southwest of Palestine. Obviously, such an arrangement could endure only in a situation of peace.

*For a brief, yet illuminating, discussion, see Elihu Lauterpacht, "Jerusalem: The Role of the U.N. (1947-1967)," *Middle East Information Series*, XVII, February 1972.

The Jewish authorities accepted the Resolution immediately, even though it contained certain provisions difficult for them to live with. For instance, the internationalization of Jerusalem, with a population of 100,000 Jews and 65,000 Arabs (including "new" and "old" Jerusalem) took away from them the visible symbol of the goal of the return to Zion. But it seemed to them that a Jewish State in part of Palestine, *with peace*, even without Jerusalem, was better than no State. For they needed an area that they could call their own, in which they could control immigration and receive Jewish refugees from the camps of Hitler and from the oppressions of Asia. The assumption they made in accepting the internationalization of Jerusalem is that the Resolution would be accepted by all parties concerned and that Jerusalem would be an open city.

A few days after the Resolution was passed, the Arabs burned a Jewish sector in the center of Jerusalem, and it soon became clear that the Arabs were intent upon possessing all of Jerusalem. Jewish Jerusalem was in a short time surrounded by Arab forces and placed under siege—with all the problems of maintaining the water supply and getting through convoys of food and supplies from Tel Aviv with great loss of life. No person who lived through the siege of Jerusalem will ever forget it. By April 1948, the Trusteeship Council gave up on the task of "elaborating" a special international regime. And despite its avowed concern for the Holy Places, the United Nations did nothing to protect Jerusalem. *Civilian* casualties were over a thousand. Marie Syrkin concludes her account of the siege of Jerusalem, "In Israel's aristocracy of valor, the highest rank was awarded to those who held Zion itself."

This is the historical background that explains why the Israelis and the inhabitants of Jerusalem will not now consider any political design that would render the Holy City dependent for protection on an international agency. The theological dimensions of the Jerusalem problem are of tremendous importance, but they are not of overriding importance, for it should be recalled that before their experience in the siege of Jerusalem, the Jews were ready, albeit with unhappy resignation, to accept the "special regime" for Jerusalem and its environs.* The case of Jerusalem illustrates what the Israelis mean when they say, rightly or wrongly, that the Arabs destroyed the validity of certain provisions of the Partition Resolution by their actions.

*The same point holds for the unification of the city that took place as a consequence of the Six-Day War of '67. For it should be noted that for eighteen years after the Jordan-Israel armistice agreement of 1949, which separated Israeli and Jordanian forces by a line going through Jerusalem, the Israelis accepted being barred from access to the Western Wall of the Temple (an access specifically provided for by the agreement). It was only after King Hussein rejected the formal offer of Israel to keep Jordan and its territory out of the fighting, and the rejection took the form of lobbing shells into Jewish Jerusalem, that the unification of Jerusalem became inevitable.

30 Some Problems of Arab-Jewish Coexistence in Israel

By Sammy Smooha and John E. Hofman

Most modern societies are pluralistic. They are composed of groups that differ significantly in cultural traditions, maintain separate institutions, and share unequally in the available resources. Pluralistic states are, by and large, undemocratic. They are held together by negative forces such as economic dependence and political domination. Some of them manage, however, to preserve democratic pluralism.

Switzerland is the best example of a stable democracy in a pluralistic society. It is possible to establish four general conditions from this remarkable case on which cooperative coexistence in multi-ethnic societies can be based:

a. *A shared ideology of partnership:* both the minority and majority accept the ideology that they are equals and partners and that their relations should be grounded in cooperative coexistence;
b. *Cultural autonomy:* the minority commands all institutional arrangements to perpetuate its cultural heritage and keep its separate identity;
c. *Equality of resources:* the minority enjoys a proportional share of the socio-economic and power resources;
d. *Interpersonal accommodation:* most members of the minority and majority hold positive and symmetric attitudes toward each other.[1]

Most minorities in the world are non-assimilating. Coexistence is, to them, either desirable or the lesser evil. As van den Berghe notes, "a separate but equal system is quite possible in a multinational state because each ethnic group can maintain a large degree of autonomy under the larger political umbrella."[2]

Dr. Smooha and Dr. Hofman are members of the Department of Sociology at Haifa University, Israel.

Israel is both pluralistic and democratic.[3] The major pluralistic divisions are those between non-European and European Jews (the demographic ratio is 55:45), religious and non-religious (30:70), Israeli Arabs and Jews (15:85), Druze, Christian and Muslim Israeli Arabs (8:16:76), and Arabs and Jews in Israel and in the occupied territories (35:65). With the exception of non-European Jews, all the other non-dominant groups are non-assimilating minorities for whom consensual coexistence has to be worked out.

In this paper we will discuss the extent to which the above conditions for cooperative coexistence prevail in the case of Arabs and Jews in Israel proper (excluding Arabs in the West Bank and Gaza Strip).[4]

A Shared Ideology of Partnership

The first condition for cooperative coexistence is a dominant ideology which views coexistence as a desired goal and as preferable to the alternative patterns of assimilation, dissociation, and domination. The two sides must see each other as integral parts of the same society and as equals and partners.

Dissociation, rather than peaceful coexistence, was the dominant force shaping Arab-Jewish relations before the establishment of the State of Israel. British Mandatory Palestine was a typical pluralistic society sharply divided into Arab and Jewish communities whose contacts were virtually confined to the marketplace and trouble areas. This reality of separation was nurtured by the separatist ideologies of both the Palestinian and Zionist national movements. Arab nationalists looked at Jews as intruders and insisted on forming an Arab state in the entire territory of Palestine. Jewish nationalists felt, on the other hand, that only a sovereign Jewish state could put an end to the Jewish people's sufferings as a permanent and hated minority and that Palestine should be divided along national lines. Neither Arabs nor Jews pursued coexistence in one political unit and the British, for their part, did little to bring the two peoples together.

The State of Israel's birth marked the failure of complete separation and the creation of an Arab minority. The Arabs rejected the 1947 U.N. Resolution and lost the ensuing 1948 war. Of the 1,200,000 Arabs living in Palestine in 1947, some 590,000 left and became refugees, some 160,000 remained in the new state and the rest were residents of the West Bank. From being a majority of about two-thirds in Palestine, Arabs became a minority of about one-seventh in Israel. Moreover, while Arabs in British Mandatory Palestine were a majority vying for dominance, they became a weak minority seeking accommodation in Israel. Because of the war and its aftermath, they also lost their professional elite and political leadership; their economy and community institutions collapsed, and their extensive family and cultural ties with the Arab world were severed.

As Arabs became an involuntary minority, Jews, inspired by their separatist Zionist ideology, became an involuntary majority. Coexistence was forced, therefore, on both sides and mutual alienation was rampant.

The Jews, as the dominant group in the State of Israel, had to act. From the very beginning, three forces became discernible in Jewish reactions toward the Arab minority. The first was that of democratic pluralism: Arabs are given full civil rights and their basic demand to maintain a separate identity is respected. The second was the fact that Israel is a Jewish state: Israel is Jewish in the state's name, emblem, flag, anthem and other national symbols. It is Jewish in its official holidays, in its Law of Return, in the predominance of the Hebrew language, etc. It is also clearly Jewish in its close relations with world Jewry. A dominant Jewish majority and a dominant Jewish-Zionist culture are Israel's *raison d'être*. As such the state is identified with its majority group and members of the Arab minority — and many Jews themselves — feel that Arabs are outsiders.

The third force was the exigencies of national security. Israel has been under seige since its inception. The Arab minority is part of the Arab world with which Israel is at war. Hence Arabs find themselves in the deplorable position of being an enemy-affiliated-minority. Initially regarded as a security risk, Arabs were put under military rule until 1966, some Arab border villagers were relocated in the interior and, with minor exceptions, Arabs are still exempted from compulsory military service.

Given these apparent contradictions, Jewish attitudes are understandably mixed. The pre-state desire for dissociation has lingered on whereas the option for coexistence once the state was established has not yet gained wide acceptance.

In the early years of the state's existence, Arabs and Jews viewed their relations as transitory, hoping that a final settlement of the Arab-Israeli dispute would eliminate the problem in one way or another. The last twenty-eight years have, however, shattered both the hopes and the fears. The trend was for recurrent wars rather than for a lasting peace and the Arab minority has neither become a fifth column nor left the country *en masse*. Israeli Arabs have grown in number, totaling over half a million and are expected to reach a million in the 1990s. This makes them a significant minority in a small country like Israel.

Both sides have now come to realize two simple facts — that Israel is a Jewish state and that an Arab minority is there to stay. It is unlikely that Israel will ever renounce its Jewish character or that the Israeli Arabs will disappear.

There are essentially two alternatives for coexistence: assimilation or domination. Assimilation is strongly rejected by both sides. Domination will not be tolerated for long by a minority undergoing continual modernization, involvement in a national movement and participation in a region-wide majority. Nor is Jewish domination compatible with the democratic pluralism to which Israel is committed.

It is doubtful whether the condition of a

shared ideology of partnership actually obtains in Israel at present. Arabs and Jews cannot be said to espouse the ideology of basing their relations on equality and partnership (Jews in particular have difficulty in viewing Arabs as full members of Israeli society). Both sides have probably not abandoned other alternatives for Arab-Jewish relations and have not wholeheartedly adopted peaceful coexistence as a common goal. Yet most now realize that coexistence is unavoidable although they continue to avoid the issues it raises.

Cultural Autonomy

A second necessary condition for consensual coexistence is cultural autonomy. Clearly, the greater the cultural differences there are between the groups, the greater the need grows for effective institutional measures to protect the separate identity of non-assimilating minorities.

The two ethnic groups exhibit pervasive cultural differences. They differ in all basic values, such as ethnic origin, religion, language, nationality and family structure. Israeli Arabs are thus a distinct minority in many respects. They are Arab by extraction, predominantly Muslim, Arabic speaking, and still largely bound to the extended family. Arabs are also distinguishable from Jews by their surnames, accent, place of residence and, sometimes, appearance.

The divergences in core-culture are multiplied by numerous subcultural variations. On the traditional-modern continuum Israeli Arabs as a whole are approaching the middle transitional section while Jews are approaching the modern pole. This tendency is exemplified by the high birth rate and low mortality rate among Arabs as compared with the low birth and mortality rates among Jews (see Table I, p. 9). Dissimilarities in mentality and lifestyle are noticeable. To name a few, Arabs possess on the average less of the Protestant ethic than do Jews; they display more of the traditional hospitality,etc., than do Jews, and they have a much stronger preference for Near-Eastern food, music, clothing and festivities.

Several lines of institutional separation ensure the perpetuation of the Arabs' distinct cultural heritage and ethnic identity. The most important one is the centuries-old *millet* system. By law, Arabs and Jews belong to separate religious communities which are granted full authority in matters of marriage, divorce and inheritance. The legislation fixing this religious division makes the separate religious statuses salient and binding and practically assures endogamy (although intermarriage is not illegal).

The other line of separation is organizational. Arabs have separate Arabic-instruction schools. They avail themselves of a network of Arabic communications media — newspapers, radio and television programs, movies, literature, etc. They also have their own social clubs, election lists, sport teams, and so on. The Government and the Histadrut (Israel Labor Federation) maintain separate departments for Arab minority affairs.

A large-scale territorial and residential isolation provides a solid base for the existing institutional and organizational separation between the two communities. Arabs are concentrated in certain parts of the country. The central section of Galilee, the Little Triangle area, and the Southern Negev are contiguous geo-cultural Arab areas. About 90% of the Arabs live in the two all-Arab towns of Nazareth and in 103 all-Arab villages (there are also 40 Bedouin encampments). The rest reside in separate quarters in seven mixed towns. The all-Arab towns and villages have Arab-elected local government.

Cultural and social pluralism between Arabs and Jews is, therefore, appreciably evident, legitimate and stable. Arabs have both the publicly recognized privilege and the institutionally supported ability to maintain their separate identity. Does this amount then to cultural autonomy?

If cultural autonomy is taken to mean only a guaranteed ethnic identity, then Arabs certainly enjoy cultural autonomy in Israel. Many Arabs, however, dispute such a narrow interpretation. For moderate Arabs, cultural autonomy means being in control of their institutions. Today, Israeli Arabs have separate but not independent organizations. The Jewish dominated Israel Ministry of Education makes the appointments and determines the curriculum in the Arab schools. The relevant Jewish-dominated institutions control the Arabic language mass media and run the special departments for Arab affairs.

More radical elements among the Arab population interpret cultural autonomy more broadly. For them it implies something reminiscent of Woodrow Wilson's right of minorities to self-determination. Many Arabs now view themselves as not just an ethnic, religious, linguistic and cultural minority but as a national minority as well. Nobody knows exactly what it means to be a national minority in a Jewish state. It may mean, for instance, that the Arabs will develop a recognized national leadership ready to negotiate terms of Arab-Jewish coexistence with the Government, or it may mean that the Arabs will form a national Arab party that will take a stand on the Palestinians issue, foster links with the Arab world, and appeal to the Arab masses for concerted action.

Much of Arab cultural autonomy in Israel can be said to conform with the principle of cultural pluralism but it is difficult to reconcile this principle with the other two principles of the fact that Israel is a Jewish state and the exigencies of Israel's national security needs. Many Jews, in the Government and outside, feel that a truly Arab cultural autonomy would erode the Jewish nature of the state by introducing bilingualism, biculturalism and binationalism. Many Jews also feel that under the present circumstances it would be a political and security liability to recognize Israeli Arabs as a national minority, since they might later demand self-rule or even become irredentist.

Equality of Resources

Equality of opportunity and rewards to be shared among constituent groups is probably the most fundamental condition for peaceful coexistence in pluralistic societies. This is also the most difficult condition to meet when considerable inequalities existed before.

The initial gaps between Arabs and Jews were substantial indeed. Those Arabs who remained in Israel were poor, rural and uneducated in disproportionate numbers. They had lost their intellectual elite, who had left Israel. They had to find their way in a culturally alien system, without the benefits which the Jews had of capital imports such as the United Jewish Appeal and German reparations.

Despite these and other difficulties, Israeli Arabs have made steady headway since 1948. They have taken advantage of the public services, employment opportunities and higher living standards of Israeli society. Their class structure has expanded to include a sizeable middle class and a small intellectual elite. Moreover, the disparities between Arabs and Jews have slowly diminished over the years.

Yet present Arab-Jewish inequalities in socio-economic status and political representation remain great. Arabs are, by and large, still on the lower rungs of the economic ladder and are virtually outside the national political structure. The distribution of resources between Arabs and Jews is so asymmetric that gaps reach ratios well over 1:2-3 (see Table 1 for selected measures).

Although Israel is committed to equality of opportunity and to reduction of intergroup inequalities, there are many complications. An ideology of democratic and egalitarian pluralism is not enough of an incentive in order to muster the enormously prohibitive investments needed to bring the underdeveloped Arab sector up to the level of the modern Jewish sector. Nor can the ideology of a Jewish state serve as a leveler. It is difficult to provide the Arabs with opportunities to achieve equal status and power in a situation where most of the sparse resources must go toward Israel's national security needs, its immigration programs and the state's overall need to maintain its Jewish character. The demands of national security pervade a great many sectors of the economy and also the political scene. Many Jews wonder if Arabs can be fully trusted as equal partners in economic and political life and whether Arabs should

TABLE 1

Demographic Characteristics, Socio-economic Status and Political Representation of Israeli Arabs and Jews, 1973-1974.

Dimension	Total	Jews	Arabs
I. DEMOGRAPHIC CHARACTERISTICS (1974)[1]			
Births and Deaths			
Rate of live births	27.7	24.7	44.6
Rate of deaths	7.2	7.5	5.4
Rate of infant mortality	23.5	19.2	37.0
Rate of natural increase	20.5	17.2	39.2
Life expectancy (of a newborn)—male		70.5	69.0
Life expectancy (of a newborn)—female		73.7	72.3
Age Distribution			
Percent of persons 0-14 years old	32.9	29.9	49.5
Median age	24.4	25.6	15.2
Family Size			
Percent of families with 6 or more persons	17.5	13.8	56.1
Average size (including single persons)	3.8	3.6	6.2
Type of Locality			
Percent rural	14.2	9.3	41.7
Percent living in cities (municipalities)	68.6	75.3	35.5
Percent living in unincorporated settlements	2.7	0.1	17.4
II. SOCIO-ECONOMIC STATUS (1974)[1]			
Education			
Median number of years of schooling		9.5	5.9
Percent illiterate		8.1	24.4
Percent with at least some college education		16.6	4.9
Students in post-primary schools per 100 persons aged 15-19 in the population	46.8	50.8	27.4
Students in higher education per 100 persons aged 20-29 in the population	7.3	8.1	1.3
Occupation (Selected Categories)			
Percent in scientific, professional, managerial and clerical jobs	38.8	41.4	14.3
Percent in non-skilled jobs	6.3	5.3	15.7
Percent in agriculture and construction	14.6	12.2	37.6
Material Well-Being			
Annual per capita income in Israeli pounds	6,282	6,308	3,515
Percent of families possessing electric refrigerators	64.2	98.3	53.8
Percent of families possessing telephone	48.0	52.2	7.0
Percent of families possessing private cars	26.1	27.6	11.5
Percent of families living in one or less persons per room	47.8	51.1	14.6

Continued on next page

Table I (cont'd)

III. POLITICAL REPRESENTATION (1973)[2]			
State			
Cabinet ministers	18	18	0
Deputy ministers	6	4	2
Knesset members	120	114	6
Supreme Court justices	10	10	0
Directors-General	18	18	0
Heads of local authorities	147	99	48
Histadrut			
Central Committee	20	20	0
Executive Committee	167	163	4
Parties			
Mapai (Israel Labor Party):			
Bureau	27	27	0
Central Committee	615	605	10
Mapam (United Workers Party):			
Steering Secretariat	9	9	0
Central Committee	351	340	11
Mafdal (National Religious Bloc):			
Secretariat	16	16	0
Broader Executive Committee	200	200	0
Herut:			
Executive Committee	31	31	0
Central Committee	254	251	3
Liberal Party:			
Executive Committe	33	33	0
Central Committee	115	115	0

Sources:

1. Central Bureau of Statistics, Statistical Abstract of Israel, 1975, No. 26.
2. Sammy Smooha, *Israel: Pluralism and Conflict*. London: Routledge and Kegan Paul, 1977.

achieve equality of rights in the absence of equality of duties (Arabs are exempted from conscription).

Interpersonal Accommodation

Our last condition for cooperative coexistence is interpersonal accommodation. The broader conditions of an ideological commitment to coexistence, cultural autonomy and equal access to national resources are not enough to ensure equality unless the members of the two groups have mutual trust and accept each other in both the public domain and in private life.

Several studies have been conducted on Arab-Jewish ethnic identity, alienation and social distance in the last ten years. Table II summarizes some of the available findings. The overall picture is rather discouraging despite signs of goodwill in the two communities.

Research on the self-identity of Arabs and Jews has revealed, time and again, that a gulf separates the two groups. National identity is the most salient in both. Jews define themselves as Jews or Israelis and regard their sub-identities as important, attractive and complementary. Arabs perceive themselves as Arab or Palestinian and feel some tension between these sub-identities and their Israeli citizenship. It is evident that Israeli sub-identity applies mostly to the dominant Jewish group and that a new all-inclusive Israeli identity, common to Arabs and Jews, has not yet emerged.[5] This wide divergence in the self-concepts of Arabs and Jews reflects the separatist ideologies of the national movements of the two ethnic groups on the one hand and the firm Jewish character of the state on the other.

Other attitude surveys reveal a lot of mutual alienation. An overwhelming majority of Jews stereotype Arabs as inferior and dishonest, suspect them of hating Jews, would like a close surveillance of Arab activities and wish that there were fewer Arabs in the country. At the same time a majority of Jews are willing to accept Arabs in ranking political positions, even as cabinet ministers. This shows that despite their deep suspicions, Jews are willing to admit (and they are indeed admitting) Arabs who accept the State of Israel as a Jewish state to high posts.

Jewish distrust could feed immensely on Arab alienation from the State of Israel. According to the figures in Table II, only a minority of Arabs accept Israel as a legitimate entity, feel at home in Israel, and have hope for Arab youths' future in Israel. Hence, most Arabs reject the State of Israel and would prefer a different political arrangement.

The alienation between Arabs and Jews is the cumulative result of two major factors. One is the persistent Israeli-Arab conflict (an overriding factor in the perceived Jewish distrust of Israeli Arabs). The other is a deep feeling of superiority among Jews as the institutionally dominant group in the Jewish state, as the modern and more socio-economically privileged sector, and probably as European in origin or at least in orientation.[6]

Studies on inter-ethnic contact disclose a number of interesting tendencies. First, readiness for social relations far exceeds actual contacts. Relations between Arabs and Jews are considered by big majorities on both sides as both possible and desirable although more desirable than possible (see Table II). In reality, Arab-Jewish relations are common in the technical fields of work, in business and the public domain, while social or intimate encounters are less frequent. There is, no doubt, a large untapped reservoir of good will underlying the gap between the readiness for and the scarcity of intergroup social relations.

Secondly, there is a diminishing asymmetry in Arab and Jewish attitudes. Arabs seek contacts with Jews much more than Jews seek contacts with Arabs. A large majority of Arabs, as compared with a small minority of Jews, say there is opportunity for contact and try to foster contact. Between 1971 and 1975, a sharp drop in Arab readiness for social relations took place. Arabs still hanker more after Jewish friendship but less than they used to. Greater Arab readiness for contact is well accounted for by the greater material and symbolic gains usually accruing to minority members in

TABLE 2

Reciprocal Attitudes of Jewish and Arab Israelis: 1967-1976.

Dimension			½ Yes
I. IDENTITY			
A. Jewish Attitudes			
Consider "being an Israeli" important or very important (1974)[1]			91%
Consider "Jewishness" as important or very important (1974)[1]			74%
B. Arab Attitudes			
The term "Israeli" describes me fairly well or very well (1974)[2]			53%
The term "Palestinian" describes me fairly well or very well (1974)[2]			85%
II. ALIENATION			
A. Jewish Attitudes			
It would be better if there were fewer Arabs in Israel (1967)[3]			91%
Every Arab hates Jews (1967)[3]			76%
Arabs will not reach the level of progress of Jews (1967)[3]			64%
The police ought to keep an eye on Arab activities (1976)[4]			92%
Accept an Arab as a minister in government (1976)[4]			69%
Accept an Arab as a top official in government (1976)[4]			76%
Accept an Arab as a top official in a mixed city (1976)[4]			85%
Believe Arab youths have future in Israel (1971)[5]			67%
Believe Arab youths have future in Israel (1976)[6]			61%
B. Arab Attitudes			
Israel has the right to exist (1967)[3]			31%
Israel has the right to exist (1974)[2]			40%
Feel more at home in Israel (1967)[3]			31%
Feel more at home in Israel (1974)[2]			25%
Favor an Arab state in the entire territory of Palestine (1967)[3]			19%
Favor a secular state where Jews and Arabs will have equal rights (1974)[2]			48%
Believe Arab youths have future in Israel (1971)[5]			54%
Believe Arab youths have future in Israel (1975)[6]			61%
III. SOCIAL DISTANCE	**1971**	**1975**	**Difference**
A. Jewish Attitudes[5,7]			
Have opportunity for contact	21%	16%	− 5%
Consider contact essential	11%	23%	+12%*
Try to foster contact	19%	25%	+ 6%
Do not avoid contact	77%	77%	0%
Consider contact possible	78%	77%	− 1%
Consider contact desirable	97%	88%	− 9%
B. Arab Attitudes[5,7]			
Have opportunity for contact	74%	34%	−40%*
Consider contact essential	80%	61%	−19%*
Try to foster contact	88%	60%	−28%*
Do not avoid contact	94%	83%	−11%*
Consider contact possible	75%	66%	− 9%*
Consider contact desirable	86%	73%	−13%*

* Change statistically significant.

Table II (cont'd)

Sources

1. A stratified sample of Jewish high school students, 1974, N=1875. See Simon Herman, Uri Farago and Ya'akov Harel, *Continuity and Change in the Identity of Student Youth in Israel* (In Hebrew) (Mimeographed). Jerusalem: Eshkol Institute, The Hebrew University, 1976.
2. A stratified sample of Arabs in the northern part of Israel, Fall, 1974, N=348. See Mark A. Tessler, "Israel's Arabs and the Palestinian Problem," paper presented at the annual meeting of the Middle East Studies Association of North America, 1974.
3. A sample of Jewish adults in Tel-Aviv, Winter 1968, N=450. See Yochanan Peres, "Ethnic Relations in Israel," *American Journal of Sociology,* 76, 6 (May 1971), pp. 1021-1047.
4. A sample of college students, May 1976, N=89. Unpublished survey, John E. Hofman, University of Haifa.
5. A sample of Arab and Jewish high school students, 1971, Arabs N=213, Jews N=140. See John E. Hofman, "Readiness for Social Relations Between Arabs and Jews in Israel," *Journal of Conflict Resolution* 16, 2, (1972), pp. 241-251.
6. A sample of Arab and Jewish university students, January 1976, Jews N=159, Arabs N=50. Unpublished survey, John E. Hofman, University of Haifa.
7. A sample of Arab and Jewish high school students, 1975, Arabs N=251, Jews N=259. Unpublished survey, John E. Hofman, University of Haifa.

---

contact with majority members. The drop in Arab readiness signifies a decrease in their unilateral dependence on Jews as well as a rise in their self-esteem and self-assertiveness following the War of 1973.

Thirdly, there is a significant discrepancy between personal and political Arab attitudes. While a majority of Arabs consider relations with Jews as possible, desirable, or even fair to excellent, the majority have reservations about or reject Israel's right to exist. In fact, this apparent "inconsistency" is even more marked among urban, educated and younger Arabs. It appears that with advancing modernization Arabs come closer to Jews on the personal level but get further away on the national level.[7]

This last finding is important for a proper perspective on the weight of interpersonal accommodation as a factor in cooperative coexistence. Interpersonal accommodation is doubtless a contributory factor but is less central than the other broader conditions and is not a substitute for them. Since interpersonal accommodation is weak in Israel it tends to reinforce rather than counteract the negative effects attendant with the adverse circumstances surrounding Jewish-Arab relations.

Conclusion

We have tried to identify some of the major conditions conducive to peaceful coexistence in a multi-ethnic and democratic society. They include a shared ideology of partnership, meaningful cultural autonomy, equal access and share in the national resources and interpersonal accommodation.

Although certain auspicious beginnings are apparent, those conditions do not, by and large, prevail in the relations between Arabs and Jews in Israel. As has been stated, Arab-Jewish relations are shaped by three major considerations: democratic pluralism, the fact of the Jewish state and the needs of national security. These forces produce pressures and cross-pressures. The present versions of the prevailing Zionist and Palestinian ideologies militate against the emergence of an ideology of partnership. The idea of the Jewish state appears incompatible with Arab cultural autonomy. The needs of national security create fundamental distrust and inequality in duties and in availability of opportunities and resources. Current institutional arrangements keep Arabs and Jews separate and unequal and thereby discourage interpersonal accommodation.

To date, the alienating factors of a Jewish state and national security far out-balance the positive effects of democratic pluralism for cooperative coexistence between Arabs and Jews. This is to be expected in view of the fact that the Jewish elements are being more emphasized in these early decades of Israeli statehood and that the Jewish state still lacks both universal recognition and secure borders. The problem of Arab-Jewish coexistence is, of course, overshadowed by the broader Israeli-Arab conflict. It is also possible that the mechanism of denial serves as a convenient way of ignoring the Arab minority as long as Israel finds itself overburdened with the problems of immigrant absorption, population dispersion, economic independence, and state-religious issues.

The status quo of involuntary coexistence is, however, slowly but surely breaking down. Israeli Arabs have become less dependent on Jews and more restive. They have already started to voice their demands and to form the necessary independent organizations to promote their interests. Jews have responded with concessions and accommodations but have continued to avoid the painful issues that are involved in the transformation of coexistence from being temporary and forced to becoming permanent and voluntary.

How Arab-Jewish coexistence will finally receive the ideological and practical attention it deserves only time will tell.

FOOTNOTES

1. Cf. Pierre van den Berghe, "The Benign Quota: Panacea or Pandora's Box?" *The American Sociologist,* 6 (Supplementary Issue), 1971, p. 41.

2. *Ibid.*, p. 42.

3. Pierre van den Berghe, "Pluralism and the Polity: A Theoretical Exploration," in Leo Kuper and M.G. Smith (eds.), *Pluralism in Africa* (Berkeley and Los Angeles: University of California Press, 1969), p. 74.

4. For a survey of Arab-Jewish relations and a selected bibliography, see Sammy Smooha, "Arabs and Jews in Israel: Minority-Majority Group Relations" (in Hebrew), *Megamot,* 1976.

5. For a summary of studies on Arab and Jewish identity, see John E. Hofman, *Identity and Intergroup Perception in Israel: Jews and Arabs* (Mimeographed). Haifa, Jewish-Arab Center, University of Haifa, 1976.

6. Although about 55% of the Jews in Israel are not European in origin, they take the European dominant group as a positive reference group. In fact, non-European Jews have, on the average, stronger anti-Arab attitudes. This is due to a variety of factors, including their need to mark themselves off from Arabs with whom they share some subcultural features, lower socio-economic status which is associated with higher ethnocentrism, and greater conflict of interests in competition for the scarce resources available for these two non-dominant groups.

7. See Yochanan Peres, "Modernization and Nationalism in the Identity of the Israeli Arab," *Attitudes Toward Jewish Statehood in the Arab Worla,* Ed. by Gil Carl AlRoy, *Middle East Area Studies* — Series IV, *American Academic Association for Peace in the Middle East,* 1971, pp. 149-164.

Israel's Population: The Legal Status

Population: 3.2 million. Of this number, 2.7 million are Jews (85.1% of the population); 359,000 are Muslims (11.2% of the population); 80,000 are Christians (2.4% of the population); 39,000 are Druzes and other communities (1.3% of the population). *(According to the last census, taken in 1972.)**

Citizenship: All those living in the newly created State of Israel in 1948 and who have continued to live there are Israeli citizens regardless of their ethnic background or religion, as are all those born in the State of Israel since 1948 and who continue to live there. Persons of all nationalities and creeds (excluding only known criminals and similar undesirables) may immigrate to Israel and may apply for citizenship, which is granted following a specific waiting period (of three years in most cases). Israel offers an expedited procedure for Jews. Under its *Law of Return,* Jews are admitted to Israel and may become citizens of the State upon application and without need for a waiting period.

Language: The official languages of the State of Israel are Hebrew and Arabic. Arab members address the *Knesset* (Israel parliament) in Arabic. All *Knesset* proceedings are conducted with simultaneous translation. Israeli citizens may use either Hebrew or Arabic in any court of law or government office.

The Media: 4 of Israel's 24 daily newspapers are in the Arabic language. There are 20 Arabic-language journals. Daily programs in Arabic are featured on radio and television. Censorship is exercised only in matters defined as involving military security.

Religion: Israeli policy adheres to Middle Eastern tradition which affords religious communities a recognized status and jurisdiction in such matters of personal status as marriage and divorce. Each community has jurisdiction over its own system of religious courts in keeping with its own specific religious laws (i.e., Rabbinical, Muslim,* Druze, Roman Catholic, etc.). All the religious communities administer their own religious endowments. The salaries of the clergy of all the faiths are paid by the State.

The Jewish Sabbath — Saturday — is Israel's legal holiday. Muslims and Christians may, by law, keep Friday or Sunday respectively as their legal holiday.

Government: Of a total of 70,000 civil service employees, some 5,000 are Arabs. Magistrates may be Jewish, Arab or Druze, etc.

Political Parties: Voters frequently cross ethnic lines. The left-wing *Mapam* Party and the Communist Party include rab members on their regular slates of candidates to the *Knesset* elections. Other parties in Israel's multiparty system — including *Mapai* (the Israel Labor Party) — offer special slates ("affiliated lists") of Arab candidates. There are several exclusively Arab parties.

Of the *Knesset's* 120 members, 4 are Arab, 1 is Druze and 115 are Jews.

Local Government: 2 municipal councils and 46 local councils are predominantly Arab or Druze. 27 Arab villages have representation in councils with mixed Arab-Jewish membership.

Police: Individual members of the Bedouin, Arab, Druze, Jewish and other communities serve in the Israel Police Force. Their duties include cooperation with the Israel Army in guarding the borders against infiltrators. In 1973 there were 1,287 Arab and Druze policemen in a total force of 13,882.

The Armed Forces: Members of the Arab and certain other ethnic and religious communities are exempted from the draft. The Druze and the Circassian communities have waived this exemption and serve in the army. Arabs and members of other non-Jewish communities may and do volunteer for army service. Jews are not exempted.

---

* 90% of Israel's Christian population is Arab. The Christian denominations include Greek Catholics, Presbyterians, Greek Orthodox, Russian Orthodox, Melkites and members of the Lutheran, Evangelical, Episcopal and Latin Churches (Roman Catholics). There are also a number of Armenians, Copts and members of the Ethiopian Church. Some 2,000 Polish and Hungarian Catholics have settled in Israel. A long-established Bahai community lives mainly in the Haifa area.

Two ancient Jewish sects, the Karaites (numbering some 12,000) and the Samaritans (numbering some 400) live in Israel and also on the West Bank.

* Polygamy is, however, banned by law despite the fact that the *Shari'a* (Muslim religious courts) permits it. The law also prohibits child marriages, setting the minimum age of marriage for women at seventeen years. A woman's agreement to marriage is statutorily required. A law also forbids divorce unless the wife's agreement is forthcoming. Divorce must be registered in a religious court. Contrary to *Shari'a* law also, Section 3(a) of the Equal Rights for Women Law entitles a mother to the custody of her children.

Freedom of Movement: All citizens may travel to all parts of Israel without licenses or permits. They are free to leave and return to Israel with routine visa requirements.

Employment: All wage-earners receive equal pay for equal work. Some 65% of all employed Arab citizens belong to *Histadrut* (the Israel General Federation of Labor).

Education: Compulsory for all to age 14, with free tuition. Arabic-language schools teach Hebrew as a second language. Almost all Hebrew-language schools teach Arabic courses. Arabic is a compulsory second language in many of these schools, with courses lasting for a period of several years. Arab history and civilization are taught in all Hebrew-language schools. The Koran, the Christian catechism and the Hebrew scriptures are part of the school curriculum for Muslims, Christians and Jews respectively. (The number of Arabic-language schools increased from 46 in 1949 to 644 in 1973.)

Muslim, Christian and Jewish students are enrolled in Israel's six universities. 1,200 Arab students were enrolled of a total student body of 50,000 in 1975.

31
The Evolution of Israeli Politics

By Michael Curtis

The Israeli political system is currently in an unusually fluid condition. One can still observe the remarkable continuity of the basic party structures, political behavior and ideological divisions that were inherited from the pre-state yishuv. Yet it is also clear that politics today has a different complexion from that of the first twenty-nine years following the establishment of the state in 1948.

Until 1977 politics was dominated by the Labor groups of which Mapai has always been the leading partner and which combined first in 1965 and then in 1969 to form the Alignment. Both in electoral politics and in control of public power Labor appeared to be not only the dominant but also the indispensable group.

The political system was shaped by Labor's pragmatic politics and consensus style of government. Ben-Gurion transformed Mapai into a left of center, rather than an ideological party. After 1948 the government nationalized most of the non-political services — including military, educational, labor exchanges, social welfare — previously performed by political groups, mostly Labor. Yet, even after supporters could no longer directly benefit from these former activities of Labor they still experienced a sense of psychological dependence on Labor as well as benefiting from Labor's use of public resources to provide jobs and housing for them. It is also worth remembering, especially at the present time, that the political system for much of the first two decades was dominated by the charisma of Ben-Gurion who attracted political support by his own personality as much as by his position as leader of Labor. Under him a national consensus seemed to exist on a mixed economy, on the boundaries of the state and on territory and on religion, with Labor agreeing to abide by the status quo. Coalitions with comfortable majorities in the Knesset were always present with the adherence to the Labor groups of the National Religious Party, the members of which have been *ministrables* in a way similar to that of the Radical Party in the French Third Republic. This arrangement provided both continuity and stability. Between 1948 and 1977, Israel had only 5 Prime Ministers. Some individuals occupied key ministries, such as defense, foreign affairs and finance, for long periods. Some ministries were traditionally allocated to a particular party: the NRP assumed that the interior and religious affairs ministries were their special preserve.

The major parties were centrally controlled by strong oligarchies. The centralized nomination procedure of all parties, and the ability of leaders to decide the order of candidates on party lists reinforced that control. In Israel's extreme electoral process of proportional representation, voting is still based on party lists rather than on individual candidates.

In the yishuv parties were not only ideologically oriented but also extended their activities to the economic, social and cultural activities of the community. Though the most significant relationship was between Labor (Achdut Ha'avoda in 1919 and Mapai in 1930) and the Histadrut set up in 1920 and the kibbutz movements, the other parties had similar arrangements, particularly with religious schools and Yeshivot. Parties therefore had economic and social power over their members and adherents who supported them in return for benefits. Though Ben-Gurion on becoming Prime Minister adopted a policy of statism *(mamlachtiyut)* by which the governmental

---

Dr. Curtis is Professor of Political Science at Rutgers University, New Brunswick. His latest publication, of which he is the editor, is *Antisemitism in the Contemporary World* (Westview Press, 1986).

functions of non-governmental bodies would be eliminated or reduced, some of these functions are still exercised, especially by the Histadrut and the Jewish Agency. Indeed, the Histadrut today with its powerful economic interests, constitutes a formidable opposition to the Likud government.

Parties have been grouped around three essential views or visions of the nature of Israel: the socialist, the religious, and the centrist-right view of the Jewish state as a refuge. These three views still remain as powerful though divisive factors in contemporary Israel. But there have always been a considerable number of combinations of parts of these three views in differing form such as the socialist religious view of Hapoel Hamizrachi. The multiple cleavages on religious, socioeconomic, defense and foreign policy issues, and on relations with Arabs and on territorial boundaries, have in the past presented and still present obstacles to party realignment into three permanent major blocs. However, until 1977 there was surprisingly little variation in voting for the three major blocs and in the number of seats in the Knesset: Labor varied between 64-69 seats, the center-right between 27 and 34, and the religious groups 15-18 seats.

The religious parties have competed among themselves and with the secular parties to gain the electoral support of the orthodox. A constant factor has been that the religious parties obtain 13-15% of the vote though about one-third of the population is observant if attendance of orthodox schools is an indicator. The NRP has always been the leading religious party (from 1956-1981 it never had less than 10 M.K.s) even in 1981 when it sharply declined to 6% of the poll. Until recently it was moderate in its policies and a comfortable coalition partner except for short periods in 1958-1959 and 1976-77. It made few demands on Labor, limiting itself to religious legislation and some public services. But the price paid by both Golda Meir and Rabin to get NRP support was a pledge that no agreement on withdrawal from occupied territory would be completed before the electorate was consulted.

During this period Israeli Arab politics appeared largely as a satellite to the major parties with attached lists. Rather than symbolizing any ideological affinity, this was in essence a simple trade off of electoral support for material benefits.

The crucial change that occurred in 1977 when Likud took the reins of power can be attributed to a number of short and long term factors.

The first, unforeseen consequence of the 1967 war, was the breakdown of the national consensus on the boundaries of the country with parties sharply divided on the future of the occupied territories and a more hawkish attitude, not only in the center-right groups, but also within part of Labor and the religious groups. The NRP, taking a harder line on the West Bank, became more nationalistic and assertive. A new younger leadership emerged within the NRP, much of it sympathetic with the actions of Gush Emunim. Social and economic concerns became less significant than security and defense matters.

Within the Labor bloc itself internal divisions took their toll. In a sense Labor took a long time to recover from the havoc wrought by Ben-Gurion who split the party over the prolonged Lavon affair, creating the dissident Rafi in 1965 and causing a crisis in succession in the party. Golda Meir was initially seen as the temporary conciliator rather than a policy-making leader. When Sapir, the old style party boss, refused to become Prime Minister in 1974, the party lost its last opportunity to combine strong party control and governmental power. A new younger group of ex-generals and senior bureaucrats competed within the party with those of a more traditional political background and the activists of the kibbutzim. The party witnessed not only an increase in intraparty factionalism and a weakening of central control but also the bitter personal fight between Rabin and Peres, which even now has not been completely settled. Rabin as Prime Minister was remote from the party. Peres suffered from becoming leader only four weeks before the 1977 election.

Criticism of Labor focused not only on the corruption or misdemeanors of prominent leaders but also on the indecisiveness of the party as a governing group. The governments of Eshkol and Golda Meir can now be seen more as dealing with crisis management than with decision-making. Political changes led, for the first time, to a minority government under Golda Meir and then to a government with a bare majority under Rabin. Labor had to bear the charges of incompetence for the Yom Kippur war and the bitterness of *mechdal* (omission) after the thorough investigation and criticism of its conduct. One significant result of the growing crisis of confidence in Labor was the creation of a government of National Unity in which Begin was included for three years and which bestowed the mantle of respectability on the previous political pariah, who had appeared to be in permanent opposition. The short-sighted dismissal of NRP ministers by Rabin in December 1976 on a relatively trivial issue was only one of a number of short term factors which led to the disastrous defeat of Labor in 1977.

In retrospect it can be seen that Labor had been steadily losing support in successive elections. In 1965 Labor and its two related parties held 63 seats but in 1977 they obtained only 32 seats. There were two warning signs for Labor in 1977. The first was that it lost votes in the wealthier parts of cities to the new Democratic Movement for Change and also in the poorer sections it lost heavily to the Likud. The other was that it did badly in the development towns, dropping from 45% to 20.5%, in the moshavim where the Likud got 41%, and in the army, where Likud got 44%.

This decline was accompanied by a similar decline in the identification of voters with the party. This was true of all parties — in 1981 only 15% of all voters were party members — but it especially handicapped Labor. Voting from 1948 to 1969 had been very stable but half of the electorate voted differently in 1977 from in 1973.

A sign of the general dissatisfaction was the rapid rise of the DMC which appeared as a centrist party in 1977, appealing to the middle class, to professionals and to those disillusioned with Labor. In winning 15 seats, the largest number for a new party, it took away a significant part of the Labor vote and indirectly brought Likud to power. But the DMC had little program other than the call for a change in the electoral system and for the democratization of the party structures. A party of "the whites and the rich," the DMC immediately split on the issue of membership of the new government. Its idealism faded before political expediency with its leader Yadin claiming, as Dayan had done in 1974, that the national emergency required his joining the government. The political ineptitude of Yadin, whom many had seen as a possible savior of the country, led to the dissolution of the party, with only the minority Shinui still in existence.

Another consequence of the Six Day War was the increase of Israeli Arab nationalism and the switch from Arab adherence to attached lists of the major parties to more extreme groups. In 1980 a poll, registering a decline in Arab radicalization from 1979, showed that only a bare majority of Israeli Arabs accepted the state's right to exist. In 1979 a considerable majority of those Arabs thought that the Zionist movement was racist, that Israel should withdraw to pre-1967 borders, and that the Law of Return should be abolished. In 1955 Mapai got 70% of the Arab vote and the Communist Rakah 22%. By 1977 Labor got only 27% and Rakah 51%. Over 90% of the Rakah vote came from Arabs. At the 1981 election the vote for Rakah declined to 46%. No firm conclusion can be drawn about the continuaton of this decline for three reasons. The first is that the difference between 1977 and 1981 was only 65,000 votes. The second is that the Arab turnout in 1981 was 70.1% compared with the 78.5% Jewish vote. The most important factor was that Arab voters evidently swung from Rakah to Labor in order to defeat Begin.

Ethnicity is currently a crucial political factor. Voting analyses as well as impressionistic views suggest that the most serious political polarization has occurred along ethnic lines, especially when this is correlated with social class or income. The outstanding feature of 1981 was that 60% of Orientals (a term used instead of Sephardim, with which it is not synonymous) voted for Likud, compared with 32% in 1969, and only 30% for Labor. Similarly, 60% of the Ashkenazi vote went to Labor (51% in 1969). Of total Labor votes 70% came from

Ashkenazim while 65% of the Likud vote came from Orientals.

In light of demographic figures that well over half of the Jewish population is of Oriental descent origin, and that Orientals are still more fertile than Ashkenazim, the danger for Labor is clear. In addition there are three uncomfortable truths for Labor. The Likud did even better among the second generation of Orientals (the young) than among the first. Labor did better among the Ashkenazim who immigrated (the older) than among their children. The resentment by Orientals of the more successful and privileged Ashkenazim was vividly expressed by the strong Likud vote in the expanding development towns against the European pioneer settlers and aristocracy of the kibbutzim which have not attracted Orientals.

The feeling of relative deprivation and of political neglect or discrimination on the part of Orientals has led to support of Likud which on economic grounds they logically should oppose. For reasons explained by the long labor dominance and the inheritance of parties from the yishuv, Orientals were largely excluded from politics. In the Knesset between 1949 and 1970 three quarters of the M.K.'s were born in Eastern Europe. Only three cabinet ministers between 1948 and 1973 were Orientals.

Two things are striking about this exclusion. One is that no national Oriental party arose, though Orientals held office at local and municipal level and by 1970 were a third of the mayors. A number of explanations can be offered: the acceptance of Zionist ideology and of the unity necessary for security reasons, the material advancement of many Orientals, the concessions made by the leading parties which met some of their demands, expressions of sympathy about other demands and the cooption of some Oriental leaders. Only in 1981 did a successful ethnic party arise since an early and small one in 1951. Formed by the flamboyant Aharon Abuhatzera, descendant of a prominent rabbinical Moroccan family, Tami drew members from a number of the other parties, ran a strong campaign and won 2-3% of the vote and 3 seats. Yet the fact that four other ethnic lists, all with similar social programs, had little success suggests that Tami benefited from its mixed political-religious appeal and the forceful character of Abuhatzera, soon to be convicted of fraud. A strong ethnic party is still possible but with better education and higher income of Orientals and with increasing intermarriage, now 20% of all marriages, it appears unlikely.

The second matter is that the ethnic differences were almost entirely contained within the system and the call for autonomy or challenge to national authority, experienced in some other multiracial and multicommunal countries, was not pronounced. If the Orientals were not attracted by the collectivism of the kibbutz and were more hawkish towards Arabs, they did not, except for occasional outbreaks such as the Black Panther movement in 1971, engage in antisystem activity.

Ethnic politics exists in the sense that all major parties have now appealed to the vote of Orientals. Individuals of Oriental descent were included in leading places on the party lists in 1981, and have gained leadership positions in the system, including the Presidency. Yet there is some irony in the nature of the Oriental vote. Though Likud has been the dominant governmental party since 1977 Orientals still see Labor as the "establishment" against which they should protest. Yet at present 14 of the 47 Labor M.K.'s are Orientals compared with only 6 of the 48 Likud M.K.'s. Likud, mostly a conservative bloc, got the bulk of the vote of the 18-30 age group, the urban areas, and blue collar workers with less education and income while Labor got support from the middle aged, better educated and white collar workers of the middle class. Will Likud retain Oriental support? If Likud remains in power it is difficult to see how it can sustain its role as the anti-establishment party. Much also will depend on whether the allegiance of Orientals has gone to Likud, a coalition of groups with diverse interests, or simply to its leader, Begin.

Structural analysis sometimes plays inadequate attention to personal factors. In 1959 Labor won its resounding victory with the slogan "Say yes to the old man." Not since Ben-Gurion's ascendancy in the first 20 years has a master politician such as

Begin emerged in Israel. He has adroitly appealed, in charismatic fashion, to many Orientals who see him as a father-figure, the object of a personality cult. He has astutely stressed and benefited from the traditional and unifying bonds of Judaism. A tough campaigner and effective orator he has used strong rhetoric to great effect. In populist fashion, feeling comfortable with and having a close relation with the masses, he has been the proponent of a strong religious nationalism, somewhat different from that of his master, Jabotinsky. Begin has been able to control the factions within his bloc in a way unlikely to be emulated by his successor. Likud may well disintegrate as an entity when Begin goes. Moreover, the immediate effect of the internal crisis over events in Lebanon has been to diminish the moral authority of Begin, a process from which he might not recover as Ben-Gurion did not over the Lavon affair.

The argument has been made that the elections of 1977 and 1981 show the overlapping of the cleavages of religion and class. Some of the evidence certainly points this way, but doubts also are pertinent. In the April 1981 Histadrut elections Labor increased its share of the vote. Economic issues appear to have played a small role in the Knesset 1981 election where the main issues were the personalities of the leaders, foreign policy and the territories. Nevertheless the paradox exists. What meaning does ideology have when the middle class votes for the center-right? Labor faces the problem that the socialist vision does not appear to capture the imagination of a substantial section of Israeli society and the irony that large numbers do not associate it with desirable social change.

The 1981 campaign was marked by violence to an unprecedented degree, causing fear of future danger to the democratic nature of Israel. In the short term the violence probably helped the Labor vote by those disturbed by signs of anti-democratic behavior. What is noticeable, however, is that, apart from Meir Kahane's Kach group, there is no extremist anti-system party. Other protest groups have been small, ineffective or not posing any political danger. Only Gush Emunim exists as a potentially significant group that can challenge political authority. Already it has contributed to the breakup of one government and obliged Begin to treat it carefully. But at the moment it can still be regarded as an extra-parliamentary rather than an anti-parliamentary force.

Is there a trend to a 2-party system? For two successive elections only 5 groups have got over 3% of the vote each. In 1981 Labor-Likud got 73.6% of the votes and 80% of the seats while 21 groups got less than 1% each. Part of the explanation may be the bitterness engendered in the campaign which caused many to vote for one or another of the two major blocs. It is unlikely that the trend to two blocs will continue for a number of reasons. The electoral system itself still guarantees a certain multiplicity of parties. The extraordinary volatility of electoral views as shown by public opinion polls during 1981 indicates the weakening of voter ties to any major bloc. Both of the major blocs suffer from internal divisions, each of which may lead to future factions going off on their own. The overlapping of cleavages may be a temporary phenomenon. The different visions of Israel and of Judaism still remain sufficiently strong to prevent a coalescence of political opinion. One can expect the continuation of different and changing combinations.

There are always unknown elements in politics. Can Israel be regarded as a prime ministerial or as a cabinet government system? Relations between Begin and his ministers, and the life of his government, may depend on the answer. Has the appointment of about a quarter of the M.K.'s to the government unduly strengthened the hand of the executive in regard to the Knesset? Whatever the answer, the current open dialogue in Israel, the challenging criticism of the actions in Lebanon of its leaders constitute an extraordinary example of democracy at work. The electoral poll has been sustained at a high level of almost 80%. Civilian control over the military has been maintained as has adherence so far to an accepted code of moral behavior and political rules. The democratic fabric of the country is not in danger though its politics may present some uncomfortable moments for its friends and allies.

32

Zionist Diplomacy and Israeli Foreign Policy

By Aaron S. Klieman

Among the many profound transformations brought about by Israeli statehood was the new state's opportunity to exercise one of the principal attributes of sovereignty: the independent conduct of foreign relations. In reviewing Israel's performance in the international arena after three decades, it is important to appreciate the basic factors which have affected her behavior. Two of these are immediately apparent: the situational constraints imposed from without, such as Arab hostility and the overshadowing superpower rivalry, and domestic priorities and limitations. Less appreciated is the extent to which recent policy bears the imprint of pre-state experience with global statecraft.

Few leaders of newly emergent states in the postwar period have had as much exposure to the realities of world politics as the Zionist founders of the State of Israel. In 1948, Weizmann, Ben Gurion and Sharett were eminently qualified and prepared to fulfill this cardinal function of Israeli security by their own previous experience. And behind them was a long period of Zionist diplomacy dating back to Herzl and the close of the nineteenth century. At the moment of formal statehood there already existed an established set of policy goals, standard operating procedures, preferences and suppositions, as well as a corps of diplomatists schooled in *realpolitik*. These values and preferences have continued to color and guide Israeli foreign policy, both for better and for worse.

Policy Objectives

The contrast between initial policy goals and the more modest ones imposed upon Israel by the overriding struggle with her Arab neighbors is striking. Certainly one popular assumption in May 1948, was that acquisition of full statehood alone might resolve, permanently and honorably, the enduring Jewish problem both for the Jews and for the rest of the world. Only thus could the Jewish people be converted from an anomaly, a nation without a territorial home of its own, into a proper nation-state capable of ingathering its exiles and supporting and protecting them. This formula, aiming at enjoyment of unexceptional status under international law, to be sure, was in keeping with the mainstream of Zionist political thought.

Moshe Sharett, Israel's first Minister for Foreign Affairs, gave eloquent expression to this deep longing for normalcy when Israel's flag was raised outside U.N. headquarters on 12 May 1949. Those left bereaved by the War of Independence should find comfort in knowing that their sacrifice, and that of the fallen, had not been in vain. They had given of themselves, "in order that the Jewish people shall find life, freedom and equality within the family of nations," and so that "the nation of Israel should have the opportunity to express its full creative capacity."[1] Israel and her people were gaining international respectability at last, in the tangible form of *de jure* recognition, exchange of envoys, ratifica-

---

Dr. Klieman teaches International Relations at Tel Aviv University. His publications include *Soviet Russia and the Middle East* (The Johns Hopkins Press, Baltimore, 1970), *Foundations of British Policy in the Arab World* (The Johns Hopkins Press, Baltimore, 1970), and *Israel's Global Reach: Arms Sales as Diplomacy* (Pergamon Press, 1985).

tion of bilateral agreements and admission to world bodies.

It was perhaps only natural that these official actions were seized upon in Jerusalem and Tel Aviv as proof positive of the willingness of other states to accept Israel on the basis of equality, reciprocity and comity, thereby vindicating the fundamental thesis of Zionism. Thirty years later, this original image of Israel among the nations seems illusory, or at least premature. Both founders and sons had wished to perceive Israel as being "like all the nations" *(k'mo chol hagoyyim)* and as so judged to be by others, but political developments have only conspired to emphasize Israel's uniqueness in the international sphere.

Israel is the only member of the world community unable to identify with another state according to at least one of the following criteria: shared language, culture, or religion. Of over 150 countries, she is one of the few not formally affiliated with an existing bloc, pact, regional grouping or alliance. Finding herself in the Middle East geographically, but not entirely *of* the Middle East, she is regarded at times as part of Europe, of Asia or, indeed, of neither. In addition, there is the fact that she is the only state that has to deal with a permanently hostile environment and, Israel's Arab adversaries, by possessing a much greater power potential, merely reinforce this further unenviable distinction.

No other country suffers from a combination of quite so many unfavorable geopolitical factors. In the midst of fighting for what is nothing less than self-preservation, Israel's consternation becomes all the more pronounced, therefore, when critics condemn her foreign policy as imperialistic, and as aiming at nothing less than hegemony over others.[2] This sharp disparity in cognition between how Israelis see their policy priorities and how outsiders see them also extends to how the nature of the Arab-Israeli struggle is defined.

To Israeli leaders this does not imply that there are merely differences of opinion about conventional and secondary issues, such as over territory, economic rivalry or opposition to a particular form of domestic regime. Israel continues to regard herself, and to predicate foreign policy, in terms of a total and sustained struggle for sovereign existence — even more, for her very right to exist juridically no less than physically. This state of affairs tends to foster, among Israelis, a feeling of isolation and vulnerability. The result is a strong sense of national insecurity which runs like a strand through the thirty years of Israeli diplomacy.

It was certainly not with this in mind that the Israeli Knesset, on 11 March 1949, approved the original five principles for Israeli foreign policy. Yet these principles still remain unrealized and indeed seem further than ever from fulfillment.

The five principles elaborated in 1949 were the following:

1. *Loyalty to the fundamental principles of the United Nations Charter and friendship with all peace-loving states, especially the United States and the Soviet Union:* Over the years, Israel has increasingly come in for severe criticism by the U.N. Her policy of strong and immediate retaliation against acts of violence originating from the neighboring Arab countries has been criticized since the early 1950s. Anti-Israel resolutions condemning her presence and administration in areas occupied since June, 1967 have been passed by the Security Council and the General Assembly. The U.N.'s inability to provide an impartial forum where Israel is concerned has resulted in Israel's estrangement from that international organization (although not from its fundamental principles.) Similarly, Cold War ideological differences and the intrusion of subjective considerations like Muslim solidarity or the persuasiveness of Arab monetary aid, have frustrated Israel's efforts to achieve amicable relations with the Soviet Union, the Communist bloc countries and a majority of the Afro-Asian states. In January, 1973 Israel had 81 embassies among her missions abroad, i.e., in approximately one-third of the international community. In 1977 Israel could claim formal diplomatic ties with only some 52 countries.

2. *Efforts to achieve an Arab-Jewish alliance based on economic, social and cultural cooperation within the United Nations*

framework: Any discussion of close Arab-Jewish ties, founded upon mutual understanding and projections of the benefits to be reaped by regional cooperation are still greeted with skepticism by many Israelis, despite the Sadat initiative. The predominant pattern of relations between the two peoples has been almost exclusively one of bitter conflict; the experience of thirty years does not fade away easily. In their blueprint for peace, Israel's spokesmen repeatedly dangled before the Arabs the prospect of technical and financial aid in fostering development. Today, the Arabs feel they can afford to dismiss this offer. Sophisticated technology, they say, is readily available from European and other sources. They view Israel as reduced to pauper status by its dependence on American aid while Saudi Arabia and the other Arab oil-exporting countries have money to spare and to share.

3. *Support for all measures strengthening peace and Human Rights:* Here, too, events ran counter to aspirations. Because of its intractability, the Middle East conflict (and, by implication, Israel's position on the conflict) became one of the main points of friction between the two rival superpowers, impairing rather than strengthening international peace. Charges have constantly been brought against Israel for violating human rights: initially those of the Arab population inside Israel and, since 1967, the rights of the Arabs in the West Bank and Gaza under military government. Such accusations culminated in the U.N. resolution on 11 November 1975 labeling Israel and Zionism "a form of racism and racial discrimination." Whether these charges are groundless is immaterial. The fact is that Israeli diplomacy must still expend a great deal of energy in repudiating them. In the eyes of the world Israel has yet to prove herself.

4. *Insistence on the right of Jews to settle in Israel — and to leave their present country of residence:* One of the crueler transformations to have taken place in terms of principles for the conduct of foreign policy lies in this area of *aliya* (immigration). The right of Jews to immigrate to Israel had been more or less recognized in principle: openly, by many countries, tacitly, in the case of Soviet Russia. Adept diplomacy, however, cannot provide an antidote for the unwillingness of Jews to exercise this right — a fact reflected in the declining annual rate of immigration (there were 19,754 immigrants in 1976 as against 54,886 in 1973) and the clusters of Israeli expatriates who prefer to reside abroad.

5. *Effective preservation of the independence and sovereignty of Israel:* Significance may or may not have been attached to the order in which the five principles of Israeli foreign policy were listed in 1949. If there was, who could have guessed that as late as 1978 this fifth tenet, stressing the essentials of independence and sovereignty, would remain at the top of Israel's priorities? It is this primacy of national security which has dictated foreign policy, and which serves to explain (without necessarily excusing) many of its procedural as well as substantive features. Security considerations are the prism through which national policy options, both strategic and tactical, are filtered. They also account for the heavy criticism to which general policy, as distinct from specific acts, has been subjected.[3]

Despite the prevailing image of Israel as an assertive state actor (defiant to the point of arrogance, according to some) what we in fact find is a reigning spirit of conservatism in the handling of foreign policy. Certainly this spirit reflects the imperative need for caution deriving, as already noted, from the security situation. Given the narrow margin for error, everything has to be reduced to its essentials in terms of potential costs or benefits. Yet policy conservatism should also tell us something about the manner in which decisions are reached, as well as why Israeli expectations from diplomacy are not great.

Pre-state Doctrines Still in Force

At least four constants have been retained from the pre-state period: the "one Great Power" doctrine; a preference for abstaining from involvement in Middle Eastern politics; maintenance of a centralized authority for policy making, and political realism. The first two are of a substantive nature; the latter fall more into the category of procedural characteristics, on *how* policy tends to be made.[4]

The "one Great Power" doctrine: This finds clear expression in the "special relationship" with the United States which Israeli leaders consciously sought to cultivate, especially since 1967, and which they cited with pride as the greatest achievement in Israeli foreign policy. This can be explained in several ways. First, it became impossible to maintain the early policy of non-identification for long. The very fact of Israel's special needs and place within the larger regional and global configuration quite possibly denied her the privilege afforded other small states of playing both superpowers against each other in accordance with the unwritten rules of neutralism and nonalignment. Second, are ideological considerations, which placed Israel squarely in the Western camp. Third, has been the fundamental divergency of interests as seen from Moscow since the early 1950s, given the pro-Arab emphasis of Russian policy in the eastern Mediterranean.

To this list I would add a fourth aspect which is rooted in the pre-state assumptions of Zionist diplomacy and which, moreover, does not see identification with a particular Great Power as necessarily detrimental. On the contrary, Zionist leaders from Herzl to Weizmann appreciated how important the support, moral and political, of a leading world power could be for their cause. Such a major actor's patronage might prove decisive in three ways: a) in giving Zionism legitimacy; b) in protecting the national home in Palestine and encouraging its economic growth, and c) in making the Arabs realize that opposition — especially violent opposition — to Zionism was no longer an option worth pursuing.

With this in mind, Weizmann and the others sought to foster a "British connection" during those formative years which coincided with the British mandate period in Palestine proper. The intention was boldly to make Zionism an ally of Great Britain by linking the fate of the nationalist movement with that of empire and equilibrium. In those years much effort went into reminding British officials in London of the original Balfour commitment and in pushing for its being honored in the only way possible: through greater support and closer association with the Zionist enterprise. When, by 1945, the British connection was no longer possible, the Zionist leadership turned to the United States.

It soon became clear to Weizmann's successors, starting with Ben Gurion and continuing through Eshkol, Meir and Rabin that multilateral diplomacy, based on the U.N. and its institutions, could not be an adequate substitute for the assured support and understanding of one Great Power patron, and they reverted to the older practice of concentrating on relations with one Power. This is readily apparent in Israeli efforts toward the U.S. since 1965.[5] There had been earlier disappointments. Ben Gurion's initiative in seeking a mutual defense treaty had been rebuffed by Washington in 1955; so, too, were requests for formal security guarantees in 1957; the U.S. had failed to honor previous informal commitments to the freedom of navigation during the 1967 crises. Nevertheless, subsequent governments (including the present Likud government) have given top priority to strengthening ties with the U.S. — and for precisely the same four reasons that earlier motivated Zionist diplomacy in the search for: legitimacy, protection, tangible assistance and to act as a deterrent to Arab enmity.

For each of these reasons, and so long as the benefits far outweigh the discomforts of dependency, Israel can be expected to devote herself to promoting the relationship established with the U.S. in recent years, and thus the "one Great Power" doctrine will continue to serve as an accurate guide for Israeli foreign policy well into the fourth decade of statehood. This policy, however, ignores the American side of the equation and possible future U.S. interests.

Israel's Role in Middle East Politics

Non-interference in regional Arab politics is a second durable feature of both Zionist and Israeli foreign policy. While the reasons may be somewhat different in each of the respective periods, this does not alter the fact that policy makers have shown neither a flair for trying to influence the affairs of the neighboring countries nor even any real desire to do so. This holds true for the Arab domestic political scene and for the overall regional balance between conservative and radical Arab forces, or between those advocating a pro-Soviet or a pro-American policy. Such considerations have tended to be only secondary and indirect: for example, the deep-penetration sorties by the Israel air force during the war of attrition in 1970 drove Egypt to strengthen her ties with the Soviet Union.

This pattern of aloofness and of refusing to participate in regional intrigues and political alignments — whether out of disdain or as the result of rational calculation — says something about prevailing attitudes and assumptions before statehood and at present with regard to Israel's place in the Middle East. The fact that Israel was poised to intervene against Syria in the 1970 Jordan civil war and her open support of the Lebanese Christian community are really exceptions which only prove the rule. The general pattern is perhaps again indicative of the constraints which exist. To adopt a clear position on regional issues exposes Israel to the charge of exploiting the Arab world's centrifugal pressures with the aim of dominating her neighbors. The irony is that by this very political abstinence first the *yishuv* (Hebrew community in Palestine) and then Israel have exposed themselves to the Arab complaint that this is a foreign body alien to the region and insensitive to its rhythms, its passions and concerns. From this perspective, events since the Sadat visit to Jerusalem, emphasizing the possibility of a separate accord with Egypt, signal the onset of a fundamentally different Middle Eastern political context for Israel, fraught with obvious hazards but also with tremendous opportunities for possible alliances on the regional and global levels.

Diplomacy by the Few

One reason why President Sadat's November 1977 initiative first appealed to the Government of Israel is that it fitted in so perfectly with the Israeli leaders' preference for direct personal diplomacy at the highest level. Subsequent complications at the Cairo conference, at Ismailiya and in Jerusalem only served to reaffirm this prejudice. Prime Minister Begin attributed the slackening of the momentum to petty-mindedness on the part of Egyptian officialdom: core issues like peace are best dealt with by heads of State or of Government, and should not be held back by bureaucratic considerations. It therefore follows that through direct talks, in an atmosphere of personal trust and commitment, outstanding differences have a better chance of resolution. The Camp David experience will leave a deep imprint upon Israeli premises on how policy making should be made, both at home and vis-a-vis negotiating partners.

If its future now seems assured, this preference for summitry has a long tradition. Early Zionist contacts with other states were also maintained through great leader-personal diplomacy. Appreciation of the need to cut through red tape and to dispense at times with the niceties of diplomatic protocol, to go right to the top, finds a precedent in the efforts of Theodor Herzl, in Zangwill's phrase, "the first Jewish statesman since the destruction of Jerusalem," and Herzl's diaries reveal how with little or no backing he negotiated single-handedly with the rulers, statesmen and financiers of Europe and the Near East. By far the most successful practitioner of personal diplomacy was Chaim Weizmann. A consummate diplomat and prolific correspondent, he was the only Zionist leader who could meet world statesmen as an equal, making important friends for the Zionist cause. His close relationship with British Cabinet members, especially in the negotiations which preceded the Balfour Declaration but also throughout the mandate period, are well-known. His greatest achievement came in 1947-48.

The personal approach owed its origins to the informal, structured and experimental nature of a state as yet in the making. Statehood did not put an end to free-wheeling, idiosyncratic diplomacy by placing it on an organizational rather than personal basis. Israeli foreign policy-making, instead of becoming structured along institutional lines, still emphasizes direct leader involvement in interpersonal statecraft. And this is perhaps best reflected in the permanent downgrading of the Ministry of Foreign Affairs, although it can also be seen in the secondary role played in the making of foreign policy by both the Cabinet and the Knesset through its Committee on Foreign Affairs and Security.

Pragmatism

The external relations of a nationalist movement are one matter, those of a sovereign state, another. In the case of Israel this transition has been softened by a fourth feature of continuity: pragmatism. Flexibility and pragmatism were also the hallmarks of Zionist activity during the forty years of pre-state diplomacy. Weizmann and his colleagues were not above playing off the respective belligerents, Germany and England, during the First World War. There was concern in London lest England be preempted by a unilateral German pledge of support for Zionist aspirations in Palestine. By reinforcing this British concern the Zionist leaders helped to insure issuance of the Balfour Declaration. In 1921-22, appreciation of political realities led the leadership to acquiesce, albeit grudgingly and without prejudice to the ultimate Zionist claim, to Churchill's conversion of Transjordan into an exclusively Arab province within the Palestine mandate. Pragmatic Zionists preferred to concentrate their energies on developing and expanding the *yishuv*, west of the Jordan.

In the 1930s, although personally identified with a pro-British policy, Weizmann conducted negotiations with Mussolini. In August 1937, the proposal made by Great Britain to partition Palestine led to a major internal crisis, yet a majority of Zionists followed Weizmann and Ben Gurion in endorsing the principle of an independent though truncated Jewish state in but a small part of Palestine. Sharett (then Shertok) argued the "historical necessity" of accepting partition; Zionism's ultimate success lay in "the maximum exploitation of historic opportunities" as they arose. In another instance of strategic pragmatism, Ben Gurion defined Zionist policy toward the British mandatory power during the Second World War as: "We shall fight the war (against Nazi Germany) as if there were no (1939) White Paper, and we shall fight the White Paper as if there were no war." Toward the climax of the struggle for statehood, Weizmann in particular showed himself capable of making the requisite political shift dictated by circumstances. His orientation and energies moved from England to the ascendant world power, the United States.

In sum, it can be argued that pragmatism in Israeli foreign policy has helped to compensate for what might otherwise have proved a fatal overemphasis, and reliance, upon great leader or "lone wolf" diplomacy. Sensitivity for the limits of the possible largely balances the accident of personality by moderating the impulsive, affective side of individual leaders and their selective perceptions of the world.

Conclusion

Attitudes change slowly while strategies are prisoners of actual situations. There is no reason to expect any abrupt shift in Israel's traditional diplomatic posture. Yet certain breaks with the past — which are in her power to effect — would be commendable if Israeli diplomacy is to make its maximum contribution to Israel's security. Whatever the long-term repercussions of the 1977 diplomatic upheaval, it has become possible, really for the first time, to contemplate an Israel actively and directly participating in Middle East politics. At an early stage in the shaping of Israel's diplomatic tradition Zionist leaders were quick to profess their conviction that ". . . a Jewish renaissance in this country can only have a strong and invigorating influence upon the Arab nation."[6] They felt confident that the "two brother nations, Jews and Arabs, working together in peace and harmony, are destined to bring about the cultural and economic revival of the awakening peoples of the Near and Middle East."

These words were written over a half century ago. If realized now this in itself would be a major source of discontinuity, representing a break with the past and relieving Zionist-Israeli statecraft from its greatest constraint: the absence of a framework for Arab-Jewish peace and cooperation.

FOOTNOTES

1. Moshe Sharett, *At the Threshhold of Statehood*, (Tel Aviv: Am Oved, 1966), p. 359.

2. Samuel Roberts, *Survival or Hegemony? The Foundations of Israeli Foreign Policy*. The Washington Center of Foreign Policy Research of the John Hopkins University School of Advanced International Studies (Studies in International Affairs No. 20, 1973).

3. See, for example, Michael Brecher, *The Foreign Policy System of Israel* (New Haven: Yale University Press, 1972), p. 562; and Lewis Brownstein, "Decision Making in Israeli Foreign Policy: An Unplanned Process," *Political Science Quarterly*, Vol. 92, No. 2 (Summer 1977), p. 260. Probably the most controversial critique is that by George Ball, "How to Save Israel in Spite of Herself," *Foreign Affairs*, Vol. 55, No. 3 (April, 1977), pp. 456-563. More thoughtful and constructive is Stanley Hoffmann's, "A New Policy for Israel," *Foreign Affairs*, Vol. 53, No. 3 (April, 1975), pp. 405-431.

4. These four components of the Zionist legacy are dealt with by the author in greater detail in Alan Arian (ed.), *Israel Society in the Making* (tentative title), (forthcoming).

5. These efforts are the subject of two recent major studies: Bernard Reich, *Quest for Peace. United States-Israel Relations and the Arab-Israeli Conflict*, (New Brunswick: Transaction Books, 1977), and Nadav Safran, *Israel, The Embattled Ally*, (Cambridge: Harvard University Press, 1978).

6. Memorandum submitted by representatives of the Jewish community in Palestine on 28 March 1921 to Winston Churchill, then Colonial Secretary, during his visit to Jerusalem. The text can be found in Aaron S. Klieman, *Foundations of British Policy in the Arab World* (Baltimore: The Johns Hopkins Press, 1970), pp. 275-8.

33 Assessing Israel As a "Strategic Asset"

A Quantitative Comparison with Other Prepositioning Sites

By Jay Adams

The debate over how best to defend the Persian Gulf and its oil against the possibility of Soviet aggression is warming up, and as it does, it becomes increasingly clear that an issue as simple as geography is at the heart of the problem. The Soviet Union borders on Iran and is within 1000 miles of the main oilfields of the Middle East, while the distance from the United States is about 9000 miles by air and considerably longer by sea. Moreover, unlike Europe, the Far East, and Southeast Asia, there is no intact U.S. military basing structure to provide support in the event of a conflict, and since the fall of the Shah, no nation of the Gulf region is prepared to extend to the United States full-scale basing privileges. The closest U.S. base, on the Indian Ocean island of Diego Garcia, is still 3000 miles from the assumed locus of conflict, and this base is in any case limited in scale by the smallness of the island.

These simple facts create quite a problem for U.S. planners. A Soviet standing army of perhaps fourteen divisions sits astride the region across the border with Iran, in addition to the force of nearly a hundred thousand stationed in Afghanistan, while a single American division of about 25,000 would, if airlifted from the United States with its 70,000 tons of equipment, take about four weeks to get there using all U.S. airlift resources (and over twice as long using half the available airlift). It might well be a case of "too little too late," and if the Soviets perceived this in advance, they might be tempted to exploit their advantage.

Both the defense of the region and deterrence of a Soviet attack therefore require energetic remedial measures to enhance our "projection" capability. In part, this may take the form of expanding our small fleet of airlift and sealift vessels, procuring such items as additional C-5s or CXs. But at a $60 million program unit cost, there are severe limits on the number of strategic air transporters that can be procured. A second solution is to "lighten the load" to be lifted by developing lighter armored forces, thereby reducing the number of flights ("sorties") and transporters needed. But this would, at best, result in a saving of perhaps 20 percent in terms of time or the required size of the lift fleet. While there is much to be said for both measures, additional solutions clearly are required.

The most obvious solution is to have the equipment in the theater of conflict, or at least near it, when you need it, rather than moving it only after an aggression begins. By moving the heavy equipment to "prepositioning sites" in peacetime, and flying in just the men to "marry up" with the equipment if a conflict contingency develops, considerable time can be saved. The prepositioned equipment poses no threat in peacetime, but serves as a notice to the Soviets that a rapid response to aggression is possible, and thereby enhances the deterrent threat to enhance the stability of the region.

With this in mind, the Carter Administration negotiated a set of "access arrangements" to permit prepositioning in Oman, Somalia, Egypt, and Kenya on a limited scale, and the Reagan Administration has submitted to Congress appropriation requests for funding to flesh out these arrangements. There are, however, several problems with the prepositioning sites negotiated to date. Kenya is over 2500 miles from assumed conflict areas by the most direct route, and Somalia about 1600. Somalia is demanding a king's ransom in aid in exchange for access, and has problems of

---

Jay Adams is a student of defense issues.

political stability. Neighboring Ethiopia is a virtual colony of the Soviet Union, and has openly threatened to employ its air force against U.S. facilities in Somalia (with which Ethiopia is at war). As if this weren't enough, Somalia and Kenya are antagonists, and Kenya is informally allied with Ethiopia against Somalia. Kenya objects to U.S. cooperation with Somalia. Neither Kenya nor Somalia is in a position to provide an air defense umbrella for the security of American equipment and personnel against air attack, so anything prepositioned at these locations will be vulnerable unless the scarce air defense assets of the United States are devoted to the task and permitted by the host government to operate.

Oman is the best site of all in terms of distance, lying at the mouth of the Persian Gulf, but as an access opportunity it suffers from some of the problems already mentioned. It is within strike range of Soviet aircraft stationed in Afghanistan as well as the increasingly sophisticated air force of South Yemen (another Soviet colony), yet the host government cannot provide air defense. This alone will limit the amount of materiel the United States can put at risk in a vulnerable environment. In addition, the Omani government, not wishing to be seen as a "cat's paw" of a superpower in the region, intends to limit the conditions under which facilities can be used by United States forces. For example, Sultan Qaboos was so outraged by the reported use of Omani facilities on Masirah Island in support of the (failed) Iran hostage rescue mission that he threatened to withdraw all American privileges. While the latter did not happen, it is clear that American access in Oman will be less than 100 percent reliable over time under the present government. Nor is the survival of the Omani regime a foregone conclusion, although there are few signs of instability at the moment. In addition, Masirah Island and the other Omani sites mooted in the press are among the hottest and most inhospitable places on the planet Earth, and the effects on U.S. armed forces personnel retention could be a real problem.

It is also worth noting that Oman, while it is close to the Gulf, is quite distant from Europe (as are Somalia, Kenya, and Diego Garcia). This means that equipment stationed there is dedicated to Persian Gulf contingencies but poorly located for NATO. Ideally, prepositioning sites would be suited to a "swing force" that could be deployed *either* to Europe or the Gulf, to limit the adverse impact of Persian Gulf security arrangements on the already-precarious NATO alliance capability.

In these terms, Egypt has a considerable advantage over Kenya, Somalia, Oman, and Diego Garcia. For example, the distance from Ras Banas, Egypt to Munich is about half that of Masirah, Oman. Egypt can also provide general air defense against any adversary but Israel, and can provide security against other forms of attack on the facilities that have been discussed. Moreover, Egypt is forthright in its support for a strengthening of U.S. capability in the region, and clearly intends to cooperate in plans to build the Rapid Deployment Force.

Yet, even the sites in Egypt raise problems. Cairo's isolation in the Arab world is unnatural, and should the current or a future Egyptian government seek to rejoin its historic allies, the price might include a weakening of the alliance with Washington. This might come, for example, after Egypt repossesses the Sinai in April 1982, under the terms of the peace treaty with Israel. Moreover, the evolution of the domestic political situation in Egypt could lead to a change of policy or even a change of government. After the bitter experience with Britain and then the USSR, Egyptians have a considerable antipathy to foreign troops and equipment on their soil. Egypt was one of the founders of the nonaligned movement, and foreign installations by whatever name are bound to become a target for Arab nationalist "Third Worldist" criticism of the regime. While, at the present time, the Egyptian/American alliance seems secure, Egyptian policy five and ten years hence is unpredictable.

Given this array of problems and reasons to worry, American planners are obligated to "spread the risk" by distributing American commitments among the access sites. Of the sites discussed, Egypt emerges as the "dominant solution," but conditions there too will limit the scale of American military investment. Basically, something more is needed.

Israel as a Prepositioning Site

Given the problems of each of the sites already explored, attention is beginning to turn to Israel. Israel offers several distinct advantages as a "steppingstone" access site, which, taken together, comprise an attractive package:

1. *Location*. The distance from Israel to the Gulf is less than one-seventh that from the U.S. It is also half the distance of Diego Garcia, and closer than Kenya, Somalia, or Turkey (assuming, in the last case, that overflight of Syria, Iraq and Iran is excluded). At the same time, it is half the distance to Europe (Munich) compared to the East Coast of the United States, and also about half the distance to Europe compared to Diego Garcia, Oman, Somalia, and Kenya. Of states willing to provide regional access for the RDF, only Egypt is competitive as a location for a "swing force" that could be sent either to Europe or the Gulf.

2. *Political Stability*. While the future political structures and policy orientations of Oman, Somalia, Kenya, Egypt, and Turkey are subject to radical change, the basic political structure and policy of Israel are stable and predictable as they affect that country's policy toward regional security. Virtually all Israeli leaders in the major parties support a strengthening of the United States role in the region, an enhancement of U.S. capability to deter and, if need be, defeat Soviet aggression, and an enhancement of U.S. force projection capabilities to support these objectives. The leadership of both major Israeli parties has forthrightly endorsed the provision of strategic access arrangements to the United States under appropriate conditions. Sites in Israel would be intrinsically less vulnerable to revolutions, coups, and domestic disorders.

3. *Political Reliability*. No sovereign nation in the modern world will extend basing privileges to a foreign power completely without restriction. But the political limitations that would be imposed in the Israeli case probably would be less severe than those on which Oman, Egypt, Somalia, and Kenya will insist, for the simple reason that there is a closer congruence between Israel's own interests and those of the United States as regards force projection contingencies. If, for example, an Iraqi threat to Kuwait or Iran called for an American response, the policies of Oman and Egypt could be limited by inter-Arab politics, while Israel would, in almost all scenarios, find its interests aligned with those of the U.S. The contrast might be still more pronounced in a European scenario, from which the Arab states might wish to divorce themselves while Israel, given its strategic position, could not. While there are differences between Israeli and American policies in the local diplomatic arena, their postures in regional strategic military affairs are generally in agreement.

4. *Air Defense*. U.S. materiel prepositioned in many states of the region could be subject to conventional and guerilla attacks, yet few of the host nations have the capability to provide a secure defense umbrella. Israel is a clear exception. The primary mission of the Israeli Air Force is to defend that nation's own air space, and the IAF's mastery of the skies is almost uncontested. While the United States might have to provide its own air defense in such locations as Masirah or Berbera, allocating scarce F-15 wings or I-Hawk SAM batteries, security of "prepo" against air attack in Israel would be provided implicitly by the host government. The same applies to security against large-scale guerilla operations, which the Israelis have brought almost completely under control.

While these differences between Israel and other sites, taken together, might be regarded as a considerable, even commanding advantage, there has been comparatively little American interest in strategic cooperation with Israel until recently. The notion of Israel as a strategic asset has been a subject of considerable interest in American Jewish and Israeli circles, but until recently it has been regarded with official indifference if not contempt, particularly by the Carter Administration. Indeed, it is said that the name "Israel" was not, until recently, permitted even to appear in official exploratory discussions of prospective access sites, and that, having been rejected from the start as a serious candidate for the regional security system, Israel's potential contribution was

Table 1
AIRLIFT TO THE PERSIAN GULF (DHAHRAN)
(using half of strategic lift)

From	Days to Transport One Mechanized Division
United States	77 days
Israel (Tel Aviv)	11
Diego Garcia	27
Somalia (Berbera)	14
Kenya (Mombasa)	22
Oman (Masirah)	8
Egypt (Ras Banas)	10
Turkey (Izmir) (no overflight of Iraq, Syria, or Iran)	17

Table 2
AIRLIFT TO EUROPE (MUNICH)
(using all of strategic lift)

From	Days to Transport One Mechanized Division
United States	24 days
Israel (Tel Aviv)	11
Diego Garcia	29
Somalia	20
Kenya	23
Oman	20
Egypt	12
Turkey	8

Table 3
DIRECT COSTS OF AIRLIFTING ONE MECHANIZED DIVISION
(as in Tables 1 and 2)

From	To Dhahran	To Munich
United States	$391 millions	$247 millions
Israel	63	125
Diego Garcia	138	294
Somalia	76	198
Kenya	124	232
Oman	43	208
Egypt	54	140
Turkey	99	87

not studied by Carter officials in any systematic way.

The Reagan Administration brings to the issue a different perspective. Repeatedly during the 1980 Presidential campaign, the Republican candidate called attention to Israel as a concrete strategic asset and ally, and the new Administration is reported to have a serious interest in exploring potential forms of strategic cooperation with the government of Israel.

Reagan is of course aware that the Arabs (with the possible exception of Egypt) do not look kindly upon U.S./Israeli cooperation, but, unlike his predecessor, he does not take this as an absolute limit to U.S. freedom of action. Since the very founding of the Jewish state, the U.S. has played both sides of the street successfully (in spite of heckling from certain elements in the Washington bureaucracy who endlessly warned that it couldn't be done). It is probably even the case that the U.S. has had more rather than less influence with the Arabs exactly because it also has had (most of the time) influence with Israel too. Ironically, Arab opinion already takes it as given that the U.S. is in cahoots with Israel, which Washington supports with considerable economic and military aid. The incremental diplomatic cost of expanded strategic cooperation could, for this very reason, be minimal if the problem were managed intelligently during the transitional period.

Still, there will be political costs to be measured against strategic benefits. It is worthwhile, therefore, to assess in closer detail the strategic value of Israel, to quantify the military advantages that should be compared to any political disadvantages. What follows, then, is a more detailed statistical excursion to compare Israel with other prepositioning sites in military and economic terms, to quantify the value of cooperation or the "opportunity cost" of non-cooperation, in the expectation that this may provide a criterion by which to assess future policy.

Comparing Deployment Times

For the military planner, the central consideration of any prospective arrangement affecting the Rapid Deployment Force is its impact on force effectiveness. In the case of a prospective access site, this means that the central measure of effectiveness is the contribution that a "stepping stone" can make to shorten the time that it takes to deliver and deploy forces to assumed conflict locations, by comparison with sending forces from the continental United States (CONUS) or from other regional access sites.

The methodology by which such comparisons are made is complex, and includes the following factors:

1. distance;
2. the number and types of transport aircraft available;
3. the portion of this lift fleet assumed to be available for a given contingency;
4. utilization factors, sortie rates, speed, and productivity; and
5. the weight and bulk of the materiel to be lifted.

These factors can be estimated from such public sources as the Defense Marketing Service databook, *Rapid Deployment Force* (Greenwich, Connecticut, DMS, 1980), on the basis given in the appendix to this paper. Assuming that the equipment for a mechanized infantry division is to be lifted from prepositioning sites to Dhahran, Saudi Arabia (from which they would move overland to participate in a Persian Gulf conflict), and that half of the available U.S. transporters were used for a Persian Gulf scenario (the other half being held in reserve for European contingencies), prepositioning in Israel compares to prepositioning at other sites or lift from the continental U.S. as in Table 1 (p. 46).

The advantage of prepositioning in Israel is substantial compared to sending forces from the U.S.; the first whole division would get to the Gulf 2½ months earlier! Forces from Diego Garcia or Kenya would take twice as long to arrive, and forces from Turkey 50 percent more time (assuming that overflight of radical countries is excluded). Only Oman and Egypt offer shorter deployment times, and in both cases the advantage is marginal.

If a war erupted in Europe instead of the Gulf, major U.S. reinforcement would be required for NATO to hold the line against the vastly larger Warsaw Pact armies. It

Table 4
NUMBER OF C-5As REQUIRED TO MATCH DEVELOPMENT TIME FROM ISRAEL

To Dhahran			
	from	United States	168.37 more
		Diego Garcia	39.00
		Berbera	6.68
		Mombasa	30.67
		Izmir	17.84
		Masirah	10.06 fewer
		Ras Banas	4.48 fewer
To Munich			
	from	United States	69.28 more
		Diego Garcia	89.88
		Berbera	40.66
		Mombasa	57.82
		Masirah	45.81
		Ras Banas	7.44
		Izmir	20.05 fewer

Table 5
ADDITIONAL COST (SAVINGS) OF CAPABILITY TO DEPLOY MECHANIZED DIVISION TO DHAHRAN IN 11 DAYS

(as in Table 4)

From	$ millions
United States	$9,429 million
Israel	0
Diego Garcia	2,185
Somalia	374
Kenya	1,718
Turkey	999
Oman	(563) savings
Egypt	(251) savings

could, in such a contingency, be necessary to lift materiel prepositioned for Persian Gulf contingencies to Europe instead of Dhahran. Assuming that the equipment for a mechanized infantry division were to be lifted from these prepositioning sites to Munich, Germany, and that all the available U.S. transporters were used, Table 2 (p. 46) shows how Israel compares to the other sites:

Forces prepositioned in Israel could be in Europe in half the time it would take those from the continental United States to arrive, and Israel is closer than any of the other regional prepositioning sites except Turkey (which is, of course, a member of NATO). It is also worth noting that Diego Garcia, which is the anchor of the RDF prepositioning system, is even further from Europe than the continental United States. Forces prepositioned in Diego, Somalia, Kenya, or Oman are in effect dedicated to Persian Gulf contingencies, while Israel, Egypt, and Turkey are superior as sites for a "swing force" suited to either Gulf or European scenarios.

In addition to the swing force concept,

Egypt, Israel, and Turkey also have importance for Mediterranean contingencies, from which Diego, Oman, Somalia, and Kenya are remote. The "beefing up" of our navy in the Indian Ocean has been accomplished partly at the expense of the Sixth Fleet in the Mediterranean, and any comparison of allocation of U.S. forces to alternative access sites should also take Mediterranean conflict into account.

Comparisons in Terms of Cost

So far we have compared prepositioning sites exclusively in terms of military effectiveness and deployment time. But in the real world of force planning, choices are constrained by budgetary impact as well. For example, if the cost of deploying a given unit to a particular location within a required time can be reduced, the budgetary resoures "liberated" can be used to strengthen other elements of the overall force structure. Conversely, spending more to achieve a given objective implicitly weakens other elements of the force structure.

How, then, would Israel compare to other access sites in terms of cost, holding military effectiveness constant? One way to make such a comparison is to compare the direct costs of the airlifts of equipment for one mechanized infantry division to Dhahran or Munich, as above, on the simple principle that miles translate into airfleet sorties which cost money (see Appendix). Table 3 (p. 46) gives the direct costs for the airlifts enumerated in Tables 1 and 2.

Combining these comparisons (i.e., using the imaginary case in which one division was lifted to Dhahran and a second division to Munich), a "swing" force would cost a half billion dollars less to lift from Israel compared to the U.S.: $350 million less than Diego Garcia; $170 million less than Kenya; $90 million less than Somalia; and $60 million less than Oman. Again, only Egypt and Turkey are competitive in terms of cost, both being essentially identical to Israel.

But comparison of cost on this basis ignores a critical dimension of effectiveness, which is the time required to deploy. The very purpose of an airlift is to reduce the time that otherwise would be required to move forces at less expense but more slowly by sea. Indeed, even airlift deployment times like those given in Tables 1 and 2 are considered much too slow by officials responsible for U.S. national security planning, and procurement of additional C-5s or CXs is considered essential to the RDF.

One way to correct for deployment time in our comparisons, then, is to take into account the number of aircraft that would have to be procured to meet a given lift time requirement from the various prepositioning sites. To permit such a comparison, let us take as our deployment time standard the times required to lift the equipment for a mechanized division from Israel to Dhahran (11 days) and Munich (also 11 days), and take as the unit of cost the number of additional (or fewer) C-5A's that would need to be procured to match this time from the other sites. The number of aircraft, derived from the calculations in the Appendix, is shown in Table 4 (p. 48).

Using the $56,000,000 program unit cost of the C-5A as a standard, equalization of deployment times will reveal considerable "hidden" cost differences between the access sites, differences much greater than the direct costs of the lifts ignoring time (Table 3) or the costs of facilities on the ground in the host countries. (see Appendix). Table 5 (p. 48) compares the C-5A procurement costs to make it possible to lift one mechanized division to Dhahran in 11 days from the various sites.

By this measure, prepositioning in Israel is the equivalent of 168 C-5As or almost ten billion dollars compared to sending forces to the Gulf in the same time from the continental United States. Diego, Somalia, Kenya, and Turkey would also cost substantially more.

Only Oman and Egypt are superior to Israel for prepositioning in terms of cost to deploy to Dhahran in 11 days. If we add the comparison to Munich, on the other hand (see Table 4 and Appendix), Turkey is superior but Egypt would require 7 additional C-5s ($417 million) and Oman 46 ($2.6 billion). Finally, on a combined cost basis, Israel emerges as the least expensive alternative for a swing force if the cost of C-5s for both Munich and Dhahran is taken as the criterion, since in the three cases where there is an additional expense to one location and a saving to the other the additional expense is greater.

Conclusions

Israel offers clear and substantial advantages as a prepositioning site for U.S. projection forces, in terms of both force effectiveness and cost. Many of these advantages derive from its geographic position at the crossroads of the Mediterranean and Southwest Asian strategic zones. There is more political support for an American presence among the Israeli public than any other state of the region, and more support among the competing political elites. A U.S. decision to preposition materiel in Israel could be taken with a higher degree of confidence that access would in fact be available in a conflict contingency some years down the road than in most of the other host nations now under discussion. In addition, Israel is in a position to provide a security umbrella for prepositioned materiel, while in some of the other sites such security would have to be provided by U.S. forces. Overall, prepositioning in Israel would be a useful complement to other access arrangements, and would strengthen overall force effectiveness at substantially lower cost than other alternatives.

It is true that prepositioning in Israel also will entail political costs, in that certain of the Arab states will be strongly opposed. But these costs are containable if handled firmly, particularly during the transitional period. From the Arab point of view, the principal objection is surely to United States military and economic aid to the government of Israel, aid which will continue regardless of the degree to which Israel is developed as a regional strategic asset. Moreover, Arab publics already assume that the United States is engaged in a strategic alliance with Israel; the concept is more novel to Americans than to the peoples of the region.

In any case, the possibility of prepositioning in Israel should not be rejected a priori, without a careful accounting of costs and benefits. If, on balance, a decision is taken not to develop the strategic benefits of cooperation with Israel, it should, at the minimum, be taken with a clear-eyed awareness of the strategic and economic advantages that are being foregone.

APPENDIX

Basis of Calculations, Additional Data and Sources

TABLES I & II (pp. 52, 53)

1. The following inventory of primary aircraft available was used:

70	C5A
234	C141
234	C130

Any airlift under 3000 miles is assumed to utilize C130 aircraft as well as C5A and C141 aircraft.

2. A down factor of 15% was applied to the above numbers and then: (1) all available aircraft were employed in the Munich lift; (2) 50% of all available aircraft were employed in the Persian Gulf lift. The number of aircraft employed in any actual airlift would be highly scenario dependent, the above usage rate was chosen to provide a means for comparison.

3. All figures assume transport of all cargo from the on-loading point stipulated. The U.S. figures do not allow for a possible mix of CONUS and POMCUS locations, nor do any others.

4. After transporting all outsize cargos, C5As are assumed to continue to tranport bulk and oversize cargo until the lift is completed.

5. No limitations have been placed on run-through capability of either the on-loading or off-loading point. It is assumed that any location chosen to serve as a future site will be built up as necessary to permit operations. It is also assumed that no limitation has been placed for national security reasons. In the 1973 lift to Israel, the Secretary of Defense limited the number of aircraft permitted on the ground at Tel Aviv at any given time for security reasons. These figures do not allow for such a limitation.

6. Mileage has been calculated as the most direct flight with over-flight restrictions as follows: no overflight of the Soviet Union or any Soviet bloc state; no overflight of a Soviet controlled or allied state; no overflight of Iraq, Iran, Libya, Syria, Ethiopia, or Yemen.

7. Overflight of Jordan and Saudi Arabia is permitted on the assumption that regardless of the originating point, if Saudi Arabia is permitting off-loading in Dhahran, overflight will also be permitted.

8. Non-U.S. pre-positioning sites assume the first leg of the airlift originates on the U.S. East Coast, and that airlift aircraft are based in the U.S.

9. The divisional tonnage figures represent a division and support as follows:

Airborne	
Outsize	13,775
Bulk and Oversize	48,300
	62,075 tons
Mechanized	
Outsize	34,655
Bulk and Oversize	60,948
	95,603 tons
Infantry	
Outsize	20,942
Bulk and Oversize	56,399
	77,341 tons

The figures for an armoured division were not calculated. It is assumed (1) this division would be transported by sea due to its extreme weight; and (2) this division would be the last division transported.

The source for these tonnage figures is Defense Marketing Service, *Rapid Deployment Force*, 1980.

10. The cost figures given are based on the peace-time operating cost per flying hour for each aircraft. The following figures were used:

C5A	$6,793/hour
C141	2,087/hour
C130	763/hour

It is acknowledged that in an actual lift scenario there would be additional ground support expenditures which are not included in the given figures.

The source of these figures is *Hearings Before a Subcommittee of the Committee on Appropriations*, House of Representatives, 96th Congress, 2nd Sessions, Part 8, *Department of Defense Appropriations* for 1981, p. 418.

The following formula was used to compute airlift capability in short tons/day*:

$$\mathbf{L} = \frac{\mathbf{N \times U \times S \times R \times P}}{\mathbf{D}}$$

where:

- **L** = lift capacity for a particular force, for a particular aircraft
- **N** = the number of aircraft utilized
- **U** = utilization rate of aircraft; utilization rate is determined by maintenance requirements, aircrew availability, and the fleet-wide average of the number of hours per day that each type of aircraft can fly
- **S** = block-in speed of the aircraft: averaging the cruising speed with the slower take-off and landing speeds
- **R** = productivity factor for the aircraft, allowing for empty return
- **D** = distance travelled in airlift
- **P** = payload of aircraft in cargo of specified force

The following factors were used for the specific aircraft and specified divisions.

C5A	**U** = 12.5
	S = 428 mi/hour
	R = .445
	P = 54.6 Airborne
	68.5 Mechanized and Infantry
C141	**U** = 12.5
	S = 407
	R = .445
	P = 18.07 Airborne
	27.04 Mechanized
	23.14 Infantry

NOTE: The calculations assumed the C141B aircraft was used. This craft has been stretched to permit greater capacity before "cubing out". Actual figures for the C141B are not yet available; the Air Force estimate of a 30% increase cited in *Hearings Before the Subcommittee of the Committee on Appropriations,* House of Representatives, 96th Congress, 2nd Sessions, *Department of Defense Appropriations for 1981,* Part 6, p. 413, was used. Unofficial reports indicate the C141 capacity has been increased by more than 30%.

C130 **U** = 8.0
S = 260 mi/hour
R = .445
P = 13.8 all divisions

*Source for the formula and factors is Defense Marketing Service, *Rapid Deployment Force,* 1980.

TABLE I
Airlift to the Persian Gulf (Dhahran)

From	Miles	Days to Transport	Cost (M$)
United States (East Coast)	8739		
Airborne Division		69.38	350.0
Mechanized Division		77.44	390.7
Infantry Division		68.17	343.9
Israel (Tel Aviv)	1284		
Airborne Division		9.77	55.2
Mechanized Division		11.18	63.2
Infantry Division		9.88	55.8
Diego Garcia	3012		
Airborne Division		24.52	123.7
Mechanized Division		27.30	137.7
Infantry Division		24.11	121.6
Somalia (Berbera)	1580		
Airborne Division		11.79	66.6
Mechanized Division		13.52	76.4
Infantry Division		11.92	67.3
Kenya (Mombasa)	2642		
Airborne Division		19.05	107.6
Mechanized Division		21.95	124.0
Infantry Division		19.27	108.9
Oman (Masirah)	839		
Airborne Division		6.73	38.0
Mechanized Division		7.65	43.2
Infantry Division		6.80	38.4
Egypt (Ras Banas)	1086		
Airborne Division		8.41	47.5
Mechanized Division		9.61	54.3
Infantry Division		8.50	48.0
Turkey (Izmir)	2074		
Airborne Division		15.17	85.7
Mechanized Division		17.45	98.6
Infantry Division		14.30	80.8

TABLE II
Airlift to Munich

From	Miles	Days to Transport	Cost (M$)
United States (East Coast)	5530		
Airborne Division		21.76	221.4
Mechanized Division		24.31	247.4
Infantry Division		21.38	217.5
Israel (Tel Aviv)	2543		
Airborne Division		9.62	109.5
Mechanized Division		11.01	125.3
Infantry Division		9.73	110.8
Diego Garcia	6418		
Airborne Division		25.88	263.3
Mechanized Division		28.84	293.5
Infantry Division		25.44	258.9
Somalia (Berbera)	4296		
Airborne Division		17.52	178.3
Mechanized Division		19.50	198.4
Infantry Division		17.23	175.3
Kenya (Mombasa)	5036		
Airborne Division		20.44	208.0
Mechanized Division		22.75	231.5
Infantry Division		20.09	204.4
Oman (Masirah)	4518		
Airborne Division		18.40	187.2
Mechanized Division		20.48	208.4
Infantry Division		18.09	184.1
Egypt (Ras Banas)	2864		
Airborne Division		10.71	121.9
Mechanized Division		12.27	139.7
Infantry Division		10.83	123.3
Turkey (Izmir)	1679		
Airborne Division		6.69	76.2
Mechanized Division		7.61	86.6
Infantry Division		6.76	77.0

TABLE III
Cost of Equalizing All Options

TO DHAHRAN

from United States	$9,428.72	M cost
Diego Garcia	2,185.12	
Berbera	374.08	
Mombasa	1,717.52	
Izmir	999.04	
Masirah	$ 536.36	M savings
Ras Banas	250.88	

TO MUNICH

from United States	$3,879.68	M cost
Diego Garcia	5,033.28	
Berbera	2,276.96	
Mombasa	3,237.92	
Masirah	2,565.36	
Ras Banas	416.64	
Izmir	$1,122.80	M savings

*The program unit cost of $56M for the C5A aircraft is used. The unit fly-away cost cited in the same source is $29.7 M. Source: Defense Marketing Service.

**The cost for the C5A was used on the assumption that any actual procurement in any number, would be C5A aircraft. The CX was not used because it is still in the developmental stages.

TABLE IV
Construction Costs for Basing Options

Site	FY '81	FY '82	FY '83	Program Total
Diego Garcia		317.6		317.6
Somalia	.4	24.0		24.4
Kenya	19.1	26.0		45.1
Oman	85.5	81.5	44.6	211.6
Egypt		148.5		148.5

Turkey: no figures available.
Israel: no figures available.

Source: DD 1391, Military Construction Project Data

34 Jerusalem's Unity and West Bank Autonomy — Paired Principles

By Saul B. Cohen

The Shatterbelt characteristics of the Middle East belie the hope that the resolution of any single issue or conflict will assure regional harmony and stability. The region, like Southeast Asia, is a Shatterbelt because it is internally fragmented and subject to continuing external pressure by major powers because of its unique geographical, resource, cultural and historical conditions.[1] Thus, lasting peace between Arabs and Jews will no more ensure overall tranquility than would single accomplishments of rebuilding the Lebanese nation, fulfillment of Kurdish homeland ambitions, agreement upon the Shatt-al-Arab boundary, radicalization of Persian Gulf states, merger of geographically and culturally disparate countries, or stabilization of petroleum output and prices.

Nevertheless, not all of the issues that keep the Middle East in turmoil have the global impact of the Arab-Israeli conflict or the petroleum crisis. And nearly every other issue that besets the region has some relationship to these global problems. Thus, war between Iraqi and Iranians, however rationally unconnected with the Arab-Israeli conflict, nevertheless prompts both sides to lay blame on Israel and Zionism, and involvement of other parties on Iraq's behalf affects Israel's security. Also, oil politics, jockeying by the United States, Maritime Europe and the USSR inevitably influences the fate of Israel. What resolution of the Arab-Israeli conflict will accomplish, then, is not to bring peace to the entire Middle East, but to enable the other serious issues that plague the region to be addressed directly, candidly and without needless diversion of political and military energies.

Certainly a major contributory factor to the global and regional character of the Arab-Israeli conflict is Jerusalem. In many ways Jerusalem is as much at the political center of the conflict, as it was at the military center during Israel's War of Independence. And any new outbreak of the conflict, if it were to be accompanied by an uprising in the West Bank, would surely have as profound an impact upon Jerusalem as did the events of the June, 1967 War.

It is because Jerusalem is so much at the heart of the dispute that those committed to the proposition of step-by-step diplomacy have been so reluctant to deal with the issue. But because Jerusalem is so central, no other diplomatic steps that have been or might be taken can have an enduring affect until Jerusalem is confronted.

Despite the past history of diplomatic avoidance efforts, Knesset passage of the Jerusalem Law during the summer of 1980 and the announced plan to transfer the Prime Minister's office to East Jerusalem propelled the Jerusalem issue onto the international scene with explosive force. These actions triggered a storm of opposition from Israel's friends and foes alike. Moreover, important segments of Israeli and World Jewish leadership variously criticized the Law as redundant, untimely, provocative, a legislative freak and folly. That many Knesset members who voted for the measure were also among its critics is sad testimony to the triumph of political expedience over principle. Those castigating M. K. Geula Cohen, the bill's sponsor, for ideological zealotry are reminded that had Knesset critics shown the same political courage as adherents, it would not have been enacted.

Avowed purpose of the Jerusalem Law, which affirms the united city as Israel's

---

Dr. Cohen is a member of Graduate Center, City University of New York.

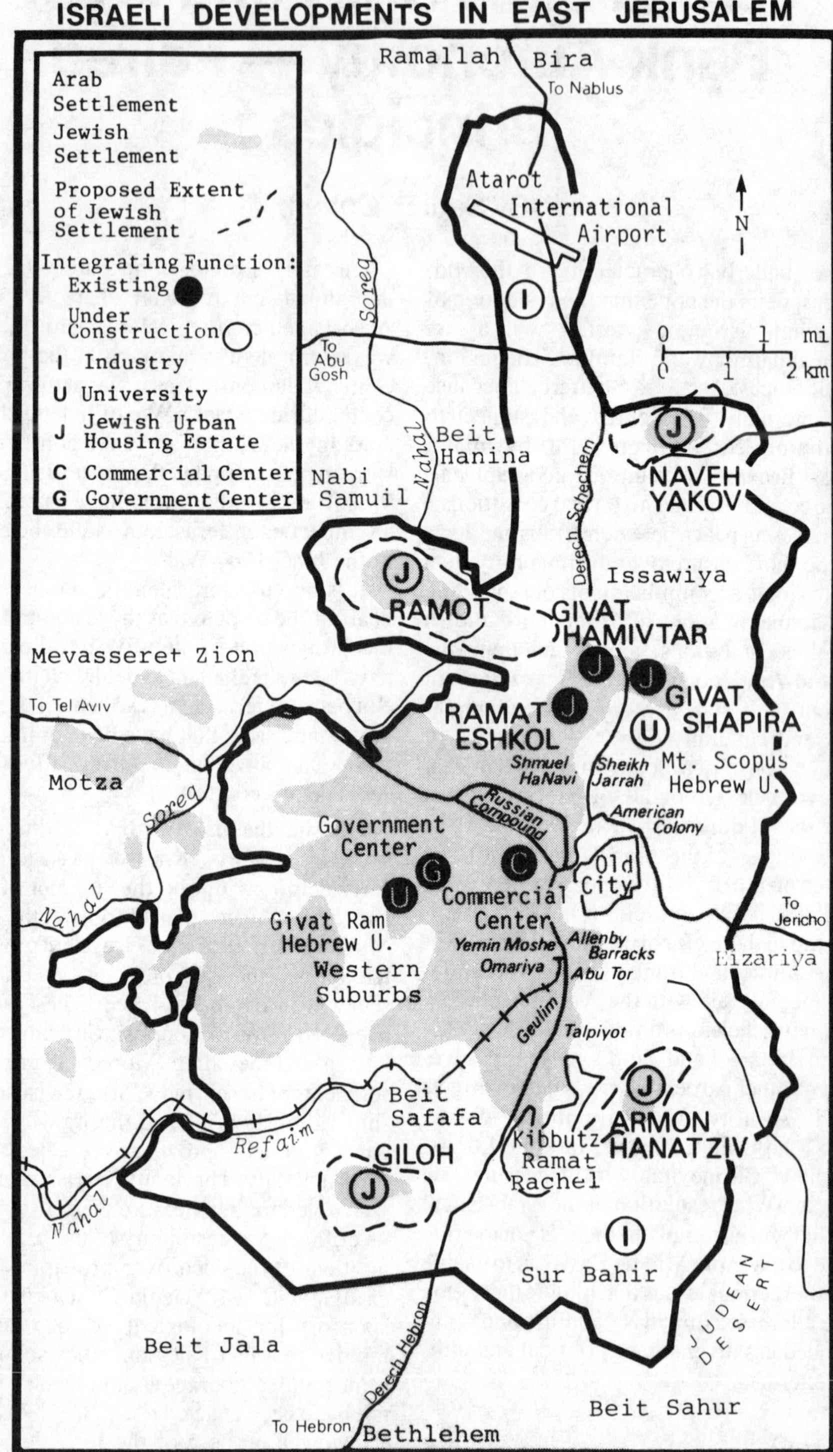
ISRAELI DEVELOPMENTS IN EAST JERUSALEM
Arab Settlement
Jewish Settlement
Proposed Extent of Jewish Settlement
Integrating Function:
Existing
Under Construction
I Industry
U University
J Jewish Urban Housing Estate
C Commercial Center
G Government Center
Ramallah
Bira
To Nablus
Atarot
International Airport
N
0 1 mi
0 1 2 km
To Abu Gosh
Soreq
Nahal
Beit Hanina
Nabi Samuil
Derech Schechem
NAVEH YAKOV
Issawiya
RAMOT
GIVAT HAMIVTAR
Mevasseret Zion
To Tel Aviv
RAMAT ESHKOL
GIVAT SHAPIRA
Motza
Shmuel HaNavi
Sheikh Jarrah
Mt. Scopus Hebrew U.
Russian Compound
American Colony
Government Center
Old City
Commercial Center
To Jericho
Givat Ram Hebrew U.
Yemin Moshe
Allenby Barracks
Eizariya
Western Suburbs
Omariya
Abu Tor
Geulim
Talpiyot
Beit Safafa
Refaim
ARMON HANATZIV
GILOH
Kibbutz Ramat Rachel
Sur Bahir
JUDEAN DESERT
Beit Jala
Derech Hebron
Beit Sahur
To Hebron
Bethlehem
CLARK UNIVERSITY CARTOGRAPHICS - WILLIAM GRAFF

Figure 1

eternal capital, is to remove Jerusalem from the negotiating table. Instead, tragically, the action has moved Jerusalem to the head of the agenda under diplomatic circumstances negative to Israel.

It was predictable that the biased United Nations General Assembly and Security Council would denounce Israel. That President Sadat would initially react by suspending already-stalled West Bank autonomy talks should also have been foreseen. The diplomatic setback that was not anticipated was removal from Jerusalem to Tel Aviv of all of the thirteen embassies located in Israel's capital — a serious blow undermining years of patient effort by Israel to affirm the legitimacy of Jerusalem as its capital.

Whatever the motives of the Law's proponents and reluctant backers, there has been one saving feature to the unhappy sequence of events — the Jerusalem debate has been joined in the open, despite Israel's and America's diplomatic efforts to defer the solution to the very end of the negotiations. American strategy derives from the sterile commitment to step-by-step diplomacy that would whittle away at Israel's position until the 1967 status-ante-quo had been restored. Israel's strategy stems from two erroneous premises — that Sinai's return would persuade Egypt to soft-pedal autonomy, and that Egypt would defer the Jerusalem issue indefinitely. Egypt, on the other hand, has now brought into the open its insistence that both East Jerusalem and the West Bank settlements be placed directly on the negotiating table.

It has been argued that the Camp David agreements could not have been consummated, had Jerusalem been directly faced. If true, then the basis for the Camp David agreement is fundamentally flawed. By not "pairing" the principles of West Bank autonomy and Jerusalem's unity, Camp David can lead only to Israel's withdrawal from Sinai, not to peace, for the conflict's central issue — relations between Jew and Arab in the Holy Land, will not be confronted.

In accepting the principle of Palestinian autonomy, Israel agreed to negotiate a compromise which, if effectuated, is likely to lead to full self-determination for the Arabs, whether through federation with Jordan, or independently in truncated, demilitarized mini-state form.

Without the matching principle of Jerusalem's unity, what bargaining power will Israel have to secure Arab compromises on Jerusalem? And what lasting value will any autonomy agreement have, if the Jerusalem problem would afterwards not be resolved?

Pairing the principles of West Bank autonomy and Jerusalem's unity was proposed by this writer prior to Camp David.[2] Subsequent events have shown that each side has much to trade-off in the negotiating process.

For national survival, Palestinian Arabs need the West Bank as a territorial homeland. The PLO has been driven out of Jordan and kept on a tight leash in Syria. Moreover, former "Fatahland" has been reduced to a small area in Lebanon that Israel attacks at will, squeezed between Major Hadad's Christian mini-state, Phalangist-controlled territory from East Beirut north, and the Syrians, so that PLO freedom of action is more restricted than ever. Without a viable PLO base for continuing the conflict, and with Egypt's renunciation of the war option, negotiations become the only viable way for Palestinians to attain their homeland. For its part, Israel cannot renounce autonomy negotiations, both because of the strategic risks incurred by the Sinai withdrawal, and international pressures.

On the other hand, any form of Palestinian self-determination, if followed by repartition of Jerusalem, would gravely undermine Israel's security, as well as the rights of all peoples to full access to all of Jerusalem. Under Jordanian occupation, so-called East Jerusalem and its outlying villages forged a 270° noose around Jewish Jerusalem, and denied Jews the right of worship in their holy places. Israel has since incorporated and populated empty areas at all four compass points to break this noose. Understanding this map reveals the bankruptcy of the geographical concept of East Jerusalem, and the impossibility of redivision into the "West" and "East" that never existed strategically (see Figure 1, p. 28).

Historic claims aside, the current Israeli presence in Jerusalem's eastern, northern and southern reaches is not a de novo settlement process. Jews played a pioneering role in expanding the new city on its north-south axis from the very start of the Mandatory period. Thus in 1920 the village of Atarot was established by Socialist Zionist workers organized in *Gdud HaAvoda* (the Labor Brigade) at the northern extremity, adjoining the village and later the airport of Kalandia. To the south of Atarot, the farm settlement of Kfar Ivri (Naveh Yakov) was established in 1924. To the northeast of the Old City, the Jewish presence on Mount Scopus was affirmed through the founding of the Hebrew University there in 1921. To the south, in 1923 *Gdud HaAvoda* members created a base camp which three years later became organized into the kibbutz of Ramat Rahel.

Atarot and Kfar Ivri were lost in 1948 at the outbreak of war. They were evacuated on the day of the establishment of the State because of the failure of a Hagana attempt to capture Mount Nabi Samuil, from which protective cover the two villages could be secured. Mount Scopus, on the other hand, never fell to Arab attacks, nor did Ramat Rahel. After the armistice, the boundary was drawn so that Ramat Rahel was incorporated within Israeli Jerusalem and adjoined by the Government House (Armon Ha Natziv) Demilitarized Zone. Mount Scopus, while remaining in Israeli hands as a demilitarized zone, was cut off from free access to the rest of Jewish Jerusalem in a flagrant violation of the armistice agreement that endured throughout the Jordanian occupation.

The large Israeli residential estates that have been built at Naveh Yakov in the northeast, at French Hill (Giva Zarfatit) on the edge of Mount Scopus, and at Armon Ha Natziv in the southeast, as well as the renewed Mout Scopus campus of the Hebrew University, are therefore not post-1967 settlement "intrusions." They are, rather, a settlement return to which Israel has very special moral and political right. At the other points of the compass, the new major residential suburbs of Ramot in the northwest and Gilo in the southwest safeguard pre-1967 Jewish Jerusalem by settling high elevations from which Arabs had previously shelled and otherwise endangered the Israeli population of modern Jerusalem.

The complexity of the Jerusalem problem derives from the Holy City's special character, history, geographical setting and recent demographic changes. The very name Jerusalem conjures up a series of worlds — myth, symbol, dream and reality. For some these worlds are isolated, for others integrated; for some sequentially connected, for others randomly linked.

Jerusalem tugs at the hearts, minds and emotions of men. Its uniqueness is mythic and symbolic, of course, but it is also real. Jerusalem is a place set on the knife's edge of the "sown and the desert." Its summer days may alternately be choked by dust-laden desert winds, or cooled by strong Mediterranean breezes. Its winter may be blasted by continental wind and torrential storms which overflow storm sewers, and leave streets and pavements slick. They may be made radiant by warming sun that belies the season or melts very rare snowfalls before one's eyes. Jerusalem is a place whose hills and valleys provide unexpectedly different views of one another — views that then change in alternating sunlight, shadow and darkness. It is a place with remarkable man-made diversity, from high-gloss luxury hotels and modern box-like apartments to the stately dignity of tree-lined streets bordered by half century-old, grand Arab-built houses and modest Jewish-built apartments; to the quaint charm of century-old restored Turkish-style houses and Jewish communal stone barracks. Jerusalem is replete with mosaics of scenes, tastes, smells, sounds and touch — and with memories. It is ever changing, and ever the same.

The Jerusalem of such rich images is more than a city, yet at the contemporary political level, it is a city. Elsewhere in this world torn cities straddle national provincial/state or ethnic/religious borders. Mostly they have achieved a level of transborder integration that permits easy movement of persons, goods and ideas. This was not the case for Jerusalem during its 1949-67 period of disunity, when the Jordanian-imposed wall of hostility exceeded even the Berlin Wall or Belfast's neighborhood barricades as a barrier to movement. Removal of the barbed wire and concrete has made possible the full flow of persons and goods throughout every corner of the city; however, Israeli sovereignty has not lifted the veil of separation of ideas. This boundary of the mind will remain until there is mutual acceptance of each people's political status. Jerusalem's Arabs regard themselves as Palestinians, just as most of its Jews view themselves as Israelis. For the city to be as one, and at peace, the Arab residents must either experience an ideological *volte face* and accept Israelization, as have the Arabs of the Galilee or the Little Triangle, or they must find their political fulfillment in a new status — that of "Citizens of Jerusalem."

Such status requires a new kind of political configuration in which Arabs and Jews can attribute salience to the political sphere of their choice. "Spheres" include the intra-urban, urban, regional, national-cultural, sovereign state and international. In most Western societies, the national state dominates and permeates all other levels of government. For Jerusalem's Arabs, the normal hierarchy would have to be reversed, with the intra-urban, city and region transcending the state in many political functions, and having primary call upon group identification and loyalty.

From an Israeli standpoint, the Arabs must make the greater compromises in Jerusalem, just as for the Arabs, Israelis must make the greater compromises on the West Bank. Since Israelis are unanimous on maintaining sovereignty over a unified city, the Arabs cannot achieve its redivision by any means short of war. Defeat in war raises the spectre of Arab flight or expulsion from the city. So the Arabs of Jerusalem and the West Bank might be increasingly inclined to cast aside stale slogans, and search for a "50% solution" that in time can evolve into the "90% solution." They can trade claims in Jerusalem for Israeli claims on the West Bank.

Solutions for Jerusalem cannot be based on a single formula — e.g., Boroughs or Vaticanization. Only a complex formula will permit the highest level of Arab political and Muslim/Christian self-rule (see Table I). At the city level, Arabs could enjoy unprecedented local autonomy through political units, territorially-organized as neighborhoods and communities. Residents of such units could possess administrative powers free of the city's Jewish majority-controlled government. Another level of government, the regional (city-regional) could provide an administrative-territorial framework for Arabs and Jews living within and outside Jerusalem. City-regional administrative authorities should have appeal to the Arabs who would enjoy numerical parity in a city-region whose boundaries extend into heavily populated parts of the West Bank, as well as the Jewish-settled Jerusalem Corridor. The city-region's functions would be conducted across the borders of Israel and a West Bank entity. On a national level, the Arab "citizens of Jerusalem" could hold dual citizenship with a West Bank entity (in the same way that Jewish settlers on the West Bank could hold Israeli citizenship and permanent West Bank residence rights), and could be linked to the West Bank entity by geographical corridors.

Still one more level of the political hierarchy could meet the needs not only of Jerusalem's citizen-residents, but of world communities as well. The Arab and Jewish peoples, distinct from specific sovereign states, and Christians organized through their ecclesiastic bodies, could have a formal share in the city's destinies through control of religious and certain cultural institutions, including extra-territorial enclaves within the Old City. Indeed, a class of "Jerusalem World Citizen" could be created, with individuals contributing a special tax to support specific institutions. In this way, "Jerusalem the Sacred" whose boundaries are not affixed by metes and bounds or concrete markers could find modern political expression.

While Jerusalem's Arabs have more to gain from compromise in Jerusalem than do Jews there, surely Jews cannot ignore Arab aspirations. However, Jerusalem's fate can and should be linked to the Palestinian struggle for a West Bank homeland. Indeed, as long as Israel controls a unified Jerusalem militarily, dividing the West Bank into three parts — Samaria, Judea and the Jordan Valley, a truncated Arab entity will be a limited direct military threat. It is because there is great division within Israel over the future of the West Bank and because territo-

TABLE I

JERUSALEM'S MULTI-TIER GOVERNMENTAL STRUCTURE

Unit of Governance	*Functions*	*Source of Revenue*	*Structure of Government*
State	Physical security (army, police); Social security; Hospitals and other health facilities; Labor exchanges and unemployment benefits; Financing of housing, industrial plants, utilities and transportation infrastructure; School construction, salaries and national curriculum standards	National taxation system	Israel parliament appointed sub-committee on Jerusalem
Kehillot (Nations)	Ideological guidance in education, cultural and religious matters	Religious institutional taxes; National and world philanthropic bodies	Citizen-bodies, appointed by city as special delegations to national parliaments and world organizations
City Council	Operation of fire, transport, water, electric, sanitation and sewerage companies; Constabulary; Road construction and maintenance;	State support	Popularly-elected municipal council, weighted by size of Communities; City-wide election of mayor

	Developing and maintaining public housing and markets; Centralized land use planning services; Setting environmental quality standards		
Communities (Boroughs)	Building permits and enforcement of land use and environmental quality codes; School personnel administration and hiring, and educational program direction; Operation of parks and recreational programs	State support and community-levied real estate taxes	Direct elections within Community
Neighborhoods	Pre-school education; cultural, youth and sports activities; small parks	Community support	Administrative wards
Metropolitan Authorities	Transportation; waste disposal; recreation; highways; building; markets	National support (Israel and West Bank)	Joint Israeli-Arab Authorities
City-regional Authorities	Industrial development; agriculture; tourism; recreation; settlement; transportation; labor exchange; electric company; water company	National support (Israel and West Bank)	Joint Israeli-Arab Authorities

rial compromise has characterized the philosophy of mainstream Zionism from the 1930s to 1977, that possibilities for a negotiated trade-off exist.

The Lord gave Jerusalem to the Jewish people and to the world. While guardianship of Islamic and Christian sites is the moral responsibility and right of Muslim and Christian peoples from all over the world, guardianship of the city as a whole is the moral responsibility and right of the Jewish people. Since 1967, Israelis have been proven worthy guardians of the Holy City by their deeds and actions. Their stewardship of a city undivided has responded to the religious sensitivities of peoples of all faiths by providing free and secure access to every single building, shrine and site in every part of the city. When Arabs and Christians seized the city's stewardship, the former from 1948 to 1967, the latter during the British Mandatory period, they violated this sacred trust.

Guardianship of Jerusalem means more than guaranteed access — it means investing human and fiscal resources in a city beautiful, in edifices faced by Judean stone, in gardens and parks, in archeologic and historic restoration, in rational planning for growth, and in an unsullied urban environment. The eternal city where man and environment are one, and live with the spirit of the Lord, is no more divisible in spiritual terms than it is in contemporary geopolitical terms. Israel has proven that it can maintain Jerusalem as both a Jewish and a global city.

The city that throughout its history has known glory and war, magnificence and poverty, beauty and disease, can achieve renewed harmony and splendor through the political principles of pairing that are the basis for resolution of the Arab-Israeli conflict.

Jews must choose between historic/religious ties to Hebron and Shechem, and Jerusalem's centrality in Judaism. Palestinian Arabs must choose between sovereignty over part of Jerusalem where religious and cultural rights can be secured through other political means, and aspirations for a territorial homeland on the West Bank. For Israel, unity and sovereignty in Jerusalem transcends in strategic and spiritual value the risks of a territorial solution for the Palestinian Arabs. For the latter, a national homeland has priority over all other aspirations. On these two principles, negotiations can go forward and peace on the basis of compromise becomes a possibility.

FOOTNOTES

1. S. Cohen, *Geography and Politics in a World Divided,* New York: Oxford University Press, rev. second edition, 1973.

2. S. Cohen, *Jerusalem – Bridging the Four Walls,* New York: Herzl Press, 1977, 221 pp., and S. Cohen, *Jerusalem Undivided,* New York: Herzl Press, 1980, 70 pp.

35 Some Guidelines for Positive Thinking on Jerusalem

By Meron Benvenisti

I

Recent events have proved again that Jerusalem is the key to peace between Jew and Arab, and without a solution to the Jerusalem question there can be no durable solution to the Israeli-Arab conflict. Attempts, such as the Camp David accords, to sweep the problem under the rug have failed. The lump was simply too big.

The renewed realization of the centrality of Jerusalem in the peace process has led people of good will to try their hand at the old game of devising ultimate solutions. Not all of them are aware of the fact that since Jerusalem became an international political problem, sixty years ago, no fewer than forty plans for "ultimate solutions" have been officially presented. Most of them were brilliant, even-handed and logical, but none of them could be implemented. The parties simply refused to accept them, even as a basis for negotiation.

The comprehensive approach is based on two premises: first, the problem is acute, so much depends on its solution, it is in the interest of all parties to look for a way out, therefore it will be found. Second, the conflict can be resolved by devising a compromise in the middle.

It seems that both premises are not applicable to Jerusalem.

The sense of urgency is not shared by all the conflicting parties. The Arabs, indeed, regard the problem as acute and are doing everything in their power to solve it by taking Jerusalem away from the Israelis. The Israelis, however, attach no urgency to the problem, because they are relatively content with the *status quo* and do not believe that a compromise can improve their situation.

The notion of a compromise in the middle is rejected *prima facie* by both sides. They claim that their present positions are already painful compromises and no further concession is conceivable.

The difficulty is clearly not in devising logical and objective solutions, but in coping with the perceptions of the conflicting parties. The dispute is perceived by both sides as a struggle to attain and preserve basic human needs.

Jerusalem represents for Israeli and Arab alike certain basic interests: *identity*, a sense of belonging to one's home town and motherland; *control* over their destiny; *recognition* and self-esteem; *security* and *welfare*. The political expression of these basic interests is national sovereignty and the symbols of sovereignty are flags, army, capital city, national institutions. Therefore, sovereignty and its symbols are "non-negotiable," as one cannot give up or compromise on basic human needs.

Third parties tend to underestimate the "zero sum" nature of the game. They refuse to accept the perception, equally shared by both Israelis and Arabs, that what one side can win equals what the other side must lose. Frustrated peace-seekers insist that both sides can gain from a peaceful solution, but they fail to convince the parties.

The Israelis and the Arabs, for their part, refuse to face the symmetry of their perceptions. They choose to dismiss the positions of the other side as mere propaganda, or to ignore them completely. This attitude causes many false assumptions on the nature of the conflict and, in turn, results in wrong conclusions.

Meron Benvenisti is a former Deputy Mayor of Jerusalem and the author of *Jerusalem: The Torn City* (University of Minnesota Press, 1976).

Part I of this article originally appeared in *Jewish Chronicle*, October 17, 1980, under the title, "Towards the Peace of Jerusalem." It is reprinted by permission. Part II originally appeared in *The Jerusalem Post Magazine*, February 22, 1980, under the title, "Status and Sovereignty." It is reprinted by permission.

Many believe that the conflict will vanish or will solve itself. Given the centrality of Jerusalem in the eyes of Israeli and Arab alike, this is wishful thinking. The problem will not only endure, but the cost of the continued strife will increase, for both sides. It has already cost countless lives; its continuation is bound to degenerate into ugly inter-communal armed struggle with a vicious circle of resistance-coercion-terrorism-retaliation.

The conflict is often depicted as a clash of material interests that can be solved by "practical arrangements." Economic progress, equal services and even-handed allocation of "public goods" will reconcile most interests. The remainder will be left for future generations to cope with. This is an attempt to turn the conflict upside down.

While it is true that people are ready to be flexible on material interests, they insist that concessions will be made under the umbrella of their own political system. First, they insist on attaining symbolic gratification in the form of sovereignty and flags. Only then can they discuss material arrangements.

The Jerusalem question is often defined as an inter-religious dispute. The solution, therefore, lies in granting religious freedom, ensuring free access and establishing extra-territorial status for the Holy Places. In fact, there is no religious dispute between Jew and Muslim over any holy place, nor is there a conflict between both and Christians. The conflict is between Israeli and Arab (Muslim or Christian) over the political control of Jerusalem. Both are ready to grant the other religious freedom provided that they retain political control.

Some would like to reduce the national conflict to inter-ethnic tension. They maintain that a system that will safeguard the cultural and communal autonomy of the minority will solve the conflict. The preservation of ethnic heritage and safeguarding of the political rights of the minority are definitely important elements. However, both sides refuse to define their political objectives as such. They consider themselves an integral part of their respective national movements; their goal, therefore, is self-determination and national sovereignty, not cultural and communal autonomy.

A common notion is that one can isolate the Jerusalem question from the general conflict over Palestine. It is argued that Jerusalem, being the most difficult issue, should be dealt with only after all other outstanding problems have been solved. This is a sound tactical approach, but it should not be construed that there can be a political solution to Jerusalem that, basically, will be different from the solution to the Palestine question. For example, political partition of Palestine with the internationalization of Jerusalem will be rejected by both sides.

In devising political solutions for Jerusalem one is tempted to regard it as a border dispute. Such disputes are usually solved by drawing demarcation lines that define absolute political jurisdictions. Absolute sovereignty in Jerusalem is impossible and both sides clearly understand that, as manifested by the universal agreement to keep the physical unity of the city. The Israelis insist on exclusive political control over the united city, but recognize that they must limit their control, at least as far as the Holy Places and local autonomy of the Arab inhabitants are concerned.

The Arabs, insisting on the political partition of Jerusalem, are nevertheless suggesting a united municipality, which indicates willingness to restrict their control.

As long as the conflicting parties maintain their subjective perceptions of the reality and remain entrenched in their unyielding positions, the conflict will remain insoluble.

Those who belong to the "ultimate solution" school dismiss partisan perceptions as childish misconceptions. The issues are for them real, objective and quantifiable; therefore they can be solved. They regard the conflict as a chess game in which one can move all the pieces at once. If the parties will not listen to reason, external pressure should be applied. Such attempts at this stage of the conflict are not only doomed to failure, they are counter productive.

It is a well-known fact that when a conflict escalates, perceptions become stereotyped, every move is interpreted as a menace, views that do not fit the established political line are rejected, those who try to present alternatives are considered traitors, moderates are intimidated and fall silent. Under such circumstances, any comprehensive plan will be regarded as a hostile act and will exacerbate the conflict even further.

A different approach is clearly needed. It should be a gradual process in the course of which the parties will be called upon to make only the decisions that seem to them reasonable within the framework of their perceptions.

They should be faced with a series of clear and legitimate choices, each involving specific action that they are capable of making and which will render desirable results. A choice, presented now, between Jerusalem and peace is clearly illegitimate in the eyes of the Israelis and will be rejected. A choice between further deterioration of internal security or some concessions to the local inhabitants would seem fair.

Bearing in mind the nature of the Jerusalem question we all know that at some point the equation "Jerusalem = peace" will be posed as a solution. A gradual approach would prepare the parties to regard it as a legitimate choice. By then peace will assume such positive value that its preservation will create enough incentive to seek alternative arrangements for Jerusalem. These arrangements can be at the same time flexible and nevertheless safeguard the basic needs of both communities in the city.

Some guidelines for positive thinking in the first phase of this gradual process would include the following elements:

To deal with and resolve only those issues which are relevant and essential to each stage of the peace process. There is no point in arguing the issue of sovereignty when it has been agreed already to postpone the debate on sovereign claims over the West Bank for five years;

Both sides to acknowledge publicly the sensitivity of the Jerusalem problem to the other side (and it will be constructive if both will recognize the importance of Jerusalem to the world. First, it is true; second, it creates a spirit of good will without compromising any interests; third, it teaches the lesson that one can understand another's viewpoint without having to accept it);

To maintain flexible formulae concerning Jerusalem. Instead of saying Jerusalem is "non-negotiable" and fortifying such statements by Acts of Parliament, both sides should indicate willingness to negotiate "questions concerning Jerusalem" within the context of a final peace agreement. There is no real difference between willingness to conduct negotiations "without prior conditions" and "strong claims made by either side." But the tune makes the music;

To strive to contain the conflict and stop its deterioration. One way to achieve this is by devising an interim agreement. Such an interim agreement may include the points listed in Part II.

II

- Residents of United Jerusalem who are Jordanian subjects may vote for and be elected to the institutions of the Self-Governing Authority (SGA).
- The Israel government is prepared to recognize the Muslim inhabitants of United Jerusalem and the Muslim inhabitants of the West Bank as one religious community. The institutions of this community, its courts and the management of its endowments (Wakf) may have their seat in Jerusalem and be based on Shari'a laws. The community will have complete control of its Holy Places and its religious life, and will enjoy freedom of worship.
- The *status quo* on the Temple Mount, as enunciated by the government in the Knesset in 1968 and in the High Court ruling of October 1970, and as observed in the existing practical arrangements with the Muslim authorities, will be maintained.
- Residents of United Jerusalem who are Jordanian subjects will be eligible to vote for and be elected to the municipality of Jerusalem. The government will decree that "local councils" be established in areas presently administered by the municipality, in accordance with the character and needs of the various localities. The powers of the local councils will be determined on a functional basis.
- There will be no change in the existing

curriculum in East Jerusalem public schools and their examination system will continue to be supervised by the West Bank education committee or the body that replaces it upon the withdrawal of the military government from the West Bank.

- All official printed matter in Jerusalem will be in Hebrew and Arabic. Arab residents will be able to correspond with the authorities in Arabic.
- The present status and functions of the Arab Chamber of Commerce will be officially recognized.
- There will be no land expropriations for public purposes in Jerusalem, except those required by specific town planning schemes.

Most of these points are based on the existing reality; the novelty would lie in their formalization.

There is a difference between formal and binding arrangements taken in the context of practical steps towards a settlement, and *de facto* arrangements such as have existed in Jerusalem since 1967, which Israel can abrogate unilaterally.

The practical arrangements envisaged here would assume political significance. They could be interpreted as a transitional solution, guaranteeing basic Arab interests in the city pending future discussions.

The concentration of all the components in a binding statement transforms them into a comprehensive program covering the lives of the Arab population without harming Israeli interests. Moreover, the proposals are totally in keeping with Israeli law.

Now for an analysis of each point.

Elections. The Arabs in Jerusalem comprise more than 10 percent of the electorate of the West Bank and Gaza. Without them, autonomy will not be established. Giving them the right to vote for and be elected to the institutions of the SGA might seem to conflict with the principle of Israeli sovereignty. But this difficulty disappears if we take into account the minimalist Israeli approach, which sees autonomy as a question of residence rather than territory: Jerusalem is under Israeli sovereignty, while its Arab residents belong to the ethnic community of Palestinian Arabs. The Arabs, for their part, can interpret this linkage as implying that Jerusalem is part of the West Bank.

The proposal answers real needs, contributes to the establishment of self-government and is not contrary to the position of either side. It seems to us to be the only feasible method of satisfying both parties.

Religious Institutions. The Supreme Muslim Council of Jerusalem created a de facto Muslim community of Jerusalem and the West Bank when in 1967 it declared itself to be "responsible for Muslim affairs on the West Bank, including Jerusalem, until the termination of the occupation." The annexation of East Jerusalem made all aspects of religious life in that part of the city subject to Israeli law. The law regulates the appointment of Qadis, the establishment and powers of the Shari'a courts, the Wakf, so that their legal status is quite different from that of the West Bank. But the decision to apply Israeli law remained a dead letter and institutions continued to function without interference.

The clause recognizing Jerusalem and West Bank Muslims as one community is possible because Israeli law grants internal autonomy to all the country's religious communities, regardless of any question of sovereignty. Nor is there any political significance in the location of their common institutions in Jerusalem. When the SGA is set up, the religious organization established in 1967 will have to be adjusted.

Status Quo on the Temple Mount. This is one of the most sensitive matters because of its symbolism, but the proposal regarding it should not be difficult to implement. Since 1967, the Muslim Council has in practice controlled the mosques on the Temple Mount and all but one of the gates to the Mount. Public order is kept by guards of the Muslim Council and a unit of the Israeli police force composed of Muslim and Christian Arabs. Access is guaranteed to all, though non-Muslims pay an entrance fee.

Since 1967, Jewish public prayers have been forbidden in the area of the Mount both by religious law and in the interests of public order. This has been affirmed by the Supreme Court, and despite attempts by extremists to contravene it, it is accepted by virtually all concerned.

Municipal Administration. The question of what is the best municipal organization for Jerusalem in view of the ethnic conflict, has been raised many times over the past half century, irrespective of the sovereignty issue. It has always been a problem of establishing a city council that would provide efficient services, with elected institutions that would reflect the ethnic composition of the population and avoid conflicts over the control and distribution of resources.

The idea of dividing the city into boroughs under one roof body in order to give the Arab population some degree of municipal autonomy has been raised a number of times since 1967, but has not gained support from either the Israeli or the Arab side.

Israeli opposition to the borough plan resulted from unwillingness to introduce special legislation for Jerusalem, which might be interpreted as readiness to set it apart from other cities in Israel. Another reason for opposition was the requirement of defining as an Arab borough a district that would encompass all the Arab neighborhoods beyond the former "green line" (the 1967 border). This might be interpreted as a "division" of the city.

The first fear is unfounded, since there is already a precedent in the recent establishment of a local council with wide responsibilities within the area of the Haifa Municipality. The authority of the local councils could be gradually extended, as political fears are dissipated and experience accumulates.

The fear of division of the city is deeper and more difficult to dispose of. One possible solution would be to establish a local council that would include only politically insensitive areas of East Jerusalem, leaving out some Arab neighborhoods and the Old City. Outlying Jewish neighborhoods could be organized into additional local councils.

When political fears concerning the partition of the city have been alleviated, and when it becomes clear that the local councils deal only with municipal and community matters, it will be possible to establish more of these bodies.

Elections for the local councils will not, of course, take the place of elections to the municipal council. The Arabs will be entitled to participate in the latter in accordance with Israeli law, but they are unlikely to exercise the right until a satisfactory political solution for the city is found.

Educational Autonomy. After much trial and error, an arrangement concerning education in Arab public schools of Jerusalem was reached in 1975. It provided that pupils from the seventh grade onwards could choose between the Israeli and the West Bank curriculum. They have all chosen the latter, which is identical to that of Jordan. They take the examinations of the Arab League *(Tawjihi).* These are prepared and supervised by the West Bank Education Council, which operates within the framework of the Military Government and in accordance with Jordanian law.

This arrangement was approved by the Israel Education Ministry, in accordance with the provision of the State Education Law that the curriculum of non-Jewish educational institutions is to be adapted to their special conditions. Given the political situation, it is satisfactory to all sides.

The Arabic Language. In many mixed cities in the world with ethnic or linguistic-cultural conflicts, the right of the minorities to use their language freely, and the duty of the authorities to respect this right, are guaranteed by law.

Economic and Business Institutions. Many East Jerusalem businesses and economic institutions work closely with the economic system of the West Bank and Jordan. The Arab Chamber of Commerce, the quasi-official institution which organizes this activity, is a member of the Organization of Chambers of Commerce of the West Bank set up in 1968, and regularly and directly represents its Jerusalem members in Amman.

It also acts as the virtual Jordanian Consulate in Jerusalem, dealing with such matters as passport requests, Jordanian identity cards, land sales registry, transfers of car ownership, authentication of transactions, guarantees and mortgages.

While the Arab Chamber of Commerce has never been given official recognition by the Israeli authorities, there has been no interference with its activities — its vital importance is recognized. Without the Chamber, the "open bridges" policy would not work. Its activities do not conflict with Israeli law or commercial practice.

Land Policy. The purpose of this part of the declaration is to ease the fears of the Arab population regarding the possible establishment of new Jewish neighborhoods on Arab-owned land. The Israeli public will oppose the declaration, even though it has no serious, practical implications because land already reserved for public building is sufficient for the completion of 5,000 housing units during each of the years 1978 to 1982. Thus, this declaration does not limit development in Jerusalem.

Three components of the Jerusalem problem, (political) sovereignty, religious (holy places, religious organizations), and ethnic-municipal matters are interrelated, but not identical, and a solution for one is not necessarily a step towards a solution for the others.

The suggestions presented above relate only to the last two components of the problem and not to the question of sovereignty. This, on the assumption that all sides agree that the decision on this is to be deferred for five years. But short-range solutions will be unacceptable if they do not at least point to permanent solutions.

For example, the Israelis can judge that the unilateral measures leave options open for international recognition of Israeli sovereignty over Jerusalem, while solving the political, religious and ethnic problems of the Arab residents.

The Arabs can see in the Israeli declaration a recognition of their religious and ethnic interests in Jerusalem, a guarantee that options for a return to their political status in the city are not closed. They can view the plan as a defusion of the explosive differences between Jerusalem and the West Bank and even as proof that Jerusalem is part of the West Bank.

The mediator or the objective onlooker can see how the seeds of long-term solutions are sown in practical arrangements.

The problem lies in devising a process in which the parties are brought gradually and slowly to the point where they could conceivably agree on a specific settlement. Each step in this process should be devised so that the parties can perceive it as not contradictory to their stated principles. If successful, the process will gradually become more manageable and the decisions with which the leaders and the people are faced will seem reasonable. The risks of compromise will seem tolerable to each side and the two governments will move towards a final agreement.

This is the approach suggested here. It needs a delicate sense of timing, and should be initiated only if and when the Jerusalem issue becomes a stumbling block that may result in the collapse of the entire peace process.

Every suggestion will definitely be opposed by Israelis as being too much and by the Arabs as being too little. But this is welcome, because it will lead inexorably to the parties creating their own solution. The danger to progress lies in the impatience of frustrated peace-seekers: those who are tempted to believe that they can formulate the best comprehensive formula and that if the parties do not agree, they should simply impose it.

The fact that since 1917 no fewer than 40 official plans for the solution of the Jerusalem problem have been suggested and thousands have died in battle in the meantime should serve them as a warning.

36
Zionism and the Future of Israel

By Daniel J. Elazar

Both the Bible and the Greeks early attested to the fact that none of us escape the patterns established at the founding. At best there can be refoundings under certain conditions that may somewhat alter those patterns and their direct consequences, but they are rare enough. Zionism was an effort at refounding the Jewish people. As such it had to develop at least partly in relation to earlier refoundings and a much earlier founding. This in itself has dictated many of the parameters and paradoxes of the Zionist movement and much of the dynamic which has animated it. In its pre-state years, Zionism not only involved a general ideology but specific ones as well. Today, there is no longer the firm belief in particular ideologies of the kind that existed until the establishment of the state. These ideologies have lost their ability to compel.

In the 1950s and 1960s, the "end of ideology" decades, the non-ideological types clearly had the upper hand within both the Zionist movement and the State of Israel. Today they are being challenged again, albeit in a still very modest way, since the proponents of the ideological reinvigoration do not have an ideology to propound. Moreover, the seekers after ideological invigoration are limited in their ability to present an acceptable ideology by the fact that any such ideology would probably have to include some sense of the negation of the diaspora to satisfy them and this would have immediate practical repercussions to the detriment of the unity of the Jewish people, something which they themselves would not like to see jeopardized.

At the same time, the day to day business of maintaining the Jewish state is such that those responsible for conducting that business are not likely to be particularly interested in or concerned with development of a new ideology. The most that can be said is that, coming out of ideologically oriented traditions, they pay lip service to the need for ideology for what are fundamentally aesthetic reasons; it makes them feel that the world is somehow better put together when there is an ideological base underneath their essentially pragmatic response to daily problems.

At the same time, the three trends or camps within the Zionist movement which grew out of the earlier ideological years continue to exist as the basis of Israeli politics. With all the changes that have taken place, including the great weakening of concern with parties and ideologies within the Israeli body politic, these three trends persist undiminished. They persist partly for natural political reasons and partly as a reflection of the real divisions that separate the men and women of affairs in Israel, even if they are unideological.

Contrary to the conventional wisdom, the three camps do not relate to each other on a left-right continuum but stand in something like a triangular relationship to one another (Figure 1, p. 18). For a long time, preoccupation with European modes of political thought prevented us from seeing that, even though there never was a time when we did not operate on that basis. Thus for certain purposes, each of the camps is more to the left or more to the right than any of the others. What each has staked out for itself is a particular vision of what the Zionist enterprise and its creations, the Jewish state and a reconstituted Jewish people, are all about.

The camps themselves divide into parties, some of which are quite antagonistic to one another within the same camp (it is within the camps that left-right divisions do exist). The size of each camp is not fixed, either in relation to the total Jewish popula-

Dr. Elazar is the Chairman of the Department of Political Studies at Bar-Ilan University, directs the Center for the Study of Federalism at Temple University, and heads the Center for Jewish Community Studies. His most recent book is *Kingship and Consent: The Jewish Political Tradition and its Contemporary Uses* (University Press of America, 1983).

tion or in relation to one another, but whatever the fluctuations, the camps themselves persist. Their persistence is reflected in the relative stability of Knesset elections.

In the last analysis, it is the existence of the three camps and the institutions which they have built over three generations that has led to the biggest change in Zionism since the establishment of the state, namely, the establishment of a permanent Zionism. Immediately after 1948, when the most obvious and visible task of the Zionist movement had been achieved, it was widely suggested that the movement should simply fold its tents, amid its well-deserved laurels, and those people within it who were interested in continuing their public careers should move on to other things. Indeed, many of the Zionist leaders in Israel did just that, moving into leadership positions in the new state.

Zionism itself came to be either ignored, as it was in much of the diaspora, or made a matter of some ridicule, as it was among large segments of the Israeli population. The Israeli political leadership was quite ambivalent toward Zionism in these years. On the one hand, as a movement, it was maintained by the conscious efforts of that leadership who saw it as a vehicle for forging certain links to the diaspora, while, on the other, they were perfectly willing to bypass the organized Zionist movement in the diaspora to reach out to a different leadership which was built into pre-eminence in the Jewish world as a result.

Nevertheless, it was during this period that institutionally the Zionist movement regrouped and settled down for the long haul. Then the victory of 1967 and the shock of 1973 revived Zionist sentiments among Israelis. It became apparent that, particularly for those Israelis outside of the religious camp, Zionism was the faith of their fathers — the only faith they knew — and hence, the faith they turned to in hours of crisis.

This is a common enough phenomenon, a variant of the "foxhole religion" experienced by soldiers in wartime. To say this is not to dismiss it. Quite to the contrary, reliance upon the faith of one's fathers is a natural human expression and the particular faith involved tells us a great deal about the aspirations of the people involved. It is highly significant that in the course of both wars, American Jews flocked to their synagogues in record numbers and Israelis began talking about Zionism. Both were manifestations of latent belief made manifest in the hour of emergency.

It is not far-fetched to suggest that, *de facto,* Zionism has become another branch of Judaism, parallel in its own way to Orthodoxy, Conservatism, Reform, or Reconstructionism in the United States and other diaspora communities. Albeit, like Communism, it is a secular rather than a theistic religion in its fundamentals (not that religious Zionists are not Zionists, but their Zionism plays a different role for them, representing as it were, an extension of a larger set of religious beliefs). Zionism serves as the basis for the Jewish self-definition of a majority of the Jewish population of Israel just as Conservative Judaism (according to the studies) serves a majority of the Jewish population in the United States. The one is primarily an Israeli phenomenon today with some diaspora outposts while the other is primarily an American Jewish phenomenon with some strength in other diaspora communities.

As a branch or expression of Judaism, Zionism has its own rituals and symbols, which, because of its particular character have become part of the civil religion of Israel. Like every religious movement, Zionism in its first stages was utterly messianic in that its proponents expected that it would achieve a rapid success which would in turn bring about the full achievement of its goals, namely, the redemption of the Jewish people in their own land through political means. In fact, Zionism was successful enough to capture a major share of the Jewish people as its adherents and a central place for itself among modern Jewish institutions. It did succeed in creating a Jewish state and transforming the Jewish people in the process, but like every other religious movement, its messianic expectations were not realized.

•

Zionism then entered the next stage in the development of religious movements, in which its proponents argue that the achievement of its immediate goal (in this case, the state) is only the prelude to the achievement of its ultimate goals and that the movement is needed in both its ideological and institutionalized forms to pursue those ultimate goals over the long haul. Should peace indeed be achieved this need will not diminish but will become even greater in the eyes of most Israelis as the sheer struggle for physical survival no longer is suffered but to maintain their sense of themselves.

Once we understand Zionism as another branch of Judaism, rather than as an all encompassing revolutionary movement or a strictly organizational phenomenon, its present condition and needs can be clarified.

The revival of Zionist concern in the past decade has given rise to a new generation of Israeli thinkers and ideologists whose work is just now beginning to capture the attention of the Jewish people. They have taken it upon themselves to grapple with these problems. It is significant that, just as the thought being produced by North American Jewish thinkers moves from theology to the concerns of politics, if not politics itself, Israeli Zionist thought moves from politics to the concerns of theology — if not theology itself. That is because of the particular character of the Jewish people as a theopolitical phenomenon. This concern with both politics and theology is likely to grow as more Israelis search for the transcendent meaning of their experience.

In essence, the rebirth of Jewish political independence has brought with it a rebirth of the classic partisan division within the Jewish people associated with Jewish statehood. That division found its classic expression in the Hasmonean state in the existence of Sadducees, Pharisees and Essenes but, in fact, can be traced back to the division that appeared in the First Commonwealth with the rise of the Davidic monarchy between supporters of the Davidic house, supporters of the prophetic tradition of Elijah, and Kenites or Rechabites. Today, the religious camp carries on the Pharisaic tradition, which for some eighteen hundred years emphasized the halakhic dimensions in Jewish life and through the halakha had dominant if not exclusive control over the Jewish people. The other two camps together represent a revival of the Sadducean approach to Jewish life, one which emphasized the political dimension as the basis for Jewish unity and which tied the other dimensions to it. To round out the picture, we can see in the kibbutz movement a current expression of an old Jewish instinct for messianic expression through communal living which in the past was expressed by the Kenites and the Essenes.

From our present perspective, Zionist Israel can be seen as the first step toward the revival of a Sadducean dimension in Jewish life. One of the reasons for its great success was that such a dimension was exactly what was needed at the time, given the breakdown of Jewish religious belief and observance on the one hand, and the problems of Jewish physical survival on the other. While those Jews, including many Zionists, who seek a monistic Judaism or a Jewish people committed to a single ideology may be appalled by the existence of the three parties or camps, in many respects it represents the true normalization of the Jewish people, not in the way that certain Zionist theorists sought Jewish normalization, namely to make the Jews "like all the nations," but in the sense that a diversity of approaches to Jewish existence has been normal to Judaism in every period of full Jewish national existence.

In understanding the emergence of Sadducees (and, to a lesser extent, Essenes), and the way in which the normalcy they create differs from the normalization sought by earlier Zionist theory, we can begin to understand the direction which Zionism is likely to take to meet the challenges of contemporary Jewish life in Israel. With a few exceptions, classical Zionist theory suffers from some very real deficiencies stemming from the fact that it was created in the late 19th century and emerged out of the particular milieu of that period. It additionally suffers from the fact that it was primarily a polemic against assimilation designed to restore political awareness to the Jews, but had little to say about political life once a Jewish political self-consciousness was in existence. Both of these deficiencies make it difficult for Israel today to build upon classical Zionist theory. Israel needs a true political theory, not a nationalist polemic, and it must be a theory that squares with Jewish tradition in the broadest meaning of the term.

•

Classical Zionist theory is permeated with late 19th century romantic nationalism based upon biological analogies, utopian expectations and socialist slogans derived from the current applications of Darwin, Marx and other revolutionary theorists. Both the premises of those theories and the expectations they generated have dissipated in the course of the 20th century. With this critique, it is important to recall that the same reasons which have since made those theories so obsolete were the ones that made them so effective at the time. If the theories suffer in comparison with other, deeper expressions of political thought, they were most effective as political polemics, which indeed was their primary purpose, whether so perceived or not.

In the era of emancipation, Jews had lost even that sense of the political character of the Jewish people which had been preserved within the framework of halakhic Judaism until the modern era. As a result, a major dimension of Jewish life had been abandoned, and the Jewish people itself was threatened with disintegration in the face of one attractive universalism or another. The first task of Zionist theory was not to develop an understanding of the polity, even of the Jewish polity, or of the power relationships within it. Rather, it was to convince doubting Jews that there was a political dimension to Jewish life in the first place, and to stimulate them to desire to recreate the Jewish polity. For that reason alone, it would have been incumbent upon Zionist theorists to speak in the political language that was the common coin of the realm at that time, even at the sacrifice of eternal validity. It is unlikely that they consciously made that choice — they were, after all, products of their environment and, as such, believed in the eternal validity of the theories they espoused — even though that was the end result.[1]

Israelis are beginning to recognize that the task of Zionist theory in Israel today follows more along the lines of classical political theory. Zionist theory must address itself to questions of the character of the Jewish polity and the power relationships within it. At the same time, it must contribute to the development of a new or renewed vision of Israel and its place in the world.

The Jewish people is a product of both kinship and consent.[2] The Torah defines Jews as both an *Am* and an *Edah*. In their technical meaning, *Am* (people) refers to a relationship established by kinship, and *Edah* literally refers to the political relationship which is established as a result of consenting to the Covenant. Between the exodus from Egypt and the covenant at Sinai, the Bible tells us, a family of tribes was transformed into both an *Am* and an *Edah*. The combination of *Am ve'Edah* persisted unbroken down the years until the modern era, when, under the impact of emancipation, first the Jews ceased to be a coherent *Edah,* and shortly thereafter began to lose their sense of kinship — of being an *Am* — as well.

The Zionist revolution was instrumental in restoring the sense of kinship to a very substantial segment of the Jewish people. Today there is a wide-spread sense of kinship upon which can be built a new sense of political consent. One is reminded of the late Leo Strauss' distinction between ancient and modern liberalism to note that a similar distinction exists between ancient and modern consent. Ancient consent involved *consentio,* like thinking within a tradition. Modern consent involves agreeing to think alike or to think together. Nevertheless, the continuity of consent is at least as important as the continuity of tradition.

•

Here, Israelis are faced with a problem that goes back to the roots of Zionism itself. As a revolutionary movement, Zionism had to break away from the continuity of Jewish history at least to a certain extent. I need not elaborate on the reasons for that here. It is sufficient to indicate that the Jewish people, whose history had been dominated for so many centuries by the Pharisaic tradition, was faced with a major crisis as tradition broke down in the wake of emancipation. Without some other galvanizing force of revolutionary dimensions, the Jewish people faced continued assimilation and erosion. Yet in order to create such a new force, the existing tradition had to be vigorously assaulted and its hold on the definition of what constituted Jewish life had to be broken.

At the same time, with the exception of a few extremists the Zionist movement did not seek to abandon its Jewish past, but radically to transform the Jewish future. So, for example, it devoted considerable effort to absorb certain Jewish traditions by reinterpreting them. The end result of these efforts in cultural and moral terms was that two generations of Jews have now grown up in the land of Israel cut off from any real knowledge of 3,000 years of Jewish tradition, but possessing in its place a kind of Zionist-Israeli civil religion which focuses on a re-interpreted Jewish calendar and makes use of many traditional Jewish symbols, but which has led to a growing separation of large numbers of Israelis from crucial dimensions of their Jewish roots.

Ironically, it may be that Zionism as the faith of the fathers is still the only vehicle through which non-religious Israelis will be able to overcome that separation, but Zionism as it exists today, is in itself still suffering from the discontinuity problem. The original Zionists were Jewishly authentic because most of them came out of Jewishly authentic environments. Thus their revolution against those environments, no matter how extreme, could not damage their own Jewish authenticity. But the generations which they produced, which may be far less hostile to the same Jewish traditions against which their fathers revolted, lack their fathers' authenticity, by virtue of being their fathers' sons and grandsons. Many of the sons and grandsons of the fathers are desparately searching for this authenticity today, and some are working at it quite vigorously.

It is clear that the Pharisaic tradition offers a way to reach out for Jewish authenticity. It is not yet clear whether the Sadducean or Essenian traditions do, although they did in the past, under certain conditions. The possibility is clearly one to be explored. One thing is clear however: neither the Sadducean or Essenian traditions of the past nor their predecessors were secular in the way that the mainstream of the Zionist revolution sought to be secular as part of its revolutionary break with the Jewish past. All three streams had as their starting point *yir'at shamayim* (awe of Heaven).

•

The Jewish national revival of our times led first to the restoration of Jewish political consciousness, then to the reestablishment of the Jewish polity. The next step in the process is the rediscovery of the Jewish political tradition. I would suggest that there is indeed a Jewish political tradition with all that it implies in the way of a continuing dialogue regarding practical or acceptable modes of political behavior, institutional forms, and political cultural norms. To suggest that there is a Jewish political tradition is not to suggest that there is a single uniform, monolithic "Jewish way of politics." A tradition by its very nature is multifaceted, even dialectic in character. Like a river, it has currents within it that are united because they are within the same banks, and in the long run flow in the same direction.

A tradition is, in fact, a continuing dialogue based upon a shared set of fundamental questions. For Jews, this dialogue began with the emergence of the Jewish people as a body politic. It has continued ever since, at times — particularly when the Jews have lived independently in their own land — resonating strongly and at other times, less so. The emancipation of the Jews in the modern era nearly brought it to a close but precisely at its weakest moment it was revived, as the political character of the Jewish people became clear once again.

The enduring foundations of the Jewish

political tradition are to be found in the Bible. In one sense, this is because the foundations of all Jewish tradition are to be found there. In many respects, however, the Jewish political tradition has been more enduringly influenced by the Bible than by other aspects of the Jewish tradition. While all of the tradition has been filtered through the Talmud, the efforts of the rabbis after the Bar Kochba revolt to diminish the political tradition in the wake of the disastrous Roman wars (the effort in itself was a political act of the first magnitude) meant that the Talmud was least transformed by the political events. So much so that with the revival of explicit political inquiry in the middle ages, Jewish thinkers and leaders who otherwise relied on the Talmud for all things went back to biblical sources for ideas with regard to the proper political behavior and even institution building. Centuries later, we find a fainter echo of that process in the way that Zionists sought to base their quest for Jewish statehood (albeit, not their institutions) in the land of Israel on biblical sources.

While Jews have been unconcerned with their political tradition, as such, since the Pharisees triumphed over the Sadducees, it is a tradition that continues to live in the way Jews behave politically — even in the way the State of Israel is shaped politically, for better or worse — even when Israeli (and other) Jews are unaware that they are living by and within that tradition.

FOOTNOTES

1. There were a handful of Zionist theorists, or Zionists who theorized, who may have escaped from this dilemma. First and foremost among them were Martin Buber and Louis Dembitz Brandeis, but both have been ignored by subsequent generations of Zionists for reasons that have more to do with their personal politics rather than the quality of their thought. Significantly, both addressed themselves at least as much to the kind of polity that should be built in the land of Israel as to the polemic of convincing Jews that one should be built.

2. See Daniel J. Elazar, ''Kinship and Consent in the Jewish Community: Patterns of Continuity in Jewish Communal Life'' in *Tradition,* Vol. 14, No. 4 (Fall 1974).

PART VII
THE ROLE OF THE SUPERPOWERS

37

The Philosophy Behind Recent American Policy in the Middle East

By Steven L. Spiegel

In recent years the Middle East has been changing rapidly and the shocks administered to American policy makers have been occurring at a startling pace. Only since the onset of the Carter administration American leaders have had to adjust to such events as the Egyptian-Israeli peace process, the continuing disintegration of Lebanon, the overthrow of the Shah, the hostage episode in Iran, the Soviet invasion of Afghanistan, disturbing incidents inside Saudi Arabia, the wars between the Yemens and between Morocco and the Algerian backed *Polisario* over the future of the former Spanish Sahara, between Somalia and Ethiopia and between Iran and Iraq. But even allowing for this pace of altering regional developments, it has still been difficult for the U.S. to adjust to the changes as suggested by the many twists and turns and tortured adjustments which ultimately became a trademark of the Carter administration. The reasons for the confusion lie in the basic assumptions of policy makers, and it is therefore necessary to examine the philosophy of the most recent administration to experience a full four year term in order to understand why the high level of intellectual discomfort has been occurring.

The Global Policy

The Carter administration entered office with ideas and influences which soon crystallized into a policy based on the following fundamental assumptions:

1. The administration de-emphasized relations with the Soviet Union; no longer was the U.S.-Soviet relationship the central organizing feature of American foreign policy. The result was a benign interpretation of the activities of the Soviets and their proxies in such areas as the Middle East and Africa. This policy resulted in a high degree of inconsistency in American policy toward Moscow, because the Soviets or their clients occasionally engaged in local activity that even the well-intentioned Carter administration could not stomach (e.g., the 1978 invasion of Zaire by Cuban-backed rebels based in Angola; the South Yemeni invasion of North Yemen in early 1979; and the Russian invasion of Afghanistan in December).

2. The corollary of lessened concentration on the Soviet Union was a diminished preoccupation with communism worldwide and an increased willingness to deal with radical and anti-American regimes.

3. A new stress on the importance of the Third World as a force in international politics was a further element in the new approach. The administration's national security advisor, Zbigniew Brzezinski, was fond of discussing such "new fundamentals" as India, Brazil, Nigeria, Venezuela, and Saudi Arabia. The United Nations again became an important focus of American diplomacy.

4. A fourth component of the new strategy included a diminished reliance on the use of force as a means of achieving diplomatic objectives.

5. The concomitant of less reliance on the use

Dr. Spiegel is Professor of Political Science at the University of California, Los Angeles. He is the author of *The Other Arab-Israeli Conflict: Making America's Middle East Policy from Truman to Reagan* (University of Chicago Press, 1985).

An earlier and more extended version of this paper was published under the title "Does the United States Have Options in the Middle East?" which appeared in the Summer 1980 issue of *Orbis*.

The author wishes to thank the UCLA Center for International and Strategic Affairs for assistance in the preparation of this essay.

of force was a greater emphasis on international interdependence, economic matters, the dynamics of North-South relations, issues raised by OPEC and most specifically, the energy crisis.

6. These policies were accompanied by an intensive human rights campaign.

7. Many of these policies precipitated tensions with many traditional friends of the United States because the crux of the policy was to appeal to the types of regimes that had not hitherto been close to Washington.

The Regional Policy

The problems and issues raised in the Middle East were ideally suited to this new foreign policy conception, and it is therefore not surprising that the region soon received top priority from the President and high-ranking officials of the new administration. On every level of the new policy, the Middle East could serve as a model. Thus:

1. The Soviet Union was perceived as a potential ally in achieving an Arab-Israeli settlement, and thus was the October 1, 1977, Soviet-American communique brought into being.

2. With the diminished concern for ideology and with a fascination for previously anti-American regimes, the administration was "liberated" conceptually to begin wooing Syria, Iraq, Algeria, and the PLO.

3. This approach meshed well with the stress on the "new influentials," focusing on Saudi Arabia in particular, Moreover, since the Palestinian question had become a symbol of Third World aspirations, it is not surprising that the administration proceeded further than its predecessors in identifying American policy with the objective of a Palestinian homeland. U.S. diplomats repeatedly sought to associate the United States with UN Security Council resolutions that would enshrine the new approach and were apparently at times even prepared to risk the demise of UN Security Council Resolution 242, which has been the centerpiece of Middle Eastern diplomacy for over a decade.

4. The aversion to the use of force in international affairs laid the grounds for a preoccupation with a comprehensive Arab-Israeli settlement as the key to Middle East stability in the belief that such an accord would both protect local regimes and prevent the necessity for U.S. intervention.

5. Similarly, a comprehensive Arab-Israeli settlement was perceived as the means by which the energy situation might be stabilized in the region and an even more acute global energy crisis averted.

6. The human rights issue was used as a political weapon; in particular, that weapon was employed against Iran in keeping with Washington's new interest in the Third World, where the Shah was unpopular. Israel, too, served as a target, thus demonstrating sympathy with the Palestinian cause and encouraging Israeli concessions in the West Bank.

7. Therefore, although for very different reasons, the administration soon found itself frequently at odds with the two countries that had previously been America's most reliable allies in the region — Israel and Iran.

These general policy conceptions soon confronted the harsh realities of the Middle East. Despite efforts to effect a comprehensive accord through a Geneva Conference and Soviet collaboration, the outcome was doomed by a formula that permitted the most negative Arab party (in this case, Syria) to veto the plans for participation of the most moderate (in this case, Egypt). Within the United States, domestic criticism of the emerging Carter Middle East policy was rising, especially among key Congressmen and within the American Jewish community.

The entire framework of Carter's initial thrust in the Middle East was overturned by President Sadat's visit to Jerusalem. Henceforward, the administration pursued a schizophrenic policy: confronted by the reality that it must even sponsor the Egyptian-Israeli connection if peace were to be seriously pursued, the administration nevertheless clung to its initial conception of a comprehensive accord as a basis for achieving regional stability and a resolution of the energy crisis. Thus Jerusalem and even Cairo were repeatedly prodded by American officials to make advances in the direction of Palestinian self-determination as a way of gaining the involvement of Arab parties who remained in the sidelines. Yet, even major arms deals with Saudi Arabia and repeated verbal and diplomatic thrusts in the direction of Arab dissenters were insufficient to bring any Arab party (besides Egypt) to the negotiating table.

Even more disturbing to the original policy conception was the gradual disintegration of the American position in the

Persian Gulf. Despite the continuing notion that the Arab-Israeli dispute is central to overcoming the energy crisis, the principal threat to the security of energy supplies has come from a pervasive regional instability and from Russian gains in such peripheral countries as Ethiopia, South Yemen, and Afghanistan. Rather than constituting a stable regime that could alter its policies in response to pressure on human rights, the Shah's government collapsed, significantly weakening the security of the American presence in the Gulf. Even "new influential" Saudi Arabia turned out to be susceptible to internal corruption and instability, as demonstrated by a dissident assault on the holiest of Islamic shrines in Mecca and by Shi'ite rioting in the country's oil-producing region — both occurring in late 1979.

The Challenge in Iran and Afghanistan

The two most devastating challenges to the Carter approach to foreign affairs came in Southwest Asia near the end of 1979 — the takeover of the American embassy in Iran and the Soviet invasion of Afghanistan. Toward the Iranian hostage situation the administration gravitated between a policy of confrontation (as in the aborted April 1980 raid to rescue the hostages) and one of conciliation (hoping at times to achieve cooperation with Iran against Soviet actions in Afghanistan). On the surface, the Afghan invasion transformed American policy. The President himself admitted that it altered his conception of Soviet intentions more drastically than any other previous event in his presidency. In his promulgation of a "Carter doctrine" in January 1980, he stated bravely that "an attempt by any outside force to gain control of the Persian Gulf region will be regarded as an assault on the vital interests of the United States of America and such an assault will be repelled by any means necessary, including military force."

Yet, the Carter administration had previously castigated the Soviet Union only to moderate its stand later. The reaction to Afghanistan should be examined in the light of specific administration actions which can be revealed to have been directly consistent with its initial foreign policy assumptions, with some tactical adjustments to deal with altered circumstances. Thus, despite the invasion of Afghanistan, the Carter administration was still seeking to appeal to anti-American regimes, to solve the problems of the area by settling the Palestinian question, and to avoid, if at all possible, the appearance of relying on force as a tool of international diplomacy. Once this strategy is comprehended, the indirect approach to the Soviet Union adopted after Afghanistan is revealed as in harmony with the original Carter conception and hardly a dramatic revolution in the administration's approach to the world.

Yet, if the original policy remained intact, so did its weaknesses. For example, it was never clear how Olympic boycotts or grain embargoes would resolve the loss of American credibility throughout the Middle East — the consequence of U.S. setbacks from Ethiopia to Afghanistan — or how the USSR would be dissuaded by these actions from proceeding with an offensive foreign policy strategy in the region once its position in Afghanistan was consolidated. Thus, despite the rhetoric of change, the Carter administration proceeded with a policy framework that was consistentently proven inadequate in the light of continuing developments throughout the Middle East. Even the rhetoric was not always altered. In case any observer might doubt the administration's consistency, it is worth quoting from Brzezinski's interview with the *Wall Street Journal* on January 15, 1980 — barely a week before the proclamation of the "Carter doctrine": "Let me add, the United States wishes friendly relations with all Moslem countries. This explicitly includes Iraq and Libya, countries with whom we don't have irreconcilable differences."

The Alternatives

Are there alternatives? Certainly fundamental to the conceptions of the Carter administration was that there were no conceivable options available that could better serve American policy. The sense of inevitable constraint was itself central to the Carter approach to foreign affairs.

The way to free American policy from this strait jacket is to conceive of different guiding principles that can lead to an alternative set of policies. These principles might be described as follows:

1. The United States cannot afford to ignore its competition with the Soviet Union, especially when Moscow and its proxies are actively encircling the Persian Gulf, the heartland of the West's oil supply.

2. While the United States should cooperate with regimes embracing a divergent political ideology, a simple criterion must be met — the willingness of a regime to collaborate with American objectives and to work toward the achievement of mutually beneficial interests.

3. Much of the Third World is in a state of chaos and upheaval. Therefore, it is folly to assume that the protection of American interests can be structured around "new influentials" whose regimes are frequently unstable and whose foreign policy objectives are often opposed to those of the United States.

4. The experience of Vietnam illustrates starkly the perils of an unwise reliance on the use of force in foreign affairs. Yet, an opposite policy which ignores the role of military power and which is mired in passivity, can be just as dangerous. If regimes that are dependent on the United States for their security conclude that Washington is unwilling or unable to afford them protection, they will seek to make alternate arrangements even at the expense of American interests.

5. Therefore, energy policy cannot be separated from the military tools of diplomacy, for American credibility, a reputation for reliability, and international respect are critical to effective negotiations with oil producers.

6. A successful human rights campaign must uphold the centrality of democratic values and institutions.

7. Similarly, the United States cannot conduct a credible foreign policy when nations that associate closely with Washington are not assured of continued support. Otherwise, only the weak and the desperate will be left with any incentive to pursue coalition politics with America.

When these principles are applied, the basic approach to the crises in Iran and Afghanistan and indeed the Persian Gulf as a whole is transformed. The alternative strategy is based on the assumption that specific, strong steps must be taken. Means must be found in order to accomplish the following goals:

a. The Russians must be signaled that there are limits to the aggressive steps they can take without meeting an active and effective American response.

b. The Persian Gulf oil producers must be convinced that the United States is willing and able to provide protection against external threats.

c. The key Persian Gulf states must be shown that the United States is capable of developing a coherent strategy in the wake of local wars, internal instability and revolutionary Marxian and fundamentalist Islamic political movements.

The recognition of American goals is only the first step in developing a new approach — and the easiest. The critical problem confronting the United States today in the Middle East is to identify and to implement tactics that will work. In addressing the new challenges it will be necessary to avoid two contrasting pitfalls: (1) The temptation to declare sweeping new activist policies while actually pursuing passive options highlighted by little practical succor to frightened regimes: (2) The temptation to overreact by sole reliance on huge military expenditures and installations. The first fallacy would result in a serious loss of credibility and prestige in the region, as the poverty of American inability to provide protection and support would be painfully obvious to local regimes. The second fallacy would result in either precipitating crises by the sheer visibility of the American presence or would cause the United States to become mired in every local disturbance. The answer — more easily stated than practiced — is for the United States to adopt an activist policy in which it relies on qualitative rather than quantitative instruments of providing assurances. In the use of weaponry, manpower, types of armed forces and diplomatic strategies, the U.S. must employ a selective approach, relying on visible but delicate means of activity without overreacting with huge emplacements that will only destabilize the local political balance of forces. Only if this type of strategy is devised will the economic and the political collapse of Western interests in the Middle East and the Persian Gulf be avoided.

38

United States Decision-Making in Middle East Crises: 1958, 1970, 1973

By Alan Dowty

Is there a consistent pattern in American responses to crisis in the Middle East? If there is, identification of such continuity might help us anticipate responses to future crises, and facilitate substantive criticism of policies chosen. What can we, in fact, learn from case studies of past decision-making during periods of Middle East turbulence?

The three case studies summarized here do not constitute an analysis of U.S. decision-making in all Middle East crises. They span a fifteen-year period and involve two different presidential administrations, but the conclusions may apply only to the cases studied. Nevertheless, a close look at three major crisis periods, using the perspective and tools of decision-making theory, may reveal consistencies of more than purely historical interest. And indeed, as the analysis below shows, there are some rather striking common features among the three cases.

The cases in question are the Lebanese crisis of 1958, the Syria-Jordan crisis of 1970, and the Yom Kippur War of 1973, three episodes involving U.S. decision makers in crucial questions of diplomatic and military intervention, the survival of dependent regimes or states, and confrontation with the Soviet Union. We will begin with questions regarding the impact of crisis conditions on the decision-making process, and then proceed to points of particular interest regarding the substance of U.S. Middle Eastern policy.[1]

The Decision-Making Process

The following observations regarding U.S. decision-making in 1958, 1970, and 1973 deal with the way policy was formulated, rather than the substance of U.S. policy toward the Middle East. They represent the sorts of questions political scientists ask generally about crisis decision-making. In this regard, U.S. decision-makers in the three cities tended to react in the following ways:

1. *Closing out external influences:* As the crisis intensified, decision-making groups became more closed to the influence of interest groups, domestic politics, Congress, the media, public opinion, and other pressures from outside the executive branch. In 1958, the crucial decision to intervene in Lebanon was taken within a few hours of receipt of the news of the coup in Iraq; during that time of frenzied consultations within the government, the only consultation with "outsiders" was a meeting with 22 Congressional leaders, who were given to understand that the decision had in fact already been taken.[2] Even this nicety was missing in 1970, as Nixon shared neither Eisenhower's desire to observe form by consulting Congress, nor the latter's felt need to explain his actions to the American public (as Eisenhower did after his decision, at least). The Nixonian approach to crisis management put stress on keeping the crisis insulated from public excitement and hysteria and maintaining a calm, low-key posture. At the height of the 1970 crisis, Nixon even

Dr. Dowty is Professor of Government and International Studies at the University of Notre Dame. He is the author of *Middle East Crisis: U.S. Decision-Making in 1958, 1970, and 1973* (University of California Press, 1984).

avoided following the public media, in order not to be influenced by "the hot words of television."[3] The 1970 crisis was in fact purposely muted, as it was felt that "going public" would make it more difficult for the other side to retreat and that public support was uncertain in any event. In general, U.S. policy in the critical days of the 1970 crisis was determined without consultation of public or congressional opinion.[4]

The 1973 crisis could not be shielded as effectively from outside pressures, if only because of the higher activity level of lobbying groups, Congress, and others during the war. But the weight of evidence suggests that while Congressional pressures played some role in the decision to resupply Israel by military airlift, in general decisions were made with only marginal reference to such pressures. The activities of lobbying groups tended to offset each other, and Secretary of State Kissinger was not overly moved by the possibility of Israel's supporters "going public," according to the testimony of those most intimately involved.[5]

There has been a lingering suspicion that Nixon's domestic political problems had an impact on U.S. policy during the 1973 War, and especially on the world-wide alert called the night of October 24-25. There is little doubt that Nixon personally was distracted by the Saturday Night Massacre and Vice President Agnew's resignation, both of which occurred during the crisis. According to all testimony, however, Kissinger picked up the slack and coordinated the decision process without much reference to domestic politics, considering it important to demonstrate that Watergate had not deflected the country's course.[6] In fact, public charges that the alert of October 24 was motivated by a desire to distract attention from Watergate came as a shock to top decision-makers, and testified to the extent to which the "tunnel vision" of crisis had isolated them from public thinking.[7]

Since both the 1958 and 1970 crises came shortly before Congressional elections, it would be surprising if electoral considerations were entirely absent from the minds of policy-makers. But such considerations are rarely mentioned; they are apparently internalized and operate as unspoken constraints, to the extent they are influential at all. All in all, Quandt offers a fair summary of domestic pressures in 1973 that could apply to all three cases:

> The key decisions of the crisis, however — the cease-fire proposals, the airlift to Israel, and the alert — were not responses to domestic politics . . . Crisis periods, especially, tend to isolate policy makers from domestic pressures. Decisions are often made rapidly, before public opinion can be mobilized. Information is closely held, depriving interest groups of the means for more effective action. The stakes are high and the public tends to be deferential to presidential authority, even when that authority has been weakened, as Nixon's has been.[8]

2. *Centralization of decision-making:* It is no surprise that crucial decisions in time of crisis should be made by the top policy-maker and his closest advisors. While subordinate officials might be consulted, the ultimate decisions in all three cases were made by one or two people. Eisenhower observed the forms of collective decision-making by convening the National Security Council but, as he admitted later, "this was one meeting in which my mind was practically made up regarding the general line of action we should take, before we met."[9]

During the Nixon years crises were coordinated by the Washington Special Action Group (WSAG), chaired by Kissinger and usually including the Undersecretaries or Deputy Secretaries of State and Defense, the Director of the CIA, the Chairman of the Joint Chiefs of Staff, and the senior State and Defense Department officials responsible for the relevant region. WSAG's "recommendations" were conveyed to the President by Kissinger, who thus served as the link between Nixon and other top advisors. In both 1970 and 1973 the focus of decision-making passed from WSAG to the critical consultations between Nixon and Kissinger, with Kissinger then speaking in the President's name (this was particularly marked in 1973, with Nixon isolated and distracted). In 1970, some of the top decision-makers were even unaware of the critical agreement on Israeli intervention that Kissinger negotiated with Israeli Ambassador Yitzhak Rabin. In 1973, with

Kissinger holding the post of Secretary of State as well as National Security Advisor, centralization had proceeded to the point that high State and Defense officials later claimed that only Kissinger, and some of his closest NSC aides, had a complete picture of what was going on.[10]

3. *Consensus on basic policy:* Despite the concentration of authority at the top, there was a widespread perception among subordinates that the decision-making process was a harmonious effort (with the partial exception of 1973). One explanation for this is that, despite being closed out, lower-level advisors were not in disagreement with the basic thrust of policy decisions and thus could feel they had contributed to them. The degree of consensus is striking. A crisis atmosphere is expected to evoke sharp debate, given the importance of decisions taken and the high level of tension, and in all three cases there were indeed heated arguments and sharp dissents. But on closer examination, these debates appear to involve the means to be employed rather than basic policy. As one WSAG member in 1970 remarked, in a crisis one is preoccupied with problems of the moment — getting forces in place, the infrastructure, etc. — and there is little inclination for reconsideration of basic aims.[11]

In the Lebanese case, there was apparently no dissent from within Eisenhower's official family to the view that prevention of a Nasserist victory in Lebanon was an American interest, and that only direct military action would suffice in the aftermath of the Iraqi coup. There was conflict later between political and military authorities responsible for executing the intervention, but this involved questions of how, rather than whether, to land U.S. troops.[12]

Likewise in 1970 there was virtual unanimity on the need to save the Jordanian regime; earlier anti-Hussein voices were not heard. The perceived need for quick action, after the Syrian armored "incursion" into Jordan, led to an immediate focus on the best means of coming to Hussein's rescue should it become necessary, with the basic options being direct U.S. action or support of Israeli action. In the end there was even considerable consensus on this level; many who had regarded the Israeli option with distaste came to view it as the lesser of two evils.[13]

The basic consensus in 1973 has been somewhat obscured by the noisy debate over "who delayed the airlift," a debate apparently fed by personal conflict between the Secretary of State and Secretary of Defense. Extensive interviewing of partisans and neutrals leads to the conclusion that there was, in fact, little conflict between political and military decision-makers on the question of resupply to Israel. To some extent there were indeed "technical problems" that delayed the airlift, especially with regard to the ill-fated but apparently sincere effort to charter civilian airplanes. But basically, U.S. policy during the first week of the Yom Kippur War was to maintain a low profile on resupply of Israel. There was no significant dissent from this policy, nor any open support for a U.S. military airlift, from any top policy-makers, until perceptions of the military situation changed toward the end of the first week. The real technical problems were, in some degree, overplayed in order to protect the low profile policy, thus laying the foundation for stories of Pentagon obstructionism. In truth, while there were anti-Israel voices in the Department of Defense (as elsewhere), they did not delay the airlift, and there was little dissent even from these circles over the military airlift to Israel, once evaluations of the military situation changed.[14]

4. *No re-examination of basic beliefs:* Decision-making theorists are interested in the dominant mode of decision-making in a given case. Do the decision-makers behave as normative theory would have them behave, searching for all relevant information and options, evaluating alternatives in terms of cost and benefit as objectively as possible, and then choosing on that basis (the "analytic" model)? Or do decision-makers tend to rely on standard operating procedures, reducing problems to bureaucratic routine in which established programs and precedents are decisive and the policy-maker's role is largely to keep the machine running smoothly (the "cybernetic" model)? Or do decision-makers simply accommodate in-

formation to their prevailing perceptions, activating their basic values, instincts, and belief system so as to impose order on a complex and uncertain reality (the "cognitive" model)?

The evidence at hand underlines the importance of cognitive factors in setting general policy aims. In none of the three crises does there appear to be any tendency to analyze the basic assumptions upon which policy rested. The importance of preventing the Nasserist take-over of Lebanon in 1958, of saving Hussein in 1970, and of preventing either Israeli defeat or total Israeli victory in 1973, were axiomatic in policy discussions. The explanation for these undebated decisions lies in the perceptual frameworks then dominant, typically expressed in terms of recent historical analogies and experiences. In 1958 Eisenhower and Dulles were convinced that Nasser was consciously or unconsciously the tool of Soviet policy in the Middle East. Crises in Jordan (Feb., 1957) and Syria (August, 1957) seemed to confirm the pattern and accustom policy-makers to consideration of intervention. The Lebanese situation itself had already led twice to serious consideration of intervention (in May and June, 1958). A series of blows to American "prestige" in various spots had apparently created in Eisenhower a feeling that "enough is enough." All of this contributed to Eisenhower and Dulles making what one observer called "a quick intuitive judgement." Eisenhower himself expressed the feeling that "doing something was better than doing nothing," and began his public defense of the action with a long list of "analogies," beginning with Greece in 1947 through Korea and Indochina in the 1950s.[15]

The perceptual universe of Nixon and Kissinger in 1970 also created a proclivity to action. The state of U.S.-Soviet relations at the time, reinforced by recent Soviet actions in the Middle East, led policy-makers to regard the crisis basically as a Cold War confrontation rather than as a localized Middle East conflict. There was a sense of forward Soviet thrust, shown in Soviet rejection of the Rogers Plan, increasing military involvement in Egypt, and Egyptian violation of the standstill cease-fire in August, 1970 (demonstrating Soviet perfidy). The sense of being "tested" by the Soviet Union was further reinforced by the Vietnamese situation, by Soviet "stalling" in SALT, Berlin, and European Security Conference negotiations, and the construction of a Soviet nuclear submarine base in Cuba.[16]

The 1973 crisis began with a mistake that can only be explained cognitively: the failure to foresee the Egyptian-Syrian attack despite an abundance of evidence. Signs of war were minimized because of prevailing assumptions that the Arab states could not and would not risk a full-scale war. This complacency had been reinforced by Egyptian acceptance of the 1970 cease-fire, by the expulsion of Soviet experts from Egypt in 1972, and by the previous Egyptian mobilization, without attack, in May, 1973. Once war broke out, of course, U.S. policy was dominated by the perceptions of a single figure, to the extent that any analysis tends to revolve around the question of "what was on Henry's mind."[17]

5. *Rationality in operational decision-making:* While decisions on basic policy directions were firmly rooted in the perceptions and instincts of top policy-makers, operational decisions were made on a more analytic basis. In these decisions more open debate and disagreement took place, and subordinates played a more active role. With basic policy guidelines assumed, the deliberative machinery of decision-making focussed on the practical problems of carrying the policy out.

The Lebanese crisis is a partial exception to this. The choice of military means on July 14 was strongly linked to the overall perception of a Soviet-backed Nasserist plot to dominate the Middle East; in fact, the original troop deployments were aimed more at meeting an invasion from Nasserist Syria than at influencing domestic Lebanese politics. But with the dispatch of Robert Murphy to Lebanon, the U.S. government came to realize that the cause of stability in Lebanon could best be served by dealing with internal Lebanese factions rather than focussing on external threats. Thus, in the end, a closer analysis of the situation led to a shift in means, from military action (U.S. troops in Lebanon were not used to suppress Chamoun's opponents, much to his disappointment) to diplomatic support of a new compromise Lebanese government.

In 1970, the U.S. reaction to Syria's incursion was intense internal debate over the best means of forcing a Syrian withdrawal from Jordan. Diplomatic means — pressuring the Soviets to exert their influence — were invoked, and military options, as a last resort, were discussed intensively and with attention to all the ramifications. Sober judgements of military capabilities, including painful judgements on U.S. incapacities, were reached with expert advice. The political and diplomatic consequences of different options were assessed; the risks of using Israel to save Hussein were taken into account. According to report, Nixon and Kissinger even "war gamed" the options at the height of the crisis.[18]

In 1973, the basic aim of U.S. policy — to prevent Israeli defeat but likewise avoid too great an Israeli victory — remained constant for the duration of the crisis. What changed were appreciations of the military situation, and the appropriate tactical moves based on this intelligence. Once expectations of a quick Israeli victory were put to rest, policy-makers began tuning their responses more closely to changes on the battlefield. Thus the gradual shift in resupply policy (too gradual, in Israel's eyes) paralleled the evolution in military evaluations. Knowing and appreciating the costs (in U.S.-Arab and U.S.-Soviet relations) of open resupply for Israel, the United States also carefully searched first for low-level options that would maintain Israeli capability without such a cost. What one observer described as the "minuet" with the Soviet Union on a cease-fire was likewise very closely related to calculations (on both sides) of the most advantageous point at which to stop the fighting. Even the U.S. alert of October 24, while perhaps appearing more dramatic than policy-makers intended, was the result of a careful weighing of options and a careful reading of the relative risks of action and inaction.[19]

Characteristics of Crisis Behavior

In addition to common features in the policy-making process, there are regularities in the content of American responses in 1958, 1970, and 1973. Four of these patterns can be briefly identified at this point, along with some speculation on their relationship to the decision-making process:

1. *Intelligence failure:* In all three cases the key event in the crisis was unanticipated. The Iraqi coup in 1958, the Syrian invasion of Jordan in September, 1970, and the Egyptian-Syrian attack of 1973 all caught policy-makers by surprise. In addition, inadequate information was a constraint on decision-making throughout all three crises, according to the testimony of participants. We must be careful not to demand the impossible of intelligence analysts; no one can foresee every contingent event. But it seems likely that the centralization of policy-making, inadequate representation of local expertise, and tendencies to perceptual consensus all contributed to faulty intelligence. Good policy-making begins with reliable information from the field, and in the cases examined it cannot be said that U.S. Policy-makers understood the Middle East.

2. *Dominance of global perspectives:* In all three cases, local and regional forces were seen as a function of U.S.-Soviet relations. In 1958 Eisenhower noted that "if (Nasser) was not a communist, he certainly succeeded in making us very suspicious of him."[20] In 1970, Nixon and Kissinger saw the Syrian incursion as proof of Soviet duplicity if not complicity, and believed that their response must establish American credibility on a world-wide basis. And in 1973 some observers thought the American airlift was as much a signal to the Soviet Union as a response to Israel's needs; in any event, American policy was clearly geared to Soviet actions, as the hasty cease-fire of October 22 and the alert of October 24 both demonstrated. To be sure, in both 1958 and 1973 the United States turned, in the post-crisis period, to an active diplomatic effort tuned to local and regional factors. But the initial perception was always global. To some extent, of course, this is because the top decision-makers were generalists, not specialists; local expertise tends to be closed out as crisis decision-making is centralized. Also, Americans have traditionally tended

to perceive the international system globally, whether in ideological terms (the Eisenhower-Dulles style) or in a traditional Great Power framework (i.e., Kissinger).

3. *Lack of political-military coordination:* Far from dominating crisis decision-making, military spokesmen played secondary roles in 1958 and 1973 and were influential in arguing *against* direct U.S. military intervention in 1970. Military advisors tended to complain, as a result, that civilian policy-makers made decisions with inadequate attention to military factors. In any event, political and military planning often worked at cross purposes, nearly leading to disaster in Lebanon,[21] and causing unnecessary complications in 1973. The American tendency to divorce military and political considerations has been noted often, and is reinforced in the crises studied by centralization of decision-making. But as military constraints become more important in crisis decision-making (and the trend from 1958 to 1973 was toward greater limitations on U.S. capabilities in confrontations with the Soviet Union), better integration and coordination would seem imperative.

4. *Achievement of immediate ends:* Despite flawed perceptions, faulty intelligence, defective political-military coordination, and other shortcomings that characterized U.S. decision-making, in each case the immediate American aims were achieved. Lebanon was stabilized with a non-Nasserist regime, Hussein survived after suppressing the PLO in Jordan, and the Yom Kippur War ended in a way that opened diplomatic vistas. In each case U.S. policy was at least partly instrumental in achieving these results, even when this policy was based on perceptions not closely tuned to local complexities. Both Kerr, analyzing the 1958 crisis, and Quandt, speaking of 1970, make a strong case for the appropriateness of U.S. policy, even while criticizing the perceptions on which it was based.[22] A similar argument could be made for 1973.

Perhaps American policy-makers have a lucky habit of doing the right thing for the wrong reasons; on the other hand, there may be some explanation for the pattern. By converting Middle East crises to U.S.-Soviet confrontations, the United States puts stress on its strategic military capabilities, where it is in a stronger position, rather than on local capabilities that are often more problematic. Moreover, holding the Soviet Union responsible for the behavior of a local client may work even if the assumption of Soviet complicity was originally incorrect. As one NSC staff member in 1970 and 1973 argues, as a working hypothesis the assumption of Soviet responsibility may be the best course of action whatever the Soviet role in instigating the crisis; pressure on the Soviet Union is likely to be more effective than trying to deal with the local client.[23]

Implications

Any implications drawn from these cases must be tentative. But if the patterns described above should prove to be typical, what should be our concerns regarding U.S. decision-making in future Middle Eastern crises?

There is little need to comment on failures of intelligence or the tendency to define basic policy aims by instinct and belief rather than open-minded examination of options. These are well-known problems, common to other areas of human endeavor, that have well-known if infrequently practiced solutions.

The continuing ability of decision-makers to "do the right thing for the wrong reasons" is, however, another kind of problem. It may work only so long as the United States has a large margin of power in which to err. When such a margin exists, an action based on a perception of global struggle may be incorrectly addressed, but may incidentally meet the needs of the situation.

In a situation of strategic parity among the superpowers, however, and with local military balances even more questionable from the U.S. perspective, such a margin for error may no longer exist. The risks will increase as the margin for error decreases, and actions that are based on misperceptions or ignorance of local conditions may no longer turn out happily in spite of everything.

On the other hand, one can make a case

that the "closing out" and centralization of decision-making may, on balance, be positive. Crisis decision-making needs a global context, though not exclusively global perceptions. Regional experts tend inevitably to feel that their advice is inadequately respected, but any policy-maker who tried to please all his ambassadors simultaneously would surely commit even more grievous follies. Furthermore, it was the regional experts in all three cases who failed to alert their superiors to impending crisis. The solution would not seem to be increasing the role of the regional experts, but rather improving the quality of their input. It is apparent, in the cases before us, that those responsible consistently failed to convey to top policy-makers an accurate sense of Middle Eastern thinking and political behavior.

FOOTNOTES

1. The study from which this paper is drawn is an integral part of the International Crisis Behavior Research Project, under the direction of Michael Brecher. The ICB project uses a common framework across a large sample of cases in order to create a data base for a general theory of crisis decision-making.

2. Dwight D. Eisenhower, *Waging Peace* (New York: Doubleday and Company, 1965), pp. 271-272; Herbert K. Tillema, *Appeal to Force: American Military Intervention in the Era of Containment* (New York: Thomas Y. Crowell Company, 1973), pp. 104-105; *New York Times*, July 15, 1958; *U.S. News and World Report*, July 25, 1958. According to Eleanor Dulles (*American Foreign Policy in the Making*, New York: Harper and Row, 1968, p. 275), Secretary of State John Foster Dulles consulted with 70 (governmental) officers and experts during the five hours before the decision was made.

3. "The Mideast: Search for Stability," *Time*, Oct. 5, 1970 p. 12.

4. William Quandt, "Case Studies: Lebanon 1958 and Jordan 1970," in Barry Blechman and Stephen Kaplan, *The Use of the Armed Forces as a Political Instrument* (Washington, Brookings Institution, 1978); interview with Senator J. William Fulbright, Chairman, Committee on Foreign Relations, U.S. Senate (all positions listed for interviewees are those held at the time).

5. Interviews with Fulbright: Senate legislative aide; House administrative aide; Simha Dinitz, Israeli Ambassador to U.S.; I.L. Kenen, Director, America-Israel Public Affairs Committee; David Korn, Country Director, Lebanon, Jordan Syria, and Iraq, Department of State; James Akins, U.S. Ambassador to Saudi Arabia. See also Marvin Kalb and Bernard Kalb, *Kissinger* (New York: Dell Publishing Company 1975), pp. 525-529.

6. See the published account of one NSC staff member, William Quandt: *Decade of Decisions* (Berkeley: University of California Press, 1977) pp. 172-173, 199, 203. Also, interviews with three NSC staff members.

7. Interviews with William Colby, Director, CIA; Admiral Thomas Moorer, Chairman, Joint Chiefs of Staff; NSC staff members.

8. Quandt, 1977, p. 203

9. Eisenhower, p. 270. According to Robert Cutler, Eisenhower's National Security Advisor, the President considered the meeting such a formality that he almost forgot to call on Dulles for an opinion. Cutler, *No Time for Rest* (Boston: Little, Brown and Company, 1966), pp. 262-364. See also Townsend Hoopes, *The Devil and John Foster Dulles* (Boston: Little, Brown and Company, 1973), p. 435.

10. Interviews with WSAG members and other officials; Harry Brandon, *The Retreat of American Power* (New York: Dell, 1973), p. 136; Quandt, 1977, pp. 204-205; Kalb and Kalb, esp. pp. 538-539.

11. Personal Interview.

12. See the account by Ambassador Robert McClintock, "The American Landing in Lebanon," *U.S. Naval Institute Proceedings*, Vol. 88 (October, 1962): 65-79.

13. Interviews with participants, including Moorer, Admiral Elmo Zumwalt (Chief of Naval Operations), and U. Alexis Johnson (Undersecretary of State for Political Affairs); Quandt, 1978.

14. Interviews with participants, including Helmut Sonnenfeldt and three other members of the NSC staff; two high State Department officials; Maj. Gen. Gordon Sumner, Jr. Director, Near Eastern and South Asian Affairs, Department of Defense; Richard Peyer, Near Eastern and South Asian Affairs, Department of Defense; Edward Luttwak, Consultant, Department of Defense; Moorer; Zumwalt; Gen. George Brown, Chief of Staff, U.S. Air Force; two legislative aides, U.S. Senate. The standard pro-Kissinger version of the debate is in Kalb and Kalb, pp. 509-540; among the anti-Kissinger accounts are Tad Szulc, "Is He Indispensable? Answers to the Kissinger Riddle," *New York*, July 1, 1974; and Matti Golan, *The Secret Conversations of Henry Kissinger,* (New York: Bantam, 1976). Two accounts that generally confirm the findings of this article are Quandt, 1977, pp. 165-206, and Nadav Safran, *Israel: The Embattled Ally* (Cambridge and London: The Belknap Press of Harvard University Press, 1978), pp. 476-505.

15. Eisenhower, esp. pp. 274-275; Tillema, pp. 77-78; Hoopes, pp. 435-439; E. Dulles, *John Foster Dulles: The Last Year* (New York: Harcourt, Brace and World, 1963), p. 132; Malcolm Kerr, "The Lebanese Civil War," in Evan Luard, ed., *The International Regulation of Civil War* (New York University Press, 1972), p. 78.

16. Interviews with Sonnenfeldt and Johnson; interviews with Samuel Hoskinson, William Hyland, and Harold Saunders, all on the NSC staff. See also Quandt, 1978; and Kalb and Kalb, pp. 241-244.

17. Interviews with participants; Kalb and Kalb, pp. 504-564; Quandt, 1977, pp. 165-206.

18. Interviews with most participants, including Moorer, Sonnenfeldt, Saunders, Hyland, Hoskinson, Johnson, Melvin Laird (Secretary of Defense), and Robert Pranger (Deputy Assistant Secretary of Defense, Near East and South Asian Affairs).

19. Interviews with Sonnenfeldt, Moorer, Zumwalt, and Colby; Quandt, 1977, pp. 195-198; Safran, pp. 477-495.

20. *Waging Peace*, p. 265.

21. McClintock, *op. cit*.

22. Kerr, p. 79: "This writer happens to be convinced that the Lebanon intervention was not a mistake, however foggy the thinking that determined it." Quandt, 1977, pp. 119-127.

23. Interview with Sonnenfeldt.

39

American Interest and The Middle East

By Michael Curtis

It was always an unreasonable expectation that the personal diplomacy of Secretary of State Kissinger in Middle Eastern affairs would meet with uninterrupted success. American foreign policy is being framed today not only in a period of economic difficulty that warrants close attention to internal issues and at a time of political competition between an increasingly assertive Congress and a relatively weak President but also in a climate of declining enthusiasm for foreign undertakings, foreign aid programs or binding commitments. The American debacle in Southeast Asia and the frustrations caused by the overextension of American power in the past have understandably produced a mood in which retrenchment seems the wisest, safest and economically most profitable policy. But the U.S. cannot renounce its position as the major world power and retreat into an isolationist fortress concerned only with short term gain. It remains the indispensable element in the maintenance of world order and the preservation of world peace.

The view held in the early years of the Nixon administration that the constellation of forces in the world had moved from a bilateral to a pentagonal relationship in which Europe, Japan and China had joined with the two superpowers and in which the United States could maneuver among the other four powers, has proved not to be an accurate analysis of power and influence in contemporary international affairs. The bilateral relationship between the U.S. and the Soviet Union remains the key factor in world politics even at a time when the power of Arab oil and petrodollars has become potent, the influence of the Third World countries felt especially in international organizations, and the activity of multinational corporations prominent in economic affairs. Though the Cold War is over and the idea of anti-communism as the guiding spirit behind American foreign policy is long outmoded, the U.S. must remain alert to the danger of Soviet expansion in areas vital to American national interest and to the threat posed by the oil cartel to the world economy.

•

Dr. Curtis is Professor of Political Science at Rutgers University, New Brunswick. His latest publication, of which he is the editor, is *Antisemitism in the Contemporary World* (Westview Press, 1986).

It has long been recognized that the Middle East is potentially the most explosive area in the world. Not only has a state of belligerency existed for twenty-eight years since the attack on Israel by the Arab states whose implacable hostility to its existence has led to continual escalation of the conflict, but any contemplated amelioration of that hostility has been prevented by the highly volatile relationships among the Arab states and population which make a unilateral initiative by a single Arab state difficult. In addition, the possibility of the conflict igniting a wider conflagration has been a real one because of the danger of the involvement of the two superpowers.

Both the U.S. and the Soviet Union recognize the significance of the Middle East, not only in terms of its natural resources, but as the bridge between Europe and Africa, as a vital point in the security of the Mediterranean area and the southern flank of Europe and as an access to the Persian Gulf and the Indian Ocean. For the United States moral considerations and strategic concerns intersect and overlap with political, economic and geographical interests. In the kaleidoscope of American concerns—the preservation of the links between the Mediterranean and the Indian Ocean and between NATO and SEATO, the ensuring of the flow of Arab oil, the requirement of political stability, the maintenance of good relations with the moderate Arab regimes, the need to contain Soviet influence while preserving détente and avoiding conflict with the Soviet Union, American political and material support for Israel remains crucial.

In essence American objectives in the Middle East comprise five elements: the moral and political commitment to Israel; the preservation of a balance of power in the area; the continuation of friendly relations with the Arab states and expansion of opportunities for trade with them; the prevention of Soviet domination of the area, and the fostering of a peaceful settlement on the basis of U.N. Security Council Resolutions 242 and 338.

Since Woodrow Wilson recognized in 1919 that "the foundations of a Jewish commonwealth" should be laid in Palestine and authorized "the historical claims of the Jewish people in regard to Palestine," the United States has been concerned with the fulfillment of promises made to the Jewish people. Though no formal document exists, the U.S. has maintained its support and aid to the State of Israel. "America cannot be true to itself" wrote Henry Kissinger "without moral purpose." The commitment to Israel has been a major illustration of that purpose. As recently as April 1976 Kissinger stated: "The survival and security of Israel are unequivocal and permanent moral commitments of the United States." At a time when only 19% of the world's population lives in a state of full freedom, the commitment has been deepened by the liberal and democratic character of Israel's politics and society with which the U.S. shares common values and a similar approach to political issues.

Whatever the troubling nature of U.S. policy in South East Asia, Israel is neither Vietnam nor Cambodia. Its political stability, democratic polity, moral strength, social integration, scientific and technological ability, its ethical vitality, provide it with an ability and assurance to defend itself and to remain a reliable friend of the U.S. The whole concept of American deterrence would be discredited if the moral commitment to maintain the security of Israel were not upheld.

There is a coincidence of American and Israeli interests on certain issues: the avoidance of war in the area, the maintenance of a military balance, the reduction of the role of the Soviet Union. But the global interests of the United States may make the American conception of a desirable settlement differ from that of Israel with its more regional concerns. A number of recent events—the Saunders testimony, the agreement to the participation of the Palestine Liberation Organization at the Security Council in January 1976, the resignation of Moynihan as Ambassador to the U.N., the Scranton statement on Israeli settlements, the refusal to sell Pershings to Israel and the decision to sell military supplies to Egypt—all suggest awareness of that difference. It is essential that the United States engage in no punitive action against Israel for any lack of consonance in the policies of the two countries.

The qualities that Israel possesses and the contribution it makes to a dynamic and a progressive world order are intangible compared with the concrete assets of oil, markets and wealth of the Arabs. This has led to passive acquiescence in the Arab political position in the conflict on the part of some European countries, Japan and many countries of the Third World and to a deferential attitude on the part of some American companies dazzled by the possibilities of greater trade. But there are three caveats to be made. One is that the energy problem, difficult though it is at the present moment, is a short term problem that will be solved within the next two decades and it would be absurd to sacrifice long term strategic interests for short term gains. The second is that the pattern of Arab trade in the last two years has shown that the Arabs are more concerned with comparative prices, quality and delivery terms for their imports than with the foreign policy of the supplier country. American exports to the Arab countries increased 109% in 1974 and 82% in the first nine months of 1975. By contrast, France, in spite of its change to a pro-Arab position, has been disappointed by its lack of success in exports to the Arabs. The third is the inter-Arab rivalries and the struggle for hegemony in the Arab world, the potential instability of Arab regimes, the uncertainty of the retention of power by present rulers and the futility of relying on supposedly moderate Arab states for support. The assassination of King Feisal of Saudi Arabia, the civil war in Lebanon, the increasingly vigorous Arab verbal attack on Sadat, adequately illustrates the precariousness of such reliance. Moreover, the oil agreements have been discarded at will by all the Arab countries. Feisal, the supposed friend, had promised not to use oil as a political weapon bud did nothing to prevent the oil embargo in 1973. At a time when storage tanks were full and the demand for oil tankers was weak, the reduction of production by Saudi Arabia in February-March 1975 by 25% to a level of 6.5 million barrels per day prevented other members of OPEC from being pressured and indicated how minimal was the concern of Saudi Arabia to be helpful to the West.

•

The Arab-Israeli conflict has always been asymmetrical in character, in manpower, military equipment, relationship of clients to patrons and real objectives of the participants. Currently Israel is at least at a 3-1 disadvantage in planes and tanks, 9-1 in artillery, 12-1 in all types of missiles, 10-1 in surface-to-surface missiles and 5-1 in active manpower. Moreover there is no guarantee that military equipment sold by the U.S. to one Arab state will not be transferred to another. The Soviet Union has unstintedly supplied the Arab confrontation countries with military and economic assistance and replaced all military losses with ever more up-to-date and sophisticated equipment, including batteries of SA-2, SA-3, and SA-6 missiles and surface-to-surface anti-tank missiles, 350 Scud missiles, T-62 tanks, MIG 23 fighters, and even some MIG 25s, which are more maneuverable and faster than the American F4 Phantoms, the best planes in the Israeli air force. In 1974 alone Syria and Egypt received $4 billion worth of equipment from the Russians. The oil producing Arab states have given $8.4 billion in grants to Syria and Egypt. Moreover the Arab states between 1946 and 1972 received from the United States $1.92 billion in economic loans, $2.33 billion in grants, $394 million in military assistance credits and $309 million in military grants. The Russian delay in sending spare parts to Egypt has led not only to the abrogation by the latter of its treaty of friendship with the Soviet Union in March 1976 but also to a diversification of its sources of military and economic assistance in which the United States, France, Italy and Britain have joined. The Western sale of sophisticated equipment to the Arabs means they are benefiting from American, European and Russian technology, thus reducing the Israeli qualitative superiority.

Israel is currently spending 36% of its GNP on defense and imposing a 70% level of taxation on its citizens. The asymmetry in resources can only be corrected by American supplies and economic assistance to create a balance of power in the area. Minimizing the possibility of confrontation can only result from sufficient credible deterrence in the hands of Israel. The experience of Munich is familiar. Refusal to support the state being threatened is an inducement to greater aggression in the future, which in the present era might lead to nuclear disaster. The U.S. arms lift to Israel in the 1973 war led to an amelioration not a worsening of relations with the Arabs.

A sincere desire for closer and more harmonious relations with the Arab countries does not necessitate political obeisance to them nor does the rapid accumulation of wealth by the Arab oil producing countries and the increase in trade with them require acceptance of their ethnic or religious views. In October 1974 Sheik Yamani of Saudi Arabia warned of the renewal of war within six months if the U.S. did not force Israel to withdraw from all occupied Arab territory and promised reduction of oil prices if the U.S. pressure was successful. But the energy problem will not be solved by a sacrifice of Israel or by a supine West accepting as axiomatic the foreign policies of an exultant Islam. On the contrary, the U.S. in collaboration with other oil-consuming nations must frame policies which reduce or eliminate the potentialities for political blackmail by the OPEC countries. A comprehensive alternative energy policy is still lacking. But a variety of methods—reduction of consumption, rapid development of alternative sources, a quota on oil imports and the sale of import licenses by competitive bidding, the creation of a governmental agency to make all foreign purchases of crude oil and refined products, safeguards over the long term use of Arab money—can be used. Approval for a show of strength of this kind may also be gained from those Third World countries which have been so adversely affected by the OPEC increase of the price of oil and who may be righteously indignant about the $116 billion in oil revenues going to the OPEC countries in 1974, of which $69 billion went to the Arab countries. In particular the U.S. must strengthen the resolve of the Western European nations, Japan and Canada within the International Energy Agency, even though France has refused to be a member and prefers a policy of "concertation" which seems coincidental with the views of Iran.

Similarly a firm stand by both political and legal means must be made against other forms of Arab pressure. The U.S. cannot accept the commands of the Arab Boycott office determining which American officials may be sent to Arab countries, or tolerate the blacklisting of business interests and the imposition of Arab religious discrimination against U.S. citizens and corporations as Saudi Arabia has done or permit restrictive trade practices. The fact that the value of U.S. exports to the Arab countries has increased must not seduce the U.S. into acceptance of blackmail. Nor can Arab investments in the U.S. be allowed unless they are in accordance with the laws and mores of the country. The Justice Department must watch for violations of civil rights and anti-trust laws and uphold the policy of opposition to boycotts against friendly countries, and the President might be given authority to forbid large investments by foreigners in U.S. companies if he believes this to be harmful to American interest. In academia the universities and high schools of the country must not accept the available bountiful Arab money if it is proferred on conditions which seriously qualify academic integrity and autonomy.

•

A brooding presence in the Middle East conflict has been the Soviet Union. Historically, Russia has tried to gain control of the Dardanelles, thus obtaining an outlet for its naval forces and strategic mobility. Opportunistically, the Soviet Union has probed the whole Middle East, providing assistance for regimes of different political colorations, support for either communist parties or nationalist groups, changing its relations with individual leaders and governments, providing technical assistance for a variety of projects, and signing treaties of friendship as with Egypt in 1971 and Iraq in 1972 to the detriment and sometimes peril of local Arab leftists, in its erratic attempts to gain influence and expand its power. It now supports every Arab position on the conflict and helps coordinate Arab diplomatic strategy.

The expansion of the Soviet navy in recent years has been dramatic and its logistical facilities in the area formidable. The Soviet Union is now a Mediterranean as well as a Black Sea power. Its considerable Mediterranean force can provide protection for the Arab confrontation countries. Combined with its naval forces, the Soviet air transport system and strike forces provide a capability to intervene in conventional conflicts.

The Soviet Union is well supplied with bases or facilities in the area, even in Egypt, from which its military mission was expelled in 1972, until 1976. It has a foothold in Somalia and Southern Yemen which control the southern access routes to the Suez Canal. In Somalia the Soviet use of airfields at Uanle Uen for long range reconnaissance over the Indian Ocean and its facilities at the deep water port of Berbera, at which a Soviet nuclear powered attack submarine armed with missiles called in the winter of 1975, have made that country a virtual satellite. In Aden in Southern Yemen the Russians use both the submarine base and the former British airfield for reconnaissance. In Socotra, an island in the Gulf of Aden, Soviet marines conduct exercises. In the Persian Gulf itself, Soviet minesweepers based at Basra in Iraq have undertaken intelligence activities and a Soviet naval port is being built at Um Qasr, twenty miles from Basra. From Iraq Soviet pilots have been flying reconnaissance missions over Iran and the Persian Gulf.

Unquestionably the reopening of the Suez Canal will greatly benefit the Soviet Union, allowing expanded naval missions in the Persian Gulf and in the northwest approaches of the Indian Ocean, and shortening the journey from the Black Sea to the south coast of Arabia from 11,500 to 3,200 nautical miles. Since the reopening of the Canal in June 1975 the Soviet Union has sent more ships through Suez than has any other country.

The disparity between Soviet and American resources and facilities in the Middle East and the Indian Ocean is growing. By contrast with the Soviet Indian Ocean fleet which has varied from 8 to 15 ships, the United States has only two destroyers and a command ship with occasional deployment of ships from the seventh fleet based in the Phillipines. The base at Bahrain is the only known American naval station between the Mediterranean and Diego Garcia, the British atoll in the Indian Ocean, where the U.S. has communication facilities. The U.S. has been obliged to make a sixfold increase in payments for the use of the port and has been threatened by the termination of the arrangement if the American political position is not sufficiently favorable to the Arab cause. The U.S. facilities in Asmara, Eritrea, are endangered by the civil war in the country. A small base at Masirah Island off the coast of Oman has not yet been completed.

The American strategic position has been weakened by developments in the NATO countries: the fratricidal relationship between Greece and Turkey over Cyprus—which at one stroke made the communications facilities in Kyrenia precarious, has led Greece to withdraw from NATO military commands and has produced the strong possibility that the Turkish bases will no longer be automatically available to the U.S. The dramatic changes in Portugal make the use of the bases in the Azores uncertain in the future, and the continuing intransigence of France poses an obstacle to Western unity. Israel remains the only stable friendly state in the area on whose continued cooperation the U.S. can count, and which asks in return only for diplomatic support, economic aid and military supplies for its own defense.

•

During the October 1973 war a constant anxiety of the State Department was that the growing harmonious relationship between the Soviet Union and the United States might be endangered and therefore the action of the U.S. must be considered in the light of their effect on that relationship. But this was an incorrect perception of the situation. In the war it was Russia which was responsible for the strain in relationships and which exploited the atmosphere of détente by its strong political commitment to the Arab position and by its immediate resupply of some 225,000 tons of military equipment after initially providing the confrontation Arab countries with $5.3 billion in hardware including surface-to-air missiles, anti-tank missiles and bridging equipment to cross the Suez Canal. Only belatedly in the second week of the war did the U.S. respond with an airlift of 22,300 tons to help compensate for Israeli losses. The Russian behavior was a violation of the Soviet-American understandings of May 1972 and June 1973 which spoke of the desirability of joint or separate action by each power to help alleviate tension in conflict areas. It is for the Soviet Union to show by its actions in the Middle East that it is observing the underlying assumptions of détente and the avoidance of conflict if it is to benefit from American concessions on other issues.

•

The Soviet Union must join the U.S. in helping prepare the basis for a peaceful settlement. Such a settlement can be based only on the lines of the Security Council Resolutions 242 and 338 and can result only from negotiations between the parties concerned. A compromise agreement must end the state of belligerency on the part of the Arabs and ensure the acknowledgement of the sovereignty, territorial inviolability, and political independence of states living within secure and recognized boundaries if it is to require withdrawal from occupied land by Israel. American national interest is best served by an agreement that allows a strong and viable Israel to coexist with its Arab neighbors in an atmosphere of mutual respect.

Such an agreement can now be reached only within the context of a reconvened Geneva conference. A less flamboyant policy by the U.S. does not in itself constitute a diplomatic disaster. Valuable though the Kissinger step-by-step approach was in obtaining the initial disengagement agreements, it suffered from four major deficiencies.

The first is that Israel is called on to surrender territory, most immediately in 1975 the two strategic passes and the Abu Rodeis oilfield, in return for intangible or unmeasurable concessions which would become perceptible only after the passage of time. Necessarily, Israel would require long intervals between partial agreements in order to ensure that the elements of non belligerency whether a lowering in the level of propaganda, reducing the economic and diplomatic boycott or allowing free navigation in the Suez Canal, were being put into practice.

The Israeli reluctance to yield to U.S. pressure and make concessions in the face of Arab refusal to talk of non-belligerency or "an end to the state of war" is understandable.

The second difficulty is that the step-by-step approach not only depends on the continuing magic and success of the trusted negotiator who shuttles between the parties, but also leads increasingly to the U.S. being regarded as the guarantor of Israeli good will on the one hand and of Egyptian willingness to make peace on the other. But it does not allow the parties to the conflict itself to start negotiating a just and durable peace as required by Security Council Resolutions 242 and 338. It is essential that the two parties, in a climate of mutual acceptance and recognition, participate directly in the framing of their future relationship within the context of the Security Council decisions. Any American formal guarantee, difficult to envisage in any event, can be meaningful only after a peace agreement has been signed and the Arab states have renounced their state of belligerency. The token group of 200 technicians in the Sinai cannot be regarded as embodying such a guarantee.

Reluctance to reconvene the Geneva conference has been partly due to the fear that the Soviet Union might not be helpful and that the presence of Palestinian extremists might produce deadlock. But the opportunity for Soviet mischief has always existed. Understandably, the Russians have felt slighted by their removal from the step-by-step process and annoyed at the prestige gained by the U.S. The Soviet Union at any stage of this process could encourage one of the Arab parties to the conflict to raise obstacles. On balance it would seem the better part of wisdom to have the Soviet Union as a participant in negotiations at Geneva and to convince them that their interests are better served by peace than war in the Middle East.

Russian relations with the PLO have grown increasingly official since the secret visit of Arafat to Moscow in July 1968. The Soviet Union has supplied the PLO with weapons as well as with political support and tactical advice. It is likely to support the presence of the PLO at Geneva as part of one of the delegations whose membership has been approved by all the others. But the U.S. should argue that the true voice of the Palestinian Arab population on the West Bank should be heard.

Above all, the reconvening of Geneva is necessary because it is the best way to deal with the basic cause of the Middle East conflict, the refusal of the Arab states to end the state of war with Israel and to recognize the legitimacy of the state. The Arab insistence that the state of war would end only after Israel had withdrawn from all occupied territory on the three fronts precluded any possibility of diplomatic success. Peace is still the only objective of an Israel with secure and recognized borders. Withdrawal as a unilateral act cannot be the basis of negotiations while Scud missiles in the hands of both Egypt and Syria could cause unacceptable damage to the civilian population as well as to the airfields and military installations of Israel. The difficulty with the slogan of "a piece of territory for a piece of peace" is its very intangibility. Peace, as Litvinov used to say in the 1930s, is indivisible. Geneva is now the place where the major effort to gain peace can be made.

There are three main dangers in all of this. The Russians may indeed take advantage of a reconvened Geneva meeting to reap political benefits by encouraging Arab reluctance to sign an agreement and providing the Arabs with unconditional support thus creating an asymmetry in the negotiating process. The U.S. can be expected to provide political support for the Israeli position but not to the same degree as the Soviet support of the other side.

The second problem is that almost every formal gathering of Arab leaders has led to the acceptance of an extremist formula as shown at Khartoum in 1967 and Rabat in 1974. It will take great skill on the part of U.S. diplomats to prevent another such formula and an intransigent Arab position being adopted as each Arab party strives to become the standard bearer of Arab nationalism.

The third obstacle is that neither Israel, the United States and Jordan nor the Rejection Front within the PLO itself is prepared to agree to a PLO delegation. The framework of the Geneva conference precludes the invitation of additional parties without the consent of all the present members. But a Palestinian voice of some kind must be heard.

The end of the step-by-step process does not automatically imply a resort to force. Negotiating possibilities exist either in the form of yet another attempt at the Kissinger shuttle service in Golan, an interim agreement with Jordan or in the kind of proximity talks envisaged by Secretary Rogers in 1970. But on balance, Geneva seems the best road to peace.

40

What's In It For Us? America's National Interest in Israel

By Aaron Wildavsky

My argument will be that America's highest national interest is preservation of what gives it its own sense of self-worth — religious liberty, democratic institutions, moral character, and western culture. If the idea of America became illegitimate to Americans, nothing else would much matter, for our people would have lost both their ability to identify interests and their will to support them. Well and good, one might say, but where does Israel fit in? In the past, our forebears used to refer to America as their Zion, their promised land. In the present, it is hard to find a single objection to Israel (other than its small size) that does not apply equally to America. Israel alone raises questions of the legitimacy of immigration, the value of religion, the desirability of democracy, and the viability of western culture. To ask if Israel deserves support is to ask the same question about America.

Dr. Wildavsky is Professor of Political Science and a member of the Survey Research Center, University of California, Berkeley. His numerous publications include *Presidential Elections,* with Nelson Polsby (Charles Scribner's Sons); *The Great Détente Disaster: Oil and the Decline of American Foreign Policy,* with Edward Friedland and Paul Seabury (Basic Books, 1975); *Budgeting: A Comparative Theory of Budgetary Processes* (rev. ed., Transaction Books, 1986). He was made Honorary Doctor of Law, Brooklyn College, 1977, and received the Charles A. Merriam Award, presented by the American Political Science Association in 1975, among other honors.

Can there be a concept of national interest that does not include concern for a nation's cultural heritage, its liberties, and its religious and moral character? The answer is "no" because even the narrowest definition — national interest as vital to the physical survival of the country — includes a moral preference for the survival of the nation's way of life. If this were not so, if existence alone were the aim of national policy, then either pure passivity or unlimited aggression would be adequate. On one hand, armies could be abolished and the nation laid open to all comers; alternatively, all efforts could concentrate on national defense even if morality, liberty, and culture fell by the way. But no one, presumably, argues that survival should be America's only interest, or that either pure passivity or all-out aggression is the best way to achieve it. No, the argument is always that the things we care about most are compatible with survival. Like the lady in the lifeboat who refuses to choose which of her children to save, Americans try to make all basic values compatible with surviving to enjoy them. The question here is whether they go along with support for Israel.

Criteria for American National Interest in Israel

To become operative, interests must be embodied in actions. In order to choose among actions, we need criteria to let us identify policies that serve American interests and to rule out those that do not. Now criteria may be plausible or helpful, but not necessarily correct or true. In action, interests embody values — and values are not neutral. No particular set can be absolutely right or wrong, therefore, criteria, like interests themselves, necessarily are subjective. We are looking for criteria that will be helpful — few enough to be manageable; focused, so they are useful in distinguishing among alternatives; and congruent with American values, in order to command general support. I propose three to help us decide what kind of policies best serve America: (1) America's interest in its own self-worth (legitimacy); (2) its interests in having allies (solidarity); and (3) its interest in being able to choose its own future interests (autonomy).

The first criterion, *legitimacy,* suggests that any reason for rejecting Israel must not apply equally well to the United States. If Israel is judged unreliable because governments there change, it should be remembered that the United States also, as a democratic regime, practices alternation in office. If Israel is deemed unworthy because its founders displaced native inhabitants, how much greater must have been our offenses in regard to Indians and Mexicans. If it were accepted, furthermore, that no nation whose founders were born elsewhere could be judged as legitimate, there would be even less rationale for putting America's legitimacy above that of Israel, whose people have been in Palestine from the beginning of recorded history.

The second criterion, *solidarity,* implies that arguments against Israel must not be such as to apply equally well to most of America's allies, for then we would not be talking about America's lack of interest in Israel in particular, but about why the United States did not need (or should not want) allies in general. For example, opponents of Israel claim that Israel does not possess substantial military forces; would this not rule out Japan and Canada? Or, the argument is made that there are no contiguous borders between the United States and Israel; with the exceptions of Mexico and Canada, what allies would that leave us? Which allies would feel safe if the same principles used for abandoning Israel were applied to them? If democracy and a common cultural heritage were not enough, what would it take to stay on America's most-favored-nation list? Greece and Italy, for instance, have little going for them other than cultural affinity and awkward attempts at democratic politics. The United States gives them more than it gets in economic support; and their reliability, in terms of political cleavages, is suspect. Britain is better off politically but not economically. Small fry, like Belgium and the Netherlands, acceptable on those grounds, are not rich enough to be worth protecting on that ground alone. How about Canada, Japan, and Norway? Serious questions can be raised about each. Norway has oil but can hardly defend itself; Japan is rich but far away, hence difficult to defend; and Canada is close but suffering from internal political conflict.

Nevertheless, even if a few nations did merit American support, would they, alone and exposed, think it worth carrying on? In the absence of recent experience it is easy to underestimate the demoralization of being left with few culturally compatible nations in one's world. In such circumstances, might not Americans themselves begin to question the worth of their own existence? The choice of cultural isolation is not one America should want to make. The moral of the story is all too clear: if the United States tries hard enough, it can find ample reasons to reject any ally as unworthy or indefensible — and end up alone.

The third criterion is *autonomy,* the ability of the United States to decide in future circumstances whether and how far to intervene in a Middle East conflict. Whatever the rationale for adopting a "trip-wire" situation in Europe, created by the presence there of American troops, such an automatic reaction system would not be a good idea in the more volatile Middle East. The number of conflicts, after all, is likely to be large and their direction (who is fighting against whom) and duration (who will be involved for how long) hard to predict. Even with the willingness to get involved, the United

States would prefer to choose the form (military, diplomatic, economic) and the forum (the United Nations, a Geneva conference, bilateral negotiations) before committing itself to specific actions. Who argues otherwise? Almost everyone who suggests that the United States impose and/or guarantee a settlement stipulates in advance what it would do if or (more likely) when the agreements broke down.

Few argue that legitimacy, solidarity, and autonomy are unimportant as generalized national interests. It remains to be seen what happens when they are measured against the specific mix of military and economic interests with which the United States must also be concerned.

Military Interests

If national interest in the Middle East were determined solely by military factors the United States would do well to back the side that can defend itself with American weapons but without American troops. If the Soviet Union intervened, it could not do so simply by sending weapons; in fact the regimes it supports, as history shows, lack the internal cohesion necessary to sustain military effort should the tide turn against them. Whenever its allies or proteges are defeated, the USSR must face the difficult choice between letting them go down or risking the use of its own soldiers far away from home. By contrast, the United States, as it were, can meet the situation by remote control. Turn the matter around: What would American public reaction be if our government had to send soldiers in support of undemocratic, unstable, and untrustworthy states whose support could not be guaranteed even after they were saved?

Some people, perhaps too friendly to Israel for its own good, view Israel as strategically important, thus constituting *ipso facto* a vital American national interest. This position in part is just loose talk: the Middle East somehow is strategic in that it lies between East and West—next door to Africa, near the Indian Ocean, and along the Mediterranean—thus leaving open a path to the sea and thence to Southern Europe. What is left is tough talk: Israel becomes a strategic interest by providing the United States with bases for its troops and nuclear weapons. With friends like this, however, Israel would need few enemies, saving itself, so to speak, only to become an occupied country. The rationale for its very existence—the struggle for cultural identity and independent national life —would be lost in its defense.

Only in desperation would America wish to use Israel as a military base. The United States would have to be unable to refuel its planes or berth its ships or keep its weapons anywhere in Europe and the Mediterranean. Israel would have to remain the only friendly patch of ground in a hostile world. The thrust of American foreign policy is to avoid such situations, not to bring them about.

The future military importance of one country to another is determined, not by the resources that exist in some passive sense (like a lump of clay), but by those resources that the country is (a) willing and (b) able to employ with (c) consistency over periods of time. The combined wealth and manpower of the Middle East is much greater than that of Israel. But Israel neutralizes this advantage because its government can mobilize far more of its national resources. As all Israelis know, their government is a good tax collector; it is also a superb conscriptor of men and women. When one takes a dynamic rather than a static view of national resources, Israel is more desirable as an ally.

Suppose we compare Israel with its Middle Eastern neighbors as potential American allies by trying a gruesome but instructive mental experiment. What would be the effect (in these countries) of losing the national leader, the top ten, and the next hundred leaders, or the top thousand, and ten thousand public officials? In Egypt, Syria, Jordan, Libya and Iran, for instance, the assassination of the national leader might drastically alter the nation's politics. No one knows what would happen after a Qadhafi, a Sadat, a Hussein, an Assad, or a Shah left the scene. Even if one person were not crucial, the removal of ten or one hundred at the top might well topple an entire political regime. Only in Israel can we confidently expect that any government which took office, even after all leading public officials had been removed, would be similar—in political structure and in public policy—to its predecessor. That concensus on fundamentals among virtually all political factions is the true meaning of stability. Dictatorships are good at appearing stable while democracies are better at hiding stability beneath surface intrigues. Only when the surface calm of a dictatorship is shattered does it become clear that so few people make the difference between continuity and chaos.

Nothing, as we know, comes for free; there is also no ally, stable and steadfast though it may be, that is incapable of resisting influence from abroad. A common objection to alliance with Israel, after all, is that its difficult, often recalcitrant leaders make necessary numerous compromises. How could it be otherwise? The very closeness of the relationship between the leaders and the led stems from its democratic character. Such a relationship is based on consent, not coercion: and we know it will last even if the current set of leaders is replaced.

Economic Interests

A quantitative estimate of Israel's economic worth may be had from the latest (fall of 1976) OPEC conference. Those we may designate as commercial nations, because they want to maximize their oil income, wanted a 15 percent price increase. Saudi Arabia offered 5 percent for six months on the condition that the United States follow a favorable policy in the Middle East. Can we not say, then, that the existence of Israel is worth approximately 10 percent of the OPEC oil bill in America ($3.4 billion), a sum exceeding the $2 billion plus that the United States now gives. Even in pure economic terms, Arab need for American assistance in regard to Israel may be worth more than it costs to supply Israel.

I do not say this to argue that America can gain economically from Israel, but only to point out that economic loss is not automatic. In fact, economic interests cut both ways. Obviously the Arab oil-producing nations are much richer than Israel. They are more important now to America than ever before because of their impact on its economy. Whether this impact would be lessened by friendlier foreign relations, or by actions designed to drive down the price of oil, is not self-evident. More important, even if the flow and price of oil are paramount, America needs a strong and friendly Israel so that oil producers interested in gaining concessions from Israel will have a need for America to intercede for them. America needs Israel in order to be able to bargain with Arab oil producers.

But what about the threat of an oil embargo? It is a double-edged sword, of greater potential threat to those who use it than to those against whom it is aimed. Embargo is far better as threat than as practice, for it would simultaneously divide OPEC (the Arab and non-Arab members) and unify its opponents. The unifying force in OPEC is the common interest of its members in making far more money together than they could singly, and thus in competition with each other. Based on past practice, there is little reason to believe that non-Arab members—Iran, Venezuela, Indonesia, Nigeria—would join an embargo. By receiving supplies through these producers, as well as by using stockpiles, we could blunt the force of any embargo.

Those who submit to open "oilmail" may influence others to take advantage of this weakness. When Saudi Arabia made its case for imposing a five percent oil price increase (one percent equaling a mere billion dollars), it also wanted the United States to make commercial concessions on various other valuable international commodities. An important precedent always implicit in "oilmail" has now been made public: Oil prices as well as oil embargo can be used for additional political and economic purposes. Once the target of "oilmail" is not limited to U.S. policy with regard to Israel, it becomes a general purpose weapon that can be used to achieve a variety of objectives. If

America does not support Israel in the face of "oilmail," then it had better ask which of its other interests are worth more than Israel; those which are not, then, would be subject to the same threat: If the United States does (or fails to do) X or Y the price of oil will rise to Z. "We wouldn't stand for it," you say. Who ever would have thought that tiny, feudal, and despotic regimes could be pressuring the United States in public?

Cultural Interests

To have interests implies willingness (up to a point), to sacrifice something for them. Unless there are things one is prepared to give up, interests are only unfocused desires. Asked to lay it on the line, how much would Americans be willing to sacrifice for what interests?

My list would include religious liberty, political freedom, economic opportunity, and such other practices as ethnic pluralism, and freedom to travel and choose goods, which define our way of life. Put the matter the other way: Who among us would want to defend an America which lacked these aspects of what is loosely called culture? Indeed, it is this cultural complex that we call the American way of life. If its legitimacy were undermined—if political liberty were a farce, if ethnic pluralism were a delusion, if advancement depended wholly on political favoritism—America would collapse from within long before it was threatened from without. America's first national interest, therefore, is to solidify its own sense of self-worth.

Translated into international terms, America's primary interest is to foster an environment hospitable to its culture. "Fortress America" might be a military goal, but it could never be the cultural one, for that requires a number of nations sharing sites where Western culture is (and historically has been) practiced. Foremost among these, because of the critical part they played in creating our culture, are Jerusalem, home of Judaism and Christianity, and Athens and Rome, originators of our secular civilization.

I presume to remind us of the child's ABC's of Western culture because the cultural importance of these places is not matched in this era by their economic or military significance. Greece and Italy hardly could defend themselves against external attack. They have little to offer economically, and their loans, likely to be succeeded by larger loans, are unlikely to be repaid to the United States and other Western creditors. Much the same, I might add, could be said of Britain, which is not without cultural-historic value among ourselvès and other English-speaking states.

Now, in regard to Israel, it is said that sentiment is no substitute for substance. Israel is outnumbered in the Middle East. It is poor while its neighbors grow rich. Israel lacks oil because it is badly located. America would profit materially by being on the good side of the Arabs; it has nothing to gain from Israel. America's interest in Israel, they say, is idealistic—the kind of interest that cannot survive without a material base. Thus, to borrow a phrase from Trotsky, Israel's opponents consign it to the dung-heap of history. And without a material base ("How many divisions does the Pope have?" as Stalin was reported to have asked) America, according to this logic, can have no national interest in Israel.

Need I say that Americans would be devastated if London, Rome, Athens, or Jerusalem fell into hostile hands? Deprived of cultural ties and affectionate memories, we could hardly help but wonder if our days were numbered, and whether cultures like ours were doomed to disappear. Let us just say the decline of the West would not be good for American morale.

Presumably it is this cultural interest that is called "ideal" as opposed to "material." Why things worth fighting for should be separated from what it takes to fight for them is beyond me. Would the capacity to use force not be affected by the strength (or lack of it) of the belief in self-worth that underlies the will to defend oneself?

Culture alone, considered as pure preference, is not enough without the means for its realization. As Jung says, "The man who promises everything is sure to fulfill nothing, and everyone who promises too much is in danger of using evil means in order to carry out his promises, and is already on the road to perdition." Interests may become delusions if they are incapable of being realized in actions. America's cultural interest in Israel must be supportable. How, then, might it be managed?

Procedural Rules for Expressing American National Interests

Goals for America, we now see, lie in preserving a compatible culture in Israel as well as in the Western world, and reducing the probability of any being drawn into war. To secure these aims the United States needs not only a formula for an immediate settlement but also rules to enhance the prospect of permanent peace. These rules should be designed to provide the parties at conflict with incentives not only to settle, but also to monitor agreements reached so that the need for American intervention is reduced.

The first rule is that crime (read, moving armed forces across boundaries) should not pay. This means both that the United States will help negate gains won by aggression and that it will not intervene to prevent losses sustained by the aggressor. The superpowers must not provide insurance policies against the risks of aggressive war. So long as the parties believe they can attack each other with impunity (if they win, they win, but if they lose, they are rendered able to try again) violence will grow. However promising any settlement that the United States might help negotiate, inevitably it will break down if one side can significantly better its position by force.

The rule of force is essential, but it cannot stand alone, for then those who gain by the *status quo* could prevail by doing nothing. Thus our second rule is one of reciprocity: Each side gets as much as it gives; for each degree of peace conceded by Egypt, Syria, Jordan and their allies, Israel must make a corresponding territorial concession. The most is given for normalization of relations—trade, travel, diplomatic relations, etc.—and the least, but still something, for nonbelligerency. The more Israel and its neighbors yield to each other, the more they should expect to get.

Our third rule is to leave room for error by segmenting and separating solutions. If an overall settlement means that each element is tightly linked to each other, the malfunction of a single part can destroy the entire edifice. By building up agreements part-by-part, all parts will not have to be assembled anew if only one fails to function. Breakdowns thus can take place without imperiling an entire structure of agreements and without resulting in the movement of armies immediately next to Israel's heartland or in the need for a U.S. presence in local disputes.

The United States should be as much concerned about repairing breakdowns as about initial agreement. That agreements may have to be concluded simultaneously does not mean that all have to collapse at the same time. If assaults took place across the Lebanese border, for example, the United States would not wish this relapse to be followed by fighting along the Eygptian, Jordanian, and Syrian borders as well.

The fourth rule, that all agreements should be self-policing, is aimed in part at avoiding unwanted American involvement. Specifically it means that joint Israeli-Egyptian-Syrian-Jordanian patrols are to be made responsible for various regulatory tasks such as maintaining demilitarized zones. For one thing, these exercises will provide practice in living together. For another, joint involvement means that the parties must at least try to repair breakdowns before calling for outside help. It is not in America's interest to get credit for an agreement that will lead to direct (and quite possibly armed) U.S. involvement every time something goes wrong. Alternatively, it would be morally debilitating to America and its allies to look the other way when obvious violations of the peace accords take place, perhaps because there are so many violations it is difficult to justify intervention in each and every situation.

The fifth and final rule is to implicate others. The Soviet Union should be included in (not kept out of) negotiations so that it shares responsibility for the results. Since there can be no viable agreement without the USSR, its participation is essential for its consent. Credit for a settlement should be shared to avoid discredit for a dissolution of all that has gone before.

Are there no limits to this American national interest in Israel? In other parts of the world there are limits to American action. If Canada were invaded, the United States presumably would intervene. But in some situations—if internal discord rendered Canada militarily indefensible, or its alleged oppression against its French-speaking countrymen rendered it morally culpable, or it was trying to involve the United States in an unwanted war—the United States might well take no action. No commitment is (or should be) total. Therefore America's desire for a speedy settlement in the Middle East should not lead to its being sucked in unawares. To go on dreaming that every problem can be solved—an old American illusion—could prove especially unfortunate in the Middle East. A settlement in the Middle East is in America's interest only if it initiates and sustains a process through which contending parties maintain the incentive to solve their own disputes.

The Process is the Purpose

It may not be in America's interest to seek a comprehensive, once-and-for-all solution to the Israeli-Arab dispute. Why? Because the process of negotiating a single solution could lead to overexposure and over-commitment. Overexposure is inevitable because the United States would have to negotiate each and every point in public. Over-commitment comes from overexposure: Since American prestige would then be visibly attached to a settlement, the party over whom the U.S. has most leverage (and of whom it is asking the greatest sacrifice—no doubt Israel, but possibly the Palestinians as well) will ask for guarantees. Thus the United States will find itself saddled with treaty commitments requiring it to move in if Israel is invaded or to coerce Israel if it reneges. By promising Arab Palestinians a state of their own, the United States (and what is worse, its soldiers) would be in the middle of the Middle East, directly involved in the numerous violations of the settlement that are bound to occur when an imposed rather than a mutually (un)satisfactory solution is negotiated.

Thus there can be no permanent peace in the sense of a solution that remains entirely stable. How, then, can conflict be limited and structured so that its creative elements are retained and its destructive tendencies minimized? By making it worthwhile for the parties directly involved in the dispute to make and to maintain their own agreements. And how might this be done? By reinforcing the rules of force, reciprocity, error, self-policing, and implication that enhance mutual accommodation.

Here lies the American dilemma in the Middle East; autonomy is ultimately at odds with solidarity. To support solidarity it is necessary to let others know in advance that the United States will not allow Israel to be invaded with impunity. To preserve autonomy, the United States should not commit itself to specific actions in advance. No doubt history will tell us how this trade-off is likely to be made. As Al Smith used to say, let's look at the record: America has intervened before. America, under different Presidents and parties, has pledged itself to preserve Israel; both parties' national platforms include these pledges. President Carter has reinforced them. So has Congress. Of course, there is risk even in a general commitment; but so is there risk in its absence and, worst of all, in vacillation, for that tempts the worst impulses without having decided one will not thwart them. There is no easy way out—one single decisive act to assure permanent peace—but only the steadfast application of rules that cannot eliminate but can reduce risk.

If there is risk in over-commitment there is equal danger in the other direction: Because it has managed so well in the past, because its deeds of "derring-do" are only too well-known, Israel's capacity to go on confronting adverse conditions may be overestimated. How long can its people live with the constant awareness that they may be invaded and over-run with few friends to help them? How long can they cope with a super-heated, overinflated economy in which it is unwise to save, and with which it is impossible to keep up? Morale good enough to sustain a single heroic effort may be dissipated by too many small sacrifices. The result could be sudden collapse, followed by a precipitous rescue effort—much more dangerous for them (and us) than continuous support. If Israel is worth preserving, the United States should stick to rules that will make it less necessary to take risks when it is very late or very dangerous.

The Moral Objection

The interests I have discussed are self-interests for America. Having allies or even supporting similar cultures are interests the United States maintains because it believes they are good ones, not because they necessarily represent universal moral principles. That support of Israel is in America's interest does not ipso facto make it right.

Is it arguable that Israel has no moral right to survive? In America, to be sure, the question is always raised the other way around: as ex-Senator Fulbright said, "It is in our interest for Israel to survive because we *wish* Israel to survive,"[1] suggesting that Israel's survival is morally right but materially wrong. Yet if the moral justification for Israel is so obvious, why is it so often challenged abroad? Why indeed?

If Israel truly is all that we know it to be — politically free, morally humane, an expression of the best in Western civilization — why does it have so many enemies? This apparent anomaly must be faced. Surface answers suggest themselves. Arabs regard Israelis as intruders and dispossessors, Europeans see them as an inconvenience in making arrangements with Arabs, for the sins of Europe during the holocaust have been transferred to the Middle East. The Soviet Union sees an opportunity to gain a foothold by exploiting enmity against a nation based on a different political system. African and Asian nations see Israel opposed to their "third world" compatriots. At a deeper level, however, we must all recognize that Israel is an anomaly in the world that has taken shape since the Second World War.

This incongruity has been well-expressed by a respected student of Middle Eastern affairs, Professor George Lenczowski, who observes that Israel is the only major exception to the "movement of liberation and anti-colonialism promoted on a world-wide basis by the United Nations and practiced by the major Western powers." Lenczowski says that Israel is a state established

> . . . by immigrant alien colonists in the teeth of native opposition . . . Israel and its supporters in the United States have often argued that opposition to Jewish settlement in Palestine is artificially spurred by self-seeking Arab politicians and that the ordinary Arabs of Palestine stand to gain from Jewish immigration by being exposed to better agricultural techniques, greater employment opportunities, and improved health standards . . . These assertions might have been correct, and yet the world today has repudiated them, recognizing instead the right to independence as a higher value.[2]

It does no good to say that the United States and the Soviet Union have been far more expansionist in their time, or that Israel has paid for its land whereas others have simply seized what they wanted, or even that Arab Palestinians would have a state if Israel had not been attacked in 1948. True but irrelevant. If self-determination circa 1945 is the standard, Israel wasn't there and the Arabs (though not of course the Palestinians, whose sense of national identity was created by the conflict with Israel) were. The basic argument against Israel is not strategic or material but moral and cultural. Israel is attacked because it represents a different kind of culture—Western culture in a non-Western area of the world.

Whether anyone likes it or not, Israel is of, by and for the West. By deciding for development, Israel feels, smells, and looks like a Western country. Unlike Vietnam or Korea or Angola or Jamaica or wherever you want, Israel is not part of the periphery but contains the core of the West. For better or for worse, Israel is us.

America's national interest in the security and prosperity of Israel rests on this: any moral argument which condemns Israel applies equally to America itself and any cultural argument against Israel applies to all of Western civilization. In Israel we Americans are brought face to face with our own origins. By acting as if there were no American national interest in Israel, the United States would simultaneously be rejecting its own religious, moral, political, and cultural identity. America has a national interest in Israel precisely because no other nation invokes at one and the same time so many basic American values. What's in it for us?—Our own purposes, values, self-worth, and any other reasons we Americans have for believing in ourselves. When we ask whether we have an interest in Israel we are really asking about ourselves.[3]

FOOTNOTES

1. J. William Fulbright, "United States Interests in the Middle East," (*Middle East International,* December 1975) p. 6.

2. George Lenczowski, "United States Interests in the Middle East," (*American Enterprise Institute for Public Policy Research,* October 1968) p. 110

3. This substitution of Israel for America—one promised land for another—may explain a phenomenon I have often observed: Show me someone who believes Israel is not worth defending and I will show you one who thinks America is unworthy.

41

"Common Sense" About Middle East Diplomacy: Implications for U.S. Policy in the Near Term

By Adam M. Garfinkle

Introduction

Since this is written in 1984, I may be forgiven if I quote George Orwell: "We have now sunk to such a depth at which the restatement of the obvious is the first duty of intelligent men."

My purpose here is to restate what I take to be obvious propositions about the character of Middle East peace diplomacy, especially the U.S. role in that diplomacy, and then to draw out some modest policy-relevant implications for the United States in the near term.

Admittedly, what is obvious to one person may be disputable to another. Moreover, "obvious" truths sometimes turn out to be not only wrong but damaging if used as bases for action. This is well illustrated by an alternative set of "obvious" propositions that nowadays pass for common knowledge in many circles, not only in Europe — where the common knowledge is so pervasive as to be impervious to reasonable dissent[1] — but also in certain offices of the U.S. Departments of State and Defense. It is the application of this "common sense," indeed, that has brought U.S. Middle East diplomacy to its current nadir. Since it is more difficult to see the truth when the landscape is littered with falsehood, perhaps it is best to state and discuss some of this "common sense" before proceeding further.

Dr. Garfinkle is Research Associate and Coordinator of the Political Studies Program at the Foreign Policy Research Institute and a Lecturer in Political Science at the University of Pennsylvania. He is the author of numerous articles on Middle Eastern and U.S. defense policies.

The Common Knowledge, According to NEA[2]

The reigning common knowledge on Middle Eastern affairs may be summed up in ten propositions:

(1) The main impediment to peace in the Middle East is the chronic non-solution of the Palestinian Arab national problem. If Palestinian Arab national rights are recognized by all parties, especially Israel, then an honorable compromise "two-state" solution can be found.

(2) Peace cannot be envisioned, therefore, without an Israeli territorial withdrawal from the West Bank and the Gaza Strip (Latrunean adjustments only) and the establishment of a Palestinian state; it is a hoax to suggest that the Palestinian national problem could or should be settled east of the river, i.e., at Jordan's expense.

(3) The Palestine Liberation Organization is the only near-universally recognized spokesman for Palestinian nationalism within the Arab world and among the Palestinian people, and is therefore a proper and legitimate interlocutor in Middle East diplomacy.

(4) Israel is a powerful state whose territorial ambitions have been largely satisfied. Since the Arabs are weak and divided, Israel has no incentive to make peace. Therefore, only considerable pressure and the invocation of material sanctions by the United States can bring Israel to make the necessary concessions to achieve peace.

(5) Applying such sanctions to Israel has up to now been prevented by the disproportionate power of the Jewish lobby in U.S. domestic politics.

(6) A shift to a more "even-handed" policy would benefit the United States because good relations with more than a dozen Arab states, with over 100 million people (and much oil), are clearly more important geostrategically than good relations with a single Jewish state with three million people.

(7) The Arab-Israeli conflict and the more crucially important security of the Persian Gulf are inextricably linked politically, and no solution to the latter problem can be imagined without progress in the former problem.

(8) Since U.S. relations with the most important Arab states (the "moderates" and the "oil producers") can only be improved at the expense of the "unnatural" and "artificial" closeness of U.S.-Israeli relations, Israel *cum* ally is a strategic liability to the United States.

(9) The step-by-step approach to peace is too slow (thanks to Israeli negotiating tactics) and worse, too fragile, because such an approach divides the Arabs, making each successive "step" harder. Only a comprehensive package solution with full international backing (read Soviet backing) is adequate.

(10) The Soviet Union has neither the will nor the ability to obstruct a fair comprehensive solution if its local allies favor it.

There *is* a grain of truth in some of these propositions. But taken together as a sort of policy *gestalt*, as it almost always is, it is seriously flawed, containing errors both of commission and omission, as well as sometimes masking certain visceral inclinations that have no relevance to policy analysis.

Calling Common Knowledge to Account

(1) The non-solution of the Palestinian national problem is clearly troublesome, particularly for the Arab states that have hosted large numbers of Palestinians — Syria, Kuwait, Saudi Arabia, and especially Lebanon and Jordan. Ideally, too, a settlement premised on compromise and co-ownership of western Palestine[3] is the accepted solution of the world community at large, as attested by the 1947 United Nations partition resolution, United Nations Security Council Resolution 242 of 1967, and many other resolutions since then. But the foreign policy of a superpower cannot be framed around the ideal; it must be framed around the possible. What is best lies outside of time; what is possible always lies ahead, not behind. Thus, the resurrection of the 1947 partition borders is not possible, nor is, as will be seen below, the precise territorial *status quo ante* of June 5, 1967.

Even if the non-solution of the Palestinian national problem were the main impediment to peace, it does not follow that the burden for removing that impediment should fall so heavily, or exclusively, on Israel. It was not Israel's fault that no Palestinian state was set up in 1948-1949; it was King Abdallah's, who had the tacit acquiescence of the Arab League and the support of Great Britain. The Palestinian national problem is an Israeli *and* an Arab problem; both must have a hand in settling it.

Finally, the recognition by Israel of Palestinian Arab national rights, even if simultaneous with the Palestinian recognition of Israel's legitimacy, is not necessarily a harbinger of a just settlement. It may instead be a harbinger for the solution of the Palestinian national problem at the cost of recreating the Jewish national problem. There are many who claim that more Arabs today than ever before, including Palestinians, accept Israel's existence and that Israeli recognition of Palestinian national rights would cause a veritable avalanche of Arab moderation. But in many parts of the world, political concessions are viewed not as an indicator of a willingness for pragmatic compromise but as an indication of weakness and decaying willpower. There is a great deal of difference between "accepting Israel" as a fact of life — which an increasing number of Arabs do — and "accepting Israel" as a legitimate expression of Jewish national rights to even part of Palestine — which almost no Arabs do. The latter kind of acceptance is a matter of principle, the former is a function of the transient balance of power. It reminds one of the traditional Arab Muslim notion of *darura*, an honorable truce born of necessity. The Palestine National Covenant still stands, and powerful forces throughout the Arab (and Muslim) world still refuse to come to terms with an Israel within any borders whatsoever. Between 1949 and 1967, when the Arab states successfully contained the Palestinian national movement and when there was no question about Israeli "occupied territory," there was also no peace. And though it is seldom spoken of in public, there is still considerable latent and not-so-latent anti-Semitism in the world. So the frustration of Palestinian nationalism is only half the problem at best, the protection of Jewish national rights in the longer term being an issue of equal significance.

(2) As to the matter of an Israeli territorial withdrawal, it is true that no stable and formal peace on Israel's eastern frontier is imaginable that does not require renewed Arab sovereignty over major parts of the West Bank (and perhaps Gaza). It is also true that the "Jordan is Palestine" argument of the Israeli right is something of a hoax. Only in a narrow and artificial sense is it legally proper to speak of Jordan as Palestine, the reference being to the brief period between the Balfour Declaration and the Churchill White Paper of 1922.[4] (And why any Arab, any Zionist, or anyone else for that matter, should accept British imperial *diktats* as the source of legal legitimacy for any contemporary Middle Eastern state is truly a mystery.) Finally, it is true that any "returned" territory probably cannot revert to the exact political condition that obtained before the June 1967 War, i.e., to exclusive Jordanian sovereignty. But this is where the truth of this proposition stops.

Withdrawal does not necessarily and cannot practically mean total withdrawal, as posited by the common knowledge. Nor, simply because Jordan is *not* in fact Palestine, is Jordan irrelevant to the future of any territories that Israel may agree to relinquish. In reality, of course, Palestinians, like Jews, are attached to Palestine between the river and the sea. In reality, too, Hashemite Jordan's destiny and that of the Palestinians are inseparable, a conspiracy of history and demography if there ever was one. This is why there will not be an independent Palestinian state in the West Bank, for even if Israel were not determined to prevent it, Jordan would be. So, there must be withdrawal in order for there to be peace, but the withdrawal cannot be total, and there is a nearly wall-to-wall consensus in Israel against returning to the exact lines of June 5, 1967. There must be Palestinian participation in the governing of whatever is returned, but it must be something less than exclusive Palestinian sovereignty and it cannot ignore Jordan's interests.

(3) As for the PLO, there is much truth in the assertion that the Arafat wing, at least, is more or less legitimate in the eyes of Palestinians, if not also the Arab states. That the PLO leadership is not democratically elected is irrelevant; what Arab government is? That the PLO's status has been gained by default — a consequence of Israeli occupation policies since 1967 more than anything else — is also irrelevant. What is not irrelevant is that Israel cannot be expected to parley with an organization whose *raison d'être* is Israel's destruction. Moreover, the PLO is incapable of coming to practical decisions as an organization, and is in fact not *an* organization at all. Indeed, each time something goes wrong for the PLO, a process of internal escalation takes place which seems further to mortgage the future of the organization to its most extreme and recalcitrant elements. Even if the PLO heals its internal wounds, to insist on explicit PLO participation in peace negotiations is to insist on paralysis.

As for U.S. policy, there are other factors to consider. The PLO does have limited power to obstruct progress toward peace, and it also participates in inter-Arab politics. U.S. diplomacy cannot ignore the PLO. But "talking to" the PLO, which the last four U.S. administrations have done, is not the same thing as "recognizing" the PLO, thereby explicitly endorsing its claims of legitimacy. Those who have urged the United States to "recognize" the PLO, including most of our erstwhile European allies, fail to see that recognition is itself a diplomatic concession and have failed, too, to consider which side is weaker and ought to be forced to give something in return for the establishment of a formal relationship.[5] To its credit, the United States has so far resisted this bad advice.

This is not to say, however, that the only policy choice the United States has is to try to bend the PLO toward moderation through an extensive informal relationship. This has been tried; it has not worked. Instead, the United States could elect to wait until the PLO is displaced or destroyed, and could give at least modest help in this direction. We are told that the PLO "is a fact," but just as nothing seems to endure like the provisional in international relations, facts can be and are occasionally undone. That Israel is also "a fact" is not usually an influential argument within most Palestinian councils. At the start of the al-Fatah mutiny in the late spring of 1983, Nicholas Veliotes, then Assistant Secretary of State for Near Eastern and South Asian (NEA) Affairs was asked his view of the mutiny. He answered that insofar as the mutiny made it more difficult for the PLO to reach a positive unified decision on the Reagan Plan, it was an unfortunate development.[6] But the PLO never had taken, and as then constituted, never would or could have taken a unified policy decision that might have advanced U.S. policy objectives. It did not occur to NEA until much later that a weakened PLO might facilitate the development of an alternative Palestinian political "voice" in conjunction with local West Bankers and Jordan that would take a far more pragmatic view toward both Israel and the Reagan Plan. As it happened, the development of such a "voice" did advance in the wake of the war in Lebanon and drew Mr. Arafat toward it, only to be opposed and successfully suppressed (temporarily?) by Syria. Had the United States not consistently misread Syrian ambitions and capabilities from June of 1982 to October of 1983, the Syrians might have failed instead.

(4) The contention that Israel has no incentive to make peace owing to its great power is a malicious half-truth. Israel is strong today by many measures. But Israel was not always so strong militarily, and the local power balance is subject to swift change owing to the advance of modern military technology and the eagerness of the world's arms merchants.[7] Moreover, Israel's increased strength is roughly proportional to its increased dependence on the United States. Israelis remember well their betrayal by France in 1967, and for these two reasons, Israel does not *feel* its strength, particularly in the aftermath of the Lebanese War.

It is true that the Likud government of 1977-84 had no intention of withdrawing from the West Bank or from the Golan Heights. Since even Israel's greatest benefactor opposed Likud's attitude toward the West Bank and Golan, it is fair to say that in the final analysis Israel's unwillingness to negotiate the return of these territories, or even parts thereof, has rested on the plain fact that no one could wrest them away. It is also true that even a Labor government willing to negotiate peace on the basis of territorial withdrawal and compromise would have its diplomatic program bolstered by military strength. But that is where the truth ends.

If Israel is strong enough not to need peace, then how does one explain the withdrawal from Sinai? Why do its people so ardently desire peace? And why does at least half its electorate favor peace even at the expense of land? Israeli foreign policy cannot be explained away as a kind of mechanical *Machtpolitik*. It is at the same time sad and amusing to hear the argument from Third World countries and their sympathizers that the United States should force a strong Israel to make peace. What is implied by U.S. pressure if not peace by imposition, a kind of post-colonial gunboat diplomacy? To hear Indians and Pakistanis, Iraqis and Iranians, Somalis and Ethiopians all calling for such an imposed settlement is to be reminded that we can all endure the misfortunes of others.[8] But it is perhaps too much to expect "citizens" of military dictatorships, sham democracies, and other petty tyrannies to see foreign policy as anything other than *Machtpolitik*, or to understand how foreign policy is formulated in a true democracy.

(5) The so-called Jewish lobby *is* strong in the United States. It tries to influence policy and sometimes it succeeds. The same is true of the Greek lobby, the AMA, the AFL-CIO, the "peace lobby," and many other groups. And like these other issue-oriented pressure groups, the Jewish lobby is

patriotically American by its own lights. What is wrong with that? The arguments that pro-Israeli groups make about the strategic value of Israel to the United States may be correct or incorrect, but their right to make them is not open to question as long as the United States remains a free society. Moreover, there is good reason for government decision-makers to accept many of the arguments of the pro-Israel lobby, whatever their feelings about religion or about Jews.

(6) It is undeniable that U.S. material and geopolitical interests in the Arab world are important and diverse, but the proposition that the Arabs are more important than the Israelis is without substance. The Arab countries are politically distinct and are often, if not always, in contention with one another. Even if Israel did not exist, advancing U.S. interests in the Arab world would not be easy. For similar reasons, the numerical disparity between Arabs and Israelis is almost meaningless in practice. It is after all, not a matter of choosing between Israel and the "Arab world" but between Israel and say, Jordan (3 million people), or Syria (9.3 million people), or Saudi Arabia (5 million people).

Finally, on a different level, the United States, like Israel, has interests and motives that transcend geopolitics, narrowly construed. The United States has not only material and geopolitical interests, but more broadly political and, yes, even ethical interests to consider. Israel is the only true democracy in the Middle East and the only country in the Middle East for whom the United States is truly a friend of the spirit, not merely a friend of convenience. It is true that the foreign policies of democracies tend to be less capricious and less subject to erratic shifts than those of dictatorships, but that is not the only reason we ought to and do prefer to consort with them. Those who gainsay such factors altogether are more than cynical — they are mistaken.

(7) The assertion that the politics of the Persian Gulf and those of the Levant are linked to one another is true as spoken but false as usually intended. As intended, the argument says: if you of the western industrial world want the oil to flow at reasonable volume and price, then you must make a good faith effort to solve the Palestinian problem in a way that suits the Arab Persian Gulf states, notably Saudi Arabia. The linkage argument lives a double life, one as a statement of fact, one as a statement of intended blackmail. If the former, it is an example of the phenomenology of fools, for anyone can assert that everything is related to everything else in one way or another. If the latter, it is to say that Arab politicians will *create* a linkage between the problems of the Persian Gulf and those of the Arab-Israeli conflict by words and deeds for the sake of pursuing a common goal vis-à-vis Israel and the West.

Now blackmail of this sort has a long, history in interstate relations, and even if we do not normally hold the principle in esteem, there is no reason to doubt its efficacy. But can the linkage be produced and sustained, or is it a bluff? The linkage is not a natural fact of Arab politics but requires the gullibility of the intended target to bring it into existence. It is a bluff that succeeds only when aimed at the faint hearted, the myopic, or the unprincipled. Thus, political blackmail and political terrorism have this in common: both require the intended victim to conspire unknowingly in his own undoing.

As far as the United States is concerned, there clearly is a relationship between the Arab-Israeli "theatre" and the Persian Gulf "theatre." The point of policy, however, is to keep them separate when circumstances suggest doing so, and to force them together when circumstances suggest doing that. U.S. policy in either area cannot be a substitute for policy in the other, and events in one area should not be allowed to dictate the timetable for U.S. diplomacy in the other.

By way of example, it will be recalled that during the AWACs debate of 1981-82, the United States insisted that the primary threat to the Gulf region was the Soviet Union. Not wishing to antagonize the Russians needlessly, the Saudis averred that Israel was the main threat, implying that that was why it wanted the AWACs. In the end, of course, it was neither Israel nor the Soviet Union but Iran that quickened the pace of U.S.-Arab cooperation in the Gulf. The point is that one must look beyond the rhetoric to the real priorities that motivate the Arab Gulf states. Even if we grant that Persian Gulf Arab leaders feel deeply about the Palestinian problem (and some do not grant it), the question remains: given their own vulnerabilities and their own agenda of needs and complaints vis-à-vis the United States, what action are they prepared to take that involves any risk or sacrifice on their part? The record is clear: nothing. There is no reason to believe that U.S. support for Israel has had a deleterious effect on U.S. interests in the Persian Gulf except perhaps at the margin, in the realm of atmospherics. If that were not already clear before the Gulf War, it certainly should be clear now.

(8) This proposition states the intuitively appealing postulate of the zero-sum: that there is necessarily an inverse relationship between the degree of amity in U.S. relations with Israel and the Arabs. Intuitively sensible though it may be, it is also wrong.

In the first place, the choice is never between Israel and "the Arabs" but between Israel and the Arab states as individual entities. When the United States favors Saudi Arabia, it is not only Israel that is concerned, but also Iraq, the Yemens, and Iran. When the U.S. does something for Jordan, it is not only Israel that is concerned, but also Syria. The relationship is not symmetrically zero-sum because there are more than two sides.

But an even more important point is that somewhat close U.S.-Israeli relations are actually a goad to improved U.S.-Arab ties for those states willing to contemplate peace. Pragmatic Arab statesmen know that in serious negotiations, only the persuasiveness, the generosity, and the strength of the United States can convince Israel to yield on important concerns. The Arabs lose interest in the United States to the degree that U.S.-Israeli relations deteriorate so badly that U.S. offices cannot produce the desired pressure. This is a relationship within limits, of course. If U.S.-Israeli relations were to be too good, the Arabs would despair even of getting Washington's ear. If they were to be too bad, then the prospect of tough sanctions and the imposition of a settlement could indeed hearten the Arabs without their having to do anything for the United States. Under such circumstances acting coy and aloof would serve them best. But Middle East diplomacy since 1973 has no experience with either extreme, nor is it likely to in the foreseeable future. Sadat exaggerated when he said that the United States holds 99 percent of the cards. But the United States holds no cards if it forces the Israelis away from the table, because if that happens, the Arabs won't want to play either.

(9) The argument against the incremental step-by-step strategy for peace and for the comprehensive, all-at-once package deal approach, is in some respects an outgrowth of proposition 4. If there is going to be an imposed settlement instead of a negotiated one, why not impose a complete rather than a partial settlement? Clearly, for many of its advocates a "comprehensive" approach is not really a negotiation at all; it is a euphemism for a superpower *Diktat*. For a *negotiated* comprehensive settlement to succeed, Israel must agree freely to make concessions not only to the pragmatists, like Jordan, but to the rejectionist ideologues like Syria and the PLO. Only strong Israeli faith in a foolproof package of international guarantees could produce acceptance of such a settlement that would expose it to so many risks. But there is no such package. Moreover, the comprehensive negotiations approach makes the incredible assumption that all the major actors involved — including Syria and the PLO — want peace even if they have to compromise and negotiate directly with Israel to get it. It also presumes a more or less unified Arab position. In practice, the comprehensive approach allows the most extreme and recalcitrant elements to sabotage any progress whatsoever. Indeed, this is what Sadat concluded in 1977 from the Carter Administration's early obsession with a comprehensive solution. He went to Jerusalem because he believed that the U.S. approach had made Egyptian interests hostage to individuals such as Yasir Arafat and Hafez al-Asad.

The charge that step-by-step agreements divide the Arabs and make each step harder reverses the truth. The step-by-step approach is not the source of contemporary divisions among the Arabs; it is the division among the Arabs that is the source and *raison d'être* of the step-by-step approach. The step-by-step process does not make each *successive* step harder; it makes possible any steps at all.

(10) It is a theoretical question what the Soviet attitude would be if peace were at hand between Israel and one of its local allies — notably Syria. Whether the Soviets *could* obstruct peace is an open question; Syria is not a Soviet puppet. Whether it would wish to do so is another matter. For the last thirty years, the conflict with Israel has been the chief Soviet entry point into the Arab world. Without that conflict, what interest would Syria or any other Arab state have in such close relations with the Soviet Union? And if peace were primarily the outcome of an American endeavor, what incentive would there be for Moscow to crown the achievement? Given the imponderables, it makes sense to invite the Soviet Union into Middle East diplomacy only after it has lost the capability to spoil the proceedings, but before their final international blessing is asked.

The Obvious

As an alternative to the common knowledge, the following five propositions should be weighed.

(1) Given the depth of mistrust between the parties (and not only between Israel and the Arab states, but also among the Arab states), the good offices of the United States are a necessary condition to progress toward a fuller peace. Only the United States enjoys full and friendly relations with states on both sides; only the United States can offer sufficient incentives and threaten sufficient sanctions to move reluctant parties toward each other.

(2) U.S. mediation *is* a necessary but *not a sufficient condition* for progress. There must be a local inclination to progress, or at least not a strong disinclination. The application of strong U.S. pressure at unpropitious moments is both counterproductive to the peace process and damaging politically to any U.S. administration stricken with such illusions of omnipotence. For the United States, the Arab-Israeli conflict is an irritant but not a mortal threat. For the local states, it *is* a mortal threat, and no amount of superpower pressure can make Israel or Jordan or Syria do anything that runs against its sense of survival.

(3) The regional inclination to progress is largely a function of domestic politics. More than one government must conclude either that the possible rewards for progress outweigh the risk of failure, or that the risk of doing nothing exceeds the risk of failure at doing something. More than one government must conclude that testing the water is not an all-at-once proposition, that one can retreat to shore before drowning.

(4) When the domestic requisites for local inclinations toward progress are absent — as they are now — the alternative U.S. policy is *not* to do nothing, watching passively as retrograde motion sets in. Public negotiations are not always the best venue and formal, explicit peace treaties are not always the best proximate goals of diplomacy. When countries are unwilling or unable to take big risks in public view, their own sense of frustration may incline them to take more modest risks in private. The United States can help them. It will be objected that this implies hypocrisy on the part of governments and undue secrecy from their own people. Perhaps, but on more than one occasion hypocrisy has been the advanced wave of a new truth.

(5) The Soviet Union should be excluded from Middle East negotiations — public and private — unless and until its general attitude toward international order and law changes in such a way as to willingly tolerate ideological diversity and to respect the interests of other powers. Since this is improbable, the United States should assume that Soviet policy will be obstructive unless it has firm evidence to the contrary.

Implications for the Near Term

The prospect for indigenous local progress toward peace in the near term is dim. The Syrian regime is apparently about to begin a difficult period of leadership transition. The regime is in any case so narrowly based on the Alawis that dramatic, unpopular initiatives are unlikely even if Syria were inclined — which is doubtful — to move toward peace under an American aegis. The Lebanese can do nothing important without Syrian permission.

The PLO is fragile and divided. Some of its groups are heavily influenced by Syria; those groups more moderately inclined need either the West Bankers or the Hashemites to force their hand. At this point, neither seems willing or able to do so. Arafat is still walking his familiar tightrope and this consumes all of his energies. No dramatic proclamation from al-Fatah is likely, and if it did occur, a new PLO civil war would be inevitable.

Progress hinges on Jordan, a country whose leadership may be inclined to be more flexible than its situation permits. The constraints on Jordanian policy are a consequence of three related conditions. The first concerns the relationship between the ruling Hashemite hierarchy and Jordan's largely Palestinian "political demography," a relationship that influences most if not all of Jordan's public policy choices. The second concerns Jordan's economic well-being, which depends heavily on external subventions of various sorts, and which has a direct bearing on Jordan's internal political health. The third concerns Jordan's internal and external security problems, which are exacerbated by the first condition but whose easement is financed through the second. Hussein is not about to risk the displeasure of his own population, the loss of major sources of revenue which help pacify that population, and waves of Syrian and Palestinian terrorism in Amman in order to enter into a negotiation with Israel whose chances of ending successfully are unknown and probably scant. On the other hand, a successful negotiation with Israel that satisfies at least in part Palestinian desires and regains occupied lands is the only way that Hussein can have peace with Israel, peace with the Palestinians in his realm, the return of at least part of the West Bank, and ample economic and security assistance from the United States all at the same time.

There is no assurance that Hussein will ever take the plunge toward peace, however much he may desire it. Jordan is thus in the unenviable position of fearing to do something and fearing to do nothing simultaneously.[9] There are good reasons why the latter fears might one day propel King Hussein into a decision to act, but U.S. failure in Lebanon, local Syrian ascendancy, Hussein's general mistrust of the United States, and the third successive failure of the Israeli Labor Party to win a strong electoral mandate have counselled the King to be patient for the moment.

Nothing significant can be expected from Saudi Arabia, Iraq, Morocco, and other Arab countries. They do not border Israel and are more interested in other matters.

Even if an Arab party were interested in serious progress toward peace, the Israeli domestic political scene is not conducive to bold action and the making of painful choices. The July 23 election produced a national unity government which is unlikely to be able to agree on a comprehensive vision of peace and on the sacrifices required to obtain peace. The opportunity for progress in the near term is absent. Far more likely is a war between Israel and Syria.

Although these dire prospects should deter the United States from bold public diplomacy, they may not do so. Washington periodically turns its gaze upon the Middle East with highmindedness and high ambition as if by reflex. The United States is correct to pursue Arab-Israeli peace both for its own sake and because a multitude of other western interests are better served by peace than war. Nevertheless, it is crucial that the second Reagan administration be fully aware of the vicissitudes of regional politics before launching itself into another high stakes diplomatic campaign to solve the Arab-Israeli conflict.

Although there is little hope of imminent indigenous movement toward peace, this does not mean that the best U.S. policy is one of benign neglect. An active and ambitious diplomacy does not have to be an open diplomacy whose main objective is a formal treaty of peace. Even in the absence of local movement toward peace, the United States can help lay the groundwork for peace in advance of the day when local conditions change for the better. The United States has in the past been successful at quiet diplomacy; U.S. aid in helping Israel and Syria reach an understanding about their respective security concerns in Lebanon in 1976 is a case in point.[10] But such diplomacy has never been given highest priority and, as such, the scope of its ambitions has been modest. Since it is far better to succeed at modest tasks than to fail at grand ones, the United States should consider the benefits of a strategy of building a quiet peace.

The central area of opportunity in this respect concerns relations between Israel and Jordan, two countries that for most of the past thirty-five years have maintained a *de facto* peace with one another. It is well known, too, that before the Likud's coming to power in 1977, many informal contacts existed between Israel and Jordan. Most of these contacts have ceased, and the United States could be instrumental in resuscitating some of them. A plethora of modest, apolitical problems between Israel and Jordan that are far below the line of political sight might yet be solved in private. Navigation in the Gulf of Aqaba, the mining of potash at the Dead Sea, currency exchange, tourist traffic, overflight rights for national air carriers, pest control, water control, oil pipeline security, certain intelligence functions, and the facilitation of pilgrimage for Israeli Muslims are only some of the many subjects that could be taken up with American urging and assistance. Progress on such minor apolitical issues could in time build up a modicum of trust between the parties and, in the event of a change for the better in local conditions, supply an avenue of contact that could be used for larger purposes.

Even with respect to Israeli-Egyptian, Israeli-Lebanese, and Israeli-Syrian relations, there may be some opportunity for a quiet U.S. diplomacy to arrest negative trends at the very least. There are dangers in a strategy of quiet diplomacy, the most harmful being perhaps the disingenuous use of U.S. mediation by one party to avoid direct contact with another or to embroil the United States in conflict with a regional partner. But no diplomacy is riskless. A strategy of building a quiet peace is preferable to doing nothing, and far more preferable to noisy failure.

Such a strategy may be doomed for political reasons. Politicians are not often interested in good deeds unless they can take credit for them. To succeed in the world, governments, like people, do everything they can to appear successful. And it is not as if things are likely to be dull in foreign affairs after January 1985; the United States will not need to seek out windmills at which to tilt. If nothing else, the United States will have Central America to deal with. Nevertheless, if helping in the Middle East is as important as is universally claimed, then there is still hope. On a different level, finally, it will be said that small successes on apolitical points can never amount to anything significant. But a modern American philosopher, Casey Stengel, once remarked: "They say you can't do it, but sometimes that doesn't always work." Let us take heart from that.

FOOTNOTES

1. For signs that this may finally be changing, see Martin Peretz, "Oxford Diarist," *The New Republic*, November 26, 1984, p. 43.

2. It is perhaps unfair to single out NEA (the Bureau of Near Eastern and South Asian Affairs in the Department of State). The mini-"State Department" within the office of the Joint Chiefs of Staff is also a victim of this "common knowledge."

3. "Western Palestine" refers to Palestine west of the Jordan river, as opposed to the "Palestine" of the Balfour Declaration, which included all of present day Jordan, as well.

4. For a short discussion, see my chapter "Genesis," in Alvin Z. Rubinstein, *The Arab-Israeli Conflict: Perspectives* (New York: Praeger Publishers, 1984), pp. 18-21.

5. See my "The Politics of a Palestinian State," *Orbis*, Spring 1983, pp. 215-216.

6. See my "Sources of the al-Fatah Mutiny," *Orbis*, Fall 1983, p. 631.

7. See my *Western Europe's Middle East Diplomacy and the United States* (Philadelphia: Foreign Policy Research Institute, 1983), p. 88.

8. This witticism is attributed to Francois, Duc de La Rochefoucauld (1613-1680).

FOOTNOTES

9. See my "Jordanian Foreign Policy," *Current History,* January 1984.

10. The full story of the "red line" policy has yet to be told — it may have to await the next volume of Henry Kissinger's memoirs. In the meantime, see the account of former Israeli Prime Minister Itzhak Rabin in *Yedi'ot Aharonot* (Tel Aviv), September 30, 1977, and interviews of Shimon Peres and Menachem Begin in *Foreign Broadcast Information Service* (FBIS), Daily Report (Middle East and Africa), May 5, 1981, p. 15, and May 6, 1981, p. 12.

42
U.S. Policy and the West Bank

By James R. Kurth

I. The Need for a New Look at U.S. Policy

Recent events have provided an opportunity and a necessity to reexamine some of the basic perceptions and assumptions underlying the policies of the United States toward Israel. The United States and Israel each held national elections in 1984 which will set the course of their countries for several years to come. The period after these elections, particularly early 1985, could provide an opportune time to reconstruct U.S.-Israeli relations on a foundation that accords with new conditions, on a basis that will be more mature and realistic than has been the case in recent years.

The collapse of the Reagan Administration's policy in Lebanon revealed grave errors in the way U.S. policy makers perceived the politics of that hapless Middle Eastern country, just as the collapse of the Carter Administration's policy in Iran had earlier revealed similar errors about the politics of that apparently solid Middle Eastern ally.[1] The repercussions from the advance of Syria and the retreat of Israel in Lebanon in turn raise anew the question of U.S. policy toward the disputed territories of the West Bank (Judea and Samaria), East Jerusalem, the Golan Heights, and the Gaza District.

The essential commonality of interests between the United States and Israel is well known, and the fundamental basis of U.S.-Israeli relations is quite sound. The U.S. values Israel as a strategic asset, one that provides a wide range of military and intelligence benefits for the U.S. policy of containing the military expansion of the Soviet Union in the Middle East.[2] The U.S. also values Israel as a political democracy, one with which Americans share political, cultural, and religious norms and practices. From time to time, of course, there have been disputes about a variety of issues, such as sales of U.S. advanced weapons to Arab countries, the amount of U.S. aid to Israel, and the Israeli invasion of Lebanon. But these disputes have generally been short-lived, and after the issue has been decided the fundamental equilibrium of U.S.-Israeli cooperation has been restored.

There is indeed only one major and continuing issue of dispute in U.S.-Israeli relations, and this concerns the territories that Israel acquired as a result of the 1967 Arab-Israeli War: the West Bank (Judea and Samaria), East Jerusalem, the Golan Heights, and the Gaza District. It is the argument of this essay that the position of the United States on these territories rests upon assumptions which no longer correspond to the realities of the Middle East, and that the time is ripe for bringing this dispute to an end.

II. The New Realities of the Territories

A generation has passed since Israel entered these territories. By now, Israel has ruled the West Bank and East Jerusalem almost as long as did Jordan, and the Gaza District almost as long as did Egypt. It is usually forgotten that the Jordanian occupation, like the Israeli one, was never recognized by other Arab states. Indeed, the only states that recognized Jordanian rule in these territories were Britain and Pakistan.[3]

For almost a generation U.S. administrations have been fruitlessly objecting to the continuing, expanding, and maturing Israeli presence within the territories. This presence now comprises a dense network of many strands — economic integration,

Dr. Kurth is Professor of Political Science at Swarthmore College. He is currently on leave as a Visiting Professor at the Center for Naval Warfare Studies at the Naval War College, Newport, R.I. His recent publications have focused on U.S. foreign policy and the politics of industrializing countries.

political administration, military security, and permanent Jewish settlements — and it is now highly institutionalized. Indeed, in the view of many sober and responsible analysis of this presence — including both those who support it and those who criticize it — it is now irreversible.[4]

Of these strands, the permanent Jewish settlements in the West Bank (Judea and Samaria) have been especially controversial from the perspective of the United States. But these settlements have also become especially important in establishing the irreversibility of the Israeli presence in the disputed territories. They now compose an ensemble of considerable variety and great extent[5]: (1) towns and settlements surrounding Jerusalem; (2) settlements on the western ridges of the Samarian mountains overlooking the coastal plain; (3) settlements in the Jordan River Valley; and (4) settlements in the heartlands of Judea and Samaria adjacent to Arab cities, such as Nablus, Ramallah and Hebron.

Of these categories of settlements, the first three are overwhelmingly supported by all major groups and parties in Israel, including both the Likud and the Labor coalitions. The settlements surrounding Jerusalem and on the Samarian ridges are natural extensions, indeed suburbanizations, of the cities of Jerusalem and Tel Aviv. Many of these settlements are bedroom communities that are within a thirty-minute commute from the city. They rest upon a solid base of economic and social realities. It is precisely their suburban quality, their very ordinariness, which will make them an enduring presence, whatever the ebbs and flows of Israeli party politics. Indeed, they will become a solid mass that will help guide that ebb and flow; in the multiparty Israeli political system, even a small group, if it represents a concentrated and consistent interest, can acquire substantial leverage, or at least a veto power, as an indispensable element of the governing coalition in the Knesset. The suburban voters on the West Bank are likely to become such an interest.[6]

The settlements in the Jordan River Valley grow out of the Allon Plan of the Labor Party as well as the supporting policies of Likud. Lying between the Jordan River itself and the hills rising to the west, they result from the recognition that the most, indeed the only, viable eastern strategic frontier for Israel is the river and its hills. These frontier settlements form a line reaching from the Red Sea to the Sea of Galilee; two-thirds of this distance lies in the West Bank territory acquired in 1967. Without the settlements in the Jordan River Valley and on the western ridges of the Samarian mountains, central Israel around Tel Aviv is only nine to thirteen miles wide. With them, the width of central Israel quadruples to about forty-five miles. These settlements rest upon a solid base of obvious military necessity.

Indeed, in Israel the only controversial category of settlements is the fourth, those in the heartlands of Judea and Samaria adjacent to Arab cities. But even these settlements are now supported by such powerful and committed political constituencies that even a new Labor government is most unlikely to abandon them.

Given these new realities about the disputed territories, why have U.S. policy makers persisted in their increasingly sterile and counterproductive opposition to the Israeli presence?

III. The American Conception of the Territories

At one level, the motives behind the U.S. position have been to maintain good ties with the "moderate Arab states," to appear "even-handed" in the Arab-Israeli conflict. This has especially been the case in regard to Saudi Arabia, with its obvious oil wealth; Jordan, with its presumed strategic potential (for example, a possible strike force for use in the Persian Gulf); and even Syria, which U.S. State Department officials have perennially hoped to wean away from the Soviet Union.

This view of the importance of the Arab-Israeli conflict for U.S. relations with the moderate Arabs might have been a plausible enough approach in the first few years after 1967. But today, it is now clear that the policies of different Arab states will vary over time for a host of reasons completely unrelated to the issue of the territories.[7] Does anyone really think that any Arab state gives high priority to the PLO, given the fate of the PLO in Arab politics in the past two years? Or that the Jordanian monarchy would be any less rickety and its policy any less vacillating if it had the responsibility to govern the West Bank or had a neighbor in an independent Palestinian state? Or that the Syrian regime would be any less a Soviet client if the Golan Heights were returned to it?

There is another, more fundamental level of perception, however, which better explains the persistence of the U.S. opposition. Here, the motive behind the U.S. position on the territories has been the idea or premise that the Israeli presence in them is somehow unnatural, that the occupation of the territory of one people by the state of another is not feasible in the contemporary world, that "nationalism" is the relevant issue and the inevitable reality. This premise behind the U.S. opposition to Israeli policy in the territories rests upon the misapplication of European and American conceptions of politics to Middle Eastern realities.

People in the West view the Middle East through the prisms of their own political experiences. For Europeans, this is especially the prism of the nation-state; for Americans, it is especially the prism of the pluralist democracy (although by now, most U.S. policy makers have recognized that this idea is wildly irrelevant to the Middle East, and they have retreated to the European notion). But in the real Middle East, there are no nation-states (other than Turkey), and there are no pluralist democracies (other than Israel itself).

It is true that for about two generations — from about 1945 to about 1975 — there was among some Arabs a hope, and among most Europeans and Americans an expectation, that there would soon be real nation-states in the Middle East, perhaps even one great, unified Arab nation-state. But this idea largely faded away in the 1970s, with the death of President Abdul Nasser of Egypt, with the failure of every attempt at unity between Arab states, and with the Islamic revolution in Iran.[8] And the fading of this idea allows us to see what was always the real political structure of the Middle East, which had been operating there all the time beneath the fog of Arab nationalism.

IV. The Middle Eastern Reality of Millet Societies

The reality of the Middle East always has been a series of political and military *centers*, or cores, constructed by peoples who are more organized and more militant than their neighbors. Each center, or core, is surrounded by a series of other peoples or ethnic communities who are less organized, less militant, or perhaps merely less numerous than those in the core. Together, the core and the associated peoples form a society. The core people organize the state structure and the military security which in turn surrounds and provides the framework for the entire ensemble of disparate peoples. The associated peoples and their leaders, however, assume many of the other political and administrative tasks involving their own ethnic community.[9]

At its best, this is a system of shared authority and communal autonomy such as prevailed in Lebanon in its "Golden Age" from 1946 to about 1970. More commonly, as with Egypt under Sadat, it is a system of bureaucratic authoritarianism and precarious autonomy. And at its worst, as in contemporary Syria and Iraq, it is a system of secret police and state terror.

In Ottoman times, this Middle Eastern reality could be called by rather accurate terms; there was what was known as the "Ottoman ruling institution," which ordered a complex society of ethnic communities, known as "millets." In modern times, however, Westerners have give this reality their own misleading terms; they try to see in the Middle East a series of actual and potential nation-states.

It would be impossible, however, to redraw the map of the Middle East or of any particular state within it so that all or even most ethnic communities have their own states, as in much of contemporary Europe. The ethnic communities of the Middle East are, and always have been, condemned to live several of them together in a wider society and under a "ruling institution," a state structure organized primarily by one of them.

There is today, however, one major political system whose ethnic components are organized very much in the way of the Ottoman Empire and of the Byzantine Empire before it. That is the Soviet Union, like the Russian Empire before it. In the Soviet Union, the Russians (more precisely, the Great Russians as distinct from the Little Russians or Ukrainians and the White Russians or Byelorussians) have always been more organized and more militant than their neighbors, have organized the state structure and the military security which, in turn, has surrounded the ensemble of disparate peoples, ranging from the Estonians to Kazakhs. In regard to this particular multi-ethnic system, of course, one would not say that the associated peoples and their leaders assume many of the other political and administrative tasks involving their own ethnic community. Rather, in the Soviet Union, we have something of a worst-case analysis, i.e., secret police and state terror.[10]

It is, however, this very way of organizing an ensemble of ethnic communities, a multinational empire, that makes the Soviet Union such a relevant and useful political model for certain authoritarian regimes in the Middle East. This is especially the case where the regime represents a militant but minority ethnic community, as with the Alawi-based regime of Hafez Assad in Syria (based on the Alawis, who represent a variation of Shiism) and the Sunni-based regime of Saddam Hussein in Iraq. In Syria, the Alawis comprise some 12 percent of the population; in Iraq, the Sunnis comprise some 45 percent. A minority regime tends to compensate for its smaller numbers of natural supporters with greater intensity of repression and terror. Such regimes are natural admirers and consumers of Soviet secret police organization, methods and advisors.[11]

V. The Israeli Practice Within the Territories

The Israeli policy towards the territories they acquired in 1967 is in accord with these enduring Middle Eastern military and social realities of "ruling institutions" and "millet societies," but in relatively benign form.

A glance at the map quickly and clearly shows that any viable framework for military security for the land between the Mediterranean Sea and the Jordan River would have the military security border be at or near the river and on the Golan Heights. As the core people in that land, the Israelis organize the military security of the area, including the disputed territories. Each core people has always had its political and even spiritual center, the center of the center, so to speak. For the Israelis, of course, this is Jerusalem, an integral part of the system we have described.

The Israelis also provide a wider range of economic and social services than normally has been provided by other core peoples in the Middle East. Many other political, administrative, economic, and social functions in the territories are either shared with or assumed by other authorities, such as local councils of Arab communities and even the Jordan government.[12]

Different Palestinians respond to this structure in different ways. Some Palestinians see their primary concerns as economic, and their political concerns as primarily local. For them, Middle Eastern practice, economic interests, and political focus converge in making communal and personal autonomy within the Israeli military security framework a viable and acceptable situation.

Other Palestinians assign less value to concrete economic interests and more to abstract political ideas. They could come to find their natural political arena to be within Jordan, for, in large measure, Jordan has become a Palestinian society within a Hashemite or Transjordanian state.[13] Amman, the capital of Jordan, is now the largest Palestinian city in the world. The time is not far off when the cores in Jordan could be reversed with the Palestinians themselves organizing the state structure within Jordan.

The overall system, then, is composed of (1) an Israeli-organized realm composed of Jewish and Palestinian peoples and (2) a Jordanian- (or potentially a Palestinian-) organized realm of Jordanian and Palestinian peoples. This system, of course, is not a stable one in the sense that nation-states, such as France, or pluralist democracies, such as the United States, are stable (although even here there have been times, such as in 1968, when "stable" was not the first adjective that came to mind). The point, however, is that this is the most stable political system for these lands that the social realities can produce.

More particularly, no Israeli government can accept either a pure American or a pure European model for Israel. Pluralist democracy, American-style, would result in an Israeli state that was no longer distinctively Jewish. A nation-state, European-style, one composed only or overwhelmingly of Jews, would shrink to frontiers even less viable and defensible than those before 1967. For a Jewish state in the Middle East to be secure against its enemies in the Middle East, it must have a state-community structure, Middle Eastern style.

VI. Implications for U.S. Policy

These considerations about millet society in general, and the disputed territories in particular, suggest that the U.S. would be wise to develop a new policy toward the Israeli-Palestinian conflict, a policy more in accord with these Middle Eastern realities. The U.S. could contribute to a more realistic environment in the Middle East by no longer opposing and disputing the Israeli presence in the territories. It would also be sensible, although now obviously controversial, for the U.S. to align its diplomacy with this reality by recognizing Jerusalem as the capital of Israel and by moving the U.S. embassy from Tel Aviv to Jerusalem.

In addition, a new U.S. foreign policy that recognized and accepted the realities of the territories, including the centrality of Jerusalem within the territories and within the wider Israeli realm, would liberate political and intellectual energies within the American foreign policy community. For too long, American policy makers and policy analysts have squandered their talents in vain attempts to reconstruct the ever-unstable and now-vanished conditions that existed before 1967, or to construct a European or American fantasy-state among the Palestinians in the West Bank. However, if these talents and energies can be harnessed to build on the rock of reality, rather than on the sand of fantasy, the United States, Israel and the more reasonable and constructive Palestinians will together be able to work out a political order that will be as stable, humane and authentic as possible, given the Middle East's doleful history.

FOOTNOTES

1. On U.S. misperceptions of Lebanon, see John Keegan, "Shedding Light in Lebanon," *The Atlantic* (April 1984), pp. 43-60; also David Ignatius, "How to Rebuild Lebanon," *Foreign Affairs* (Summer 1983), pp. 1139-1156.

2. Steven Spiegel, "The U.S. and Israel: A Reassessment," in Steven L. Spiegel, editor, *American Policy in the Middle East: Where Do We Go From Here?* (New York: Josephson Research Foundation, 1983) pp. 139-155.

3. Sasson Levi, "Local Government in the Administered Territories," in Daniel J. Elazar, editor, *Judea, Samaria, and Gaza: Views on the Present and Future* (Washington, D.C.: American Enterprise Institute for Public Policy Research, 1982), pp. 105-106.

4. Meron Benvenisti, *The West Bank Data Project: A Survey of Israel's Policies* (Washington, DC: American Enterprise Institute for Public Policy Research, 1984) (a summary is given in Benvenisti, "The Turning Point in Israel," *The New York Review of Books* (October 13, 1983), pp. 11-16); Arthur Hertzberg, "Israel and the West Bank: The Implications of Permanent Control," *Foreign Affairs* (Summer 1983), pp. 1063-1077; Daniel J. Elazar, "Present Realities in Judea, Samaria, and the Gaza District," in Spiegel, editor, *American Policy in the Middle East*, pp. 111-122. For a comprehensive background, see the essays in Elazar, editor, *Judea, Samaria, and Gaza: Views on the Present and Future*.

5. The following section is drawn from Elazar, "Present Realities in Judea, Samaria, and the Gaza District," in Spiegel, ed., *American Policy in the Middle East*, pp. 114-117.

6. Benvenisti, *West Bank Data Project*, pp. 57-60; Walter Reich, "A Stranger in My House: Jews and Arabs in the West Bank," *The Atlantic* (June 1984), pp. 57-60.

7. Haim Shaked, "The U.S. and the 'Moderate Arab States'," in Spiegel, editor, *American Policy in the Middle East*, pp. 77-83.

8. Daniel Pipes, "How Important is the PLO?"

FOOTNOTES

Commentary (April 1983), pp. 17-25; Bernard Lewis, "The Return of Islam," in Michael Curtis, editor, *Religion and Policies in the Middle East* (Boulder, Colorado: Westview Press, 1981), pp. 9-29. The fading of Arab nationalism is also discussed in several other essays in the Curtis compendium.

9. The pattern of Middle Eastern politics and society is discussed in Ernest Gellner, *Muslim Society* (Cambridge: Cambridge University Press, 1981), especially chapters 1-2; Daniel Pipes, *In the Path of God: Islam and Political Power* (New York: Basic Books, 1983), especially chapters 1, 7-9; James A. Bill and Carl Leiden, *Politics in the Middle East* (Boston: Little, Brown, 1979). Gellner reviews Pipes' book in his "Mohammed and Modernity," *The New Republic* December 5, 1983), pp. 22-26.

10. Daniel Pipes, "The Third World Peoples of Soviet Central Asia," in W. Scott Thompson, editor, *The Third World: Premises of U.S. Policy*, revised edition (San Francisco: ICS Press, 1983), pp. 155-174.

11. Karen Dawisha, "The U.S.S.R. and the Middle East," *Foreign Affairs* (Winter 1982/83), pp. 438-452.

12. Daniel J. Elazar, "Present Realities in Judea, Samaria, and the Gaza District," in Spiegel, ed., *American Policy in the Middle East*, pp. 118-119; Levi, "Local Government in the Administered Territories," in Elazar, ed., *Judea, Samaria, and Gaza*..., pp. 103-122.

13. Mordechai Nisan, "The Palestinian Features of Jordan," in Elazar, ed., *Judea, Samaria, and Gaza*..., pp. 191-209.

43 The Soviet Union's Imperial Policy in the Middle East

By Alvin Z. Rubinstein

Soviet analysts frequently use the word "complexity" *(slozhnost')* to describe a situation of great fluidity, uncertainty, and danger, in which the policymaker must choose from among equally unattractive dilemmas that throw into question previously accepted assumptions and options. Looking ahead, they see a time of complexity for Soviet policy in the Arab world as well as developments that could undermine Moscow's long-nurtured and costly (not just economically and militarily, but also politically in terms of relations with the United States) courtship of Arab countries.

Ever since Sadat expelled 20,000 Soviet military personnel in July 1972 and then unceremoniously plumped his eggs in Washington's diplomatic basket — despite the October War in which Moscow had risked a confrontation and deterioration of detente with the United States in order to protect Egypt from defeat — the Soviet leadership has found its options narrowed to support for a smorgasbord of Arab regimes, whose common denominator was an anti-U.S. policy. Moscow's main attractions were supplies of arms (for cash) and an implicit guarantee of protection from defeat by a U.S.-backed regional rival. In this way, the USSR sought to develop closer ties with Syria, Iraq, Libya, Algeria, and the People's Democratic Republic of Yemen (PDRY). After Sadat's historic visit to Jerusalem in November 1977 and conclusion of a peace treaty with Israel in March 1979 (in return for Israel's return of Sinai and readiness to negotiate a grant of "autonomy" to the Arabs of the West Bank and Gaza), these Arab regimes, and the Palestine Liberation Organization, constituted the core of the Steadfastness or Rejectionist Front, which was committed to war against Israel and disruption of the Egyptian-Israeli treaty. In the opposition of these Arab leaderships to the Camp David peace process, Moscow sensed a new opportunity to consolidate its relationships, frustrate U.S. policy, and perhaps even alienate the oil-rich Arabs of the Arabian Peninsula from the United States. It believed the Israeli-Egyptian accord would repolarize Arab politics, with Egypt dependent on the United States and all the other Arab regimes relying on the Soviet Union. And, skeptical that Israeli Prime Minister Menachem Begin would really give up all of Sinai, it also expected trouble between Egypt and Israel.

The Soviet line of reasoning was plausible, but somewhat oversimplified, reducing Arab politics as it did to the Arab-Israeli variable. In the aftermath of Camp David, Moscow strengthened ties with members of the Rejectionist Front, notably, Syria, the PDRY, and the PLO. Syria has long held pride of place in the USSR's political-ideological effort to establish a sound relationship with a leading Arab country. The first to receive Soviet arms (in the fall of 1954, though admittedly on a small scale), it was attractive because of its radical secular anti-Western political tradition, its toleration of communist party activity, and its bitter opposition to any compromise with Israel. In the early 1970s arms flowed to President Hafez Assad, to whose defense Moscow rallied during the October War and whose obduracy toward U.S. efforts to promote a

---

Dr. Rubinstein is Professor of Political Science at the University of Pennsylvania, and Senior Fellow of the Foreign Policy Research Institute. He is the author of numerous publications, including *Soviet Policy Toward Turkey, Iran, and Afghanistan* (Praeger, 1982).

Syrian-Israeli agreement was rewarded with a major arms buildup. Moscow was unhappy with Syria's intervention in Lebanon in 1976, but did nothing to pressure Assad to withdraw, on the contrary, continually upgrading its commitments and transfers of weapons. By October 1980, Moscow had the friendship treaty with Syria that it had sought for more than a decade.

The People's Democratic Republic of Yemen was another showpiece of Soviet diplomatic handiwork, in many ways the most valuable strategic-military asset that Moscow has to show after more than a generation of increasing involvement in the Arab world. The PDRY entered into close relations with the USSR shortly after it became independent in late 1967. Soviet assistance, military and economic, started almost immediately and increased steadily. In the early 1970s, the PDRY's attempt to foment a revolution through support of the insurgency in the Dhofar province of neighboring Oman was possible only because of Soviet supplies and logistical support. To discourage a PDRY rapprochement with Saudi Arabia, Moscow has provided ever increasing support. PDRY leaders make frequent trips to Moscow, and the joint communiques reflect closeness not only at the government-to-government level but at the party-to-party level as well. For the Soviets, the rewards have been substantial: the use of the excellent port facilities at Aden, the base at Khormaksar, air fields for flying reconnaissance missions over the Red Sea and Indian Ocean, and an anchorage off the PDRY's island of Socotra at the entrance to the Gulf of Aden and the Red Sea. Without these military privileges, the Soviet Union would have found it very difficult to intervene on Ethiopia's behalf in the 1977-78 Ethiopian-Somalian War.

In June 1978 the assassinations of top leaders in the PDRY and the Yemen Arab Republic (YAR) ended the PDRY's efforts to normalize relations with Saudi Arabia and push Yemeni unity — aims Moscow opposes. Another result was the entrenchment of Abd al-Fatah Ismail al-Jawfi, the militantly pro-Soviet ideologue. Fatah Ismail proceeded in October to establish, doubtless with Soviet encouragement, a vanguard Marxist-Leninist party, the Yemeni Socialist Party (YSP). A year later, during a visit to Moscow, he signed a 20-year treaty of friendship and cooperation in which the two governments declared "their determination to strengthen the indestructible friendship between the two countries and to steadily develop political relations and all-round cooperation ... and to develop cooperation in the military sphere ... in the interests of strengthening their defense capability."[1]

In April 1980, Fatah Ismail was forced to resign and was replaced by his Defense Minister, Ali Nasir Muhammad, who has maintained close relations with the Soviet Union, in no way reducing either the PDRY's dependence on Moscow or the USSR's privileged military position. There is some speculation that Moscow managed Fatah Ismail's downfall, because his belligerent stance toward the Yemen Arab Republic jeopardized the Soviets' renewed courtship of the conservative Yemeni government in Sana,[2] but the evidence remains fragmentary and often contradictory. It is just as possible that the showdown was an internal affair, linked to clashes of personality, differences of approach to domestic problems, and regional policy. What is unmistakable is the USSR's continued extensive military advantages in the PDRY — its most impressive in the Arab world.

Elsewhere in the Arab world Soviet attainments have fallen far below expectation. For example, in the case of Iraq, relations, good until the mid-1970s, have turned sour, despite the 1972 treaty of friendship and cooperation. Once it possessed vast earnings from oil exports and price hikes, the Ba'thist regime of Saddam Hussein preferred to diversify its arms suppliers and import Western, not Soviet, technology and equipment. The relationship has also been strained by far-ranging differences: "over the Arab-Israeli problem, Iraq refusing even to accept UN Resolutions 242 and 338 as a basis for possible settlement; over clients in the Horn of Africa, where Iraq supports Eritrean separatists against the Moscow-backed Ethiopian regime; over Iraqi Communists, who are represented in the Ba'th government but are periodically executed for organizing party cells in army units; and over Moscow's quest for "privileged treatment," which the Ba'th has refused.[3] Even more devastating to the relationship has been Moscow's coolness to Iraq's requests for arms, since its invasion of Iran in September 1980.

Despite the USSR's negligible influence in most of the Arab world, in October 1981, the assassination of Egyptian President Anwar Sadat seemed to vindicate Moscow's policy of catering to the cross-currents of anti-Americanism in the Arab world, funneling enormous amounts of modern weaponry to Arab clients able to pay for them, doing nothing to encourage an Arab-Israeli settlement, and thus demonstrating a willingness to protect the hardline, militant regimes in the Arab world from defeat at the hands of an American-backed regional rival. Moscow's intent is to supply the diplomatic support and military hardware that enable hostility to an Arab-Israeli settlement to be a feasible political option.

But 1982 has so far not been a good year for the Soviet Union in the Arab world. First, on April 25, Israel withdrew from Sinai, in accordance with the Egyptian-Israeli treaty, disproving the alarmist predictions of those who feared (wanted?) a rupture of the Egyptian-Israeli reconciliation. The treaty has taken hold, thanks to far-sighted U.S. policy. Egyptian President Hosni Mubarak has apparently effected a smooth assumption of power, and remains committed to the Camp David process, though full normalization is confined, primarily because of the lack of progress toward autonomy for the Palestinians on the West Bank and Gaza.

Second, the Iraqi-Iranian War has intensified the fears of the Lower Gulf Arabs over Khumayni's militant Islamic fundamentalism and has opened the way for their reconciliation with Egypt. The effect of such a development would be to stymie the polarization that Moscow had hoped to use to consolidate its position and frustrate U.S. policy. Third, Israel's invasion of Lebanon in June, if at all as successful politically as it has been militarily, may remove Lebanon as a confrontation state, destroy the military pretensions and political prestige of the PLO, isolate Syria and perhaps force it to rethink its unregenerate hostility to Israel, and, coupled with consolidation of the Egyptian-Israeli relationship, virtually eliminate the possibility of another Arab-Israeli war, thereby depriving Moscow of one of its principal attractions for Arab Rejectionist states. If the United States does not pressure Israel into a premature withdrawal, it stands to be, with Lebanon, a prime beneficiary of this potentially momentous restructuring of Arab politics.

Too much should not be made of the USSR's failure to do anything militarily to help the PLO resist the Israeli army; after all, neither has any Arab country. A preliminary assessment of the fighting in Lebanon between Israel and the PLO (this essay is being written at the end of July) suggests the following about Soviet relations with the PLO:

1) Moscow's support for the PLO has been tactical, a function of the USSR's perceived need to adapt to the policies of the hardline states it courted. One analyst described the situation thusly:

> **...both in the realm of Soviet-U.S. relations and Soviet-Arab relations, that is, the regional conflict dominated by the superpower competition, the Soviet position vis-a-vis the PLO remained a tactical one. Although the Soviets may have had certain fundamental positions on such matters as the borders of a Palestinian state or the use of international terror or the political leadership of the Palestinian cause, based on considerations of practicality and what Moscow justifiably termed "realism," they were willing to adjust their stand, assume a new one, or even avoid any stand on various issues such as a government-in-exile, Palestinian link with Jordan, PLO participation in the Geneva Conference, and others, depending upon the circumstances of the negotiating process, inter-Arab and Arab-U.S. relations.**[4]

2) Moscow may support the PLO, but it never agreed to act as its protector; it has no obligation, moral or legal, to defend the PLO.

3) The USSR has, judging by Israeli

reports of captured caches of weapons, provided the PLO with an enormous quantity of weaponry, but it has done so in exchange for money.

4) Soviet influence in the PLO is minimal: on no issue of significance to the PLO did Arafat accede to Moscow's preferences — not in a willingness to acknowledge the right of Israel to exist with secure and recognized boundaries in accordance with UN Resolutions 242 and 338, and not in the matter of curbing terrorist activities in favor of intensified political initiatives. The PLO's support for Moscow's policy in Afghanistan is political recompense for Soviet favors, but does not entail any compromise on the PLO's core policies.

5) Moscow's credibility is not on the line in Lebanon or in its attitude toward the PLO. As long as Syria, with which it has a treaty relationship, is not threatened, Moscow is not obligated to intervene.

It would also be premature to see in the current Lebanese crisis an *inevitable* or *permanent* setback for the Soviet Union and its Arab clients. The landscape in the Middle East is dotted with the sands of ephemeral triumphs. One Western journalist, reporting from Moscow, observed:

> **Some diplomats believe that the Kremlin's passivity reflects a shrewd perception that it can do well enough in the current crisis by staying on the sidelines. Those espousing this view say that the excesses of the Israeli invasion could revise the political equation in the Middle East by driving moderate Arab states such as Jordan into common cause with their more radical neighbors and further away from the Camp David approach and the United States. Especially if the consensus widened to include such current American friends as Egypt and Saudi Arabia, the Kremlin could find that in the long run, it had gained greatly by doing nothing at all.**[5]

Though inactive for the moment, the Kremlin is not silent. Angered by allegations that Soviet weapons supplied to the Arabs were inferior to the U.S. arms used by Israel, stymied by Arab divisiveness, and frustrated by the Arabs' unwillingness to stand up for the PLO, the Soviets lash out at the United States, Egypt, and Israel, and chide the PLO for its political rigidity. Their propaganda seeks to refute "the assertions of some circles in the Arab world that allegedly the Soviet Union renders insufficient support for the Arab cause."[6] It resorts to the familiar communist tactic of currying to the anti-Jewish animosities, in this instance accusing Israel of planning genocide and the extermination of the Arabs.[7] By cleverly blurring the line between religious affiliation and nationality, Soviet propaganda tries to make common cause abroad with all the groups and forces opposed to an Arab-Israeli settlement based on UN resolutions and the Egyptian-Israeli treaty.

•

If, compared to a decade ago, the Soviet Union has little to show in the Arab world for its extensive and expensive efforts to acquire influence in key Arab countries (the PDRY, as said earlier, being a notable exception), the situation is vastly different with respect to the non-Arab Muslim countries on its southern border. Turkey, Iran, and Afghanistan are strategically the centerpiece of Soviet policy in the Third World, contiguity accounting for continuity and centrality in an imperial foreign policy.[8] The fall of the Shah and the Soviet occupation of Afghanistan have altered the regional environment in these rimland states in ways conducive to the Soviet Union's long term strategic advantage, "bringing the Soviet ground and air forces closer to the Indian Ocean and to the oilfields and oil transport routes of the Persian Gulf, and increasing Soviet pressure on Iran and Pakistan;" and irrespective of the reasons for the Soviet move into Afghanistan, "the rest of the world had to deal with the fact that the military frontier of the USSR had been moved southward and that a former buffer state had been absorbed."[9] These cataclysms have produced permanent changes in the region, and the adverse consequences for U.S.-Soviet relations are sure to be long term.

In the period from Stalin's death to the late 1970s, Soviet aims in the non-Arab sector of the Middle East were: first, to thwart containment and undermine the U.S. military position in the region; second, to normalize and improve political and economic relations with Turkey, Iran, and Afghanistan; third, to foster congenial nonalignment rather than communism and diminish fears in these countries of threat from the Soviet Union; fourth, to isolate China, the Brezhnev collective security proposal of June 1969 being directed toward isolating Peking rather than organizing the countries of the region into a special Soviet-oriented grouping; fifth, to become a participant in the imperial management of regional affairs; and finally, to oppose all U.S. efforts to establish a military presence in the Persian Gulf and Indian Ocean. In different ways and for different reasons, most of these aims have been realized. Indeed, Soviet successes in the non-Arab sector of the Middle East alone have more than vindicated Moscow's overall effort made toward the region as a whole.

Since the upheavals of 1979 in Iran and Afghanistan, the Soviet Union has sought to allay regional anxieties over its intentions by making a variety of proposals for arms limitation, demilitarization, and nuclear-free zones, and by contrasting its putative desire for peaceful coexistence with the USA's alleged bellicosity. The Soviet net has been cast wide and Moscow has often become tangled in its own diplomatic mesh.

First, to offset its takeover of Afghanistan, Moscow intensified its courtship of India, offering extensive arms and economic packages at bargain rates. During Brezhnev's visit to New Delhi in December 1980 he made a five point proposal for neutralization of the Persian Gulf and Indian Ocean that aims at deflecting criticism from Soviet policy in Afghanistan and that serves as the basis for Soviet initiatives, none of which has found any takers. Second, Soviet propaganda in the region has hammered at U.S. responsibility for the region's arms races and conflicts and at Washington's desire to control the region's oil.

Third, Moscow has attempted to normalize relations with Khumayni's Iran, thus far unsuccessfully. The prime beneficiary of Iran's drastic political turnabout and anti-American animus, it would like to restore the close economic relationship that existed during the halcyon period of Soviet-Iranian relations under the Shah in the 1968 to 1978 period, but its unwillingness to pay Iran world market prices for Iranian natural gas, coupled with the anticommunism of the mullahs running the ruling Islamic Republican Party and their hostility toward Soviet policy in Afghanistan and interference in Iranian domestic affairs, have kept relations chilly. But Moscow is patient, and, judging from its professed neutrality on the Iraqi-Iranian War, it deems Iran rather than Iraq the strategic prize in the region. The war put Moscow in a quandary: how to improve relations with Khumayni's theocratic Iran without jeopardizing relations with Iraq's radical secularist regime, with which it has a treaty of friendship and cooperation.

Fourth, Moscow keeps reassuring the Arabs of the Gulf of its peaceful intentions, hoping to persuade Saudi Arabia to normalize Soviet-Saudi relations. Frequent Soviet commentaries insinuate that the Saudis should use their "Soviet card" in order to gain additional leverage in Washington on the Arab-Israeli issue.

Finally, Moscow is in Afghanistan to stay. This political development has enormous significance for the region as a whole, and its consequences will become more apparent in the years ahead, especially when the Sovietization of Afghanistan, which may well take another decade, is completed.

As the Middle East enters a period of political and diplomatic uncertainty, Moscow may be expected to continue to aggravate regional tensions, oppose initiatives that might serve Western interests, and exploit the opportunities that are bound to emerge.

FOOTNOTES

1. For the text of the treaty, see Foreign Broadcast Information Service/USSR International Affairs, October 29, 1979, H2-H5.

2. Amos Perlmutter, "The Yemen Strategy," *The New Republic* (July 5-12, 1980), 16.

3. Alvin Z. Rubinstein, "The Soviet Union and the Arabian Peninsula," *The World Today*, Vol. 35, No. 11 (November 1979), 444.

4. Galia Golan, *The Soviet Union and the Palestine Liberation Organization: An Uneasy Alliance* (New York: Praeger, 1980), 248-249.

5. John F. Burns, *The New York Times*, July 4, 1982.

6. *The New York Times*, July 2, 1982, 5.

7. For example, *The Times* (London), June 7, 1982; Soviet Foreign Minister Andrei Gromyko at a press conference in New York, *The New York Times*, June 22, 1982; and Leonid Brezhnev in a letter to President Ronald Reagan, made public on July 8, used the phrase stressed by the Soviet propaganda apparatus, namely, "the extermination of the Arab people of Palestine." *The New York Times*, July 9, 1982.

8. Alvin Z. Rubinstein, *Soviet Policy Toward Turkey, Iran, and Afghanistan* (New York: Praeger, 1982), *passim*.

9. John C. Campbell, "The Gulf Region in the Global Setting," in Hossein Amirsadeghi (ed.), *The Security of the Persian Gulf* (London: Croom Helm, 1981), 8.

According to the *Voice of Lebanon*, October 7, 1982, among the "illegal aliens" arrested that week, 18 were Palestinians and the rest were foreign volunteers. Fourteen were from Egypt, 11 from the Bader-Meinhof gang, 3 from the Italian Red Brigades, 12 from the Secret Armenian Army and from *Saiqa*, the Syrian-sponsored terrorist organization.

Also arrested, according to *Davar* (Israel), October 7, were volunteers from Turkey, India and Pakistan.

44

Soviet-American Rivalry in the Middle East

By Alvin Z. Rubinstein

A post-World War II phenomenon, Soviet-American rivalry in the Middle East developed fitfully in the wake of the systemic polarization in Europe and the Far East. A weakened Britain, a harassed Greece threatened by Communist subversion, and a relentless Soviet pressure against Iran and Turkey prompted the enunciation of the Truman Doctrine in March 1947 and the American involvement in the Eastern Mediterranean, heretofore the preserve of the European powers. With the partition of Palestine in 1948, Soviet and American foreign policy interests spread to the Arab world as well. Stalin, however, had little to show for his efforts. Stymied in Greece and Turkey by timely American aid, outfoxed by the Iranians, and castigated by the Arabs for supporting the partition of Palestine and the creation of Israel, Moscow found itself excluded from Middle Eastern affairs.

In the mid-1950s the new Soviet leadership skillfully exploited the regional polarization in the Middle East, a development that had crystallized in large measure as a consequence of the U.S. policy of globalizing and militarizing the strategy of containment. By misjudging the attraction of nonalignment for new nations and by pressuring Arab countries to join Western-sponsored military pacts, Washington sowed the seeds for the erosion of the West's once preeminent position and paved the way for Soviet penetration. Syria and Egypt opposed the Baghdad Pact and sought to counter the Western buildup of Iraq, their regional rival. Moscow quickly seized the opportunity, and used arms as its key to entry into the Arab world.

Soviet aims were unmistakable: to exploit Arab nationalism and undermine the Western political-military position in the Arab world, particularly the U.S. network of military bases that had been established

---

Dr. Rubinstein is Professor of Political Science at the University of Pennsylvania, and Senior Fellow of the Foreign Policy Research Institute. He is the author of numerous publications, including *Soviet Policy Toward Turkey, Iran, and Afghanistan* (Praeger, 1982).

along the southern tier of the U.S.S.R.;[1] and to implant a Soviet presence in the Arab world and encourage a pro-Soviet orientation among Arab nationalist movements. In time, the quest for military bases and the exploitation of Arab oil were to be added.

Both superpowers recognized the importance of Egypt. Though Moscow did improve its relations with Cairo in the aftermath of the 1955 arms deal, Washington exaggerated the extent to which the Soviets could exploit Nasser for their own purposes. Nasser demonstrated that a weak state could bargain successfully with a powerful one, a modus operandi Tito helped him perfect.[2] Indeed, one of the most important lessons that emerges from the past two decades of superpower rivalry in the Middle East is that, whatever their intended behavior, it is the superpowers who more often than not react to the local actors, and not the other way around: it is not the powerful patrons but the putative pawns who set the pace for the game. For example, in 1955 Moscow reacted quickly when Nasser broached the matter of arms purchases; in 1957 the Eisenhower Doctrine was a response more to Nasser's radical nationalism and the threat it posed to pro-Western governments in Iraq, Jordan, and Lebanon than to the alleged danger from "international communism," Eisenhower's justification to the U.S. Congress; and in 1967 and 1973 the local actors took initiatives that compelled far-reaching superpower responses.

Excepting 1958, when the Iraqi revolution provided the U.S.S.R. with new opportunities to develop close ties to an anti-Western, Arab nationalist regime, the decade from 1957 to 1967 found Soviet-American rivalry in the Middle East in low key. The Arab-Israeli conflict was relatively quiescent. The Sino-Soviet rift was a distracting problem for Moscow, which was interested in stabilizing the superpower relationship in Europe.

Moscow had headaches in its dealings with its Arab clients. For a time, it backed Iraq's Kassem against Nasser because in contrast to Nasser's repeated expressions of interest in improving relations with the Western countries, Kassem was militantly critical; in contrast to Nasser's crackdown on local Communists and assertions that communism was incompatible with Arab nationalism and unity, Kassem brought Communists into the government and relied on their support against his Nasserite opponents; and in contrast to Nasser's ambitions to unify the Arab world under his leadership, Kassem represented a force for retaining the existing nation-state system, which afforded Moscow more room for diplomatic maneuver and lessened the likelihood of Arab nationalism's taking on a bourgeois complexion that might entrench the position of conservative groups in Arab societies.

Shrewdly, Khrushchev kept Moscow's mini-Cold War with Cairo from interfering with the expansion of economic ties, as exemplified by the Soviet commitment in October 1958 and January 1960 to help build the Aswan Dam. Moreover, by 1961-1962, he had become disenchanted with Kassem because of his suppression of Iraqi Communists. Even more important, Albania's May 1961 eviction of the Soviets from the naval base they had enjoyed at Vlone since 1945, and the imminent U.S. deployment of Polaris submarines in the Mediterranean, prompted reconciliation with Nasser and intensified Soviet efforts to obtain naval facilities in Egyptian ports.[3] This quest for tangible military concessions increasingly absorbed Moscow and led to muting the political differences with Nasser and to subsidizing the Egyptian intervention in the Yemeni civil war after 1962. Despite increasing Soviet assistance, Moscow did not obtain its privileged position in Egypt until after the June War.

In the decade after the 1956 Suez War, the United States worked to improve relations with Nasser and to come to terms with Arab nationalism, quite apart from any concern over Soviet inroads, which were still of modest proportions. Washington's effort to maintain nonpartisan detachment in local Arab disputes, to adopt a policy of "American nonalignment," if you will, was not equal, however, to the complexities of the Middle East and came a cropper over Nasser's move into Yemen. Concern over stability in the Persian Gulf area moved Washington to support Saudi Arabia against Egypt's Moscow-backed intervention. By late 1966-early 1967, the National Security Council advised President Lyndon Johnson that the Soviet role in the Yemeni fighting and in the restiveness in Aden, coupled with Moscow's construction of a "blue water" fleet, signified a Soviet policy of challenge to the Western position in the Persian Gulf and Mediterranean regions.

Soviet American rivalry in the Middle East was significantly affected by the third Arab-Israeli war in June 1967. First, in contrast to the previous decade, it was now shaped by the Arab-Israeli conflict and not by intra-Arab alignments. The result (until after the October War) was a deterioration of American standing in the Arab world, a situation Moscow was nonetheless unable to exploit for any length of time because its arms could not bring victory over Israel. Second, the rivalry fueled the regional arms races, and an ever increasing quantity of sophisticated weaponry poured into the Middle East. This turned the "War of Attrition," launched by Nasser in the spring of 1969, into a bitter struggle that inexorably enmeshed the superpowers. A prologue to 1973, the war of attrition was a warning of the vast destructiveness that Middle East countries are capable of wreaking one on the other. Third, Moscow's response to the June War showed that it had no intention of cutting its losses and leaving the Middle East field to the United States; that it was determined to compete in every way possible.

Both superpowers watched as Israel smashed the Arab armies. Even if Moscow had contemplated intervention, the military outcome had been decided too quickly for its aid to have been effective. Besides, in 1967, Moscow lacked, as it no longer did in 1973, a major airlift capability and a Mediterranean fleet that could seriously threaten the U.S. Sixth Fleet. Contenting itself with rebuilding Arab armies, cultivating their dependency, and supporting Arab initiatives in the United Nations, the U.S.S.R., faced in 1968 with a crisis in Czechoslovakia and in 1969 with a worsening of relations with China, did not want war in the Middle East. The United States, too, preoccupied with a searing struggle in Vietnam, preferred to let the dust settle. Moreover, the interest of both superpowers in promoting strategic arms limitation talks and détente in Europe strengthened their preference for the status quo in the Middle East.

Nasser's war of attrition upset their calculations. A crisis atmosphere developed in early 1970 as Egypt's military pressure on Israel backfired. Heavy losses along the canal and Israeli deep penetration raids, which by mid-January 1970 had extended to the outskirts of Cairo itself, impelled Moscow to accede to Nasser's request and raise the ante of aid sharply, to commit Soviet missile crews, pilots, and air defense teams for the protection of Egypt's heartland. The cease-fire of August 7, 1970, quelled this conflagration. But Arab politics, meanwhile, entered a period of flux, highlighted by the defeat of Palestinian forces in the Jordanian civil war and the death of Nasser on September 28, 1970.

For the next three years, until the outbreak of the Fourth Arab-Israeli War on October 6, 1973, the Middle East was again relatively low on the list of Soviet and American priorities, as the superpowers concentrated on their other problems. Indeed, Soviet difficulties with Sadat, epitomized by the stunning expulsion of Soviet military personnel from Egypt in July 1972, encouraged American officials to believe that the evolving détente relationship would persuade Moscow to maintain a prudent restraint and discourage its Arab clients from starting a war.

The October War marked a watershed in Soviet-American rivalry in the Middle East. For the first time both superpowers were equally involved in a crisis each viewed with the utmost seriousness, not only with regard to their respective client states but with regard to their relationship with each other; for the first time they were locked in direct conflict in a Middle East crisis; for the first time they found themselves on a collision course there, even though elsewhere they were trying to restructure and stabilize their global relationship; and this was their first crisis in a period when the Soviet Union enjoyed military equivalence, both nuclear and conventional. Furthermore, neither was constrained by any pressing problem elsewhere. And oil intruded itself into the consciousness of both American and Soviet decisionmakers. The post-October War diplomatic calculations of the United States, particularly, were influenced by the economic and strategic implications of this essential commodity. A confrontation was avoided, but pressures in the United States arising out of the near showdown with Moscow forced the administration to modify its position on issues that were of great interest to the U.S.S.R., namely, SALT, trade, and credits. Détente, it turned out, was not a linear process.

Perhaps the one aim that top decisionmakers in the Soviet Union and the United States shared during the crisis (apart from the understandable desire to avoid nuclear war) was to prevent an Israeli victory: Moscow, it is obvious, would have been placed in an untenable position vis-à-vis the Arabs and could not have tolerated such a state of affairs, unless it was prepared to write off the area; Washington would have been unable to improve relations with the Arab governments, assure a steady flow of Persian Gulf oil to the West and Japan, or act as a credible go-between in its attempt to bring the local protagonists from the battlefield to the conference table.

In assessing the post-October War fortunes of the Soviet Union and the United States, one could say that nothing fails like success. Moscow had saved Egypt and Syria from military defeat and enabled them to emerge with a political triumph of sorts, yet no sooner had the fighting stopped than Egypt turned to Washington, not Moscow. Whereas in 1967 the Arab states broke off diplomatic relations with the United States even though it had not aided Israel, in 1973 they restored diplomatic ties even though Washington had intervened on behalf of Israel. The Geneva Conference, which was co-sponsored by the Soviet Union and the United States and was to have legitimized Soviet participation in the process of arranging a settlement and in the management of Middle Eastern affairs — a key Soviet objective — was adjourned less than forty-eight hours after it had convened, with Moscow clearly the odd capital out.

The American position in the Arab world was strengthened. Secretary of State Henry Kissinger fashioned disengagement agreements between Egypt and Israel and between Syria and Israel without Soviet participation, to Moscow's ire. The Sinai Agreement between Egypt and Israel in September 1975 reinforced the American argument that only the United States could deliver the return of Israeli-held Arab territory. Elsewhere, in the Persian Gulf area, American strategy seeks to keep the Soviet Union out of the mainstream of that crucial region's politics.

For the moment, Moscow's options are limited. The deterioraton in Soviet-Egyptian relations dramatically came to a head on March 15, 1976, when Egypt unilaterally abrogated the 1971 Soviet-Egyptian Treaty of Friendship and Cooperation, and several weeks later when Sadat terminated Soviet naval facilities in Egyptian ports. Moscow's Palestinian card has been severely frayed by the fratricidal bloodletting in Lebanon and the cleavages that have reappeared in Arab ranks. Soviet weapons remain a potential trump, but the oil-rich Arab states prefer to underwrite arms purchases from Western suppliers. Soviet economic aid, such as it is, is accepted but not crucial. At the moment, Moscow is in search of a role to play in the Middle East tragedy. It is patient, believing that opportunities will again be forthcoming.

The superpower rivalry in the Middle East is more than the mere total of specific national interests and ambitions; it is an intricate web whose threads are global as well as regional. U.S. interests are fairly easy to identify: an assured flow of oil from the Persian Gulf-Saudi Arabian peninsula region to Western Europe, Japan, and the United States; the support of pro-Western oriented governments in the Arab world; an independent Turkey and Iran, linked to the West; the preservation of Israel as an independent country; the prevention of another Arab-Israeli conflict, which could seriously jeopardize the first two objectives noted above; and the containment of Moscow's presence and influence in the region.

Though Kissinger has often spoken of the linkages in American-Soviet relations between regional and global issues, Washington has, in practice, shown little inclination to apply such conceptual formulations to the Middle East. Neither in 1955, when it did not attempt to link the easing of tension in Europe to demanding Soviet restraint in feeding the arms race in the Middle East, nor in 1976, when it sought agreement on SALT and Europe, has Washington been willing to barter away its opposition to Soviet ambitions in the Mediterranean-Persian Gulf areas. Concern over the growing Soviet challenge serves to exacerbate the dilemmas the U.S. faces in responding to Egypt's legitimate needs in the wake of Sadat's latest imbroglio with Moscow; in reconciling Israel's quest for security with the Palestinian demand for an independent state; in selling arms to oil rich Saudi Arabia, Kuwait, and Iran and thereby tacitly encouraging regional arms races whose outcome can only prove destabilizing and contrary to U.S. objectives in the area; and in stimulating expectations among the Arabs that cannot be indefinitely held in abeyance without damaging the improved relationships newly forged.

Soviet objectives in the Middle East have changed considerably since the Stalin period. The current level of Soviet interest is determined primarily by the character of Soviet imperial ambitions and not by any serious concern over the presence of the U.S. Sixth Fleet in the Mediterranean or the deployment of Polaris submarines in the Indian Ocean, both of which are constants of American global strategy. In the mid-1950s and early 1960s, when the United States had major military installations in Turkey and Pakistan, and Iran seemed on the verge of granting permission for U.S. missile sites, Moscow's fears for its security were understandable and its "forward policy" in the Middle East was a sound diplomatic strategy designed to undermine and outflank the offensive network of bases being developed nearby by its adversary. But that is past. Though these countries remain formal allies of the United States — a type of cheap insurance — they have opted for a de facto nonaligned position, and no U.S. military force of consequence exists in the countries lying south of the Soviet Union. The threat to the U.S.S.R. from Polaris has nothing to do with the ups and downs of political fortunes in the Middle East itself or with the scale of Soviet activity. Soviet polaris-type submarines now plying the waters off the American coasts constitute as much of a threat (or deterrent) as their American counterparts in the Mediterranean and Indian Ocean. Moscow can no longer talk of any American military threat to the Soviet Union stemming from American activities in the Middle East.

Moscow is in the area for the long haul. As a superpower, the U.S.S.R. wants to become an integral and permanent member of any Great Power consortium that develops for mediating Middle Eastern disputes. It seeks naval "facilities" (the post-colonial euphemism for de facto bases) for reasons of state unrelated to the Arab-Israeli dispute. It does so in order to outflank NATO and to better position Soviet forces for possible use in the Third World arena.

Though Moscow may not want war, neither does it press for peace, which, in any event, it considers most unlikely in the foreseeable future; given the region's endemic instability and deep-rooted varied animosities, this bleak assessment is shared by many observers in the non-Communist world as well. No original peace proposals issue from Moscow. Those proposals that do are carefully tailored to the cut of courted Arab centers of power. Two examples may be given. In April 1975, when Kissinger's effort at a second Egyptian-Israeli disengagement agreement had temporarily failed, Soviet diplomats busily explored with Arab and Israeli officials the possibility of reconvening the Geneva Conference, the one objective that Moscow can be said to have consistently sought since December 1973. The Soviets held out the prospect of renewed diplomatic ties to Israel, and Gromyko implied, but never explicitly stated as some newspapers reported at the time, that Moscow would accept Israel's 1967 borders as legitimate. Opposition from the PLO, however, led Moscow to backtrack. To date, the Soviet government has never come out openly in favor of a settlement based on the 1967 borders, for to do so would be to alienate the Palestinians and the so-called "confrontation states" — Libya, Syria, Algeria, and Iraq, on whom Moscow places its hopes for a solid presence in the area. An official Soviet government statement on the Middle East issued on April 28, 1976, purporting to offer a general framework for a settlement, turns out on examination to be nothing more than a rehashed formulation that could have been drafted by any intransigent Arab group.[4]

To paraphrase Kierkegaard, policy formulation is future-oriented, but it can only be formulated looking backward. At the heart of Soviet strategy in the Middle East lies the goal of undermining the U.S. position and thereby of promoting the fragmentation of the Western world. Events of the past few years clearly indicate that Soviet-American rivalry has become a permanent part of the volatile and unpredictable Middle East scene.

FOOTNOTES

1. Andrei D. Sakharov, *My Country and the World* (New York: Vintage Books, 1975), p. 81. Sakharov cites Khrushchev as his source, in mentioning Soviet objectives in the Middle East in 1955.
2. For an analysis of the Nasser-Tito relationship, see Alvin Z. Rubinstein, *Yugoslavia and the Nonaligned World* (Princeton: Princeton University Press, 1970), Chapter VII.
3. George S. Dragnich, "The Soviet Union's Quest for Access to Naval Facilities in Egypt Prior to the June War of 1967," in Michael McGwire, Ken Booth, and John McDonnell (eds.), *Soviet Naval Policy: Objectives and Constraints* (New York: Praeger Publishers, 1975), pp. 252-269.
4. FBIS/USSR International Affairs, April 29, 1976, pp. F2-F4.

PART VIII
THE EXTERNAL WORLD

45
Africa, Israel and the Middle East

By Michael Curtis

International politics frequently demonstrates the validity of Walter Lippmann's observation that people respond as powerfully to fictions as they do to realities.[1] Nowhere is this as demonstrable as in the changing international perceptions of the policies of Israel and its relations with Black African countries and with South Africa.

Black African countries have been interested primarily in the right of national self-determination, development as independent nations, and the elimination of discrimination on the African continent. Israel has been concerned with survival in the midst of hostile neighbors who have tried to undermine its legitimacy by a variety of means, including a policy of deliberate distortion of its actions. This distortion has aimed at changing the perception of Israel held by Black Africans and the rest of the international community by equating Zionism with racism and by depicting Israel as a close associate of South Africa.

Few political issues today strike such strong emotional chords or enjoy such universal consensus as the condemnation of the South African political regime. Though this regime has recently made certain minimal changes and promises to make others, it still denies political rights to 21 million black citizens and consigns them to an inferior status in law and therefore deserves to be criticized for its policies of *apartheid*. Everyone sincerely concerned with the issue of human rights in South Africa must therefore be troubled about the misuse of the opposition to *apartheid* for partisan, irrelevant, and self-interested motives.

Representatives of Arab countries and the Communist bloc, in which human rights are sadly lacking, indulge in the luxury of anti-Zionist rhetoric and even occasional antisemitic incitement. They also make it their duty to denounce Israel not only as a racist state but even as the fount of racism. In their eagerness to misrepresent, exaggerate, and distort the actions and policies of Israel, these countries are apparently not troubled by the fact that their actions are weakening, indeed betraying, the valid anti-*apartheid* cause.

The Arab-Communist coalition, in a mixture of cynicism and opportunism, has skillfully used international forums, especially the United Nations and its specialized agencies, to pass resolutions linking Israel and South Africa. In true Orwellian fashion it has attempted to expunge the memory of the historic Jewish opposition to racism in all its forms and the record of Jewish willingness to fight and suffer for the civil rights of blacks. These resolutions obfuscate the reality that the state of Israel is founded, as its Declaration of Independence says, on the principle of complete equality of social and political rights. The anti-*apartheid* cause, in which South African Jews were prominent in disproportion to the total white population,[2] and which Israel supported in the United Nations until 1972, when the cause became linked with the opposition to Zionism, has been misused by the Arab-Communist coalition rather than honestly employed against its proper target. Consensus exists that the Arab countries support African-sponsored resolutions at the U.N. only if they are linked to the Palestinian question. Even Ali Mazrui argues that the Organization of African Unity (OAU) has become "a mechanism by which the Arabs can politically influence black Africans."[3] As a result of this Communist-Arab effort,

---

Dr. Curtis is Professor of Political Science at Rutgers University, New Brunswick. His latest publication, of which he is the editor, is *Antisemitism in the Contemporary World* (Westview Press, 1986).

Israel's previously cordial relations with Black Africa have been undermined.

Israel and Africa

One of the most impressive features of the early decades of Israeli policy was its concern for and interest in humanitarian action in Third World countries, especially in Black Africa.[4] To some extent this was a policy of enlightened self-interest whereby Israel sought to win friends and gain political support in the international community. But more significantly, its actions were an illustration of the concept of social justice that underlay the regime and a demonstration of genuine sympathy for other new developing nations engaged in nation-building. These new nations, seeking non-obligating guidance and support, were able to benefit from Israel's own unique development experience, especially in agriculture, regional planning, zone development, water management, cooperatives, community development, education, health and youth programs. Because of Israel's limited capital funds, most of the early aid was in the form of technical assistance.

Israeli policy was based on certain guidelines. Diplomatic relationships and mutual recognition were essential. Israel would assist in administration and development if formally requested and if action could be taken quickly, without long-term study. The host country would cover expenses if there was local participation. And the Israeli presence would be phased out at the completion of the project.

On this basis, relations between Israel and Black Africa took a number of forms: expert help, trainee programs, cooperative efforts, military aid, and diplomatic relations.

1) Experts. The prominence of Africa in Israeli aid programs is obvious from the statistics. From 1958 to 1969 some 1,525 Israelis went on long- or short-term assignments to Black Africa. By the 1960s, Israeli experts were helping develop projects in over 30 African countries. Israel's own experience as a developing country proved valuable in the African context for such activities as planting trees, expanding agricultural production through reducing soil erosion and introducing new methods of irrigation, raising livestock, and eliminating malaria. Attempts at creating organizational structures, such as cooperative institutions, on the *kibbutz* and *moshav* models, proved less successful though the Rehovot model of integrated rural planning has been much admired.

2) Trainees. In Black Africa, Israeli instructors trained several thousand African students. In Israel itself, about 9,000 Africans attending various training institutions studied a variety of subjects and participated in vocational and management programs. Most were given scholarships at the Afro-Asian Institute at Tel Aviv, the Mount Carmel International Training Center for Community Services in Haifa, and the Hadassah Medical School in Jerusalem.

3) Joint Cooperation. Additional assistance was provided by joint endeavors in various ventures, most of which were construction projects in conjunction with Solel Boneh, the Israeli construction firm. The earliest significant venture was the Black Star Shipping Line set up in 1957 by Zim Lines in Ghana, the first Black African country to gain its independence and the leader of African nationalism at that time. Different needs were attended to in different countries: low cost housing in the Ivory Coast, roads to previously inaccessible places in Nigeria, cotton plants in Swaziland, pharmaceutical works in Ethiopia. Between 1957 and 1973, 21 African countries signed cooperative agreements with Israel; another 11 received economic assistance, while loans and credits were provided to 7 countries.

4) Military Aid. Israeli assistance in this area took a number of forms: the training of pilots, military and police officers; the establishment of a military academy in Sierra Leone; the paramilitary training of youth organizations; and direct military aid to 10 countries.

5) Diplomatic Relations. Beginning in 1956, Israel established a total of 27 embassies and 33 missions throughout Africa except in the five Arab states in the North and the Muslim states of Sudan, Mauritania, and Somalia. In these relations both the Africans and the Israelis recognized a mutual interest and even a certain ideological affinity.

For Israel this set of relationships meant enlarging its circle of international contacts with the hope that African countries would support — or at least not oppose — Israel's struggle for existence. Israel recognized the strategic value of the African countries along the Red Sea for its own security, and the importance of protecting shipping in the Gulf of Aqaba passing through Bab-el-Mandeb to the Indian Ocean. Trade between the Black African countries and Israel, largely an exchange of raw materials and finished products, was important not only in itself, but also in that it constituted a significant check on the Arab boycott of Israeli products. The Labor Zionist ideology of many of the Israeli leaders led them to a genuine concern to aid new, developing nations in the Third World, some of which seemed to rest on political aspirations similar to those of Israel. Golda Meir herself saw Israel's African policy as "a continuation of our own most valued traditions and as an expression of our own deepest historic instincts."[5]

For their part, African countries saw Israel as an example of a newly independent nation pointing a way to economic modernization and political development that they could follow. From Israel they could obtain technical assistance without danger of a neo-colonialist presence or fear of being drawn into a military alliance or being pressed for military bases. They recognized a new nation with which they shared some common features: a history of past persecution, a mixed economy that was neither capitalist nor socialist, a country facing danger of intervention by external forces, and a certain political balance in international East-West relations in the early years.

Israel frequently voted in the United Nations against the system of *apartheid* and in 1961 supported the call for sanctions against South Africa. Parenthetically, Israel also voted in favor of the decolonization of Portuguese territories in Africa.[6] In 1963 Israel reduced its diplomatic representation in South Africa to consular level, and in 1966 voted against South Africa's mandate over Namibia. Black African countries did not vote alike on Middle East questions. Some, especially the Francophone countries, tended to vote in support of Israel until the 1970s. Significantly, countries which received aid from Israel did not automatically vote in its favor.[7] But most Black African countries did not accept the Arab argument that Israel had cooperated with South Africa and Portugal, the two main enemies of Africa.

The Breakdown of the Relationship

After 1967 this harmonious relationship between peoples of different races began to change for a variety of reasons. Some had little connection with Israel as such and were more related to the problems of development that African countries were experiencing and to the changes in some of their political regimes. Other factors, such as the changing image of Israel as a result of its 1967 military victory and the lessening of French Government sympathy for Israel, had an impact.

But more important, if not always publicly discussed and sometimes even denied, were the direct pressures of Arab states on Black African states to which the Arabs addressed a mixture of appeals, promises and threats. Appeals for Islamic unity were made to African countries which were predominantly or significantly Muslim. Afro-Arab solidarity was called for as a part of Third World consciousness in which the principles of self-determination and opposition to colonialism were important. Promises of economic assistance and oil supplies at reduced prices were attractive, especially after 1973 with the immediate quadrupling of oil prices and the unprecedented increase in wealth of the Arab oil-exporting countries. Threats against some African political regimes and even the lives of individual leaders were not unknown.

During this period two general arguments related to actual or alleged Israeli actions surfaced and became prominent in various United Nations and other international forums where Israel was castigated on countless occasions. The first held that because Israel after the Six Day War in June 1967 had occupied territory of Egypt, a member of the OAU, Israel was guilty of violating the boundaries and territorial integrity of an African state. Resolutions calling for Israeli withdrawal from Egyptian territory were introduced at OAU meetings, and the Israeli occupation of Sinai was termed "a serious threat to the regional peace of Africa." The first country to break relations with Israel was Guinea, in 1967; it was followed by seven others between 1972-73. The "violation of African integrity" argument was used more intensively after the Yom Kippur War in 1973 when Israeli forces crossed the Suez Canal and, for a short time, actually held a small part of the African mainland. More Black countries broke off relations; in all, 29 of 33 Black African states interrupted relations with Israel. The only exceptions were Malawi, Swaziland, Lesotho, and Mauritius (until 1976). Many African states went beyond the issue of territorial integrity, and lent support to criticism of Israel in its conflict with the Arab states, which was irrelevant to that issue. On the November 10, 1975, "Zionism is racism" resolution in the General Assembly, twenty African states voted in favor, twelve abstained and only five voted against. Yet even so, some African states, courageously resisting the farther reaching demands of the Arabs, rejected the 1975 OAU summit's call for the expulsion of Israel from the U.N. and an economic boycott against it.[8] Some were disturbed by the refusal of Arab countries to support Sadat's peace initiatives. None of the Black African countries broke relations with Egypt after it concluded its treaty with Israel. The moderate African countries still strove to prevent the linking of Zionism with racism.

Unquestionably, the concern for territorial integrity of African states is deeply felt, but that feeling has not been fully extended to the continuing Libyan occupation of a considerable part of the territory of Chad. It is ironic that Libya's claim to some of Chad's territory resembles that made by Fascist Italy when it controlled Libya.

One would expect that the withdrawal of Israeli forces from any part of the territory of an African state would be plausible justification for restoring African-Israeli relations. Yet, even after the Sinai withdrawal agreements in 1975, and especially after the 1979 Egyptian-Israeli peace treaty and the consequent withdrawal of Israeli troops from the whole of Sinai, that restoration did not occur.

The United Nations Battleground

The second argument for the breaking of African-Israeli relations is the alleged close tie and affinity between Israel and South Africa. At the General Assembly and the various agencies of the United Nations, and at U.N.-sponsored meetings such as the *United Nations Decade for Women,* this tie has been alleged and denounced in one resolution after another as a result of pressure by the Communist-Arab lobby. The two countries have been equated as the world's most blatant examples of racism or have been linked by Israel's alleged approval of the racial policies of South Africa.

A particularly flagrant and sustained attack on Israel has come from the Special Committee on the Policies of Apartheid of South Africa set up by the United Nations in 1962. This body, now generally known as the Special Committee against Apartheid, issues both annual and special reports. The selective morality of the Committee has been amply illustrated not only by repeated references to "systematic collaboration between South Africa and Israel," a formula only recently amended to include on occasions "certain Western powers," but also by the disproportionate number of the special reports (9 out of 18 between 1976 and 1984) which were devoted to relations between Israel and South Africa.

The Special Committee Against Apartheid in 1983 engaged in political activity that appears to exceed the authority given it by the General Assembly, which itself had already tolerated extravagant polemical declarations from the Committee. In cooperation with the Afro-Asian Peoples' Solidarity Organization, the Organization of African Trade Union Unity and the World Peace Council (generally accepted as a Communist front controlled by the Soviet Union), the Committee organized an *International Conference on the Alliance between South Africa and Israel* which was held in Vienna in July 1983. The conference concluded that the "alliance" had assumed very serious proportions, was a menace to the people of southern Africa, and posed a challenge to the United Nations.[9]

The Special Committee itself, meeting in August 1983, was anxious to publicize the deliberations of the Conference, some of whose membership overlapped with that of the Committee. It even requested that the formal declaration of the Conference, which was a strong condemnation of the Government of Israel for "its collaboration with the racist regime of South Africa," be published as a document of the General Assembly, though this seems to be a violation of the rules of the United Nations itself. In the incestuous political networks within the U.N. the work activities and anti-Israeli rhetoric of the Special Committee have also been interrelated with the work and recommendations of the *Decade for Action to Combat Racism and Racial Discrimination.*

For some years, meetings of the United Nations and its various agencies have been deluged with similar resolutions denouncing "the close relationship between South Africa and Israel." The volume of rhetoric and the amount of time consumed on the issue are so extravagantly disproportionate, the content so blatantly false, that the normal ritual of self-indulgent verbiage at the U.N. on other issues seems by comparison like penitential abstinence.

African representatives are becoming increasingly aware of the harm done to their own cause by the extraneous injection of Arab antagonism to Israel into the issue of human rights in Africa. The *1973-83 Decade for Action to Combat Racism and Racial Discrimination* was proclaimed by the General Assembly; national, regional, and international action was to eliminate racism and racial discrimination in all its forms. The *First World Conference to Combat Racism and Racial Discrimination* held in Geneva in August 1978 proposed to end discrimination and the dissemination of ideas based on racial superiority. But in February 1983, U.N. Assistant Secretary General James Jonah, the Secretary General of the *Second World Conference,* held in August 1983, observed that the achievements of the decade had been quite minimal because of political difficulties, that the "Zionism is racism" resolution of November 1975 had led to "serious questioning of the motives for the Decade," and that a number of countries had walked out when the Arab countries had brought the Middle East issue into the *First Conference.*[10]

At the *Second Conference* itself, Ambassador Jonah, arguing that Zionism was intrinsically anti-racist, helped prevent yet another resolution equating Zionism with racism, though he could not prevent the final resolution of that Conference from including condemnation of Israel's "racial discrimination against Palestinians" in the occupied territories, and an attack on Israel's growing relations with the "racist regime" of South Africa.[11]

Ambassador Jonah's sensible advice was disregarded with the convoking of the August 1984 Tunis *Conference of Arab Solidarity with the Struggle for Liberation in Southern Africa,* organized by the Special Committee against Apartheid in cooperation with the League of Arab States. Predictably, this Conference "strongly condemned the close alliance which has developed between the racist regimes in Pretoria and Tel Aviv in their common hostility to genuine freedom of African and Arab peoples. The growing collaboration between these regimes in the military, nuclear, economic and cultural fields represents a menace to both Africa and the Arab States and people." The Conference also commended African states which "have refrained from any relations with Israel because of its alliance with the racist regime in South Africa and its hostility toward the Arab people and the inalienable rights of the Palestinians."[12]

These themes have been incessantly repeated in the halls of the U.N., including most recently the General Assembly meetings to discuss *apartheid* in November 1984. During the long debate, representatives of the Communist and Arab countries engaged in a similar litany. Israel was charged with an alliance in all fields or with open collaboration with South Africa. It was termed "racist," occasionally "Nazi"; was depicted as a colonial regime wallowing in military pride. It was accused of committing acts of genocide against the Palestinians; with seeking to apply the Nazi concept of *lebensraum* and with using the same repressive methods as the *apartheid* regime. Moreover, it was alleged to be a conduit of arms to South Africa and to be actively assisting it in the enhancement of its nuclear capacity. The style of this debate, one instance of dozens, exemplifies the fact that the U.N. has been used to exacerbate disputes rather than to resolve them. It can only be regretted that the concern of many representatives about the alleged curtailment of human rights by Israel has not yet extended to ways in which their governments might contribute to greater fulfillment of those rights in their own countries.

The only comic relief in the November debate was the attack of the Albanian representative on "Soviet social imperialism," which he regarded as almost as harmful as Israel and the United States in its impact on African affairs.[13] Less amusing was the reckless tossing around of statistics. At one point, for example, the Ukranian delegate charged that South Africa received 70 percent of Israel's arms exports. Fifteen minutes later, the Soviet delegate reduced the figure to 35 percent of Israel's arms sales in 1983.[14] (This may well be the only recorded instance of a publicly expressed difference between these two member states.) Logic too was often in short supply. Mr. Khalifa, speaking as Special Rapporteur appointed by the Sub-Commission on Prevention of Discrimination and Protection of Minorities included in his analysis of the "racist and colonialist regime of South Africa" the view that South Africa was nothing but the "Israel of Africa" and that "Israel was the South Africa of the Middle East."[15]

Yet, an interesting development is noticeable in the current debates. The ritualistic formula of condemnation is now "the continued collaboration of certain Western states and Israel with the racist regime of South Africa." But only the Communist and Arab countries engage in the vitriolic attacks on Israel or the invidious comparisons of it with South Africa. At the last General Assembly meeting, moderation appears to have surfaced in that the non-Arab and non-Muslim African countries, with rare exceptions, refrained from similar condemnation.

Israel and South Africa

This change in attitude suggests that the fantasy created by Arab and Soviet political legerdemain is starting to fade. Rational analysis of the real relationship between the two countries may dispel the phantasmagoria of "close cooperation" or "infamous alliance" in trade, military, nuclear, diplomatic and cultural matters.

Trade. From any objective point of view the attacks on the supposed close relationship between South Africa and Israel are patently absurd. While it is true that trade has increased in the decade since the 1973 Yom Kippur war, the total volume remains small, even allowing for the fact that some figures, such as sales of diamonds, are routinely excluded from official figures. The trade figures can be stated simply. In 1983 Israel's imports from South Africa amounted to 0.8 percent of the latter's total exports, and its exports to South Africa were 0.5 percent of that country's total imports. On the other hand, Israel's imports from South Africa in 1983 amounted to 1.7 percent of its total imports, while its exports to South Africa amounted to 1.8 percent of its total exports.

Trade between the two countries (Tables 1 and 2) is between one-fifth and one-sixth of that between South Africa and the countries of Black Africa, which in 1983 amounted to $772 million in exports and $288 million in imports; indirect, unpublicized trade through third parties makes these figures considerably higher. The extent of this trade by Black Africa is even more surprising when one remembers that these states are members of the OAU, which officially maintains a trade boycott against South Africa. It is understandable that the African states must trade where they can, but the double moral standard so much in evidence in these matters has meant that the African countries have no-

Table 1:

A. Direction of South African Trade ($ million)

	Exports		Imports	
	1982	**1983**	**1982**	**1983**
World	17,647	18,881	17,026	14,392
United States	1,220	1,551	2,484	2,207
Japan	1,533	1,390	1,711	1,765
France	415	353	708	544
Germany	785	703	2,503	2,003
Britain	1,300	1,219	2,029	1,697
Non-oil producing countries	1,732	1,748	1,032	1,208
Africa	834	772	305	288
Asia	494	638	437	438
Latin and Central America	166	83	193	376
Israel	140	142	66	69
Arab Oil Exporters		not reported		
Soviet Camp	15	24 (most not reported)	60	22

B. Per Cent Distribution of Trade

	Exports		Imports	
	1982	**1983**	**1982**	**1983**
Industrial Countries	44.0	44.3	68.7	71.4
Oil Exporting Countries	0.4	0.2	—	—
Non-Oil Exporting Countries	9.8	9.3	6.1	8.4
Africa	4.7	4.1	1.8	2.0
Israel	0.8	0.8	0.4	0.5
Asia	2.8	3.4	2.6	3.0
Europe (Non-industrial)	0.6	0.6	0.2	0.3
Latin and Central America	0.9	0.4	1.1	2.6
Soviet Camp	0.1	0.1	0.4	0.2

Source: *Direction of Trade Statistics*, IMF 1984 Yearbook

where been condemned for conducting almost ten times as much trade with South Africa as does Israel.

Of the 52 member states of the OAU, at least 46 now have some commercial relationships with South Africa including trade in a variety of industrial products, machinery, food and basic raw materials. For many African states South Africa is the cheapest source of needed goods; it is the foremost trading partner of Zimbabwe and Zambia. (The latter takes 16 percent of its total imports from South Africa.) Other links exist among the African countries. South African airlines have flights to at least 12 African states. Mozambique, through the port of Maputo, handles over 15 percent of South Africa's total trade. Moreover, several of the Black African countries rely on South Africa for service

Table 2:
A. Direction of Israel Trade ($ million)

	Exports		Imports	
	1982	**1983**	**1982**	**1983**
World	4,186	5,067	9,763	9,336
United States	1,119	1,319	1,542	1,626
United Kingdom	404	395	618	666
Germany	354	348	895	1,038
Oil Exporting countries	64	38	0.9	1
Non-Oil Exporting Countries	769	735	578	570
South Africa	78	86	166	168
Rest of Africa	44	36	25	14
Asia	310	334	96	107
Egypt	25	7	0.8	7
Latin and Central America	109	82	156	141
Soviet Bloc	6	10	12	12

B. Per Cent Distribution of Trade

	Exports		Imports	
	1982	**1983**	**1982**	**1983**
Industrial Countries	65	71	57.4	68
Oil Exporting Countries	1.2	0.8	—	—
Non-Oil Exporting Countries	14.6	14.5	5.9	6.1
South Africa	1.5	1.7	1.7	1.8
Other Africa	0.8	0.7	0.3	0.1
Asia	5.9	6.6	1.0	1.1
Europe (Non-industrial)	3.8	3.7	1.4	1.4
Middle East	0.5	0.1	—	0.1
Latin and Central America	2.1	1.6	1.6	1.5
Soviet Bloc	0.1	0.2	0.1	0.1

Source: *Direction of Trade Statistics*, IMF 1984 Yearbook

of their aircraft and railroad equipment and occasionally for the purchase of armored cars. In addition, South Africa is an important source of employment for citizens of Black Africa; some 80 percent of the South African mining force is drawn from neighboring Black countries.

Official figures do not list South African trade with specific African or Middle Eastern countries apart from Israel. However, it is known that a number of Arab states have sold South Africa large quantities of oil in exchange for gold, diamonds, foodstuffs, and building materials. Until 1973 Saudi Arabia provided about a quarter of South Africa's oil, and this trade continues.

In spite of a supposed embargo, reaffirmed in 1983, by the Organization of Arab Petroleum Exporting Countries (OAPEC), on the sale of oil to South Africa, a substantial part of that country's oil imports come from the Arab countries. Though the origin of the oil shipped to South Africa is concealed, it can be traced through the data of the Shipping Research Bureau in the Netherlands, which monitors tankers delivering oil, and the Lloyds Voyage Records, which publish the actual shipments.

The results provide interesting instruction in the art of duplicity. In 1984 the Dutch Bureau traced 49 shipments of oil to South Africa. Of these, 37 (76 percent) came from four Arab countries. The majority of this, 39 percent, came from Saudi Arabia in 19 shipments. The rest came from the United Arab Emirates (24 percent) in 12 shipments; Oman (10 percent) in five shipments; and Bahrein (2 percent) in one shipment. Another 6 percent came from Islamic Iran. It is worth noting that the Arab proportion of oil exports to South Africa increased from 38 percent in 1981 to 76 percent in 1984. Moreover, since the Dutch Bureau could trace only about half of the South African imports, it is likely, on the assumption that the proportions of untraced oil correspond to those of the known amounts, that Arab oil exports to South Africa would reach almost $2.5 billion a year. On the basis of these estimated figures, Arab trade with South Africa would be larger than that of Britain ($1.6 billion), Japan ($1.7 billion) and even that of the United States ($2.2 billion). Typical of the fantasy world of the U.N., General Assembly Resolution 39/72 of December 13, 1984 commends "the decisions of oil exporting countries that have declared it their policy not to sell oil to South Africa."

The extent of the commercial relationship between the Arab states and South Africa is officially left obscure. But it would seem that these states account for more than a third of total foreign investment in South Africa. Kuwait is known to hold a controlling interest in the Lonrho Corporation, one of the world's largest multinational businesses. Although the destination of South Africa's gold sales is unstated, because gold is sold both on the open market in London to undeclared buyers and to banks in Zurich which in turn sell to customers, the amount going to the Arab countries is believed to be considerable. In communication links, a significant development is the new air route between South Africa and Jedda, via Moroni, the Comoran capital, and Mogadishu, Somalia, for pilgrims to Mecca. Though South Africa's Muslim population is only 177,000 and the *hajj* takes place just once a year, the new air service makes weekly flights.

In all, South Africa has over 140 trading partners in the world, and these include a number of the members of the *Special Committee against Apartheid*. One expects South African trade with the developed countries in Europe and elsewhere to be substantial. As a basis for comparison: in 1981 Japan bought $1,574 million and sold $2,266 million to South Africa, Britain bought $1,313 million and sold $2,500 million, and France bought $638 million and sold $1,046 million. The nine members of the Common Market in 1979 were responsible for 52.7 percent of South Africa's imports and for 36.7 percent of its exports. More surprising has been South African trade with the East European countries, including the Soviet Union, which in 1981 amounted to $22.4 million and in 1983 to $24 million in exports and $51.2 million in 1981 and $22 million in 1983 in imports. Taking account of South Africa's secret trade (much of it conducted in Antwerp and Amsterdam) with the Communist countries would almost certainly make those figures much larger. The Soviet Union is also known to have been a substantial buyer of chrome from South Africa. Thus the figures belie the Soviet Union's repeated claims that it does not trade with South Africa. Therefore its frequent calls for a trade embargo can only be regarded with suspicion.

On related economic issues, many in the international community have applied a double standard. Israeli investment in South Africa, in desalination plants and electronic equipment, is criticized, yet it accounts for only 0.1 percent of the total investments in South Africa and only 0.01 percent of Israel's own total annual investment.[16] South Africa has invested in Israeli housing, hotels and port development. An interesting contrast is that Black Africa has invested $570 million, Asia $400 million and Western Europe $13.5 billion in South Africa. French investments in South Africa amount to over 7 percent of its total foreign investments.

Some joint South African-Israeli companies and ventures have been set up, mostly in iron and steel processing and chemical and fertilized manufacturing. Air and shipping exchanges have taken place, and the sale of Krugerrands is permitted in Israel. Some small scale trade exists between Israeli businessmen and the South African homelands, but Israel has officially refused to recognize any of these homelands and has frowned on the trade relationships. This small trade fades into insignificance compared with the extent of trade involved in the Soviet Union's diamond output, which is marketed through the South African firm of De Beers.

Military. The thunderous condemnations in the U.N. often allege a close military relationship between South Africa and Israel in arms sales, military advice and nuclear cooperation. Allegations of this kind, repeated by sources in this country hostile to or frequently critical of Israel are based on little hard evidence or documentation. The most absurd recent allegation apeared in the Soviet daily *Selskaya Zhizn* (picked up by *Kenya Times,* April 3, 1985), which averred that Israel and South Africa were developing chemical weapons that would kill only Arabs and non-whites.

Between 1963 and 1975, over $1 billion in arms and war material was sold to South Africa, with France as the largest supplier. Other arms have been sold not only by Western countries but also by the Soviet Union, Czechoslovakia and Bulgaria, sometimes through German and Austrian agents; and by Jordan, which in 1974 sold British Centurion battle tanks and the Tiger surface-to-air missile system together with support and maintenance equipment.[17]

Military trade between South Africa and Israel has been a very small part of the former's arms trade, and all of it has been related to defense purposes. Israel is known to have supplied six *Reshef*-class fast attack missile boats which protect the South African coast line, and is reported by the Stockholm International Peace Research Institute to have sold Gabriel-2 missiles for these craft. Some remotely-piloted drone scouts and a number of Ramata patrol boats have been sold, as has electronic surveillance equipment, radar stations and alarm systems. South Africa is believed to have a Belgian license to manufacture Uzi sub-machine guns. These past Israeli sales are insignificant, from both a financial and military point of view, in contrast to the arms sales of other countries.

Despite a 1977 United Nations Security Council resolution reaffirming a 1963 UN arms embargo declaration, sales of arms to South Africa have continued, although in a more surreptitious manner than heretofore. Israel has stated on many occasions that it will abide by the 1977 Security Council Resolution. But France sold South Africa 360 air-to-surface missiles in 1980, and granted licenses for production of Landmobile surface-to-air missiles, and

Mirage F-1A fighter aircraft and armored cars. Italy has supplied attack trainer aircraft.

Allegations of nuclear cooperation or collusion between South Africa and Israel have frequently been raised in international forums. Yet, a U.N. study in 1980 on "Implementation of the Declaration on the Denuclearization of Africa" found no evidence to substantiate these allegations. On the other hand, it is undeniable that France has built South Africa a nuclear power station with two reactors and two turbine generators near Cape Town and that China has supplied South Africa with enriched uranium.

Even more important, because it is much more dangerous for the whole of Africa, is Libya's pursuit of nuclear weapon capability. Qadhafi, an apostle of the "Islamic bomb," is determined that Libya shall "have our share of the atomic weapon." Though Libya failed to persuade China to sell it an atomic device in 1971, Qadhafi persisted in his efforts and in 1974 succeeded in getting Argentina to sign a secret agreement for uranium prospecting. Libya then turned to the Soviet Union and in 1975 signed an agreement under which the Soviets built the Libyans a 10-megawatt research reactor outside Tripoli and, in addition, supplied them with a 440-mw power reactor. More recently, Libya has not only imported Arab scientists to work on nuclear research, but has also bought uranium from Niger, some of which has been diverted to Pakistan for the manufacture of *its* bomb. The Aouzon strip in northern Chad, which Libya has occupied since 1975, apparently contains uranium. This suggests that the occupation of the area by Libya is directly connected with its desire to secure its own reliable supply of uranium ore.

African countries are increasingly aware of the Libyan threat in nuclear weapons. They have also realized that the danger of military aggression emanates not from Israel, as the Communist-Arab bloc argues, but from the ambitions of the Libyan dictator, who has already sent troops to Chad, Tunisia, and Uganda; and from the Communist countries, such as Cuba with 38,000 troops in Angola and Ethiopia, and the Eastern European countries which have stationed contingents in several African countries, thereby exposing their governments to destabilization.

Diplomatic and Cultural. Diplomatic and political relationships between South Africa and Israel have fluctuated in response to the warmth which Black Africa has manifested towards Israel. In 1949 Israel established a diplomatic and consular mission in South Africa, but this was not upgraded to an embassy until 1974. South Africa did not set up a consulate general in Tel Aviv until 1971, and this did not become an embassy until 1975. Whatever the level of the relationship, Israel has always made clear that the existence of diplomatic relations does not imply Israeli support for the policy of *apartheid* either in the forums of international organizations or in direct representations to the South African government. A particularly significant symbolic gesture was made in 1978 when the Israeli Ambassador, boycotting the premiere of the play *Golda* because Africans were not admitted to the theatre in Pretoria, explained that by attending "I would commit an act of infidelity to our heritage." This heritage, which includes opposition to racism in all its forms, was expressed with contemporary relevance by Theodor Herzl eighty years ago in his novel *Altneuland* when he wrote that "once I have witnessed the redemption of the Jews, my people, I wish also to assist in the redemption of the Africans."

As a consequence of the diplomatic exchanges, Prime Minister Vorster visited Israel in 1976, President Botha paid a two-day visit in 1984; and Israeli leaders, including Simcha Erlich, Moshe Dayan and Ariel Sharon, visited South Africa. In the international lexicon these meetings have been accorded an awesome significance while the many other political visitors from all over the world go uncommented upon. In the case of these other countries, 26 of which have diplomatic missions in South Africa, it is accepted that normal relations do not require acceptance of each other's policies, nor do they prevent criticism of these policies. Israel and South Africa are not allies, and no *entente cordiale* exists between them. They are associated, as are other nations, for mutual convenience. It is therefore regrettable that some Black African countries perceive that association as one of high visibility and profess to be disturbed by the diplomatic activities of Israel, a country that was once an exemplary symbol for them.

Though the Communist-Arab bloc has continued to depict the two countries as "racist," the argument is belied by the asymmetrical motives for this portrayal. On the one hand, South Africa is denounced because of its internal policies of racial discrimination and its political structure. But Israel is attacked because of its very existence. Distorted arguments, incorrect data and inflamed rhetoric are then employed to justify the condemnation.

Israel's relationship with South Africa, low-level though it is in reality, has not gained much admiration for Israel. Yet its basic motivations are understandable as a defensive policy after the disappointment over the breaking of relations by Black Africa. Both countries are confronted by threats to their regimes and, in the case of Israel, to its existence. But for Israel there is also the troubling problem of the Jewish community of 120,000 in South Africa, which is no longer subject to acute discrimination or harassment and which since 1967 can again supply financial support to Israel.

African Disillusion with the Arab Countries

Why did Black Africa reverse its cordial relationship with Israel? To some extent the reversal can be ascribed to ideological conversion or religious identification. Some African states genuinely accepted the Arab position in Middle East affairs, saw Israel as an outpost of imperialism, and called for justice for the Palestinians whose image changed dramatically to that of victims of aggression. A considerable part of the Sub-Saharan population — perhaps over 100 million — is Muslim. It is understandable that countries like Senegal, Mali, Guinea and Niger, with populations that are 80 percent Muslim, may be predisposed to be sympathetic to the Arab point of view.

Black African criticism of Israel is traceable to a variety of reasons. For example, Israel overextended itself in its early African projects, some of which were unsuccessful, others too expensive or inappropriate, as in Tanzania. Moreover, it raised excessive African expectations for its development aid program. As a result the various countries found it convenient to blame Israel for their own indigenous economic, political, and institutional difficulties.[18] One can also understand African unhappiness at the failure of the mission of the four African "wise men," the heads of state who in November 1971 visited Egypt and Israel under OAU auspices to try to revive the Jarring peace mission to the Middle East. Heavy Arab pressure at the next OAU meeting in 1972 led many African countries to condemn Israel.

But the Arab diplomatic offensive against Israel, starting with the visits of King Feisal to Africa in 1966 and 1972, coupled with the Arab use of money and oil as weapons of persuasion, has been the most significant factor. Though some have attempted to deny that African countries were ever promised assistance in return for political support, most observers agree with Mazrui that "some black Africans expected special rewards from the Arabs following their break with Israel."[19]

If this was indeed the case, the results have been disappointing for the Africans. Before 1973 the volume of Arab aid was relatively modest. Essentially it was limited to grants and loans by Kuwait, Libya, and Saudi Arabia to Jordan, Syria and Egypt.[20] Between 1973 and 1977, 83 percent of Arab aid went to other Arab countries; Sub-Saharan Africa received only about 8 percent.[21] The largest amount of aid still goes to the Arab League countries of Africa (Mauritania, Sudan and Somalia), to mainly Muslim countries

(Guinea and Niger), and to those that have politically supported the Arab position.[22]

Official reports now acknowledge that the "rather low level of aid" to non-Arab Africa contrasts with repeated Arab statements alleging the importance of Arab-African cooperation.[23] Moreover, Arab commitments to non-Arab African countries have been less than one-tenth of Western official aid.[24] During 1975-78, the Arab OPEC countries provided $640 million (2.5 percent) of the total of $25.4 billion received by Black Africa from all sources. The extravagant promise of $1.45 billion made at the first Afro-Arab summit meeting in Cairo in 1977 has not been kept. In recent years net aid disbursements by OPEC to all countries have fallen by one-third. In 1982 this represented 1.22 percent of GNP, the lowest since 1971.

Bilateral concessional aid from OPEC to Sub-Saharan Africa fell from $1191.8 million in 1980 to $914.4 million in 1982. Even if one adds the amounts coming from multinational bodies, such as the Arab Bank for Economic Development in Africa (BADEA), the Arab Fund for Economic and Social Development, the OPEC Special Fund, the Special Arab Aid Fund for Africa, the Islamic Development Bank and international bodies, the total remains considerably lower than the commitment. The program of BADEA, though significant, has come nowhere near meeting the targets projected by its own leaders in 1975.[25] By the end of 1982 only $235 million had actually been disbursed.

African countries are aware of the negative consequences of the rise in oil prices which resulted from OPEC action. Arab aid has not come close to compensating them for their increased expenditures on imports of oil and other products, such as fertilisers and insecticides, based on petrochemicals.[26]

This has affected them adversely in three ways: they are paying a higher direct price for oil; they are paying higher world prices for manufactured goods due to inflation; and they are suffering declining demand for their primary products as Western consumption has fallen in response to the oil price rise.[27]

It has been calculated that African countries have paid the Arab OPEC (AOPEC) countries $35 billion for oil while receiving only $2 billion in aid.[28] AOPEC refused to agree on a two-tier pricing system for oil to help the Africans. The real cost of oil imports can be seen in the following table.

Oil Import Costs as a Proportion of Total Exports and Imports

	Exports		Imports	
	1973	**1979**	**1973**	**1979**
Kenya	13.6	31.8	11.7	18.5
Tanzania	14.3	31.6	10.6	15.6
Madagascar	9.5	18.6	10.7	11.3

Source: Yearbook of International Trade Statistics, UN, 1979; IMF International Financial Statistics, 1981.

This has hurt in two ways. Oil accounts for between a fifth and a third of all imports in Africa. The price rise meant that oil consumption went up by only 2.8 percent between 1973 and 1979, as compared to 5.9 percent for the entire Third World.[29] As a consequence, development has been slowed. Secondly, because of the oil price rise, oil imports, which average about 15 percent of total imports, have increased as a share of exports, and African countries have had to forego other imports.

Non-Oil Sub-Saharan Africa Imports of Oil

	1970	**1973**	**1979**
Barrels (thousands)	55,664	57,355	79,794
Value ($ million)	178	297	1,676

Source: Yearbook of World Energy Statistics, UN, 1980; Statistical Survey of Non-OPEC Developing Countries, OPEC, 1979.

In addition this has meant a worsening of their balance of payments position, together with an increase of indebtedness.[30] This results from the higher price of manufactured goods, again due to oil price increases, which have accelerated inflation and has led to increased rates of interest at the international level. All this has meant not only a threat to African economies and the depletion of the foreign exchange reserves of several African countries, but also the stagnation or disruption of their socio-economic development plans. The reality today is that African countries are poorer now than they were in 1970, and the pressures of population, already over 500 million, are mounting. As a result of these crises of development, internal conflict has been sharpened, causing a generally higher proportion of scarce resources to be spent on the military and in some extreme cases, to governments being taken over by the military.[31] The Arab countries are less interested in the labor-intensive projects of Africa than in their own capital-intensive projects. Moreover, Arab countries trade with the West rather than provide markets for African goods.[32]

The Winds of Change

The November 1984 *apartheid* debate in the UN General Assembly serves as a barometer of changing African views of the Arab-Israel conflict. African states are evincing a new unwillingness to introduce irrelevant anti-Israeli declarations in the context of their own affairs. This phenomenon is attributable to a number of factors.

Some African states have acknowledged that the ostensible reason for breaking relations — Israeli occupation of African soil — no longer obtains. Some are anxious to support the pacific policy of Egypt. After the exchange of ambassadors between Egypt and Israel, full relations with Israel were reestablished by Zaire in 1982 and by Liberia in 1983, and Israeli diplomatic "interest offices" have been set up in six other countries.

Economic relations between Israel and 22 black African countries exist in a variety of forms.[33] Even after formal relations were broken, other ties, in trade and training programs, were never fully ended. Trade in imports and exports increased from $57 million in 1972 to $132 million in 1981-92. Israeli companies, such as Solel Boneh and Koor, and Israeli consulting firms are active in fields such as road construction, public housing and industrial development. Israeli assistance programs have restarted with the return of advisers to Black Africa — over 1000 Israelis currently work in Nigeria — and the training of Africans in Israel.

These new Afro-Israeli relations are different in character from those of the 1960s. The Israeli presence is now more low key and less ambitious, Trade, economic and cultural ties are stressed more than aid and diplomacy. The links between the countries, less diffused and often concentrating on the more economically advanced black nations, have as their key figures businessmen and managers rather than diplomats and technical experts.[34] Israel and Black Africa both need institutions and collective habits in which tradition and modernity can coexist.[35] But both sides appreciate that the Israeli model of development is not easily transferable to Black Africa.

The African countries have also understood that economic realities, of which the Arab boycott is a major element, oblige Israel to trade where it can just as they themselves do. Such trade implies neither close cooperation nor commitment to similar social and political values. Indeed, they can recognize that the sincerity of the Israeli rejection of *apartheid* is the result of Jewish historic suffering from racist policies to which Jews were subject.

Designating Israel in the international organizations as "racist" or equating it with South Africa rests on inappropriate analysis at best and on deliberate obfuscation at worst. Legitimate differences may exist regarding the treatment of Arabs inside Israel and the condition and destiny of the Palestinian population in the territories administered by Israel. But rational criticism of Israeli actions and policies ought to fall far short of attacking it as a "racist" state. To say that Israel was founded as a *Jewish* state is not to say that it has a separatist ideology; the crucial determining fact is that the 18 percent non-Jewish part of its current population possesses full legal, religious, civil and political rights. From an ideological point of view, Zionism, a national liberation movement calling for the ingathering of Jews, is totally different from *apartheid,* which is based on racial distinctiveness and the superiority of some races to others. Zionism is a philosophy related to the Jewish people; it is not related to race in any way. The people is composed of individuals from widely different backgrounds and races. Ethnic demands have been made in Israel, and inequality exists — as it does in all countries — in the distribution of economic resources and political power.[36] But Israel is a democratic society with a population of all different colors, and its political system is open to a variety of pressures: between different ethnic Jewish groups, between the Arab minority and the Jewish majority, between the religious orthodox and the non-religious, and within all of these groups.

If no rational argument is sufficient for those who have labelled Israel as a "racist" state or who refuse to see the Law of Return as religious and moral, not exclusive, in character, the example of Operation Moses, the extraordinary and successful transporting of over 10,000 Ethiopian Jews to Israel in late 1984 and early 1985 ought to show unmistakably the falsity of accusations of colonialism, racism or color prejudice. Immediately on arrival in Israel these black Jews, self-styled members of *Beta Israel* (the House of Israel) were given citizenship as part of a common people.

African countries have registered disappointment at and disillusion with Arab actions. They do not relish the hypocrisy of the Arab nations which engage in trade with South Africa in a volume at least ten times greater than Israel's trade with that country. They have expressed disappointment at the amount of AOPEC aid, which has not been sufficient to offset the huge rise in oil prices. The countries are aware of the cost in cash, in reduced development and food production, and in the increase of national debt consequent to the rise in the price of oil.[37] Nigeria in particular, though a member of OPEC like Gabon, has diverged from the oil-price and other policies of Saudi Arabia. With the present world oil glut, the Arab "oil weapon" has lost its edge if not its effectiveness. The Arab Oil Exporting Countries have less money available and are now less able to exert pressure on African countries to share these countries' views on a Middle East issue that is not of central concern to them and that, indeed, may handicap their own struggle to develop. In his speech at Geneva in August 1983, U.N. Assistant Secretary Jonah reminded the *Second World Conference to Combat Racism and Racial Discrimination* that the Secretary-General of the United Nations had recommended that governments adopt measures with a view to making the deliberative organs of the U.N. credible forums, for negotiation even encouraging them "to eschew rhetoric in preference to the search for practical solutions to difficult international problems."[38]

Notwithstanding all these factors, Arab pressure and influence still remains a force in African-Israeli relations. Most African countries have supported the call for Palestinian self-determination, a policy they distinguish from hostility to Israel itself. Though the first — and so far the only — Afro-Arab summit meeting was not held until 1977, such meetings, arranged by the permanent committee on Arab-African cooperation, are available for political interchange. Arab pressure was brought to bear in 1982 when all aid to Zaire was cut off and several Arab nations broke relations with that country after it reestablished ties with Israel. African countries which are wholly or significantly Muslim are not soon likely to look favorably on Israel, though in some cases (notably Nigeria and Cameroon) direct and indirect commercial ties have been maintained despite Arab pressure. In any case, restoration of relations with Israel is not a high priority item for Black Africa.[39] Agricultural expertise from Israel is more welcome at the present time of drought and food crises in Africa.

A number of factors — geopolitical, religious, economic, common association with African themes — have helped strengthen Arab organizational efforts and rhetorical appeals to influence and gain support from Black Africa.[40] Nine members of the Arab League are in the African continent and are therefore members of the OAU as well. The slogan of Afro-Arab solidarity and the desire of African countries to strengthen OAU have been used to link Middle Eastern and African issues. In return for African support, the Arab countries have backed the Africans not only on the South Africa issue but also on Third World issues such as global redistribution of wealth and a new world information order.[41] Muslims now constitute perhaps well over a third of the African population and Arabic is the most important single language, spoken by about a fifth of the continent.[42] Between 1973 and 1982 Africa received committments for about $5.7 billion in Arab aid, though only a small portion was actually received.

Ideologically, some radical African leaders view the Arabs as partners in the struggle against colonialism and imperialism. For Israel, a particular difficulty arises because the chief African liberation movements are revolutionary Marxist and are linked with the Soviet Union in a number of ways. They tend to link Israel and South Africa as outposts of monopoly capitalism, and therefore of racism. The African National Congress of South Africa is allied to the Communist Party; its publications since the late 1960s have held that the racial policies of Israel and South Africa are similar.[43]

The combination of Arab oil wealth and Communist political and diplomatic activity has influenced the outcome of Afro-Arab meetings at both official and nongovernmental levels. Since 1976, diplomatic representation of Arab countries in Africa has increased; some sort of Arab representation in now present in every African country.

The result has been the series of international resolutions in which Israel is portrayed as an aggressor, a racist state, an ally of South Africa and a threat to the African continent. Though many African countries at first objected to the linking of unrelated issues, Arab persistence succeeded in wearing down resistance. At the 1977 Afro-Arab summit, discrimination was condemned in "South Africa, Palestine, and other Arab and African occupied territories." The meeting of the OAU "radical" states, attended by only 24 members, in Tripoli in August 1982 called for an international economic and military embargo on "the Zionist entity." The most recent OAU summit, in Addis Ababa in June 1983, decided against resumption of diplomatic relations with Israel.

Nevertheless, the winds of change are blowing more strongly. Some Africans remain opposed to Arab insistence on extreme resolutions condemning Israel. Africans are not unaware that the Arabs are exploiting them for Arab political ends. African reservations on this score are mounting as the result of a number of factors: the high price of oil, African memories of the Arab slave trade, the distinction between "white" Arabs in North Africa and Black Africa, the fear of the spread of fundamentalist Islam, the possibility that Christianity might be imperilled, the lessons from the prolonged civil war in Southern Sudan, the hostility between Ethiopia and Eritrea, the conflict in Western Sahara and the Arab political machinations in Angola and Chad, all have reinforced African concern. At the 1981 Arab League conference, President Moi of Kenya, then chairman of the OAU, indicated that the Arab-Israeli conflict "should not be allowed to overshadow other issues calling for solutions."

In general the African countries are now less fearful of Arab threats or the efficacy of Arab sanctions against them on issues connected with the Middle East. They are more aware of the military threat to the continent as a whole posed by the unpredictable behavior of Colonel Qadhafi. His occasional calls for a *jihad* against Christianity in Africa have reminded Africans of past days of enslavement when, as Joseph Nyerere, the brother of the Tanzanian President, said in June 1974 "... the Arabs, our former slave-masters, used to drive us like herds of cattle and sell us as slaves." In similar fashion, President Banda of Malawi argued that the Arab participation in the African slave trade excluded them from being considered genuine friends of Africa.[44] The story of black slavery in the Arab countries generally, and in Saudi Arabia until 1962, and the indignity implied by the colloquial Arab use of the word for slaves *(Abid)* in referring to blacks are not forgotten.[45] This African collective memory of Arab slave traders, and the proselytization of Islam, by the sword as well as by trade, have left Black Africans with a negative attitude towards Arabs.[46]

African countries have become aware that the issue of racism, on which they rightly feel so strongly, has been exploited for the political advantage of others. They understand that the Arab-Israeli conflict is a political problem having no connection with the elimination of racial discrimination in Africa. They can perceive the irony of President Assad, who slaughtered 20,000 of his own people in Hama in 1982, writing of "the racist-Zionist regime's inexplicable crimes, atrocities and acts of aggression" to the *1983 Second World Conference to Combat Racism and Racial Discrimination.*[47] Everyone genuinely concerned with that combat must help ensure that political hatred and vituperative rhetoric will not destroy the ability of international bodies to correct injustice.

FOOTNOTES

1. Walter Lippmann, *Public Opinion*, Harcourt, Brace, New York, 1922, p. 14.

2. Gideon Shimoni, *Jews and Zionism: The South African Experience 1910-1967*, Oxford University Press, Cape Town, 1980, p. 227.

3. Ali A. Mazrui, *Africa's International Relations: The Diplomacy of Dependency and Change*, Westview Press, Boulder, 1977, p. 157

4. Michael Curtis and Susan A. Gitelson, *Israel in the Third World*, Transaction Press, New Brunswick, 1976.

5. Moshe Decter, *To Serve, To Teach, To Leave*, American Jewish Congress, New York 1977, p. 9

6. Olusola Ojo, "Israeli-South African Connections and Afro-Israeli Relations," *International Studies*, Vol. 21, No. 1, January-March 1982, p. 37.

7. Farouk A. Sankari, "The Cost and Gains of Israeli Pursuit of Influence in Africa," *Middle East Studies," Vol. 15, May 1979, p. 275.*

8. Ethan A. Nadelman, "Israel and Black Africa: A Rapprochement?," *Journal of Modern African Studies*, Vol. 19, No. 2, June 1981, p. 216.

9. United Nations Document, A/38/311, July 25, 1983.

10. James Jonah, *Objective*, February 3, 1983, United Nations Department of Public Information, pp. 24-32.

11. James Jonah, speech at World Jewish Congress, Vienna, January 29, 1985.

12. United Nations Document, A/39/450, August 31, 1985.

13. United Nations Document, A/39/PV.68, November 23, 1984, p. 47.

14. United Nations Document, A/C.3/39/SR.14, October 25, 1984, pp. 10, 13.

15. United Nations Document, A/C.3/39/SR.8, October 15, 1984, p. 5.

16. Naomi Chazan, "The Fallacies of Pragmatism: Israeli Foreign Policy Towards South Africa," *African Affairs*, Vol. 82, No. 327, April, 1983, p. 179.

17. Stockholm International Peace Research Institute, *Yearbook 1975*, p. 239.

18. Victor T. Le Vine and Timothy W. Luke, *The Arab-African Connection: Political and Economic Realities*, Westview Press, Boulder, 1979, pp. 9-11.

19. Ali A. Mazrui, "Black Africa and the Arabs," *Foreign Affairs*, No. 4, July 1975, p. 739.

20. Andre Simmons, *Arab Foreign Aid*, Fairleigh Dickinson University Press, Rutherford, N.J., 1981, p. 25.

21. *Middle East Yearbook*, 1977. p. 66, quoted in Simmons, p. 27

22. Susan A. Gitelson, "Arab Aid to Africa: How Much and at What Price?" *Jerusalem Quarterly*, Spring, 1981, pp. 120-127.

23. *Aid from OPEC Countries*, OECD, Paris, 1983, p. 34.

24. *Development Cooperation,* OECD, Paris, 1978, 1979, 1980.

25. Willard R. Johnson, "The Role of the Arab Bank for Economic Development in Africa," *Journal of Modern African Studies,* Vol. 21, No. 4, December 1983, p. 644.

26. Simmons, *op. cit.*, p. 166.

27. Michael Lyall, "Arab Aid to Black Africa: Myth versus Reality," in Dunstan M. Wai, ed., *Interdependence in a World of Unequals,* Westview Press, Boulder, 1982, p. 189.

28. Kunirum Osia, "Arab Aid to Black African States and Their Relations with Israel," *Journal of African Studies,* Vol. 10, No. 3, Fall 1983. p. 111.

29. Dunstan M. Wai, "African-Arab Relations: Interdependence or Misplaced Optimism?" *Journal of Modern African Studies,* Vol. 21, No. 2, June 1983, p. 200.

30. Philippe Hugon, "Le système financier mondial et l'endettement des Etats africains," *Afrique Contemporaine,* April-June 1984, p. 27.

31. Robin Luckham, "African-Arab-OECD Military Relations: The Recycling of Imperialism," in Wai, *Interdependence in a World of Unequals,* p. 51.

32. Victor Le Vine, "The Arabs and Africa: a Balance to 1982," *Middle East Review,* Spring/Summer 1982, p. 59.

33. Naomi Chazan, "Israel in Africa," *Jerusalem Quarterly,* No. 18, Winter 1981, pp. 31-34.

34. Naomi Chazan, "The New Politics of Participation in Tropical Africa," *Comparative Politics,* Vol. 14, No. 2, 1982.

35. Dan V. Segre, "Colonization and Decolonization: The Case of Zionist and African Elites," *Comparative Studies in Society and History,* Vol. 22, No. 1, January 1980, p. 40.

36. Yael Yishai, "Responsiveness to Ethnic Demands: the case of Israel," *Ethnic and Racial Studies,* Vol. 7, No. 2, April 1984, p. 298.

37. Chedly Ayari, "The Reality of Afro-Arab Solidarity," *African Report,* Vol. 20, No. 6, November-December, 1975, p. 8.

38. *Report of the Second World Conference to Combat Racism and Racial Discrimination,* UN.A/CONF./119/26, p. 41.

39. Arye Oded, "Africa, Israel and the Arabs: On the Restoration of Israeli-African Diplomatic Relations," *Jerusalem Journal of International Relations,* Vol. 6, No. 3, 1982-83, p. 69.

40. *Ibid.*, pp. 51-52.

41. Le Vine, *Middle East Review,* p. 57.

42. Ali A. Mazrui, "The Semantic Impact on Black Africa: Arab and Jewish Cultural Influences," *Issue,* Vol. XIII, 1984, p. 4.

43. Richard L. Sklar, "Africa and the Middle East: What Blacks and Jews owe to each other," Paper presented at the Afro-American Studies Program, March 25-27, 1982.

44. *Zambia Daily Mail,* June 21, 1974; Aryeh Oded, "Slaves and Oil: The Arab Image in Black Africa," *Wiener Library Bulletin,* 27, 1974, pp. 34-47; Basil Davidson, *The African Slave Trade: Pre-Colonial History, 1450-1850,* Little, Brown, Boston, 1961, pp. 192-193.

45. Dunstan M. Wai, African-Arab Relations from Slavery to Petro-Jihad," *Issue,* Vol. XIII, 1984, p. 9.

46. *Ibid.*, p. 9.

47. *Report of the Second World Conference,* p. 54.

46 The Arabs and Africa: A Balance To 1982

By Victor T. LeVine

The bloom is definitely off the rose. The Arab-African alliance, largely created in the heat of the 1973-74 oil crisis and the October 1973 Arab-Israeli war, now remains more a marriage of convenience than the great and indissoluble bond of friendship its founders had hoped it would become. Based as it was on combinations of coercion and persuasion, principle and political opportunism, greed and economic realism, all evoked by the extraordinary events of the June 1976-October 1973 period rather than by long-standing, recognized affinities, the alliance was bound to begin disintegrating once the special circumstances which had brought it into being had either vanished or begun to change dramatically. Unquestionably, what remains of the alliance still provides some useful returns to both sides: for the Arabs, there are some forty nearly-automatic votes in the UN (and other international bodies) on Palestinian issues, denunciations of Israel, and other matters of interest to the Arab bloc. There are also the symbolic rewards of alignment with the "Third World," which has permitted the Arab oil producers to pose as champions of the poor countries and blame the West for the latter's troubles. For the Africans, there are still sizeable amounts of development aid, energy-related balance of payments support, some capital investment, as well as Arab votes in the UN and elsewhere on issues related to Namibia, Southern Africa, and demands for the global redistribution of wealth. However, recent developments now offer a much more somber picture of the relationship, not the least of which is a shared perception — for radically different reasons, to be sure — that the alliance has become excessively asymmetrical and that in any case, it has lost much of its original raison d'être. The cracks in the foundation are by now large enough to be easily visible, so much so that they can no longer be papered over by declarations of mutual concern and solidarity. These cracks are, moreover, largely exposed by the Africans themselves, and include, for example, increasingly open statements about Arab stinginess in aid and investment, a more frequent willingness by African leaders to ascribe many of their current economic difficulties to high oil prices, muted (and now, some open) talk about reestablishing diplomatic relations with Israel, the visible anger and frustration over Colonel Qadhafi's Chadian *Anschluss*, the controversy at the 1981 Nairobi OAU summit over siting the 1982 meetings in Tripoli, and the demand — as yet unmet — by Black African foreign ministers at Nairobi for another Arab-African summit to sort out their grievances. Anthony Sylvester, an observer particularly sympathetic to the Arab side of the relationship, has suggested that some of these problems are "technical" in nature, and in no way affect the amity and basic community of interests between Africans and Arabs.[1] The weight of evidence suggests otherwise. What, then, is the nature of the Arab-African alliance, and how has it evolved?

The Alliance Forms: 1967-1974

The growth and complexity of the relationships between the peoples and states of Black Africa and those of the Arab world of the Mediterranean littoral and the Near East have been traced elsewhere in detail;[2] for our purposes only a few main points are pertinent:

1. Despite the very considerable Arab-

Dr. LeVine, who is Professor of Political Science at Washington University, St. Louis, is this year on a Fulbright Scholarship at the University of Yaoundé, Cameroon. He is the co-author, with Timothy Luke, of *The Arab-African Connection: Political and Economic Realities* (Westview Press, 1979).

Muslim cultural presence in sub-Saharan Africa, the traditional Arab-African cultural and religious linkages generally have not been translated into close political and economic ties. There are perhaps 100 million Muslims in sub-Saharan Africa, and in at least ten African countries Muslims comprise over 50% of the population. Mecca receives about 200,000 pilgrims from sub-Saharan Africa every year, and the famous Islamic university of El-Azhar, in Cairo, regularly enrolls over 3,000 students from sub-Saharan countries. The Arab states of north Africa (Morocco, Algeria, Tunisia, Libya and Egypt) are all members of the Organization of African Unity (OAU). Despite all this, and for the reasons to be noted later, relations between Arab and African countries tend to reflect heuristic, pragmatic considerations rather than the older social affinities. There are two, perhaps three exceptions: Somalia (99% Muslim) joined the Arab League, as did Mauritania (96% Muslim). Both of these countries are officially "Islamic republics," which in practical terms means that Islam is the state religion, that all top government positions are reserved to Muslims, and that the two countries will almost automatically vote for League-sponsored initiatives in the UN and elsewhere. Unconfirmed reports suggest that Guinea (65% Muslim) will also become an Islamic republic,[3] though it is unlikely to become a member of the Arab League.

2. Political links between Arab states and sub-Saharan Africa before 1963 tended mainly to center on projections of Nasserist revolutionary ideology, as well as on the sponsorship of various African Liberation groups, including a number violently opposed to the African elites who were soon to take power in such countries as Senegal, Upper Volta, Niger, Ivory Coast and Cameroon. Morocco, Egypt, and (after 1962) Algeria, joined by the "radical core" of African states (Ghana, Guinea and Mali), so managed to antagonize their more moderate African neighbors that, when the third Conference of Independent African States took place in Addis Ababa in 1963, Arab concerns about the Middle East received short shrift. (The conference launched the Organization of African Unity — north African Arab states became members.)

3. Arab political influence in sub-Saharan Africa between 1957 and 1970 tended to be largely offset by a considerable and generally successful Israeli program of providing technical assistance and other aid to over two score African states. The net effect of the Israeli effort, coupled with an already well-developed African reluctance to become involved too deeply in Arab affairs, operated to maintain a visible political distance between most of the new African states and the Middle East conflict.

The June 1967 Arab-Israeli war marked the beginning of the African change of attitude — away from support of Israel and toward espousal of Arab theses on the Middle East conflict. Though the Israeli victory in 1967 was quietly hailed in Africa, it was not long before a combination of astute Arab diplomacy (continual stress on the "Tel Aviv-Johannesburg axis," two African tours — 1966 and 1972 — by Saudi Arabia's King Feisal, a number of visits by African heads of state to Arab capitals between 1967 and 1972) increased and large-scale Arab munificence to Africa, plus maladroit Israeli behavior (the tendency to become arrogant about its June 1967 victory) began to have its effects in Africa. Only Guinea broke with Israel in 1967. However, in 1971 the failure of a special OAU presidential commission (Ahidjo of Cameroon, Mobutu of Zaire, Senghor of Senegal and Gowon of Nigeria) to mediate between Israel and Egypt was immediately translated — with Arab prompting, to be sure — into evidence of Israeli intransigence and lack of sympathy for the Palestinian cause. In 1972, both Uganda and Chad broke relations with Israel and within days, Israel closed its embassies in Niger and the Congo Peoples' Republic. There is strong evidence that all four African countries, particularly the first two, were offered extraordinary financial inducements to make the break;[4] at the time, however, these developments were seen in the light of a pattern of increasing willingness by African states to endorse Arab positions.

By the end of 1973, all except four African states (Malawi, Lesotho, Botswana and

Swaziland) had renounced their ties with Israel and the Arab-African alliance was proclaimed. Again, there is no need to recapitulate here the details of the transformation; suffice it to summarize the complex of reasons underlying the African shift by noting (1) that by September, 1973 (during which month OPEC met in Vienna and the "non-aligned" states, in Algiers), pro-Arab sentiment was already quite strong in the African camp; (2) that the Israeli seizure of part of the west bank of the Suez during the latter part of the October 1973 war offered an African rallying point for the potent political charge that Israel had seized "a portion of African soil;" (3) that the October war offered the Arab oil producers an unprecedented opportunity: to tie massive increases in the price of oil (which they had intended to do all along, but more slowly) to the politics of Arab and Palestinian nationalism; (4) that the Arabs strongly encouraged the African shift by explicit and implicit promises that the African states would not be disadvantaged by the embargo and oil-price increases, and (5) that the African states themselves were under strong cross-pressures from their own neighbors to display unity in the situation.[5]

To what extent did the new Arab-African alliance reflect genuine conversion to the Arab cause? To what extent political and economic pragmatism? Granted, by 1973 African sentiment had begun to shift toward the Arabs, but the shift was by no means universal and, indeed, until mid-year 1973 most African states neither thought of breaking with Israel or, if asked, denied they had anything of the like in mind. In 1979, in a study of Arab-African relations, Timothy Luke and I concluded that

> ...(1) the early converts indisputably displayed more economic and political opportunism than ideological affinity, and (2) the circumstances under which most of the rest switched suggest that they did so as a consequence of extreme pressure — it was not moral, religious, or political conversion.[6]

Senegal's President Senghor, unwittingly speaking for most African countries, put the situation bluntly and clearly: "The Arabs have numbers, space and oil. . .; they outweigh Israel."[7] Little can be added to a 1975 editorial comment in Paris' *Le Monde* (July 7, 1975): "The continued presence of the Israelis in the occupied territories weighed a good deal less than the enormous potential financial aid of the Arab oil producers."[8]

Fruits of the Alliance

Unquestionably, Arab aid in various forms (project loans and grants, balance of payment loans, loans for petroleum purchases, etc.) have been generous. Between 1973 and 1980 ca. $4.71 billion in bilateral and multilateral concessional aid from Arab sources was committed to non-Arab African countries; of that total, ten countries (Guinea, Senegal, Zaire, Kenya, Uganda, Zambia, Mali, Niger, Tanzania, and Cameroon) accounted for ca. $3.46 billion. These figures do not include the value of scholarships offered Africans to attend such centers of learning as El Azhar University, bilateral technical assistance (in 1981 there were at least 3,000 Egyptian technicians in Nigeria and the Ivory Coast alone), and private Arab investment in African industrial and commercial sectors (not including, of course, the much older and established activity by Lebanese, Syrian, Iraqi, Egyptian and Sudanese merchants).[9] In Cameroon, for example, Arab sources contributed $60 millions of the ca. $203 million costs of the large Songloulou Dam on the Sanaga River; the Saudis alone contributed $36 million to the dam, in addition to about $33 million for road building, railway maintenance and the construction of schools and mosques.[10]

Among the intangible benefits to the Africans, there were, as noted previously, Arab support in international forums for African causes (particularly those involving southern Africa), and strong Arab endorsement of African demands relating to the global redistribution of wealth, the New International Economic Order, the proposed UNESCO New World Information Order (NWIO), and the like.

For the Arabs, though the returns on the alliance were mainly intangible, they were nonetheless politically significant. At least until 1979 the Arab League and the hard-line

Arab states on the Middle East conflict could count on a solid phalanx of African votes in various world bodies on all questions relating to such favored themes as the rights of the Palestinians, the Arab-Israeli conflict, and condemnation of Israel for everything from archaeological malfeasance to raids on PLO centers in Lebanon. Less noticed, but also important, the alliance opened the doors to the proliferation of Arab diplomatic and commercial missions to Africa, provided greatly enhanced opportunity for Islamic proselytization, and offered improved fields for the spread of anti-Israeli and anti-semitic propaganda.[11]

It did not, however, take very long before the alliance began to fray at the edges. African criticism, even as early as 1974, tended to center on claims that Arab promises — explicit or implicit — of preferential treatment on oil prices had not been kept, that expectations of Arab largesse had proven illusory, and that instead of becoming active partners in the alliance, Africans had been relegated to the role of an unwilling, supporting chorus to Arab plays staged in other, mainly non-African theaters. Above all, African irritation centered, and still focuses, on the severe — and in the African view, largely unredressed — economic impact of precipitously higher energy costs on their developing economies. Given the fact that oil is not available at concessional prices to African buyers, for the non-oil producing African states[12] the effects have been calamitous, forcing extensive public and private borrowing to meet oil bills, redeployment of scarce development resources, and mounting debt and balance of payments difficulties. Fuel costs, for example, have risen to almost 70% of export earnings for Kenya, 60% for Tanzania, and over 30% for Ghana.[13] Byproducts of the steep rise in the price of oil have been, of course, worldwide galloping inflation — particularly in the so-called MSA (most seriously affected) countries — and much higher prices for imported goods. "It now takes 250% more jute, 180% more sugar, 101% more copper to buy one barrel of oil than it did in 1975."[14]

Yet, the devastating impact of high oil prices on the sub-Saharan non-oil producing developing countries (NODCs) is difficult to capture in the bald statistics usually presented as evidence. In most cases it has meant a net deterioration in the terms of trade (the prices of imported goods rising faster than the revenue for exports), drastic revisions in development plans, and a decline in the living standard for the affected populations. Not even the world oil glut that became apparent in 1980, and which carried into 1982, has given the African NODCs much relief. The $34 a barrel floor reference price adopted by OPEC on Oct. 20, 1981, though welcomed by Western consumers, did not help the African NODCs since it represented an *increase* of $2 per barrel over the previous price level. That increase was absorbed by the industrialized countries because, for them, the figure actually meant a *drop* in the very high prices charged by some of the producers such as Iran, Libya, and Algeria. Not so for the African NODCs: each additional dollar per barrel meant an additional $2 billion balance of payments deficits for them as a group. In 1973 the African NODCs paid about $700 million for their imported oil; in 1976 that figure had risen to $6 billion, in 1980 it was ca. $11 billion, in 1981 it was an estimated $13 billion, and in 1982, it may go as high as $15 billion. Nor is this all. During late 1981 and early 1982, the French franc (on which the currencies of the French-speaking NODCs are based) was devalued, and the British pound (which backs the currencies of most English-speaking African NODCs) lost considerably in value compared to the US dollar and the German mark. Since oil bills have to be paid *in dollars*, the loss in exchange value increased even further the net costs of these countries' oil bills, as well as their balance of payments deficits.

The problem for the NODCs might not have been as acute had the Arab oil producers delivered (at least according to African sources) on promises to sell them oil at reduced or concessionary prices after the first round of increases had taken effect during the winter of 1973-74. No such preferential prices were ever offered by any OPEC country, the African NODC's pleas notwithstanding. At one time, Nigeria did consider selling oil at cheaper prices to its African neighbors with refineries, providing they not resell it below the fixed OPEC price. Nothing came of the matter, and no subsequent requests for concessionary prices, such as those voiced by OAU President Daniel Arap Moi of Kenya during 1981, have had any effect. The OPEC countries, Nigeria and Gabon included, have always argued that (a) concessionary prices would mean a two-tier pricing system which would undermine the strength of OPEC and thus make it less able to help the NODCs, (b) concessionary prices would permit Western consuming countries to pressure the NODCs into becoming conduits for cheaper oil, thus further exploiting the latter, and (c) the developmental priorities of the oil producers do, after all, have first claim — a decrease in oil revenues for the oil producers would help nobody, least of all the NODCs. It need hardly be added that these arguments do not convince the African NODCs, to say the very least.

The prevailing African view was openly and well expressed in *Jeune Afrique*, a weekly journal on African affairs widely read in Francophone Africa and usually sympathetic to Arab causes:[15]

> It has been said before, but it cannot be repeated too often: one of the causes of the continent's economic stagnation is the double oil shock administered by OPEC in 1973 and 1979. On the eve of the (Franco-African) summit (in Paris in November 1981), the cartel of oil exporters delivered another blow by raising average price of "crude" by one dollar. An apparently minimal increase, which, however, translates into an additional oil bill of $1.8 billion for the members of the Third World who are not members of OPEC, which will itself stand to gain about $60 billion (by the raise). These figures are all the more cruel since Algeria, Libya, Nigeria, and Gabon are OPEC members; moreover, the new (African) producers, Ivory Coast, Cameroon, Congo and Angola, will also profit from the increase imposed by the cartel. Yet in practice, these privileged (countries) display no solidarity with the other so-called "fraternal" African states.

African criticism of Arab aid to and investment in Africa has also grown more explicit since 1974. Gabon's president, Omar Bongo, himself a convert to Islam, expressed the common sentiment: "The Arab states must understand that the African countries broke with Israel solely out of solidarity with them [the Arabs]. They should [the Arabs], in turn, put their money in our countries and not in Geneva or the United States!"[16]

The evidence cannot have escaped African eyes. The vast bulk of Arab petrodollar surpluses (estimated to have reached over $400 billion in 1981) have been invested in European and North American commercial ventures or in liquid assets available on loan through Eurodollar, private and public international banks, and Arab-led investment, banking and insurance consortia. Arab aid commitments to non-Arab Africa never exceeded 15% of all Arab concessional assistance (in 1979, for example, it was $527.9 million, or 12.6% of a total of $4.7 billion); around 60% of the total regularly went to such Middle East states as Syria, Jordan and (before 1977) Egypt. Moreover, compared to Western aid, the Arab contribution is even smaller: in 1979 (the last year for which complete data is available) Arab aid commitments to non-Arab African countries only amounted to ca. 10.5% of all Western official development aid (ODA) *to the same countries*. Other jagged edges in the relationship became visible as well: Arab aid disbursements often lagged behind commitments by as much as 35 to 45%; Arab aid appeared all too frequently to be distributed on the basis of political and religious considerations rather than need; and on the whole, according to African sources, the "return" on the alliance — in the form of loans, grants, investments, etc. — has not exceeded 25% of the vastly increased amounts African states have had to pay out for oil since 1973-74. Finally, not only has the alliance unwillingly drawn African states into inter-Arab quarrels, but when Arab and African interests become directly opposed, the Arabs — in African eyes — appear willing to forget the fraternal aspects of the relationship. Some recent African involvements of this kind have proven highly unpleasant; one need only cite the cases of the Western Sahara conflict, the continuing Ethiopian-Somali confrontation, and Colonel Qadhafi's ventures in Chad. Equally disturbing have been Palestinian terrorist activities in Africa (in Ethiopia, Khartoum, Nairobi, and Entebbe), the inter-Arab conflict over Egypt's role and position (which spilled over into the 1981 OAU meetings in Nairobi), and Libya's export of subversion and terrorism to its Arab and African neighbors.

Back to Square Two: The New Relationships

The Afro-Arab alliance reached its apogee at an extraordinary summit meeting of African and Arab leaders held in Cairo in March 1977.[17] It was the first and only such meeting; neither the Standing Commission, created to examine ways of implementing the summit's resolutions, nor any of the other organs set up by the summit, functioned beyond 1978 because Arab members of these bodies refused to sit with an Egypt that had made peace with Israel. In any case, given the inability of its institutional appendages to operate, and — even more important — the growth of African disillusion with the Arab link, the alliance simply fell apart. Understandably, the fact has not been publicly acknowledged by either side. The point remains, however, that the summit, which was supposed to meet every three years, did not do so in 1980; and an African attempt at the 1981 Nairobi OAU conference to revive the Standing Commission was simply brushed aside by the Arab states in attendance. What is left of the alliance are periodic bursts of ideological rhetoric which maintains that it is alive and thriving, somewhat more restrained African support for Arab and Palestinian causes, and (perhaps paradoxically) continued Arab assistance, now increasingly oriented toward the poorest African countries.[18]

What has changed, and changed markedly, is the behavior of African governments in their dealings with the Arab world. The increasing willingness of African leaders to criticize Arab and Arab-OPEC actions was noted earlier. Of even greater significance is the simple fact that bilateral arrangements have once again become the preferred African mode in dealing with the Arab world. Instead of the frustrations of seeking Arab concessions at summits, congresses, or the meetings of African and Arab international organizations, African countries now make their own deals and feel free to distinguish between "friendly" and "unfriendly" Arab interlocutors. The new orientation facilitated strong African reaction to Libya's Chadian ventures: at Lomé (Togo), in January 1981, 14 African states condemned Quadhafi and Libya and seven of them (Mali, Sudan, Liberia, Mauretania, Nigeria, Niger and Somalia) either broke diplomatic relations with Tripoli or expelled its embassies-turned-"peoples' bureaux." It also appears to have encouraged an 11-country African trip by Algeria's President Chadli Benjedid (April 1981), and a similar six-country tour of Somalia's Siad Barre (June 1981).

Once a vital sponsor of the alliance, and then later a catalyst for its dissolution, Egypt remains a critical factor in the new African orientation. There is no need here to dwell on the fact that Egypt, particularly since the Islamization of substantial populations south of the Sahara, has been a traditional pole of African attraction. El Azhar has trained many thousands of African Muslim theologians, and Egypt has always been and remains today one of the principal African gates to the *Hajj*. In recent times the personality and visions of Nasser commanded widespread attention and respect in Africa; his pretensions to leadership of the African nationalist struggle may not always have commended him to moderate African leaders, but there was no gainsaying his influence. And it is not too far from the truth to state, as did *West Africa* magazine recently, that some African states broke with Israel out of loyalty to Egypt.[19] Thus, when Sadat, Nasser's successor, made his dramatic peace with Israel, he not only split the Arab world, but drove deep wedges into the Arab-African alliance. Not only were most African states embarrassed and confused by the attempt to exclude Egypt from Arab-African councils, but they reacted with shocked indignation at the way Sadat's murder was received in some Arab capitals. Even before that event, in Nairobi, at the 1981 OAU summit, an Arab resolution to condemn the Camp David Accords was turned aside; Nigeria (January 1981) pointedly joined the Egyptian-sponsored "League of Arab and Islamic Peoples;" and in November 1980, Senegal's President Senghor undertook a well-publicized visit to Egypt and Sadat. The stated intention of Ghana, Nigeria and Liberia to boycott the 1982 OAU meetings in Tripoli owed as much to Libya's unwillingness to commit itself to inviting Egypt as it did to a desire to rebuke Colonel Qadhafi. And after Sadat was assassinated on October 6, 1981, Africans by the thousands came to sign the *cahiers des condoléances* (mourners' registers) at Egyptian embassies throughout the continent.[20]

If Egypt was one of the main catalysts of the alliance, it was Israel, after all, which symbolized its raison d'être. A break with Israel — closing its missions, expelling its diplomats and technicians — was the ticket which entitled the African bearers to enter the new Arab-African fraternity and share its promised benefits. Thus, it is hardly surprising that one of the clearest indications of the new African orientation — and of the end of the alliance — has been the quiet but steady renewal of Israeli-African ties.

Certainly, Sadat's peace with Israel helped since it simultaneously removed loyalty to Egypt as a reason to shun Israel, and provided a rationale for doing more openly what already had become commonplace by 1978. As one observer noted, "new forms of interaction have been devised, marginal contacts have been elaborated, and a complex network of relationships have been woven in a situation where formal diplomatic ties are absent."[21] Since 1977 African-Israeli links have multiplied, and though only four African states recognize Israel, Israel has trading connections with (possibly) as many as thirty. Israeli private and parastatal companies (such as Solel Boneh, Coor, and Motorola-Israel) are active in various African countries.[22] It is useful to recall that the Israeli rescue of the Entebbe hostages in June 1976 would not have been possible without the active collaboration of the Kenyan government, and worth noting that Israeli diplomats and politicians (most recently, Israel's Defense Minister Ariel Sharon) now more or less openly criss-cross the continent every year. Though occasional African voices raise the possibility of resuming diplomatic links with Israel — as did Liberia's foreign minister Bacchus Matthews at the UN — a wholesale move in that direction is unlikely in the near future because the present arrangements continue to serve all sides concerned. The Israelis appear in no hurry to reopen their embassies in Africa — though they would ultimately like to do so — and Israel's African collaborators like things as they are because it preserves the illusion of the alliance with the Arabs and enables them to continue to receive Arab aid.

Given their preoccupation with events in the Middle East, the Arabs seem to have made little fuss about the new African-Israeli relationships, though when they occasionally do so, are politely told to mind their own business. So long as the Arabs continue to derive some benefits from what is left of the alliance — and so long as the African states do not antagonize their Arab friends by reopening Israeli embassies — the African states can probably continue to enjoy the current odd, though profitable state of affairs. In Africa, at least, and in the new pragmatic relationship among Arabs, Africans, and Israelis, we may have witnessed another small triumph of enlightened self-interest over ideology.

FOOTNOTES

1. Anthony Sylvester, *Arabs and Africans, Cooperation for Development* (London: The Bodley Head, 1981), pp. 183-219, *passim*.

2. Notably, Joseph Cuoq, *Les Musulmans en Afrique* (Paris: Maisonneuve et Larose, 1975); I.M. Lewis, *Islam in Tropical Africa* (London: Oxford University Press, 1966); Vincent Monteil, *Islam Noir* (Paris: Ed. du Seuil, 1964); and John S. Trimmingham, *The Influence of Islam Upon Africa* (New York: Praeger, 1968). The above works deal principally with the historical, cultural, and religious aspects of the relationship. For discussions of economic and political relationships since World War II, see Sylvester, *op. cit.*; E.C. Chibwe, *Afro-Arab Relations in the New World Order* (London: Julian Friedman, 1977); and Victor T. Le Vine and Timothy Luke, *The Arab-African Connection: Political and Economic Realities* (Boulder, Colo.: Westview Press, 1979). The most extensive bibliography is by Samir M. Zoghby, *Islam in Sub-Saharan Africa* (Washington, D.C.: U. S. Government Printing Office, 1978), which contains 2,682 entries, a glossary of Arabic terms, and a detailed index of authors and subjects.

3. *Jeune Afrique*, No. 1087 (4 Nov. 1981), p. 42. It should be added that Mauretania's membership in the Arab League has not prevented her from coming into direct conflict with its northern neighbor, with which it once divided the Western Sahara. After Mauretania made its peace with the Polisario forces and ceded its part of the Western Sahara to Morocco, relations soured with Morocco, who accused Nouakchott of providing sanctuary to Polisario troops. In 1981, Morocco even sent its war planes over the Mauretanian border in "hot pursuit" of Polisario units.

4. Following a visit to Libya by Chadian President Tombalbaye in December 1972, two weeks after the break with Israel, a $91 million Libyan loan to Chad was announced. *(West Africa*, no. 2900:55). The Parisian daily *Le Figaro* (Jan. 6, 1974) set "more than $30 millions" as the "price" for the break, and noted that Tombalbaye had demanded, and was refused, a $6 million Israeli military assistance package. Uganda's Idi Amin was promised ca. $59 million by Libya and Saudi Arabia after the Israelis had similarly refused him military aid. *(Africa Confidential* 13:5, October, 1972).

5. For details, see LeVine and Luke, *op. cit.*, pp. 9-18. See also S. A. Gitelson, "Israel's African Setback in Perspective," in *Israel in the Third World*, edited by Michael Curtis and S. A. Gitelson (New Brunswick: Transaction, 1976), pp. 182-99.

6. *Op. cit.*, p. 15. No new evidence has surfaced since the book was published to persuade us to change our judgment.

7. Cited by B. Rivlin and J. Fomerand, "Changing Third World Perspectives and Policies Toward Israel," in Curtis and Gitelson, eds., *Israel in the Third World, op. cit.*, p. 347.

8. "Le maintien des Israeliens dans les territoires occupés à pesé d'un bien moindre pids que l'enorme potentiel d'aide financière des pays arabes producteurs de pétrole." Cited by Yehoshua Rash in "Les années israéliennes en Afrique: un bilan," *Le Mois en Afrique*, vol. 16, no. 182-183 (Feb.-March, 1981), p. 40.

9. Sources: Sylvester, *op. cit.*, p. 227; *1980 Report* of the Arab Bank for Economic Development in Africa (BADEA); Saudi, Algerian, and Egyptian embassies in Yaoundé, Cameroon.

10. Source: Saudi Embassy, Yaoundé On the Songloulou project, the Saudi Fund for Development contributed $35.28 m., the Kuwait Fund, $16.0 m., and the Islamic Development Bank, $7.0 m. The other participants were the European Investment Bank, the EEC fund, and a consortium of Cameroonian banks.

11. The Saudi embassy in Yaoundé, for example, distributes a 1967 French-language Beirut edition of the old, viciously anti-Semitic tract, *The Protocols of the Elders of Zion*. The Saudi cultural attaché was pleased to give me two copies "for study and reflection." The Libyan embassy gave me a copy of the report of a conference in Tripoli which discussed and endorsed the "Zionism is racism" theme as well as newspapers and pamphlets containing violent anti-Zionist and anti-Israeli diatribes by Colonel Qadhafi. It should be added that anti-Semitism does not do well in Africa since most Africans have never met a Jew, and Judaism is usually favorably associated (among Christians) with the Old Testament and Jesus. Israelis tend to be identified *as Israelis*, not Jews.

12. In sub-Saharan Africa, this group now includes all African states except Nigeria, Congo, Gabon, Ivory Coast, Cameroon and Angola.

13. *Africa Research Bulletin*, Economic, Financial, and Technical Series, Vol. 18, No. 6 (July 31, 1981).

14. Ulf Lantzke, Executive Director of the International Energy Agency, speaking at the UN Conference on the Sources of New and Renewable Energy, Nairobi, Kenya, 10-22 August, 1981. Quoted in *Afrique*, No. 52 (October, 1981), p. 72. Translation is mine. See also Le Vine and Luke, *op. cit.*, pp. 31-41, for a discussion of the economic consequences on African countries of the 1973-74 oil crisis; and the World Bank's *World Development Report 1981* (Washington, D.C., August, 1981) for analyses of the problems associated with the continuing energy crisis, especially Chapters 4 (pp. 35-48) and 6 (pp. 64-96).

15. "Pétrole: la supercherie du siècle?" (Oil, the swindle of the century?) *Jeune Afrique*, No. 1088 (11 Nov. 1981) p. 58. The translation is mine.

16. Cited by Rash, *op. cit.*, p. 40. The translation is mine.

17. For discussions of the Afro-Arab Summit, see Sylvester, *op. cit.*, pp. 203-209; Chibwe, *op. cit.*, pp. 137-146; and LeVine and Luke, *op. cit.*, pp. 64-67.

18. In September, 1981, after a review of conditions on the continent, the Arab Bank for African Economic Development (BADEA), announced that 49 percent of its total funding activities would be devoted to 19 of Africa's 21 oil-importing developing countries. *Jeune Afrique*, No. 1082 (30 Sept. 1981), p. 11.

19. No. 3350 (12 October 1981), p. 2368. For an insightful, though somewhat biased, look at the Egyptian role in Africa, see Pierre Mirel, ''L'Egypte et l'Afrique: piège de l'aventure,'' *Le Mois en Afrique*, No. 184-185 (April-May, 1981), pp. 38-54.

20. Four such large registers were filled in Yaoundé, the capital of Cameroon, and sent on to Cairo. I signed one of them, and observed that my name was preceded by those of a number of high-ranking government officials. I was told that all but four African heads of state (I was not told which ones) had sent long messages of sympathy to Cairo; eulogies or sympathetic editorials appeared in almost all West and East African official newspapers. A number expressed open revulsion at the celebrations in Tripoli, Beirut, Damascus, and Baghdad which followed the assassination.

21. Naomi Chazan, ''Israel in Africa,'' *The Jerusalem Quarterly*. No. 18 (Winter 1981), p. 29. The article is the best assessment thus far available of the new Israeli relationships with Africa.

22. Israel does not publish detailed information on its African links, for obvious reasons. Israelis are not, however, invisible in Africa. Israeli companies (such as *Solel Boneh*) have been taking an active part in construction projects in Nigeria and the Ivory Coast, and Israeli businessmen are actively bidding on government projects throughout Francophone Africa. I was reliably told that African leaders have been making quiet trips to Israel for the last several years; I recently met two who admitted as much, but asked not to be identified.

We voice our support for the coup which took place against the bourgeois government in Ghana, because the person who led the coup is a friend of ours and he is Flight-Lieutenant Rawlings. He is our friend, he is a believer in the Third Universal Theory* and in people's power, and indeed he is one of the members of the [Libyan] External Revolutionary Committees.

Col. Mu'amar Qadhafi, in a speech to the General People's Congress, January 5, 1982.

*As expounded by Col. Qadhafi *(Eds.)*.

---

47 South Asia and the Gulf: Linkages, Gains, and Limitations

W. Howard Wriggins

I. INTRODUCTION

During the past fifteen years India and Pakistan, each in its own way, have been drawn into remarkably close involvement with the Gulf. The meshing of interests and interactions between the two South Asian states and those of the Gulf has been particularly marked since the secession of Bangladesh in 1971 and the surge in oil prices following 1973.[1]

On the surface, policy in Islamabad and New Delhi was determined by the need to import indispensable energy supplies and to find the means to pay for them. But, as we hope to show, these changed relationships were driven as much by elements of statecraft as by market imperatives. Geopolitical and security considerations, the balancing of power internationally, new patterns of trade, employment opportunities with their consequent emigrant remittances — all these combined to shape the South Asians' policies and to make the Gulf highly consequential to both these states. As a result, the fates of Pakistan and India remain closely linked with those of the relatively small — and in some instances even miniscule — states to the west.

Thucydides argued that statesmen's choices emerge from a combination of fear, ambition and interest. To reconstruct the fears, ambitions and interests of the statesmen who have led the major states in both South Asia and the Gulf, this paper explores the way Pakistan and India developed their respective relationships with the principal states of the Gulf, Iran, Iraq and Saudi Arabia. Inescapably speculative in parts, it draws not only on extensive reading but also on interviews in most of the capitals of these states or with their representatives or former officials available in the United States.

Many analyses of politico-diplomatic activity in these regions place superpower competition at the center, as if the states of these regions were mere pawns of the major outside powers. In fact, however, much that happens derives mainly from indigenous forces. Therefore, as we investigate the way these states of South Asia and the Gulf have related to one another, we will apply a useful corrective to many Western analyses by downplaying the role of the superpowers and China.

II. INDO-PAKISTAN RELATIONS IN SOUTH ASIA

The approach of both India and Pakistan to their neighbors in the Gulf is difficult to understand without some appreciation of how these two have dealt with each other within South Asia. Since independence, each has tended to eye the other with exaggerated anxiety, much like France and Germany prior to World War I. Relations between the two form a near-

Dr. W. Howard Wriggins, a former U.S. ambassador to Sri Lanka, is Professor of International Politics at Columbia University and a Research Associate of Columbia's Institute of War and Peace Studies and its Southern Asia Institute.

The writer expresses his appreciation to the Ford Foundation for its support of a research seminar at Columbia University which focused on the subject of this article; to the members of the seminar (including Zalmay Khalilzad, Gary Sick, Tom Thornton, Razi Wasti, Myron Weiner, and Warner Schilling) for assisting in the evolution of this article by their comments or critiques; and to graduate students (including Ted Hopf, Shireen Mazari, and Deepa Olapally) for their stimulating comments in class discussions. Particular thanks go to research assistant Mark DuBois for his countless searches for data and for his painstaking preparation of the tables.

perfect instance of the "security dilemma," an action-reaction relationship whereby the steps one party takes to improve his security could not have been better designed to frighten the opponent; and the steps the latter takes in turn to compensate for his worsened circumstances only intensify the anxieties of the former.[2]

Centuries of Moghul and British rule left a legacy dividing Hindus from Muslims. After World War II, the protracted three-cornered constitutional debate preceding partition not only resulted in each successor state being committed to quite different principles of political organization but also poisoned the personal relations between leaders of the two communities. The territorial quarrel over Kashmir, which had international security implications for each side, also came to play a part in each state's domestic politics as the new governments were just gaining their feet.

Moreover, each state had a different vision of its role. The leaders in New Delhi believed their part of the subcontinent was the natural inheritor of Britain's role in the entire region; they often gave the impression that they expected Pakistan and the others to defer to India.[3] Pakistan, however, was not inclined to give automatic acknowledgement to India's claim to preeminence. The leaders of the Islamic state of Pakistan saw themselves a part of the Middle East as well as of South Asia. Cultural ties linked many of its leading families to Iran. Just as smaller states next to large ones will often do, Pakistan attempted to balance its larger neighbor by seeking assistance from a number of states outside its immediate region. First it reached toward the Arab states and Iran; then to the United States in the mid-50's; and after the Indo-Pakistan war, toward China in the mid-'60's.[4] It was the Pakistani search for further balancing support in the direction of the Gulf, an effort urgently renewed after 1971, which led both India and Pakistan to attribute to the Gulf a significance that went beyond economic factors.

III. SOUTH ASIA AND THE GULF: POLITICO-DIPLOMATIC RELATIONS

Pakistan and the Gulf

Pakistan's orientation toward the Gulf comes into focus when we consider Islamabad's relations with the two principal actors in the Gulf — Iran and Saudi Arabia.

Pakistan and Iran. From the beginning of Pakistan's independence in 1948, the governments of Iran and Pakistan had worked closely together, notably during the early UN debates on the Soviet presence in Azerbaijan, and later, from the mid-1950s, in CENTO. Afghanistan's efforts to foment unrest among their Baluchi tribes were troublesome to both Iran and Pakistan. Although both these states were weak in the 1950s, it became clear in the 1960s that Iran could be of greater help to Pakistan than *vice versa.*[5] The 1971 secession of Bangladesh further demonstrated Pakistan's weakness. The oil price hikes in 1970 and 1973, which sharply improved Iran's income, hurt India and for several years adversely affected Pakistan also.

The Shah's Iran and Qadhafi's Libya were among the first to come to the assistance of Mr. Bhutto's new government after the 1971 breakaway of Bangladesh.[6] At a time when Iran's ambitions to increase her power in the Gulf required a stable security environment vis-à-vis the subcontinent, tribal unrest in Pakistan's Baluchistan might excite Iranian Baluchis and possibly other disgruntled minorities. Wider geostrategic concerns also enhanced the importance of Islamabad. Despite some detente achieved with Moscow, the Soviet Union remained the Shah's most urgent long-run security worry.[7] The Soviet presence bore heavily upon Iran's northern frontier and its generous transfers of Soviet military equipment to Iraq on the south created an "encirclement" of Iran that it was bound to view as dangerous. Moreover, in case the Soviets should move into Iran, a solid Pakistan might help deter their further advance to the Mekran coast or the Strait of Hormuz, whence they could effectively squeeze Iran by threatening to constrict the flow of oil through that critical choke point.[8]

The Shah, therefore, had good domestic and international political reasons for supporting Pakistan, and his ability to do so improved markedly in the late 1960s and early 1970s. The Nixon/Kissinger "Guam Doctrine" sharply increased Tehran's ability to buy modern weapons, while Pakistan's trained military manpower proved useful when seconded to Tehran to help manage logistical and maintenance systems.

Following the breakup of Pakistan, the Shah in 1973 publicly warned that any threat to Pakistan's integrity from outside would be seen as a threat to Iran itself.[9] Pakistanis may not have had a very high opinion of the fighting qualities of the Iranian army, but support from any quarter at the time was welcome. Commercial relations also improved as increased quantities of Pakistani foodstuffs and textiles were exchanged for larger amounts of Iranian oil.[10]

On the other hand, there were constraints on the development of Iranian-Pakistani accord. Pakistan sought to maintain good relations with Saudi Arabia as well as Iran, even though the two were separated by the Arab/Persian, Shia/Sunni division and by their competition for influence in the Gulf. From the mid-70s, the Shah's initiatives toward India made clear that Iran's goals were far from identical with those of Pakistan. Nevertheless, the Shah's economic resources, Iran's apparent stability, and its diplomatic and security support were important to Pakistan.[11]

Pakistan and Saudi Arabia. It was with Saudi Arabia, however, that Pakistan developed a truly "special relationship." In the 1960s there were already a number of senior Pakistanis in responsible positions within the Saudi administration. With the price hikes of the early 70s, the Saudi armament program surged, and Riyadh's construction and administrative needs expanded rapidly.

The Pakistanis had substantial advantages as plausible security partners.[12] Their trained military manpower were Muslims, who easily accommodated to Saudi religious and social disciplines. Moreover, since they knew little Arabic, they did not possess the inclination to meddle in their partner's domestic affairs that most Arabs are said to have. The Pakistan army and police have a solid reputation from longstanding contract service throughout the Gulf, as in Jordan, where a brigade under Zia ul-Haq helped save Hussein's throne. After the fall of the Shah, more Pakistani troops were brought into Saudi Arabia, and by 1984 some 20,000 had been organized into two units facing Iraq and South Yemen; others performed service and maintenance functions, as well as guarding some members of the royal family.[13] Economic assistance also increased after the oil price hike. In 1976 alone, Riyadh transferred some $500 million to Pakistan, or more even than Egypt received that year.[14] Amounts transferred in several subsequent years were still larger.

In contrast to the Shah, who talked of a grand design for the region, the Saudis appeared to be responding more to the urgings of Pakistan's leaders than to a design of their own.[15] Decisions were often slow, and administration was said to have been unreliable.[16] By the time the Reagan administration negotiated its aid package in 1981, however, Riyadh was able to make firm commitments to cover perhaps half the cost of Pakistan's F-16 aircraft purchases from America.[17] Both parties saw advantage in this security collaboration. Close links between Pakistan and Saudi Arabia confirmed the Islamic legitimacy of Islamabad's government, helping sustain domestic support for the regime among the rural and urban masses.[18] Riyadh could see Pakistan's need for economic assistance, help it modernize its aging military equipment, and even plead Pakistan's case in Washington during the difficult early years of the Carter Administration.[19]

There were constraints on both sides, however. The Saudis were understandably wary. With some 750,000 to 1 million Pakistani civilian workers in the country, 20,000 well-trained Pakistani soldiers might, in the event of domestic disturbance, decisively tip the political balance in favor of either the 35,000-man Army or the 25,000-man National Guard.[20]

For his part, Mr. Bhutto did not want to risk his newly won non-aligned status by too intimate an association with such a close ally of the U.S. For Bhutto's successor it was easier, as the Soviet invasion of Afghanistan turned virtually all the non-aligned except India publicly against the Soviet Union, thus giving fresh legitimacy to those non-aligned who developed closer relations with America's friends and allies.

Accordingly, Pakistan found in both Iran and Saudi Arabia neighboring Muslim countries with whom collaboration was both natural and supportive. The overthrow of the Shah, coupled with the Soviet invasion of Afghanistan, brought a new unpredictability to Islamabad's relations with Tehran while further consolidating Pakistan's relations with Saudi Arabia.

India and the Gulf

India and Iraq. Until the mid-70s, New Delhi, like Nasser's Cairo, had been openly critical of the Shah's rule, his support for Pakistan, and his connections with the United States. India has also generally supported Iraq's anti-imperialist positions, and both were enthusiastic participants in the Non-Aligned Movement. After the price hikes of the early 1970s, Iraq became important to India less for these diplomatic interests than as a source of concessional oil deliveries, preferential trade arrangements, and investment and consultancy opportunities.[21]

Placed between the larger Iran and the wealthier Saudi Arabia, the leaders of Iraq had their own agenda. Defensively, they sought to overcome quite classic fears about the intentions and capabilities of both of their major neighbors. Just as Pakistan and India had both sought to counterbalance the weight of their principal opponents by seeking support from an outside power, so too did Iraq seek support from Moscow to counterbalance the growing strength of Iran and Saudi Arabia.[22] In an almost ideal-type reflection of Kautiliyan principles, India found itself working closely with Iraq, the state that was a regional rival of Pakistan's two closest friends, Iran and Saudi Arabia.

Iraq and Iran both sought control over the Shatt-al-Arab, that shared waterway that also marked the historical religio-cultural faultline separating the Persian Shi'ite from the Arab Sunni realms.[23] Each used the Kurdish minority in the other's territory to promote unrest and dissidence.[24]

Baghdad also had ambitions to induce change in its neighbors. At least until the mid-1970s, successive Ba'athist governments were intensely radical, pushing economic transformation at home while encouraging unrest and radical regime changes in its conservative neighbors — Iran, Saudi Arabia and the sheikdoms of the Gulf.

After the oil price hike, Iraq's income, like that of Iran and Saudi Arabia, rose sharply. Economic connections with India became more intimate. A number of Indian contractors were hired to improve Iraq's railroads and her water and sewage systems, and Indian entrepreneurs undertook joint industrial enterprises with Iraqi counterparts.[25] And concessional oil transfers and credits softened the effects of the price hike to some extent.

India and Iran. As New Delhi saw it, the Shah was an anachronism; he had always supported Pakistan, was allied with the United States, and opposed Nasser and the non-aligned.[26] Following the Guam Doctrine and the oil price hike, the Shah sharply expanded his military establishment, and his obviously growing ambitions could be seen as leading to potential Indo-Iranian rivalry in the Indian Ocean.[27] Less hypothetical was the supply and price of petroleum. Before the price hike, Iran had been providing some two-thirds of India's petroleum, and the quadrupling of oil prices had been a hard blow to India.

Despite this longstanding coolness of relations between India and Iran, from the mid-1970s until the revolution their relations considerably improved. Economic and geopolitical interests seemed about equally engaged. Iran began to import more industrial and inexpensive consumption goods from India, and complex iron ore and other projects were taken up. The Shah even spoke of a Common Market encompassing Iran, Pakistan, India, etc. Delhi saw the obvious economic advantages to India.

At the same time the Indians, like the Shah, saw possible political advantages as well. Iran was by far the most influential country in the Gulf region. Now that Pakistan had been reduced by the breakaway of Bangladesh, India was by all odds now preeminent in South Asia. Both were in effect seeking to succeed to the former British preeminence in their respective regions. If India and Iran were to contend against each other, each would be the weaker in his own region. On the contrary, if they were to cooperate, each might expect to exert greater influence in his own bailiwick.[28]

As seen from Tehran, easing some of India's economic problems might induce New Delhi to depend less on the Soviet Union, reduce its enthusiasm for Iraq, and lead to greater understanding of Pakistan's problems. On the other hand, in light of Mrs. Gandhi's worries about Pakistan, she could equally well hope that closer Indian relations with Tehran might help to undercut the Shah's support for Pakistan.[29] Here again, New Delhi sought to deal with a diplomatic problem in South Asia by improving its relations with Iran as it had done earlier with Iraq, by much the same course that Pakistan had already taken by improving its relations with both Iran and Saudi Arabia.

IV. 1979/80: YEAR OF ERUPTION

In 1979/80, this nascent diplomatic collaboration between these two major regional powers was abruptly terminated when the Shah was overthrown. His imperial pretensions were replaced by Khumayni's destabilizing efforts to promote fundamentalism among Shi'ias in Iraq, Bahrein and the eastern provinces of Saudi Arabia. Fears mounted that Muslims in Pakistan and India might become affected. Complex industrial arrangements with India, and security and economic support for Pakistan were abruptly discontinued.

The Soviet invasion of Afghanistan in December 1979 worsened Pakistan's security exposure. However, it brought military assistance from the United States, strengthened Zia's ability to use Islamic issues to rally domestic support, and understandably reduced the boldness of his opposition. India's virtual acquiescence in the invasion only intensified Pakistan's fears of collusion between New Delhi and Moscow, and, for a time, alienated India from the other Muslim states in the region. These developments enhanced the importance of Pakistan for the Islamic states in the Gulf, and led Riyadh, Kuwait and the UAE to bolster Pakistan by providing additional foreign exchange support. In return, Pakistan increased the numbers of its skilled security personnel in the area.

The outbreak of the Iran-Iraq war drew the Arab states more closely together in shared opposition to Iran and promoted the beginning of the Gulf Cooperation Council while Iraq was distracted. The war complicated Pakistan's efforts to keep lines open to the Ayatullah's Tehran while remaining close to Riyadh. Moreover, it sharply contracted petroleum shipments from Iran and gradually reduced the resources the Arab states were able to spare for subsidizing Pakistan. Yet, as we shall see, the economic costs of these changes after 1982 were not as severe in South Asia as they seemed after the major price hikes of 1973 and 1980.

V. ECONOMIC RELATIONS

Trade

Economic and manpower issues also drew South Asia and the Gulf together. Petroleum was the first imperative. By 1973, India was producing domestically some 35 percent of its petroleum requirements while Pakistan, though producing substantial supplies of gas, managed to meet only 10 percent of its petroleum needs.[30] So long as the price of oil remained low through the 1960s, India's petroleum imports absorbed roughly 15 percent and Pakistan's some 10 percent of foreign exchange earnings. Hard currency was scarce, even to meet these bills. But the year following the 1973 price hike India was required to expend some 40 percent and Pakistan 30 percent of their respective earnings on petroleum from the Gulf![31]

After the first very difficult years, new trade and economic activities, aid flows and migration patterns sharply reduced the pain, particularly for Pakistan. As might have been expected, Indians were active principally in Iraq and the UAE, and Pakistanis largely in Saudi Arabia, the UAE and the other emirates. Remarkably quickly, these new activities brought undreamed-of opportunities to those South Asians willing to migrate to the Gulf as temporary laborers and specialists, while their homelands experienced important domestic political side effects.

Prior to the 1973 price hike, the Gulf was hardly a factor in official Pakistani or Indian export efforts, and only a few trading communities had longstanding business relationships. Within a year, however, both governments made intensive efforts to increase shipments to the Gulf, often risking shortages at home to do so.[32] Exports of light industrial goods from India, and food and other consumer goods from both countries rapidly increased. New activities were undertaken, such as construction, joint ventures, consultancy, management and other service contracts. Between 1971 and 1981, for instance, India increased her earnings from exports of all types to Iran fourfold, from $35 million to $140 million; to Saudi Arabia nearly twelve times, moving from $20 million to $250 million; and to the UAE 20 times, to $220 million. During the same period Pakistan increased her earnings from trade with Iran by a factor of 30 ($153 million); and with Saudi Arabia and the UAE by a factor of 17. Even discounting for inflation, these represented remarkable increases.[33]

The newly rich Gulf states also engaged in various substantial though unpredictable and inconspicuous aid programs to South Asia. There is some evidence that by mid-1976, the Arab countries and Iran had provided loans to Pakistan of nearly $1 billion.[34] There were reiterated rumors of concessional government-to-government medium-term oil contracts which spared both India and Pakistan some of the rigors of the increased world price.[35]

As a result of this increasingly close economic interaction, officials in both New Delhi and Islamabad became more attentive to the views of the oil states. Indeed, prior to the Iranian revolution, Indian commentators hoped that growing economic links with Iran as well as Iraq would also lead to useful international political side effects for New Delhi.[36]

Migration

Emigrant jobs and remittances represent an additional strand drawing India and Pakistan closer than ever to the Gulf states. The actual numbers who have emigrated to the Gulf are not known with any certainty. Figures vary sharply.[37] Informed estimates, however, based on a variety of sources, suggest the following magnitudes for 1985. In the UAE, 1,500,000 Indians and 250,000 Pakistanis; in Saudi Arabia, 750,000 to 1,000,000 Pakistanis and 80,000 Indians; in Kuwait, 100,000 Pakistanis and 80,000 Indians; in Bahrein, 50,000 Pakistanis and 254,000 Indians; in Iraq, 50,000 Pakistanis and 30,000 Indians; and in Oman, there are estimated to be some 50,000 Pakistanis and 65,000 Indians.[38]

The bulk of these migrants have arrived since the oil price hike of 1973. They are participants in one of the largest economic migrations in the Indian Ocean region since the Chinese emigrated into Southeast Asia. The crucial importance of this migration to the host states is suggested by the fact that over half the workers in most Gulf countries are foreigners, and in Kuwait and the UAE they comprise over 80 percent![39] To protect the indigenous population from being numerically and politically swamped, the states have had to control immigration carefully and set strict working and living conditions. In most cases, the average foreign worker leads a harsh, strictly disciplined, unpleasant and makeshift life.[40] Moreover, precisely because laborers' pay at home in South Asia was so low, they were prepared to put up with the onerous, barrack-like existence in exchange for the 6- to 10-times increase in their take home pay.[41]

One issue that bedeviled relations of both governments with the host states was the harsh working conditions of the migrants. New Delhi's efforts to block the flow of emigrants until working conditions improved only angered prospective workers who were eager to pay a year's salary for the privilege of going. As Myron Weiner pointed out,

> **"The asymmetrical dimensions of policy making are well understood by all. For all practical purposes, the power to regulate is primarily in the hands of the labor importing, not the labor exporting countries."[42]**

Three years of hard labor in the Gulf would allow them to return with a nest egg the likes of which they could never even have dreamed of had they stayed at home. In certain areas, such as Pakistan's Northwest Frontier Province, perhaps as many as 10 percent of the families have had their incomes at least quadrupled.[43] As a result of this unprecedented infusion of economic resources and new skill on the district and village level, a new dynamism is apparent in certain districts. New methods are being tried, restrictive social status structures are under challenge, and there is an air of optimism and of new individual possibilities hitherto virtually unknown. Spontaneous development is thus transforming certain districts, despite government planners' neat designs. In the process, however, the political order in the affected areas becomes hostage to continued prosperity in the Gulf.[44]

Remittances

For the individual migrants it has been a hard won but enormous bonanza. Nor is it any less so for the sending governments. Indeed, the flow of remittance income has been a critical aspect of their balance of payments position. The exact amounts remitted must remain estimates, since there are many ways that individuals can send resources home without going through the formal banking structure. Nevertheless it is reliably estimated that in recent years remittances equivalent to \$2.-\$2.5 billion flowed to Pakistan while petroleum imports cost the country roughly \$1.45 billion, a clear net gain.[45] Indian remittance income from the Gulf is considerably less, while energy import needs are roughly three times greater. Nevertheless, remittances in some years account for some 15 to 20 percent of India's merchandise exports.[46]

These data suggest that as Pakistan derives greater relative advantage from these economic activities than India, it is in like measure more vulnerable to the adverse effects of a possible secular decline in OPEC prosperity.

Economic Effects of 1979/80 Eruptions

The Iranian revolution and the Iran-Iraq war have altered specifics of these economic relationships, but they have not changed the fundamentals as much as one might expect. The incipient Indo-Iranian industrial ventures and a number of Pakistani projects were abruptly halted by the revolution; and the war eventually forced Iraq to cancel many commitments to Indian contractors. Sources of petroleum for both South Asian countries responded quickly to wartime interruptions as imports from Saudi Arabia substituted temporarily for disrupted Iranian shipments. From 1977, Riyadh replaced Tehran in providing nearly two-thirds of Pakistan's oil. By 1983, both Iran and Iraq — despite their conflict — reportedly were again India's two principal suppliers, though at a lower level, while the Soviet Union stepped in to provide some 15 percent of India's oil imports.[47] For some time, the Arab states were able to sustain their support for Iraq's war effort while continuing to assist Pakistan, but by the third year of the war, as oil prices began to slip, less was heard of identifiable Arab assistance for Pakistan beyond the Saudi commitment to specific procurement needs of Islamabad.

Contrary to expectations when oil prices softened, South Asian personnel in countries other than Iran and Iraq have not yet markedly declined, although their tasks are changing, with fewer unskilled construction jobs and more need for maintenance and operations. Moreover, the needs of war increased the demand in Iran and Iraq for imported consumption and light industrial goods from both countries. In other Arab states, some decline in oil income encouraged them to buy more in South Asia where landed costs were sometimes lower than for Western goods. To be sure, there has been a leveling off in the total numbers of South Asians going to the Gulf, and in 1984 some 10 percent reduction in their remittances, in part because more are managing to take their families with them. But the time is yet to come when the mesh of connections we have been considering will have materially weakened as a result of fewer migrants.[48]

VI. CONCLUSION

Politico-diplomatic relations between India and Pakistan on the one hand and the states of the Gulf on the other were initially driven by classic considerations of international politics. Indo-Pakistan rivalry within South Asia found its parallel manifestation in the Gulf with Pakistan seeking to counterbalance the weight of India, and India hoping to limit the support Pakistan might find there. At the outset, economic issues were important but not critical. The oil price hike of 1973, however, brought such intense economic pressures to bear that the character of relationships changed. The urgent need to promote exports and the reciprocal desires of South Asian laborers and prospective host countries induced a huge migration and brought about a many-sided economic interaction. As a result, the Indo-Pakistan subcontinent can no longer be considered the separate and distinctive politico-diplomatic arena that it used to be.

For a number of reasons, Pakistan has derived an asymmetrical advantage from these relationships, profiting proportionately more than India, both politically and economically. On the one hand, precisely because it is more dependent upon the Gulf than India, Pakistan will be more susceptible to influences originating in the Gulf and more vulnerable to future economic or political difficulties there. On the other hand, there is no reason to think that India's diversified economy will not find a rich field for economic relationships in the future.

Even though oil prices should soften further, there will be a continued need for large numbers of competent South Asians for maintenance, services, and supervision. The nature of political relations is harder to predict.[49] Much will depend on the policies adopted by Iran and Iraq after the war.

Many other questions remain. Will the security ties to Riyadh drag Pakistan too deeply into inter-Arab or Saudi family rivalries, or impede long run relationships with Tehran? Will India be able to counterbalance Pakistan's political advantages by relationships of its own with any one of the principal Gulf states? Will not a post-Khumayni Iran, like the Shah, find collaboration with India a fruitful long run possibility? Regardless of the answers history may provide us in the future, one thing is clear: India and Pakistan in South Asia and the Islamic states of the Gulf are now linked to each other as never before.

FOOTNOTES

1. For more details, see my "Changing Power Relations between the Middle East and South Asia", *Orbis,* Vol. 20, No. 3, Fall 1976, pp. 785-803.

2. John R. Herz, *International Politics in the Atomic Age* (New York, Columbia University Press, 1959), Ch. 10; Robert Jervis, *Perception and Misperception in International Politics* (Princeton University Press, 1976), pp. 66, 75-76, and articles by the same author. See also an earlier formulation by Nicholas Spykman, who described the familiar dynamic in Western Europe's diplomatic history: "the margin of safety for one is the margin of danger for the other; and alliance must, therefore, be met by counter-alliance and armament by counter-armament in an eternal competitive struggle for power." *America's Strategy for World Politics* (New York, Harcourt Brace, 1942), p. 24.

3. For a suggestive discussion of the historical sources of this often unexamined assumption, see Ainslie Embree, "Pakistan's Imperial Legacy" in Masuma Hasan (ed), *Pakistan in a Changing World,* Karachi, Pakistan Institute of International Affairs, 1978, esp. pp. 15-18. See also Surjit Mansingh, *India's Search for Power* (New Delhi, Sage, 1984), p. 38.

4. See Wriggins, "The Balancing Process in Pakistan's Foreign Policy," Ziring, *et al., Pakistan, The Long View* (Chapel Hill, Duke University Press, 1977), Ch. 11.

5. S. Tahir-Kheli, "Iran and Pakistan in an area of conflict", *Asian Survey* (Vol. XVII, No. 5, May 1977), p. 477.

6. Amir Taheri, "Policies of Iran in the Persian Gulf Region", in Abbas Amirie (ed.), *The Persian Gulf and the Indian Ocean in International Politics* (Teheran, Institute of International Political and Economic Studies, 1975), p. 270.

7. S. Chubin, "Soviet Policy Toward Iran and the Gulf," (London, IISS, *Adelphi Papers,* No. 157, Spring 1980), pp. 18-22.

8. For some of these points, Amir Taheri, *op. cit.,* pp. 269-270.

9. *Ibid.*

10. Abdul Majid Khan, "Foreign Trade with Iran," *The Muslim* (Islamabad) Jan. 18, 1984.

11. Tahir-Kheli, *op. cit.,* p. 476.

12. W. B. Quandt, *Saudi Arabia in the 1980's,* pp. 40-41.

13. W. B. Quandt, *op. cit.,* p. 41; also IISS, *The Military Balance 1983-1984* (London, 1983), p. 97.

14. Adeed Dawisha, "Saudi Arabia's Search for Security," *Adelphi Paper No. 158* (IISS, Winter 1979-1980).

15. For a report on the Shah's design, see R. K. Karanjia, *The Mind of a Monarch* (London, Allen and Unwin, 1977), esp. ch. 14.

16. Interviews in Riyadh and Islamabad, 1982.

17. Interviews, Washington, 1982.

18. Zubeida Mustafa, "Pakistan and the Middle East," *Pacific Community,* vol. 7, July 1976, p. 613.

19. This perspective very much worried Indian observers, as reported by Mohammed Ayoob, "Indo-Iranian Relations: Strategic, Political and Economic," *India Quarterly,* Vol. 33, Jan.-Mar. 1977, pp. 1-13.

20. Figures from IISS, *The Military Balance, 1983-1984,* pp. 61-62; the point from S. Tahir-Kheli, "The Saudi-Pakistani Military Relationship," *op. cit.,* p. 160.

21. For a detailed discussion of the political and economic relations that developed between the two, see P. Visalakshi, *India and Iraq: From Cordial Political Relations to Close Economic Relations,* Dissertation prepared at the University of Hyderabad, 1981 (unpublished).

22. The "security dilemma" was at work here, too. See footnote 3.

23. For a detailed discussion of the successive treaties applied to this issue and other sources of the conflict, see Tareq Y. Ismael, *Iraq and Iran: Roots of Conflict* (Syracuse, Syracuse University Press, 1982).

24. G. S. Harris, "The Kurdish Conflict in Iraq", in Astri Suhrke and L. G. Noble (eds.), *Ethnic Conflict in International Relations* (New York, Praeger, 1977), Ch. 4.

25. Visalakshi, *ibid.*

26. Mohammed Ayoob, *op. cit.*

27. For the Shah's view of his wider ambitions, see Alvin J. Cottrell, "The Foreign Policy of the Shah," *Strategic Review,* Fall 1975, p. 37; for a discussion of the Soviet view of these ambitions, see S. Chubin, "Soviet Policy Towards Iran and the Gulf," *Adelphi Papers,* No. 157 (London, IISS, 1980), pp. 10-13.

28. Mohammed Ayoob, *op. cit.*

29. Bhabani SenGupta, "Waiting for India: India's Role as a Regional Power," *Journal of International Affairs,* Vol. 29, #2, Fall 1975, pp. 171-183; Shirin Tahir-Kheli, "Iran and Pakistan: Cooperation in an Area of Conflict," *Asian Survey* v. 17, May 1977; G. S. Bhargava, "India's Security in the 1980's," *Adelphi Paper,* No. 175 (London, IISS, 1976).

30. See Note 1 in Appendix. Calculated from 1981 *Yearbook of World Energy Strategies* (United Nations, 1983).

31. Data from James E. Howse, *Agenda for Action* (Overseas Development Council, New York, 1975), pp. 238-239.

32. Bhabani Sen Gupta, "India's Relations with the Gulf Countries," *op. cit.,* p. 157.

33. See Note III for details and sources. For 1970-74, *Direction of Trade Annual (IMF/IBRD);* for 1982/84, *Direction of Trade Statistical Yearbook (IMF).*

34. M. G. Weinbaum and G. Sen, "Pakistan Enters the Middle East," *Orbis,* Fall 1978, p. 602.

35. See, for instance, *Quarterly Economic Review— India, Nepal* (London, The Economist Intelligence Unit, Annual Supplement, 1982); Visalakshi, *op. cit.,* pp. 54-60.

36. K. R. Singh, *IRAN: Quest for Security* (New Delhi, Vikas, 1980), pp. 181-183; Visalakshi, *ibid.*

37. Jonathan Adelton, "The Impact of International Migration on Economic Development in Pakistan," *Asian Survey,* Vol. XXIV, No. 5, May 1984, pp. 576-577 for discussion of different estimates and sources.

38. Perhaps 5-10% of migrants to Saudi Arabia, 20-25% to the UAE include non-working family members. I am grateful to staff of the IBRD for advice on these magnitudes, particularly Shahid Javed Burki.

39. I. S. Birbas and C. A. Sinclair, *Arab Manpower: The Crisis of Development* (New York, St. Martin's Press, 1980).

40. One of the most useful discussions is Myron Weiner's "International Migration and Development: Indians in the Persian Gulf," *Population and Migration Review,* Vol. 8, No. 1 (March 1982), pp. 1-36.

41. Tsakok, Isabelle, "The Export of Manpower from Pakistan to the Middle East, 1975-1985," *World Development,* vol. 10, no. 4, pp. 219-325, p. 319.

42. Myron Weiner, *op. cit.,* p. 7.

43. Shahid Javed Burki, "What Migration to the Middle East May Mean for Pakistan," *Journal of South Asian and Middle Eastern Studies,* Vol. III, No. 3, Spring 1980, pp. 55, 64. Much the same can be said for India's west coast.

44. To be sure, all is not positive. Land values are skyrocketing; a share of resources goes into conspicuous family rituals rather than productive investment, and envy on the part of those who did not go generates another cleavage. Expenditure preferences run something like this: (1) improve family diets, (2) begin paying off debts, (3) improve sister's dowry, (4) upgrade home, (5) start small business or buy land. Writer's interviews in Pakistan.

45. Shahid Javed Burki, *Pakistan's Labor Migration: Social and Economic Implications at Home* (A comment), Columbia University Seminar on Migration, October 26, 1984.

46. Gurushri Swamy, *International Migrant Workers' Remittances: Issues and Prospects* (World Bank Staff Working Paper No. 481, 1981), p. 9. Burki reported to the writer that in 1984, they equaled merchandise exports for Pakistan and amounted to nearly 15 percent for India.

47. Calculated from *Yearbook of World Energy Statistics: 1979 and 1981. For 1982--1983* (United Nations, Energy Unit, UN Statistical Office).

48. Javed Burki, IBRD, consultation June, 1985.

49. For a theoretically promising approach to this problem, see Barry Buzan, "A Framework for Regional Security Analysis," forthcoming.

STATISTICAL APPENDIX

Table 1.

Domestic Production of Crude Oil as Percentage of Total Consumption

	1970	1973	1975	1978	1979	1980	1981
India	37%	35%	38%	44%	45%	37%	51%
Pakistan	10%	10%	8%	12%	12%	11%	11%

Source: Calculated from 1981 *Yearbook of World Energy Statistics*, United Nations, 1983.

Table 2.

Principal Suppliers of Crude Oil to India and Paksitan 1971-1983 (Thousands of Metric Tons)

	1971	1973	1975	1977	1979	1981	1983
To India							
Iran	9,960	9,620	6,500	6,870	2,350	2,360	4,250
Iraq			3,120	1,860	6,690	6,710	4,450
Saudi Arabia			4,040	2,870	3,030	3,210	2,500
UAE				960	1,410	1,420	1,400
USSR		280	980	1,650	1,770	2,610	2,500
To Pakistan							
Iran	1,500	2,470	2,400		40		
Iraq					520		
Saudi Arabia	570	370	400	2,270	1,750	3,140	
UAE	1,430	60	800	1,000	680	1,190	

Sources: For 1971-1974: *World Energy Supplies: 1950-1974*, (Statistical Papers Series J, No. 19) United Nations, New York, 1976); for 1975-1980: *Yearbook of World Energy Statistics: 1979 and 1981;* for 1982-1983: Energy Unit, UN Statistical Office, United Nations, New York.)

Table 3.

Exports from India and Pakistan to Principal Gulf States (In Millions of US Dollars)

	1971	1973	1975	1977	1979	1981
From India						
Iran	30	39	351	165	92	137
Iraq	17	18	91	70	67	76
Saudi A.	15	23	63	130	189	247
UAE	9	18	66	177	158	221
From Pakistan						
Iran	5	15	20	92	57	154
Iraq	12	14	43	50	63	80
Saudi A.	11	20	67	61	111	190
UAE	10	21	42	45	112	169

Source: *Direction of Trade Annual*, 1970-1974 (IMF and IBRD); *Direction of Trade Statistics Yearbook*, 1982 and 1984 (IMF).

48 Arab Oil and Japanese Foreign Policy

By Roy Licklider

The conventional view of Japan's Middle East policy is that it did not exist before 1973 and that it then became strongly pro-Arab because of the impact of the oil weapon. I want to suggest a modification which stresses the continuity in Japan's policy rather than the changes over the postwar period.

Background

Japan has practically no historical connection with the Middle East or with the Arab-Israeli dispute, although diligent researchers have found evidence of indirect contact as early as the sixth century.[1] It had no colonial links with the area, and it was not involved in the Holocaust. It also has no Jewish community of its own. This lack of ties makes it unique among the developed democracies.

Japan was the OECD country most dependent on Middle Eastern oil. Valerie Yorke notes that imported oil supplied 37 percent of Japan's energy needs in 1960, 71 percent in 1970, and 76 percent by 1978. The figure had dropped by 66 percent by 1980, but it was not expected to fall rapidly; the national goal for 1990 was 49 percent, and Japan has had great difficulty establishing a realistic national energy program, despite its vaunted business-government cooperation.[2] In 1980 over 70 percent of Japan's imported oil came from the Gulf. On the other hand, much of this oil came from Iran, which was not a member of OAPEC. Thus Japan was less dependent on *Arab* oil at the time than these figures would suggest; it got about 40 percent of its oil from the Arabs.[3] Japanese dependence on Arab oil may have actually increased since 1973 due to the Iranian Revolution and the Iraq-Iran war.[4]

Japan was uniquely doubly dependent:

> . . . on Middle East oil for a crucial margin (80 percent) of its indispensable oil imports and an even broader dependence on the United States as a supplier of a variety of essential imports including food, feed, raw materials, and high technology, as Japan's most important and profitable export market, and as the ultimate guarantee of Asian-Pacific peace and the military security of the Japanese homeland.[5]

As a result of the traumas of World War II and its high level of economic dependence, Japan has generally stressed economic relations in its foreign policy and has tried to stay out of political controversies, as one author says, "being friendly with everybody, or at least not making serious enemies anywhere."[6]

Before 1973, as Michael Yoshitsu puts it, Japan had a Middle Eastern policy based on the "twin pillars" of two United Nations resolutions, but no diplomacy to implement it.[7] Japan had helped draft United Nations Security Council Resolution 242 in 1967 (it had chaired the Security Council at the time) and remained strongly committed to it;[8] this resolution "set the tone for the limited role Japan took."[9]

Less well-known was a 1970 General Assembly resolution (2628) which asserted that "respect for the rights of the Palestinians is an indispensable element in the establishment of a just and lasting

---

Dr. Roy Licklider is Associate Professor of Political Science at Rutgers University, New Brunswick. His published works include "The Failure of the Arab Oil Weapon in 1973-1974" in *Comparative Strategy,* 3 (1982). He is author of a book-length manuscript, *Targets of the Oil Weapon,* which analyzes the impact of the oil weapon on the industrial countries' foreign policies toward Israel. The present article is taken from that manuscript's chapter on Japan.

peace in the Middle East." Yoshitsu correctly notes that Japan voted with the UN majority on 2628,[10] but overlooks the fact that the only other Western countries which did so were France, Greece, and Spain;[11] for a country which supposedly refused to take the lead in foreign policy, this vote was rather daring. On May 23, 1971, the Japanese government referred to the "lawful rights" of the people of Palestine during a visit by King Faisal. Valerie Yorke notes that Japan "was well in advance of other industrial states in the West" in supporting self-determination for the Palestinians.[12] However, it was so quiet about the policy that it failed to reap any political benefits.

> Senior officials had constructed these twin pillars of Persian Gulf policy, believing them to be the minimal requirements for peace in the region. Nevertheless, they had refrained from fusing the two elements into one comprehensive statement . . . Moreover, Tokyo planners had informed only one Persian Gulf leader, King Faisal of Saudi Arabia, of their views on Israeli withdrawal and the Palestinian issue. As a result, "the Arab countries were largely unaware of [Japan's] recognition of the legitimate right of Palestinian self-determination."[13]

The Oil Crisis

The fourth Arab-Israeli War broke out on October 6, 1973. On October 17, the Arab oil producers embargoed oil shipments to the United States and the Netherlands and reduced their total oil exports. They also linked shipments to other countries to these governments' positions on the Arab-Israeli conflict. Japan's initial response was to reiterate its support for Resolution 242 and express its hopes for peace. However, on October 24 the Arabian Oil Company (the major Japanese oil producer in the Middle East) was required to reduce production by 10 percent, twice the "normal" cut imposed on companies,[14] and BP, Gulf, and Exxon all announced that they would cut their shipments to Japan significantly.[15] Apparently this caught the Japanese by surprise.

On November 4, the Arab position became clearer with the declaration that production would be cut by 25 percent, escalating 5 percent per month, and that countries "would have to take a more specifically positive attitude toward the Arab cause" in order to be classified friendly.[16] On November 6 the European Economic Community (EEC) issued an elegantly crafted statement in Brussels. It called for Israel to end "the territorial occupation" resulting from the 1967 war; this formulation avoided the problem of whether to withdraw from all the territory or only some of it, the central ambiguity of Resolution 242. (I disagree with Garfinkle's contention that this was equivalent to requiring Israel to withdraw from all occupied territories.[17]) It also asserted that the "legitimate rights" of the Palestinians should be taken into account in any peace settlement in the Middle East but did not specify those rights.

On the same day, the chief secretary of the Japanese Cabinet, Susumu Nikaido, issued a statement reiterating the government's previous position, which was very similar to that of the EEC. It (1) opposed territorial expansion by force and supported Resolution 242; (2) supported U.S.-Soviet mediation of the dispute; and (3) supported the right of self-determination and equality for the Palestinians as set forth in "the United Nations Resolution" (presumably 2628 and its successors, since 242 does not address this issue). However, this statement did not help Japan as the equivalent EC statement helped Europe. The Arabs were apparently disappointed that Israel had not been explicitly condemned.[18] The Saudi and Kuwaiti governments declared Japan a "non-friendly" country the next day.[19] On November 18 the OAPEC oil ministers announced in Vienna that the EEC would be exempted from the 5 percent December cuts; the Japanese were pointedly not given the same favorable treatment. "The sense of panic which some government officials had experienced by late October now became pervasive."[20]

Apparently a series of further demands were made on Japan which, although never formally acknowledged by either side, were widely known. Japan was reportedly asked to (1) break diplomatic relations with Israel, (2) sever all economic ties with Israel, (3) provide military assistance to the Arabs,[21] and (4) pressure the United States to alter its policy toward the Arab-Israeli dispute.[22]

These demands plunged the Japanese government into an intensive internal debate. The Japanese sent three separate envoys to the Middle East. Henry Kissinger came to Japan and argued against acceding to the Arab demands. The Foreign Ministry and bureaucrats at the Ministry of International Trade and Industry (MITI) opposed a policy change which might alienate the United States. However, the increasing public concern and internal political rivalries brought politicians into the dispute. The role of Yasuhiro Nakasone, then MITI minister and now prime minister, seems to have been decisive. The result was a new position.[23]

On November 22, 1973, Nikaido issued a three-part statement. (1) Israel should withdraw from all territories it had occupied during and after the 1967 war. Japan thus went further than the November 6 EEC statement which was unclear whether "all" territories were included; it also modified its support of 242 which, like the EEC statement, was deliberately vague on this point. (2) Palestinian self-determination should be a precondition of any peaceful settlement in the Middle East. (3) The Japanese government would reconsider its policy towards Israel if Israel refused to accept these preconditions.[24] This statement has been widely seen as the first independent foreign policy initiative by the Japanese since World War II.[25]

Japan, however, did not meet any of the four Arab demands. It did not break diplomatic relations with Israel and consistently refused to clarify the rather vague language about when this might be done.[26] Economic ties with Israel were also not severed. Because of its constitution, Japan claimed to be unable to supply sophisticated weapons to the Arabs. Apparently, however, its substitution of money and personal diplomacy was successful. On November 28 Japan was exempted from the 5 percent cut scheduled for December, but the earlier cuts remained in effect, and it wasn't clear whether the November 22 statement would be sufficient.[27] On December 10, as Miki was preparing to go to the Middle East, the Arabs announced another 5 percent cut for January for the European Community and Japan, which did not seem like a good sign. However, on December 25 Japan was formally reclassified as a "friendly" country by OAPEC, while Miki was still in the Middle East.[28]

While in the Middle East, Miki had promised $127 million to help rebuild the Suez Canal and $100 million additional aid to Egypt. Sources differ as to whether this was at his own initiative or at the suggestion of Foreign Minister Ohira,[29] but the fact that the noted international economist and later Foreign Minister Saburo Okita was included in his entourage suggests prior planning. Miki was followed to the Middle East by Nakasone in January and a number of other Japanese government leaders later, each of whom promised more money; one source estimated the total amount of Japanese credits pledged during the crisis at $3.3 billion.[30]

Japanese Middle Eastern Policy Since the Crisis

In her analysis of U.N. voting patterns on Arab-Israeli issues, Janice Stein distinguished three different coalitions in 1974, just after the crisis. The U.S. opposed acknowledging Palestinian rights while all of its allies, including Japan, abstained. The U.S. was joined by most of its European allies in opposing recognition of the PLO; France, Italy, and Japan abstained.[31] All voted against a resolution condemning Zionism and racism except Japan, which abstained. Thus, with the possible exception of Greece after the overthrow of the colonels, Japan remained the most pro-Arab industrial country, as it had been before the oil crisis. This pattern has continued.

The level of agreement between Japan and other members of the alliance is significantly lower than among all other allies. On the other hand, Japan clearly remains within the Western consensus on the Middle East, albeit at the pro-Arab end; for example, Japan abstained on the 1974 General Assembly Palestinian resolutions because they did not reaffirm Resolution 242 and did not explicitly affirm Israel's right to exist.[32] Thus, in relative terms, Japan continued to occupy almost precisely its pre-crisis position vis-a-vis its Western partners.

In 1975 the Japanese government invited the Palestinian Liberation Organization to begin talks on establishing an office in Tokyo, although it firmly resisted pressure to extend formal diplomatic recognition. After extensive negotiations, the office opened in 1976.[33]

Another aspect of Japanese foreign policy was a deliberate shift of trade and investment policy. One "lesson" learned by Japanese elites from the crisis was that they had an enormous stake in the Middle East, while the Middle East had no equivalent stake in Japan. The result was to greatly increase investment in the Middle East, particularly in Iran[34] and, after the Iran-Iraq war began, in Saudi Arabia.[35] Ironically one result was the abortive $1.5 billion investment by Mitsui in an Iranian petrochemical complex which cannot be completed because of the Iran-Iraq war.

The Iranian Revolution and resulting oil crisis in 1979 weakened the Japanese confidence that they could bargain money and technology for oil in a relatively non-political manner.[36] On August 6, Foreign Minister Sonoda said that Middle Eastern peace must be comprehensive (an implicit criticism of the Camp David process), must involve recognition of Palestinian rights, including self-determination, and must include the PLO as negotiators. He also condemned Israeli occupation of the 1967 territories and its settlement policy. The Japanese diplomatic position was to ask the Israelis for self-restraint, with a strong commitment to Israeli security behind the 1967 borders, and to ask the PLO to accept UN Resolution 242 in return for self-determination. Following a Japanese initiative in 1979 and complex negotiations, Japan in 1981 became the first Western country to have talks with the PLO at the prime ministerial level.[37]

Japan reacted negatively to the Israeli invasion of Lebanon in 1982; indeed the head of the Foreign Ministry's Middle East-Africa Bureau urged Israel to withdraw and explicitly did not make the same request of Syria on the grounds that Syrian troops were in Lebanon by invitation of the Arab League.[38] In March 1983, the chief of the Tokyo office of the PLO was invited to the Emperor's birthday party, a step one observer called "extraordinary."[39] It is not clear whether Japan is leading the Western alliance or being pushed by it, but it has remained just a little bit in front on the Arab-Israeli issue.

Dimensions of Change in Japanese Middle Eastern Policy

We can trace two different kinds of policy shift toward the Arab-Israeli conflict during and after the oil crisis. Rhetorically Japan went further than any other Western country in supporting the Arab position on Israeli withdrawal from the occupied territories and threatened to "reconsider" its policy toward Israel if this did not occur. Economically the Japanese promised huge amounts of financial assistance to Middle Eastern countries. These acts were widely seen as Japanese capitulation to Arab pressure, readily explained by the "supply theory" of economic sanctions since Japan is more dependent on Middle Eastern oil than any other industrial country.

However, this is too simple an explanation. The supply theory would predict that Japan would yield to practically any demand which did not threaten its basic national interests, but in fact the Japanese refused to accede to most of the Arab demands. Japan did not break diplomatic relations with Israel, even though this would have been merely a rhetorical gesture without any substantive impact whatsoever. It did not terminate economic relations with Israel, even though they were not particularly important to Japan. It did not supply weapons to the Arabs. It also does not seem to have tried to pressure the United States to change its Middle Eastern policy.[40]

Japan's actual deeds were more shadow than substance. Israel did not withdraw from the occupied territories, but Japan has not noticeably "reconsidered" its policy as a result. Even Japanese economic promises were in many cases not kept.[41]

Japan has supported the PLO more strongly rhetorically than any other Western country, but in fact it did so before the oil crisis as well. As the industrial nations have shifted toward a more pro-Arab position, Japan has essentially maintained its relative position within the Western alliance. Thus continuity seems more important in Japanese Middle Eastern policy than change, even though the supply theory would have predicted major changes as a result of the oil weapon.

The Impact of the Oil Weapon on Japanese Middle Eastern Policy

It seems to me that there are two separate issues to explain: (1) why did Japan adopt a public position which was more pro-Arab than other industrial states and (2) why did Japan not meet further Arab demands? Most discussions of the case have focused on the first issue, but in some ways the second is more interesting. Sherlock Holmes was intrigued by the dog that didn't bark; similarly the supply theory of economic sanctions leaves the observer wondering why the Japanese did not accede to most of the Arab demands.

Japan seemed to be the "perfect target" for the oil embargo. It was the most dependent OECD country on Middle Eastern oil, it had no historic interest or involvement with the Middle East, there was no internal Jewish pressure group working for Israel, and it had a reputation of a low-profile foreign policy which yielded readily to external pressure. Thus it is not hard to see why Japan has been the most pro-Arab of the Western countries. Indeed Japan is generally seen as the major success of the oil weapon.

The central question of the Japanese case, however, is why there was so little policy change when the embargo seemed to have such enormous power. Undoubtedly one major reason was the offsetting external pressure of the United States, the major ally of both Japan and Israel. Henry Kissinger made a serious effort to keep the Japanese government from adopting a pro-Arab stance. Ironically he feels that he failed, while my analysis suggests that he succeeded. Japan remains within the general Western consensus of supporting the existence of Israel, not recognizing the PLO, and leaning on 242 (albeit a different interpretation of the resolution) as the cornerstone for a negotiated settlement. Arab oil leverage has been unsuccessful in moving it away from these positions.

The U.S. was in an unusually strong position to influence Japan because pro-American positions had become practically second-nature to most Japanese bureaucrats, in MITI as well as the Foreign Ministry. Thus even the relatively innocuous pro-Arab rhetoric of the November 22 statement would probably never have been approved except for the involvement of leading politicians, particularly Nakasone, because of public concern caused by the embargo. (Yoshitsu attributes this change to decisions within the Foreign Ministry.) Thus the embargo does seem to have produced this rhetorical change of policy. However, as soon as the crisis dissipated, the bureaucrats took over again, and their attitudes do not seem to have been changed much by the experience.

On the other hand, while the direction of Japan's position has not changed much, it is clear that the embargo moved Middle Eastern policy from a relatively minor aspect of Japanese policy to a much more important position.[42] Moreover, given the general difficulty of changing Japanese policy, there is some reason for this shift being seen as significant by the Japanese themselves, as indeed they do, although to outsiders it may seem fairly trivial.

Lastly, we are left with the question of how the Japanese would have reacted if the oil weapon had been continued and had been successful in severely cutting back oil supplies to Japan. Respondents felt that Japan, more than any other country in this study, would have been willing to make further concessions to the Arabs under such circumstances. But it is hard to escape the sense that Japan's political vulnerability has been overestimated, given its lack of real change in the face of very impressive threats.

In some other countries the long term shift in Middle Eastern policies seems best explained by the "new wealth" of the Arabs and the consequent increases in Arab export markets and capital investment. This explanation seems less applicable to Japan, both because of its greater dependence on Middle Eastern oil and because of its more impressive general economic performance. Economic activities with the Middle East seem to have remained a means to an end for the Japanese, a way to increase access to oil supplies in the future, while in the European countries such activities became a key part of their economies. There is no doubt that new Arab wealth facilitated the Japanese policy shift,[43] but for Japan, unlike the other countries studied, the issue of oil supplies remained paramount.

The Japanese diplomatic response, however, was not to break ranks with other Western countries and desperately seek to curry Arab favor by irresponsible gestures. Instead, the Japanese have essentially continued their earlier policy of staying just a little more pro-Arab than any other Western country. The oil weapon didn't really "teach" the Japanese anything new. They already knew they were dangerously dependent on Middle Eastern oil, and they had already taken steps, albeit very quietly, to try to rectify this situation by diplomatic gestures. The oil crisis had major short-term effects on Japan, but in the longer run it seems to have merely confirmed to the Japanese the wisdom of their earlier strategy.

FOOTNOTES

1. Yasumasa Kuroda, "Japan and the Arabs: The Economic Dimension," *Journal of Arab Affairs*, 3 (1974) p. 1.

2. Louis Turner, *Oil Companies in the International System* (London: George Allen & Unwin, 1978), pp. 107-108 and Ronald A. Morse, "The Politics of Japan's Energy Strategy: Resources — Diplomacy — Security" (Research Papers and Policy Studies #3, Institute of East Asian Studies, University of California, Berkeley, 1981).

3. Valerie Yorke, "Oil, the Middle East, and Japan's Search for Security" in Nobutoshi Akao, *Japanese Economic Security: Resources in Japanese Foreign Policy* (New York: St. Martin's Press, in press), pp. 10-11.

4. Martha Ann Caldwell, "The Dilemmas of Japan's Oil Dependency" in Morse, pp. 81-82.

5. Kiichi Saeki, "Japan's Energy-Security Dilemma" in J. C. Hurewitz, *Oil, the Arab-Israeli Dispute, and the Industrial World* (Boulder, Colorado: Westview Press, 1976), p. 258.

6. Saburo Okita, "Natural Resource Diplomacy and Japanese Foreign Policy," *Foreign Affairs*, 52 (July, 1974), p. 723.

7. Michael Yoshitsu, *Caught in the Middle East: Japan's Diplomacy in Transition* (Lexington, Massachusetts: D. C. Heath & Company, 1984), p. 1.

8. Michael Baker, "Grappling With Dependence: Japanese Oil Policy, 1970-1974," East Asian Institute Certificate Essay, Columbia University, New York, New York, Spring, 1978, p. 28.

9. Martha Caldwell Harris, personal interview.

10. Yoshitsu, p. 1.

11. Dusan J. Djonovich, *United Nations Resolutions*, Series I Resolutions Adopted by the General Assembly, Volume XIII 1970-1971. (Dobbs Ferry, New York: Oceana Publications, Inc. 1976), pp. 221 and 52.

12. Yorke, in Akao, pp. 37-38n.

13. Yoshitsu, p. 1; the quotation is from his interview with "a high-ranking Japanese official."

14. Yuan-li Wu, *Japan's Search For Oil: A Case Study on Economic Nationalism and International Security*, Hoover Institution Publication 165. (Stanford, California: Hoover Institution Press, 1977), pp. 1-2.

15. Kenneth Juster, "Japanese Foreign Policy Making During the Oil Crisis," B.A. thesis, Department of Government, Harvard College, Cambridge, Mass., 1976, pp. 52-53; Yoshitsu, 2.

16. Baker, p. 30.

17. Adam M. Garfinkle, "Western Europe's Middle East Diplomacy and the United States," Philadelphia Policy Papers, Foreign Policy Research Institute, Philadelphia, Pennsylvania, 1983, p. 3.

18. Juster, p. 55.

19. Baker, p. 31.

20. Juster, p. 55.

21. "Using the Oil Crisis," *Oriental Economist*, 41 (December, 1973), p. 10; J. B. Kelly, *Arabia, the Gulf and the West* (New York: Basic Books, Inc., 1980), p. 409; George Lenczowski, "Middle East Oil in a Revolutionary Age," National Energy Study No. 10, American Enterprise Institute for Public Policy Research, Washington, D.C., 1976, p. 21; Economist Intelligence Group, *Quarterly Economic Review: Saudi Arabia, Jordan*, 4 (November 17, 1973), p. 5; and Gaston Sigur in U.S., Congress, House of Representatives, Committee on Foreign Affairs, Subcommittee on Asian and Pacific Affairs, *Hearings: Oil and Asian Rivals: Sino-Soviet Conflict; Japan and the Oil Crisis*, 93rd Congress, 1st and 2nd Sessions (1973-1974), p. 37.

22. Henry Nau, "Japanese-American Relations During the 1973-74 Oil Crisis" in Michael Blaker, "Oil and the Atom: Issues in US-Japan Energy Relations," Occasional Papers Series, Project on Japan and the United States in Multilateral Diplomacy, East Asian Institute, Columbia University, New York, New York, 1980, p. 16.

23. This process is discussed at length in the Japanese chapter of my larger manuscript, "Targets of the Oil Weapon."

24. Wu, pp. 3-4.

25. Yoshi Tsurumi, "Japan" in Raymond Vernon, *The Oil Crisis* (New York: W. W. Norton & Co., 1976), p. 124; Baker, p. 46; Yorke in Akao, p. 13; Robert Pfaltzgraff, Jr., "Energy Issues and Alliance Relationships: The United States, Western Europe and Japan," Special Report, Institute for Foreign Policy Analysis, Inc., Cambridge, Massachusetts, 1980, p. 20.

26. Martha Ann Caldwell, "Petroleum Politics in Japan: State and Industry in a Changing Policy Context," Ph.D. dissertation, University of Wisconsin, Madison, 1980, pp. 215-216.

27. Kenneth Juster, "Foreign Policy-making During the Oil Crisis," *Japan Interpreter*, 11 (Winter, 1977), p. 305.

28. Kazushige Hirasawa, "Japan's Tiling Neutrality" in Hurewitz, p. 141.

29. *Ibid.;* also, Yoshitsu, p. 7.

30. *Japan Petroleum Weekly*, 9, (January 28, 1974), p. 2, cited in Wu, p. 5; cf. Caldwell, p. 228 and Yorke in Akao, p. 14.

31. Janice Stein, "Alice in Wonderland: The North Atlantic Alliance and the Arab-Israeli Dispute," in Steven Spiegel, *The Middle East and the Western Alliance* (London: George Allen & Unwin, 1982), pp. 57-59.

32. Yoshitsu, pp. 13-14.

33. *Ibid.*, pp. 14-22.

34. Henry Nau, personal interview.

35. Yoshitsu, p. 85.

36. Morse, pp. 10-11.

37. Yorke in Akao, pp. 23-26, 33, and 41; Yoshitsu, pp. 24-37 and 74-75; Caldwell in Morse, pp. 75-78; Yasumasa Kuroda, "Japan's Middle East Policy: Changing Relationships between Japan and West Asia," paper for the International Studies Association-West, Berkeley, California, March 25-27, 1983, p. 29.

38. Kuroda, "Japan's Middle East Policy," pp. 23 and 26-27.

39. W. R. Campbell, "Japan and the Middle East" in Robert S. Ozaki and Walter Arnold, *Japan's Foreign Relations: A Global Search for Economic Security* (Boulder, Colorado: Westview Press, 1984), p. 149.

40. Henry A. Kissinger, *Years of Upheaval* (Boston: Little, Brown & Company, 1982), pp. 741-742.

41. Juster, "Japanese Foreign Policy Making During the Oil Crisis," p. 81.

42. Henry Nau, personal interview.

43. *Ibid.*

49

Through a Glass Darkly: Western Europe and the Middle East

By Linda B. Miller

How have the Iran-Iraq war and the Israeli intervention in Lebanon altered the Middle East landscape with respect to West European foreign policies? What roles are the individual states and the European Community equipped to play? To answer these questions in the midst of rapidly unfolding events is speculative at best, foolhardy at worst. Yet there is value in assessing the likely impact of these two dramatic and violent episodes, compared with reactions to the fall of the Shah of Iran and the ensuing hostage crisis, the incident in Mecca, the assassination of President Sadat, or the Soviet invasion of Afghanistan. Observers who were initially certain that entrenched attitudes would shatter are now more tentative in their judgments and correctly so.

As will be shown, elements of continuity rather than change are evident in national foreign policies and in the stance of the Community. While major shifts in European perspectives occurred in 1973-74, the years since the oil "crisis" have witnessed an elaboration of now familiar themes, a deepening of now familiar anxieties. Thus the most useful way to assess the current situation is to consider the factors that shape Middle East policies in Western Europe and the differences between West European and American approaches. The scope for European activity in the turbulent area will emerge more clearly as a result.

Dr. Miller is Professor of Political Science at Wellesley College. She is the author of numerous works on world politics, American foreign policy and European affairs.

I

The Western Europe that confronts the Middle East today is neither the United States of Europe the founders of the European Communities hoped the disparate nation-states might become, nor the fragmented region some critics foresee, if relations within NATO deteriorate further. The major and lesser powers are preoccupied with an array of domestic economic and political problems that threaten most advanced industrial countries, including persistent inflation, recession, and rising unemployment. Within each country, problems of internal cohesion or external status plague policymakers who must balance national requirements and regional or alliance obligations.

Of course, the West European countries vary widely in terms of relative prosperity, resource endowment and the presence of domestic groups with salient foreign policy concerns in the Middle East. Ties are felt most acutely in Britain and France, the two countries with both the longest imperial tradition and the largest Jewish communities. In the continuing contest for European support in Middle East conflicts, local parties there used to assume that France and Italy were "pro-Arab," while Holland, Denmark and West Germany were "pro-Israel." Other governments were labeled "undecided". These categories have become increasingly obsolete as the West Europeans have competed with one another and the superpowers to sell arms and manufactured goods to both Arab countries and Israel in order to provide employment for their populations and funds for imported oil.

After enlargement of the European Community from Six to Ten, it has become more difficult to go beyond the rhetorical definition of common security and economic interests. The transfer of wealth from the OECD countries to the OPEC countries has taken place as the Community has become less efficient and more heterogeneous. Although splits in the membership on agriculture, budgets, monetary policy, defense and detente have not produced either the much maligned "finlandization" or "neutralism", these divisions have contributed to the weakness of West European middle-rank states in an unruly world of superpowers and "third world" countries with their own agendas.

Ironically, in the Middle East, long a center of European rivalries, the collective interests, fears, sentiments and principles of both the states and their Community have created at least the impression of a unified policy. The content of that policy derives from the fact that West European economic wellbeing is still highly dependent on imported petroleum, almost a decade after the first oil "shock". Despite somewhat successful attempts at conservation and the diversification of supply from non-OPEC sources, the Community lacks a common energy policy. The frantic scrambling for favorable bilateral deals with the Arab oil producers throughout the 1970s underscored the heightened sense of vulnerability representatives of the once proud and independent "patron" states of Europe sensed in dealing with "clients" who now appeared to dictate the terms. This psychological trauma, while difficult to analyze, has had a deleterious effect on the capacity of West European governments to make political choices in the Middle East.

Already sensitive to perceptions of declining power after decolonization, the West Europeans understandably place the highest value on "stability". For countries whose leaders are concerned that their diplomatic influence is waning, that their military stature is slipping and that their economic standard is falling, the Iran-Iraq war would be especially worrisome. Despite the fact that the conflict has been fought inconclusively, during an oil glut, without extensive media coverage, the residuum of 1973-74 has affected the European response. Eager to avoid any real or imagined threat to oil supplies, the West Europeans as a group have endorsed the impartial mediation efforts of Olof Palme and others, while at the same time they have provided weapons to both sides.

In part, the analysis behind this apparently ambiguous behavior is sound, for the war does jeopardize serious Western interests, including containment of the USSR. If America's allies have seemed unconcerned about Moscow's ability to aid Iraq directly or Iran indirectly, via its proxies, Libya and Syria, it is because they realize that there is not much they could do about it. Similarly, while the rise of Islamic fundamentalism gives the Europeans pause, political leaders regard the development as one that the former metropoles are unlikely to affect. After a period of some uncertainty, the West Europeans have begun to downgrade Iran's capacity to export its ideology and to stress the constraints on the Ayatullah Khumayni if he aspires to regional hegemony.

Because European attitudes are not likely to be decisive in the outcome of the fighting, a more important question is whether a faulty connection has been made between the Iran-Iraq war and the Arab-Israeli conflict. Since the Yom Kippur war of 1973, the West Europeans' overriding preoccupation with oil supplies has severely limited European freedom of action. By stating constantly that a resolution of that conflict would inevitably ease the continent's energy problems, the West Europeans have chosen to neglect the abundant evidence that the oil weapon is less potent in 1983 than in 1973, given newer technologies and alternative sources. They have also been reluctant to acknowledge that Saudi Arabia's pricing decisions are governed by economic rather than political priorities. The Europeans have denied themselves the chance to exploit more fully the disputes within OPEC that might give them additional room for maneuver in times of slower demand for petroleum.

The link between energy dependence and economic growth is real. Nevertheless, perceptions of disadvantage *vis a vis* oil exporters may be more important as restrictions on European political choices than actual statistics would warrant. This dilemma is a major factor shaping the content of West European policies in the Middle East. A restoration of European influence is not excluded by it, but neither is it facilitated.

II

In few parts of the world do the West European states, especially Britain and France, assert more of a proprietary interest than they do in the Middle East. Because the area is beyond the geographical boundaries of NATO, efforts to coordinate alliance policies directed from Washington have proved fruitless. After the Suez debacle, perhaps due to the maladroit fashion in which America played its hand in 1956, Britain and France have resisted common policies that seemed based on a distinction between the "regional" dimension of post-imperial Europe's objectives and the "global" nature of America's commitments. The West Europeans wish to present themselves to local parties as offering an alternative to the superpowers, with different ideas of how to use diplomatic, economic, political and cultural instruments to attain foreign policy goals.

To others, European desires to conduct a subtle game in the Middle East have often backfired. The West Europeans have looked self-serving, displaying no unusual understanding of inter-Arab politics, despite claims of superior insight derived from the colonial past. The Europeans handling of the Camp David accords typified a short-sighted, self-defeating posture. When they opposed the American initiative that promised and achieved the first real peace between Israel and an Arab state, they were unable to substitute anything of substance. Their ritualistic expressions of sympathy for the Jewish state had a hollow ring. When the Community issued the Venice Declaration in June 1980, which called for a Palestinian state on the West Bank and Gaza, the Europeans put themselves squarely on one side of an exceedingly complex issue and effectively terminated any remaining influence on Israel.

If the pronouncement reflected French policy preferences, its terms surprised no one. The peculiar brand of romanticism and cynicism that characterized the French position on the PLO and the Palestinian question was already well known. That the Community as a whole supported such a statement revealed again a widespread, misguided, view that a solution to the Arab-Israeli conflict on Arab terms was crucial to the steady flow of Persian Gulf oil, and perhaps sufficient to assure it. After Venice, the European governments have shown little inclination to question whether it has been wise or necessary for them to accept the PLO as the "legitimate representative" of the Palestinian people. In calling the PLO "moderate", in allowing it to open offices in some European capitals and in meeting its leaders, Europeans, essentially the French, have appeared to condone both terrorism and the PLO Covenant that calls for Israel's destruction. European credibility sank further when the British applauded the Fahd plan, essentially a restatement of old Arab claims. The British, who with the French, the Italians and the Dutch, wished to join the multinational force in Sinai, effectively disqualified themselves when they included a restatement of the Venice Declaration in their grudging acceptance of Camp David.

For a brief period, it looked as if the new French socialist president, Francois Mitterrand, could help the Europeans break out of the vicious circle their convoluted Middle East policies had become. As the self-styled champion of third world causes, Mitterrand's France would aid the Nicaraguans, flirt with Castro and court the PLO, all to Washington's annoyance. At the same time, M. Mitterrand would personally strengthen the fragile relationship with Israel by undertaking the first state visit of a French president to Jerusalem. The reversal of French policy was short-lived. It could not survive the Israeli intervention in Lebanon. Predictably, the French and other Europeans led a chorus of criticism and insisted on the preservation of the PLO as a political force, even in the face of Arab disenchantment with a militarily defeated movement they could no longer control. The upsurge of terrorist acts in France itself exposed not only lax security but also latent anti-Semitism in the predominantly Catholic country.

Together with Greece, the Community's newest member, France has pressed the Ten and the United Nations to take strong measures against Israel, including a ban on arms sales. Lacking any direct influence on the Begin government, the French have worked closely with Egypt on UN resolutions for cease fires and have tried to persuade Washington to implement sanctions. Although the Europeans were hesitant to employ sanctions against Iran during the hostage crisis or against the Soviet Union after the invasion of Afghanistan or the imposition of martial law in Poland, for fear of damaging commercial relations, their willingness to propose such measures against the Jewish state indicates that they expect Israel to pay a high price for peace in the Middle East. It also reveals that the Europeans are less sanguine than the Americans that a reconstruction of a stronger Lebanon may follow the expulsion of the PLO from Beirut and the anticipated departure of Syrian and Israeli forces.

Paradoxically, the war, with its exaggerated casualty figures, may well have narrowed differences between America and Western Europe on the next steps to pursue in the peace process in the Middle East. With Alexander Haig's departure from the State Department, the United States has abandoned its ill-conceived notion of a "strategic consensus" formed of its own allies, Israel, Egypt and Saudi Arabia, though not its equally problematic concept of a Rapid Deployment Force in the Persian Gulf. Washington's interest in restarting the stalled autonomy talks would find the Europeans eager to take part, just as France and Italy were pleased to join the multinational force to supervise the PLO evacuation of Beirut.

Whether American and European approaches might become more harmonious depends more on the Reagan Administration than on the Europeans. If the United States adopts the view that official contacts with a reconstituted Palestinian leadership serve Washington's interests in seeking an accommodation on the West Bank and Gaza, the gap between the NATO allies will shrink. Nevertheless, American leverage on Israel, given its position as chief arms supplier and source of foreign loans and credits, will substantially outweigh that of the Europeans, individually and collectively. For the United States, if not for Europe, the ultimate question is still Israel's fate, not the occupied territories' destinies.

•

There is little reason to believe that the Iran-Iraq war, frequently ignored by the international media, or the Israeli intervention in Lebanon, reported in great and often inaccurate detail, will fundamentally alter the roles that the West European states and their Community are equipped to play in the Middle East. To be sure, in elite opinion, calls for the more active participation of Western Europe and Japan in the Indian Ocean and Persian Gulf are heard. Theoretically, European ground and sea forces could share defense burdens with the U.S., thereby stressing the political and economic stake of the entire Western alliance in the Middle East. Practically, at the government level, a tendency for the Europeans to rely on now well established, if confined, roles as arms suppliers, traders, oil importers, and supporters of the Palestinian cause, is evident.

For Western Europe, the name of the game is political influence, as a means and as an end. Their present roles, some forced upon them, others self-chosen, are what yield such influence and also circumscribe it. In the last decade, the cost of moving from ambiguity to equivocation on the subject of the Arab-Israeli conflict has been large, for the West Europeans now find themselves on the periphery of events in the Middle East rather than at the center, a foreign policy goal they did not seek yet seem powerless to change.

50

Israel and the Third World

By Dan V. Segre

Israel's relations with the Third World are today the subject of controversy. To some they constitute a very successful example of international cooperation. To many others they serve as an example of neo-colonialism and imperialism. The distinction between these two approaches is obviously a personal one, and it would be very difficult to reach any sort of agreement on them if one took the short-term view of the problem. It is a fact that Israel does not operate in the Third World for charitable reasons; it operates for political reasons, like any other state. It is also a fact that Israel tries to foster, in these countries, its own national interests. Since these interests are linked with the profound, deepseated and prolonged crisis with which the Afro-Asian countries are involved, it is inevitable that, if we take the short-term view of the problem, the Middle East conflict will reverberate on the whole effort of Israeli-Third World cooperation.

To extract the substance, however, of this cooperation, one must take a long-range view, and ask what will remain,

---

Prof. Segre is with the Department of Political Science at Haifa University, and the Van Leer Institute, Jerusalem. His latest work is *A Crisis of Identity: Israel and Zionism* (Oxford University Press, 1980).

what will be said of this effort of international cooperation of a small, developing state with other small—and not so small—developing states, twenty, thirty or forty years hence.

I think that what will remain will be an acknowledgement by Israel of the evolution of a number of comprehensive techniques of development, which I would define under the general term of micro-cooperation, as opposed to other techniques of development practiced mainly by the great powers, which are usually termed *macro-cooperation.*

The distinction between micro-cooperation and macro-cooperation is not only in size—although that is, of course, very important—but also in strategy of development. Macro-cooperation tends to change the environment, in the hope that people will eventually adapt to a new environmental condition and therefore modernize their habits. Micro-cooperation, on the other hand, concentrates its efforts on the attempt to change people's habits, in the hope that eventually, because of this change, they will be more open to accept innovation. There is also another difference. In practice macro-cooperation is an activity which tends to groom "Generals" of development. Micro-cooperation — the type of cooperation which Israel has been developing over the last ten or fifteen years—is, on the contrary, mainly concerned with the training of the "Non-Commissioned Officer" of development.

It is in this perspective that I would like to retrace the history of Israeli cooperation with the Third World, the reasons which have brought it about, the conceptual structures behind it, and some of its major—as I view them—failures and successes.

This history begins with the Bandung Conference of 1955 to which Israel was initially invited, only to have the invitation revoked. The Conference decided (on behalf of two and a quarter billion people belonging to the Afro-Asian family) that the people of Israel (at that time numbering 2.2 million) not only did not belong to the Afro-Asian nations but were, in fact, the spearhead of all the evils besetting the Afro-Asian countries—racialism, colonialism, imperialism, etc.

The shock of this resolution was deeply felt in Israel and was, in all probability, the beginning of the new Israeli appraisal. Then came the Suez war of 1956, which opened the Gulf of Aqaba to Israeli navigation and thereby created new opportunities for contact and trade in the Red Sea, East Africa and the Indian Ocean. Starting from 1959, new states in Africa obtained their independence and consequently Israel became interested in establishing immediate relations with them. The period from 1961 to 1966 marked the peak of this cooperation between Israel and mainly African, but also several Asian, states—relations which developed in the field of agriculture, military cooperation, in much diplomatic contact and in joint deliberations (mainly at the U.N.). There was even, for a moment, some talk of an "Israeli-African Bloc for Peace" at the U.N. General Assembly of 1961 and 1962. The proposals which this bloc put forward with a view to fostering direct talks between Arabs and Israelis, were not accepted, but they indicated the closeness of the cooperation. And of course there was recognition of Jerusalem as the capital of Israel by the majority of those African states which had sent their presidents to visit Jerusalem.

Then came the war of 1967, which registered as a great traumatic experience in the relations between Israel and the Afro-Asian states as a whole, but mainly with Africa. This was because Israel found herself victorious over an Arab-African state—Egypt, and because this war seemed, to the Africans, to have encroached on one of the fundamental principles of the Charter of African Unity—that no border should be changed by force.

It is probably one of the proofs of the solidity of the relations between Israel and the Afro-Asian countries that only one African country (Guinea) broke off relations with Israel at the time, and that it took 5 years of direct Arab pressure and large Libyan financial grants to persuade two others — Uganda and Chad—to follow suit.[1] In fact, Israel's cooperation with the Third World still continues and is perhaps greater than before, although with a change in focus developing today toward the Latin American states.

In 1971 there was intense political activity on the part of the African states, who sent a delegation of four presidents[2] to Cairo and Jerusalem that December to try to find a compromise formula that would, somehow, reactivate the Jarring mission. It was not very successful. Then came the crisis of 1972, between Israel and Uganda, which has had a traumatic effect and will, I think, still have much influence and impact on the future of Israeli-African relations. We shall return to this topic later in the paper.

Reasons for Cooperation

What are the reasons for the intense activity of cooperation reflected by some 17,000 Afro-Asian trainees in Israel today, and some 2,500 Israeli experts in these countries? On the Israeli side, as we have mentioned, there are diplomatic reasons — the necessity of being present on the spot; collaboration with African countries at the U.N.; there are economic interests — promoting the import of some very important raw materials, promoting exports and investment. (The whole of the Israeli diamond industry, for example, which is Israel's major export, depended at a certain moment upon supplies of diamonds from Africa.) There was certainly also a deep psychological urge to break out of that claustrophobia, that feeling of being besieged, that Israelis had been suffering from, and to go to a world which was free of prejudices about the Israeli-Arab conflict. To all these reasons I would add one minor, but at the time relevant, fact: some of Israel's new immigrants, mainly those coming from French-speaking North African states, were young intellectuals, available for service, who found themselves during 1964-65 in difficulties with regard to their own internal assimilation in Israel. The fact that they could go out as experts to the French-speaking, former colonies of France in Africa was a kind of creation of a new Negev for them in Africa, beyond the frontiers of Israel. All these things were important.

From the point of view of the recipients, I would point out, firstly, that most of these states viewed Israel as a small state which provided aid based on its own experience of development, which was very congenial for geographical and historical, as well as ideological reasons; Israel was not an impressive power — there were no strings attached to its aid; there was also a strong religious attraction for a country which has Jerusalem as its capital. The major political reason for this interest, however, was that Israel could, it was felt, be used as lever by those Afro-Asian states who could not turn to the communist bloc in order to pressure the western bloc. These states could use Israel as a lever, that is, to obtain concessions from the old metropolitan countries.

The Conceptual Structure of Cooperation

Israel's aid to the developing countries has undergone many changes. There was, at first, the intense and sentimental need to help others; there was a sense of mission which has not died out even today; there was the idea that Africans and Jews had something in common (slavery and Auschwitz); there was the idea that Israel could, perhaps, produce a new type of technique that would suit developing countries.

1. Since the delivery of this paper, 3 more countries broke their diplomatic relations with Israel: Congo Brazzaville, Niger and Mali.

2. Presidents El Harj Ahmadon Ahidjo (Cameroon); Yakubu Gowon (Nigeria); Lt.-Gen. Joseph Desire Mobutu (Zaire); Leopold Sedar Senghor (Sengal).

All the factors were important to begin with, but they did not cut very deep into the problems of cooperation. In this field, one of the ideas which Israel really brought forward — and this, I think, is still operative — is that poverty is not only a matter of economics: it is above all a matter of social structures, of adequate bureaucracies, of dedicated elites. Efforts, therefore, must be made on a comprehensive scale to combat poverty, and not in single packages, only in one direction or the other.

The second idea on which Israeli cooperation founded its strategy was that development — the process of catching up — must create hope. Hope can be instilled through ideology and through example. Israel could export some ideological jargon of a socialist type, but not a revolutionary ideology. It did, however, have a large reserve of people who could set an example in the field of cooperation, a real "army" of trained carriers of know-how, of innovation, who could help to stimulate imitations and activate the potential skills of the local traditional elites, who would, in turn, influence their own societies. This idea, that one can find ways and means of "manipulating" the traditional elites through an appropriate carrier of an innovation, had been tested in Israel over a long period. It was embodied in the person of the *madrich* (lit. "guide"). The *madrich* is a young (or sometimes not so young) man (or woman) who takes charge mainly of young people. These may be immigrants from Aliyat HaNoar[3] (Youth Immigration) who have come to Israel in the main as orphans and who were helped, prior to the creation of the State of Israel and immediately thereafter, to become integrated into Israeli society. The *madrich*, thus, has had to be a leader, teacher, father and — what is more important — he has had to adapt himself to the changing condition both of his charges and of their environment.

At a later stage, the *madrich* turned into the technical instructor of the new immigrant. In the development towns and villages he became, of necessity, much more than an instructor: he had to set a personal example if he wanted his instruction to be followed in, for example, the fields of agriculture, cooperative work or artisanship.

The *madrich* as a "commodity" was produced in Israel in considerable quantities. But just because he seemed to be so linked with the very special social and historical situation of the Jewish return to their homeland, no one dreamt that he could be used beyond the borders of the Israeli environment. It was only when Israel began going out to the new countries of Africa and looking for the right men to send there, that it realized the value of *madrichim* for technical cooperation and made them one of its resources in the field of assistance to development.

Furthermore, it was through the work of the *madrichim* that Israel was able to work out practical development schemes which tended to activate the traditional elites for the purpose of legitimating the acceptance of an innovation. Let me give an example drawn from personal experience. In Madagascar, the social structure of the indigenous society is based on the belief that dead ancestors take an active part in the existence of the living. If, therefore, one wants to introduce some change into village life — for instance, to start a weaving cooperative — one must have the agreement not only of the inhabitants, but also of their dead ancestors, through the latter's appointed "speakers" in the village. Otherwise one will achieve no practical results, or — as in my own case — see the new income realized from cooperative work being spent on improving the tombs of the

3. A Jewish Agency Department and movement originally created by Reha Frayer and Henrietta Szold to rescue Jewish youth from Nazi Europe, this body was also responsible for the rescue of Jewish youth from the Arab states after 1948, and today is in charge of the rehabilitation of underprivileged youth in Israel.

ISRAELI EXPERTS ABROAD IN 1970 (By Continent and Purpose)

	Agriculture	Youth Organization	Medicine and Health	Education	Construction and Building	Management and Public Service	Social Work and Community Development	Cooperation	Science and Technology	Miscellaneous	Number of Experts	Total man/months
Africa	53 (309)	74 (551½)	28 (159½)	17 (105½)	6 (31½)	28 (206½)	5 (16½)	3 (11½)	15 (78)	17 (25½)	246	1495
Asia	29 (187½)	1 (3)	1 (1)		2 (9)	9 (25½)	1 (6)	4 (5½)	3 (10½)	13 (20)	63	268
Latin America and the Caribbean	42 (311½)	11 (57½)		3 (5)	2 (3½)	23 (110½)		1 (12)	3 (2)	10 (46)	95	548
Mediterranean Area and others	10 (36½)		2 (1)	6 (3)	1 (1½)	2 (2)			1 (1)	3 (5)	25	50
Total	134 (844½)	86 (612)	31 (161½)	26 (113½)	11 (45½)	62 (344½)	6 (22½)	8 (29)	22 (91½)	43 (96½)	429	2361

Figures in brackets show man/months

TRAINEES IN ISRAEL IN 1970 (By Continent and Profession)

	Agriculture	Cooperation	Community Development	Academic Studies	Health and Medicine	Management and Public Service	Vocational Training	Study Tours	Miscellaneous	Number of Trainees	Total study/months
Africa	120 (344½)	99 (322)	59 (226)	36 (184½)	52 (445)	36 (98)	15 (90)	10 (5)	7 (9)	434	1724
Asia	33 (78)	31 (108½)	127 (713)	44 (208½)	1 (10)	2 (2)	18 (18)	18 (2½)	3 (5)	277	1145½
Latin America and the Caribbean	32 (67½)	69 (145½)	9 (9)	55 (167)	25 (93)	21 (42)	–	13 (5)	2 (1½)	226	530½
Mediterranean Area and Others	47 (64½)	2 (7)	3 (3)	29 (84)	8 (96)	1 (1)	–	34 (11)	3 (2)	117	268½
Total	232 (554½)	201 (583)	198 (951)	164 (644)	86 (644)	60 (143)	33 (108)	65 (23½)	15 (17½)	1054	3668½

Figures in brackets show study/months

Development Data. Israel's Program of International Cooperation. Basic Statistics. Israel Ministry for Foreign Affairs. International Cooperation Division, Jerusalem, 1971 dead rather than the conditions of the living.

So much for the main conceptual structures behind Israel's international cooperation. Let us now turn very briefly to some of the results.

Evaluating Israel's Activities

Israel's major success, and the reason for her outstanding position in Africa and Latin America (where she is indeed considered a major factor in the field of aid) is that she has never had the financial resources to spend on large projects. Whenever she did have funds for large projects, the results were usually poor — as is generally the case elsewhere. Israel's greatest opportunity, therefore, and major source of success, was the poverty of her material resources and the richness of her human resources. Yet this was also sometimes a source of failure.

Just because some of these carriers of innovation were so successful on occasion, they engaged their government in activities which went beyond the original goals. This was the case in Uganda, where the success of the Israeli military experts on the spot drew Israel into political involvements quite beyond the limits of her original political objectives. After years of intense cooperation, when General Amin's extravagant requests for military aid had to be rejected, the African disappointment was as great as its hopes had been. Helped by Arab money and propaganda, and aware of a very delicate local political situation, the Ugandan government found it convenient to turn its irritation into violent hostility which forced all Israelis out of the country. For the Israelis this was a deep, but to some extent a salutary shock.

What will remain of the Israeli effort? Some people think it will all boil down to a few diplomatic gimmicks. I think that eventually there will be something more. This experience has lasted almost 15 years already, it continues to grow and is unlikely to stop for some time to come. I cannot foresee whether this effort will eventually be seen as an original breakthrough in the field of cooperation, but it will certainly be remembered as one of the most successful efforts so far made in this field. More than any other country Israel has proved the validity of the old Chinese proverb which says that if you give a man a fish to eat, you will satisfy his appetite for one day. If you teach him how to fish, you will satisfy his appetite for much longer.

DISCUSSION

Question:

Is it not true that the major reason for the success of Israeli programs is that Israelis have learnt to improvise and adapt whatever know-how that has accumulated in their own nation-building to the problems of the developing countries, and that they did this in a diversity of ways, such as by establishing dozens of study courses and seminars, using the best Israeli institutions at all levels, inviting local experts to attend courses in Israel, etc.? And that this aid involved establishing large companies and creating large construction projects, such as hospitals and apartment buildings?

Prof. Segre:

In the field of investments and financing it is sometimes found that the borders between a simple financial investment, and aid, is very thin. Simple business transactions become aid just because they are carried out in underdeveloped countries. In the case of Israel, I was merely asserting that the amount of money available for aid is very limited. The whole of the 1971 aid budget — and I do not mean for investment — was IL 16 million, or slightly below $4 million. I do not think that Israel has made large loans. I can think of only three cases when it has done so, on a limited scale. What Israel did, in the early days, was to give credits for exports and for purchases in Israel of Israeli goods. The government-supported "Vered" Company, which engaged in large construction projects in various parts of the world, is an example—when money was made available, the result was failure. The main reason why this money was made available in the first place was because "Vered" went into large enterprises abroad in 1965-66, when there was a recession in Israel, and it was felt that if Israeli engineers and technicians could be used in such projects there would be no emigration of technicians from Israel. But if one looks into "Vered"'s mismanagement of this money, one sees that when public capital is available for investment, the results may not be very good, in Israel as in any other country.

I agree entirely about the advantages of Israel's gift for improvization and techniques, and that some of Israel's best aid to Africa or Asia was inside Israel itself. It was in Israel, and particularly in those areas which, from the climatic point of view were most similar to parts of Africa and Asia, that cooperation with the Third World was most intensive and consistent. Israel could offer, in its own territory, innumerable laboratories for technical cooperation which bigger and more powerful states (for instance, the European countries) could not, because the structure of the European countries is so different. They could not show people from underdeveloped countries how the process of development started — for the very simple reason that in Germany or Switzerland or England this process began some two hundred years ago, whereas in Israel it began only a few years ago—and in parts of the country was actually only just starting when Afro-Asians arrived in Israel. This was certainly one of the major sources of Israel's strength and success in the underdeveloped world.

Question:

Do you think there is any conscious Israeli policy to contain the geographical expansion of the Arab world — something similar to the American containment in Europe after the Second World War — the idea of finding friends along the periphery of the Arab world, and then militarily assisting such countries?

Prof. Segre:

The temptation to interpret Israeli military aid activities in terms of containment — and I would go beyond that, in terms of a "James Bond" operation — is great. Such an interpretation has found a place not only in the totality of Arab, Soviet, and New Left press, but sometimes even in the Israeli press. I think one must make a clear distinction between military interests and involvements which have a direct bearing on the military crisis in the Middle East, and those which are beyond, on the periphery, and examine every case individually. There have been reports, mainly in *Le Monde,* about an Israeli presence in the Sudan. If these are correct I think that this would be a situation of military logic, which is linked with the very core of the Middle East crisis. But as far as I know this purported Israeli presence in the Sudan has never been substantiated. Israel's military cooperation activities must be divided into two different areas: 1) Those which have no direct interest in and no relevance to the military situation in the Middle East, for instance, the presence of military instructors in Sierre Leone or the Ivory Coast. The reason why there have been Israeli military experts there is because these countries have asked for this type of assistance, in their own interests. This is true also of Chad. In view of the distances and the logistic problems involved, any direct military interest is simply impossible. 2) In the Congo, on the other hand, Israel supplied military aid at the request of the United Nations. There were certainly those—both outside and inside Israel—who thought that it was a good thing to have some Israeli military experts in areas which might be regarded as a strategic danger by the Arab States (mainly Egypt) and thus create, if not a real, at least a psychological diversion. I think that this whole type of reasoning has crumbled since the Six Day War because of the Israeli presence in Sinai. Israel has no need to be in Africa in order to have a strong military presence in the Red Sea. Thus, the shock of Uganda's expulsion of Israeli technicians has not only had repercussions on relations between Israel and Uganda (which have proved disastrous), but has also dampened the enthusiasm of Israeli policymakers for extending military aid in general, and to East Africa in particular. My guess is that we will see a progressive withdrawal of Israel from such activities. In the long run they are dangerous, and militarily speaking they are useless.

Question:

Have not the Arabs succeeded in effecting the ostracization of Israel in Asia?

Prof. Segre:

Historically speaking. Arab ostracization of Israel started *before* Israel had anything to do with the Third World. One of the direct effects of the Israeli involvement in the Third World, and one of the reasons for it, was to limit this ostracization in the newly emergent countries. Israel has been ostracized in Asia for the very good reason that it was not present in any of the Asian countries at the moment of its creation. The Arabs were. There was also an element of Islamic identity which kept many countries (for instance, Indonesia) away from Israel. I don't think this has much to do with the efforts of technical aid. I have mentioned the importance of the Bandung Conference, which really brought home to the Israelis what they had not realized. They were very much surprised by the results of that conference. One reason for the lack of an Israeli presence in large parts of the so-called Third World (and the terminology "Third World" is so vague, so comprehensive and such a difficult tool to use that it may be misleading) has been not the Arabs but the Jews themselves. For example, Israel rejected China's proposal to establish diplomatic relations in 1953—after recognizing Peking in 1950. Israel had a sort of "psychological callousness" towards a very large part of the world, partly because she felt herself at the time to be small and very weak, but also because there were no Jewish communities in those areas. Because of the urgency of problems inside Israel itself, and because of the images which the Israeli leadership had of the Asian and African worlds, there was also not enough perception at the time, not enough Israeli alertness regarding the immense importance of these relations.

But there is another problem. Israel has not been able to make use of the liberationist rhetoric of the Third World, despite the fact that it was one of the first countries to spill the blood of its people in an anti-colonialist fight. This is because the fight between the Israelis and the metropolitan colonial power (Britain) was a fight between white men. In most of the Third World the rhetroic used concerns a war between races. For this reason the Jewish struggle for the liberation of colonial Palestine has not made an impact on the rest of the world. We have a similar situation in the case of Israel's relations with the Marxist world. Fundamentally, Israeli socialism is based on the rationalistic and humanitarian concepts of the American Revolution and on the agrarian concepts of the 1905 Russian Revolution. Thus Israeli socialism found itself in total opposition to Soviet Communism. One could perhaps say that Israel is regarded by Moscow with the antipathy one would expect from Soviet Russia for what probably looks like the only successful Menshevik state in history.

Question:

The Third World also extends to Latin America. I understand there has been some significant Israeli technical assistance there which is somewhat different from that extended to Africa and Asia —these people share the Judaeo-Christ-

ian heritage, including possibly, a common mentality?

Prof. Segre:

Israeli cooperation with Latin America is a rather late development, and is apparently going to grow and overshadow all other Israeli aid activities. Politically, one of Israel's preoccupations in Latin America is to avoid a hostile stand by these generally Christian - conscious countries over the Jerusalem question. Cooperation itself has developed in two main ways. Israelis are working there mainly within the framework of international organizations. Bilateral cooperation is limited. Israel is also trying to export to South America methodologies of development, rather than development itself. For instance, in cases where Israel has been asked to help with the realization of projects of agrarian reform, intensive study courses on the special methodologies of development are being offered as much as new seeds for crops.

Question:

It was not that Israel was successful but because Libya would not give more funds to Uganda that brought about the break in relations. The whole history of the development of Israeli aid to African and Asian nations started at a time when these peoples had no freedom or experience of a trade union movement. The Afro-Asian trade union movements were also the liberation movements in their countries. Trade union leaders met Israeli trade union leaders at various international conferences. When their countries became independent these leaders turned to the Histadrut (*Israel Trade Union Organization*) *for help. I don't know whether the* Histadrut *has helped the African countries politically, but I am sure that it has helped in these countries' development. Then, also, many of these countries have voted against Israel at the U.N. and other places, and yet Israel has not cut off its aid or cooperation with them. As for the* Histadrut's *Afro-Asian Institute, since the Six Day War more Moslems from these countries have come to it than ever before.*

Prof. Segre:

It is true that both the *Histadrut* and the Israeli Socialist movement have played a large and significant role in the development of Israel-Third World relations.

51 Reviewing the United Nations

By Paul Seabury

"Toto, I have the feeling we're not in Kansas anymore...." Dorothy, in *The Wizard of Oz*

The United Nations was conceived on New Year's Day, 1942, in what Churchill would have called a fit of terminological inventiveness — though for reasons other than might come to mind today.

The occasion was Churchill's visit to Washington, three weeks after Pearl Harbor. He and Roosevelt then hastily searched for a name to give the new wartime anti-Hitler coalition, so that a statement on its behalf could greet the world in the New Year. Preoccupied with global strategic questions in that dark hour, they still found time to compose a Declaration to be signed by representatives of countries then at war with Nazi Germany. But as Churchill reported back to London, naming it had posed terminological problems for Roosevelt. Churchill — inclined to grand Marlborough showmanship — wanted it to be called the Grand Alliance, but any suggestion of an alliance for Roosevelt was out of the question. It raised for him, as it had for his predecessor Wilson, the ugly bugbear of Senate constitutional prerogatives. The other (Wilsonian) term, "Associated Powers," was far too innocuous for present exigencies. Roosevelt then conjured up the "United Nations." Churchill recalled later that

> The Presidet was wheeled in to me on the morning of January 1. I got out of my bath, and agreed to the draft.

As for Roosevelt's "United Nations," Churchill thought the name a splendid one:

> I showed my friend the lines from Byron's *Childe Harold:*
>
> *Here, where the sword the United Nations drew*
> *Our countrymen were warring on that day!*
> *And this is much – and all – which will not pass away.*[1]

Dr. Seabury is Professor of Political Science at the University of California, Berkeley, and the author of, among others, *America's Stake in the Pacific*, (Ethics and Public Policy Center, Washington, D.C. 1981).

I

So, the UN was conceived in an upstairs White House bathroom by two Western liberals. A long gestation followed, however, before this war-making coalition was transformed into a universal peacekeeping organization. The UN Charter was signed on June 25, 1945. By then, Roosevelt was dead and Churchill near the end of his term.

Between these dates, however, the U.S. government in wartime played far more than a midwife role to this organization. It was an *idee fixe* to some American officials. When Secretary of State Cordell Hull, for instance, went to Moscow in 1944, and Ambassador to the USSR Averell Harriman urged him to have Soviet Foreign Minister Molotov talk about Soviet plans for Poland, Hull responded: "I don't want to deal with these piddling little things. We must deal with the main issues."[2] As the British Embassy wrote to London from Washington in early 1945, Americans showed

> ...a certain permanent tendency... to put faith in declarations and blueprints, as capable by themselves to cure most of the ills of the world; this, naturally enough, leads to a sharp sense of 'let down' whenever events refuse to conform to the aspiration of men of good will...[3]

Each stage of the UN's growth, during the war, saw ceaseless U.S. proddings and initiatives; postwar planners busily devised schemes for all sorts of world organizations. Certain it is that without these relentless initiatives the chief world organizations we know would never have come into being or been revived. The UN and its affiliates all started from American-sponsored R.S.V.P. parties.

To further illustrate this obvious point, another vignette comes to mind: Canadian diplomat Lester Pearson's account of the first full-fledged United Nations conference (this on food and agriculture) convened, at Roosevelt's invitation, in Hot Springs, Virginia, in early 1943.

> It was in March 1943 [Lester Pearson wrote in his memoirs] that we first heard of the President's plans for this initial U.N. conference. He announced them, rather vaguely, at a White House press conference, explaining that no date had been set for the meeting because replies to the invitation had not all come in. There was good reason for this: none at the time had been sent out. Indeed, the State Department knew nothing about the President's plans.[4]

Pearson recalled the Hot Springs opening session as having been as American as apple pie.

> The chairman, a good Democrat from Texas, tried to blend dignity with bonhomie; to combine the Congress of Vienna with a Rotary meeting. We opened with a silent prayer and ended by singing ... the 'Star Spangled Banner.' ... (N)one of the foreigners knew the words of the American national anthem.[5]

Truman, succeeding Roosevelt, had at least as much enthusiasm for the new organization as his predecessor. Addressing the United Nations conference in San Francisco on June 26, 1945, he said:

> Let us not fail to grasp this supreme chance to establish a world-wide rule of reason — to create an enduring peace under the guidance of God.[6]

It is said that Truman carried in his coatpocket a dogeared card with a snippet from Tennyson's "Locksley Hall" — a rambling Victorian poem:

For I dipped into the future, far as human eye could see,
Saw the Vision of the world, and all the wonder that would be..
Till the war-drum throbbed no longer, and the battle-flags were furled
In the Parliament of man, the Federation of the world.

II

One can quibble about the historical significance of these vignettes. In that bathroom, on that day, Roosevelt coined an expression, not a grand design; it was intended as a label for swords, not ploughshares. The idea for a postwar international organization was not Roosevelt's. He and Hull encouraged schemes for a postwar system of collective security, but both were operating out of a Wilsonian tradition; furthermore, Wilson's earlier design for a League certainly was not an American idea — it was an American *invention*. Its roots (as students of international politics should know) go back to "grand designs" of Dante, Sully, Rousseau, etc. Nevertheless, neither a League of Nations nor a UN could have come into being in the twentieth century *had not an American President insisted upon them*.

III

This was more true of the UN than of the League. After the League had collapsed in the late 1930s, among Europeans there remained little enthusiasm for (and much hostility to) the prospect of breathing fresh life into it as a postwar system. By then the League was regarded as having been worse than nothing, a feeble reed or a dangerous will-'o-the-wisp; it had fostered a kind of wishful thinking in Western liberal minds, giving rise to misplaced confidence in a toothless forum which could hardly act as surrogate for both the balance of power and national security. As in 1919, so during World War II, shrewd Europeans humored this American enthusiasm; it was one way of prying the U.S. out of its isolation carapace so that it could be a co-guarantor of some postwar peace settlement favorable to the victors.

Yet how can we account for such American enthusiasm at the time, when set against such European cynicism? The enthusiasm seems all the more remarkable when one recalls the stubborn American opposition to the League as late as the late 1930s — an opposition which Roosevelt scarcely bothered to challenge during his first two terms of office. It is even more remarkable, considering that the League's failures seemingly confirmed Cassandra-like warnings of American critics about it long before. Anyone familiar with the League's history could have seen the obvious — that the liberal publics (at least in the West— who were its chief supporters — placed such confidence in collective security as to neglect or ignore the sinister realities of power politics which it was supposed to replace; to see the League as substitute for national power, by consigning to it the world's difficulties for resolution, was (as the saying goes) "to let George do it," and George, when tested, proved no more than the sum of George's uncoordinable parts. The totalitarian states at the time, no friends to collective security, operated according to far different rules.

IV

Americans have a way of radically reinterpreting their past in light of current conditions. This was particularly true during the Second World War. It was true both of Americans' wartime reassessment of their nation's general role in world politics in the interwar years, and also of the reasons provided for the League's failure. The world order of Versailles collapsed (the argument now went) because the U.S. had failed to support it! The League had failed, not due to internal flaws, but to American abstention from it. Here is where domestic politics came in: the League, furthermore, failed because Wilson had been betrayed by Republican isolationists, and particularly by Senator Henry Cabot Lodge, *eminence grise* of the "wilful little men" who had blocked Senate ratification of the Versailles Treaty and the League Covenant. Had America joined it, the League would have worked, the peace been saved. And so, *mirabile dictu,* the collapse of world order could be attributed in part to reactionary Republicans! Roosevelt's enthusiasm for a new international organization could in part be attributed to his canny political instincts. The Republicans in 1944 could not only be made out as enemies of domestic reform, but of world peace also.

V

But these reflections cannot explain in any sufficient way the extraordinary, and enduring, support which the United Nations had when it was ultimately ratified by the American Senate, or the public support the organization received even after the Cold War had shown the organization's incapacity to deal with the most severe threats to peace, and to America's security, which came from the Soviet Union. From the start, the very financial existence of the organization; its New York headquarters; its very capacity to exist; depended upon American benefactions and Congressional appropriations. The American contribution to the annual UN budget towered (and continues to tower) over payments from any other government in the world. Congress, always sensitive to public mood changes, nevertheless continued to fund the organization over the decades. It is still true, by and large, that public opinion polls continue to show approval of the organization. One must conclude that whatever changes have occurred in the United Nations, the Organization has remained a symbol of the kind of world which decent Americans have wanted to see come about: a candle of hope set against the darkness of a dangerous world environment.

VI

This fact of American parentage from the beginning invested the organization with a symbolism closely connected with America's self-esteem and prestige; for if it did not and does not today represent the aspirations of some other beasts in the jungle at least it has represented the best *American* ones for a better world. This fact of parentage, however, as time wore on has helped sustain a certain patronizing attitude toward the organization, which became incongruous and even embarrassing as the offspring developed characteristics distinctly offensive to its progenitor — as a mother, in company of guests, might silently avert her eyes from the misbehavior of a grown-up child to avoid the mortification of stooping publicly to reprimand him. For how, given the radical changes in the demeanor of the United Nations, could one possibly admit in public to *arrieres pensées,* when one's own ego (not to mention one's aspirations) had been so deeply involved in a noble experiment? Many Americans who follow these matters scarcely today dare to think the unthinkable: is this organization — product of our own liberal culture — compatible any more with liberal values? Has it betrayed the principles of its own Charter?

VII

Tennyson's *Locksley Hall* now would seem to have become a "dangerous place" — as Daniel P. Moynihan has pointed out in his book bearing that title. Its outward features remain much the same as they were at the outset — even with three times as many tenants and flags; it is what occurs inside which is very different. There, in its many mansions, the Parliament of Man's liberal character is vanishing. One might say, so what? The membership is changed; a majority has become a minority; the majority can redefine the agenda, as in any majoritarian body.

VIII

Let us stop and look back, for a minute, at the much-abused League of Nations, which so miserably failed to keep the peace of the world. However ineffective the League proved, in one respect it had a redeeming virtue of remaining, to the end, true to its convictions even if incapable of doing much for them. As child of the rosy months of hope which followed the Allied victory in 1918, the League both at birth and throughout its short life was conceived and dominated by the liberal democracies (minus the United States). Not a single diplomat who helped draft its Covenant in 1919 represented a non-democratic state; through all its existence the democracies continued to dominate its agenda. No matter how feeble the League was, when beset by the tests of the 1930s, its covenantal philosophy was not turned upside down; states members of the organization which by their aggressions violated the Covenant's canons of collective security *left* the organization in a huff (Japan, Germany and Italy), or were actually expelled (the Soviet Union, for invading Finland in 1939).

The League, of course, "failed" when its chief members refused, in the crunch, to live up to its principles *not* because they turned these principles upside down to use the organization as engine of assault against the world order. The League's last major act, ironically, was to expel the Soviet Union — for invading a small country which chose to fight rather than forfeit its sovereignty. (It was for this reason alone that Stalin, during the war, had absolutely no interest in establishing a new collective security organization.) But there can be fidelity even in despair; at the end, the League at least died faithful to its Covenant. Can the same fidelity to principle today be found in the General Assembly of the UN — as far as its vast majority is concerned? A dour remark might here be made: now it is almost as though, by analogy, the Fascist states had managed to *seize* the League in the 1930s, rather than merely walk out on it.

IX

Most Americans today probably still like the UN for the nice things it claims to do, or actually does, such as those projects depicted on its stamps: helping refugees, stamping out diseases and illiteracy, helping the women of the world get their rights and children to get their food, promoting "development," and so on. The League, too, had similar projects going in *its* time,[7] if on a more modest scale. However well these tasks were pursued, they hardly could be called the central purposes of the organization. (*The* central purpose of the organization then was and now is to "save succeeding generations from the scourge of war," and to do so with regard to the integrity of its member states.) When the central (i.e., the political) functions fail (as did those of the League), then the organization and all that goes with it fails too, *regardless of* how well its "functional" tasks were performed in specialized agencies. When and if the central purposes are so perverted as to actually sabotage convenantal principles, one might imagine that the foxes had taken over the henhouse. The League failed, however, not because it principles were perverted to ends opposite to those which its founders had intended, but because it failed, in crisis, to defend its principles.

X

Observers of the UN should note an incongruous aspect of the organization *as it has evolved* since the 1960s. In its many assemblies — the Security Council, the General Assembly, and the many councils of its "functional" organizations (ECOSOC,

UNESCO, the ILO, and the like) — the UN operates in procedural ways akin to those of representative assemblies in free societies. (So did the League.) Issues are debated; votes are taken; majorities and qualified majorities decide momentous issues in public sessions. (Until recently, when South African diplomats have been denied the General Assembly's podium) all member states have had the right to speak up. Thus these bodies have the outward appearance of the parliaments of the democracies. They have listening galleries, and the press has access to the proceedings, if it chooses to come. Moreover, the language of debate and resolutions — UNese — has the same monotonous flavor of the parliaments, tempers checked by Senatorial courtesy.

An odd aspect of all of this is that now the vast majority of states members do not permit such procedures at home (where, if parliamentary bodies exist at all, they exist unanimously to ratify decisions taken by the authorities). The idea of public opposition is not tolerated; thus the anomaly: the UN is a free debating society composed largely of states which forbid debate at home. The number of these regimes members of the organization now is more than two-thirds the UN's total membership.

While *pro forma* respect for open debate and parliamentary practice still characterizes the UN bodies, in a *de facto* sense heavy inroads have already been made into these procedures, and this by no means bodes well for the future of Roberts' Rule of Order in *Locksley Hall*. Many anti-Western resolutions routinely and regularly introduced and adopted by the UN bodies do not arise in ordinary parliamentary fashion. Rather, they are prepacked products of extra-mural conferences and organizations of anti-Western states — the Non-Aligned, in particular, now comprising 92 of the organization's 153 members. Resolutions are framed in such organizations, and they are simply *transferred to* UN bodies. In these previous sessions (as though the Non-Aligned now represent a UN house of first instance), democratic centralism is normally the rule. In them, the forms of parliamentarism (including the democratic custom of acting in public opposition) are supplanted by procedures of pressure aimed at a result of full public unanimity. If one wished to see what the UN *can* become in the future, one might possibly wish to inspect the procedures and practices of the Non-Aligned, anti-Western conferences of Lusaka (1970), Algiers (1973), Colombo (1976) and, in plenum most recently, Havana (1979).

An odd custom of such Non-Aligned meetings is to grant the host regime the privilege of drafting agendas and first drafts of conference declarations and resolutions. Thus at Havana in 1979, it fell to Castro (both Soviet puppet and host) to perform the task of drawing up the conference agenda and of shaping its results; for that spell of time, Castro in effect *was*, pretty much, the United Nations — pouring vitriol on the usual enemies of mankind — colonialists, neo-colonialists, Zionists, crypto-Zionists, monopoly-capitalists, racists, imperialists and other exploiters of the world's masses. The vocabulary of the Non-Aligned is scarcely distinguishable from that of Soviet propagandists. One scarcely bothers, anymore, to comment on the hypocrisy of Non-Alignment. But one can at least understand why such totalitarian congregations strive for public uniformity and democratic centralism: that is how their systems work at home. The result of this is to cast a heavy aroma over Turtle Bay.[8]

These practices are not confined to the General Assembly; they have spread to agendas of specialized agencies as well — notably, UNESCO, UNCTAD, and the ILO. Here, the specialized agencies' bureaucracies can be of use. (Recently, the Director General of UNESCO, the Honorable Amadou M'Bow has become notable for *himself* organizing caucuses to develop UNESCO rule for licensing and controlling newsmen. Soviet diplomats play a significant part in abetting such designs.)

XI

How to explain why Americans have paid so little attention to the deformations of the UN at the hands of its New Majority? There are no simple explanations, and probably a number of them weightily scrambled together. Probably the most obvious is that, when this process of degeneration commenced, in the 1960s (I would date it probably around the two assassinations, of Dag Hammarsjold and John Kennedy), Americans were distracted by other things: our own cultural revolution, the Vietnam war, and all the other media sensations of the time.

Probably, another reason was that then (as now) there were quite a number of highly placed figures in Washington — in both parties, for that matter — who viewed the organization with contempt. Dean Acheson was dean of this school of thought.[9] This view was not that of the John Birch Society; it was of those Realists who thought along the lines propounded by the late Professor Hans Morgenthau; it was not that this school saw (or sees) the organization as a threat to the Republic, but as a distraction from weighty affairs of state. And the fact that year after year, succeeding Administrations appointed media celebrities as public delegates to United Nations General Assembly sessions, testified in part to the degree of esteem accorded the organization in succeeding Republican and Democratic Administrations.[10]

A second hypothesis not unrelated to the previous one, is the "so what?" school: if the United Nations had begun to misbehave, and its councils now rang with tirades against American imperialism, so what? Who, after all, should stoop to reply to such slander? One might discern a certain patronizing attitude in all this: after all, what can one expect of such people? If the debates in Turtle Bay Hall were often intellectually and morally idiotic, so what? Who in their right mind could take them seriously? If the organization was dominated by fools, why not suffer them lightly? Furthermore, if the honorable delegates to UNESCO conferences decide to proclaim the virtues of global press censorship on behalf of authoritarian regimes, so what? Such idiocy will not signal the death knell of a free press; even if *Reuters,* the *United Press,* and *Agence France Presse* are replaced in a majority vote with some giant system of regulatory journalism, the market principle will still be around; after all, even Idi Amin from time to time needed *some* Western newsman to get his points across to a listening world. If, some day, the UN credentials the PLO as a member, with some future Andrew Young approving or abstaining, also so what? Israel will not collapse, like Jericho, to these trumpeters of righteousness. And even if the General Assembly finally were to declare the people of Puerto Rico free from U.S. imperialism, it is to be assumed that those people may still have their say, as have the people of Gibraltar, whom the UN tried to liberate some years ago from their British oppressors, by majority vote. (Intolerably, Gibraltarians for some odd pernicious reason seem actually to *like* their oppressors: an infuriating defiance of the UN anti-colonialists who try to force them to be free, or at least "returned" to their one-time Spanish masters). Finally, if and when the General Assembly proclaims the New International Economic Order, the world of trade and finance will not obligingly knuckle under. Again, so what?

The trouble with this line of reasoning is that many of those who now display private contempt at these games, in all these committees, councils and plenums, seem with all their realism to be rather naive. If the organization is a "toothless forum," it is a forum nevertheless, and one in which obstinately, from year to year, ideas about how the world should be reorganized, nations invented, subverted or even destroyed, are drilled into the minds of those who take such matters seriously. Much foolishness, if incessantly repeated, can be actually taken seriously even by its potential victims. (In fact, as far as the Western liberal public is concerned, the nonsense about the New International Economic Order *is* being taken seriously, in the sense that it gained wide acceptance.[11] Ideas have consequences. Israel is not made the safer for the rhetorical defamation heaped upon it year after year as being the successor state to Nazi Germany. Even though General Assembly resolutions for the most part have no binding effect on member states, they can have a profound cumulative effect in *conditioning* men's minds.

What is even more risky about such a complacent attitude is that, publicly ventilated, such absurdities have the effect of pouring vitriol on already troubled waters; the UN was not created in order to create trouble, but to create conditions of peace. It is odd that, as the organization became dominated by those pursuing trouble creation, intrinsically desirable projects in such causes as hunger, food, trade union rights of labor, and human rights, have been poisoned by ideological crusades. (For example, the Rome Food Conference in 1973, called by the United States to discuss methods of coping with the very real dangers of food shortages, became a stage on which "First World" food producers, the U.S. in particular, were accused of oppressing the poor of the world.) It is not likely that such polemics will encourage such sponsors to think seriously about again arranging conferences to offer solutions, *and paying for them*. Whatever the already lopsided voting record of states in the UN's councils, the danger of such packed proceedings is that the convening of such conferences in itself creates or strengthens the polarization of monolithic groups. Certainly it does not — one might say — create an atmosphere of cooperation.[12]

XII

In recent years a quite different set of considerations may have entered the minds of American policy makers observing these sorry spectacles: Could we really *afford* to fight back in these "toothless forums" when, in a time of growing vulnerability, America needed as few enemies as possible? Why show our teeth, or even our tooth, when prudence would suggest turning the other cheek? For example, Algerian oil was more important than making a court case against some ridiculous Algerian Third World resolution. Once such a state was reached, we might sense that trouble was ahead, yet good-humored sportsmanship served as a disguise for real misapprehension as to the implications of what was going on. Now, here was a *real* policy dilemma: Ought we to be polite, when politeness might now be perceived, not as the patronizing posture of superiority, but as the prudence of the weak? To accept continuing defeats with "grace" could ill conceal the defeats themselves, while (a real Catch 22) it continued to infuriate some who still perceived, in such feigned courtesy, the same old pretentious gentility of the superior colonialist exploiter. A trace of possible cowardice could be seen when everyone notes that the wind of "rhetoric" blows from quarters we do not at all wish to antagonize. A consequence of such a Bre'r Rabbit pose on the part of Uncle Sam (particularly during the Carter Administration) was not only to leave the forum to our philosophical enemies, but to confirm a suspicion on their part that they could press their causes with even greater determination and prospect of success.

Especially for those Americans who still retain enthusiasm or respect for the United Nations, such pious posturing should especially be regarded as a very risky strategy. It may be surmised that one consequence of such patronizing false friendliness is to risk having member states which pursue antagonizing pressure gravely misjudge possible American reactions in the future, at such time as the American public again returns to paying attention to them. There is no reason, especially in this new Administration, that a policy of passive resistance followed by friendly tete-a-tetes in the UN bar, may not continue to be overlooked. John Birchers may not be alone in wondering why the U.S. heavily subsidizes these assaults on American interests and policies.

XIII

Why not defend the Charter against the Charter's enemies?

If the attempt were actually made, what might be done to try to turn the vessel around? What might be done, in other words, in a principled fashion? Certain principles could be simply reaffirmed:

> 1) The United Nations was formed as a peacemaking and peacekeeping organization, above all. If it degenerates into a simple anti-Western forum, or a forum designed to mobilize forces against certain select member states, then it not only betrays the Charter; it turns the Charter upside down.
>
> 2) There must be consistent rules about membership. From the beginning the United States was an organization of *states;* states presumably belong to it in order chiefly to

safeguard their interests in an anarchic world. Viewed in this fashion, the organization cannot allow the representation of revolutionary movements (such as the PLO) whose aims include the destruction of a member state; if these are accorded representation, the representational base of the organization is wrecked.

3) As a universal (or nearly universal) organization, the UN cannot arbitrarily determine, by majority vote, which states' internal characteristics warrant continued membership, not even South Africa, especially when attempts to do so result in total hypocrisy and a transparent double standard. Nor can its laudable pursuit of human rights be manipulated (again, with a double standard) to turn on certain regimes' alleged or real misdemeanors, while shielding others, including others far worse. (One of several shameful episodes, for instance, of Andy Young's regime at the U.S. Mission, was when a U.S. and a Cuban delegate jointly drafted a resolution condemning the Chilean government.)

4) The principle of national self-determination cannot long be permitted also to be a double standard, where *some* nationalities are favored and others neglected or abused, or where the UN seeks to *require* that certain nationality groups become "free" even though they do not want to be. This tactic surely represents a travesty of the very idea of the right of peoples to choose their own government — witness Puerto Rico and Gibraltar. (One could easily — in the Gibraltar issue — observe the naked Emperor, Spanish imperialism, in place of British colonialism). The cause of human rights, in particular, should not be allowed to be applied in ways which endorse threats to the existence of nation-states; the life and death of nations should not be a subject of debate or action on the agenda of any UN council.

5) True to its principles, the organization (as Reagan Administration spokesmen have emphasized)[13] should not attempt to actually *subvert* human rights in nations where they are generally respected, or to make the internal nature of states a test of membership.

6) Finally, since advice should begin at home, it would seem as though a basic beginning, in reaffirming such principles, should be to ensure that United States representatives do not engage in such violations of Charter provisions, as occurred during the Carter Administration; it would be a true irony if America, which bore the chief responsibility in drafting the Charter, ended up condoning or abetting its subversion.

It might be said in conclusion that the eclipse, collapse or subversion of the United Nations, while it would not necessarily be a disaster, would be a tragedy with symbolic effects of a far-reaching nature. Among decent persons the world around, it has represented a hope. It would be a pity if at some moment the civilized world had to concern itself with being safe against the United Nations, rather than being safer through it. To paraphrase Byron,

This is much which should not pass away.

FOOTNOTES

1. Churchill, *The Grand Alliance,* pp. 683-684.

2. Cited in Willian Widenor, "American Planning for the United Nations," unpublished ms., p. 16.

3. *Ibid.*, p. 9.

4. Lester Pearson, *Memoirs*, Vol. I, p. 246.

5. *Ibid., p. 247.*

6. *Widenor, op. cit.*, p. 2.

7. A very paunchy but theatrically talented Assembly interpreter, during a debate on women's rights in the League, when translating the passionate appeal of a women delegate, flailed his hands on his stomach, crying, "Speaking as a woman and a mother..." The story is apocryphal, but shows the continuity of mankind's concerns.

8. See Ariah Eilan, "Soviet Hegemonism and the Non-Aligned," *The Washington Quarterly,* Winter 1981, pp. 97-106. As Eilan remarks, "Essentially, the right to dissent, inherent in the voting system of the United Nations, is frowned upon in the Non-Aligned movement." (p. 101)

9. Following an afterdinner speech in Berkeley, after his retirement from public office, Acheson was asked, by a faculty member, "Mr. Secretary, if you had your career to do over, and could either be Secretary of State or U.S. Ambassador to the U.N., which post would you choose?" Acheson looked at the man putting the question and replied haughtily, "Are you *serious*? Why if I had only the latter option, like Seneca I would retire to my bath and open my veins." In another context, he remarked of the organization: "The ass that went to Mecca was still an ass."

10. In Ford's Administration, these luminaries included such persons as Pearl Bailey and Shirley Temple Black. One might infer that, judging by such appoint-

ments, Washington regarded the U.N. for a long time as the distaff zone of foreign policy: tough matters of *Realpolitik* were handled in Washington; matters of health, children, poverty and hunger were assigned to — well, women, as in traditional post-dinner parties, where husbands separate from their wives, with cigars and brandy, to discourse on weighty matters.

11. The recent report of the Brandt Commission on North-South relations is one such example, which, whatever else happens to it, will be displayed in reading rooms of United Nations Associations and seriously studied in seminars from California to Stockholm.

12. Another feature of such global conferences is that (wholly apart from the polemics they encourage) they inspire the delusion that such problems are "global" and unitary, requiring "global" solutions. So inspired was the U.S. delegation at the Bucharest Population Conference of such a global perspective that they proposed a global limitation goal of two children per family. (Intelligent demographers know that such a rate of procreation would lead to extinction of the race).

13. See *Rethinking Human Rights,* by Michael Novak and Richard Shifter, Foundation for Democratic Education, Washington, D.C., 1981.